THE FABER BOOK OF MURDER

Simon Rae was born in 1952 and educated at Sedbergh, the University of Kent and Lincoln College, Oxford. He won a major Gregory Award in 1981 and a Southern Arts Literature Bursary in 1982. A freelance writer and broadcaster, he presents Radio 4's request programme *Poetry Please!*, and contributes weekly topical poems to the *Weekend Guardian*, of which a selection was published under the title *Soft Targets* in 1991.

Also by Simon Rae

Poetry
Soft Targets (Bloodaxe Books, 1991)

Anthology
The Faber Book of Drink, Drinkers and Drinking (1991)

The Orange Dove of Fiji:
Poems for the Worldwide Fund for Nature
(Hutchinson, 1989)

The Faber Book of

MURDER

Edited by

SIMON RAE

faber and faber

LONDON · BOSTON

First published in Great Britain in 1994
by Faber and Faber Limited
3 Queen Square London WC1N 3AU

This paperback edition first published in 1995

Photoset by Wilmaset Ltd, Birkenhead, Wirral
Printed in England by Clays Ltd, St Ives plc

A CIP record for this book
is available from the British Library

ISBN 0-571-17494-9

2 4 6 8 10 9 7 5 3 1

GHOST: List, Hamlet, list, O list!
If thou didst ever thy dear father love –
HAMLET: O God!
GHOST: Revenge his foul and most unnatural murder.
HAMLET: Murder?
GHOST: Murder most foul, as in the best it is,
But this most foul, strange, and unnatural.

William Shakespeare, *Hamlet*

ANGEL: Who shall heal murder? What is done, is done.

Lord Byron, 'Cain: a Mystery'

Murders are exciting and lift people into a heart-beating awe as religion is supposed to do, after seeing one in the street young couples will go back to bed and make love, people will cross themselves and thank God for the gift of their stuporous lives, old folks will talk to each other over cups of hot water with lemon because murders are enlivened sermons to be analyzed and considered and relished, they speak to the timid of the dangers of rebellion, murders are perceived as momentary descents of God and so provide joy and hope and righteous satisfaction to parishioners, who will talk about them for years afterward to anyone who will listen.

E. L. Doctorow, *Billy Bathgate*

The world in general, gentlemen, are very bloody-minded; and all they want in a murder is a copious effusion of blood; gaudy display in this point is enough for *them*. But the enlightened connoisseur is more refined in his taste; and for our art, as from all the other liberal arts when thoroughly mastered, the result is, to humanise the heart.

Thomas De Quincey, 'On Murder Considered as One of the Fine Arts'

I met Murder in the way –
He had a mask like Castlereagh –
Very smooth he looked, yet grim;
Seven blood-hounds followed him:

All were fat; and well they might
Be in admirable plight,
For one by one, and two by two
He tossed them human hearts to chew
Which from his wide cloak he drew.

Percy Bysshe Shelley, 'The Mask of Anarchy'

Contents

D

E

F

Introduction

'Murder? Eugh!' A repressed shudder. 'Murder?' A cocked eyebrow. 'When's it coming out?' Those really have been the only responses I have had to this book during its preparation, and I find both equally understandable. Murder is indeed a sordid, ugly, brutal, horrible crime. 'Of all the offences man may commit against his fellow, murder is without question the cruellest, since it deprives man of the single asset he has received from Nature, and its loss is irreparable.' And having said that, possibly adding 'Murder most foul' for good measure, is there any more to be said? Certainly one might question the validity of a whole anthology devoted to murder. But as I have indicated, murder, in addition to being uniquely repulsive, is also strangely fascinating. It is, to use a phrase coined by James Fenton, one of those subjects which is 'intrinsically interesting'. And Fenton himself explores aspects of this intrinsic interest in his poem, 'A Staffordshire Murderer': 'Every fear is a desire. Every desire is fear.' Murder is a very intimate thing, not just physically, but psychologically as well. It makes its appeal – and there's no doubting it has an appeal ('I do like a good murder') – on a number of grounds. There's a curiosity as to how circumstances contrived to bring murderer and victim together, as to how the murderer could bring himself to commit the deed – and whether there was any course of action by which the victim could have saved him- or herself. The omnipotence of the writer's pen both exposes us to the horror, and at the same time controls and tames it for us. And there is also, if we are honest, a further identification. For as Freud points out on more than one occasion, the strength of the taboo against homicide is a measure of the strength of its attraction. 'Men are not gentle creatures who want to be loved, and who at the most can defend themselves if they are attacked; they are, on the contrary, creatures among whose instinctual endowments is to be reckoned a powerful share of aggressiveness . . . *Homo homini lupus* (Man is wolf to man).' Whether we like it or not, murder is a regrettable scarlet thread running through the human tapestry. It has been with us from the very beginning – from almost before the beginning, if we accept Freud's theory of the primal killing when *Homo sapiens* was almost indistinguishable from his cousins the apes. And it has provided a subject for writers from the earliest days of literature. As P. D. James comments in an interview, 'Crime stories certainly go back before the Bible. It is rather interesting, isn't it, that you get Cain and Abel in the first stories in the Bible and this is the story of a murder.'

According to Zola, 'Love and death, possessing and killing, are the dark foundations of the human soul.' Andrea Dworkin is even more forceful: 'Men love death. In everything they make, they hollow out a central place for death. Men especially love murder. In art they celebrate it. In life, they commit it.' For Joyce Carol Oates, 'Art is built around violence, around death; at its base is fear.' It's not surprising, therefore, that so much literature – and so much of the greatest literature – is fixated on death, violence, murder. Some authors clearly derive a vicarious excitement from such themes. As John Carey brilliantly demonstrated in *The Violent Effigy*, what inspired Dickens was not the depiction of Victorian middle England triumphing over wickedness, but the rampages of its sworn enemies. It is Quilp not Little Nell who stimulates the creative fission for Dickens. As Carey notes, 'Riot, murder, savagery have to be there before Dickens's imagination is gripped.' Shakespeare reveals far less of himself in his work than Dickens, and no one could say that his writing soars when he deals with murder and sinks when he depicts love (though as the extract from *A Midsummer Night's Dream* shows, the two worlds overlap more than one might suspect). But who can doubt, either, that in imagination he crept with Macbeth into Duncan's bedchamber, or felt the release of pent-up energy in that horror-filled cry, 'Let it come down!'?

Murder is the extreme crime, and, as such, acts as a prism through which character is refracted. As De Quincey says, the writer throws 'the interest on the murderer [so that] our sympathy must be with him, our sympathy of comprehension, not approbation.' No writer has performed this task more attentively than Dostoyevsky, most notably in *Crime and Punishment*. Raskolnikov's crime in itself is no less sordid than a million other squalid bludgeonings and would be of no great interest had the supposed motive – pecuniary gain – been the real one. But although he goes through the motions of stealing, Raskolnikov derives no benefit from his pitiful haul, hiding the loot under a stone and abandoning it. His real motive is very different: the murder is, in reality, a personal dare, a testing of the self, an attempt to forge an identity superior to the slovenly and mediocre society which he despises and on which, to his shame, he depends. The murder is an existential gesture, in other words.

It is perhaps the aftermath of murder that gives the greatest scope for the writer's powers of empathy. For the murderer is changed almost as radically as his victim by his irreversible act. He may at first experience exhilaration, a sense of freedom or power, but from Cain down, the killer has been ostracized by society, an outcast. He may even be said to have killed himself along with his victim. Fear of detection, and, even more dreadful, a deep and all-pervasive guilt, infect every aspect of his life. Zola's portrait of the two murderer-lovers in *Thérèse Raquin* is almost unbearable: their crime has brought them everything they wanted – each other – and yet from it springs a barrier of razor-sharp thorns across the marriage bed. Dickens scourges Sykes out into the fields surrounding London after the murder of Nancy, but there is nowhere for him to escape from the treadmill of his remorse, and he slinks sullenly back into the metropolis for his final act of aggrieved and self-destroying defiance. And after her superhuman efforts to wind her husband to the sticking point to fulfil her hard-nosed ambition, Lady Macbeth fades away into guilt-haunted madness, while Macbeth himself charts the gradual callousing of his soul down to its last leaden indifference to life and death alike.

The working of conscience is a challenging study for the writer. But of course many murderers clearly have none – the eighteenth-century killer Williams, for instance, so vividly evoked in all his cunning, brutality and ultimate stupidity by De Quincey. And Patricia Highsmith has written a series of novels in which her (anti-)hero Ripley finds himself obliged repeatedly to dispose of people who stand inconveniently between him and the things he wants. His crimes are committed out of a cool appraisal of self-interest, not at the height of passion. Highsmith describes him as 'amoral' rather than 'immoral', and we follow his exploits with interest without ever feeling we could behave in a similar fashion.

Robert Louis Stevenson's story, *The Strange Case of Dr Jekyll and Mr Hyde*, perhaps touches us more closely, for all its Gothic fantasy. Stevenson's parable of the double man could be said to have anticipated some of the major discoveries of psychoanalysis, and his descriptions of the id-like Hyde certainly ring true to the violent side of our nature normally expressed only in wishful thinking.

The main focus of this book is the personal, the domestic, murder. However, as a gesture towards inclusiveness, I have included passages on murder in, as it were, the mass. Mankind seems to have grown out of human sacrifice, but massacre, genocide, judicial murder and public executions are still with us, along with the perennially irresistible call to arms. My selections are representative only. It might be objected that to leave the Chinese out when space is given to the Soviet and Nazi atrocities is to distort the record of our own barbarous century. Certainly, had space permitted, I would have included material on the Communist regime's assaults on its own people, and on those of its betrayed neighbour, Tibet. And beyond China queues a whole host of ignominious governments forming the role of dishonour charted so depressingly and so necessarily by such organizations as Amnesty International.

There are whole libraries devoted to the subject of murder, and I have largely ignored the 'professional' shelves: works by criminologists, psychologists, sociologists, etc. I have aimed to produce an anthology that, while covering as large an area as possible, also has variety – 'light and shade' as De Quincey puts it. The alphabetical scheme, as arbitrary as the alphabet itself, provides, I hope, some interesting juxtapositions, if not a logical progression. There is no intention of swelling the long catalogue of encyclopaedias of crime (though I have pillaged two extracts from Oliver Cyriax's excellent addition to that catalogue). The categories are by no means comprehensive; some are positively spurious; and as the reader will see, the letter Y gave me particular problems.

It would be wrong-headed to pretend our reactions to violent death are always of the same seriousness. A whole sub-genre of jokes revolves around the grimmer misfortunes the flesh is heir to, and scholarly papers have been written on the therapeutic role of the sick joke. I make no apology for including Ambrose Bierce and Saki, W. S. Gilbert and P. G. Wodehouse, even though it means their rubbing shoulders with Shakespeare and Sophocles.

I made a decision very early on in this project to exclude from consideration all contemporary murders of a private nature. As though to confirm the rightness of this decision, on the day that I first met my editor to discuss the book, there appeared an article in the *Independent* written by a murder victim's father saying that the pain never goes away. Any serious study of crime must of course consider new cases as they occur, which must presumably be the justification for the burgeoning of 'True Crime' accounts of murders, kidnappings, and so forth. But I felt there was no requirement to include such material here (the assassinations of President Kennedy and Michael X are two high-profile and historic crimes, very much in the public domain). This self-imposed restriction accounts for some of the omissions, without which, as a kindly reviewer remarked of my last, no anthology is complete, and I would mention three works which would otherwise have made an appearance: Blake Morrison's 'The Ballad of the Yorkshire Ripper', Gordon Burns's account of the same story, *Somebody's Husband, Somebody's Son*, and Brian Master's *Killing for Company*.

'True Crime' is not excluded entirely, however, and after some deliberation, I have decided to include a few short sections from the recently published document purporting to be Jack the Ripper's Diary. I allow myself that note of scepticism because I believe that the diary will probably prove to be a fake. This is not to call into question the good faith of those responsible for its publication, and I have great admiration for the way Shirley Harrison has argued the case for her identification of the Liverpool cotton magnate, James Maybrick, as the Ripper. However, two major obstacles seem to present themselves. The authenticity of the diary depends, of course, on whether the handwriting is genuine. I can believe that Maybrick's will, which is in a different hand from the diary, could have been forged by his scheming brothers (who stood by while Mrs Maybrick was successfully, though unjustly, prosecuted for the murder of her husband). But in the course of an active business career, Maybrick must have left other examples of his handwriting: letters, notes, receipts. And on the day that a message from Maybrick about cotton prices turns up in a different hand, the case for the diary collapses. The second major stumbling-block is the question of blood. The Whitechapel murders were, notoriously, brutal, and the last in particular reduced a very small, and ill-lit, room to a butcher's shambles. The murderer must have emerged from that ghastly place splashed from head to foot. For Maybrick to have escaped back to Liverpool undetected, without help, would have been extraordinary. But he makes nothing of it in the diary.

The speculation about the diary (especially about its provenance) will continue, but I offer one, rather mischievous, observation. In Gordon Honeycombe's magisterial book, *The Murders of the Black Museum, 1879–1970*, the chapter dealing with the unsolved mystery of the Ripper's identity is followed immediately by the case of the Maybrick murder. Wilder flights of fancy have been stimulated by less. But of course on the day that the diary is exposed as a fake, if such a day dawns, it will simply cross over the border that divides fact from fiction, and whether fact or fiction, I feel it has a place in this anthology.

P. D. James has called the modern detective story 'a kind of morality play', and Joan Didion in *The White Album* remarked, 'We look for the sermon in the suicide, for the social or moral lesson in the murder of five.' Whatever secondary lessons the following pages contain, the overwhelming one would seem to be that the injunction 'Thou shalt not kill' remains the human race's greatest ethical breakthrough. It also remains the injunction we find most difficult to comply with.

A Note on the Text

Nearly all the passages are taken from readily available sources, for the most part in paperback. The one glowing exception is the extract from Crabbe's 'The Voluntary Insane', which, courtesy of my friend and fellow anthologist, Felix Pryor, appears in print for the first time. A full scholarly text will be published in due course, but in the meantime I am delighted to be bringing a substantial excerpt from this important poem to public notice. My first thanks must therefore go to Felix Pryor for allowing me this publishing coup.

Other friends whose help in suggesting sources has born fruit in the following pages are: Viv Beeby, Mark Bland, Richard Boston, David Buxton, Marie-Claude Chapuis, Tony Lurcock, Andrew McAllister, David MacGregor, Susan Roberts, John Whitworth, Gary Yershon.

My editor, Christopher Reid, gave me many invaluable suggestions, and I must thank him for his supportive enthusiasm and, indeed, for his occasional forbearance. Justine Willett was my desk editor, and Jane Feaver was also unfailingly helpful. Finally, I would like to thank Mary Dortch for her painstaking copy-editing, and Val Glenn for clearing the copyright permissions.

Dates: I tend to the Sellar and Yeatman view of dates (i.e. that English history gets by quite comfortably on two 'genuine' dates, 55BC and 1066) and have therefore decided to exclude the distraction of publication date at the bottom of each extract. Dates of works still protected by copyright will be found in the Acknowledgements pages, and an index gives authors' dates. I accept that there are some instances where a date of publication or composition of out of copyright material might be of particular interest. 'The Voluntary Insane', for instance, was probably written in 1822; *Ramseeana*, or *A Vocabulary of the Peculiar Language used by the Thugs* was published in 1836, and William Wood's pamphlet 'Remarks on the Plea of Insanity' was printed in 1851. I have used the 1850 version of *The Prelude* for the gibbet episode. Scot's *The Discovery of Witchcraft* was first published in 1584, and *Coke's Institutes* date from 1628 to 1644.

Simon Rae

Devizes, 1994

A

Aboriginal

There is, of course, no place for the beginnings of totemism in Darwin's primal horde. All that we find there is a violent and jealous father who keeps all the females for himself and drives away his sons as they grow up. This earliest state of society has never been an object of observation. The most primitive kind of organization that we actually come across – and one that is in force to this day in certain tribes – consists of bands of males; these bands are composed of members with equal rights and are subject to the restrictions of the totemic system, including inheritance through the mother. Can this form of organization have developed out of the other one? and if so along what lines?

If we call the celebration of the totem meal to our help, we shall be able to find an answer. One day the brothers who had been driven out came together, killed and devoured their father and so made an end of the patriarchal horde. United, they had the courage to do and succeeded in doing what would have been impossible for them individually. (Some cultural advance, perhaps, command over some new weapon, had given them a sense of superior strength.) Cannibal savages as they were, it goes without saying that they devoured their victim as well as killing him. The violent primal father had doubtless been the feared and envied model of each one of the company of brothers: and in the act of devouring him they accomplished their identification with him, and each one of them acquired a portion of his strength. The totem meal, which is perhaps mankind's earliest festival, would thus be a repetition and a commemoration of this memorable and criminal deed, which was the beginning of so many things – of social organization, of moral restrictions and of religion.

Sigmund Freud, *Totem and Taboo*, trans. James Strachey

Ambush

Had she come all the way for this,
To part at last without a kiss?
Yea, had she borne the dirt and rain
That her own eyes might see him slain
Beside the haystack in the floods?

Along the dripping leafless woods,
The stirrup touching either shoe,
She rode astride as troopers do;
With kirtle kilted to her knee,
To which the mud splash'd wretchedly;
And the wet dripp'd from every tree
Upon her head and heavy hair,
And on her eyelids broad and fair;
The tears and rain ran down her face.
By fits and starts they rode apace,
And very often was his place
Far off from her; he had to ride
Ahead, to see what might betide
When the roads cross'd; and sometimes, when
There rose a murmuring from his men,
Had to turn back with promises;
Ah me! she had but little ease;
And often for pure doubt and dread
She sobb'd, made giddy in the head
By the swift riding; while, for cold
Her slender fingers scarce could hold
The wet reins; yea, and scarcely, too,
She felt the foot within her shoe
Against the stirrup; all for this,
To part at last without a kiss
Beside the haystack in the floods.

For when they near'd that old soak'd hay,
They saw across the only way
That Judas, Godmar, and the three
Red running lions dismally
Grinn'd from his pennon, under which,

In one straight line along the ditch,
They counted thirty heads.

So then,
While Robert turn'd round to his men,
She saw at once the wretched end,
And, stooping down, tried hard to rend
Her coif the wrong way from her head,
And hid her eyes; while Robert said:
'Nay, love, 'tis scarcely two to one,
At Poictiers where we made them run
So fast – why, sweet my love, good cheer.
The Gascon frontier is so near,
Nought after this.'

But, 'O,' she said,
'My God! my God! I have to tread
The long way back without you; then
The court at Paris; those six men;
The gratings of the Chatelet;
The swift Seine on some rainy day
Like this, and people standing by,
And laughing, while my weak hands try
To recollect how strong men swim.
All this, or else a life with him,
For which I should be damned at last,
Would God that this next hour were past!'

He answer'd not, but cried his cry,
'St George for Marny!' cheerily;
And laid his hand upon her rein.
Alas! no man of all his train
Gave back that cheery cry again;
And, while for rage his thumb beat fast
Upon his sword-hilts, some one cast
About his neck a kerchief long,
And bound him.

Then they went along
To Godmar; who said: 'Now, Jehane,
Your lover's life is on the wane
So fast, that, if this very hour

You yield not as my paramour,
He will not see the rain leave off –
Nay, keep your tongue from the gibe and scoff,
Sir Robert, or I slay you now.'

She laid her hand upon her brow,
Then gazed upon the palm, as though
She thought her forehead bled, and – 'No',
She said, and turn'd her head away,
As there were nothing else to say,
And everything were settled: red
Grew Godmar's face from chin to head:
'Jehane, on yonder hill there stands
My castle, guarding well my lands:
What hinders me from taking you,
And doing that I list to do
To your fair wilful body, while
Your knight lies dead?'

A wicked smile
Wrinkled her face, her lips grew thin,
A long way out she thrust her chin:
'You know that I should strangle you
While you were sleeping; or bite through
Your throat, by God's help – ah!' she said,
'Lord Jesus, pity your poor maid!
For in such wise they hem me in,
I cannot choose but sin and sin,
Whatever happens: yet I think
They could not make me eat or drink,
And so should I just reach my rest.'
'Nay, if you do not my behest,
O Jehane! though I love you well,'
Said Godmar, 'would I fail to tell
All that I know.' 'Foul lies,' she said.
'Eh? lies my Jehane? by God's head,
At Paris folks would deem them true!
Do you know, Jehane, they cry for you,
"Jehane the brown, Jehane the brown!
Give us Jehane to burn or drown!" –
Eh – gag me Robert! – sweet my friend,

This were indeed a piteous end
For those long fingers, and long feet,
And long neck, and smooth shoulders sweet;
An end that few men would forget
That saw it – So, an hour yet:
Consider, Jehane, which to take
Of life or death!'

So, scarce awake,
Dismounting, did she leave that place,
And totter some yards: with her face
Turn'd upward to the sky she lay,
Her head on a wet heap of hay,
And fell asleep: and while she slept,
And did not dream, the minutes crept
Round to the twelve again; but she,
Being waked at last, sigh'd quietly,
And strangely childlike came, and said:
'I will not.' Straightway, Godmar's head,
As though it hung on strong wires, turn'd
Most sharply round, and his face burn'd.

For Robert – both his eyes were dry.
He could not weep, but gloomily
He seem'd to watch the rain; yea, too,
His lips were firm; he tried once more
To touch her lips; she reach'd out, sore
And vain desire so tortured them,
The poor grey lips, and now the hem
Of his sleeve brush'd them.

With a start
Up Godmar rose, thrust them apart;
From Robert's throat he loosed the bands
Of silk and mail; with empty hands
Held out, she stood and gazed, and saw,
The long bright blade without a flaw
Glide out from Godmar's sheath, his hand
In Robert's hair; she saw him bend
Back Robert's head; she saw him send
The thin steel down; the blow told well,

Right backward the knight Robert fell,
And moan'd as dogs do, being half dead,
Unwitting, as I deem: so then
Godmar turn'd grinning to his men,
Who ran, some five or six, and beat
His head to pieces at their feet.
Then Godmar turn'd again, and said:
'So, Jehane, the first fitte is read!
Take note, my lady, that your way
Lies backward to the Chatelet!'
She shook her head and gazed awhile
At her cold hands and a rueful smile,
As though this thing had made her mad.

This was the parting that they had
Beside the haystack in the floods.
William Morris, 'The Haystack in the Floods'

When hares were caught by stableboys with bells
And saints journeyed with eyes reversed in prayer,
When chivalrous men with servants were depicted
Disporting on a flowered field of gold,
This nasty contrivance was all too often seen
Being galloped about by some long-suffering horse.

Herzmund ('Baron') was inside, lapped in sweat.
Flexing the hinged and riveted shell, he peered
For prey through slits above an iron snout.
At night – the takings tossed into a chest –
He dined grossly and aired his views on death
While someone helpless screamed in a deep basement.

Charming vignette; but why, you say, be morbid?
Consider the craftsmanship, the Vulcan skill,
The arabesques engraved on the cuirass,
The nimble patterns – and the entertaining
Protection provided for the Baron's genitals;
Think of it, if you like, as abstract sculpture.

Quite; but I think mainly of the confronted
Traveller impaled by terror or in earnest,
The mounted devil-dress glimpsed in the gloaming,
The cornering and the wordless savagery.
Yes, hung in public, armour is fair monument
For those who see if not for those who look.

Fergus Allen, 'A Suit of Armour'

Amontillado

The thousand injuries of Fortunato I had borne as I best could; but when he ventured upon insult, I vowed revenge. You, who so well know the nature of my soul, will not suppose, however, that I gave utterance to a threat. *At length* I would be avenged; this was a point definitely settled – but the very definitiveness with which it was resolved precluded the idea of risk. I must not only punish, but punish with impunity. A wrong is unredressed when retribution overtakes its redresser. It is equally unredressed when the avenger fails to make himself felt as such to him who has done the wrong.

It must be understood that neither by word nor deed had I given Fortunato cause to doubt my good will. I continued, as was my wont, to smile in his face, and he did not perceive that my smile *now* was at the thought of his immolation.

He had a weak point – this Fortunato – although in other regards he was a man to be respected and even feared. He prided himself on his connoisseurship in wine. Few Italians have the true virtuoso spirit. For the most part their enthusiasm is adopted to suit the time and opportunity – to practise imposture upon the British and Austrian *millionaires*. In painting and gemmary Fortunato, like his countrymen, was a quack – but in the matter of old wines he was sincere. In this respect I did not differ from him materially; I was skilful in the Italian vintages myself, and bought largely whenever I could.

It was about dusk, one evening during the supreme madness of the carnival season, that I encountered my friend. He accosted me with excessive warmth, for he had been drinking much. The man wore motley. He had on a tight-fitting parti-striped dress, and his head was surmounted by the conical cap and bells. I was so pleased to see him that I thought I should never have done wringing his hand.

I said to him – 'My dear Fortunato, you are luckily met. How remarkably well you are looking to-day! But I have received a pipe of what passes for Amontillado, and I have my doubts.'

'How?' said he. 'Amontillado? A pipe? impossible! And in the middle of the carnival!'

'I have my doubts,' I replied; 'and I was silly enough to pay the full Amontillado price without consulting you in the matter. You were not to be found, and I was fearful of losing a bargain.'

'Amontillado!'

'I have my doubts.'

'Amontillado!'

'And I must satisfy them.'

'Amontillado!'

'As you are engaged, I am on my way to Luchesi. If any one has a critical turn, it is he. He will tell me – '

'Luchesi cannot tell Amontillado from Sherry.'

'And yet some fools will have it that his taste is a match for your own.'

'Come, let us go.'

'Whither?'

'To your vaults.'

'My friend, no; I will not impose upon your good nature. I perceive you have an engagement. Luchesi – '

'I have no engagement; – come.'

'My friend, no. It is not the engagement, but the severe cold with which I perceive you are afflicted. The vaults are insufferably damp. They are encrusted with nitre.'

'Let us go, nevertheless. The cold is merely nothing. Amontillado! You have been imposed upon. And as for Luchesi, he cannot distinguish Sherry from Amontillado.'

Thus speaking, Fortunato possessed himself of my arm. Putting on a mask of black silk, and drawing a *roquelaire* closely about my person, I suffered him to hurry me to my palazzo.

There were no attendants at home; they had absconded to make merry in honour of the time. I had told them that I should not return until the morning, and had given them explicit orders not to stir from the house. These orders were sufficient, I well knew, to insure their immediate disappearance, one and all, as soon as my back was turned.

I took from their sconces two flambeaux, and giving one to Fortunato, bowed him through several suites of rooms to the archway that led into the vaults. I passed down a long and winding staircase, requesting him to be cautious as he followed. We came at length to the foot of the descent, and stood together on the damp ground of the catacombs of the Montresors.

The gait of my friend was unsteady, and the bells upon his cap jingled as he strode.

'The pipe,' said he.

'It is farther on,' said I; 'but observe the white web-work which gleams from these cavern walls.'

He turned towards me, and looked into my eyes with two filmy orbs that distilled the rheum of intoxication.

'Nitre?' he asked, at length.

'Nitre,' I replied. 'How long have you had that cough?'

'Ugh! ugh! ugh! – ugh! ugh! ugh! – ugh! ugh! ugh! – ugh! ugh! ugh! – ugh! ugh! ugh!'

My poor friend found it impossible to reply for many minutes.

'It is nothing,' he said, at last.

'Come,' I said, with decision, 'we will go back; your health is precious. You are rich, respected, admired, beloved; you are happy, as once I was. You are a man to be missed. For me it is no matter. We will go back; you will be ill, and I cannot be responsible. Besides, there is Luchesi – '

'Enough,' he said; 'the cough is a mere nothing; it will not kill me. I shall not die of a cough.'

'True – true,' I replied; 'and, indeed, I had no intention of alarming you unnecessarily – but you should use all proper caution. A draught of this Médoc will defend us from the damps.'

Here I knocked off the neck of a bottle which I drew from a long row of its fellows that lay upon the mould.

'Drink,' I said, presenting him the wine.

He raised it to his lips with a leer. He paused and nodded to me familiarly, while his bells jingled.

'I drink,' he said, 'to the buried that repose around us.'

'And I to your long life.'

He again took my arm, and we proceeded.

'These vaults,' he said, 'are extensive.'

'The Montresors,' I replied, 'were a great and numerous family.'

'I forget your arms.'

'A huge human foot d'or, in a field azure; the foot crushes a serpent rampant whose fangs are imbedded in the heel.'

'And the motto?'

'*Nemo me impune lacessit.*'

'Good!' he said.

The wine sparkled in his eyes and bells jingled. My own fancy grew warm with the Médoc. We had passed through walls of piled bones, with casks and puncheons intermingling, into the inmost recesses of the catacombs. I paused again, and this time I made bold to seize Fortunato by an arm above the elbow.

'The nitre!' I said; 'see, it increases. It hangs like moss upon the vaults. We are below the river's bed. The drops of moisture trickle among the bones. Come, we will go back ere it is too late. Your cough – '

'It is nothing,' he said; 'let us go on. But first, another draught of the Médoc.'

I broke and reached him a flaçon of De Grâve. He emptied it at a breath. His eyes flashed with a fierce light. He laughed and threw the bottle upwards with a gesticulation I did not understand.

I looked at him in surprise. He repeated the movement – a grotesque one.

'You do not comprehend?' he said.

'Not I,' I replied.

'Then you are not of the brotherhood.'

'How?'

'You are not of the masons.'

'Yes, yes,' I said, 'yes, yes.'

'You? Impossible! A mason?'

'A mason,' I replied.

'A sign,' he said.

'It is this,' I answered, producing a trowel from beneath the folds of my *roquelaire*.

'You jest,' he exclaimed, recoiling a few paces. 'But let us proceed to the Amontillado.'

'Be it so,' I said, replacing the tool beneath the cloak, and again offering him my arm. He leaned upon it heavily. We continued our route in search of the Amontillado. We passed through a range of low arches, descended, passed on, and descending again, arrived at a deep crypt, in which the foulness of the air caused our flambeaux rather to glow than flame.

At the most remote end of the crypt there appeared another less spacious. Its walls had been lined with human remains, piled to the vault overhead, in the fashion of the great catacombs of Paris. Three sides of this interior crypt were still ornamented in this manner. From the fourth the bones had been thrown down, and lay promiscuously upon the earth, forming at one point a mound of some size. Within the wall thus exposed by the displacing of the bones, we perceived a still interior recess, in depth about four feet, in width three, in height six or seven. It seemed to have been constructed for no especial use within itself, but formed merely the interval between two of the colossal supports of the roof of the catacombs, and was backed by one of their circumscribing walls of solid granite.

It was in vain that Fortunato, uplifting his dull torch, endeavored to pry into the depth of the recess. Its termination the feeble light did not enable us to see.

'Proceed,' I said; 'herein is the Amontillado. As for Luchesi – '

'He is an ignoramus,' interrupted my friend, as he stepped unsteadily forward, while I followed immediately at his heels. In an instant he had reached the extremity of the niche, and finding his progress arrested by the rock, stood stupidly bewildered. A moment more and I had fettered him to the granite. In its surface were two iron staples, distant from each other about two feet, horizontally. From one of these depended a short chain, from the other a padlock. Throwing the links about his waist, it was but the work of a few seconds to secure it. He was too much astounded to resist. Withdrawing the key I stepped back from the recess.

'Pass your hand,' I said, 'over the wall; you cannot help feeling the nitre. Indeed it is *very* damp. Once more let me *implore* you to return. No? Then I must positively leave you. But I must first render you all the little attentions in my power.'

'The Amontillado!' ejaculated my friend, not yet recovered from his astonishment.

'True,' I replied; 'the Amontillado.'

As I said these words I busied myself among the pile of bones of which I have before spoken. Throwing them aside, I soon uncovered a quantity of building stone and mortar. With these materials and with the aid of my trowel, I began vigorously to wall up the entrance of the niche.

I had scarcely laid the first tier of the masonry when I discovered that the intoxication of Fortunato had in a great measure worn off. The earliest indication I had of this was a low moaning cry from the depth of the recess. It was *not* the cry of a drunken man. There was then a long and obstinate silence. I laid the second tier, and the third, and the fourth; and then I heard the furious vibrations of the chain. The noise lasted for several minutes, during which, that I might hearken to it with the more satisfaction, I ceased my labors and sat down upon the bones. When at last the clanking subsided, I resumed the trowel, and finished without interruption the fifth, the sixth, and the seventh tier. The wall was now nearly upon a level with my breast. I again paused, and holding the flambeaux over the masonwork, threw a few feeble rays upon the figure within.

A succession of loud and shrill screams, bursting suddenly from the throat of the chained form, seemed to thrust me violently back. For a brief moment I hesitated – I trembled. Unsheathing my rapier, I began to grope with it about the recess: but the thought of an instant reassured me. I placed my hand upon the solid fabric of the catacombs, and felt satisfied. I reapproached the wall. I replied to the yells of him who clamored. I re-echoed – I aided – I surpassed them in volume and in strength. I did this, and the clamorer grew still.

It was now midnight, and my task was drawing to a close. I had completed the eighth, the ninth, and the tenth tier. I had finished a portion of the last and the eleventh; there remained but a single stone to be fitted and plastered in. I struggled with its weight; I placed it partially in its destined position. But now there came from out the niche a low laugh that erected the hairs upon my head. It was succeeded by a sad voice, which I had difficulty in recognizing as that of the noble Fortunato. The voice said –

'Ha! ha! ha! – he! he! – a very good joke indeed – an excellent jest. We will have many a rich laugh about it at the palazzo – he! he! he! – over our wine – he! he! he!'

'The Amontillado!' I said.

'He! he! he! – he! he! he! – yes, the Amontillado. But is it not getting late? Will not they be awaiting us at the palazzo, the Lady Fortunato and the rest? Let us be gone.'

'Yes,' I said, 'let us be gone.'

'*For the love of God, Montresor!*'

'Yes,' I said, 'for the love of God!'

But to these words I hearkened in vain for a reply. I grew impatient. I called aloud –

'Fortunato!'

No answer. I called again! –

'Fortunato!'

No answer still. I thrust a torch through the remaining aperture and let it fall within. There came forth in return only a jingling of the bells. My heart grew sick – on account of the dampness of the catacombs. I hastened to make an end of my labor. I forced the last stone into its position; I plastered it up. Against the new masonry I re-erected the old rampart of bones. For the half of a century no mortal has disturbed them. *In pace requiescat!*

Edgar Allan Poe, 'The Cask of Amontillado'

Anger

And him beside rides fierce reuenging *Wrath*,
  Vpon a Lion, loth for to be led;
  And in his hand a burning brond he hath,
  The which he brandisheth about his hed;
  His eyes did hurle forth sparkles fiery red,
  And stared sterne on all, that him beheld,
  As ashes pale of hew and seeming ded;
  And on his dagger still his hand he held,
Trembling through hasty rage, when choler in him sweld.

His ruffin raiment all was staind with blood,
  Which he had spilt, and all to rags yrent,
  Through vnaduized rashnesse woxen wood;
  For of his hands he had no gouernement,
  Ne car'd for bloud in his auengement:
  But when the furious fit was ouerpast,
  His cruell facts he often would repent;
  Yet wilfull man he neuer would forecast
How many mischieues should ensue his heedlesse hast.

Full many mischiefes follow cruell *Wrath*;
  Abhorred bloudshed, and tumultuous strife,
  Vnmanly murder, and vnthrifty scath,
  Bitter despight, with rancours rusty knife,
  And fretting griefe the enemy of life;
  All these, and many euils moe haunt ire,
  The swelling Splene, and Frenzy raging rife,
  The shaking Palsey, and Saint *Fraunces* fire:
Such one was *Wrath*, the last of this vngodly tire.

Edmund Spenser, *The Faerie Queene*

Anger, a perturbation, which carries the spirits outwards, preparing the body to melancholy, and madnesse it selfe: *Ira furor brevis est:* and as *Piccolomineus* accounts it one of the three most violent passions. *Areteus* sets it downe for an especiall cause (so doth *Seneca ep. 18. lib. 1.*) of this maladie. *Magninus* gives the reason, *ex frequenti ira supra modum calefiunt*, it over-heates their bodies, and if it bee too frequent, it breakes out into manifest madnesse, saith *S. Ambrose*. 'Tis a knowne saying, *furor fit læsa sæpius patientia*, the most patient spirit that is, if he be often provoked, will be incensed to madnesse, it will make a Divell of a Saint. And therefore *Basil* belike in his Homily *de Ira*, calls it *tenebras rationis, morbum animæ, & dæmonem pessimum:* the darkning of our understanding and a bad Angell. *Lucian in Abdicato, Tom. 1.* will have this passion to worke this effect, especially in old men and women, *anger and calumny* (saith he) *trouble them at first, and after a while breake out into open madnesse: many things cause fury in women, especially if they love or hate overmuch, or envy, be much grieved or angry: these things by little and little lead them on to this malady.* From a disposition they proceed to an habit, for there is no difference betwixt a mad man, and an angry man, in the time of his fit: Anger, as *Lactantius* describes it, *lib. de Ira Dei ad Donatum cap. 5.* is *sæva animi tempestas, &c.* a cruell tempest of the minde, *making his eyes sparke fire and stare, his teeth gnash in his head, his tongue stutter, his face pale, or red, & what more filthie imitation can be of a mad man.*

Ora tument ira, fervescunt sanguine venæ,
Lumina Gorgonio sævius angue micant.[1]

They are void of reason, inexorable, blinde, like beasts and monsters for the time, say and doe they knowe not what, curse, sweare, rayle, fight, and what not? How can a mad man doe more? as he said in the Comedy, *Iracundia non sum apud me*, I am not mine owne man. If these fits be immoderate, continue long, or be frequent, without doubt they provoke madnesse. *Montanus consil 21.* had a melancholy *Jew* to his patient, he ascribes this for a principall cause, *Irascebatur levibus de causis*, he was easily moved to anger. *Ajax* had no other beginning of his madnesse; and *Charles the 6.* that Lunatick French King, fell into this misery, out of the extremity of his passion, desire of revenge & malice, incensed against the Duke of *Britaine*, he could neither eat, drinke, nor sleepe for some daies together, and in the end about the Calends of July 1392, he became mad upon his horse backe, drawing his sword, striking such as came neere him promiscuously, and so continued all the daies of his life, *Æmil. lib. 10. Gal. hist. Ægesippus de excid. urbis Hieros. lib. 1. cap. 37.* hath such a story of *Herod*, that out of an angry fit, became mad, leaping out of his bed, he killed *Josippus*, and plaied many such Bedlam prankes, the whole Court could not rule him, for a long time after: sometimes he was sorry and repented, much grieved for that he had done, *postquam deferbuit ira*, by and

1 They swell with extreme anger, the blood boils in their veins,
Their eyes flash like the fierce Gorgonian snakes. (Ovid)

by outragious againe. In hot cholericke bodies, nothing so soone causeth madnesse, as this passion of Anger, besides many other diseases, as *Peletius* observes, *cap. 21. lib. 1. de him. affect. causis: sanguinem imminuit, fel auget:* and as *Valesius* controverts, *med. controv. lib. 5. contro. 8.* many times kills them quite out. If this were the worst of this passion, it were more tolerable, *but it ruines and subverts whole townes, citties, families, and kingdomes; Nulla pestis humano generi pluris stetit*, saith *Seneca de Ira lib. 1.* No plague hath done mankinde so much harme. Looke into our histories, and you shall almost meet with no other subject, but what a company of hare-braines have done in their rage. Wee may doe well therefore, to put this in our procession amongst the rest: *From all blindnesse of heart, from pride, vain-glory, and hypocrisie, from envy, hatred and malice, anger, and all such pestiferous perturbations, good Lord deliver us.*

Robert Burton, *The Anatomy of Melancholy*

I was angry with my friend:
I told my wrath, my wrath did end.
I was angry with my foe:
I told it not, my wrath did grow.

And I water'd it in fears,
Night & morning with my tears;
And I sunned it with smiles,
And with soft deceitful wiles.

And it grew both day and night,
Till it bore an apple bright;
And my foe beheld it shine,
And he knew that it was mine,

And into my garden stole
When the night had veil'd the pole:
In the morning glad I see
My foe outstretch'd beneath the tree.

William Blake, 'A Poison Tree'

Anticipation

Even in his nausea he could not help wondering what it was that Abiatha Swelter was doing. He raised his head from the wall and brought it by degrees to its former position.

This time Flay was surprised to find that the room appeared empty, but, with a start at its dreadful nearness, he found that the chef was sitting on a bench against the wall and immediately below him. It was not easy to see him clearly through the filth and cobwebs of the window, but the great pasty dome of his head surrounded by the lamp-tinted whiteness of his swollen clothes seemed, when Flay located them, almost at arm's length. This proximity injected into Mr Flay's bones a sensation of exquisite horror. He stood fascinated at the pulpy baldness of the chef's cranium and as he stared a portion of its pale plush contracted in a spasm, dislodging an October fly. Nothing else moved. Mr Flay's eyes shifted for a moment and he saw a grindstone against the wall opposite. Beside it was a wooden stool. To his right, he saw two boxes placed about four feet apart. On either side of these wooden boxes two chalk lines ran roughly parallel to each other, and passed laterally along the room below Mr Flay. Nearing the left-hand wall of the room they turned to the right, keeping the same space between them, but in their new direction they could not proceed for more than a few feet before being obstructed by the wall. At this point something had been written between them in chalk, and an arrow pointed towards the wall. The writing was hard to read, but after a moment Flay deciphered it as: *To the Ninth Stairs*. This reading of the chalk came as a shock to Mr Flay, if only for the reason that the Ninth Stairs were those by which Lord Sepulchrave's bedroom was reached from the floor below. His eyes returned swiftly to the rough globe of a head beneath him, but there was still no movement except perhaps the slight vibration of the chef's breathing.

Flay turned his eyes again to the right where the two boxes were standing, and he now realized that they represented either a door or an entrance of some sort from which led this chalked passageway before it turned to the right in the direction of the Ninth Stairs. But it was upon a long sack which had at first failed to attract his attention that he now focused his eyes. It lay as though curled immediately between and a little in advance of the two boxes. As he scrutinized it, something terrified him, something nameless, and which he had not yet had time to comprehend, but something from which he recoiled.

A movement below him plucked his eyes from the sack and a huge shape arose. It moved across the room, the whiteness of the enveloping clothes tinctured by the lime-green lamp above. It sat beside the grindstone. It held in its hand what seemed, in proportion to its bulk a small weapon, but which was in reality a two-handed cleaver.

Swelter's feet began to move the treadles of the grindstone, and it began to spin in its circles. He spat upon it rapidly three or four times in succession, and with a quick movement slid the already razor-keen edge of the cleaver across the whirr of the stone. Doubling himself over the grindstone he peered at the shivering edge of the blade, and every now and then lifted it to his ear as though to listen for a thin and singing note to take flight from the unspeakable sharpness of the steel.

Then again he bent to his task and continued whetting the blade for several minutes before listening once more to the invisible edge. Flay began to lose contact with the reality of what he saw and his brain to drift into a dream, when he found that the chef was drawing himself upwards and travelling to that part of the wall where the chalk lines ended and where the arrow pointed to the ninth staircase. Then he removed his shoes, and lifted his face for the first time so that Mr Flay could see the expression that seeped from it. His eyes were metallic and murderous, but the mouth hung open in a wide, fatuous smile.

Then followed what appeared to Flay an extraordinary dance, a grotesque ritual of the legs, and it was some time before he realized, as the cook advanced by slow, elaborate steps between the chalk lines, that he was practising tiptoeing with absolute silence. 'What's he practising that for?' thought Flay, watching the intense and painful concentration with which Swelter moved forward step by step, the cleaver shining in his right hand. Flay glanced again at the chalk arrow. 'He's come from the ninth staircase: he's turned left down the worn passage. There's no rooms right or left in the worn passage. I ought to know. *He's approaching the Room.*' In the darkness Flay turned as white as death.

The two boxes could represent only one thing – the doorposts of Lord Sepulchrave's bedroom. And the sack . . .

He watched as the chef approached the symbol of himself asleep outside his master's room, curled up as he always was. By now the tardiness of the approach was unendingly slow. The feet in their thick soles would descend an inch at a time, and as they touched the ground the figure cocked his head of lard upon one side and his eyes rolled upwards as he listened for his own footfall. When within three feet of the sack the chef raised the cleaver in both hands and, with his legs wide apart to give him a broader area of balance, edged his feet forward, one after the other, in little, noiseless shiftings. He had now judged the distance between himself and the sleeping emblem of his hate. Flay shut his eyes as he saw the cleaver rise in the air above the cumulous shoulder and the steel flared in the green light.

Mervyn Peake, *Titus Groan*

Apache

'Cracking form, W.G.?' said Raffles, flattening a wormcast with the bottom of his bat.

'More like it indeed,' replied the Doctor.

'A goodly crowd, too,' continued Raffles, 'and still a-coming.'

'Yes', said W.G. Carriages ringed the ground. Top hats and parasols bobbed and weaved. 'I shall delay my century until the gates are closed. Foolish to pass the hat round at less than capacity.'

'There's certainly money about today, Doctor,' said Raffles, not inexperienced in these matters. 'Hello, I think you are about to enjoy yourself.' He beamed happily and winked. 'A change of bowling.'

So there was – and high time too in the Doctor's opinion. *And* the new bowler was Castor Vilebastard, no less. Oh, it will certainly give me great pleasure, he thought, to make mince-meat of this fellow. W.G. expressed very few intense dislikes, but in his view, C. Vilebastard was a fully-qualified *bounder*.

'The italics,' he announced to a startled umpire, 'are my own.'

Undoubtedly it was this rotter's presence at Lord's that lay at the root of his melancholy.

A. J. Raffles turned the first ball of the over neatly to leg, and they walked a sedate single. Vilebastard was still quick, W.G. reflected as he flexed his shoulders, adjusted his beard, tweaked his red-and-yellow-striped cap and spun his vast bat in the air as King Arthur might have whirled Excalibur aloft on such a Saturday afternoon centuries earlier, when battle was to be joined. He revolved slowly on his heel, searching for suitable gaps in the massed ranks of white-flannelled Philadelphians. Suddenly and violently the ball whistled through the Champion of All-England's voluminous beard like a grenade, fizzed past the unsuspecting wicket-keeper and all three long-stops and exploded against the sight-screen.

'None of us was ready, Vilebastard!' boomed the Doctor, scarlet with rage.

'Villibart!' cried Vilebastard, 'It is pronounced "Villibart", as you bloody well know! As in "Cholmondleigh".'

'It is pronounced Vile Bastard,' pronounced the Doctor, 'as in totally unacceptable and unsportsmanlike behaviour!'

Vilebastard marched back towards the Nursery end, seething. Behind him in the Pavilion, W.G. could hear the outraged snorting of the claret-faced members.

'He's no Gentleman of Philadelphia,' said the wicket-keeper apologetically.

'He *is* a member of the MCC,' replied the Doctor, 'or *was*.'

'There's a rotten apple in every barrel,' said the wicket-keeper.

'Ready *now*?' called Vilebastard from the distance.

'Get on with it!' roared W.G. and Vilebastard began to approach at pace. The Doctor raised his bat in readiness, and tapped his left foot impatiently on the wicket. He was going to smite this ball into the next county, where it belonged. Essex that would be.

As Vilebastard reached the crescendo of his unnecessarily long run-up and rose into the air, arms flailing, preparatory to unleashing the thunderbolt, he emitted a shrill shriek, began to fall, and, falling, was propelled by his own momentum into a series of cart-wheels and somersaults towards the middle of the pitch, where with a final jerk, a quiver and a bubbling moan, he lay still. A breathless hush fell over the ground, as the ball dropped from his hand and trickled across the grass until it halted at the Doctor's feet.

'Fore!' he cried, and banged the ball away towards the Tavern to the evident delight of the drunken Thespians and Men of Letters quaffing there.

'Come on!' he called to Raffles and set off for a quite unnecessary run as the umpire was already signalling a boundary. However, it gave W.G. the opportunity as he returned to his crease to tread on the recumbent Vilebastard's outstretched right hand.

'He's not budging sir,' said an umpire. 'He don't look at all perky.' Anxious Philadelphians were gathered about the fallen bowler. The umpire turned towards the Pavilion.

'Is there a doctor in the House?' he shouted.

'I'm a doctor!' boomed the Doctor. 'Let's have a look at him.' As he was about to leave his crease, he insisted that the umpire shouted 'Dead ball!' as he certainly would not trust young Castor further than he could throw him. W.G. pushed his way through the ring of fieldsmen and prodded Vilebastard vigorously with his bat.

'Get up!' he prescribed sharply. There was no response. W.G. turned the body over with his boot. Diagnosis was quite simple.

'Aha!' he said, nodding wisely, 'Here's your problem!'

There was an arrow embedded between his patient's shoulder-blades.

'Ye Gods, Doctor,' gasped the opposing skipper, George S. Patterson, no less. 'What, in Heaven's name is that?'

W.G. Grace knelt and broke off the end of the arrow. He peered knowledgeably at the feathers and looked slowly round the circle of bewildered faces.

'Apache,' he announced.

'Is he dead?' asked one of the umpires, the colour of flannels.

'In my book, as a doornail,' vouchsafed the Doctor.

William Rushton, *W. G. Grace's Last Case*

Apprentice

There was no sleep for me that morning. Mr Berman sent me out to a phone booth and I dialed the number he gave me, let it ring three times and hung up. I brought back coffee and rolls. The cleaning women came in and did up the club. It was now nice and peaceful in there with all the lights out except one light over the bar and whatever silt of the morning sun managed to drift in through the curtains on the front doors. Part of what I was learning was when to be on hand and visible, as opposed to being on hand and invisible. The second was the expedient I chose now, perhaps from no more evidence than Mr Berman's disinclination at this time to talk to me. I sat upstairs at the bar all alone in the dusk of the morning tired as hell and not without pride in myself for having made what I knew was a useful identification. But then all of a sudden there was Irving, which meant Mr Schultz was somewhere nearby. Irving stood behind the bar and put some ice in a glass, then he cut a lime in quarters and with his fingers squeezed lime juice into the glass, and then filled the glass with a spritz from the seltzer bottle. When all this was meticulously done, with not so much as a ring left on the bar surface, Irving drank off his lime soda in one draft. He then washed the glass and dried it with a bar towel and replaced it under the counter. At this moment it occurred to me that my self-satisfaction was inane. It consisted in believing I was the subject of my experience. And then when Irving went to the front door, where someone had been knocking on the glass for some minutes, and admitted the improvident city fire inspector who had picked just this time, and why, except that the words in the air of the great stone city go softly whispering in the lambent morning that this sachem is dead and that one is dying, as if we were some desert blooming in the smallest flowers with the prophecies of ancient tribes, I saw even before it happened what an error of thought could lead to, that presumption was dangerous, that the confidence of imperception was deadly, that this man had forgotten what a fire inspector was, his place in the theory of inspections, his lesser place in the system of fires. Irving was ready with money from his own pocket and would have had the guy out of there in another minute but that Mr Schultz happened to come upstairs from the office with the morning's news. At another time Mr Schultz might have genuinely admired the man's gall and peeled off a few dollars. Or he might have said you dumb fuck you know better than to walk in here with this shit. He might have said you got a complaint you talk to our department. He might have said I'll make one phone call and have your ass you stupid son of a bitch. But as it happened he gave this roar of rage, took him down and mashed his windpipe and used the dance floor to make an eggshell of his skull. A young man with a head of curly hair is what I saw of him alive in that light, maybe a few years older than me, a wife and kid in Queens, who knows? who like me had ambitions for his life. I had never seen anyone being killed close up like that. I can't tell even now how long it took. It seemed like a long time. And what is most unnatural is the sounds. They are the sounds of ultimate emotion, as sexual sounds can sometimes seem to be, except they are shameful and degrading to the idea of life, that it can be so humiliated so eternally humiliated. Mr Schultz arose from the floor and brushed his pants knees. There was not a spot of blood on him although it was webbed out in strings and matter all around the head on the floor. He hitched up his pants and smoothed his hair with his hands and straightened his tie. He was drawing great gasping breaths. He looked as if he was about to cry. 'Get this load of shit out of here,' he said including me in the instruction. Then he went back downstairs.

I couldn't seem to move. Irving told me to bring an empty garbage can from the kitchen. When I got back he had folded the body and tied it head to ankles with the guy's jacket. I think now he must have had to crack the guy's spine to get him doubled so tight. The jacket was over the head. That was a great relief to me. The torso still had heat. We inserted the folded body ass-down in the galvanized-iron garbage can and stuffed the space around with wooden straw of the kind that protects French bottles of wine in their cases, hammered the lid on with our fists and put the can out with the night's refuse, just as the carter came along on Fifty-sixth

Street. Irving had a word with the driver. They are private companies that take away commercial refuse, the city only does citizen garbage. Two guys stand on the sidewalk and heave the can up to the fellow standing in the truck on top of all the garbage. That fellow dumps out the contents and tosses the empty can back over the side to the guys in the street. All the cans came back except one, and if a crowd had been standing around, which there wasn't, for who in the fresh world of the morning wants to watch the cleanup of the night before, the truck motors grinding, the ash cans hitting the sidewalk with that tympanic carelessness of the profession, nobody would have noticed that the truck drove away with one packed garbage can imbedded in all that odorous crap of the glamorous night, or dreamed that in an hour or two it would be shoveled by tractor deep below the anguished yearnings of the flights of seagulls wheeling over the Flushing Meadow landfill.

E. L. Doctorow, *Billy Bathgate*

Assassination

And the children of Israel did evil again in the sight of the LORD: and the LORD strengthened Eglon the king of Moab against Israel, because they had done evil in the sight of the LORD.

And he gathered unto him the children of Ammon and Amalek, and went and smote Israel, and possessed the city of palm trees.

So the children of Israel served Eglon the king of Moab eighteen years.

But when the children of Israel cried unto the LORD, the LORD raised them up a deliverer, Ehud the son of Gera, a Benjamite, a man left-handed: and by him the children of Israel sent a present unto Eglon the king of Moab.

But Ehud made him a dagger which had two edges, of a cubit length; and he did gird it under his raiment upon his right thigh.

And he brought the present unto Eglon king of Moab: and Eglon was a very fat man.

And when he had made an end to offer the present, he sent away the people that bare the present.

But he himself turned again from the quarries that were by Gilgal, and said, I have a secret errand unto thee, O king: who said, Keep silence. And all that stood by him went out from him.

And Ehud came unto him; and he was sitting in a summer parlour, which he had for himself alone: and Ehud said I have a message from God unto thee. And he arose out of his seat.

And Ehud put forth his left hand, and took the dagger from his right thigh, and thrust it into his belly:

And the haft also went in after the blade; and the fat closed upon the blade, so that he could not draw the dagger out of his belly; and the dirt came out.

Then Ehud went forth through the porch, and shut the doors of the parlour upon him, and locked them.

When he was gone out, his servants came; and when they saw that, behold, the doors of the parlour were locked, they said, Surely he covereth his feet in his summer chamber.

And they tarried till they were ashamed; and, behold, he opened not the doors of the parlour: therefore they took a key, and opened them: and, behold, their lord was fallen down dead on the earth.

And Ehud escaped while they tarried, and passed beyond the quarries, and escaped unto Seirath.

And it came to pass, when he was come, that he blew a trumpet in the mountain of Ephraim, and the children of Israel went down with him from the mount, and he before them.

And he said unto them, Follow after me: for the LORD hath delivered your enemies the Moabites into your hand. And they went down after him, and took the fords of Jordan toward Moab, and suffered not a man to pass over.

And they slew of Moab at that time about ten thousand men, all lusty, and all men of valour; and there escaped not a man.

So Moab was subdued that day under the hand of Israel. And the land had rest fourscore years.

Judges 3: 12–30

It is yellow July evening, we say, the thirteenth of the month; eve of the Bastille day, – when 'M. Marat', four years ago, in the crowd of the Pont Neuf, shrewdly required of that Bensenval Hussar-party, which had such friendly dispositions, 'to dismount, and give up their arms, then'; and became notable among Patriot men. Four years: what a road he has travelled; – and sits now about half-past seven of the clock, stewing in slipper-bath; sore afflicted; ill of Revolution Fever, – of what other malady this History had rather not name. Excessively sick and worn, poor man: with precisely eleven-pence-halfpenny of ready-money in paper; with slipper-bath; strong three-footed stool for writing on, the while; and a squalid – Washerwoman, one may call her: that is his civic establishment in Medical-School Street; thither and not else-whither has his road led him. Not to the reign of Brotherhood and Perfect Felicity; yet surely on the way towards that? – Hark, a rap again! A musical woman's voice, refusing to be rejected: it is the Citoyenne who would do France a service. Marat, recognizing from within, cries Admit her. Charlotte Corday is admitted.

Citoyen Marat, I am from Caen the seat of rebellion, and wished to speak with you. – Be seated, *mon enfant*. Now what are the Traitors doing at Caen? What Deputies are at Caen? – Charlotte names some Deputies. 'Their heads shall fall within a fortnight,' croaks the eager People's-friend, clutching his tablets to write: *Barbaroux, Pétion*, writes he with bare shrunk arm, turning aside in the bath: *Pétion*, and *Louvet*, and – Charlotte has drawn her knife from the sheath; plunges it, with one sure stroke, into the writer's heart. '*À moi, chère amie*, Help, dear!' no more could the Death-choked say or shriek. The helpful Washerwoman running in, there is no Friend of the People, or Friend of the Washerwoman left; but his life with a groan gushes out, indignant, to the shades below.

And so Marat People's-friend is ended; the lone Stylites has got hurled down suddenly from his Pillar – *whitherward* He that made him knows. Patriot Paris may sound triple and tenfold, in dole and wail; re-echoed by Patriot France; and the Convention, 'Chabot pale with terror, declaring that they are to be all assassinated,' may decree him Pantheon Honours, Public Funeral, Mirabeau's dust making way for him; and Jacobin Societies, in lamentable oratory, summing up his character, parallel him to One, whom they think it honour to call 'the good Sansculotte', – whom we name not here; also a Chapel may be made, for the urn that holds his Heart, in the Place du Carrousel; and new-born children be named Marat; and Lago-di-Como Hawkers bake mountains of stucco into unbeautiful Busts; and David point his Picture, or Death-Scene; and such other Apotheosis take place as the human genius, in these circumstances, can devise: but Marat returns no more to the light of this Sun. One sole circumstance we have read with clear sympathy, in the old *Moniteur* Newspaper: how Marat's Brother comes from Neuchâtel to ask of the Convention, 'that the deceased Jean-Paul Marat's musket be given him.' For Marat too had a brother, and natural affections; and was wrapt once in swaddling clothes, and slept safe in a cradle like the rest of us. Ye children of men! – A sister of his, they say, lives still to this day in Paris.

As for Charlotte Corday her work is accomplished; the recompense of it is near and sure. The *chère amie*, and neighbours of the house, flying at her, she 'overturns some movables', entrenches herself till the gendarmes arrive; then quietly surrenders; goes quietly to the Abbaye Prison: she alone quiet, all Paris sounding, in wonder, in rage or admiration, round her. Duperret is put in arrest, on account of her; his Papers sealed, – which may lead to consequences. Fauchet, in like manner; though Fauchet had not so much as heard of her. Charlotte, confronted with these two Deputies, praises the grave firmness of Duperret, censures the dejection of Fauchet.

On Wednesay morning, the thronged Palais de Justice and Revolutionary Tribunal can see her face; beautiful and calm: she dates it 'fourth day of the Preparation of Peace'. A strange murmur ran through the Hall, at sight of her; you could not say of what character. Tinville has his indictments and tape-papers: the cutler of the Palais Royal will testify that he sold her the sheath-knife; 'All these details are needless,' interrupted Charlotte; 'it is I that killed Marat.' By whose instigation? – 'By no one's.' What tempted you, then? His crimes. 'I killed one man,' added she, raising her voice extremely (*extrêmement*), as they went on with their questions, 'I killed one man to save a hundred thousand; a villain to save innocents; a savage wild beast to give repose to my country. I was a Republican before the Revolution; I never wanted energy.' There is therefore nothing to be said. The public gazes astonished; the hasty limners sketch her features, Charlotte not disapproving: the men of law proceed with their formalities. The doom is Death as a murderess. To her Advocate she gives thanks; in gentle phrase, in high-flown classical spirit. To the priest they send her she gives thanks; but needs not any shriving, any ghostly or other aid from him.

On this same evening therefore, about half-past seven o'clock, from the gate of the Conciergerie, to a City all on tiptoe, the fatal Cart issues; seated on it a fair young creature, sheeted in red smock of murderess; so beautiful, serene, so full of life; journeying towards death, – alone amid the World. Many take off their hats, saluting reverently; for what heart but must be touched? Others growl and howl. Adam Lux, of Mentz, declares that she is greater than Brutus; that it were beautiful to die with her: the head of this young man seems turned. At the Place de la Révolution, the countenance of Charlotte wears the same still smile. The executioners proceed to bind her feet; she resists, thinking it meant as an insult; on a word of explanation, she submits with cheerful apology. As the last act, all being now ready, they take the neckerchief from her neck; a blush of maidenly shame overspreads that fair face and neck; the cheeks were still tinged with it when the executioner lifted the severed head, to show it to the people. 'It is most true,' says Forster, 'that he struck the cheek insultingly; for I saw it with my eyes: the Police imprisoned him for it.'

In this manner have the Beautifullest and the Squalidest come in collision, and extinguished one another. Jean-Paul Marat and Marie-Anne Charlotte Corday both, suddenly, are no more.

Thomas Carlyle, *The French Revolution: a History*

With a phalanx of Dallas police motorcycle officers clearing the way ahead, the big limousine carrying the Kennedys made a 90-degree turn from Main onto Houston in front of the Dallas County Sheriff's Office. Almost two dozen deputies and other lawmen stood on the sidewalk watching. All had been ordered not to take part in motorcade security.

The bright sun began warming the car's occupants as they approached the Texas School Book Depository. Atop the building was a large Hertz Rent-A-Car sign containing a digital time and temperature display. In front of the Depository, the limousine slowed to a crawl to make a 120-degree turn onto Elm Street, although turns of more than 90 degrees were prohibited by the Secret Service. The turn was so tight that Greer almost ran the limousine up onto the north curb near the Depository's front door, according to Depository superintendent Roy Truly.

The car continued a slow glide down the incline of Elm into Dealey Plaza, maintaining its position in the center lane of the three-lane street. The crowds thinned out as the Triple Underpass approached and security men began to relax. About three car lengths ahead of the presidential limousine in the lead car, Agent Lawson, a former Army counterintelligence man now with the Secret Service White House detail was sitting in the right front seat. He looked at his watch. It was 12:30 p.m. Picking up the car's microphone, he radioed the Trade Mart saying: 'We'll be there in about five minutes.'

In the presidential limousine, Kennedy was waving to his right at a group of people standing near a sign reading STEMMONS FREEWAY. His right arm and hand were slightly over the side of the car. Mrs Kennedy had been waving to her left, but her thoughts were on the Texas heat. Mrs Kennedy later told the Warren Commission: 'And in the motorcade, you know, I usually would be waving mostly to the left side and he was waving mostly to the right, which is one reason you are not looking at each other very much. And it was terribly hot. Just blinding all of us.' Sensing her discomfort, Mrs Connally turned and said: 'We'll soon be there.'

Mrs Kennedy recalled seeing the Triple Underpass ahead: 'We could see a tunnel in front of us. Everything was really slow then. And I remember thinking it would be so cool under that tunnel.'

Mrs Connally had been wanting to mention the warm and enthusiastic welcome for some time, but she had held back. Now she could contain herself no longer. Turning to Kennedy, she said: 'Mr President, you can't say that Dallas doesn't love you.' According to Mrs Kennedy, the President smiled and replied: 'No, you certainly can't.'

Soon after this remark, Mrs Connally heard a frightening noise off to her right. She looked in that direction and caught a peripheral glimpse of Kennedy raising both hands to his neck. She heard no sound from the President, but noticed a blank, 'nothing' expression on his face.

Kellerman, sitting directly in front of Connally and Kennedy, noticed they had just passed a highway sign when he heard a 'pop' to his right and immediately looked in that direction, surveying the easternmost slope of the Grassy Knoll. Kellerman told the Warren Commission:

as I turned my head to the right to view whatever it was . . . I heard a voice from the back seat and I firmly believe it was the President's [saying] 'My God, I am hit,' and I turned around and he has got his hands up here like this [indicating both hands up near the head] . . . [It] was enough for me to verify that the man was hit. So, in the same motion I come right back and grabbed the speaker and said to the driver, 'Let's get out of here; we're hit,' and grabbed the mike and I said, 'Lawson, this is Kellerman . . . we are hit; get us to the hospital immediately.' Now in the seconds that I talked just now, a flurry of shells come into the car . . .

Mrs Connally testified she heard Kellerman say: 'Pull out of the motorcade. Take us to the nearest hospital.' The limousine indeed pulled out of the motorcade and raced to Parkland Hospital.

Driver Greer said he was busy looking ahead to the railroad overpass when he heard a noise he thought was a motorcycle backfire. Then he heard the noise again and caught a glimpse of Connally starting to slump over. He then heard two more noises that seemed to come one on top of the other. Greer said after the second noise and a glance over his right shoulder at Connally, he stepped on the accelerator. However, a film taken that day shows the limousine brake lights remained on until after the fatal head shot to Kennedy.

Mrs Connally recalled that after the first sound 'very soon there was the second shot which hit John [Connally]'.

Connally, in testimony consistent both with that of Mrs Connally and with films made that day, confirmed he was not hit by the first shot. The governor said just after making the turn onto Elm he heard a noise he took to be a shot from a high-powered rifle. He turned to his right because the sound appeared to come from over his right shoulder, but he couldn't see anything. He began to turn to his left when he felt something strike him in the back.

Although critically wounded, Connally was conscious of shots being fired other than the one that struck him. Realizing that he had been hit a second or so after hearing a shot, Connally told the Warren Commission: '. . . there were either two or three people involved or more in this or someone was shooting with an automatic rifle.' Connally then heard a final boom and heard the bullet hit home. He later recalled: '. . . it never entered my mind that it ever hit anyone but the President . . . He never uttered a sound that I heard.'

Connally noticed blue brain tissue covering his suit and knew Kennedy was dead. He also noticed blood on the front of his shirt and realized he was hurt badly, perhaps, fatally. Crumpling into the arms of his wife, Connally screamed out: 'My God, they're going to kill us all!' Connally heard his wife saying over and over, 'Be still, you're going to be all right,' and he felt the car accelerate. He then lost consciousness.

During the initial phase of the shooting, Mrs Kennedy did not realize what was happening. She was accustomed to the sounds of motorcycle escorts backfiring and the motorcade had been a cacophony of sirens, racing motors, cheering, and shouting. She did hear Connally shout, 'Oh, no, no, no!' She heard 'terrible noises' to her right and turned to see Kennedy with his hand at his throat and a 'quizzical look on his face'. Then, the chief executive was struck in the head and fell into her lap. All she could do was cradle him and say: 'Oh, my God, they've shot my husband . . . I love you, Jack.'

Over the years a great deal of misinformation has been presented about her next actions. Many persons have stated she tried to climb out of the car in panic or to help Agent Hill. Actually, she crawled onto the trunk of the limousine and, reaching out, picked up a piece of her husband's head.

Mrs Kennedy, when talking to the Warren Commission on June 5, 1964, did not even recall this activity. But her action was captured in the films taken that day and later, sitting in Parkland Hospital, she still had the piece of skull clutched in her hand, according to a nurse who relieved her of the gruesome fragment.

Also, there is the testimony of Clint Hill, who told the Warren Commission:

Between the time I originally grabbed the handhold and until I was up on the car, Mrs Kennedy – the second noise that I heard had removed a portion of the President's head, and he slumped noticeably to his left. Mrs Kennedy had jumped up from the seat and was, it appeared to me, reaching for something coming off the right rear bumper of the car, the right rear tail, when she noticed that I was trying to climb on the car.

In the lead car, which was just about to enter the Triple Underpass when the firing began, Agent Lawson was trying to signal a policeman standing with a group of people on top of the underpass. He didn't like the idea of the President's car passing directly below these people, so he was trying to get the officer to move them to one side. The policeman never noticed him.

Just then, Lawson heard a loud report to his rear. It sounded more like a bang instead of a crack and Lawson didn't think it was a rifle shot. His first impression was that it was a firecracker. This description was to be repeated by nearly everyone in Dealey Plaza, with some notable exceptions.

Forrest V. Sorrels, head of the Dallas office of the Secret Service, like Connally was certain the first sound was a gunshot. After a brief pause, Sorrels heard two more shots coming close together. He shouted to Curry: 'Let's get out of here!'

On hearing the first burst of firing, Sheriff Decker glanced back and thought he saw a bullet bouncing off the street pavement.

Another Dallas motorcycle officer, Starvis Ellis, in 1978 told the House Select Committee on Assassinations that as he rode alongside the car in which Decker was riding he, too, saw a bullet hit the pavement. Neither Decker nor Ellis were ever questioned about this by the Warren Commission.

Motorcycle officer James Chaney told newsmen the next day that the first shot missed.

Curry saw a 'commotion' in the presidential limousine. Then a motorcycle officer drew up alongside. 'Anybody hurt?' asked Curry. 'Yes,' replied the officer. Stepping on the accelerator, Curry shouted: 'Lead us to the hospital.' Both Decker and Curry took the car's radio and ordered their men to rush to the top of the underpass and the railroad yards where they thought the shots had come from.

Like the crowd of witnesses in the Dealey Plaza, those persons deep into the plaza believed shots were fired from the Grassy Knoll, while those farther back in the motorcade – still on Houston and Main streets – believed shots came from the direction of the Depository.

Motorcycle policeman Marrion L. Baker was riding near one of the press cars. He had just turned on to Houston and his cycle was about to tip over because of a gust of wind and the slow speed. He had just returned from a deer-hunting trip and recognized the first sound as a high-powered rifle shot. He thought the sound came from either the Depository or the Dal-Tex building. Seeing pigeons fluttering off the Depository's roof, he gunned his motor and roared up to the entrance of the building. Within seconds, he and Depository superintendent Roy Truly would encounter Lee Harvey Oswald calmly standing in the second-floor lunchroom of the Depository.

Secret Service agent Paul Landis was riding in the right rear of the Secret Service follow-up car when he heard the report of a high-powered rifle. He saw Kennedy turn to look in the direction of the shot, which Landis believed came from '. . . somewhere towards the front, right-hand side of the road'.

With Landis was Secret Service agent Glen Bennett, who thought the sound was a firecracker. But then he looked at the President. In notes he said were made later that day, Bennett wrote: '[I] saw a shot that hit the Boss about four inches down from the right shoulder; a second shoot [*sic*] followed immediately and hit the right rear high [side?] of the Boss's head.'

The Secret Service agents assigned to Kennedy all acted with remarkable sluggishness when the firing began. Perhaps it was due to the visit they had paid to a 'beatnik' nightspot in Fort Worth, where they stayed until early that morning. (The club, The Cellar, was owned by an acquaintance of Jack Ruby who had connections with both big-time gamblers and police officials.)

The only agent to react with speed was Clint Hill. Hill had not been scheduled to make the Dallas trip, but came only after Mrs Kennedy made a personal request. Hill also thought the initial sound was a firecracker and began looking to his right for the source of the sound when he saw Kennedy grab at himself and lurch forward slightly. He then realized something was wrong and jumped off the follow-up car. He was racing the few feet to the limousine when he heard more shots. Hill had just secured a grip on a handhold when the car began accelerating. Looking into the back seat of the limousine, Hill saw that the right rear portion of the President's head was missing.

Nearly everyone present recalled a pause of several seconds between the first burst of fire and the final two shots, these coming rapidly one after another. It was the third and final shot, or volley of shots, that killed President John F. Kennedy. Until then, he had been immobile and quiet, only sagging slightly to his left. Then his head pitched forward violently for a split second only to be pushed hard to the left and rear. A halo of crimson liquid and tissue surrounded his head momentarily and then fell to the rear. The head shot lifted him slightly then threw him against the car's back seat. He bounced forward and over into his wife's lap.

The two Dallas motorcycle officers riding to the left rear of the limousine, Bobby W. Hargis and B. J. Martin, were splattered by blood and brain matter. Martin, who had looked to his right after the first shots, later found bloodstains on the left side of his helmet. Hargis, who was riding nearest the limousine about six to eight feet from the left rear fender, saw Kennedy's head explode and was hit by bits of flesh and bone with such impact that he told reporters he thought he had been shot.

Presidential assistant David Powers was riding with Secret Service agents in the car directly behind the President. From this vantage point, he described the entire assassination:

I commented to Ken O'Donnell that it was 12:30 and we would only be about five minutes late when we arrived at the Trade Mart. Shortly thereafter the first shot went off and it sounded to me as if it were a firecracker. I noticed then that the President moved quite far to his left after the shot from the extreme right hand side where he had been sitting. There was a second shot and Governor Connally disappeared from sight and then there was a third shot which took off the top of the President's head and had the sickening sound of a grapefruit splattering against the side of a wall. The total time between the first and third shots was about five or six seconds. My first impression was that the shots came from the right and overhead but I also had a fleeting impression that the noise appeared to come from the front in the area of the Triple Underpass. This may have resulted from my feeling, when I looked forward toward the overpass, that we might have ridden into an ambush.

Several persons in the motorcade smelled gunpowder as the cars swept through the lower end of Dealey Plaza.

Mrs Earle Cabell, wife of the Dallas Mayor, was riding in an open convertible six cars back from the motorcade's lead car. At the opening shots, the car in which she was riding was passing the Depository building. She told the Warren Commission she jerked her head up on hearing the first shot because 'I heard the direction from which the shot came . . .' Looking up, she saw an object projecting from one of the top windows of the Depository building. She said:

I jerked my head up and I saw something in that window and I turned around to say to Earle, 'Earle, it is a shot,' and before I got the words out . . . the second two shots rang out . . . I was acutely aware of the odor of gunpowder. I was aware that the motorcade stopped dead still. There was no question about that.

Mrs Cabell was riding beside Congressman Ray Roberts. She said he acknowledged smelling gunpowder too.

Former senator Ralph Yarborough also smelled gunpowder as the car carrying him and Lyndon Johnson drove through the plaza. Yarborough, a former Army infantry officer and an avid hunter, also failed to recognize the sound of the first shot. He told this author:

I thought, 'Was that a bomb thrown?' and then the other shots were fired. And the motorcade which had slowed to a stop, took off. A second or two later, I smelled gunpowder. I always thought that was strange because, being familiar with firearms, I never could see how I could smell the powder from a rifle high in that building.

It does seem strange that people would smell powder from a shot fired more than sixty feet in the air and behind them. However, it's not so strange, if a shot were fired on top of the Grassy Knoll less than twelve feet in elevation with a breeze from the north to carry smoke to street level.

One of the strangest omissions in the subsequent investigation by federal authorities concerns a Navy commander who was assigned to film major events involving President Kennedy. In early 1963, Thomas Atkins was assigned as an official photographer for the Kennedy White House. As such, he traveled to Texas with Kennedy and was photographing the motorcade with a quality camera, a 16 mm Arriflex S.

He was riding six cars behind Kennedy and filming as the motorcade moved through Dealey Plaza.

In a 1977 article, Atkins said the car he was in had just turned onto Houston Street and was facing the Texas School Book Depository, and

. . . Kennedy's car had just made the left turn heading toward the freeway entrance. Although I did not look up at the building, I could hear everything quite clearly. . . . The shots came from below and off to the right side from where I was [the location of the Grassy Knoll]. . . . I never thought the shots came from above. They did not sound like shots coming from anything higher than street level.

After returning to Washington on *Air Force Two*, Atkins assembled his film into a movie he entitled *The Last Two Days*. That film was described as 'terribly damaging to the Warren Commission finding that Lee Harvey Oswald was the lone assassin.' Perhaps this explains why neither Atkin's testimony nor his film were studied by either of the federal panels investigating the assassination. Atkins said in 1977: 'It's something I've always wondered about. Why didn't they ask me what I knew? I not only was on the White House staff, I was then, and still am, a photographer with a pretty keen visual sense.'

Obviously, the federal authorities didn't want to hear from a man with a 'keen visual sense' and strong credentials who might have told them things they did not want to hear.

But if the stories of the motorcade witnesses differed from the later official version of the assassination, that was nothing compared to the stories to come from the crowd of bystanders.

• • •

Summary

In reviewing the experiences of the people in Dealey Plaza the day Kennedy died, it is apparent that not one single person saw the assassination as it was described by the Warren Commission.

In the motorcade, Governor Connally's testimony – totally corroborated by the Zapruder film – indicated that both he and Kennedy could not have been struck by the same bullet.

Many people, including Sheriff Decker, Royce Skelton, and Austin Miller, saw one bullet strike Elm Street. Others, like Policeman Foster, saw a bullet hit the grass on the south side of Elm.

Many people heard shots coming from at least two separate locations, while those on the Triple Underpass even saw smoke drift out from under the trees on the Grassy Knoll.

The motorcade had difficulty negotiating the sharp turn onto Elm that the Secret Service advance men had failed to properly scrutinize. The Secret Service also refused additional security offered by Dallas police.

An unexplained change in the motorcade lineup moved press photographers far back in line, preventing them from photographing the assassination.

Motorcade riders heard shots from separate locations, but the majority believed shots came from the direction of the Triple Underpass. Both

Sheriff Decker and Police Chief Curry ordered their men to rush to the railroad yards behind the Grassy Knoll.

The only Secret Service agent to react quickly to the assassination was Clint Hill, who was not originally scheduled for the Dallas trip and was assigned to Mrs Kennedy.

Mrs Cabell and former senator Yarborough, among others, reported smelling gunpowder while passing through Dealey Plaza.

Some members of the crowd, such as Phillip Hathaway, Julia Ann Mercer, Julius Hardie, and the Arnold Rowlands, saw men with rifles in the area of Dealey Plaza long before the Kennedy motorcade arrived.

Several bystanders, their testimony suported by at least two films made that day, claimed to have seen more than one man on the sixth floor of the Texas School Book Depository moments before the assassination.

Some witnesses – Phil Willis, Jean Hill, Julia Mercer, and Dallas policeman Tom Tilson – even claim they saw Jack Ruby in Dealey Plaza at the time of the assassination.

People standing in front of the Depository thought shots came from down near the Triple Underpass.

Others, such as A. J. Millican, the John Chisms, and Jean Newman, who were standing between the Depository and the Underpass, believed the shots came from the Grassy Knoll.

Two of the most suspicious men in Dealey Plaza – subsequently nicknamed the 'umbrella man' and the 'dark-complected man' – were never identified or even mentioned by the Warren Commission. Yet both men made visual signals just as Kennedy drew opposite them. Moments later the dark man appeared to be talking into a radio.

The House Select Committee on Assassinations claimed to have located the 'umbrella man', but the man they found told a story totally inconsisent with the activities of the 'umbrella man' as recorded on film that day. And the Committee never bothered to mention the man with what appeared to be a walkie-talkie.

Neither could the Warren Commission seem to locate a woman filming the assassination who came to be known to researchers as the 'babushka lady'. The House Committee took testimony from this woman after she was identified by researchers as Beverly Oliver, but never mentioned her in its report.

Oliver, an acquaintance of Jack Ruby, has told researchers she was introduced by Ruby to 'Lee Oswald of the CIA' prior to the assassination.

Jean Hill, who was standing beside Mary Moorman on the south side of Elm Street at the moment of the assassination, said she saw a man fire from behind the wooden picket fence on the Grassy Knoll and saw smoke drift from this location.

Hill's story is supported by the testimony of railroad supervisor S. M. Holland, who told government investigators, he, too, saw smoke drifting from the Knoll. Holland's account is corroborated by other men on the Triple Underpass, such as Richard Dodd, James Simmons, Austin Miller, Frank Reilly, and Thomas Murphy – none of whom were asked to testify before the Warren Commission.

Even employees of the Depository, both inside and outside that building, stated shots came from the direction of the Grassy Knoll.

Three employees – Bonnie Ray Williams, Harold Norman, and James Jarman – were sitting just below the sixth-floor window later identified as the sniper's window. Despite their later testimony that they heard shots right above their heads, they all said they ran to the west side of the building because they believed that shots had come from west of the Depository.

Less than sixty seconds after shots were fired, Dallas policeman Marrion Baker and Depository superintendent Roy Truly encountered another Depository employee – Lee Harvey Oswald – in the building's second-floor lunchroom holding a Coke in his hand and appearing calm and unperturbed.

At least one Depository employee, Joe Molina, was intimidated by authorities and lost his job soon after the assassination.

One man, James Tague, was the third man wounded in Dealey Plaza when his cheek was bloodied by cement sent flying by a bullet striking the curb just east of the Triple Underpass.

Apparently it was reports of Tague's wounding that forced the Warren Commission to revise their account of the assassination. Where they had originally concluded that one shot hit Kennedy in the upper back, another struck Governor Connally, and a third struck Kennedy's head, they finally settled on the 'single-bullet theory', which states that one bullet passed through both Kennedy and Connally, another missed altogether, striking the curb near Tague, and a third shot struck Kennedy fatally in the head.

Despite great efforts on the part of authorities to establish the Depository as the source of all shots, public attention – both in 1963 and today – kept returning to the infamous Grassy Knoll.

Photographer Abraham Zapruder clearly stated that the shots came from the Knoll behind him. His testimony is corroborated by Dealey Plaza groundskeeper Emmett Hudson, who reported that shots came from the Knoll above and behind him.

Lee Bowers, a railroad employee who was in a railroad tower overlooking the back of the Knoll, told of seeing men with radios in strange cars cruising the area just prior to the assassination. He also reported seeing a flash of light and smoke from behind the fence on the Knoll at the time of the shooting.

Gordon Arnold, a young soldier, said he was chased from behind the wooden picket fences shortly before Kennedy arrived by a man showing Secret Service identification. He said he was in front of the fence on the Knoll filming the motorcade when a shot was fired from over his left shoulder from behind the fence. He said moments later two policemen took his film and he fled.

A gunman behind the picket fence may have been captured in a photograph taken by Mary Moorman. A recent enlargement of the Knoll area in her photo seems to reveal a man firing a rifle. The man is dressed in what appears to be a police uniform. The existence of this gunman is further confirmed by the acoustical studies commissioned by the House Select Committee on Assassinations in 1979. The results of these tests forced the Committee to reluctantly conclude that a second gunman fired on Kennedy from behind the Knoll fence.

The deaf-mute Ed Hoffman tried to inform the FBI after the assassination that he had witnessed a man with a rifle behind the picket fence on the Grassy Knoll. However, Hoffman was warned to keep quiet or 'you might get killed' by an FBI agent, and reports of his sighting were hidden from the public for twenty-two years.

Conclusions to be drawn from the wide range of testimony by people in Dealey Plaza on November 22, 1963, include:

- There was much confusion and panic among the people watching the presidential motorcade.
- The majority of witnesses originally believed the shots came from the area of the Grassy Knoll.
- The preponderance of evidence indicates shots came from two different directions – the Grassy Knoll and the direction of the Depository.
- There is nothing in the available evidence that rules out the possibility that more shots from other directions were fired.
- The activities of the federal authorities, especially the Secret Service and FBI, before, during, and after the assassination, have raised serious suspicions in the minds of researchers.

Jim Marrs, *Crossfire*

Assassins

The Sheikh was called in their language Alaodin. He had had made in a valley between two mountains the biggest and most beautiful garden that was ever seen, planted with all the finest fruits in the world and containing the most splendid mansions and palaces that were ever seen, ornamented with gold and with likenesses of all that is beautiful on earth, and also four conduits, one flowing with wine, one with milk, one with honey, and one with water. There were fair ladies there and damsels, the loveliest in the world, unrivalled at playing every sort of instrument and at singing and dancing. And he gave his men to understand that this garden was Paradise. That is why he had made it after this pattern, because Mahomet assured the Saracens that those who go to Paradise will have beautiful women to their hearts' content to do their bidding and will find there rivers of wine and milk and honey and water. So he had had this garden made like the Paradise that Mahomet promised to the Saracens, and the Saracens of this country believed that it really was Paradise. No one ever entered the garden except those whom he wished to make Assassin. At the entrance stood a castle so strong that it need fear no man in the world, and there was no other way in except through this castle. The Sheikh kept with him at his court all the youths of the country from twelve years old to twenty, all, that is, who shaped well as men at arms. These youths knew well by hearsay that Mahomet their prophet had declared Paradise to be made in such a fashion as I have described, and so they accepted it as truth. Now mark what follows. He used to put some of these youths in this Paradise, four at a time, or ten, or twenty, according as he wished. And this is how he did it. He would give them draughts that sent them to sleep on the spot. Then he had them taken and put in the garden, where they were wakened. When they awoke and found themselves in there and saw all the things I have told you of, they believed they were really in Paradise. And the ladies and damsels stayed with them all the time, singing and making music for their delight and ministering to all their desires. So these youths had all they could wish for and asked nothing better than to remain there.

Now the Sheikh held his court with great splendour and magnificence and bore himself most nobly and convinced the simple mountain folk round about that he was a prophet; and they believed it to be the truth. And when he wanted emissaries to send on some mission of murder, he would administer the drug to as many as he pleased; and while they slept he had them carried into his palace. When these youths awoke and found themselves in the castle within the palace, they were amazed and by no means glad, for the Paradise from whch they had come was not a place that they would ever willingly have left. They went forthwith to the Sheikh and humbled themselves before him, as men who believed that he was a great prophet. When he asked them whence they came, they would answer that they came from Paradise, and that this was in truth the Paradise of which Mahomet had told their ancestors; and they would tell their listeners all that they had found there. And the others who heard this and had not been there were filled with a great longing to go to this Paradise; they longed for death so that they might go there, and looked forward eagerly to the day of their going.

When the Sheikh desired the death of some great lord, he would first try an experiment to find out which of his Assassins were the best. He would send some off on a mission in the neighbourhood at no great distance with orders to kill such and such a man. They went without demur and did the bidding of their lord. Then, when they had killed the man, they returned to court – those of them that escaped, for some were caught and put to death. When they had returned to their lord and told him that they had faithfully performed their task, the Sheikh would make a great feast in their honour. And he knew very well which of them had displayed the greatest zeal, because after each he had sent others of his men as spies to report which was the most daring and the best hand at murdering. Then, in order to bring about the death of the lord or other man which he desired, he would take some of these Assassins of his and send them wherever he might wish, telling them that he was minded to dispatch them to Paradise: they were to go accordingly and kill such and such a man; if they died on their mission, they would go there all the sooner. Those who received such a command obeyed it with a right good will, more readily than anything else they might have been called on to do. Away they went and did all that they were commanded. Thus it happened that no one ever escaped when the Sheikh of the Mountain desired his death.

The Travels of Marco Polo, trans. R. E. Latham

Axe

Lizzie Borden took an ax
And gave her mother forty whacks.
When she saw what she had done,
She gave her father forty-one.

4 August 1892, Fall River, Massachusetts
Lizzie Borden was acquitted after a thirteen-day trial.

The door was as before opened a tiny crack, and again two sharp and suspicious eyes stared at him out of the darkness. Then Raskolnikov lost his head and nearly made a great mistake.

Fearing the old woman would be frightened by their being alone, and not hoping that the sight of him would disarm her suspicions, he took hold of the door and drew it towards him to prevent the old woman from attempting to shut it again. Seeing this she did not pull the door back, but she did not let go the handle so that he almost dragged her out with it on to the stairs. Seeing that she was standing in the doorway not allowing him to pass, he advanced straight upon her. She stepped back in alarm, tried to say something, but seemed unable to speak and stared with open eyes at him.

'Good evening, Alyona Ivanovna,' he began, trying to speak easily, but his voice would not obey him, it broke and shook. 'I have come . . . I have brought something . . . but we'd better come in . . . to the light . . .'

And leaving her, he passed straight into the room uninvited. The old woman ran after him; her tongue was unloosed.

'Good heavens! What is it? Who is it? What do you want?'

'Why, Alyona Ivanovna, you know me . . . Raskolnikov . . . here, I brought you the pledge I promised the other day . . .' And he held out the pledge.

The old woman glanced for a moment at the pledge, but at once stared in the eyes of her uninvited visitor. She looked intently, maliciously, and mistrustfully. A minute passed; he even fancied something like a sneer in her eyes, as though she had already guessed everything. He felt that he was losing his head, that he was almost frightened, so frightened that if she were to look like that and not say a word for another half-minute, he thought he would have run away from her.

'Why do you look at me as though you did not know me?' he said suddenly, also with malice. 'Take it if you like, if not I'll go elsewhere. I am in a hurry.'

He had not even thought of saying this, but it was suddenly said of itself. The old woman recovered herself, and her visitor's resolute tone evidently restored her confidence.

'But why, my good sir, all of a minute . . . What is it?' she asked, looking at the pledge.

'The silver cigarette-case; I spoke of it last time, you know.'

She held out her hand.

'But how pale you are, to be sure . . . and your hands are trembling too? Have you been bathing, or what?'

'Fever,' he answered abruptly. 'You can't help getting pale . . . if you've nothing to eat,' he added, with difficulty articulating the words.

His strength was failing him again. But his answer sounded like the truth; the old woman took the pledge.

'What is it?' she asked once more, scanning Raskolnikov intently and weighing the pledge in her hand.

'A thing . . . cigarette-case . . . Silver . . . Look at it.'

'It does not seem somehow like silver . . . How he has wrapped it up!'

Trying to untie the string and turning to the window, to the light (all her windows were shut, in spite of the stifling heat), she left him altogether for some seconds and stood with her back to him. He unbuttoned his coat and freed the axe from the noose, but did not yet take it out altogether, simply holding it in his right hand under the coat. His hands were fearfully weak, he felt them every moment growing more numb and more wooden. He was afraid he would let the axe slip and fall . . . A sudden giddiness came over him.

'But what has he tied it up like this for?' the old woman cried with vexation and moved towards him.

He had not a minute more to lose. He pulled the axe quite out, swung it with both arms, scarcely conscious of himself, and almost without effort, almost mechanically, brought the blunt side down on her head. He seemed not to use his own strength in this. But as soon as he had once brought the axe down his strength returned to him.

The old woman was as always bareheaded. Her thin, light hair, streaked with grey, thickly smeared with grease, was plaited in a rat's tail and fastened by a broken horn comb which stood out on the nape of her neck. As she was so short the blow fell on the very top of her skull. She cried out, but very faintly, and suddenly sank all of a heap on the floor, raising her hands to her head. In one hand she still held 'the pledge'.

Then he dealt her another and another blow with the blunt side and in the same spot. The blood gushed as from an overturned glass, the body fell back. He stepped back, let it fall, and at once bent over her face; she was dead. Her eyes seemed to be starting out of their sockets, the brow and the whole face were drawn and contorted convulsively.

He laid the axe on the ground near the dead body and felt at once in her pocket (trying to avoid the streaming blood) – the same right-hand pocket from which she had taken the key on his last visit. He was in full possession of his faculties, free from confusion or giddiness, but his hands were still trembling. He remembered afterwards that he had been particularly collected and careful, trying all the time not to get smeared with blood . . . He pulled out the keys at once, they were all, as before, in one bunch on a steel ring. He ran at once into the bedroom with them. It was a very small room with a whole shrine of holy images. Against the other wall stood a big bed, very clean and covered with a silk patchwork wadded quilt. Against a third wall was a chest of drawers. Strange to say, so soon as he began to fit the keys into the chest, so soon as he heard their jingling, a convulsive shudder passed over him. He suddenly felt tempted again to give it all up and go away. But that was only for an instant; it was too late to go back. He positively smiled at himself, when suddenly another terrifying idea occurred to his mind. He suddenly fancied that the old woman might be still alive and might recover her senses. Leaving the keys in the chest, he ran back to the body, snatched up the axe, and lifted it once more over the old woman, but did not bring it down. There was no doubt that she was dead. Bending down and examining her again more closely, he saw clearly that the skull was broken and even battered in on one side. He was about to feel it with his finger, but drew back his hand and indeed it was evident without that. Meanwhile there was a perfect pool of blood. All at once he noticed a string on her neck; he tugged at it, but the string was strong and did not snap and, besides, it was soaked with blood. He tried to pull it out from the front of the dress, but something held it and prevented its coming. In his impatience he raised the axe again to cut the string from above on the body, but did not dare, and with difficulty, smearing his hand and the axe in the blood, after two minutes' hurried effort, he cut the string and took it off without touching the body with the axe; he was not mistaken – it was a purse. On the string were two crosses, one of Cyprus wood and one of copper, and an image in silver filigreee, and with them a small greasy chamois leather purse with a steel rim and ring. The purse was stuffed very full. Raskolnikov thrust it in his pocket without looking at it, flung the crosses on the old woman's body, and rushed back into the bedroom, this time taking the axe with him.

He was in terrible haste, he snatched the keys, and began trying them again. But he was unsuccessful. They would not fit in the locks. It was not so much that his hands were shaking, but that he kept making mistakes; though he saw for instance that a key was not the right one and would not fit, still he tried to put it in. Suddenly he remembered and realized that the big key with the deep notches, which was hanging there with the small keys, could not possibly belong to the chest of drawers (on his last visit this had struck him) but to some strong-box, and that everything perhaps was hidden in that box. He left the chest of drawers, and at once felt under the bedstead, knowing that old women usually keep boxes under their beds. And so it was; there was a good-sized box under the bed, at least a yard in length, with an arched lid covered with red leather and studded with steel nails. The notched key fitted at once and unlocked it. At the top, under a white sheet, was a coat of red brocade lined with hareskin; under it was a silk dress, then a shawl, and it seemed as though there was nothing below but clothes. The first thing he did was to wipe his blood-stained hands on the red brocade. 'It's red, and on red blood will be less noticeable,' the thought passed through his mind; then he suddenly came to himself. 'Good God, am I going out of my senses?' he thought with terror.

But no sooner did he touch the clothes than a gold watch slipped from under the fur coat. He made haste to turn them all over. There turned out to be various articles made of gold among the clothes – probably all pledges, unredeemed or waiting to be redeemed – bracelets, chains, earrings, pins, and such things. Some were in cases, others simply wrapped in newspaper, carefully and exactly folded and tied round with tape. Without any delay, he began filling up the pockets of his trousers and overcoat without examining or undoing the parcels and cases; but he had not time to take many . . .

He suddenly heard steps in the room where the old woman lay. He stopped short and was still as death. But all was quiet, so it must have been his fancy. All at once he heard distinctly a faint cry, as though someone had uttered a low broken moan. Then again dead silence for a minute or two. He sat squatting on his heels by the box and waited, holding his breath. Suddenly he jumped up, seized the axe, and ran out of the bedroom.

In the middle of the room stood Lizaveta with a big bundle in her arms. She was gazing in stupefaction at her murdered sister, white as a sheet, and seeming not to have the strength to cry out. Seeing him run out of the bedroom, she began faintly quivering all over, like a leaf, a shudder ran down her face; she lifted her hand, opened her mouth, but still did not scream. She began slowly backing away from him into the corner, staring intently, persistently at him, but still uttered no sound, as though she could not get breath to scream. He rushed at her with the axe; her mouth twitched piteously, as one sees babies' mouths, when they begin to be frightened, stare intently at what frightens them, and are on the point of screaming. And this hapless Lizaveta was so simple and had been so thoroughly crushed and scared that she did not even raise a hand to guard her face, though that was the most necessary and natural action at the moment, for the axe was raised over her face. She only put up her empty left hand, but not to her face slowly holding it out before her as though motioning him away. The axe fell with the sharp edge just on the skull and split at one blow all the top of the head. She fell heavily at once, Raskolnikov completely lost his head snatching up her bundle, dropped it again, and ran into the entry.

Fear gained more and more mastery over him, especially after this second, quite unexpected murder. He longed to run away from the place as fast as possible. And if at that moment he had been capable of seeing and reasoning more correctly, if he had been able to realize all the difficulties of his position, the hopelessness, the hideousness, and the absurdity of it, if he could have understood how many obstacles and, perhaps, crimes he had still to overcome or to commit, to get out of that place and to make his way home, it is very possible that he would have flung up everything, and would have gone to give himself up, and not from fear, but from simple horror and loathing of what he had done. The feeling of loathing especially surged up within him and grew stronger every minute. He would not now have gone to the box or even into the room for anything in the world.

But a sort of blankness, even dreaminess, had begun by degrees to take possession of him; at moments he forgot himself, or rather forgot what was of importance and caught at trifles. Glancing, however, into the kitchen and seeing a bucket half full of water on a bench, he bethought him of washing his hands and the axe. His hands were sticky with blood. He dropped the axe with the blade in the water, snatched a piece of soap that lay in a broken saucer on the window, and began washing his hands in the bucket. When they were clean, he took out the axe, washed the blade, and spent a long time, about three minutes, washing the wood where there were spots of blood, rubbing them with soap. Then he wiped it all with some linen that was hanging to dry on a line in the kitchen and then he was a long while attentively examining the axe at the window. There was no trace left on it, only the wood was still damp. He carefully hung the axe in the noose under his coat. Then as far as was possible, in the dim light in the kitchen, he looked over his overcoat his trousers, and his boots. At the first glance there seemed to be nothing but stains on the boots. He wetted the rag and rubbed the boots. But he knew he was not looking thoroughly, that there might be something quite noticeable that he was overlooking. He stood in the middle of the room, lost in thought. Dark agonizing ideas rose in his mind – the idea that he was mad and that at that moment he was incapable of reasoning, of protecting himself, that he ought perhaps to be doing something utterly different from what he was now doing. 'Good God!' he muttered, 'I must fly, fly,' and he rushed into the entry. But here a shock of terror awaited him such as he had never known before.

He stood and gazed and could not believe his eyes: the door, the outer door from the stairs, at which he had not long before waited and rung, was standing unfastened and at least six inches open. No lock, no bolt, all the time, all that time! The old woman had not shut it after him perhaps as a precaution. But, good God! Why, he had seen Lizaveta afterwards! And how could he, how could he have failed to reflect that she must have come in somehow? She could not have come through the wall!

He dashed to the door and fastened the latch.

'But no, the wrong thing again! I must get away, get away . . .'

He unfastened the latch, opened the door, and began listening on the staircase.

He listened a long time. Somewhere far away, it might be in the gateway, two voices were loudly and shrilly shouting, quarrelling, and scolding. 'What are they about?' He waited patiently. At last all was still, as though suddenly cut off; they had separated. He was meaning to go out, but suddenly, on the floor below, a door was noisily opened and someone began going downstairs humming a tune. 'How is it they all make such a noise?' flashed through his mind. Once more he closed the door and waited. At last all was still, not a soul stirring. He was just taking a step towards the stairs when he heard fresh footsteps.

The steps sounded very far off, at the very bottom of the stairs, but he remembered quite clearly and distinctly that from the first sound he began for some reason to suspect that this was someone coming *there*, to the fourth floor, to the old woman. Why? Were the sounds somehow peculiar, significant? The steps were heavy, even, and unhurried. Now *he* had passed the first floor, now he was mounting higher, it was growing more and more distinct! He could hear his heavy breathing. And now the third storey had been reached. Coming here! And it seemed to him all at once that he was turned to stone, that it was like a dream in which one is being pursued, nearly caught and will be killed, and is rooted to the spot and cannot even move one's arms.

At last when the unknown was mounting to the fourth floor, he suddenly started, and succeeded in slipping neatly and quickly back into the flat and closing the door behind him. Then he took the hook and softly, noiselessly, fixed it in the catch. Instinct helped him. When he had done this, he crouched, holding his breath, by the door. The unknown visitor was by now also at the door. They were now standing opposite one another, as he had just before been standing with the old woman, when the door divided them and he was listening.

The visitor panted several times. 'He must be a big, fat man,' thought Raskolnikov, squeezing the axe in his hand. It seemed like a dream indeed. The visitor took hold of the bell and rang it loudly.

As soon as the tin bell tinkled, Raskolnikov seemed to be aware of something moving in the room. For some seconds he listened quite seriously. The unknown rang again, waited, and suddenly tugged violently and impatiently at the handle of the door. Raskolnikov gazed in horror at the hook shaking in its fastening, and in blank terror expected every minute that the fastening would be pulled out. It certainly did seem possible, so violently was he shaking it. He was tempted to hold the fastening, but *he* might be aware of it. A giddiness came over him again. 'I shall fall down!' flashed through his mind, but the unknown began to speak and he recovered himself at once.

'What's up? Are they asleep, or murdered? D-damn them!' he bawled in a thick voice. 'Hey, Alyona Ivanovna, old witch! Lizaveta Ivanovna, hey, my beauty! Open the door! Oh, damn them! Are they asleep or what?'

And again, enraged he tugged with all his might a dozen times at the bell. He must certainly be a man of authority and an intimate acquaintance.

At this moment light hurried steps were heard not far off, on the stairs. Someone else was approaching. Raskolnikov had not heard them at first.

'You don't say there's no one at home,' the newcomer cried in a cheerful ringing voice, addressing the first visitor who still went on pulling the bell. 'Good evening, Koch.'

'From his voice he must be quite young,' thought Raskolnikov.

'Who the devil can tell? I've almost broken the lock,' answered Koch. 'But how do you come to know me?'

'Why! The day before yesterday I beat you three times running at billiards at Gambrinus'.'

'Oh!'

'So they are not at home? That's queer. It's awfully stupid though. Where could the old woman have gone? I've come on business.'

'Yes; and I have business with her, too.'

'Well, what can we do? Go back, I suppose. Aie – aie! And I was hoping to get some money!' cried the young man.

'We must give it up, of course, but what did she fix this time for? The old witch fixed the time for me to come herself. It's out of my way. And where the devil she can have got to, I can't make out. She sits here from year's end to year's end, the old hag; her legs are bad and yet here all of a sudden she is out for a walk!'

'Hadn't we better ask the porter?'

'What?'

'Where she's gone and when she'll be back.'

'Hm . . . Damn it all! . . . We might ask. . . . But you know she never does go anywhere.'

And he once more tugged at the door-handle.

'Damn it all. There's nothing to be done, we must go!'

'Stay!' cried the young man suddenly. 'Do you see how the door shakes if you pull it?'

'Well?'

'That shows it's not locked, but fastened with the hook! Do you hear how the hook clanks?'

'Well?'

'Why, don't you see? That proves that one of them is at home. If they were all out, they would have locked the door from outside with the key and not with the hook from inside. There, do you hear how the hook is clanking? To fasten the hook on the inside they must be at home, don't you see? So there they are sitting inside and don't open the door!'

'Well! And so they must be!' cried Koch, astonished. 'What are they about in there?' And he began furiously shaking the door.

'Stay!' cried the young man again. 'Don't pull at it! There must be something wrong . . . Here, you've been ringing and pulling at the door and still they don't open! So either they've both fainted or – '

'What?'

'I tell you what. Let's go and fetch the porter, let him wake them up.'

'All right.'

Both were going down.

'Stay. You stop here while I run down for the porter.'

'What for?'

'Well, you'd better.'

'All right.'

'I'm studying the law, you see! It's evident, e-vi-dent there's something wrong here!' the young man cried hotly, and he ran downstairs.

Koch remained. Once more he softly touched the bell which gave one tinkle, then gently, as though reflecting and looking about him, began touching the door-handle, pulling it and letting it go to make sure once more that it was only fastened by the hook. Then puffing and panting he bent down and began looking at the keyhole: but the key was in the lock on the inside and so nothing could be seen.

Raskolnikov stood keeping tight hold of the axe. He was in a sort of delirium. He was even making ready to fight when they should come in. While they were knocking and talking together, the idea several times occurred to him to end it all at once and shout to them through the door. Now and then he was tempted to swear at them, to jeer at them, while they could not open the door! 'Only make haste!' was the thought that flashed through his mind.

'But what the devil is he about? . . .' Time was passing, one minute, and another – no one came. Koch began to be restless.

'What the devil!' he cried suddenly, and in impatience deserting his sentry duty, he too went down, hurrying and thumping with his heavy boots on the stairs. The steps died away.

'Good heavens! What am I to do?'

Raskolnikov unfastened the hook, opened the door – there was no sound. Abruptly, without any thought at all, he went out, closing the door as thoroughly as he could, and went downstairs.

He had gone down three flights when he suddenly heard a loud noise below – where could he go? There was nowhere to hide. He was just going back to the flat.

'Hey there! Catch the brute!'

Somebody dashed out of a flat below, shouting, and rather fell than ran down the stairs, bawling at the top of his voice:

'Mitka! Mitka! Mitka! Mitka! Mitka! Blast him!'

The shout ended in a shriek; the last sounds came from the yard; all was still. But at the same instant several men talking loudly and fast began noisily mounting the stairs. There were three or four of them. He distinguished the ringing voice of the young man. 'They!'

Filled with despair he went straight to meet them, feeling 'come what must!' If they stopped him – all was lost; if they let him pass – all was lost too; they would remember him. They were approaching; they were only a flight from him – and suddenly deliverance! A few steps from him, on the right, there was an empty flat with the door wide open, the flat on the second floor where the painters had been at work, and which, as though for his benefit, they had just left. It was they, no doubt, who had just run down, shouting. The floor had only just been painted, in the middle of the room stood a pail and a broken pot with paint and brushes. In one instant he had whisked in at the open door and hidden behind it, and only in the nick of time; for they had already reached the landing. Then they turned and went on up to the fourth floor, talking loudly. He waited, went out on tiptoe, and ran down the stairs.

No one was on the stairs, nor in the gateway. He passed quickly through the gateway and turned to the left in the street.

He knew, he knew perfectly well that at the moment they were at the flat, that they were greatly astonished at finding it unlocked, as the door had just been fastened, that by now they were looking at the bodies, that before another minute had passed they would guess and completely realize that the murderer had just been there, and had succeeded in hiding somewhere, slipping by them and escaping. They would guess most likely that he had been in the empty flat, while they were going upstairs. And meanwhile he dared not quicken his pace much, though the next turning was still nearly a hundred yards away. 'Should he slip through some gateway and wait somewhere in an unknown street? No, hopeless! Should he fling away the axe? Should he take a cab? Hopeless, hopeless!'

At last he reached the turning. He turned down it more dead than alive. Here he was half-way to safety, and he understood it; it was less risky because there was a great crowd of people, and he was lost in it like a grain of sand. But all he had suffered had so weakened him that he could scarcely move. Perspiration ran down him in drops, his neck was all wet. 'My word, he has been going it!' someone shouted at him when he came out on the canal bank.

He was only dimly conscious of himself now and the farther he went the worse it was. He remembered, however, that on coming out on to the canal bank he was alarmed at finding few people there and so being more conspicuous, and he had thought of going back. Though he was almost falling from fatigue, he went a long way round so as to get home from quite a different direction.

He was not fully conscious when he passed through the gateway of his house; he was already on the staircase before he recollected the axe. And yet he had a very grave problem before him, to put it back and to escape observation as far as possible in doing so. He was of course incapable of reflecting that it might perhaps be far better not to restore the axe at all, but to drop it later on in somebody's yard. But it all happened fortunately, the door of the porter's room was closed but not locked, so that it seemed most likely that the porter was at home. But he had so completely lost all power of reflection that he walked straight to the door and opened it. If the porter had asked him, 'What do you want?' he would perhaps have simply handed him the axe. But again the porter was not at home, and he succeeded in putting the axe back under the bench and even covering it with the chunk of wood as before. He met no one, not a soul, afterwards on the way to his room; the landlady's door was shut. When he was in his room, he flung himself on the sofa just as he was – he did not sleep, but sank into blank forgetfulness. If anyone had come into his room then he would have jumped up at once and screamed. Scraps and shreds of thoughts were simply swarming in his brain, but he could not catch at one, he could not rest on one, in spite of all his efforts . . .

Fyodor Dostoyevsky, *Crime and Punishment*, trans. Constance Garnett

B

Ballistics

Morris called only eight witnesses, including Broughton and the loyal Major Pembroke, against the prosecution's twenty. The eight were quite enough: he had already turned several of the prosecution witnesses into his own, all, except for Gwladys, testifying with impeccable politeness to Broughton's amiability and tolerance, to his lack of temper and to what Broughton called the 'unimpaired friendship' with Erroll all through the crisis. (The Crown saw this as Broughton setting a trap for Erroll; a ploy to have him always close at hand and under observation.) Among his witnesses Morris also put up his own ballistics expert, Captain Thomas Overton, to contradict the prosecution experts, although Morris had already damaged the prosecution's ballistics case by then in cross-examination.

It was in his brilliant handling of the ballistics evidence that Morris's expertise had been revealed. The technical battle that raged for days around a series of microscopic markings on a set of bullets was often confusing and difficult for a lay jury to follow. At moments, lawyers and experts were arguing only – as it seemed – for each other's benefit. Yet Morris always made sure the jury knew when he had scored a point, and the ballistics evidence on which the Crown case rested provided some of the most dramatic moments in the trial.

Briefly, Morris had two propositions to attack. The first was the confrontation that the bullets fired at Soames's farm (the 'Nanyuki' bullets) and the murder bullets came from the same gun. If these two sets of bullets could not be matched, then, Harragin said, 'The case for the Crown falls away like a pack of cards.' The second proposition was that the gun that fired all these bullets was a Colt ·32 that belonged to Broughton and which he had arranged to be stolen (with another weapon which is not relevant) from the house at Karen. This Colt ·32 was registered on Broughton's firearms certificate.

Morris proved that, given the markings on the bullets, none of them could have been shot by any Colt pistol ever manufactured – that was his 'one point' on which he hoped to defeat the Crown case. The Crown, however, might reply that Broughton had another ·32 hidden away, possibly a Smith & Wesson. To counter this Morris – using pedantry mixed with semi-terror tactics and the judicious use of ballistics textbooks – attempted to put grave doubts in the mind of the jury about the methods the prosecution experts had used in producing their conclusions that the two sets of bullets matched. There was no trace of doubt in the minds of these experts. But if the jury were at all uncertain, Broughton would have to be acquitted.

Morris dealt with the last point first. Until he began his cross-examination, the close similarities between the two sets of bullets, as demonstrated by the Government scientists, Ernest Harwich and Maurice Fox, seemed unanswerable. Fox, the chief Government chemist, had spent almost two months in the laboratory with a comparison microscope, photographing and analysing the bullets and carefully cataloguing these similarities.

A bullet passing through a barrel will pick up, in reverse, the impression of the rifling – the lands (ridges), grooves and striations, or thin lines, caused by irregularities in the barrel. Fox had photographed these features in each bullet for comparison, but through bad marking and classification, the large pile of pictures – as Morris showed – turned out to be almost useless, hopelessly confusing to a jury. Morris suggested that Fox had wasted his two months in the laboratory. From the start Fox had been defensive and pigheaded, resisting all Morris's definitions, and quibbling with his questions. (When Morris mentioned a work by a Major Burrard called *Identification of Firearms and Forensic Ballistics*, Fox said, 'It is not a book on ballistics.' 'What title would you give it then?' Morris asked. 'I would not like to give a title to another man's book,' answered Fox.)

Fox spent seven hours in the witness box for the Crown. Morris questioned him for a further fourteen hours, with many interventions from the judge when the two men seemed to be coming to blows. Their mutual antipathy brought comic relief to the court which had become bored and muddled by Morris's minute examination of lands, grooves and striations. Morris asked at one point what the letters 'S' and 'W' signified on a cartridge.

'That the cartridge is suitable for a Smith & Wesson,' replied Fox.

'Where did you get that from?' Morris asked.

'My mother told me,' said Fox.

'Are you trying to be insolent or impertinent, Mr Fox?'

'No.'

'Well, you are succeeding.'

The similarities were one thing, argued Morris, but what about the *differences*? Morris knew that there were always minute differences between two bullets fired from the same gun. He now discussed every chink and scratch visible on the bullets as if they had equal value with the Crown's universal similarities. He went into great detail, producing anarchy out of order to a jury already bemused by ballistic science. And could the comparison between different bullets really be conclusive without the firearm itself, which the Crown would never be able to produce? Under his own tireless assault from Morris, Harwich had already agreed that the identification of a bullet by its markings was 'a very complex proposition' without the actual firearm. Having got both Harwich and Fox to qualify, accept, concede certain points, Morris would then ask (turning to the jury with a look of weary exasperation), 'And you *still* maintain that the bullets are from the same weapon?'

And now Morris moved in for the kill. It had been argued, he said, that all the bullets came from a revolver whose barrel had five grooves in the rifling, which twisted along the barrel in a right-handed or clockwise direction.

MORRIS: In all these bullets, was the direction uniform?

HARWICH: Yes, it is right hand in all the bullets.

MORRIS: Is the direction in a Colt revolver right or left?

HARWICH: Left in the barrel.

MORRIS: Can you say what kind of a gun the bullets came from?

HARWICH: I can say they came from a revolver.

LORD CHIEF JUSTICE: But not a Colt.

HARWICH: As far as my experience goes, all Colt revolvers have six grooves and a left hand twist.

It was a heavy point for the defence, and the mystery remains of why, with all its ballistic experts to hand, with Fox working on the case for two months before the trial, the Crown should have ignored this flaw in its case.

There was still the problem of Soames's memory of the gun Broughton had used for target practice. He had said in evidence that he thought Broughton had shot with a Colt on his farm, although he wasn't certain. He thought, too, that it was a revolver that was hinged, in which the breech is broken – a characteristic of Colts.

Morris took the weight out of that with another question: 'If Sir Delves tells his Lordship and the Jury that his gun was not a gun that broke, but one in which the cylinder fell out, you would not dispute that?'

'I would believe him,' said Soames.

The similarity between the two sets of bullets – which nobody, not even Morris, disputed in the end – remained one of the most tantalizing elements of the mystery. There was the added similarity of the black powder marks on Erroll's wound, and the live bullets found at Nanyuki, also charged with black powder, which was extremely rare at the time of the events under discussion, but widely available before 1914.

HARRAGIN: When did you tell us you bought these revolvers?
BROUGHTON: I cannot remember the date – twelve or fifteen years ago.
Q: Do you remember where you bought them?
A: I go to many gunsmiths and I cannot remember but I should think probably the Army and Navy Stores.
Q: Did you buy them together or separately?
A: I bought them at the same time.
Q: Can you remember why you should have suddenly bought two revolvers?
A: I cannot remember after fifteen years but you never want a revolver in England and I should think I had it in mind that I might require them if I went abroad.
Q: Did you buy ammunition at the same time?
A: I think at the same time I bought a packet of ammunition for the ·32. I rather think I had some old ·45 ammunition at home and I don't think I bought any ·45 ammunition.
Q: In any event you never used them in England?
A: No.
Q: And in fact you never used them until you went to Soames's farm where I think you used only one?
A: Yes.
Q: Did you use the same ammunition that you bought twelve or fifteen years ago?
A: Yes, it was the only ammunition I had.
Q: How many rounds had you?
A: It was an unbroken box of, I think, fifty.
Q: How many rounds were shot?
A: About forty. I think I fired about twenty or twenty-five and she [Diana] fifteen. I fired more than she.

Q: And will you agree that if any live rounds of ·32 ammunition were found there the probability is that they were yours?
A: There could not have been any of my ammunition found there.

[Why not? It is extraordinary that this reply was left unchallenged.]

Q: Were you firing with black powder ammunition?
A: I have no idea but if you go to a good gunmaker I think it is very unlikely that you would obtain black powder even fifteen years ago. It is a very old fashioned type of powder. When I was a boy I used black powder but I think it went out before the last war. I should have thought it very unusual to find it in revolver ammunition.
Q: Can you give any reason why there were black powder cartridges there, not necessarily yours?
A: I cannot give any explanation.

Broughton showed a remarkable composure in his twenty hours of testimony. Imperturbable, urbane, almost insouciant – an aristocrat before the guillotine couldn't have done better. And yet at one time Broughton's impassivity suggested Camus' *L'Étranger*. The witness was Dr Joseph Gregory:

Q: Assuming a man is charged with murder, if you noticed his extreme calm and that he was apparently quite satisfied with the position or not interested in caring, would that indicate to you any condition of the brain?
A: No Sir.
Q: If he appears to be quite indifferent to the surroundings of the prison or the court, you would say that that was quite normal?
A: I would say it would indicate he is what one normally calls a philosopher.
Q: Or a man with a clear conscience?
A: Yes, either.

James Fox, *White Mischief*

Blood

MACBETH: It will have blood, they say. Blood will have blood.
Stones have been known to move, and trees to speak,
Augurs and understood relations have

By maggot-pies and choughs and rooks brought forth
The secret'st man of blood.

William Shakespeare, *Macbeth*

She rummaged in her handbag for the key on its wooden key ring and tried to fit it into the lock. But she couldn't get it in. Puzzled, but not yet worried, she tried the doorknob and the heavy iron bound door swung open. It was already unlocked, a key in place on the other side. The passage was quiet, unlit, the oak door to the Little Vestry on the left tightly closed. So Father Barnes must already be here. But how strange that he should arrive before her. And why hadn't he left on the passage light? As her gloved hand found the switch, Darren scampered past her, up to the wrought iron grille which separated the passage from the nave of the church. He liked to light a candle when they arrived, thrusting thin arms through the grille to reach the candleholder and the coin box. Early in their walk she had handed him the usual tenpenny piece, and now she heard a faint tinkle and watched while he stuck his candle in the socket, and reached for the matches in their brass holder.

And it was then, in that moment, that she felt the first twitch of anxiety. Some premonition alerted her subconscious; earlier disquiets and a vague sense of unease came together and focused into fear. A faint smell, alien yet horribly familiar; the sense of a recent presence; the possible significance of that unlocked outer door; the dark passageway. Suddenly she knew that something was dreadfully wrong. Instinctively she called out:

'Darren!'

He turned and looked at her face. And then, immediately, he was back at her side.

Gently at first, and then with one sharp movement, she opened the door. Her eyes dazzled with light. The long fluorescent tube which disfigured the ceiling was on, its brightness eclipsing the gentle glow from the passageway. And she saw horror itself.

There were two of them and she knew instantly, and with absolute certainty, that they were dead. The room was a shambles. Their throats had been cut and they lay like butchered animals in a waste of blood. Instinctively she thrust Darren behind her. But she was too late. He, too, had seen. He didn't scream but she felt him tremble and he made a small, pathetic groan, like an angry puppy. She pushed him back into the passage, closed the door, and leaned against it. She was aware of a desperate coldness, of the tumultuous thudding of her heart. It seemed to have swollen in her chest, huge and hot, and its painful drumming shook her frail body as if to burst it apart. And the smell, which at first had been tentative, elusive, no more than an alien tincture on the air, now seemed to seep into the passage with the strong effluvium of death.

She pressed her back against the door, grateful for the support of its solid carved oak. But neither its strength nor her tightly closed eyes could shut out horror. Brightly lit as on a stage, she saw the bodies still, more garish, more brightly lit then when they had first met her horrified eyes. One corpse had slipped from the low single bed to the right of the door and lay staring up at her, the mouth open, the head almost cleft from the body. She saw again the severed vessels, sticking like corrugated pipes through the clotted blood. The second was propped, ungainly as a rag doll, against the far wall. His head had dropped forward and over his chest a great mat of blood had spread like a bib. A brown and blue woollen cap was still on his head but askew. His right eye was hidden but the left leered at her with a dreadful knowingness. Thus mutilated, it seemed to her everything human had drained away from them with their blood; life, identity, dignity. They no longer looked like men. And the blood was everywhere. It seemed to her that she herself was drowning in blood. Blood drummed in her ears, blood gurgled like vomit in her throat, blood splashed in bright globules against the retinas of her closed eyes. The images of death she was powerless to shut out swam before her in a swirl of blood, dissolved, reformed, and then dissolved again, but always in blood.

P. D. James, *A Taste for Death*

Bluebeard

Impatiently she tampered with the locks,
One by one she opened all the doors;
The music boxes and the cuckoo clocks
Stopped in alarm; dust settled on the floors
Like apprehensive footsteps. Then the stores
Of silence were exposed to her soft touch:
Mute diamonds and still exquisite ores.
She had not thought the squalid world had such
Treasure to proffer, nor so easy, nor so much.

She did not listen to the hinges' groans,
Complaints in metal, warnings in the wood,
But room by room progressed from precious stones
To tears, and at each secret understood,
Exclaimed, amused, 'How simple!' or 'How good!'
As she took up some fragile, painted jar.
Throughout the palace doors and windows stood
Whether in dread or sympathy ajar
Upon a pale horizon seeming very far.

The open doors of summer afternoons,
The scented air that passes in and out
Ferrying insects, humming with the tunes
That nature sings unheard! She could not doubt
She was unseen, no one was about,
The servants all had gone – she wondered where:
The calm within was dead as that without,
And all about her breathed the stealthy air.
She knew she was alone, that no one else was there.

Now she attained the room of artifice.
Not a thing that grew there but was made:
Venetian glass that counterfeited ice
So close it seemed to melt, and green brocade,
The wind's most subtle movements in a glade.
Nothing was modern, everything was old,
And yet it was not true that they should fade
Though time and fashion dim the emerald.
Each was at once an image and a deathless mould.

Dazzled, she shut the door, but through the next
Saw greater good than any she had seen:
A window open on the sacred text
Of natural things, whose number had not been
Created or conceived, nor did they mean
Other than what they were, splendid and strange.
One leaf is like another, and between
Them all the worlds of difference range;
The world is not destroyed and does not cease to change.

The final door resisted all her strength,
No key would fit, the bars and bolts stuck fast.
But there she pried and worried, till at length
She opened it, knowing it was the last.
They hung on hooks, their finery surpassed
Each her predecessor's, in their lives
Less fortunate than she. There hung the past,
Putrid and crowned. And thinking, 'Love survives
The grave,' she stepped inside to join the other wives.

Daryl Hine, 'Bluebeard's Wife'

Body

A solitary rock is always attractive. All right-minded people feel an overwhelming desire to scale and sit upon it. Harriet made for it without any mental argument, trying to draw a few deductions as she went.

'Is that rock covered at high tide? Yes, of course, or it wouldn't have seaweed on top. Besides, the slope of the shore proves it. I wish I was better at distances and angles, but I should say it would be covered pretty deep. How odd that it should have seaweed only in that lump at the top. You'd expect it at the foot, but the sides seem quite bare, nearly down to the water. I suppose it *is* seaweed. It's very peculiar. It looks almost more like a man lying down; it is possible for seaweed to be so very – well, so very localized?'

She gazed at the rock with a faint stirring of curiosity, and went on talking to herself, as was her rather irritating habit.

'I'm dashed if it isn't a man lying down. What a silly place to choose. He must feel like a bannock on a hot griddle. I could understand it if he was a sun-bathing fan, but he seems to have got all his clothes on. A dark suit at that. He's very quiet. He's probably fallen asleep. If the tide comes in at all fast, he'll be cut off, like the people in the silly magazine stories. Well, I'm not going to rescue him. He'll have to take his socks off and paddle, that's all. There's plenty of time yet.'

She hesitated whether to go on down the rock. She did not want to wake the sleeper and be beguiled into conversation. Not but what he would prove to be some perfectly harmless tripper. But he would certainly be somebody quite uninteresting. She went on, however, meditating, and drawing a few more deductions by way of practice.

'He must be a tripper. Local inhabitants don't take their siestas on rocks. They retire indoors and shut all the windows. And he can't be a fisherman or anything of that kind; they don't waste time snoozing. Only the black-coated brigade does that. Let's call him a tradesman or a bank clerk. But then they usually take their holidays complete with family. This is a solitary sort of fowl. A schoolmaster? No. Schoolmasters don't get off the lead till the end of July. How about a college undergraduate? It's only *just* the end of term. A gentleman of no particular occupation, apparently. Possibly a walking tourist like myself – but the costume doesn't look right.' She had come nearer now and could see the sleeper's dark blue suit quite plainly. 'Well I can't place him, but no doubt Dr Thorndyke would do so at once. Oh, of course. How stupid! He must be a literary bloke of of some kind. They moon about and don't let their families bother them.'

She was within a few yards of the rock now, gazing up at the sleeper. He lay uncomfortably bunched-up on the extreme seaward edge of the rock, his knees drawn high and showing his pale mauve socks. The head, tucked closely down between the shoulders, was invisible.

'What a way to sleep,' said Harriet. 'More like a cat than a human being. It's not natural. His head must be almost hanging over the edge. It's enough to give him apoplexy. Now, if I had any luck, he'd be a corpse, and I should report him and get my name in the papers. That would be something like publicity. "Well-known woman Detective-Writer Finds Mystery Corpse on Lonely Shore." But these things never happen to authors. It's always some placid labourer or night-watchman who finds corpses . . .'

The rock lay tilted like a gigantic wedge of cake, its base standing steeply up to seaward, its surface sloping gently back to where its apex entered the sand. Harriet climbed up over its smooth, dry surface till she stood almost directly over the man. He did not move at all. Something impelled her to address him.

'Oy!' she said, protestingly.

There was neither movement nor reply.

'I'd just as soon he didn't wake up,' thought Harriet. 'I can't imagine what I'm shouting for. *Oy!*'

'Perhaps he's in a fit or a faint,' she said to herself. 'Or he's got sunstroke. That's quite likely. It's very hot.' She looked up, blinking, at the brazen sky, then stooped and laid one hand on the surface of the rock. It almost burnt her. She shouted again, and then, bending over the man, seized his shoulder.

'Are you all right?'

The man said nothing and she pulled upon the shoulder. It shifted slightly – a dead weight. She bent over and gently lifted the man's head.

Harriet's luck was in.

It *was* a corpse. Not the sort of corpse there could be any doubt about, either. Mr Samuel Weare of Lyons Inn, whose 'throat they cut from ear to ear', could not have been more indubitably a corpse. Indeed, if the head did not come off in Harriet's hands, it was only because the spine was intact, for the larynx and all the great vessels of the neck had been severed 'to the hause-bone', and a frightful stream, bright red and glistening, was running over the surface of the rock and dripping into a little hollow below.

Harriet put the head down again and felt suddenly sick. She had written often enough about this kind of corpse, but meeting the thing in the flesh was quite different. She had not realized how butcherly the severed vessels would look, and she had not reckoned with the horrid halitus of blood, which steamed to her nostrils under the blazing sun. Her hands were red and wet. She looked down at her dress. That had escaped, thank goodness. Mechanically she stepped down again from the rock and went round to the edge of the sea. There she washed her fingers over and over again, drying them with ridiculous care upon her handkerchief. She did not like the look of the red trickle that dripped down the face of the rock into the clear water. Retreating, she sat down rather hastily on some loose boulders.

'A dead body,' said Harriet, aloud to the sun and the sea-gulls. 'A dead body. How – how appropriate!' she laughed.

'The great thing,' Harriet found herself saying, after a pause, 'the great thing is to keep cool. Keep your head, my girl. What would Lord Peter Wimsey do in such a case? Or, of course, Robert Templeton?'

Robert Templeton was the hero who diligently detected between the covers of her own books. She dismissed the image of Lord Peter Wimsey from her mind, and concentrated on that of Robert Templeton. The latter was a gentleman of extraordinary scientific skill, combined with almost fabulous muscular development. He had arms like an orang-outang and an ugly but attractive face. She conjured up this phantom before her in the suit of rather loud plus-fours with which she was accustomed to invest him, and took counsel with him in spirit.

Robert Templeton, she felt, would at once ask himself, 'Is it Murder or Suicide?' He would immediately, she supposed, dismiss the idea of accident. Accidents of that sort do not happen. Robert Templeton would carefully examine the body, and pronounce –

Quite so; Robert Templeton would examine the body. He was indeed, notorious for the sang-froid with which he examined bodies of the most repulsive description. Bodies reduced to boneless jelly by falling from aeroplanes; bodies charred into 'unrecognizable lumps' by fire; bodies run over by heavy vehicles, and needing to be scraped from the road with shovels – Robert Templeton was accustomed to examine them all, without turning a hair. Harriet felt that she had never fully appreciated the superb nonchalance of her literary offspring.

Of course, any ordinary person, who was not a Robert Templeton, would leave the body alone and run for the police. But there were no police. There was not a man, woman, or child within sight; only a small fishing-boat, standing out to sea some distance away. Harriet waved wildly in its direction, but its occupants either did not see her or supposed that she was merely doing some kind of reducing exercise. Probably their own sail cut off their view of the shore, or they were tacking up into the wind, with the vessel lying well over. Harriet shouted, but her voice was lost amid the crying of the gulls.

Dorothy L. Sayers, *Have His Carcase*

Burke and Hare

God prosper long our noble King,
Our lives and safeties all,
I'll sing of murders that till now,
Did never yet befal.

In modern Athens as it's call'd,
In Wester Portsburgh Street,
Two murderers had their horrid den,
And there did nightly meet.

These wretches' names were Burke and Hare,
Both from the sister Isle,
Their plan was to take strangers in
And them of life beguile.

Which having done, they wrapped them up
And laid them in a box,
And without either dread or fear
Sold them to Dr K—.

The first was Margaret Paterson
  Whom drink had led astray,
She fell into their wicked hands,
  Who chok'd her as she lay.

Next on the list was daft Jamie,
  Who laugh'd and sang sae crouse,
And seeking his mother was decoy'd
  Into the murderers' house.

• • •

Next was a wife who came to town
  In search of her dear son,
Was by these wicked wretches dogg'd
  And barbarously undone.

Last Burke had seized an infant dear,
  Oh! horrible disgrace,
Who while he chok'd it on his knee
  Did smile up in his face.

Such are the horrid deeds of Burke,
  Deeds never done before,
Who since his sentence has confess'd
  To twenty murders more.

His trusty friend, the wicked Hare,
  Now waits alike his fate,
And though vengeance is often slow
  It never comes too late.

Now all ye powers that rule above
  Grant we may evil shun
And that henceforth such dreadful acts
  May never more be done.

Anon., 'The Recent Murders'

C

Cain

And Adam knew Eve his wife; and she conceived, and bare Cain, and said, I have gotten a man from the LORD.

And she again bare his brother Abel. And Abel was a keeper of sheep, but Cain was a tiller of the ground.

And in process of time it came to pass, that Cain brought of the fruit of the ground an offering unto the LORD.

And Abel, he also brought of the firstlings of his flock, and of the fat thereof. And the LORD had respect unto Abel, and to his offering:

But unto Cain and to his offering he had not respect. And Cain was very wroth, and his countenance fell.

And the LORD said unto Cain, Why art thou wroth? and why is thy countenance fallen?

If thou doest well, shalt thou not be accepted? and if thou doest not well, sin lieth at the door. And unto thee shall be his desire, and thou shalt rule over him.

And Cain talked with Abel his brother: and it came to pass, when they were in the field, that Cain rose up against Abel his brother, and slew him.

And the LORD said unto Cain, Where is Abel thy brother? And he said, I know not: Am I my brother's keeper?

And he said, What hast thou done? the voice of thy brother's blood crieth unto me from the ground.

And now art thou cursed from the earth, which hath opened her mouth to receive thy brother's blood from thy hand.

When thou tillest the ground, it shall not henceforth yield unto thee her strength. A fugitive and a vagabond shalt thou be in the earth.

And Cain said unto the LORD, My punishment is greater than I can bear.

Behold thou hast driven me out this day from the face of the earth; and from thy face shall I be hid; and I shall be a fugitive and a vagabond in the earth; and it shall come to pass, that every one that findeth me shall slay me.

And the LORD said unto him, Therefore, whosoever slayeth Cain, vengeance shall be taken on him sevenfold. And the LORD set a mark upon Cain, lest any finding him should kill him.

And Cain went out from the presence of the LORD, and dwelt in the land of Nod, on the east of Eden.

Genesis 4: 1–16

Adam, now ope thine eyes, and first behold
The effects which thy original crime hath wrought
In some to spring from thee, who never touched
The excepted tree, nor with the snake conspired,
Nor sinned thy sin, yet from that sin derive
Corruption to bring forth more violent deeds.
His eyes he opened, and beheld a field,
Part arable and tilth, whereon were sheaves
New reaped, the other part sheep-walks and folds;
In the midst an altar as the landmark stood
Rustic, of grassy sward; thither anon
A sweaty reaper from his tillage brought
First fruits, the green ear, and the yellow sheaf,
Unculled, as came to hand; a shepherd next
More meek came with the firstlings of his flock
Choicest and best; then sacrificing, laid
The inwards and their fat, with incense strewed,
On the cleft wood, and all due rites performed.
His offering soon propitious fire from heaven
Consumed with nimble glance, and grateful steam;
The other's not, for his was not sincere;
Whereat he inly raged, and as they talked,
Smote him into the midriff with a stone
That beat out life; he fell, and deadly pale
Groaned out his soul with gushing blood effused.
Much at that sight was Adam in his heart
Dismayed, and thus in haste to the angel cried.
O teacher, some great mischief hath befallen
To that meek man, who well had sacrificed;
Is piety thus and pure devotion paid?

To whom Michael thus, he also moved, replied.
These two are brethren, Adam, and to come
Out of thy loins; the unjust the just hath slain,
For envy that his brother's offering found
From heaven acceptance; but the bloody fact
Will be avenged, and the other's faith approved
Lose no reward, though here thou see him die,
Rolling in dust and gore. To which our sire.
Alas, both for the deed and for the cause!
But have I now seen death? Is this the way
I must return to native dust? O sight
Of terror, foul and ugly to behold,
Horrid to think, how horrible to feel!

John Milton, *Paradise Lost*

Cain alone with the body of Abel

CAIN: What? fallen? so quickly down, so easily felled,
And so completely? Why, he does not move.
Will not he stir – will he not breathe again?
Still as a log, still as his own dead lamb.
Dead is it then? O wonderful! O strange!
Dead! dead! And we can slay each other then?
If we are wronged, why, we can right ourselves;
If we are plagued and pestered with a fool
That will not let us be, nor leave us room
To do our will and shape our path in peace,
We can be rid of him. There – he is gone;
Victory! victory! victory! My heaven,
Methinks from infinite distances borne back
It comes to me re-born in multitude,
Echoed, re-echoed, and re-echoed again,
Victory! victory! – distant yet distant,
Uncountable times repeated. O ye gods!
Where am I come, and whither am I borne?
I stand upon the pinnacle of earth,
And hear the wild seas laughing all about;
Yet I could wish that he had struggled more –
That passiveness was disappointing. Ha!
He should have writhed and wrestled in my arms,

And all but overcome, and set his knee
Hard on my chest, till I – all faint, yet still
Holding my fingers at his throat – at last,
Inch after inch, had forced him to relax:
But he went down at once, without a word,
Almost without a look.
Ah, hush! My God,
Who was it spoke, what is this questioner?
Who was it asked me where my brother is?
Ha, ha! Was I his keeper? I know not!
Each for himself; he might have struck again.
Why did he not? I wished him to. Was I
To strike for both at once? No! Yet, ah!
Where is thy brother? Peace, thou silly voice;
Am I my brother's keeper? I know not,
I know not aught about it; let it be.
Henceforth I shall walk freely upon earth,
And know my will, and do it by my might.
My God! – it will not be at peace – my God!
It flames, it bursts to fury in my soul.
What is it I have done? – Almighty God!
What is it that will come of this? Ah me!
I see it, I behold it as it is,
As it will be in all the times to come:
Slaughter on slaughter, blood for blood, and death,
For ever, ever, ever, evermore!
And all for what?
O Abel, brother mine,
Where'er thou art, more happy far than me!

Arthur Hugh Clough, from 'Adam and Eve'

Caligula

The following instances will illustrate his bloody-mindedness. Having collected wild animals for one of his shows, he found butcher's meat too expensive and decided to feed them with criminals instead. He paid no attention to the charge-sheets, but simply stood in the middle of a colonnade, glanced at the prisoners lined up before him, and gave the order: 'Kill every man between that bald head and the other one over there!' Someone had sworn to fight in the arena if Caligula recovered from his illness; Caligula forced him to fulfil his oath, and watched his swordplay closely, not letting him go until he had won the match and begged abjectly to be released. Another fellow had pledged himself, on the same occasion, to commit suicide; Caligula, finding that he was still alive, ordered him to be dressed in wreaths and fillets, and driven through Rome by the Imperial slaves – who kept harping on his pledge and finally flung him over the embankment into the river. Many men of decent family were branded at his command, and sent down mines, or put to work on the roads, or thrown to the wild beasts. Others were confined in narrow cages, where they had to crouch on all fours like animals; or were sawn in half – and not necessarily for major offences, but merely for criticizing his shows, failing to swear by his Genius, and so forth.

Caligula made parents attend their sons' executions, and when one father excused himself on the ground of ill-health, provided a litter for him. Having invited another father to dinner just after the son's execution, he overflowed with good-fellowship in an attempt to make him laugh and joke. He watched the manager of his gladiatorial and wild-beast shows being flogged with chains for several days running, and had him killed only when the smell of suppurating brains became insupportable. A writer of Atellan farces was burned alive in the amphitheatre, because of a single line which had an amusing *double-entendre*. One knight, on the point of being thrown to the wild beasts, shouted that he was innocent; Caligula brought him back, removed his tongue, and then ordered the sentence to be carried out.

Once Caligula asked a returned exile how he had been spending his time. To flatter him the man answered: 'I prayed continuously to the gods for Tiberius's death, and your accession; and my prayer was granted.' Caligula therefore concluded that the new batch of exiles must be praying for his own death; so he sent agents from island to island and had them all killed. Being anxious that one particular senator should be torn in pieces he persuaded some of his colleagues to challenge him as a public enemy when he entered the House, stab him with their pens, and then hand him over for lynching to the rest of the Senate; and was not satisfied until the victim's limbs, organs, and guts had been dragged through the streets and heaped up at his feet.

Caligula's savage crimes were matched by his brutal language. He claimed that no personal trait made him feel prouder than his 'inflexibility' – by which he must have meant 'brazen impudence'. As though mere deafness to his grandmother Antonia's good advice were not enough, he told her: 'Bear in mind that I can treat anyone exactly as I please!' Suspecting that young Tiberius had taken drugs as prophylactics to the poison he intended to administer, Caligula scoffed: 'Can there really be an antidote against Caesar?' And, on banishing his sisters, he remarked: 'I have swords as well as islands.' One ex-praetor, taking a mental cure at Anticyra, made frequent requests for an extension of his sick leave; Caligula had his throat cut, suggesting that if hellebore had been of so little benefit over so long a period, he must need to be bled. When signing the execution list he used to say: 'I am clearing my accounts.' And one day, after sentencing a number of Gauls and Greeks to die in the same batch, he boasted of having 'subdued Gallo-graecia'.

The method of execution he preferred was to inflict numerous small wounds, avoiding the prisoner's vital organs; and his familiar order: 'Make him feel that he is dying!' soon became proverbial. Once, when the wrong man had been killed, owing to a confusion of names, he announced that the victim had equally deserved death; and often quoted Accius's line:

Let them hate me, so long as they fear me.

• • •

Caligula had dared commit fearful crimes, and contemplated even worse ones: such as murdering the most distinguished of the senators and knights, and then moving the seat of government first to Antium, and afterwards to Alexandria. If, at this point, my readers become incredulous, let me record that two books were found among his papers entitled *The Dagger* and *The Sword*, each of them containing the names and addresses of men whom he had planned to kill. A huge chest filled with poisons also came to light. It is said that when Claudius later threw this into the sea, quantities of dead fish, cast up by the tide, littered the neighbouring beaches.

Gaius Suetonius Tranquillus, *The Twelve Caesars*,
trans. Robert Graves

Cannibalism

The seventh day and no wind. The burning sun
Blistered and scorched, and stagnant on the sea
They lay like carcasses, and hope was none,
Save in the breeze that came not. Savagely

They glared upon each other. All was done,
  Water and wine and food, and you might see
The longings of the cannibal arise
(Although they spoke not) in their wolfish eyes.

At length one whispered his companion, who
  Whispered another, and thus it went round,
And then into a hoarser murmur grew,
  An ominous and wild and desperate sound,
And when his comrade's thought each sufferer knew,
'Twas but his own, suppressed till now, he found.
And out they spoke of lots for flesh and blood,
And who should die to be his fellow's food.

But ere they came to this, they that day shared
  Some leathern caps and what remained of shoes;
And then they looked around them and despaired,
  And none to be the sacrifice would choose.
At length the lots were torn up and prepared,
  But of materials that much shock the Muse.
Having no paper, for the want of better,
They took by force from Juan Julia's letter.

The lots were made and marked and mixed and handed
  In silent horror, and their distribution
Lulled even the savage hunger which demanded,
  Like the Promethean vulture, this pollution.
None in particular had sought or planned it;
'Twas nature gnawed them to this resolution,
By which none were permitted to be neuter,
And the lot fell on Juan's luckless tutor.

He but requested to be bled to death.
  The surgeon had his instruments and bled
Pedrillo, and so gently ebbed his breath
  You hardly could perceive when he was dead.
He died as born, a Catholic in faith,
  Like most in the belief in which they're bred,
And first a little crucifix he kissed,
And then held out his jugular and wrist.

The surgeon, as there was no other fee,
  Had his first choice of morsels for his pains,

But being thirstiest at the moment, he
  Preferred a draught from the fast-flowing veins.
Part was divided, part thrown in the sea,
  And such things as the entrails and the brains
Regaled two sharks who followed o'er the billow.
The sailors ate the rest of poor Pedrillo.

The sailors ate him, all save three or four,
  Who were not quite so fond of animal food.
To these was added Juan, who, before
  Refusing his own spaniel, hardly could
Feel now his appetite increased much more.
  'Twas not to be expected that he should,
Even in extremity of their disaster,
Dine with them on his pastor and his master.

'Twas better that he did not, for in fact
  The consequence was awful in the extreme.
For they who were most ravenous in the act
  Went raging mad. Lord! how they did blaspheme
And foam and roll, with strange convulsions racked,
  Drinking salt water like a mountain stream,
Tearing and grinning, howling, screeching, swearing,
And with hyena laughter died despairing.

Their numbers were much thinned by this infliction,
  And all the rest were thin enough, heaven knows,
And some of them had lost their recollection,
  Happier than they who still perceived their woes,
But others pondered on a new dissection,
  As if not warned sufficiently by those
Who had already perished, suffering madly,
For having used their appetites so sadly.

And next they thought upon the master's mate
  As fattest, but he saved himself, because,
Besides being much averse from such a fate,
  There were some other reasons: the first was
He had been rather indisposed of late,
  And that which chiefly proved his saving clause
Was a small present made to him at Cadiz,
By general subscription of the ladies.

Of poor Pedrillo something still remained,
But was used sparingly. Some were afraid,
And others still their appetites constrained,
Or but at times a little supper made;
All except Juan, who throughout abstained,
Chewing a piece of bamboo and some lead.
At length they caught two boobies and a noddy,
And then they left off eating the dead body.

And if Pedrillo's fate should shocking be,
Remember Ugolino condescends
To eat the head of his archenemy,
The moment after he politely ends
His tale. If foes be food in hell, at sea
'Tis surely fair to dine upon our friends
When shipwreck's short allowance grows too scanty,
Without being much more horrible than Dante.

Lord Byron, *Don Juan*

'Twas on the shores that round our coast
From Deal to Ramsgate span,
That I found alone on a piece of stone
An elderly naval man.

His hair was weedy, his beard was long,
And weedy and long was he,
And I heard this wight on the shore recite,
In a singular minor key:

'Oh, I am a cook and a captain bold,
And the mate of the *Nancy* brig,
And a bo'sun tight, and a midshipmite,
And the crew of the captain's gig.'

And he shook his fists and he tore his hair,
Till I really felt afraid,
For I couldn't help thinking the man had been drinking,
And so I simply said:

'Oh, elderly man, it's little I know
Of the duties of men of the sea,

But I'll eat my hand if I understand
  How you can possibly be

'At once a cook, and a captain bold,
  And the mate of the *Nancy* brig,
And a bo'sun tight, and a midshipmite,
  And the crew of the captain's gig.'

Then he gave a hitch to his trousers, which
  Is a trick all seamen larn,
And having got rid of a thumping quid,
  He spun this painful yarn:

''Twas in the good ship *Nancy Bell*
  That we sailed to the Indian sea,
And there on a reef we come to grief,
  Which has often occurred to me.

'And pretty nigh all o' the crew was drowned
  (There was seventy-seven o' soul),
And only ten of the *Nancy*'s men
  Said "Here!" to the muster-roll.

'There was me and the cook and the captain bold,
  And the mate of the *Nancy* brig,
And the bo'sun tight, and a midshipmite,
  And the crew of the captain's gig.

'For a month we'd neither wittles nor drink,
  Till a-hungry we did feel,
So we drawed a lot, and accordin' shot
  The captain for our meal.

'The next lot fell to the *Nancy*'s mate,
  And a delicate dish he made;
Then our appetite with the midshipmite
  We seven survivors stayed.

'And then we murdered the bo'sun tight,
  And he much resembled pig;
Then we wittled free, did the cook and me,
  On the crew of the captain's gig.

'Then only the cook and me was left,
  And the delicate question, "Which

Of us two goes to the kettle?" arose
  And we argued it out as sich.

'For I loved that cook as a brother, I did,
  And the cook he worshipped me;
But we'd both be blowed if we'd either be stowed
  In the other chap's hold, you see.

'"I'll be eat if you dines off me," says Tom,
  "Yes, that," says I, "you'll be," –
"I'm boiled if I die, my friend," quoth I,
  And "Exactly so," quoth he.

'Says he, "Dear James, to murder me
  Were a foolish thing to do,
For don't you see that you can't cook *me*,
  While I can – and will – cook *you!*"

'So he boils the water, and takes the salt
  And the pepper in portions true
(Which he never forgot), and some chopped shalot,
  And some sage and parsley too.

'"Come here," says he, with a proper pride,
  Which his smiling features tell,
"'Twill soothing be if I let you see,
  How extremely nice you'll smell."

'And he stirred it round and round and round,
  And he sniffed at the foaming froth;
When I ups with his heels, and smothers his squeals
  In the scum of the boiling broth.

'And I eat that cook in a week or less,
  And – as I eating be
The last of his chops, why, I almost drops,
  For a wessel in sight I see!

• • •

'And I never grin, and I never smile,
  And I never larf nor play,
But I sit and croak, and a single joke
  I have – which is to say:

'Oh, I am a cook and a captain bold,
  And the mate of the *Nancy* brig,
And a bo'sun tight, *and* a midshipmite,
  And the crew of the captain's gig!'

W. S. Gilbert, 'The Yarn of the *Nancy Bell*'

'A census taker tried to quantify me once. I ate his liver with some fava beans and a big Amarone. Go back to school, little Starling.'

Hannibal Lecter, polite to the last, did not give her his back. He stepped backward from the barrier before he turned to his cot again, and lying on it, became as remote from her as a stone crusader lying on a tomb.

Thomas Harris, *The Silence of the Lambs*

They warre against the nations, that lie beyond their mountaines, to which they go naked, having no other weapons than bowes, or woodden swords, sharpe at one end, as our broaches are. It is an admirable thing to see the constant resolution of their combats, which never end but by effusion of bloud and murther: for they know not what feare or rowts are. Every Victor brings home the head of the enemie he hath slaine as a Trophey of his victorie, and fastneth the same at the entrance of his dwelling place. After they have long time used and entreated their prisoners well, and with all commodities they can devise, he that is the Master of them; sommoning a great assembly of his acquaintance; tieth a corde to one of the prisoners armes, by the end whereof he holds him fast, with some distance from him, for feare he might offend him, and giveth the other arme, bound in like manner, to the dearest friend he hath, and both in the presence of all the assembly kill him with swords: which done, they roast, and then eat him in common, and send some slices of him to such of their friends as are absent. It is not as some imagine, to nourish themselves with it, (as anciently the Scithians wont to doe,) but to represent an extreme, and inexpiable revenge. Which we prove thus; some of them perceiving the Portugales, who had confederated themselves with their adversaries, to use another kinde of death, when they tooke them prisoners; which was, to burie them up to the middle, and against the upper part of the body to shoot arrowes, and then being almost dead, to hang them up; they supposed, that these people of the other world (as they who had sowed the knowledge of many vices amongst their neighbours, and were much more cunning in all kindes of evils and mischiefe than they) undertooke not this manner of revenge without cause, and that consequently it was more smartfull, and cruell than theirs, and thereupon began to leave their old fashion to follow this. I am not sorie we note the barbarous horror of such an action, but grieved, that prying so narrowly into their faults we are so blinded in ours. I thinke there is more barbarisme in eating men alive, than to feed upon them being dead; to mangle by tortures and torments a body full of lively sense, to roast him in peeces, to make dogges and swine to gnaw and teare him in mammockes (as wee have not only read, but seene very lately, yea and in our owne memorie, not amongst ancient enemies, but our neighbours and fellow-citizens; and which is worse, under pretence of pietie and religion) than to roast and eat him after he is dead. *Chrysippus* and *Zeno*, arch-pillers of the Stoicke sect, have supposed that it was no hurt at all, in time of need, and to what end soever, to make use of our carrion bodies, and to feed upon them, as did our forefathers, who being besieged by *Cæsar* in the Citie of *Alexia*, resolved to sustaine the famine of the siege, with the bodies of old men, women, and other persons unserviceable and unfit to fight.

Vascomnes (fama est) alimentis talibus usi·
Produxere animas. Juven. *Sat.* xv. 93)

Gascoynes (as fame reports)
Liv'd with meats of such sorts.

Michel Eyquem de Montaigne, from
'Of Cannibals', trans. John Floriot

Cement

Here is what I saw in the first instant of my blinking in the harsh light of a work lamp hooked to the deckhouse ceiling: the elegant Bo Weinberg standing beside his pointed patent-leather shoes, with the black silk socks and attached garters lying twisted like dead eels beside them, and his white feet looking very much longer and very much wider than the shoes he had just stepped from. He was staring at his feet, perhaps because feet are intimate body parts rarely seen with black tie, and following his gaze, I felt I had to commiserate with what I was sure he was thinking, that for all our civilization we go around on these things that are slit at the front end into five unequal lengths each partially covered with shell.

Kneeling in front of him was the brisk and impassive Irving methodically rolling Bo's pant legs with their black satin side-stripe to the knees.

Irving had seen me but chose not to notice me, which was characteristic. He was Mr Schultz's utility man and did what he was told to do and gave no appearance of thought for anything else. He was rolling up pant legs. A hollow-chested man, with thinning hair, he had the pallor of an alcoholic, that dry paper skin they have, and I knew about drunks on the wagon what they paid for their sobriety, the concentration it demanded, the state of constant mourning it produced. I liked to watch Irving whatever he was doing, even when it was not as it was now something extraordinary. Each fold-up of the pant leg exactly matched the one before. He did everything meticulously and without wasted movement. He was a professional, but since he had no profession other than dealing with the contingencies of his chosen life, he carried himself as if life was a profession, just as, I suppose, in a more conventional employment, a butler would.

And partially obscured by Bo Weinberg and standing as far from him as I was but at the opposite side of the cabin, in his open coat and unevenly draped white scarf and his soft gray homburg tilted back on his head, and one hand in his jacket pocket and the other casually holding a gun at his side that was pointed with no particular emphasis at the deck, was Mr Schultz.

This scene was so amazing to me I gave it the deference one gives to the event perceived as historical. Everything was moving up and down in unison but the three men didn't seem to notice and even the wind was a distant and chastened sound in here, and the air was close with the smell of tar and diesel oil and there were coils of thick rope stacked like rubber tires, and pulleys and chain tackle, and racks filled with tools and kerosene lamps and cleats and numerous items whose names or purposes I did not know but whose importance to the nautical life I willingly conceded. And the tug's engine vibrations were comfortingly powerful in here and I could feel them running into my hand, which I had put against the door in order to close it.

I caught Mr Schultz's eye and he suddenly displayed a mouth of large evenly aligned white teeth, and his face of rude features creased itself into a smile of generous appreciation. 'It's the Invisible Man,' he said. I was as startled by his utterance as I would have been if someone in a church painting had started to talk. Then I found myself smiling back. Joy flooded my boyish breast, or perhaps gratitude to God for granting me at least this moment in which my fate wasn't in the balance. 'Look at that, Irving, the kid came along for the ride. You like boats, kid?' he said.

'I don't know yet,' I said truthfully and without understanding why this honest answer was so funny. For he was laughing now loudly and in his hornlike voice, which I thought was terribly careless of the solemn nature of the occasion; the mien of the other two men seemed preferable to me. And I will say something more about Mr Schultz's voice because it was so much an aspect of his power of domination. It was not that it was always loud but that it had a substantial body to it, it came out of his throat with harmonic buzz, and it was very instrumental actually, so that you understood the throat as a sound box, and that maybe the chest cavity and the nose bones, too, were all involved in producing it, and it was a baritone voice that automatically made you pay attention in the way of wanting a horn voice like that yourself, except when he raised it in anger or laughed as he was doing now, and then it grated on your ears and made you dislike it, as I did now – or maybe it was what I'd said that I disliked because I was joining in some cleverness at a dying man's expense.

There was a narrow green slat bench or shelf hung from the cabin wall and I sat down on it. What could Bo Weinberg possibly have done? I had had little acquaintance with him, he was something of a knight errant, rarely in the office on 149th Street, never in the cars, certainly not on the trucks, but always intimated to be central to the operation, like Mr Dixie Davis the lawyer, or Abbadabba Berman the accounting genius – at that level of executive importance. He was reputed to do Mr Schultz's diplomatic work, negotiating with other gangs and performing necessary business murders. He was one of the giants and perhaps, in fearsomeness, second only to Mr Schultz himself. Now not just his feet but his legs to the knees were exposed. Irving rose from his kneeling position and offered his arm, and Bo Weinberg took it, like some princess at a ball, and delicately, gingerly, placed one foot at a time in the laundry tub in front of him that was filled with wet cement. I had of course seen from the moment I had come through the door how the tubbed cement made a slow-witted diagram of the sea outside, the slab of it shifting to and fro as the boat rose and fell on the waves.

E. L. Doctorow, *Billy Bathgate*

Chinese Cuts

They did not trouble to conceal their weapons. Darkness covered them, the road was empty, and the enemy banqueted at two tables in the centre of the ground floor. The axeman was through the door first, a yard clear of the choppermen, weapon low. He arced it high and buried the blade between the shoulders of a man drinking beer. The two diners on either side veered away, left and right, and were on their feet before the axeman could lift the heavy weapon again. But in a rush and whirl of falling chairs the other raiders were there now. By the time the axeman had swung again and caught a seated man on the head with the crack of a coconut split on a frosty morning, the choppermen had cut six or seven times with their light weapons. There was blood on the tablecloth; the cries of the injured mixed with the yells of the attackers.

In these first ten seconds eight men had been put out of the fray.

The second table was still intact, the diners seated in shock. Ignoring the carnage behind him, Red Cudgel swung left-handed with his long flail. He hit two men in the face and knocked them off their chairs. He shortened his grip a hitch and was among the scattering men with his cleaver. He went low, stabbed upwards with short hooking blows to groin and abdomen, and dropped two more. The flailed men had gone over without a sound; these screamed. Steel glinted in Red Cudgel's mouth. One of the flailed men was on his knees. There were red and white beads on the carpet in front of him. His hands were over his shattered jaw. Red Cudgel pulled his hair from behind and slashed his throat. He cut two men off into a corner with long sweeps of his flail. Out of the side of his eye he was looking for the enemy enforcer. Iron Plank commanded the centre of the floor with the same intention. He had not struck yet. His two square-bladed short swords were at his side, clean. A man ran for the door. Iron Plank stepped into his path, put his blades left to right across his body in an X and then sliced outwards into the fugitive's stomach. They were relaxed, contemptuous cuts, made without hurry. As the man fell, he chopped down into his neck, so that the blades had described a broad circle with the sequence of blows. He stepped over the body to the first table. He had identified his man.

Jackie Fung, a tall and deceptively slim young man, had been at the back of the first table, his head against the wall. The men on his left and right had dived under the table to join the wounded man already there. Jackie Fung remained in his chair and waited calmly. A chopperman struck awkwardly at him across the table. Jackie Fung swayed six inches to the right. He threw the neat brandy in his neighbour's glass into his assailant's face. The misdirected blow smashed a rice bowl. He seized the man's wrist, broke the glass and scraped the jagged edge over his nose and eyes. He grabbed the man's testicles savagely and then disarmed him. Armed now with the cleaver, he pushed the table over. As he did so, a swordsman struck at his head. Fung parried late with the chopper which was jarred out of his hand but just caught his attacker's sword-arm as it went back. The man went for the knife in his belt. Jackie Fung threw his palm over the swordsman's face, found the socket with his long thumb, and gouged into the eyeball. The man fell back with a cry, covering his face. Jackie Fung now had a sword. He came into the open and a man slashed at him with a cleaver. He parried, again slightly awkwardly. Then in a short, hopping action he brought his rear right heel to the left heel and, having made the necessary ground with the half-step, simultaneously high-kicked and punched to the face with the left side as smoothly and easily as a pair of scissors opening. The crack of the clean head-shots cut over all the other sounds in the room. He stepped over the body and stabbed in the back a man who had an axe poised at the top of its swing. He thrust badly; the sword jarred on bone. Jackie Fung swore, dropped the tasselled sword, put his weight on the rear leg and smashed a left-handed reverse punch to the axeman's kidneys. The man dropped without a sound.

The other banqueters were now trying to fight back and had massed between the up-turned tables, defending themselves as best they could with a variety of improvised weapons: broken bottles, chairs, a heavy ladle. There were eight left standing. Men groaned quietly on the floor or were still. Five of the raiding party were out of the action, including the four dropped by Jackie Fung.

The spearman, who had been guarding the door, moved in on Jackie Fung. He made short, stabbing feints with the six-foot weapon. Jackie Fung surprised the man by taking the offensive. He moved in swiftly. As he anticipated, the spearman withdrew his weapon before thrusting instead of stabbing at once with the weapon uncocked. The spear came out again. Jackie Fung broke the rhythm of his rush, stepped sideways and seized the shaft six inches below the metal tip. He pulled sharply, swept the man's legs, and impaled him on the ground. He stabbed him three more times, the last in the neck.

Fifty-five seconds had elapsed since the men had come through the door.

Timothy Mo, *Sour Sweet*

Complicity

'Why dois your brand sae drap wi' bluid,
Edward, Edward,
Why dois your brand sae drap wi' bluid,
And why sae sad gang yee O?'
'O I hae killed my hauke sae guid,
Mither, mither,
O I hae killed my hauke sae guid,
And I had nae mair bot hee, O.'

'Your haukis bluid was nevir sae reid,
Edward, Edward,
Your haukis bluid was nevir sae reid,
My deir son I tell thee O.'
'O I hae killed my reid-roan steid,
Mither, mither,
O I hae killed my reid-roan steid,
That erst was sae fair and frie O.'

'Your steid was auld, and ye hae gat mair,
Edward, Edward,
Your steid was auld, and ye hae gat mair,
Sum other dule ye drie O.'
'O I hae killed my fadir deir,
Mither, mither,
O I hae killed my fadir deir,
Alas and wae is me O!'

'And whatten penance wul ye drie, for that
Edward, Edward?
And whatten penance wul ye drie for that?
My deir son, now tell me O.'
'Ile set my feit in yonder boat,
Mither, mither,
Ile set my feit in yonder boat,
And I'll fare ovir the sea O.'

'And what wul ye doe wi' your towirs and your ha',
Edward, Edward?
And what wul ye doe wi' your towirs and your ha',
That were sae fair to see O?'
'Ile let thame stand tul they doun fa',
Mither, mither,
Ile let thame stand tul they doun fa',
For here nevir mair maun I bee O.'

'And what wul ye leive to your bairns and your wife,
Edward, Edward?
And what wul ye leive to your bairns and your wife,
Whan ye gang ovir the sea O?'
'The warldis room, late them beg thrae life,
For thame nevir mair wul I see O.'

'And what wul ye leive to your ain mither dear,
Edward, Edward?
And what wul ye leive to your ain mither dear?
My deir son, now tell me O.'
'The curse of hell frae me sall ye beir,
Mither, mither,
The curse of hell frae me sall ye beir,
Sic counseils ye gave to me O.'

Anon., 'Edward'

Cross-purposes

Enter Demetrius and Hermia

OBERON: Stand close. This is the same Athenian.
ROBIN: This is the woman, but not this the man.
(*They stand apart*)
DEMETRIUS: O, why rebuke you him that loves you so?
Lay breath so bitter on your bitter foe.
HERMIA: Now I but chide, but I should use thee worse;
For thou, I fear, hast given me cause to curse.
If thou hast slain Lysander in his sleep,
Being o'er shoes in blood, plunge in the deep,
And kill me too.
The sun was not so true unto the day

As he to me. Would he have stolen away
From sleeping Hermia? I'll believe as soon
This whole earth may be bored, and that the moon
May through the centre creep, and so displease
Her brother's noontide with th'Antipodes.
It cannot be but thou hast murdered him.
So should a murderer look – so dead, so grim.

DEMETRIUS: So should the murdered look, and so should I,
Pierced through the heart with your stern cruelty.
Yet you, the murderer, look as bright, as clear
As yonder Venus in her glimmering sphere.

HERMIA: What's this to my Lysander? Where is he?
Ah, good Demetrius, wilt thou give him me?

DEMETRIUS: I had rather give his carcass to my hounds.

HERMIA: Out, dog; out, cur. Thou driv'st me past the bounds
Of maiden's patience. Hast thou slain him then?
Henceforth be never numbered among men.
O, once tell true; tell true, even for my sake.
Durst thou have looked upon him being awake,
And hast thou killed him sleeping? O brave touch!
Could not a worm, an adder do so much? –
An adder did it, for with doubler tongue
Than thine, thou serpent, never adder stung.

DEMETRIUS: You spend your passion on a misprised mood.
I am not guilty of Lysander's blood,
Nor is he dead, for aught that I can tell.

HERMIA: I pray thee, tell me then that he is well.

DEMETRIUS: And if I could, what should I get therefor?

HERMIA: A privilege never to see me more;
And from thy hated presence part I so.
See me no more, whether he be dead or no.

William Shakespeare, *A Midsummer Night's Dream*

D

Definitions

Murder is when a [person] . . . unlawfully killeth . . . any reasonable creature *in rerum natura* under the Queen's peace, with malice aforethought . . . so as the party wounded or hurt etc. die of the wound or hurt etc. within a year and a day after the same.

Coke's Institutes

The *mens rea* of murder is traditionaly called 'malice aforethought'. This is a technical term and it has a technical meaning quite different from the ordinary popular meaning of the two words. The phrase, it has been truly said,

is a mere arbitrary symbol . . . , for the 'malice' may have in it nothing really malicious; and need never be really 'aforethought'.

Thus a parent who kills a suffering child out of motives of compassion is 'malicious' for this purpose; and there is sufficient aforethought if an intention to kill is formed only a second before the fatal blow is struck. Neither ill-will nor premeditation is necessary.

Kenny's Outlines of Criminal Law

LONGVIL: Do you hear, you nonsensical owl; be gone out of the garden, or by Heav'n I'll run my sword in your guts.
BRUCE: Hold, Longvil, do not kill him; 'twill be something uncivil.
SIR SAMUEL: Uncivil! What a pox do you talk? Uncivil! Why 'twill be murder, man. Uncivil, quoth a –

Thomas Shadwell, *The Virtuoso*

'Sir,' said Mr Honeythunder, in his tremendous voice, like a schoolmaster issuing orders to a boy of whom he had a bad opinion, 'sit down.'

Mr Crisparkle seated himself.

Mr Honeythunder, having signed the remaining few score of a few thousand circulars, calling upon a corresponding number of families without means to come forward, stump up instantly, and be Philanthropists, or go to the Devil, another shabby stipendiary Philanthropist (highly disinterested, if in earnest) gathered these into a basket and walked off with them.

'Now, Mr Crisparkle,' said Mr Honeythunder, turning his chair half round towards him when they were alone, and squaring his arms with his hands on his knees, and his brows knitted, as if he added, I am going to make short work of *you*: 'Now, Mr Crisparkle, we entertain different views, you and I, sir, of the sanctity of human life.'

'Do we?' returned the Minor Canon.

'We do, sir.'

'Might I ask you,' said the Minor Canon: 'what are your views on that subject?'

'That human life is a thing to be held sacred, sir.'

'Might I ask you,' pursued the Minor Canon as before: 'what you suppose to be my views on that subject?'

'By George, sir!' returned the Philanthropist, squaring his arms still more, as he frowned on Mr Crisparkle: 'they are best known to yourself.'

'Readily admitted. But you began by saying that we took different views, you know. Therefore (or you could not say so) you must have set up some views as mine. Pray, what views *have* you set up as mine?'

'Here is a man – and a young man,' said Mr Honeythunder, as if that made the matter infinitely worse, and he could have easily borne the loss of an old one: 'swept off the face of the earth by a deed of violence. What do you call that?'

'Murder,' said the Minor Canon.

'What do you call the doer of that deed, sir?'

'A murderer,' said the Minor Canon.

'I am glad to hear you admit so much, sir,' retorted Mr Honeythunder, in his most offensive manner; 'and I candidly tell you that I didn't expect it.' Here he lowered heavily at Mr Crisparkle again.

'Be so good as to explain what you mean by those very unjustifiable expressions.'

'I don't sit here, sir,' returned the Philanthropist, raising his voice to a roar, 'to be browbeaten.'

'As the only other person present, no one can possibly know that better than I do,' returned the Minor Canon very quietly. 'But I interrupt your explanation.'

'Murder!' proceeded Mr Honeythunder, in a kind of boisterous reverie, with his platform folding of his arms, and his platform nod of abhorrent reflection after each short sentiment of a word. 'Bloodshed! Abel! Cain! I hold no terms with Cain. I repudiate with a shudder the red hand when it is offered me.'

Instead of instantly leaping into his chair and cheering himself hoarse, as the Brotherhood in public meeting assembled would infallibly have done on this cue, Mr Crisparkle merely reversed the quiet crossing of his legs, and said mildly: 'Don't let me interrupt your explanation – when you begin it.'

'The Commandments say no murder. NO murder, sir!' proceeded Mr Honeythunder, platformally pausing as if he took Mr Crisparkle to task for having distinctly asserted that they said, You may do a little murder and then leave off.

'And they also say, you shall bear no false witness,' observed Mr Crisparkle.

Charles Dickens, *The Mystery of Edwin Drood*

Disappointment

There was a shallow alcove across the passageway from the top of the stairs – and with two strides Mr Flay had reached it. From there he could watch the darkness to his left. It was purposeless to follow his enemy to the door of his master's room. He would wait for his return. How would the chef be able to aim his blow in the darkness? He would prod forward with the cleaver until it touched the panels of the door. He would take a soft pace backwards. Then, as he raised the great instrument above his head, a worm, wriggling its bliss through his brain, would bring the double-handed cleaver down, like a guillotine, the great blade whetted to a screaming edge. And as this picture of Mr Swelter's methods illumined the inside of Mr Flay's darkened skull, those very movements were proceeding. Concurrently with Flay's visualization of the cleaver falling – the cleaver fell.

The floor-board beneath Mr Flay's feet lifted, and a wooden ripple ran from one end of the passageway to the other, where it broke upon a cliff of plaster. Curiously enough, it was only through the movement of the boards beneath his feet that Mr Flay knew that the chef had struck, for at the same moment a peal of thunder killed all other sound.

Swelter had brought the cold edge downwards with such a concentration of relish that the excruciating sense of consummation had dulled his wits for a moment, and it was only when he attempted to work the steel away from what gripped its edge that he realised that something was amiss. It is true that he had expected the blade to slide through the 'prostrate' beneath him as through butter, for all the thin man's osseous character – but not, surely – not with *such* ease – such *liquid* ease. Could it be that he had given to the double-handed cleaver such an edge as set up a new sensation – that of killing, as it were, without knowing it – as lazes through long grass the lethal scythe. He had not prodded forward with his toe to make doubly sure – for it had never occurred to him that he who had lain there, night after night, for over twelve years, could be elsewhere. In any event he might have wakened the long scrag by so doing. What had gone wrong? The orgasmic moment he had so long awaited was over. The cleaver was difficult to shift. Perhaps it was caught among the ribs. He began to run his hands down the shaft inch by inch, bending his knees and trunk as he did so, hot tracts of hairless clay redistributing their undulations the while. Inexorably downwards moved his fingers until they itched for contact with the corpse. Surely his hands must by now be almost at the boards themselves, yet he knew how deceptive the sense of distances can be when darkness is complete. And then he came upon the steel. Sliding his palms greedily along either edge he gave a sudden loud, murderous hiss, and loosing his fingers from the edge of the cleaver he swung his bulk about as though his foe were close behind him – and he peered back along the passage at the faint light at the stairhead. There seemed to be no one there, and after a few moments of scrutiny he wiped his hands across his thighs, and turning to the cleaver, wrenched it from the boards.

For a short while he stood fingering his misused weapon, and during this space Mr Flay had conceived and acted, moving a few yards further down the corridor where an even more favourable ambush presented itself in the shape of a sagging tapestry. As he moved out into the darkness, for he was beyond the orbit of the candles' influence, the lightning struck again and flared bluishly through the broken window so that at one and the same moment both Swelter and Flay caught sight of one another. The bluish light had flattened them out like cardboard figures which had, in the case of the chef, an extraordinary effect. Someone with an unpleasant mind had cut him out of an enormous area of electric-blue paper the size of a sheet. For the few moments that the lightning lasted his fingers and thumbs were like bright blue sausages clasped about the cleaver's handle.

Flay, presenting no less the illusion of having no bulk, struck not so much a sense of horror into Mr Swelter as a fresh surge of malice. That he should have dulled the exquisite edge of his cleaver upon Flay-less boards, and that he who should now be lying in two pieces was standing there in *one*, standing there insolently in a kind of stage lighting as a tangible criticism of his error, affected him to the extreme of control, and a horrid sweat broke from his pores.

Mervyn Peake, *Titus Groan*

Dismemberment

'Right then,' he said too loudly. 'I'll make a start. I'll do a leg.'

But he did not move. He stared at the blanket. He could see each separate fibre of the weave, the infinite replication of its simple pattern.

'Take the shoe and sock off first,' was Maria's advice. She had the lid off the tin and was stirring the glue with a tea spoon.

That was practical. He put his hand on Otto's ankle and eased the shoe off by its heel. It came easily. There were no laces. The sock was a disgrace, matted with embedded filth. He peeled it off quickly. The foot was blackened. He was glad he was by an open window. He rolled the blanket up until the legs were exposed from just above the knees. He did not want to start alone.

He said to her, 'I want you to hold him steady with both hands here.' He indicated the upper leg. She did as he asked. They were together now, side by side. He took up the saw. It was finely toothed, and was sheathed for safety in a fold of cardboard held in place by a rubber band. He got that off and stared into the crook of Otto's knee. The trousers were black cotton and shiny from wear. He held the saw in his right hand, and with his left he held Otto's leg just above the ankle. It was colder than room temperature. It drew the heat from his hand.

'Don't think about it,' Maria said. 'Just do it.' She snatched another breath. 'Remember I love you.'

It could not be, of course, but it was important that they were together in this. They needed a formal declaration. He would have told her that he loved her too, but his mouth was so dry.

He drew the saw across the crook of Otto's knee. It snagged immediately. It was the cloth, and below that, stringy tendons. He lifted the saw out and, without looking at the teeth, put it in position again and tried to pull it towards him. The same thing happened.

'I can't do this,' he cried. 'It won't go, it doesn't work!'

'Don't push down so hard,' she said. 'Do it gently. And do the first few strokes towards you. Afterwards you can go backwards and forwards.'

She knew about carpentry. She could have made a better shelf in the bathroom. He did as she suggested. The saw was moving with lubricated ease. Then the teeth snagged again, this time on bone, and then they were engaged. Leonard and Maria had to tighten their grip on the leg to keep it still. The saw made a muffled rasping sound.

'I have to stop!' he shouted, but he did not. He kept going. He should not have been going through bone. The idea was to get between the joint. His idea of it was vague, derived from roast chicken Sunday lunches. He angled the saw this way and that, and went at it hard, knowing that if he stopped, he would never resume. Then he was through something, then it was grating bone again. He was trying not to see, but the April light exposed it all. The upper leg was oozing almost black, covering the saw. The handle was slippery. He was through, there was only skin below, and he could not get at it without sawing the table. He took the lino knife and tried to scour it with one stroke, but it puckered under the blade. He had to get in there, he had to put his hand into the chasm of the joint, into the cold mess of dark, ragged flesh and saw at the skin with the blade of the knife.

'Oh no,' he shouted. 'Oh God!' And he was through. The whole of the lower leg was suddenly an item, a thing in a cylinder of cloth, with a bare foot. Marie was ready for it. She rolled it tight in the square of waterproof cloth she had prepared. Then she glued the ends and sealed them. She tucked the package into one of the cases.

The stump was oozing heavily, the whole table was covered. The newspaper was sodden and disintegrating. Blood was seeping down the table legs and it was already all over the paper on the floor. The paper stuck to their feet when they walked over it, exposing the carpet underneath. His arms were a uniform reddish-brown from the fingertips to above the elbow. It was on his face. Where it was drying there it itched. There were spots on his glasses. Marie's hands and arms were covered too, and her dress was smeared. It was a quiet time of day, but they called to one another as though they were in a storm.

She said, 'I'm going to have a wash.'

'There's no point,' he said. 'Do it at the end.' He took up the saw. Where it had been slippery, it was now sticky. This would aid his grip.

They took hold of the left leg. She was on his right, steadying the lower leg with both hands. It should have been quicker, this one, but it was not. He began well enough, but the saw stuck halfway through, wedged tight between the joint. He had to get both hands on the saw. Marie had to stretch over him and steady the upper leg as well. Even so, as Leonard struggled with the saw, the body jerked from side to side in a mad face-down dance. When the blanket dropped away, Leonard kept his eyes off the skull. It was at the edge of vision. Soon it would have to be dealt with. They were sodden now from the waist down from where they were pushing up against the table. It no longer mattered. He was through the joint. It was the skin again, and he had to put his hand in with the lino knife. Would it have been easier, he thought, if the flesh had been warm?

The second parcel was in the case. Two gumboots side by side. Leonard found the gin. He drank from the bottle and handed it to Maria. She shook her head.

'You're right,' she called. 'We must keep going.'

They did not discuss it, but they knew they would do the arms. They started with the right, the one Leonard had tried to wrench. It was crooked and stiff. They could not pull it out straight. It was difficult finding a way in, or a place to stand to get the saw into the shoulder. Now that the table and the floor, their clothes and arms and face were bloodied, it was not that bad, being near the skull. The whole of the back of it had collapsed inwards. There was only a little brain to be seen, pushed up along the line of the fractures. After red, grey was easy. Maria held the forearm. He started in the armpit, straight into the Army jacket and the shirt underneath. It was a good saw, sharp, not too heavy, just supple enough. Where the blade met the handle was an inch or two not yet obscured by blood. The maker's crest was there, and the word 'Solingen'. He repeated it as he worked. They were not killing anyone here. Otto was dead. Solingen. They were dismantling him. Solingen. Nobody was missing. Solingen, Solingen. Otto is disarmed. Solingen, Solingen.

Between the arms he drank the gin. It was easy, it was sensible. An hour's mess, or five years in prison. The gin bottle was sticky too. The blood was everywhere, and he accepted it. This was what they had to do, this was what they were doing. Solingen. It was a job. After he had given Maria the left arm, he did not pause. He got his hands behind Otto's shirt collar and tugged. The vertebrae at the top of the spine were designed to hold a saw in place. He was through the bone in seconds, through the cord, neatly guiding the flat of the saw against the base of the skull, snagging only briefly on the sinews of the neck, the gristle of the windpipe, and through and through with no need for the lineoleum knife. Solingen, Solingen.

Otto's banged-up head clunked to the floor and settled among the crumpled pages of the *Tagesspiegel* and *Der Abend* and offered up his long-nosed profile. He looked much as he had done in the cupboard – eyes closed, skin unhealthily pale. His lower lip, however, was no longer giving him trouble. What was on the table now was no one at all. It was the field of operations, it was a city far below he had been ordered to destroy. Solingen. The gin again, the sticky Beefeater, then the big one, the thighs, the big push, and that would be it, home, a hot bath, a debriefing.

Maria was sitting on a wooden chair by the open cases. She took each part of her ex-husband onto her lap and patiently, with an almost maternal care, set about folding it away and sealing it and packing it carefully along with the rest. She was wrapping the head now. She was a good woman, resourceful, kind. If they could do this, they could do anything together. When this job was done, they would start again. They were engaged, they would resume the celebrations.

The saw blade rested snugly along the line of the crease where the buttocks met the leg. He would not aim to find the joint this time. Straight through the bone, a sturdy piece of two by two, and a good saw to cut it with. Trouser, skin, fat, flesh, bone, flesh, fat, skin, trouser. The last two he took with the knife. This one was heavy, dripping at both ends when he took it to her. His carpet slippers were black and heavy. The gin, and the other leg. This was the order of things, the order of battle: everything twice, except the head. The big lump which remained on the table to be wrapped, the clearing up, the washing and scrubbing of skin, their skin, the disposal of things. They had a system, they could do this again if they really had to.

Maria was gluing the cloth round the second thigh. She said, 'Take his jacket off.'

That was easy too, what with no arms to mess with. It just lifted off. Everything so far was fitting into one case. The torso would go in the second. She packed the second thigh and closed the lid. She had a dressmaker's tape measure. He took one end and they laid it along the piece on the table. One hundred and two centimetres from gaping neck to stumps. She took the measure and knelt down by the cases.

'It's too big,' she said. 'It won't go in. You'll have to cut it in half.'

Leonard came down, he emerged from a dream. 'That can't be right,' he said. 'Let's measure it again.'

It was right. The cases were ninety-seven centimetres long. He snatched the tape and took the measurements alone. There was surely some means of bringing the figures closer.

'We'll squeeze it in. Wrap it up and we'll squeeze it in.'

'It won't go. It's a shoulder bone here, and the other end is thick. You have to cut it in half.' It was her husband, and she knew.

Arms and legs, and even the head, were extremities that could be lopped off. But cutting into the rest was not right. He fumbled after a principle, some general notion of decency to support his instinctive certainty. He was so tired. When he closed his eyes he felt himself lifting away. What was needed here were some guidelines, a few basic rules. It simply was not possible, he heard himself telling Glass and a handful of senior officers, to make abstractions and define general principles when you were right in the middle of a job. These things had to be thought through beforehand, leaving the men free to concentrate on the work itself.

Maria had sat down again. Her sodden dress sagged in her lap. 'Do it quickly,' she said. 'Then we can get cleared up.' She had found the pack with the three cigarettes inside. She lit one, took a drag and passed it to him. He did not mind the red smudges all over the paper, he honestly did not care. But when he went to pass it back to her, the cigarette stuck to his fingers.

'You keep it,' she said, 'and let's start.'

Soon he had to change his grip to avoid getting his fingers burnt. The paper came away and the tobacco spilled out. He let it all fall to the floor and stamped on it. He took up the saw and untucked Otto's shirt, exposing the back just above the waistband of the trousers. Right on the spine was a big mole. He felt squeamish about cutting through it and positioned the blade half an inch lower. His saw cut now was the whole width of the back, and again the vertebrae kept him on track. He was through the bone easily enough, but an inch or so further in he began to feel that he was not cutting through things so much as pushing them to one side. But he kept on. He was in the cavity that contained all that he did not want to see. He was keeping his head raised so that he did not have to look into the cut. He looked in Maria's direction. She was still sitting there, grey and tired and not wanting to watch. Her eyes were on the open window and the big cumulus clouds that drifted over the courtyard.

There was a glutinous sound which brought him the memory of a jelly eased from its mould. It was moving about in there, something had collapsed and rolled onto something else. He was through to the bottom and now he faced the old problem. He could not cut through the belly skin without sawing into the wood. It was a good table too, sturdily constructed of elm. And this time he was not reaching his hand in. Instead, he turned the carcass through ninety degrees and pulled it forward by the front half, so that the saw cut was in line with the table's edge. He should have asked for Maria's help. She should have foreseen the difficulty and come to his rescue. He was supporting the top half with both hands. The lower half still rested on the table. How then was he supposed to use the lino knife to cut through the belly skin? He was too tired to stop, even though he knew he was attempting the impossible. He brought his left knee up to bear the weight and stretched forwards for the knife which was on the table. It might have worked. He could have held the upper body with his knee and his hand, and with his free hand he could have reached under and cut through the skin. But he was too tired to be balancing on one leg. He almost had the knife in his hand when he felt himself toppling. He had to put his left foot down. He tried to get the free hand back in time. But the whole thing fell from his grasp. The top half swung on its hinge of skin towards the floor, exposing the vivid mess of Otto's digestive tract, and pulling the bottom half with it. Both tipped to the floor and disgorged onto the carpet.

There was a moment before he left the room when Leonard suddenly had the measure of the distance they had travelled, the trajectory that had delivered them from their successful little engagement party to this, and how all along the way each successive step had seemed logical enough, consistent with the one before, and how no one was to blame. Before he made his run for the bathroom he had an impression of liverish reds, glistening irregular tubing of a boiled egg bluish white, and something purple and black, all of it shining and livid at the outrage of violated privacy, of secrets exposed. Despite the open windows, the room filled with the close stench of musty air, which itself was a medium for other smells: of sweet earth, sulphurous crap, and Sauerkraut. The insult was, Leonard had time to think, as he stepped hurriedly round the up-ended halves of the torso that were still joined, that all this stuff was also in himself.

Ian McEwan, *The Innocent*

Disposal

'Now, for God's sake,' said Spandrell roughly, 'pull yourself together.'

Illidge pressed his handkerchief to his mouth; he was afraid of being sick. 'I think I'll lie down for a moment,' he whispered. But when he tried to walk, it was as though his legs were dead under him. It might have been a paralytic who dragged himself to the sofa.

'What you need is a mouthful of spirits,' said Spandrell. He crossed the room. A bottle of brandy stood on the sideboard, and from the kitchen he returned with glasses. He poured out two fingers of the spirit. 'Here. Drink this.' Illidge took and sipped. 'One would think we were crossing the Channel,' Spandrell went on with ferocious mockery, as he helped himself to brandy. 'Study in green and ginger – that's how Whistler would have described you now. Apple-green. Moss-green.'

Illidge looked at him for a moment, then turned away, unable to face the steady glance of those contemptuous grey eyes. He had never felt such hatred as he now felt for Spandrell.

'Not to say frog-green, slime-green, scum-green,' the other went on.

'Oh, shut up!' cried Illidge in a voice that had recovered some of its resonance and hardly wavered. Spandrell's mockery had steadied his nerves. Hate, like brandy, is a stimulant. He took another burning gulp. There was a silence.

'When you feel like it,' said Spandrell, putting down his emptied glass, 'you can come and help me clear up.' He rose and walked round the screen, out of sight.

Everard Webley's body was lying where it had fallen, on its side, with the arms reaching out across the floor. The chloroform-soaked handkerchief still covered the face. Spandrell bent down and twitched it away. The temple which had been struck was against the floor; seen from above the face seemed unwounded.

His hands in his pockets, Spandrell stood looking down at the body.

'Five minutes ago,' he said to himself, formulating his thoughts in words, that his realization of their significance might be the more complete, 'five minutes ago, it was alive, it had a soul. Alive,' he repeated and balancing himself unsteadily on one leg, with the other foot he touched the dead cheek, he pushed forward the ear and let it flick back again. 'A soul.' And for a moment he allowed some of his weight to rest on what had been Everard Webley's face. He withdrew his foot; the print of it remained, dust-grey, on the white skin. 'Trampling on a dead face,' he said to himself. Why had he done it? 'Trampling.' He raised his foot again and pressed his heel into the socket of the eye, gently, tentatively, as though experimenting with outrage. 'Like grapes,' he thought. 'Trampling wine out of the grapes.' It was in his power to trample this thing into a pulp. But he had done enough. Symbolically, he had trodden out the essential horror from his murder; it flowed from under his trampling feet.

The essential horror? But it was more stupid and disgusting than horrible. Pushing the toe of his boot under the chin, he rolled the head over until the face was looking up, open-mouthed and with half-shut eyes, at the ceiling. Above and behind the left eye was a huge red contusion. There were trickles of blood on the left cheek, already dry, and where the forehead had rested on the floor, a little pool – hardly even a pool – a smear.

'Incredibly little blood,' said Spandrell aloud.

At the sound of his calm voice Illidge violently started.

Spandrell withdrew his supporting foot. The dead face fell back with a little thump on its side.

'It's a complete justification for Bishop Odo's mace,' he went on dispassionately. That he should find himself recalling, at this of all moments, the comical prancings of that conscientious churchman in the Bayeaux tapestry – that too was part of the essential horror. The frivolousness of the human mind! The wandering irrelevance! Evil might have a certain dignity. But silliness . . .

Illidge heard him walk into the kitchen. There was the gradually sharpening note of water running into a pail. The tap was turned off; there were foot-falls; the bucket was set down with a metallic clink.

'Luckily,' Spandrell went on, in comment on his last remark. 'Or else I don't know what we should have done about the mess.'

Illidge listened with a strained and horrified attention to the sounds that came to him from the other side of the screen. A limp and meaty thud; was that an arm lifted and dropped? The sibilant sliding of a soft and heavy object across the floor. Then the splash of water, the homely noise of scrubbing. And at these sounds, so incomparably more horrible, more profoundly significant than any words, however brutal, however calmly cynical, that Spandrell could say, he felt a recrudescence of that sinking, that heart-fluttering faintness of the first minutes, when the dead man was lying there, still twitching, at his feet. He remembered, he lived over again those moments of breathless and sick anticipation before the horrible event. The noise of the car backing down the street; the gritty scrape of feet on the doorstep, and then the knock, and then a long, long silence of heartbeats and visceral creepings and imaginative forebodings, of justifying thoughts of revolution and the future, justifying hatred of oppression and the vileness of wealth. And at the same time ridiculous, incongruous recollections, as he crouched behind the screen, of those childish games of hide-and-seek on school-treat days, among the gorse and juniper bushes of the common. 'One, two, three . . .'; the seekers covered their faces and began to count their hundred, aloud; the hiders scattered. You thrust yourself into a prickly bush, you lay in the bracken. Then came the shout of 'ninety-nine, a hundred, Cooee!'; and the seekers were off, were after you. And the excitement was so painfully intense, as you crouched or squatted in your lair, peeping, listening for a chance to make a bolt for Home, that you felt an almost irrepressible desire to 'do something', though something had been done, behind the junipers, only five minutes before. Absurd memories! And because absurd, dreadful! For the hundredth time he felt in his pocket to make sure that the bottle of chloroform was still there and safely corked. The second knock startlingly resounded and, with it, the whistle and that humorous call (you could *hear*, from the tone of his voice, that he was smiling) of 'Friend!' Behind his screen Illidge had shuddered. 'Friend!' And remembering now, he shuddered again, more violently, with all the shame and horror and humiliation which he had had no time then to feel. No time; for before his mind could realize all the implications upon implications of that laughing call, the door had creaked on its hinges, there was the noise of feet on the boards, and Webley was shouting Elinor's name. (Illidge suddenly found himself wondering if he had been in love with her.) 'Elinor!' There followed a silence; Webley had seen the note. Illidge had heard his breathing, only a foot or two away, on the other side of the screen. And then there was the rustle of a quick movement, the beginning of an exclamation and that sudden dry concussion, like the noise of a slap, but duller, deader and at the same time much louder. There followed a fraction of a second's silence, then the noise of falling – not a single sound, but a series of noises spread over an appreciable period of time; the bony collapse of the knees, the scrape of shoes sliding away across the polished floor, the muffled thud of the body and arms, and the sharp hard rap of the head against the boards. 'Quick!' had come the sound of Spandrell's voice, and he had darted out of his hiding-place. 'Chloroform.' Obediently, he had soaked the handkerchief, he had spread it over the twitching face . . . He shuddered again, he took another sip of brandy.

The sound of scrubbing was succeeded by the squelch of a wetted cloth.

'There,' said Spandrell round the screen. He was drying his hands on a duster. 'And how's the invalid?' he added in the parody of a bedside manner, smiling ironically.

Illidge averted his face. The hatred flared up in him, expelling for the moment every other emotion. 'I'm all right,' he said curtly.

'Just taking it easy while I do the dirty work. Is that it?' Spandrell threw the duster on to a chair and began to turn down his shirt cuffs.

In two hours the muscles of the heart contract and relax, contract again and relax only eight thousand times. The earth travels less than an eighth of a million miles along its orbit. And the prickly pear has had time to invade only another hundred acres of Australian territory. Two hours are as nothing. The time to listen to the Ninth Symphony and a couple of the posthumous quartets, to fly from London to Paris, to transfer a luncheon from the stomach to the small intestine, to read *Macbeth*, to die of snake bite or earn one-and-eightpence as a charwoman. No more. But to Illidge, as he sat waiting, with the dead body lying there behind the screen, waiting for the darkness, they seemed unending.

'Are you an idiot?' asked Spandrell, when he had suggested that they should go away at once and leave the thing lying there. 'Or are you particularly anxious to die of hanging?' The sneer, the cool ironic amusement were maddening to Illidge. 'It would be found to-night when Philip came home.'

'But Quarles hasn't got a key,' said Illidge.

'Then to-morrow, as soon as he'd got hold of a locksmith. And three hours later, when Elinor had explained what she had done with the key, the police would be knocking at my door. And I promise you, they'd knock at yours very soon afterwards.' He smiled at Illidge, who averted his eyes. 'No,' Spandrell went on, 'Webley's got to be taken away. And with his car standing outside, it's child's play, if we wait till after dark.'

'But it won't be dark for another two hours.' Illidge's voice was shrill with anger and complaint.

'Well, what of it?'

'Why . . .' Illidge began and checked himself; he realized that if he was going to answer truthfully, he would have to say that he didn't want to stay those two hours because he was frightened. 'All right,' he said. 'Let's stay.' Spandrell picked up the silver cigarette box, opened and sniffed. 'They smell very nice,' he said. 'Have one.' He pushed the box across the table. 'And there are lots of books. And *The Times*. And the *New Statesman*. And the latest number of *Vogue*. It's positively a dentist's waiting-room. And we might even make ourselves a cup of tea.' The time of waiting began. Heart-beat followed heart-beat. Each second the earth travelled twenty miles and the prickly pears covered another five rods of Australian ground. Behind the screen lay the body. Thousands upon thousands of millions of minute and diverse individuals had come together and the product of their mutual dependence, their mutual hostility had been a human life. Their total colony, their living hive had been a man. The hive was dead. But in the lingering warmth many of the component individuals still faintly lived; soon they also would have perished. And meanwhile, from the air, the invisible hosts of saprophytics had already begun their unresisted invasion. They would live among the dead cells, they would grow, and prodigiously multiply and in their growing and procreation all the chemical building of the body would be undone, all the intricacies and complications of its matter would be resolved, till by the time their work was finished a few pounds of carbon, a few quarts of water, some lime, a little phosphorus and sulphur, a pinch of iron and silicon, a handful of mixed salts – all scattered and recombined with the surrounding world – would be all that remained of Everard Webley's ambition to rule and his love for Elinor, of his thoughts about politics and his recollections of childhood, of his fencing and good horsemanship, of that soft strong voice and that suddenly illuminating smile, of his admiration for Mantegna, his dislike of whisky, his deliberately terrifying rages, his habit of stroking his chin, his belief in God, his incapacity to whistle a tune correctly, his unshakeable determinations and his knowledge of Russian.

Illidge turned over the advertisement pages of *Vogue*. A young lady in a fur coat priced at two hundred guineas was stepping into a motor car; on the opposite page another young lady in nothing but a towel was stepping out of a bath impregnated with Dr Verbruggen's Reducing Salts. There followed a still-life of scent bottles containing *Songe Nègre* and the maker's latest creation, *Relent d'Amour*. The names of Worth, Lanvin, Patou sprawled across three more pages. Then there was a picture of a young lady in a rubber reducing belt, looking at herself in the glass. A group of young ladies admired one another's slumber wear from Crabb and Lushington's lingerie department. Opposite them another young lady reclined on a couch at Madame Adrena's Beauty Laboratory, while the hands of a masseuse stroked the menace of a double chin. Then followed a still-life of rolling pins and rubber strigils for rolling and rubbing away young ladies' superfluous fat, and another still-life of jars and gallipots containing skin foods to protect their faces from the ravages of time and the weather.

'Revolting!' Illidge said to himself as he turned the pages. 'Criminal!' And he cherished his indignation, he cultivated it. To be angry was a distraction, and at the same time a justification. Raging at plutocratic callousness and frivolity, he could half forget and half excuse to himself the horrible thing that had happened. Webley's body was lying on the other side of the screen. But there were women who paid two hundred guineas for a fur coat. Two hundred guineas! His Uncle Joseph would have thought himself happy if he could have made as much in eighteen months of cobbling. And they bought scent at twenty-five shillings the quarter-pint. He remembered the time when his little brother Tom had had pneumonia after influenza. Ghastly! And when he was convalescent, the doctor had said he ought to go away to the sea for a few weeks. They hadn't been able to afford it. Tom's lungs had never been too strong after that. He worked in a motor factory now (making machines for those bitches in two-hundred-guinea coats to sit in); Illidge had paid for him to go to a technical school – paid, he reflected, beating up his anger, that the boy might have the privilege of standing eight hours a day in front of a milling machine. The air of Manchester wasn't doing Tom any good. There was no superfluous fat to be rolled off him, poor devil. Swinish guzzling! Why couldn't they do a little useful work instead of squeegeeing their hams and bellies? That would take the fat off all right. If they worked as his mother had done . . . She had no fat to rub off with rolling-pins, or sweat off under a rubber belt, or stew off in hot baths and brine. He thought indignantly of that endless dreary labour of housework. Day after day, year after year. Making beds, that they might be unmade. Cooking to fill bellies eternally empty. Washing up what the next meal was to make dirty again. Scrubbing the floor for muddy boots to defile. Darning and patching that yet more holes might be made. It was like the labouring of Sisyphus and the Danaids, hopeless and interminable – or would have been interminable (except by his mother's death), if he hadn't been able to send her those two pounds a week out of his salary. She could get a girl in now to help with the hardest work. But she still did more than enough to make rubber belts unnecessary. What a life! And in the world of fur coats and *Songe Nègre* they complained of boredom and fatigue, they had to retire into nursing homes for rest cures. If they could lead *her* life for a bit! And perhaps they'd be made to, one of these days (he hoped so), even in England. Illidge thought with satisfaction of those ex-officers of the Tsar driving taxis and working in factories, those ex-countesses with their restaurants and cabarets and hat-shops; of all the ex-rich of Russia, all over the world, from Harbin and Shanghai to Rome and London and Berlin, bankrupt, humiliated, reduced to the slavish estate of the common people on whom they had once parasitically lived. That was good, that served them right. And perhaps it might happen here too. But they were strong here, the fat-reducers and the fur-coated; they were numerous, they were an organized army. But the army had lost its chief. He had got his packet. Embodied beastliness and plutocracy, he lay there behind the screen. But his mouth had been open and the muscles of his face, before the reeking handkerchief had covered it, had twitched grotesquely. Illidge shuddered. He looked again for indignant distraction and justification at the picture of the young lady in the two-hundred-guinea fur, of the young lady stepping, naked but coyly towelled, out of her reducing bath. Strumpets and gluttons! They belonged to the class that Webley had fought to perpetuate. The champion of all that was vile and low. He had got what he deserved, he had . . .

'Good Lord!' exclaimed Spandrell suddenly, looking up from his book. The sound of his voice in the silence made Illidge start with an uncontrollable terror. 'I'd absolutely forgotten. They get stiff, don't they?' he looked at Illidge. 'Corpses, I mean.'

Illidge nodded. He drew a deep breath and steadied himself with an effort of will.

'What about getting him into the car, then?' He sprang up and walked quickly round the screen, out of sight. Illidge heard the latch of the house door rattling. He was seized with a sudden horrible terror: Spandrell was going to make off, leaving him locked in with the body.

'Where are you going?' he shouted and darted off in panic pursuit. 'Where are you going?' The door was open, Spandrell was not to be seen, and the thing lay on the floor, its face uncovered, open-mouthed and staring secretly, significantly, as though through spy-holes, between half-closed eyelids. 'Where are you going?' Illidge's voice had risen almost to a scream.

'What *is* the excitement about?' asked Spandrell as the other appeared, pale and with desperation in his looks, on the doorstep. Standing by Webley's car, he was engaged in undoing the tightly stretched waterproof which decked in all that part of the open body lying aft of the front seats. 'These thingumbobs are horribly hard to unfasten.'

Illidge put his hands in his pockets and pretended that it was merely an idle curiosity that had brought him out with such precipitation.

'What are you doing?' he asked off-handedly.

Spandrell gave a final tug; the cover came loose along the whole length of one side of the car. He turned it back and looked in. 'Empty, thank goodness,' he said and, stretching his hand, he played imaginary octaves, span after span, over the coach-work. 'Say four feet wide,' he concluded, 'by about the same in length. Of which half is taken up by the seat. With two foot six of space under the cover. Plenty of room to curl up in and be very comfortable. But if one were stiff?' He looked inquiringly at Illidge. 'A man could be got in, but not a statue.'

Illidge nodded. Spandrell's last words had made him suddenly remember Lady Edward's mocking commentary on Webley. 'He wants to be treated like his own colossal statue – posthumously, if you see what I mean.'

'We must do something quickly,' Spandrell went on. 'Before the stiffness sets in.' He pulled back the cover and laying a hand on Illidge's shoulder, propelled him gently into the house. The door slammed behind them. They stood looking down at the body.

'We shall have to pull the knees up and the arms down,' said Spandrell.

He bent down and moved one of the arms towards the side. It returned, when he let go, half-way to its former position. Like a puppet, Spandrell reflected, with elastic joints. Grotesque rather than terrible; not tragical, but only rather tiresome and even absurd. That was the essential horror – that it was all (even *this*) a kind of bad and tedious jape. 'We shall have to find some string,' he said. 'Something to tie the limbs into place.' It was like amateur plumbing, or mending the summer-house oneself; just rather unpleasant and ludicrous.

They ransacked the house. There was no string to be found. They had to be content with three bandages, which Spandrell found among the aspirin and iodine, the boracic powder and vegetable laxatives of the little medicine cupboard in the bathroom.

'Hold the arms in place while I tie,' commanded Spandrell.

Illidge did as he was told. But the coldness of those dead wrists against his fingers was horrible; he felt sick again, he began to tremble.

'There!' said Spandrell, straightening himself up. 'Now the legs. Thank goodness we didn't leave it much longer.'

'Treated like his own statue.' The words reverberated in Illidge's memory. 'Posthumously, if you see what I mean.' Posthumously . . . Spandrell bent one of the legs till the knee almost touched the chin.

'Hold it.'

Illidge grasped the ankle; the socks were grey and clocked with white. Spandrell let go, and Illidge felt a sudden and starlingly powerful thrust against his retaining hand. The dead man was trying to kick. Black voids began to expand in front of his eyes, eating out holes in the solid world before him. And the solid world itself swayed and swam round the edges of those interstellar vacancies. His gorge turned, he felt horribly giddy.

'Look here,' he began, turning to Spandrell, who had squatted down on his heels and was tearing the wrappings off another bandage. Then shutting his eyes, he relinquished his grasp.

The leg straightened itself out like a bent spring, and the foot, as it shot forward, caught Spandrell on the shoulder and sent him, unsteadily balanced as he was, sprawling backwards on the floor.

He picked himself up. 'You bloody fool!' But the anger aroused by that first shock of surprise died down. He uttered a little laugh. 'We might be at the circus,' he said. It was not only not tragic; it was a clownery.

By the time the body was finally trussed, Illidge knew that Tom's weak lungs and two-hundred-guinea coats, that superfluous fat and his mother's life-long slaving, that rich and poor, oppression and revolution, justice, punishment, indignation – all, as far as he was concerned, were utterly irrelevant to the fact of these stiffening limbs, this mouth that gaped, these half-shut, glazed and secretly staring eyes. Irrelevant, and beside the point.

Aldous Huxley, *Point Counter Point*

Dog

The night was clear and fine above us. The stars shone cold and bright, while a half-moon bathed the whole scene in a soft, uncertain light. Before us lay the dark bulk of the house, its serrated roof and bristling chimneys hard outlined against the silver-spangled sky. Broad bars of golden light from the lower windows stretched across the orchard and the moor. One of them was suddenly shut off. The servants had left the kitchen. There only remained the lamp in the dining-room where the two men, the murderous host and the unconscious guest, still chatted over their cigars.

Every minute that white woolly plain which covered one-half of the moor was drifting closer and closer to the house. Already the first thin wisps of it were curling across the golden square of the lighted window. The farther wall of the orchard was already invisible, and the trees were standing out of a swirl of white vapour. As we watched it the fog-wreaths came crawling round both corners of the house and rolled slowly into one dense bank, on which the upper floor and the roof floated like a strange ship upon a shadowy sea. Holmes struck his hand passionately upon the rock in front of us, and stamped his feet in his impatience.

'If he isn't out in a quarter of an hour the path will be covered. In half an hour we won't be able to see our hands in front of us.'

'Shall we move farther back upon higher ground?'

'Yes, I think it would be as well.'

So as the fog-bank flowed onwards we fell back before it until we were half a mile from the house, and still that dense white sea, with the moon silvering its upper edge, swept slowly and inexorably on.

'We are going too far,' said Holmes. 'We dare not take the chance of his being overtaken before he can reach us. At all costs we must hold our ground where we are.' He dropped on his knees and clapped his ear to the ground. 'Thank heaven, I think that I hear him coming.'

A sound of quick steps broke the silence of the moor. Crouching among the stones, we stared intently at the silver-tipped bank in front of us. The steps grew louder, and through the fog, as through a curtain, there stepped the man whom we were awaiting. He looked round him in surprise as he emerged into the clear, starlit night. Then he came swiftly along the path, passed close to where we lay, and went on up the long slope behind us. As he walked he glanced continually over either shoulder, like a man who is ill at ease.

'Hist!' cried Holmes, and I heard the sharp click of a cocking pistol. 'Look out! It's coming!'

There was a thin, crisp, continuous patter from somewhere in the heart of that crawling bank. The cloud was within fifty yards of where we lay, and we glared at it, all three, uncertain what horror was about to break from the heart of it. I was at Holmes's elbow, and I glanced for an instant at his face. It was pale and exultant, his eyes shining brightly in the moonlight. But suddenly they started forward in a rigid, fixed stare, and his lips parted in amazement. At the same instant Lestrade gave a yell of terror and threw himself face downwards upon the ground. I sprang to my feet, my inert hand grasping my pistol, my mind paralysed by the dreadful shape which had sprung out upon us from the shadows of the fog. A hound it was, an enormous coal-black hound, but not such a hound as mortal eyes have ever seen. Fire burst from its open mouth, its eyes glowed with a smouldering glare, its muzzle and hackles and dewlap were outlined in flickering flame. Never in the delirious dream of a disordered brain could anything more savage, more appalling, more hellish, be conceived than that dark form and savage face which broke upon us out of the wall of fog.

With long bounds the huge black creature was leaping down the track, following hard upon the footsteps of our friend. So paralysed were we by the apparition that we allowed him to pass before we had recovered our nerve. Then Holmes and I both fired together, and the creature gave a hideous howl, which showed that one at least had hit him. He did not pause, however, but bounded onwards. Far away on the path we saw Sir Henry looking back, his face white in the moonlight, his hands raised in horror, glaring helplessly at the frightful thing which was hunting him down.

But that cry of pain from the hound had blown all our fears to the winds. If he was vulnerable he was mortal, and if we could wound him we could kill him. Never have I seen a man run as Holmes ran that night. I am reckoned fleet of foot, but he outpaced me as much as I outpaced the little professional. In front of us as we flew up the track we heard scream after scream from Sir Henry and the deep roar of the hound. I was in time to see the beast spring upon its victim, hurl him to the ground and worry at his throat. But the next instant Holmes had emptied five barrels of his revolver into the creature's flank. With a last howl of agony and a vicious snap in the air it rolled upon its back, four feet pawing furiously, and then fell limp upon its side. I stooped, panting, and pressed my pistol to the dreadful, shimmering head, but it was useless to press the trigger. The giant hound was dead.

Sir Henry lay insensible where he had fallen. We tore away his collar, and Holmes breathed a prayer of gratitude when we saw that there was no sign of a wound and that the rescue had been in time. Already our friend's eyelids shivered and he made a feeble effort to move. Lestrade thrust his brandy-flask between the baronet's teeth, and two frightened eyes were looking up at us.

'My God!' he whispered. 'What was it? What, in Heaven's name, was it?'

Arthur Conan Doyle, *The Hound of the Baskervilles*

Dots

For an hour he waited, walking up and down to keep warm, inside the enclosure of the Great Wheel; the smashed Prater with its bones sticking crudely through the snow was nearly empty. One stall sold thin flat cakes like cartwheels, and the children queued with their coupons. A few courting couples would be packed together in a single car of the Wheel and revolve slowly above the city, surrounded by empty cars. As the car reached the highest point of the Wheel, the revolutions would stop for a couple of minutes and far overhead the tiny faces would press against the glass. Martins wondered who would come for him. Was there enough friendship left in Harry for him to come alone, or would a squad of police arrive? It was obvious from the raid on Anna Schmidt's flat that he had a certain pull. And then as his watch-hand passed the hour, he wondered:

Was it all an invention of my mind? Are they digging up Harry's body now in the Central Cemetery?

Somewhere behind the cakestall a man was whistling, and Martins knew the tune. He turned and waited. Was it fear or excitement that made his heart beat – or just the memories that tune ushered in, for life had always quickened when Harry came, came just as he came now, as though nothing much had happened, nobody had been lowered into a grave or found with cut throat in a basement, came with his amused, deprecating, take-it-or-leave-it manner – and of course one always took it.

'Harry.'

'Hullo, Rollo.'

Don't picture Harry Lime as a smooth scoundrel. He wasn't that. The picture I have of him on my files is an excellent one: he is caught by a street photographer with his stocky legs apart, big shoulders a little hunched, a belly that had known too much good food for too long, on his face a look of cheerful rascality, a geniality, a recognition that *his* happiness will make the world's day. Now he didn't make the mistake of putting out a hand that might have been rejected, but instead just patted Martins on the elbow and said, 'How are things?'

'We've got to talk, Harry.'

'Of course.'

'Alone.'

'We couldn't be more alone than here.'

He had always known the ropes, and even in the smashed pleasure park he knew them, tipping the woman in charge of the Wheel, so that they might have a car to themselves. He said, 'Lovers used to do this in the old days, but they haven't the money to spare, poor devils, now,' and he looked out of the window of the swaying, rising car at the figures diminishing below with what looked like genuine commiseration.

Very slowly on one side of them the city sank; very slowly on the other the great cross-girders of the Wheel rose into sight. As the horizon slid away the Danube became visible, and the piers of the Reichsbrücke lifted above the houses. 'Well,' Harry said, 'it's good to see you, Rollo.'

'I was at your funeral.'

'That was pretty smart of me, wasn't it?'

'Not so smart for your girl. She was there too – in tears.'

'She's a good little thing,' Harry said. 'I'm very fond of her.'

'I didn't believe the police when they told me about you.'

Harry said, 'I wouldn't have asked you to come if I'd known what was going to happen, but I didn't think the police were on to me.'

'Were you going to cut me in on the spoils?'

'I've never kept you out of anything, old man, yet.' He stood with his back to the door as the car swung upwards, and smiled back at Rollo Martins, who could remember him in just such an attitude in a secluded corner of the school-quad, saying, 'I've learned a way to get out at night. It's absolutely safe. You are the only one I'm letting in on it.' For the first time Rollo Martins looked back through the years without admiration, as he thought: He's never grown up. Marlowe's devils wore squibs attached to their tails: evil was like Peter Pan – it carried with it the horrifying and horrible gift of eternal youth.

Martins said, 'Have you ever visited the children's hospital? Have you seen any of your victims?'

Harry took a look at the toy landscape below and came away from the door. 'I never feel quite safe in these things,' he said. He felt the back of the door with his hand, as though he were afraid that it might fly open and launch him into that iron-ribbed space. 'Victims?' he asked. 'Don't be melodramatic, Rollo. Look down there,' he went on, pointing through the window at the people moving like black flies at the base of the Wheel. 'Would you really feel any pity if one of those dots stopped moving – for ever? If I said you can have twenty thousand pounds for every dot that stops, would you really, old man, tell me to keep my money – without hesitation? Or would you calculate how many dots you could afford to spare? Free of income tax, old man. Free of income tax.' He gave his boyish conspiratorial smile. 'It's the only way to save nowadays.'

Graham Greene, *The Third Man*

Double

Some two months before the murder of Sir Danvers, I had been out for one of my adventures, had returned at a late hour, and woke the next day in bed with somewhat odd sensations. It was in vain I looked about me; in vain I saw the decent furniture and tall proportions of my room in the square; in vain that I recognised the pattern of the bed curtains and the design of the mahogany frame; something still kept insisting that I was not where I was, that I had not wakened where I seemed to be, but in the little room in Soho where I was accustomed to sleep in the body of Edward Hyde. I smiled to myself, and, in my psychological way, began lazily to inquire into the elements of this illusion, occasionally, even as I did so, dropping back into a comfortable morning doze. I was still so engaged when, in one of my more wakeful moments, my eye fell upon my hand. Now, the hand of Henry Jekyll (as you have often remarked) was professional in shape and size; it was large, firm, white and comely. But the hand which I now saw, clearly enough in the yellow light of a mid-London morning, lying half shut on the bed-clothes, was lean, corded, knuckly, of a dusky pallor, and thickly shaded with a swart growth of hair. It was the hand of Edward Hyde.

I must have stared upon it for near half a minute, sunk as I was in the mere stupidity of wonder, before terror woke up in my breast as sudden and startling as the crash of cymbals; and bounding from my bed, I rushed to the mirror. At the sight that met my eyes, my blood was changed into something exquisitely thin and icy. Yes, I had gone to bed Henry Jekyll, I had awakened Edward Hyde. How was this to be explained? I asked myself; and then, with another bound of terror – how was it to be remedied? It was well on in the morning; the servants were up; all my drugs were in the cabinet – a long journey, down two pairs of stairs, through the back passage, across the open court and through the anatomical theatre, from where I was then standing horror-struck. It might indeed be possible to cover my face; but of what use was that, when I was unable to conceal the alteration in my stature? And then, with an overpowering sweetness of relief, it came back upon my mind that the servants were already used to the coming and going of my second self. I had soon dressed; as well as I was able, in clothes of my own size; had soon passed through the house, where Bradshaw stared and drew back at seeing Mr Hyde at such an hour and in such a strange array; and ten minutes later, Dr Jekyll had returned to his own shape, and was sitting down, with a darkened brow, to make a feint of breakfasting.

Small indeed was my appetite. This inexplicable incident, this reversal of my previous experience seemed, like the Babylonian finger on the wall, to be spelling out the letters of my judgement; and I began to reflect more seriously than ever before on the issues of the possibilities of my double existence. That part of me which I had the power of projecting had lately been much exercised and nourished; it had seemed to me of late as though the body of Edward Hyde had grown in stature, as though (when I wore that form) I were conscious of a more generous tide of blood; and I began to spy a danger that, if this were much prolonged, the balance of my nature might be permanently overthrown, the power of voluntary change be forfeited, and the character of Edward Hyde become irrevocably mine. The power of the drug had not been always displayed. Once, very early in my career, it had totally failed me; since then I had been obliged on more than one occasion to double, and once, with infinite risk of death, to treble the amount; and these rare uncertainties had cast hitherto the sole shadow on my contentment. Now, however, and in the light of that morning's accident, I was led to remark that whereas, in the beginning, the difficulty had been to throw off the body of Jekyll, it had of late gradually but decidedly transferred itself to the other side. All things therefore seemed to point to this: that I was slowly losing hold of my original and better self, and becoming slowly incorporated with my second and worse.

Between these two I now felt I had to choose. My two natures had memory in common, but all other faculties were most unequally shared between them. Jekyll (who was composite), now with the most sensitive apprehensions, now with a greedy gusto, projected and shared in the pleasures and adventures of Hyde; but Hyde was indifferent to Jekyll, or but remembered him as the mountain bandit remembers the cavern in which he conceals himself from pursuit. Jekyll had more than a father's interest; Hyde had more than a son's indifference. To cast in my lot with Jekyll was to die to those appetites which I had long secretly indulged and had of late begun to pamper. To cast it in with Hyde was to die to a thousand interests and aspirations, and to become, at a blow and for ever, despised and friendless. The bargain might appear unequal; but there was still another consideration in the scales; for while Jekyll would suffer smartingly in the fires of abstinence, Hyde would be not even conscious of all that he had lost. Strange as my circumstances were, the terms of this debate are as old and commonplace as man; much the same inducements and alarms cast the die for any tempted and trembling sinner; and it fell out with me, as it falls with so vast a majority of my fellows, that I chose the better part, and was found wanting in the strength to keep to it.

Yes, I preferred the elderly and discontented doctor, surrounded by friends, and cherishing honest hopes; and bade a resolute farewell to the liberty, the comparative youth, the light step, leaping pulses and secret pleasures, that I had enjoyed in the disguise of Hyde. I made this choice perhaps with some unconscious reservation, for I neither gave up the house in Soho, nor destroyed the clothes of Edward Hyde, which still lay ready in my cabinet. For two months, however, I was true to my determination; for two months I led a life of such severity as I had never before attained to, and enjoyed the compensations of an approving conscience. But time began at last to obliterate the freshness of my alarm; the praises of conscience began to grow into a thing of course; I began to be tortured with throes and longings, as of Hyde struggling after freedom;

and at last, in an hour of moral weakness, I once again compounded and swallowed the transforming draught.

I do not suppose that when a drunkard reasons with himself upon his vice, he is once out of five hundred times affected by the dangers that he runs through his brutish physical insensibility; neither had I, long as I had considered my position, made enough allowance for the complete moral insensibility and insensate readiness to evil which were the leading characters of Edward Hyde. Yet it was by these that I was punished. My devil had been long caged, he came out roaring. I was conscious, even when I took the draught, of a more unbridled, a more furious propensity to ill. It must have been this, I suppose, that stirred in my soul that tempest of impatience with which I listened to the civilities of my unhappy victim; I declare at least, before God, no man morally sane could have been guilty of that crime upon so pitiful a provocation; and that I struck in no more reasonable spirit than that in which a sick child may break a plaything. But I had voluntarily stripped myself of all those balancing instincts by which the worst of us continues to walk with some degree of steadiness among temptations; and in my case, to be tempted, however slightly, was to fall.

Instantly the spirit of hell awoke in me and raged. With a transport of glee, I mauled the unresisting body, tasting delight from every blow; and it was not till weariness had begun to succeed that I was suddenly, in the top fit of my delirium, struck through the heart by a cold thrill of terror. A mist dispersed; I saw my life to be forfeit; and fled from the scene of these excesses, at once glorying and trembling, my lust of evil gratified and stimulated, my love of life screwed to the topmost peg. I ran to the house in Soho, and (to make assurance doubly sure) destroyed my papers; thence I set out through the lamplit streets, in the same divided ecstasy of mind, gloating on my crime, light-headedly devising others in the future, and yet still hastening and still harkening in my wake for the steps of the avenger. Hyde had a song upon his lips as he compounded the draught, and as he drank it pledged the dead man. The pangs of transformation had not done tearing him, before Henry Jekyll, with streaming tears of gratitude and remorse, had fallen upon his knees and lifted his clasped hands to God. The veil of self-indulgence was rent from head to foot, I saw my life as a whole: I followed it up from the days of childhood, when I had walked with my father's hand, and through the self-denying toils of my professional life, to arrive again and again, with the same sense of unreality, at the damned horrors of the evening. I could have screamed aloud; I sought with tears and prayers to smother down the crowd of hideous images and sounds with which my memory swarmed against me;

and still, between the petitions, the ugly face of my iniquity stared into my soul. As the acuteness of this remorse began to die away, it was succeeded by a sense of joy. The problem of my conduct was solved. Hyde was thenceforth impossible; whether I would or not, I was now confined to the better part of my existence; and, oh, how I rejoiced to think it! with what willing humility I embraced anew the restrictions of natural life! with what sincere renunciation I locked the door by which I had so often gone and come, and ground the key under my heel!

Robert Louis Stevenson, *The Strange Case of Dr Jekyll and Mr Hyde*

Double Bluff

Barrett said, 'You want to blackguard somebody, Inspector, so you make it look like you're blackguarding yourself at the same time, only it turns out you aren't, but it still looks like you're trying to, only you got the date wrong or something.'

'I don't know what they teach you boys at that college.' Cox banged the end of a cigarette against a matchbox. 'Nothing's ever straight as far as you're concerned, is it? All a great mass of –'

'You must admit, Cox, it does make Langdon the less likely of the two.'

'Two? What two?'

'He was vulnerable and Hodgson evidently wasn't.'

'Double bluff, sir?' asked Barrett, purely in the hope of irritating Cox.

'What's all this about the two and double bluffs? If you ever get so's you're dry behind the ears, son, you may just possibly realize that in criminal investigation what you hardly ever get is a bluff, unless it's like a bloke with an empty gun going on as if it's loaded, and what you never ever get is a double bluff. Because why? Because it's too perishing risky, that's why. If you stab a fellow and walk out into the street with the knife in your hand, people aren't going to say, oh, he can't have been up to anything, no one could be such a mutt, showing themselves like that in broad daylight. Not them; they're going to say, there's a bugger with a bloodstained knife in his hand – grab him quick. Right?'

Kingsley Amis, *The Riverside Villas Murder*

E

Elizabethan
Er . . .

He was lyin there, so I . . . er
Stabbed him. Just the once.
In the stomach. Crashed out
on the sofa he was. After the pub.

He wasn't asleep. Some nights
he'd pass out but most nights he'd pretend.
Lie there he would, eyes closed.
Burp. Fart, like I wasn't there.

Eggin me on to say somethin.
And if I did. If ever I did,
you know, say what I thought
He'd be up in a flash.

Because that's what he wanted
Me to say somethin. Lose my temper.
I'd goaded him, you see. Asked for it.
'You asked for it,' he'd say.

Afterwards, in bed, me, sobbin.
A fresh bruise on an old swellin.
Not on the face. He never hit me
on the face. Too calculatin.

Always the body. Stomach, kidneys
He used to be one of you, see.
He knew where to hit.
Cold. Always, in control.

But tonight, I took control.
Picked up the breadknife.

He was gettin ready to let one go
I could see that.

The veins in his neck standin out
Throbbin. White against the purple.
Eyes behind closed lids, flickerin
Waiting to jump out on me.

So I . . . er stabbed him. Just the once.
He farted and screamed at the same time.
I know that sounds funny, but it wasn't
Not at the time. Not with the blood.

He rolled off of the sofa
Hunched on his knees, holdin the knife.
Not tryin to pull it out
Just holdin it. Like keepin it in.

Then he keeled over and that was that.
I put my coat on and came down here
And what I want to know is . . .
What's goin to happen to the kids?

Roger McGough, 'Fart'

Elizabethan

Quoth *Esdras*, what ever thou best at whose mercie I lye spare me, and I wil give thee as much gold as thou wilt aske. Put me to anie paines my life reserved, and I willingly will sustaine them: cut off my armes and legs, and leave me as a lazer to some loathsome spittle, where I may but live a yeare to pray and repent me. For thy brothers death the despayre of mind that hath ever since haunted mee, the guiltie gnawing worme of conscience I feele may bee sufficient penance. Thou canst not send me to such a hell, as alreadie there is in my hart. To dispatch me presently is no revenge, it will soone be forgotten: let me dye a lingring death, it will be remembred a great deale longer. A lingring death maye availe my soule, but it is the illest of ills that can befortune my bodie. For my soules health I beg my bodies torment: bee not thou a divell to torment my soule, and send me to eternall damnation. Thy over-hanging sword hides heaven from my sight, I dare not looke up, least I embrace my deathes-wounde unwares. I cannot pray to God, and plead to thee both at once. Ay mee, alreadie I see my life buried in the wrinckles of thy browes: say but I shall live, though thou meanest to kill me. Nothing confounds like to suddaine terror, it thrusts everie sense out of office. Poyson wrapt up in sugred pills is but halfe a poyson: the feare of deaths lookes are more terrible than his stroake. The whilest I viewe death, my faith is deaded: where a mans feare is, there his heart is. Feare never engenders hope: how can I hope that heavens father will save mee from the hell everlasting, when he gives me over to the hell of thy furie.

Heralclide now thinke I on thy teares sowne in the dust, (thy teares, that my bloudie minde made barraine). In revenge of thee, God hardens this mans heart against mee: yet I did not slaughter thee, though hundreds else my hand hath brought to the shambles. Gentle sir, learne of mee what it is to clog your conscience with murder, to have your dreames, your sleepes, your solitarie walkes troubled and disquited with murther: your shaddowe by daie will affright you, you will not see a weapon unsheathde, but immediately you will imagine it is predestinate for your destruction.

This murther is a house divided within it selfe: it subbornes a mans owne soule to infourme against him: his soule (beeing his accuser) brings foorth his two eyes as witnesses against him, and the least eie witnesse is unrefutable. Plucke out my eyes if thou wilt, and deprive my traiterous soule of her two best witnesses. Digge out my blasphemous tongue wyth thy dagger, both tongue and eyes wyll I gladly forgoe to have a lyttle more time to thinke on my journey to heaven.

Deferre a while thy resolution, I am not at peace wyth the world, for even but yesterdaie I fought, and in my furie threatned further vengeance: had I a face to aske forgivenesse, I shoulde thinke halfe my sinnes were forgiven. A hundred devils haunt mee dayly for my horrible murthers: the devilles when I die will bee loth to goe to hell with mee, for they desired of Christ he would not send them to hel before their time: if they goe not to hell, into thee they will goe, and hideously vex thee for turning them out of their habitation. Wounds I contemne, life I prize light, it is another worlds tranquilitie which makes me so timerous: everlasting damnation, everlasting houling and lamentation. It is not from death I request thee to deliver me, but from this terror of torments eternitie. Thy brothers bodie only I pearst unadvisedly, his soule meant I no harme to at all: my bodie and soule both shalt thou cast awaie quite, if thou doest at this instant what thou maist. Spare me, spare me I beseech thee, by thy owne soules salvation I desire thee, seeke not my souls utter perdition: in destroying me, thou destroyest they selfe and me. Eagerly I replid after this long suppliant oration: Though I knew God would never have mercy upon me except I had mercie on thee, yet of thee no mercy would I have. Revenge in our tragedies is continually raised from hell: of hell doe I esteeme better than heaven, if it afford me revenge. There is no heaven but revenge. I tel thee, I would not have undertoke so much toile to gaine heaven, as I have done in pursuing thee for revenge. Divine revenge, of which (as of the joies above) there is no fulnes or satietie. Looke how my feete are blistered with following thee from place to place. I have riven my throat with overstraining it to curse thee. I have ground my teeth to pouder with grating and grinding them together for anger when any hath namde thee. My tongue with vaine threates is bolne, and waxen too big for my mouth: my eyes have broken their strings with staring and looking ghastly, as I stood devising how to frame or set my countenance when I met thee. I have neere spent my strength in imaginarie acting on stone wals, what I determined to execute on thee: intreate not, a miracle may not reprive thee: villaine, thus march I with my blade into thy bowels.

Stay, stay exclaimed *Esdras*, and heare me but one word further. Though neither for God nor man thou carest, but placest thy whole felicitie in murther, yet of thy felicity learn how to make a greater felicitie. Respite me a little from thy swordes point, and set me about some execrable enterprise, that may subvert the whole state of christendome, and make all mens eares tingle that heare of it. Commaund me to cut all my kindreds throats, to burne men, women and children in their beds in millions, by firing their Cities at midnight. Be it Pope, Emperor or Turke that displeaseth thee, he shall not breath on the earth. For thy sake will I sweare and forsweare, renounce my baptisme, and all the interest I have in any other sacrament, onely let mee live howe miserable so ever, be it in a dungeon amongst toads, serpents, and adders, or set up to the necke in dong. No paines I will refuse howe ever proroged, to have a little respite to purifie my spirit: oh, heare me, heare me, and thou canst not be hardned against mee.

At this his importunitie I paused a little, not as retiring from my wreakfull resolution, but going backe to gather more foreces of vengeaunce, with my selfe I devised how to plague him double in his base minde: my thoughtes traveld in quest of some notable newe Italionisme, whose murderous platforme might not onely extend on his bodie, but his soul also. The ground worke of it was this: that whereas he had promised for my sake to sweare and forsweare, and commit *Julian*-like violence on the highest seales of religion: if he would but this farre satisfie me, he should be dismist from my furie. First and formost he should renounce God and his laws, and utterly disclaime the whole title or interest he had in anie covenant of salvation. Next he should curse him to his face, as Job was willed by his wife, and write an absolute firme obligation of his soule to the devill, without condition or exception. Thirdly and lastly, (having done this,) hee shoulde pray to God fervently never to have mercie upon him, or pardon him. Scarce had I propounded these articles unto him, but he was beginning his blasphemous abjurations. I wonder the earth opened not and swalowed us both, hearing the bolde tearmes he blasted forth in contempt of Christianitie: heaven hath thundered when halfe lesse contumelies against it hath bene uttered. Able they were to raise Saintes and martyrs from their graves, and plucke Christ himselfe from the right hand of his father. My joints trembled and quakt with attending them, my haire stood upright, and my hart was turned wholy to fire. So affectionatly and zealously dyd hee give himselfe over to infidelity, as if sathan had gotten the upper hand of our high maker. The veyne is his left hand that is derived from the hart with no faint blow he pierst, and with the full bloud that flowed from it, writ a full obligation of his soule to the devill: yea, he more earnestly praid unto God never to forgive his soule, than many christians do to save their soules. These fearefull ceremonies brought to an end, I bad him ope his mouth and gape wide. He did so (as what wil not slaves do for feare?) therewith made I no more ado, but shot him full into the throat with my pistoll: no more spake he after, so did I shoot him that he might never speake after or repent him. His bodie being dead lookt as blacke as a toad: the devill presently branded it for his owne. This is the falt that hath called me hether, no true Italian but will honor me for it. Revenge is the glorie of armes, and the highest performance of valure, revenge is whatsoever we call law or justice. The farther we wade in revenge the neerer come we to the throne of the almightie. To his scepter is it properly ascribed, his scepter he lends unto man, when he lets one man scourge an other. All true Italians imitate me in revenging constantly and dying valiantly. Hangman to thy taske, for I am readie for the utmost of thy rigor. Herewithall the people (outragiously incensed) with one conjoyned outcrie, yelled mainely, Awaie with him, away with him. Executioner torture him, teare him, or we will teare thee in peeces if thou spare him.

The executioner needed no exhortation hereunto, for of his owne nature was he hackster good inough: olde excellent he was at a bone-ach.

At the first chop with his wood-knife would he fish for a mans heart, and fetch it out as easily as a plum from the bottome of a porredge pot. He woulde cracke neckes as fast as a cooke cracks egges: a fidler cannot turne his pin so soone as he would turne a man of the ladder: bravely did he drum on this *Cutwolfes* bones, not breaking them outright, but like a sadler knocking in of tackes, jarring on them quaveringly with his hammer a great while together. No joint about him but with a hatchet he had for the nones he disjoynted halfe, and then with boyling lead souldered up the wounds from bleeding: his tongue he puld out, least he should blaspheme in his torment: venimous stinging wormes hee thrust into his eares to keep his head ravingly occupied: with cankers scruzed to peeces hee rubd his mouth and his gums: no lim of his but was lingeringly splinterd in shivers. In this horror left they him on the wheele as in hell: where yet living he might beholde his flesh legacied amongst the foules of the aire. Unsearchable is the booke of our destinies, one murder begetteth another: was never yet bloud-shed barren from the beginning of the world to this daie.

Thomas Nashe, *The Unfortunate Traveller*

Euthanasia

When Stangl, in his conversations with me, began to speak of his transfer to the Euthanasia Programme, I noticed for the first time an alarming change come over his face: it coarsened and became slack and suffused. The veins stood out, he began to sweat, and the lines in his cheeks and forehead deepened. This was to happen repeatedly in the days and weeks to come when he had to speak about a new and terrible phase in his life.

'Kriminalrath Werner said that both Russia and America had for some considerable time had a law which permitted them to carry out euthanasia – "mercy-killings" – on people who were hopelessly insane or monstrously deformed. He said this law was going to be passed in Germany – as everywhere else in the civilized world – in the near future. But that, to protect the sensibilities of the population, *they* were going to do it very slowly, only after a great deal of psychological preparation. But that, in the meantime, the difficult task had begun, under the cloak of absolute secrecy. He explained that the only patients affected were those who after the most careful examination – a series of four tests carried out by at least two physicians – were considered absolutely incurable so that, he assured me, a totally painless death represented a real release from what, more often than not, was an intolerable life.'[1]

'What was your first reaction, your first thought when Kriminalrather Werner said these things?'

'I . . . I was speechless. And then I finally said I didn't really feel I was suited for this assignment. He was, you know, very friendly, very sympathetic when I said that. He said he understood well that that would be my first reaction but that I had to remember that my being asked to take this job showed proof of their exceptional trust in me. It was a most difficult task – they fully recognized it – but that I myself would have nothing whatever to do with the actual operation; this was carried out entirely by doctors and nurses. I was merely to be responsible for law and order.'

'Did he specify what he meant by law and order?'

'Yes. I would be responsible for maintaining the maximum security provisions. But the way he put it, almost my main responsibility would be to ascertain that the protective regulations regarding the eligibility of patients would be adhered to, to the letter.'

'But the way you are telling about it, now, you were obviously not ordered *to do this. You were given a choice. Your own immediate reaction, quite properly, was horror. What made you agree to do it?'*

'Several times during this talk, he mentioned – sort of by the way – that he had heard I wasn't altogether happy in Linz. And then, he said, there was this disciplinary action pending against me. That would of course be suspended if I accepted this transfer. He also said I could choose either to go to an institute in Saxonia, or one in Austria. But that, on the other hand, if I chose to refuse the assignment, no doubt my present chief in Linz – Prohaska – would find something else for me to do.'

'And that decided you, did it?'

'The combination of things did; the way he had presented it; it was

1 Although the 'medical commission' did travel to some institutions, such careful medical examinations were by no means the rule. Most decisions of life or death were much more routinely made at T4, purely on the basis of a questionnaire which had been sent out by 'Amt IVg' – subsection for institutional care – of the Ministry of the Interior to all mental institutions, asking for details on all patients who were senile, retarded or suffering a variety of other mental debilities: criminally insane, under care for five years or more, of foreign or racially impure extraction, incapable of work or capable of only routine mechanical tasks such as peeling vegetables. This was sent out on the pretext of gathering information to assist in economic planning (and apparently only two men in the ministry were informed of the real purpose) but photocopies were then turned over to T4 'medical staff', who marked each case with a plus or minus sign: Life or Death.

already being done by law in America and Russia; the fact that doctors and nurses were involved; the careful examination of the patients; the concern for the feelings of the population. And then, it is true, for months I had felt myself to be in the greatest danger in Linz from Prohaska. After all, I already knew since March 13, 1938, that it was simpler to be dead in Germany than anywhere else. I was just so glad to get away from Linz.'

'*So what happened?*'

'I reported to Tiergartenstrasse 4, I think to SS Oberführer Brack who explained what my specific police duties would be.' (When Stangl said this, and for some time after, it seemed significant that he, at that point a police officer of comparatively minor formal rank, should have been interviewed and instructed by SS Oberführer Victor Brack, who was one of the top officials of the Führer Chancellery. Since then, however, I have learned from Dieter Allers, former chief administrative officer of T4, that Brack interviewed and instructed personally *all* personnel assigned to T4 – 'He even interviewed the chars,' said Allers.)

'I said I'd try to do it, and that I would like to stay in Austria where I would be nearer my family. He said that, to be effective in my new job, I had to be superior in rank to the local police chief of the nearest police authority, Alkoven – it was a man called Hartmann – and I would therefore be transferred to the uniformed branch with the rank of lieutenant.'

'*Were you to wear uniform?*'

'Yes, the green police uniform [which he continued to wear until Christmas 1942, when – in Poland – he became assimilated to the SS and was given the grey SS field uniform worn by all German SS at Treblinka]. He gave me the name of a village not too far from Linz, and a telephone number; I remember, it was Alkoven 913. I was to return to Linz, pack and tell nobody where I was going. I was to go to an inn on the outskirts of Linz – the Gasthaus Drei Kronen it was, on the Landstresse – and phone that number. And I'd be given instructions.'

('Yes, of course I remember when he was first called to Berlin,' said Frau Stangl thirty-one years later in Brazil. 'He told me he had to report to Tiergartenstrasse 4. He said, "I wonder what *that* is."')

'I only stayed at home for a day, I think,' Stangl continued, 'and then did what they had told me to do: you know, I went to the Drei Kronen and called Alkoven 913. A man answered, I told him my name and he said, "I'll come and get you" – and about an hour later a kind of delivery van drove up – the driver was in civvies, a grey suit. When I asked him where we were going he wouldn't say – he just said, "In the direction of Everding." And after an hour we got to Schloss Hartheim.'

'*How did it look?*'

'Oh, it was big you know, with a courtyard and archways and all that. It hadn't been a private residence for some time: they'd had an orphanage in it I think, and later a hospital. Almost the first person I saw – it was such a relief – was a friend: a colleague from the police, Franz Reichleitner.'

It would appear that Reichleitner,[1] whose subsequent career paralleled Stangl's, if on a slightly lower level, was equally glad to see him. 'He said they'd told him I was coming and he'd been waiting for me near the entrance. He had arranged for us to share a room. He'd show me around later, he said, but first he had to take me to meet the doctors in charge and Hauptmann [Captain] Wirth.'

This was the first appearance of Strangl's next *bête noire*, the notorious Christian Wirth – the 'savage Christian', as he was to be called. It was Wirth who carried out the first gassings of Germans certified incurably insane, in December 1939 or January 1940 at Brandenburg an der Havel. According to Reitlinger's *The Final Solution*, 'Wirth's name does not occur in any of the surviving correspondence concerning euthanasia.' It would now appear from Stangl's account, which is confirmed by one of his former subalterns, Franz Suchomel, that in mid-1940 Wirth was appointed as a kind of roving director or inspector of the dozen or so institutions of this kind in 'Greater Germany'. Suchomel says that he came to Hartheim as a '*Läuterungs-Kommissar* because the place was an undisciplined pigsty'. Less than a year later he was assigned to begin the extermination of the Jews in Chelmno, the first of the five Nazi death camps in Poland, and later again was designated supervising 'Inspector' of the three major extermination camps, Belsec, Sobibor and Treblinka. This sequence of appointments reconfirms the preparatory role played by the Euthanasia Programme for the 'Final Solution'. (In practice, if apparently not, as has also been claimed, as a formal training.)

'Wirth was a gross and florid man,' Stangl said. 'My heart sank when I met him. He stayed at Hartheim for several days that time, and came back often. Whenever he was there, he addressed us daily at lunch. And here it was again, this awful verbal crudity: when he spoke about the necessity for this euthanasia operation, he wasn't speaking in humane or scientific terms, the way Dr Werner had described it to me. He laughed. He spoke

1 Killed by partisans in Trieste in 1944.

of "doing away with useless mouths" and said that "sentimental slobber" about such people made him "puke".'

'*What about the other people there? What were they like?*'

'There were the two chief medical officers: Dr Renno[1] and Dr Lohnauer.[2] And fourteen nurses; seven men and seven women. Dr Lohnauer was a rather aloof sort of man, but very correct. Dr Renno was very nice, friendly.'

'*In the weeks and months to come, did they ever talk to you about what was being done there?*'

'Often, very often, especially Dr Renno. You know . . .' he suddenly said, sadly, 'you have no idea what the patients were like who were brought there. I had never known there *were* such people. Oh my God – the children . . .' (Dieter Allers said later that he couldn't understand this reference to children: 'No children were killed at Hartheim,' he said. 'There were special places for that'; and the Ludwigsburg Central (judiciary) Authority for Nazi Crimes confirmed that if there were children who were killed at Hartheim, it could only have been isolated cases.[3]

'*But didn't it ever occur to you to think "what if* my *mother or* my *child were in this position"?*'

'Ah,' he answered at once, 'but they had told us immediately that there were four groups who were exempt: the senile; those who had served in the armed forces; those who had been decorated with the *Mutterkreuz* [a decoration for women designed to glorify motherhood], *and* relatives of Euthanasia Aktion staff. Of course, they had to do that.'

1 Excused from euthanasia trial because of ill health; now living in the Black Forest.

2 Committed suicide.

3 'Child-euthanasia' was, on the whole, a separate programme, which began earlier and ended long after the general euthanasia *Aktion*.

It was claimed by various defendants in euthanasia trials – and Dieter Allers repeated this to me – that 'parents were asked to authorize "mercy-death"' for their children. What actually happened was that parents were informed that *Kinderfachabteilungen* – Special Sections for children – were being established all over the country. They were asked to sign an authorization for their severely disabled children to be transferred to these wards and were told that, as these were in fact intensive-care units where highly advanced experiments would be carried out, this represented a unique chance for their children's possible recovery. *This* was how the Nazis obtained authorizing signatures – which were subsequently paraded in the trials. Eleven Special Sections were involved; each of them had between twenty and thirty beds. What *is* true, however, is that – unlike the adults – children were kept in these wards for a period of observation lasting between four to eight weeks. But none of my informants was able to recall any case of a child who was returned to an ordinary hospital, or to its parents, once it had been taken to a 'Special Section'. The children were 'put to sleep' with injections and, from all accounts, were not aware of their fate.

'*But aside from that then, did you have any more scruples?*'

'For a long time. After the first two or three days I told Reichleitner that I didn't think I could stand it. By then I'd heard that the police official who'd had the job before me had been relieved upon his request because he had stomach trouble. I too couldn't eat – you know, one just couldn't.'

'*Then it was possible to ask to be relieved?*'

'Yes. But Franz Reichleitner said, "What do you think will happen if you do the same? Just remember Ludwig Werner." He knew of course about my friend Werner's being sent to the KZ.[1] No, I had very little doubt of what would happen to me if I returned to Linz and Prohaska.'

'*You say you saw your wife quite frequently: it must have become obvious to her that you were under strain – it must have shown up somehow. Didn't she ever ask you again what you were doing? That's very unlike a wife, isn't it?*'

'She asked, but only casually you know. She was used to my not being able to discuss service matters.'

'*Do you think the patients at Hartheim knew what was going to happen to them?*'

'No,' he said immediately, with assurance. 'It was run as a hospital. After they arrived they were again examined you know. Their temperatures were taken and all that . . .'

'*Why would anybody want to take the temperature of people who were mentally sick?*'

'I don't know. But that's what they did. They had two tables in a sort of hall the patients were taken to when they arrived; at one of them sat the doctors and at the other nurses. And each arriving patient was examined.'

'*For how long?*'

'Oh, it varied; some just a minute, others a bit longer.'

'*One has read of patients in these "institutes" trying to run away in terror, with nurses or guards pursuing them along the corridors . . .*'

'I don't think that ever happened,' he said, sounding genuinely surprised. 'I have certainly never heard of such a thing. You see, even Wirth said, "The people must not be allowed to realize that they are going to die. They have to feel at ease. Nothing must be done to frighten them."'

'*Were there any wards? Did it ever happen that any of them stayed – a night, or more?*'

'Oh no, never.'

1 Werner was sent to a concentration camp, the legal record shows, not for asking to be relieved but for 'having had financial dealings with a Jew'.

That patients were sent to these institutions only to die without delay was confirmed by Franz Suchomel. He, a Sudeten German, was mobilized into the SS – he says he doesn't know why (Dieter Allers was to tell me later more about the method of recruiting for T4), and was first sent to the 'institute' at Hadamar as an assistant in the photographic laboratory. Or so he said at our first meeting: later, in one of several letters replying to specific additional questions, he changed this and said that he had been assigned to work at T4 in Berlin. (The truth is that he worked in both these places.) 'The institutes,' he said, 'were designated from A to F. Hartheim was C; Hadamar was E; Sonnenstein, also called *die Sonne*, was F. They gave me a dark-room and told me to develop photos for the archives. In the four institutes where gassings took place patients never stayed for more than a few short hours. Certainly nobody ever got out.' (There were in fact six where gassing took place, but only four were operational at any one time. And this does not take into account the eleven 'special' hospitals where children were 'put to sleep' by injections.)

Suchomel said at his first meeting with me that the psychiatrist Professor Heyde had his office next to his dark-room at Hadamar. This man, who was sentenced to death *in absentia* by a German court in 1946, escaped and practised in Flensburg in Germany under the name of Sawade until 1959, when he gave himself up. He committed a slightly mysterious suicide: he was found strangled, lying on the floor, with a noose attached to the central heating pipes – in Limburg prison in 1963. According to Suchomel, 'He was the head of the whole thing, he developed it.' In a subsequent letter he says, 'Heide [*sic*] had a flat at Tiergartenstrasse 4, next to my office. He was the top expert in the mercy-killing business. He only stayed at his flat when he had official business in Berlin. He was, I was told, an authority in his field . . . I know that there was a research institute into mental illness in Strasburg; he may have run that. That's where the brains of selected mental patients were sent for research purposes.' And Dieter Allers too talked a great deal about the scientific purposes of the Euthanasia Programme. 'People have completely misunderstood: now it is constantly being misinterpreted. Just look at the world now: don't you think something very much like this will have to happen?'

Stangl was in fact intellectually and emotionally considerably more affected by the whole euthanasia issue than the other people I have talked to who were directly involved with the programme.

'*You were speaking earlier about having many doubts and many discussion about the rights and wrongs of the euthanasia programme. Can you elaborate a little on this?*' I asked him.

'Strangely enough,' he said, 'you see there was somehow more freedom to talk there than I had had in Linz. Of course, we couldn't talk to anyone outside, but amongst ourselves we discussed the fors and againsts all the time.'

'*And did you get to the point where you convinced yourself you were involved in something that was* right?'

'Of course, I wasn't "involved" in that sense,' he said quickly. 'Not in the operational sense.'

I reformulated my question. '*Did you get to the point where you convinced yourself that what was being done was right?*'

'One day,' he said, 'I had to make a duty visit to an institution for severely handicapped children run by nuns . . .' ('What the devil,' said Allers, 'was he doing going to a place like that? He had no business going to any of the hospitals: his job was death certificates.') 'It was part of my function,' said Stangl, 'to see that the families of patients – afterwards – received their effects: clothes and all that, and identity papers, certificates, you know. I was responsible for everything being correctly done.'

'*What do you mean by "correctly done"? How were the families notified?*'

'Well, they were told the patient had died of a heart attack or something like that. And they received a little urn with the ashes. But for our records, as I told you, we always had to have these four attestations, otherwise it . . . it couldn't be carried out. Well, in this case the mother of a child who had been brought from that particular institution had written to say that she hadn't received a candle she had sent the child as a present shortly before it died. That's why I had to go there: to find the candle. When I arrived, the Mother Superior, who I had to see, was up in a ward with the priest and they took me up to see her.

'We talked for a moment and then she pointed to a child – well, it looked like a small child – lying in a basket. "Do you know how old he is?" she asked me. I said no, how old was he? "Sixteen," she said. "He looks like five, doesn't he? He'll never change, ever. But they rejected him." [The nun was referring to the medical commission.] "How could they not accept him?" she said. And the priest who stood next to her nodded fervently. "Just look at him," she went on. "No good to himself or anyone else. How could they refuse to deliver him from this miserable life?" This really shook me,' said Stangl. 'Here was a Catholic nun, a Mother Superior, and a priest. And they thought it was right. Who was I then, to doubt what was being done?'

Gitta Sereny, *Into that Darkness*

The test for feeblemindedness was, they had to make up a sentence using the words *dog*, *fox* and *field*.

(Judgement at Nuremberg)

These were no leaders, but they were first
into the dark on Dog Fox Field:

Anna who rocked her head, and Paul
who grew big and yet giggled small,

Irma who looked Chinese, and Hans
who knew his world as a fox knows a field.

Hunted with needles, exposed, unfed,
this time in their thousands they bore sad cuts

for having gazed, and shuffled, and failed
to field the lore of prey and hound

they then had to thump and cry in the vans
that ran while stopped in Dog Fox Field.

Our sentries, whose holocaust does not end,
they show us when we cross into Dog Fox Field.

Les Murray, 'Dog Fox Field'

F

Failure

Westlake's grey Daimler
Rips the road puddles.
It rends hanging holes of echo in the vapour-hung woods.

It slides through the village, slows at the rectory. Accelerates down burrow lanes, grass-heads lashing the side-mirrors, as he searches.

Through fir-tree fringes at last he glimpses the blue van, parked at the house of Dunworth, a young architect, Westlake's golfing companion.

Westlake is phoning from a booth.

Dunworth, eight miles away in the city, called back into his office just as he was leaving for lunch, listens to the voice of his friend.

Dunworth moves fast, surprising himself.

And now his white Jaguar sports is tilting at corners, flattening in dips and bobbing on crests, breasting the long straights on a rising note, over the eight miles, as he gnaws his lips and fights the road's variety.

Westlake's words have supplied the single answer to many clues.
The warp and weft of hints and suspicions,
Knotted, painfully, laboriously, over a long time, into a mesh
Have suddenly dragged taut, with the bulk of a body.
A few sprinkled words
Have transformed a bitter-cored ulcer
Into something delicious.

With one glance at the blue van, he walks into the house, calling his wife's name.
He climbs the fondly designed cedar staircase to his studio
Without stealth. He returns casually

As if with some curio to show to a guest
Loading his target pistol, with which he is expert,
And without pausing strides into the lounge.

His red-haired wife
Is lying naked on the couch, almost hidden
By the naked body of Lumb
Who, half-twisting, and supported on one elbow, watches Dunworth
As if waiting for him.

Dunworth has paused.
His brisk executive plan evaporates confusedly.
The sight in front of him
Is so extraordinary and shocking
So much more merciless and explicit than even his most daring fantasy
That for a moment
He forgets himself, and simply stares.
He gropes for his lost initiative,
But what he sees, like a surprising blow in a dark room,
Has scattered him.
He raises his pistol meanwhile.
He is breathing hard, to keep abreast of the situation.
He is trying to feel
Whether he is bluffing or is about to become
The puppet
Of some monstrous, real, irreversible act.

He waits for what he will do,
As a relaxed rider, crossing precipitous gulleys
Lets his horse find its way.
He levels the pistol at his wife's face and holds it there, undecided.

Her red hair is strewn bright and waterish
Across the arm of the couch which pillows her head.
Her large eyes, mascara-smudged in her gleaming face, watch him
Moistly and brilliantly.
Her bold, crudely-cut mouth, relaxed in its strength,
Yields him nothing.
He searches her hot fixed look for some sign of reprieve,
Moving his aim from her brow, to her mouth, to her throat.
She swallows but resettles her head as if to watch him more comfortably.

Her nakedness has outstripped his reaction, incredible,
Like the sudden appearance of an arrow, sticking deep in his body,
Seconds before the pain.
It cannot unhappen, and now the pain must come.
The white swell of her stomach, welded so closely
To that other strange body, which at first he hardly notices
But which prints in his brain as something loathsome and deadly, a huge python's coils, of some alien nature and substance.
He feels a pressure inside his skull, like a long lever tightening a winch.
He sees the pistol out there in front of him
As if it were a fixture he were hanging on to, outside a window,
Over a night-drop.

His gold hair seems to sweat.
His sunlamp bronze sweats.
His pale-eyed stare is brittle and impotently severe, like the stare of a lizard.

His pistol sinks its aim
Over Lumb's powerful gymnast's shoulders.
The sweat-figured muscles
Of the half-twisted torso, and the long sinewy legs
Are an unexpected development.
Dunworth has difficulty
Adding this body to the familiar long-jowled monkish visage
That watches him unmoving, as if expecting
To see him do something typically stupid.

Those hooded heavy eyes weaken him
Like a load of ironweight.

Dunworth gazes back at his wife
Almost forgetting where he is or what he is doing.
He is helplessly in love.
He stands there, in his child's helplessness,
As if he had searched everywhere and at last somehow he had found her.
An irresponsible joy chatters to be heard, somewhere in the back of his head, as he gazes at her,
Feeling all his nerves dazzle, with waftings of vertigo,
As if he were gazing into an open furnace.
At the same time he tightens on the butt and trigger of the pistol, readjusting his grip,

As if the terrible moment were approaching of itself.
In the remaining seconds
He studies her lips and tries to separate out the ugliness there,
Which he remembers finding regrettable.
He tries to isolate the monkey-crudity of her hairline,
Her spoiled chin, all the ordinariness
That once bored him so much,
But he feels only a glowing mass.
He stands there, paralysed by a bliss
And a most horrible torture –
Endless sweetness and endless anguish.

He turns the pistol towards his own face
And puts the muzzle in his mouth.
Lumb is stepping toward him.
Dunworth closes his eyes and tries to clench his strength
Which slips from him like water.
Lumb takes the pistol out of his hand.

Dunworth
Sits in a huddle on the floor.
His eyes, squeezed close, refuse the features of his trap,
Squeezing the ball of tight dazzling blackness behind his eyes.
His face is numb as rubber,
His body sunk in a depth of happening which holds it like concrete.

The Reverend Lumb has left.
Opening his eyes, Dunworth sees his wife's stockinged ankles and shoes
Passing close.
When he looks up she is fully dressed and tugging a comb through her hair.
She ignores him and goes to her room.
He follows and tries the door but it is already locked.

He leans at the door, emptied, merely his shape,
Like a moth pinned to a board,
While the nectars of the white lilac
And the purple and dark magenta lilac
Press through the rooms.

Ted Hughes, *Gaudete*

Family

My name is Boffer Bings. I was born of honest parents in one of the humbler walks of life, my father being a manufacturer of dog-oil and my mother having a small studio in the shadow of the village church, where she disposed of unwelcome babes. In my boyhood I was trained to habits of industry; I not only assisted my father in procuring dogs for his vats, but was frequently employed by my mother to carry away the debris of her work in the studio. In performance of this duty I sometimes had need of all my natural intelligence for all the law officers of the vicinity were opposed to my mother's business. They were not elected on an opposition ticket, and the matter had never been made a political issue; it just happened so. My father's business of making dog-oil was, naturally, less unpopular, though the owners of missing dogs sometimes regarded him with suspicion, which was reflected, to some extent, upon me. My father had, as silent partners, all the physicians of the town, who seldom wrote a prescription which did not contain what they were pleased to designate as *Ol. can.* It is really the most valuable medicine ever discovered. But most persons are unwilling to make personal sacrifices for the afflicted, and it was evident that many of the fattest dogs in town had been forbidden to play with me – a fact which pained my young sensibilities, and at one time came near driving me to become a pirate.

Looking back upon those days, I cannot but regret, at times, that by indirectly bringing my beloved parents to their death I was the author of misfortunes profoundly affecting my future.

One evening while passing my father's oil factory with the body of a foundling from my mother's studio I saw a constable who seemed to be closely watching my movements. Young as I was, I had learned that a constable's acts, of whatever apparent character, are prompted by the most reprehensible motives, and I avoided him by dodging into the oilery by a side door which happened to stand ajar. I locked it at once and was alone with my dead. My father had retired for the night. The only light in the place came from the furnace, which glowed a deep, rich crimson under one of the vats, casting ruddy reflections on the walls. Within the cauldron the oil still rolled in indolent ebullition, occasionally pushing to the surface a piece of dog. Seating myself to wait for the constable to go away, I held the naked body of the foundling in my lap and tenderly stroked its short, silken hair. Ah, how beautiful it was! Even at that early age I was passionately fond of children, and as I looked upon this cherub I could almost find it in my heart to wish that the small, red wound upon its breast – the work of my dear mother – had not been mortal.

It had been my custom to throw the babes into the river which nature had thoughtfully provided for the purpose, but that night I did not dare to leave the oilery for fear of the constable. 'After all,' I said to myself, 'it cannot greatly matter if I put it into this cauldron. My father will never know the bones from those of a puppy, and the few deaths which may result from administering another kind of oil for the incomparable *Ol. can.* are not important in a population which increases so rapidly.' In short, I took the first step in crime and brought myself untold sorrow by casting the babe into the cauldron.

The next day, somewhat to my surprise, my father, rubbing his hands with satisfaction, informed me and my mother that he had obtained the finest quality of oil that was ever seen; that the physicians to whom he had shown samples had so pronounced it. He added that he had no knowledge as to how the result was obtained; the dogs had been treated in all respects as usual, and were of an ordinary breed. I deemed it my duty to explain – which I did, though palsied would have been my tongue if I could have foreseen the consequences. Bewailing their previous ignorance of the advantages of combining their industries, my parents at once took measures to repair the error. My mother removed her studio to a wing of the factory building and my duties in connection with the business ceased; I was no longer required to dispose of the bodies of the small superfluous, and there was no need of alluring dogs to their doom, for my father discarded them altogether, though they still had an honourable place in the name of the oil. So suddenly thrown into idleness, I might naturally have been expected to become vicious and dissolute, but I did not. The holy influence of my dear mother was ever about me to protect me from the temptations which beset youth, and my father was a deacon in a church. Alas, that through my fault these estimable persons should have come to so bad an end!

Finding a double profit in her business, my mother now devoted herself to it with a new assiduity. She removed not only superfluous and unwelcome babes to order, but went out into the highways and byways, gathering in children of a larger growth, and even such adults as she could entice to the oilery. My father, too, enamored of the superior quality of oil produced, purveyed for his vats with diligence and zeal. The conversion of their neighbors into dog-oil became, in short, the one passion of their lives – an absorbing and overwhelming greed took possession of their souls and served them in place of a hope in Heaven – by which, also, they were inspired.

So enterprising had they now become that a public meeting was held and resolutions passed severely censuring them. It was intimated by the chairman that any further raids upon the population would be met in a spirit of hostility. My poor parents left the meeting broken-hearted, desperate and, I believe, not altogether sane. Anyhow, I deemed it prudent not to enter the oilery with them that night, but slept outside in a stable.

At about midnight some mysterious impulse caused me to rise and peer through a window into the furnace-room, where I knew my father now slept. The fires were burning as brightly as if the following day's harvest had been expected to be abundant. One of the large cauldrons was slowly 'walloping' with a mysterious appearance of self-restraint, as if it bided its time to put forth its full energy. My father was not in bed; he had risen in his nightclothes and was preparing a noose in a strong cord. From the looks which he cast at the door of my mother's bedroom I knew too well the purpose that he had in mind. Speechless and motionless with terror, I could do nothing in prevention or warning. Suddenly the door of my mother's apartment was opened, noiselessly, and the two confronted each other, both apparently surprised. The lady, also, was in her nightclothes, and she held in her right hand the tool of her trade, a long, narrow-bladed dagger.

She, too, had been unable to deny herself the last profit which the unfriendly action of the citizens and my absence had left her. For one instant they looked into each other's blazing eyes and then sprang together with indescribable fury. Round and round the room they struggled, the man cursing, the woman shrieking, both fighting like demons – she to strike him with the dagger, he to strangle her with his great bare hands. I know not how long I had the unhappiness to observe this disagreeable instance of domestic infelicity, but at last, after a more than usually vigorous struggle, the combatants suddenly moved apart.

My father's breast and my mother's weapon showed evidences of contact. For another instant they glanced at each other in the most unamiable way; then my poor, wounded father, feeling the hand of death upon him, leaped forward, unmindful of resistance, grasped my dear mother in his arms, dragged her to the side the boiling cauldron, collected all his failing energies, and sprang in with her! In a moment, both had disappeared and were adding their oil to that of the committee of citizens who had called the day before with an invitation to the public meeting.

Convinced that these unhappy events closed to me every avenue to an honorable career in that town, I removed to the famous city of Otumwee, where these memoirs are written with a heart full of remorse for a heedless act entailing so dismal a commercial disaster.

Ambrose Bierce, 'Oil of Dog'

Dinner was laced with glass, though preparation was ticklish –
Grinding the glass for hours and easing it under the crust,
(Got the idea from a story – always one for the reading),
Sainsbury's Somerset style chicken-and-mushroom pie.
Smacking his red, wet lips, he munched with disgusting relish.
We hugged our knees on the stairs, little Kevin and I;
Prayed for his gut to pop with a whoosh of internal bleeding.
'Justice, gentle Jesus. Justice. Our cause is just.
Grant us his horrible end (though the book never actually said).'
We sat on the stairs and we prayed but he still wasn't dead.

So we boiled up purple valerian in mum's big copper jam-pan,
Then in a cocoa tin rendered it down to a mush.
Mixed with three big sugars, Kev got it stirred in his tea
And he drank. Then a roar and a spit and Kev got hit in the face:
'Heavenly God! You try that again and I'll belt you again, son.'
Next was the five pound weight balanced on top of the flush –
That took a lot of explaining. The hammer eventually.
But Kev was talking to Jesus, sat in his own dark place
With the damson jam and the blackberry jelly, shelf on shelf:
All that was left of Mum. And I did it myself.

I picked my time. The best was Monday; he watched the football
And drank (it was always the same) six cans of sweet stout,
Lining them up on the top of the gas fire. When
He was snoring on the settee in front of the late-night movie,
I hit his head with the hammer, as hard as I was able.
From his wet, red lips a channel of spit was bubbling out
And his eyelids flickered. I shut my own and hit him again.
There was a sort of a grunt and a gurgle – I can't describe it –
The sucking, snuffling sound as the water drains from the bath.
I grabbed Kev's hand and we ran down the garden path,

Over the wall at the back and out across the heather
Right to the edge of the lake and a big moon shining clear.
With a swing I threw the hammer out and into the night.
Silence. Then the splash. 'Oh Kev, don't tell on me. Promise.
They'll come if you tell.' We went on standing together.
'I'm cold as ice,' says Kev. 'There's nothing more for us here.'
Looking across to the trees, and the jinking moonlight.
'Was there a lot of blood? Will we go into a home, sis?
Why did you ask if I'd tell? What sort of noise did he make?'
Looking to Jesus and wind on the face of the lake.

John Whitworth, 'Blood Ties'

O Miller Knox, whom we knew well,
And the mill, and the floury floors,
And the corn, – and those two women,
And infants – yours!

The sun was shining when you rode
To market on that day:
The sun was set when home-along
You ambled in the gray,
And gathered what had taken place
While you were away.

O Miller Knox, 'twas grief to see
Your good wife hanging there
By her own rash and passionate hand,
In a throe of despair;

And those two children, one by her,
And one by the waiting-maid,
Borne the same hour, and you afar,
And she past aid.

And though sometimes you walk of nights,
Sleepless, to Yalbury Brow,
And glance the graveyard way, and grunt,
' 'Twas not much, anyhow:
She shouldn't ha' minded!' nought it helps
To say that now.

And the water dribbles down your wheel,
  Your mead blooms green and gold,
And birds twit in your apple-boughs
    Just as of old.

Thomas Hardy, 'At the Mill'

No man takes the farm,
Nothing grows there;
The ivy's arm
Strangles the rose there.

Old Farmer Kyrle
Farmed there the last;
He beat his girl
(It's seven years past).

After market it was
He beat his girl;
He liked his glass,
Old Farmer Kyrle.

Old Kyrle's son
Said to his father:
'Now, dad, you ha' done,
I'll kill you rather!

'Stop beating sister,
Or by God I'll kill you!'
Kyrle was full of liquor –
Old Kyrle said: 'Will you?'

Kyrle took his cobb'd stick
And beat his daughter;
He said: 'I'll teach my chick
As a father oughter.'

Young Will, the son,
Heard his sister shriek;
He took his gun
Quick as a streak.

He said: 'Now, dad,
Stop, once for all!'
He was a good lad,
Good at kicking the ball.

His father clubbed
The girl on the head.
Young Will upped
And shot him dead.

'Now, sister,' said Will,
'I've a-killed father,
As I said I'd kill.
O my love, I'd rather

'A-kill him again
Than see you suffer.
O my little Jane,
Kiss good-bye to your brother.

'I won't see you again,
Nor the cows homing,
Nor the mice in the grain,
Nor the primrose coming,

'Nor the fair, nor folk,
Nor the summer flowers
Growing on the wold,
Nor ought that's ours,

'Not Tib the cat,
Not Stub the mare,
Nor old dog Pat,
Never anywhere.

'For I'll be hung
In Gloucester prison
When the bell's rung
And the sun's risen.'

• • •

They hanged Will
As Will said;
With one thrill
They choked him dead.

Jane walked the wold
Like a grey gander;
All grown old
She would wander.

She died soon:
At high-tide,
At full moon,
Jane died.

The brook chatters
As at first;
The farm it waters
Is accurst.

No man takes it,
Nothing grows there;
Blood straiks it,
A ghost goes there.

John Masefield, from 'Lollingdon Downs'

Feud

Trudy and Walter

T: Is there any news yet?

W: Nothing has come through. If things are going right they may be back any time now.

T: I suppose they will get him?

W: It's almost certain. Nower has waited long enough.

T: I am sick of this feud. What do we want to go on killing each other for? We are all the same. He's trash, yet if I cut my finger it bleeds like his. But he's swell, keeps double shifts working all night by flares. His mother squealed like a pig when he came crouching out.
Sometimes we read a sign, cloud in the sky,
The wet tracks of a hare, quicken the step

Promise the best day. But here no remedy
Is to be thought of, no news but the new death;
A Nower dragged out in the night, a Shaw
Ambushed behind the wall. Blood on the ground
Would welcome fighters. Last night at Hammergill
A boy was born fanged like a weasel. I am old,
Shall die before next winter, but more than once shall hear
The cry for help, the shooting round the house.

W: The best are gone.

Often the man, alone shut, shall consider
The killings in old winters, death of friends.
Sitting with stranger shall expect no good.

Spring came, urging to ships, a casting off,
But one would stay, vengeance not done; it seemed
Doubtful to them that they would meet again.

Fording in the cool of the day they rode
To meet at crossroads when the year was over:
Dead is Brody, such a man was Maul.

I will say this not falsely; I have seen
The just and the unjust die in the day,
All, willing or not, and some were willing.

Here they are.

(Enter Nower, George, Sturton and others. The three speak alternately.)

Day was gone Night covered sky
Black over earth When we came there
To Brandon Walls Where Red Shaw lay
Hateful and sleeping Unfriendly visit.
I wished to revenge Quit fully
Who my father At Colefangs valley
Lying in ambush Cruelly shot
With life for life.

Then watchers saw They were attacked
Shouted in fear A night alarm
To men asleep Doomed men awoke
Felt for their guns Ran to the doors

Would wake their master Who lay with woman
Upstairs together Tired after love.
He saw then There would be shooting
Hard fight.

Shot answered shot Bullets screamed
Guns shook Hot in the hand
Fighters lay Groaning on ground
Gave up life Edward fell
Shot through the chest First of our lot
By no means refused fight Stephen was good
His first encounter Showed no fear
Wounded many.

Then Shaw knew We were too strong
Would get away Over the moor
Return alive But found at the ford
Sturton waiting Greatest gun anger
There he died Nor any came
Fighters home Nor wives shall go
Smiling to bed They boast no more.

W. H. Auden, 'Paid on Both Sides'

Flight

The housebreaker freed one arm, and grasped his pistol. The certainty of immediate detection if he fired, flashed across his mind even in the midst of his fury; and he beat it twice with all the force he could summon, upon the upturned face that almost touched his own.

She staggered and fell: nearly blinded with the blood that rained down from a deep gash in her forehead; but raising herself, with difficulty, on her knees, drew from her bosom a white handkerchief – and holding it up, in her folded hands, as high towards Heaven as her feeble strength would allow, breathed one prayer for mercy to her Maker.

It was a ghastly figure to look upon. The murderer staggering backward to the wall, and shutting out the sight with his hand, seized a heavy club and struck her down.

• • •

Of all bad deeds that, under cover of the darkness, had been committed within wide London's bounds since night hung over it, that was the worst. Of all the horrors that rose with an ill scent upon the morning air, that was the foulest and most cruel.

The sun – the bright sun, that brings back, not light alone, but new life, and hope, and freshness to man – burst upon the crowded city in clear and radiant glory. Through costly-coloured glass and paper-mended window, through cathedral dome and rotten crevice, it shed its equal ray. It lighted up the room where the murdered woman lay. It did. He tried to shut it out, but it would stream in. If the sight had been a ghastly one in the dull morning, what was it, now, in all that brilliant light!

He had not moved; he had been afraid to stir. There had been a moan and motion of the hand; and, with terror added to rage, he had struck and struck again. Once he threw a rug over it; but it was worse to fancy the eyes, and imagine them moving towards him, than to see them glaring upward, as if watching the reflection of the pool of gore that quivered and danced in the sunlight on the ceiling. He had plucked it off again. And there was the body – mere flesh and blood, no more – but such flesh, and so much blood!

He struck a light, kindled a fire, and thrust the club into it. There was hair upon the end, which blazed and shrunk into a light cinder, and, caught by the air, whirled up the chimney. Even that frightened him, sturdy as he was; but he held the weapon till it broke, and then piled it on the coals to burn away, and smoulder into ashes. He washed himself, and rubbed his clothes; there were spots that would not be removed, but he cut the pieces out, and burnt them. How those stains were dispersed about the room! The very feet of the dog were bloody.

All this time he had never once turned his back upon the corpse; no, not for a moment. Such preparations completed, he moved, backward, towards the door: dragging the dog with him, lest he should soil his feet anew and carry out new evidences of the crime into the streets. He shut the door softly, locked it, took the key, and left the house.

He crossed over, and glanced up at the window, to be sure that nothing was visible from the outside. There was the curtain still drawn, which she would have opened to admit the light she never saw again. It lay nearly under there. *He* knew that. God, how the sun poured down upon the very spot!

The glance was instantaneous. It was a relief to have got free of the room. He whistled on the dog, and walked rapidly away.

He went through Islington; strode up the hill at Highgate on which stands the stone in honour of Whittington; turned down to Highgate Hill, unsteady of purpose, and uncertain where to go; struck off to the right again, almost as soon as he began to descend it; and taking the foot-path across the fields, skirted Caen Wood, and so came out on Hampstead Heath. Traversing the hollow by the Vale of Health, he mounted the opposite bank, and crossing the road which joins the villages of Hampstead and Highgate, made along the remaining portion of the heath to the fields at North End, in one of which he laid himself down under a hedge, and slept.

Soon he was up again, and away, – not far into the country, but back towards London by the high-road – then back again – then over another part of the same ground as he already traversed – then wandering up and down in fields, and lying on ditches' brinks to rest, and starting up to make for some other spot, and do the same, and ramble on again.

Where could he go, that was near and not too public, to get some meat and drink? Hendon. That was a good place, not far off, and out of most people's way. Thither he directed his steps, – running sometimes, and sometimes, with a strange perversity, loitering at a snail's pace, or stopping altogether and idly breaking the hedges, with his stick. But when he got there, all the people he met – the very children at the doors – seemed to view him with suspicion. Back he turned again, without the courage to purchase bit or drop, though he had tasted no food for many hours; and once more he lingered on the Heath, uncertain where to go.

He wandered over miles and miles of ground, and still came back to the old place. Morning and noon had passed, and the day was on the wane, and still he rambled to and fro, and up and down, and round and round, and still lingered about the same spot. At last he got away, and shaped his course for Hatfield.

It was nine o'clock at night, when the man, quite tired out, and the dog, limping and lame from the unaccustomed exercise, turned down the hill by the church of the quiet village, and plodding along the little street, crept into a small public-house, whose scanty light had guided them to the spot. There was a fire in the tap-room, and some country-labourers were drinking before it. They made room for the stranger, but he sat down in the furthest corner, and ate and drank alone, or rather with his dog: to whom he cast a morsel of food from time to time.

The conversation of the men assembled here, turned upon the neighbouring land, and farmers; and when those topics were exhausted, upon the age of some old man who had been buried on the previous

Sunday; the young men present considering him very old, and the old men present declaring him to have been quite young – not older, one white-haired grandfather said, than he was – with ten or fifteen year of life in him at least – if he had taken care; if he had taken care.

There was nothing to attract attention, or excite alarm in this. The robber, after paying his reckoning, sat silent and unnoticed in his corner, and had almost dropped asleep, when he was half wakened by the noisy entrance of a newcomer.

This was an antic fellow, half pedlar and half mountebank, who travelled about the country on foot to vend hones, strops, razors, washballs, harness-paste, medicine for dogs and horses, cheap perfumery, cosmetics, and such-like wares, which he carried in a case slung to his back. His entrance was the signal for various homely jokes with the countrymen, which slackened not until he had made his supper, and opened his box of treasures, when he ingeniously contrived to unite business with amusement.

'And what be that stoof? Good to eat, Harry?' asked a grinning countryman, pointing to some composition-cakes in one corner.

'This,' said the fellow, producing one, 'this is the infallible and invaluable composition for removing all sorts of stain, rust, dirt, mildew, spick, speck, spot, or spatter, from silk, satin, linen, cambric, cloth, crape, stuff, carpet, merino, muslin, bombazeen, or woollen stuff. Wine-stains, fruit-stains, beer-stains, water-stains, paint-stains, pitch-stains, any stains, all come out at one rub with the infallible and invaluable composition. If a lady stains her honour, she has only need to swallow one cake and she's cured at once – for it's poison. If a gentleman wants to prove this, he has only need to bolt one little square, and he has put it beyond question – for it's quite as satisfactory as a pistol-bullet, and a great deal nastier in the flavour, consequently the more credit in taking it. One penny a square. With all these virtues, one penny a square!'

There were two buyers directly, and more of the listeners plainly hesitated. The vendor observing this, increased in loquacity.

'It's all bought up as fast as it can be made,' said the fellow. 'There are fourteen water-mills, six steam-engines, and a galvanic battery, always a-working upon it, and they can't make it fast enough, though the men work so hard that they die off, and the widows is pensioned directly, with twenty pound a-year for each of the children, and a premium of fifty for twins. One penny a square! Two halfpence is all the same, and four farthings is received with joy. One penny a square! Wine-stains, fruit-stains, beer-stains, water-stains, paint-stains, pitch-stains, mud-stains, blood-stains!

Here is a stain upon the hat of a gentleman in company, that I'll take clean out, before he can order me a pint of ale.'

'Hah!' cried Sikes, starting up. 'Give that back.'

'I'll take it clean out, sir,' replied the man, winking to the company, 'before you can come across the room to get it. Gentlemen all, observe the dark stain upon this gentleman's hat, no wider than a shilling, but thicker than a half-crown. Whether it is a wine-stain, fruit-stain, beer-stain, water-stain, paint-stain, pitch-stain, mud-stain, or blood-stain –'

The man got no further, for Sikes with a hideous imprecation overthrew the table, and tearing the hat from him, burst out of the house.

With the same perversity of feeling and irresolution that had fastened upon him, despite himself, all day, the murderer, finding that he was not followed, and that they most probably considered him some drunken sullen fellow, turned back up the town, and getting out of the glare of the lamps of a stage-coach that was standing in the street, was walking past, when he recognized the mail from London, and saw that it was standing at the little post-office. He almost knew what was to come; but he crossed over, and listened.

The guard was standing at the door, waiting for the letter. A man, dressed like a gamekeeper, came up at the moment, and he handed him a basket which lay ready on the pavement.

'That's for your people,' said the guard. 'Now, look alive in there, will you. Damn that 'ere bag, it warn't ready night afore last; this won't do, you know!'

'Anything new up in town, Ben?' asked the gamekeeper, drawing back to the window-shutters, the better to admire the horses.

'No, nothing that I knows on,' replied the man, pulling on his gloves. 'Corn's up a little. I heerd talk of a murder, too, down Spitalfields way, but I don't reckon much upon it.'

'Oh, that's quite true,' said a gentleman inside, who was looking out of the window. 'And a dreadful murder it was.'

'Was it, sir?' rejoined the guard, touching his hat. 'Man or woman, pray, sir?'

'A woman,' replied the gentleman. 'It is supposed –'

'Now, Ben,' replied the coachman impatiently.

'Damn that 'ere bag,' said the guard; 'are you gone to sleep in there?'

'Coming!' cried the office keeper, running out.

'Coming,' growled the guard. 'Ah, and so's the young 'ooman of property that's going to take a fancy to me, but I don't know when. Here, give hold. All ri–ght!'

The horn sounded a few cheerful notes, and the coach was gone.

Sikes remained standing in the street, apparently unmoved by what he had just heard, and agitated by no stronger feeling than a doubt where to go. At length he went back again, and took the road which leads from Hatfield to St Albans.

He went on doggedly; but as he left the town behind him, and plunged into the solitude and darkness of the road, he felt a dread and awe creeping upon him which shook him to the core. Every object before him, substance or shadow, still or moving, took the semblance of some fearful thing; but these fears were nothing compared to the sense that haunted him of that morning's ghastly figure following at his heels. He could trace its shadow in the gloom, supply the smallest item of the outline, and note how stiff and solemn it seemed to stalk along. He could hear its garments rustling in the leaves, and every breath of wind came laden with that last low cry. If he stopped it did the same. If he ran, it followed – not running too: that would have been a relief: but like a corpse endowed with the mere machinery of life, and borne on one slow melancholy wind that never rose or fell.

At times he turned, with desperate determination, resolved to beat this phantom off, though it should look him dead; but the hair rose on his head, and his blood stood still, for it had turned with him and was behind him then. He had kept it before him that morning, but it was behind now – always. He leaned his back against a bank, and felt that it stood above him, visibly out against the cold night-sky. He threw himself upon the road – on his back upon the road. At his head it stood, silent, erect, and still – a living grave-stone, with its epitaph in blood.

Let no man talk of murderers escaping justice, and hint that Providence must sleep. There were twenty score of violent deaths in one long minute of that agony of fear.

There was a shed in a field he passed, that offered shelter for the night. Before the door, were three tall poplar trees, which made it very dark within; and the wind moaned through them with a dismal wail. He *could not* walk on, till daylight came again; and here he stretched himself close to the wall – to undergo new torture.

For now, a vision came before him, as constant and more terrible than that from which he had escaped. Those widely staring eyes, so lustreless and so glassy, that he had better borne to see them than think upon them, appeared in the midst of the darkness; light in themselves, but giving light to nothing. There were but two, but they were everywhere. If he shut out the sight, there came the room with every well-known object – some, indeed, that he would have forgotten, if he had gone over its contents from memory – each in its accustomed place. The body was in *its* place, and its eyes were as he saw them when he stole away. He got up, and rushed into the field without. The figure was behind him. He re-entered the shed, and shrunk down once more. The eyes were there, before he had laid himself along.

And here he remained in such terror as none but he can know, trembling in every limb, and the cold sweat starting from every pore, when suddenly there arose upon the night-wind the noise of distant shouting, and the roar of voices mingled in alarm and wonder. Any sound of men in that lonely place, even though it conveyed a real cause of alarm, was something to him. He regained his strength and energy at the prospect of personal danger; and springing to his feet, rushed into the open air.

The broad sky seemed on fire. Rising into the air with showers of sparks, and rolling one above the other, were sheets of flame, lighting the atmosphere for miles round, and driving clouds of smoke in the direction where he stood. The shouts grew louder as new voices swelled the roar, and he could hear the cry of Fire! mingled with the ringing of an alarm-bell, the fall of heavy bodies, and the crackling of flames as they twined round some new obstacle, and shot aloft as though refreshed by food. The noise increased as he looked. There were people there – men and women – light, bustle. It was like new life to him. He darted onward – straight, headlong – dashing through brier and brake, and leaping gate and fence as madly as his dog, who careered with loud and sounding bark before him.

He came upon the spot. There were half-dressed figures tearing to and fro, some endeavouring to drag the frightened horses from the stables, others driving the cattle from the yard and out-houses, and others coming laden from the burning pile, amidst a shower of falling sparks, and the tumbling down of red-hot beams. The apertures, where doors and windows stood an hour ago, disclosed a mass of raging fire; walls rocked and crumbled into the burning well; the molten lead and iron poured down, white hot, upon the ground. Women and children shrieked, and men encouraged each other with noisy shouts and cheers. The clanking of the engine-pumps, and the spirting and hissing of the water as it fell upon the blazing wood, added to the tremendous roar. He shouted, too, till he was hoarse; and flying from memory and himself, plunged into the thickest of the throng.

Hither and thither he dived that night: now working at the pumps, and now hurrying through the smoke and flame, but never ceasing to engage himself wherever noise and men were thickest. Up and down the ladders, upon the roofs of buildings, over floors that quaked and trembled with his weight, under the lee of falling bricks and stones, in every part of that great fire was he; but he bore a charmed life, and had neither scratch nor bruise, nor weariness nor thought, till morning dawned again, and only smoke and blackened ruins remained.

This mad excitement over, there returned, with tenfold force, the dreadful consciousness of his crime. He looked suspiciously about him, for the men were conversing in groups, and he feared to be the subject of their talk. The dog obeyed the significant beck of his finger, and they drew off, stealthily, together. He passed near an engine where some men were seated, and they called to him to share in their refreshment. He took some bread and meat; and as he drank a draught of beer, heard the firemen, who were from London, talking about the murder. 'He has gone to Birmingham, they say,' said one: 'but they'll have him yet, for the scouts are out, and by to-morrow night there'll be a cry all through the country.'

He hurried off, and walked till he almost dropped upon the ground; then lay down in a lane, and had a long, but broken and uneasy sleep. He wandered on again, irresolute and undecided, and oppressed with the fear of another solitary night.

Suddenly, he took the desperate resolution of going back to London.

'There's somebody to speak to there, at all events,' he thought. 'A good hiding-place, too. They'll never expect to nab me there, after this country scent. Why can't I lie by for a week or so, and, forcing blunt from Fagin, get abroad to France? Damme, I'll risk it.'

He acted upon this impulse without delay, and choosing the least frequented roads began his journey back, resolved to lie concealed within a short distance of the metropolis, and, entering it at dusk by a circuitous route, to proceed straight to that part of it which he had fixed on for his destination.

The dog, though. If any descriptions of him were out, it would not be forgotten that the dog was missing, and had probably gone with him. This might lead to his apprehension as he passed along the streets. He resolved to drown him, and walked on, looking about for a pond: picking up a heavy stone and tying it to his handkerchief as he went.

The animal looked up into his master's face while these preparations were making; whether his instinct apprehended something of their purpose, or the robber's sidelong look at him was sterner than ordinary, he skulked a little farther in the rear than usual, and cowered as he came more slowly along. When his master halted at the brink of a pool, and looked round to call him, he stopped outright.

'Do you hear me call? Come here!' cried Sikes.

The animal came up from the very force of habit; but as Sikes stooped to attach the handkerchief to his throat, he uttered a low growl and started back.

'Come back!' said the robber.

The dog wagged his tail, but moved not. Sikes made a running noose and called him again.

The dog advanced, retreated, paused an instant, turned, and scoured away at his hardest speed.

The man whistled again and again, and sat down and waited in the expectation that he would return. But no dog appeared, and at length he resumed his journey.

Charles Dickens, *Oliver Twist*

Forensic

It was warm – the federally-mandated 80° – in the elevator when Crawford came down from the roof with the note, his hair blown silly by the helicopter blast. He was mopping his face by the time he reached the Hair and Fibre section of the laboratory.

Hair and Fibre is a small section, calm and busy. The common room is stacked with boxes of evidence sent by police departments all over the country; swatches of tape that have sealed mouths and bound wrists, torn and stained clothing, deathbed sheets.

Crawford spotted Beverly Katz through the window of an examining room as he weaved his way between the boxes. She had a pair of child's coveralls suspended from a hanger over a table covered with white paper. Working under bright lights in the draught-free room, she brushed the overalls with a metal spatula, carefully working with the wale and across it, with the nap and against it. A sprinkle of dirt and sand fell to the paper. With it, falling through the still air more slowly than sand but faster than lint, came a tightly-coiled hair. She cocked her head and looked at it with her bright robin's eye.

Crawford could see her lips moving. He knew what she was saying.

'Gotcha.'

That's what she always said.

Crawford pecked on the glass and she came out fast, stripping off her white gloves.

'It hasn't been printed yet, right?'

'No.'

'I'm set up in the next examining room.' She put on a fresh pair of gloves while Crawford opened the document case.

The note, in two pieces, was contained gently between two sheets of plastic film. Beverly Katz saw the tooth impressions and glanced up at Crawford, not wasting time with the question.

He nodded: the impressions matched the clear overlay of the killer's bite he had carried with him to Chesapeake.

Crawford watched through the window as she lifted the note on a slender dowel and hung it over white paper. She looked it over with a powerful glass, then fanned it gently. She tapped the dowel with the edge of a spatula and went over the paper beneath it with the magnifying glass.

Crawford looked at his watch.

Katz flipped the note over another dowel to get the reverse side up. She removed one tiny object from its surface with tweezers almost as fine as a hair.

She photographed the torn ends of the note under high magnification and returned it to its case. She put a clean pair of white gloves in the case with it. The white gloves – the signal not to touch – would always be beside the evidence until it was checked for fingerprints.

'That's it,' she said, handing the case back to Crawford. 'One hair, maybe a thirty-second of an inch. A couple of blue grains. I'll work it up. What else have you got?'

Crawford gave her three marked envelopes. 'Hair from Lecter's comb. Whiskers from the electric razor they let him use. This is hair from the cleaning man. Gotta go.'

'See you later,' Katz said. 'Love *your* hair.'

Thomas Harris, *Red Dragon*

G

Games

We knew a pale and bony girl called Coral,
About twelve maybe (she seemed grown-up to us),
Who interrupted our Meccano quarrel
And the everlasting Test match on the grass,
With games that were strict, imaginative and moral,

Taking in both the vivacity of crime
And the satisfactoriness of punishment.
It worked like this: In a well-drilled pantomime
I crashed the blunt and bloodstained instrument
Onto my brother's bonce time after time,

Eviscerating with a kitchen knife
His nearly breathless corpse. Or he might be,
In Mummy's nightie and high heels, the wife
Drowned in the water-butt. Then the murderer (me),
Quaking with fear, stood trial for his life.

Coral, in some great-aunt's big, black-veiled hat,
Did judge and executioner. The rope
Was knotted on, a prayer said, then SPLAT!
Justice triumphant. These days, where's the scope,
With videos and such, for games like that?

John Whitworth, 'Home Entertainments'

They should not have left him there alone,
Alone that is except for the cat.
He was only nine, not old enough
To be left alone in a basement flat,
Alone, that is, except for the cat.

A dog would have been a different thing,
A big gruff dog with slashing jaws,
But a cat with round eyes mad as gold,
Plump as a cushion with tucked-in paws –
Better have left him with a fair-sized rat!
But what they did was leave him with a cat.
He hated that cat; he watched it sit,
A buzzing machine of soft black stuff,
He sat and watched and he hated it,
Snug in its fur, hot blood in a muff,
And its mad gold stare and the way it sat
Crooning dark warmth: he loathed all that.
So he took Daddy's stick and he hit the cat.
Then quick as a sudden crack in glass
It hissed, black flash, to a hiding place
In the dust and dark beneath the couch,
And he followed the grin on his new-made face,
A wide-eyed, frightened snarl of a grin,
And he took the stick and he thrust it in,
Hard and quick in the furry dark.
The black fur squealed and he felt his skin
Prickle with sparks of dry delight.
Then the cat again came into sight,
Shot for the door that wasn't quite shut,
But the boy, quick too, slammed fast the door:
The cat, half-through, was cracked like a nut
And the soft black thud was dumped on the floor.
Then the boy was suddenly terrified
And he bit his knuckles and cried and cried;
But he had to do something with the dead thing there.
His eyes squeezed beads of salty prayer
But the wound of fear gaped wide and raw;
He dared not touch the thing with his hands
So he fetched a spade and shovelled it
And dumped the load of heavy fur
In the spidery cupboard under the stair
Where it's been for years, and though it died
It's grown in that cupboard and its hot low purr
Grows slowly louder year by year:
There'll not be a corner for the boy to hide

When the cupboard swells and all sides split
And the huge black cat pads out of it.
Vernon Scannell, 'A Case of Murder'

Garotte

Tom pushed the garrotte into the right-hand pocket of his jacket. 'Stay there, because I might need you.' Tom went over to the WC, saw it was empty, and went in.

Tom locked the toilet door. The garrotte wasn't even through its loop. Tom adjusted it for action, and put it carefully into the right-hand pocket of his jacket. He smiled a little. Jonathan had gone pale as a sheet! Tom had rung up Reeves the day before yesterday, and Reeves had told him Jonathan was coming but would probably hold out for a gun. Jonathan must have a gun now, Tom thought, but Tom considered a gun impossible in such conditions.

Stepping on the water pedal, Tom wet his hands, shook them, and passed his palms over his face. He was feeling a bit nervous himself. His first Mafia effort!

Tom had felt that Jonathan might botch this job, and having got Trevanny into this, Tom thought it behoved him to try to help him out. So Tom had flown to Salzburg yesterday, in order to board the train today. Tom had asked Reeves what Marcangelo looked like, but rather casually, and Tom didn't think Reeves suspected that he was going to be on the train. On the contrary, Tom had told Reeves that he thought his scheme was hare-brained, and had told Reeves that he might let Jonathan off with half the money and find someone else for the second job, if he wanted to make a success of it. But not Reeves. Reeves was like a small boy playing a game he had invented himself, a rather obsessive game with severe rules – for other people. Tom wanted to help Trevanny, and what a great cause it was! Killing a big shot Mafioso! Maybe even two Mafiosi!

Tom hated the Mafia, hated their loan-sharking, their blackmail, their bloody church, their cowardliness in forever delegating their dirty work to underlings, so that the law couldn't get its hands on the bigger bastards among them, never get them behind bars except on charges of income tax evasion or some other triviality. The Mafiosi made Tom feel almost virtuous by comparison. At this thought, Tom laughed out loud, a laugh which rang in the tiny metal-and-tile room in which he stood. (He was aware too that he just might be keeping Marcangelo himself waiting outside the door.) Yes, there were people more dishonest, more corrupt, decidedly more ruthless than himself, and these were the Mafiosi – that charming, squabbling batch of families which the Italian–American League claimed did not exist, claimed were a figment of fiction-writers' imagination. Why, the church itself with its bishops making blood liquefy at the festival of San Gennaro, and little girls seeing visions of the Virgin Mary, all *this* was more real than the Mafia! Yes, indeed! Tom rinsed his mouth and spat and ran water into the basin and let it drain. Then he went out.

There was no one but Jonathan Trevanny on the platform, Jonathan now smoking a cigarette, but he at once dropped the cigarette like a soldier who wanted to appear more efficient under the eyes of a superior officer. Tom gave him a reassuring smile, and faced the side window by Jonathan.

'Did they go by, by any chance?' Tom had not wanted to peer through the two doors into the restaurant car.

'No.'

'We may have to wait till after Strassburg, but I hope not.'

A woman was emerging from the restaurant car, having trouble with the doors, and Tom sprang to open the second for her.

'*Danke schön*,' she said.

'*Bitte*,' Tom replied.

Tom drifted to the other side of the platform and pulled a *Herald-Tribune* from a pocket of his jacket. It was now 5.11 p.m. They were to arrive at Strassburg at 6.33 p.m. Tom supposed the Italians had had a big lunch, and were not going to go into the restaurant car.

A man went into the lavatory.

Jonathan was looking down at his book, but Tom's glance made Jonathan look at him, and Tom smiled once more. When the man came out, Tom moved over towards Jonathan. There were two men standing in the aisle of the carriage, several yards away, one smoking a cigar, both looking out the window and paying no attention to him and Jonathan.

'I'll try to get him *in* the loo,' Tom said. 'Then we'll have to heave him out the door.' Tom jerked his head to indicate the door on the lavatory side. 'If I'm in the loo with him, knock twice on the door when the coast is clear. Then we'll give him the old heave-ho as fast as poss.' Very casually Tom lit a Gauloise, then slowly and deliberately yawned.

Jonathan's panic, which had reached a peak when Tom had been in the WC, was subsidising a little. Tom wanted to go through with it. Just why he did was beyond Jonathan's power to imagine just now. Jonathan also had a feeling that Tom might intend to botch the thing, and leave Jonathan holding the bag. And yet, why? More likely Tom Ripley wanted a cut of the money, maybe all the rest of it. At that moment, Jonathan simply didn't care. It didn't matter. Now Tom himself looked a bit worried, Jonathan thought. He was leaning against the wall opposite the WC door, newspaper in hand, but he wasn't reading.

Then Jonathan saw two men aproaching. The second man was Marcangelo. The first man was not one of the Italians. Jonathan glanced at Tom – who at once looked at him – and Jonathan nodded once.

The first man looked around on the platform, saw the WC and made for it. Marcangelo passed in front of Jonathan, saw that the WC was occupied, and turned back and returned to the carriage aisle. Jonathan saw Tom grin and make a sweeping gesture with his right arm, as if to say, 'Dammit, the fish got away!'

Marcangelo was in plain view of Jonathan, waiting just a few feet away in the aisle, looking out the window. It occurred to Jonathan that Marcangelo's guards, who were in the middle of the carriage, wouldn't know that Marcangelo had had to wait, so that this extra time would arouse their anxiety sooner if Marcangelo didn't come back. Jonathan nodded slightly at Tom, which he hoped Tom would understand to mean that Marcangelo was waiting near by.

The man in the loo came out and returned to the carriage.

Now Marcangelo approached, and Jonathan gave a glance at Tom but Tom was sunk in his newspaper.

Tom was aware that the dumpy figure entering the platform was Marcangelo again, but he did not look up from his newspaper. Just in front of Tom, Marcangelo opened the door of the WC, and Tom sprang forward like a person who was determined to get into the toilet first, but at the same time he flipped the garrotte over the head of Marcangelo whose cry Tom hoped he stifled as he dragged him, with a jerk of the garrotte like a boxer's right cross, into the little room and closed the door. Tom yanked the garrotte viciously – one of Marcangelo's own weapons in his prime, Tom supposed – and Tom saw the nylon disappear in the flesh of the neck. Tom gave it another whirl behind the man's head and pulled still tighter. With his left hand Tom flicked the lever that locked the door. Marcangelo's gurgle stopped, his tongue began to protrude from the awful wet mouth, his eyes closed in misery, then opened in horror, and began to have the blank, what's-happening-to-me stare of the dying. Lower false teeth clattered to the tiles. Tom was nearly cutting his own thumb and the side of his forefinger because of the force he was exerting on the string, but he felt it a pain worth enduring. Marcangelo had slumped to the floor, but the garrotte, or rather Tom, was holding him in more or less a seated position. Marcangelo was now unconscious, Tom thought, and it was impossible for him to be breathing at all. Tom picked up the teeth, and dropped them into the toilet, and managed to step on the pedal which dumped the pan. He wiped his fingers with disgust on Marcangelo's padded shoulder.

Jonathan had seen the flick of the latch that changed the colour from green to red. The silence was alarming to Jonathan. How long would it last? What was happening? How much time had passed: Jonathan kept glancing through the glass half of the door into the carriage.

A man came from the restaurant car, started for the toilet, and seeing that it was occupied, went on into the carriage.

Jonathan was thinking that Marcangelo's friends would appear at any moment, if Marcangelo was in the least long in getting back to his compartment. Now the coast was clear, and was it time to knock? There *must* have been time for Marcangelo to die. Jonathan went and rapped twice on the door.

Tom stepped calmly out, closed the door and surveyed the situation, and a woman in a reddish tweed suit entered the platform just then – a smallish, middle-aged woman who was plainly headed for the toilet. The indicator was now showing green.

'Sorry,' Tom said to her. 'Someone – a friend of mine is being sick in there, I'm afraid.'

'*Bitte?*'

'*Mein Freund ist da drinnen ziemlich krank*,' Tom said with an apologetic smile. '*Entschuldigen Sie, gnädige Frau. Er kommt sofort heraus.*'

She nodded and smiled, and went back into the carriage.

'Okay, give me a hand!' Tom whispered to Jonathan, and started for the WC.

'Another one's coming,' Jonathan said. 'One of the Italians.'

'Oh, Christ.' The Italian might simply wait on the platform, Tom thought, if he went into the loo and locked the door.

The Italian, a sallow chap of about thirty, gave Jonathan and Tom a look, saw that the lavatory said *libre*, then went into the restaurant car, no doubt to see if Marcangelo was there.

Tom said to Jonathan. 'Can you bash him with the gun after I hit him?'

Jonathan nodded. The gun was small, but Jonathan's adrenalin was at last stirring.

'As if your life depended on it,' Tom added. 'Maybe it does.'

The bodyguard came back from the restaurant car, moving more quickly. Tom was on the Italian's left, and pulled him by the shirtfront suddenly, out of view of the restaurant car's doors, and hit him in the jaw. Tom followed this with a left fist in the man's abdomen, and Jonathan cracked the Italian on the back of the head with the gun butt.

'The door!' Tom said, jerking his head, trying to catch the Italian who was falling forward.

The man was not unconscious, his arms flailed weakly, but Jonathan already had the side door open, and Tom's instinct was to get him out without spending a second on another blow. The noise of the train wheels came with a sudden roar. They pushed, kicked and poured the bodyguard out, and Tom lost his balance and would have toppled out, if not for Jonathan catching him by his jacket tails. *Bang* went the door shut again.

Jonathan pushed his fingers through his tousled hair.

Tom motioned for Jonathan to go to the other side of the platform, where he could see down the aisle. Jonathan went, and Tom could see him making an effort to collect himself and look like the ordinary passenger again.

Tom raised his eyebrows in a question, and Jonathan nodded, and Tom nipped into the WC and swung the latch, trusting that Jonathan would have the wit to knock again when it was safe. Marcangelo lay crumpled on the floor, head next to the basin pedestal, his face pale now with a touch of blue in it. Tom looked away from him, heard the rustle of doors outside – the restaurant car doors – and then a welcome two knocks. This time Tom opened the door just a crack.

'Looks all right,' Jonathan said.

Tom kicked the door open past Marcangelo's shoes which the door bumped, and signalled for Jonathan to open the side door of the train. But in fact they worked together, Jonathan having to help Tom with some of Marcangelo's weight before the side door was in a fully open position. The door tended to close because of the direction of the train. They tumbled Marcangelo through it head-first, heels over head, and Tom, giving him a final kick, didn't touch him at all, because his body had already fallen clear on to a cinder bank so close to Tom that he could see individual ashes and blades of grass. Now Tom held Jonathan's right arm while Jonathan reached for the door's lever and caught it.

Tom pulled the toilet door shut, breathless, trying to assume a calm air. 'Go back to your seat and get off at Strassburg,' he said. 'They'll be looking at everyone on this train.' He gave Jonathan a nervous pat on the arm. 'Good luck, my friend.' Tom watched Jonathan open the door that went into the carriage aisle.

Patricia Highsmith, *Ripley's Game*

Genre

A great part of our liking for detective fiction is *based* on a liking for improbability. When A is murdered, and B and C are under strong suspicion, it is improbable that the innocent-looking D can be guilty. But he is. If G has a perfect alibi, sworn to at every point by every other letter in the alphabet, it is improbable that G can have committed the crime. But he has. When the detective picks up a fleck of coal-dust at the seashore, it is improbable that such an insignificant thing can have any importance. But it will.

John Dickson Carr, *The Hollow Man*

Personally I don't care whether a detective-story writer was educated in night school or day school
So long as they don't belong to the H.I.B.K. school.
The H.I.B.K. being a device to which too many detective-story writers are prone,
Namely the Had I But Known.
Sometimes it is the Had I But Known what grim secret lurked behind that smiling exterior I would never have set foot within the door,
Sometimes the Had I But Known then what I know now I could have saved at least three lives by revealing to the Inspector the conversation I heard through that fortuitous hole in the floor.
Had-I-But-Known narrators are the ones who hear a stealthy creak at midnight in the tower where the body lies, and, instead of locking their door or arousing the drowsy policeman posted outside their room, sneak off by themselves to the tower and suddenly they hear a breath exhaled behind them,
And they have no time to scream, they know nothing else till the men from the D.A.'s office come in next morning and find them.
Had I But Known-ers are quick to assume the prerogatives of the Deity,
For they will suppress evidence that does suit their theories with appalling spontaneity,
And when the killer is finally trapped into a confession by some elaborate

device of the Had I But Known-er some hundred pages later than if they hadn't held their knowledge aloof,

Why they say Why Inspector I knew all along it was he but I couldn't tell you, you would have laughed at me unless I had absolute proof.

Would you like a nice detective story for your library which I am sorry to say I didn't rent but owns?

I wouldn't have bought it had I but known it was impregnated with Had I But knowns.

Ogden Nash, 'Don't Guess, Let Me Tell You'

A stately home where doves, in dovecotes, coo –
fields where calm cattle stand and gently moo,
trim lawns where croquet is the thing to do.
This is the ship, the house party's the crew:
Lord Feudal, hunter of the lion and gnu,
whose walls display the heads of not a few,
Her Ladyship, once Ida Fortescue,
who, like his Lordship very highborn too
surveys the world with a disdainful moue.
Their son – most active with a billiard cue –
Lord Lazy (stays in bed till half past two).
A Balkan Count called Popolesceru
(an ex-Dictator waiting for a coup).
Ann Fenn, most English, modest, straight and true,
a very pretty girl without a sou.
Adrian Finkelstein, a clever Jew.
Tempest Bellairs, a beauty such as you
would only find in books like this (she'd sue
if I displayed her to the public view –
enough to say men stick to her like glue).
John Huntingdon, who's only there to woo
(a fact, except for her, the whole house knew)
Ann Fenn. And, last, the witty Cambridge Blue,
the Honourable Algy Playfair, who
shines in detection. His clear 'View halloo!'
puts murderers into a frightful stew.

But now the plot unfolds! What *déjà vu*!
There! In the snow! – The clear print of a shoe!

Tempest is late for her next rendez-vous,
Lord Feudal's blood spreads wide – red, sticky goo
on stiff white shirtfront – Lazy's billet-doux
has missed Ann Fenn, and Popolesceru
has left – without a whisper of adieu
or saying goodbye, typical *mauvais gout*!
Adrian Finkelstein, give him his due,
behaves quite well. Excitement is taboo
in this emotionless landowner's zoo.
Algy, with calm that one could misconstrue
(handling with nonchalance bits of vertu)
knows who the murderer is. He has a clue.

But who? But who? Who, who, who, who, who, who?

Gavin Ewart, 'The Owl Writes a Detective Story'

In *Trent's Last Case* (often called 'the perfect detective story') you have to accept the premiss that a giant of international finance, whose lightest frown makes Wall Street quiver like a chihuahua, will plot his own death so as to hang his secretary, and that the secretary when pinched will maintain an aristocratic silence; the old Etonian in him maybe. I have known relatively few international financiers, but I rather think the author of this novel has (if possible) known fewer.

There is one by Freeman Wills Crofts (the soundest builder of them all when he doesn't get too fancy) wherein a murderer by the aid of make-up, split-second timing, and some very sweet evasive action, impersonates the man he has just killed and thereby gets him alive and distant from the place of crime. There is one of Dorothy Sayers' in which a man is murdered alone at night in his house by a mechanically released weight which works because he always turns the radio on at just such a moment, always stands in just such a position in front of it, and always bends over just so far. A couple of inches either way and the customers would get a rain check. This is what is vulgarly known as having God sit in your lap; a murderer who needs that much help from Provindence must be in the wrong business.

And there is a scheme of Agatha Christie's featuring M. Hercule Poirot, that ingenious Belgian who talks in a literal translation of schoolboy French, wherein, by duly messing around with his 'little grey cells', M. Poirot decides that nobody on a certain sleeper could have done the murder alone, therefore everybody did it together, breaking the process down into a series of simple operations, like assemblinge an egg-beater. This is the type that is guaranteed to knock the keenest mind for a loop. Only a halfwit could guess it.

There are much better plots by these same writers and by others of their school. There may be one somewhere that would really stand up under close scrutiny. It would be fun to read it, even if I did have to go back to page 47 and refresh my memory about exactly what time the second gardener potted the prize-winning tea-rose begonia. There is nothing new about these stories and nothing old. The ones I mention are all English only because the authorities (such as they are) seem to feel the English writers had an edge in this dreary routine, and that the Americans (even the creator of Philo Vance – probably the most asinine character in detective fiction) only made the Junior Varsity.

This, the classic detective story, has learned nothing and forgotten nothing. It is the story you will find almost any week in the big shiny magazines, handsomely illustrated, and paying due deference to virginal love and the right kind of luxury goods. Perhaps the tempo has become a trifle faster, and the dialogue a little more glib. There are more frozen daiquiris and stingers ordered, and fewer glasses of crusty old port; more clothes by *Vogue*, and décors by *House Beautiful*, more chic, but not more truth. We spend more time in Miami hotels and Cape Cod summer colonies and go not so often down by the old grey sundial in the Elizabethan garden.

But fundamentally it is the same careful grouping of suspects, the same utterly incomprehensible trick of how somebody stabbed Mrs Pottington Postlethwaite III with the solid platinum poniard just as she flatted on the top note of the Bell Song from Lakmé in the presence of fifteen ill-assorted guests; the same ingénue in fur-trimmed pyjamas screaming in the night to make the company pop in and out of doors and ball up the timetable; the same moody silence next day as they sit around sipping Singapore slings and sneering at each other, while the flatfeet crawl to and fro under the Persian rugs, with their derby hats on.

Personally I like the English style better. It is not quite so brittle, and the people as a rule, just wear clothes and drink drinks. There is more sense of background, as if Cheesecake Manor really existed all around and not just the part the camera sees; there are more long walks over the downs and the characters don't all try to behave as if they had just been tested by MGM. The English may not always be the best writers in the world, but they are incomparably the best dull writers.

There is a very simple statement to be made about all these stories: they do not really come off intellectually as problems, and they do not come off artistically as fiction. They are too contrived, and too little aware of what goes on in the world. They try to be honest, but honesty is an art. The poor writer is dishonest without knowing it, and the fairly good one can be dishonest because he doesn't know what to be honest about. He thinks a complicated murder scheme which baffled the lazy reader, who won't be bothered itemizing the details, will also baffle the police, whose business is with details.

The boys with their feet on the desks know that the easiest murder case in the world to break is the one somebody tried to get very cute with; the one that really bothers them is the murder somebody only thought of two minutes before he pulled it off. But if the writers of this fiction wrote about the kind of murders that happen, they would also have to write about the authentic flavour of life as it is lived. And since they cannot do that, they pretend that what they do is what should be done.

Raymond Chandler, 'The Simple Art of Murder'

The Milieu (Human)

The detective story requires:

(1) A closed society so that the possibility of an outside murderer (and hence of the society being totally innocent) is excluded; and a closely related society so that all its members are potentially suspect (*cf.* the thriller, which requires an open society in which any stranger may be a friend or enemy in disguise).

Such conditions are met by: (a) the group of blood relatives (the Christmas dinner in the country house); (b) the closely knit geographical group (the old world village); (c) the occupational group (the theatrical company); (d) the group isolated by the neutral place (the Pullman car).

In this last type the concealment–manifestation formula applies not only to the murder but also to the relations between the members of the group who first appear to be strangers to each other, but are later found to be related.

(2) It must appear to be an innocent society in a state of grace, i.e., a society where there is no need of the law, no contradiction between the aesthetic individual and the ethical universal, and where murder, therefore, is the unheard-of act which precipitates a crisis (for it reveals that some member has fallen and is no longer in a state of grace). The law becomes a reality and for a time all must live in its shadow, till the fallen

one is identified. With his arrest, innocence is restored, and the law retires forever.

The characters in a detective story should, therefore, be eccentric (aesthetically interesting individuals) and good (instinctively ethical) – good, that is, either in appearance, later shown to be false, or in reality, first concealed by an appearance of bad.

It is a sound instinct that has made so many detective story writers choose a college as a setting. The ruling passion of the ideal professor is the pursuit of knowledge for its own sake so that he is related to other human beings only indirectly through their common relation to the truth; and those passions, like lust and avarice and envy, which relate individuals directly and may lead to murder are, in his case, ideally excluded. If a murder occurs in a college, therefore, it is a sign that some colleague is not only a bad man but also a bad professor. Further, as the basic premiss of academic life is that truth is universal and to be shared with all, the *gnosis* of a concrete crime and the *gnosis* of abstract ideas nicely parallel and parody each other.

(The even more ideal contradiction of a murder in a monastery is excluded by the fact that monks go regularly to confession and, while the murderer might well not confess his crime, the suspects who are innocent of murder but guilty of lesser sins cannot be supposed to conceal them without making the monastery absurd. Incidentally, is it an accident that the detective story has flourished most in predominantly Protestant countries?)

The detective story writer is also wise to choose a society with an elaborate ritual and to describe this in detail. A ritual is a sign of harmony between the aesthetic and the ethical in which body and mind, individual will and general laws, are not in conflict. The murderer uses his knowledge of the ritual to commit the crime and can be caught only by someone who acquires an equal or superior familiarity with it.

The Milieu (Natural)

In the detective story, as in its mirror image, the Quest for the Grail, maps (the ritual of space) and timetables (the ritual of time) are desirable. Nature should reflect its human inhabitants, i.e., it should be the Great Good Place; for the more Eden-like it is, the greater the contradiction of murder. The country is preferable to the town, a well-to-do neighborhood (but not too well-to-do – or there will be a suspicion of ill-gotten gains) better than a slum. The corpse must shock not only because it is a corpse but also because, even for a corpse, it is shockingly out of place, as when a dog makes a mess on a drawing room carpet.

Mr Raymond Chandler has written that he intends to take the body out of the vicarage garden and give the murder back to those who are good at it. If he wishes to write detective stories, i.e., stories where the reader's principal interest is to learn who did it, he could not be more mistaken, for in a society of professional criminals, the only possible motives for desiring to identify the murderers are blackmail or revenge, which both apply to individuals, not to the group as a whole, and can equally well inspire murder. Actually, whatever he may say, I think Mr Chandler is interested in writing, not detective stories, but serious studies of a criminal milieu, the Great Wrong Place, and his powerful but extremely depressing books should be read and judged, not as escape literature, but as works of art.

The Victim

The victim has to try to satisfy two contradictory requirements. He has to involve everyone in suspicion, which requires that he be a bad character; and he has to make everyone feel guilty, which requires that he be a good character. He cannot be a criminal because he could then be dealt with by the law and murder would be unnecessary. (Blackmail is the only exception.) The more general the temptation to murder he arouses, the better; e.g., the desire for freedom is a better motive than money alone or sex alone. On the whole, the best victim is the negative Father or Mother Image.

If there is more than one murder, the subsequent victims should be more innocent than the initial victim, i.e., the murderer should start with a real grievance and, as a consequence of righting it by illegitimate means, be forced to murder against his will where he has no grievances but his own guilt.

The Murderer

Murder is negative creation, and every murderer is therefore the rebel who claims the right to be omnipotent. His pathos is his refusal to suffer. The problem for the writer is to conceal his demonic pride from the other characters and from the reader, since, if a person has his pride, it tends to appear in everything he says and does. To surprise the reader when the identity of the murderer is revealed, yet at the same time to convince him that everything he has previously been told about the murderer is consistent with his being a murderer, is the test of a good detective story.

As to the murderer's end, of the three alternatives – execution, suicide, and madness – the first is preferable; for if he commits suicide he refuses to repent, and if he goes mad he cannot repent, but if he does not repent society cannot forgive. Execution on the other hand, is the act of atonement by which the murderer is forgiven by society. In real life I disapprove of capital punishment, but in a detective story the murderer must have no future.

(*A Suggestion for Mr Chandler*: Among a group of efficient professional killers who murder for strictly professional reasons, there is one to whom, like Leopold and Loeb, murder is an *acte gratuit*. Presently murders begin to occur which have not been commissioned. The group is morally outraged and bewildered; it has to call in the police to detect the amateur murderer, rescue the professionals from a mutual suspicion which threatens to disrupt their organization, and restore their capacity to murder.)

W. H. Auden, 'The Guilty Vicarage'

DCC: It has been suggested that a crucial element in detective fiction is that the reader identifies both with the detective and the criminal; that the detective and the criminal are opposite sides of the same figure; that, as Julian Symons has said, the detective and the murderer are the light and dark sides of the reader's nature. Do you agree with that?

P. D. James: I do to one extent. I think this is what we mean when we say that detective fiction may be a substitute for the old morality plays. Certainly in detective fiction, right does triumph and wrong is punished, if not in this world, in the next, as it were. The problem is solved and this is the difference perhaps between crime fiction and detective fiction; and the detective who is a kind of avenging, judgemental figure is always successful. I can't think of any novels in which the whole of the investigation is a total fiasco. This wouldn't I think, then fall within the genre. But on a fairly low level, the detective is the light and the murderer is the dark. In modern mysteries, it is less simple because the detectives are becoming much more complicated and more psychologically interesting so that within the detective you get the dark and the light. He is no longer just a figure representing the good part of man's nature. He may have within his personality the seeds of corruption which he undoubtedly does have. He may do things that he knows himself are immoral, unethical, wrong, he may deceive and trap and betray. He may in his relationships with other people, particularly his subordinates, be less than fair. Because the detective is increasingly becoming a human being, that part of his personality which is evil has to be shown. So, to an extent, this destroys the old idea that you have the good and evil, the dark and the light.

• • •

DCC: In what way does amorality interest you in a character like Tom Ripley?

Patricia Highsmith: I suppose I find it an interesting contrast to stereotyped morality which is very frequently hypocritical and phony. I also think that to mock lip-service morality and to have a character amoral, such as Ripley, is entertaining. I think people are entertained by reading such stories. The murderers that one reads about in the newspaper half the time are mentally deficient in some way or simply callous. There are young boys, for instance, who pretend to be delivering, or who may help an old lady carry her groceries home, and then hit her on the head when she invites them in for tea, and rob her. These are forever stupid people but they exist. Many murderers are like that and they don't interest me enough to write a book about them. Somebody like Ripley, however, who is reasonably intelligent and still has this amoral quality, interests me. I couldn't make an interesting story out of some morons.

DCC: It seems to be a *sine qua non* of crime fiction that order is restored and good triumphs over evil but sometimes your murderers do get away with murder; again, Philip Carter and Tom Ripley.

PH: This is the way life is and I read somewhere years ago that only 11 per cent of murders are solved. That is unfortunate but lots of victims are not so important as the President of the United States. The police make a certain effort, and it may be a good effort, but frequently the case is dropped. And so I think, why shouldn't I write about a few characters who also go free?

DCC: You have been accused of carrying your identification with your psychotic characters to the point where you actually seem to be preferring their interesting evil to the mediocre virtue of their victims. Would you agree with that assessment?

PH: Yes. I think it is more interesting to talk about something off the beaten track than it is to talk about a so-called normal person. That's one answer to your question. Another might be, that in some of my books the victims are evil or boring individuals so the murderer is more important than they. This is a writer's remark, not a legal judge's.

DCC: Is this why you might perhaps find amorality more interesting than immorality, because it is more unusual?
PH: Yes. I suppose it is such a subtle question because it is such a subtle difference. Amorality such as Ripley's is rarer than immorality. People in the Mafia or pimps, people in any kind of wretched occupation, know that they and their work are strictly in the gutter, that their activities are disgusting, and they don't care as long as it puts a little money in their pockets. This is immoral but the Ripley type is amoral.

Diana Cooper-Clarke,
Designs of Darkness: Interviews with Detective Novelists

Gibbet

There are in our existence spots of time,
That with distinct pre-eminence retain
A renovating virtue, whence, depressed
By false opinion and contentious thought,
Or aught of heavier or more deadly weight,
In trivial occupations, and the round
Of ordinary intercourse, our minds
Are nourished and invisibly repaired;
A virtue, by which pleasure is enhanced,
That penetrates, enables us to mount,
When high, more high, and lifts us up when fallen.
This efficacious spirit chiefly lurks
Among those passages of life that give
Profoundest knowledge to what point, and how,
The mind is lord and master – outward sense
The obedient servant of her will. Such moments
Are scattered everywhere, taking their date
From our first childhood. I remember well,
That once, while yet my inexperienced hand
Could scarcely hold a bridle, with proud hopes
I mounted, and we journeyed towards the hills:
An ancient servant of my father's house
Was with me, my encourager and guide:
We had not travelled long, ere some mischance
Disjoined me from my comrade; and, through fear
Dismounting, down the rough and stony moor

I led my horse, and, stumbling on, at length
Came to a bottom, where in former times
A murderer had been hung in iron chains.
The gibbet-mast had mouldered down, the bones
And iron case were gone; but on the turf,
Hard by, soon after that fell deed was wrought,
Some unknown hand had carved the murderer's name.
The monumental letters were inscribed
In times long past; but still, from year to year,
By superstition of the neighbourhood,
The grass is cleared away, and to that hour
The characters were fresh and visible:
A casual glance had shown them, and I fled,
Faltering and faint, and ignorant of the road:
Then, reascending the bare common, saw
A naked pool that lay beneath the hills,
The beacon on the summit, and, more near,
A girl, who bore a pitcher on her head,
And seemed with difficult steps to force her way
Against the blowing wind. It was, in truth,
An ordinary sight; but I should need
Colours and words that are unknown to man,
To paint the visionary dreariness
Which, while I looked all round for my lost guide,
Invested moorland waste, and naked pool,
The beacon crowning the lone eminence,
The female and her garments vexed and tossed
By the strong wind.

William Wordsworth, *The Prelude*

My human brothers who live after me,
See how I hang. My bones eat through the skin
And flesh they carried here upon the chin
And lipping clutch of their cupidity;
Now here, now there, the starling and the sea
Gull splinter the groined eyeballs of my sin,
Brothers, more beaks of birds than needles in
The fathoms of the Bayeux Tapestry:
'God wills it, wills it, wills it: it is blood.'

My brothers, if I call you brothers, see:
The blood of Abel crying from the dead
Sticks to my blackened skull and eyes. What good
Are *lebensraum* and bread to Abel dead
And rotten to the cross-beams of the tree?

Robert Lowell, 'France'

Gift

We met the British in the dead of winter.
The sky was lavender

and the snow lavender-blue.
I could hear, far below,

the sound of two streams coming together
(both were frozen over)

and, no less strange,
myself calling out in French

across that forest-
clearing. Neither General Jeffrey Amherst

nor Colonel Henry Bouquet
could stomach our willow-tobacco.

As for the unusual
scent when the Colonel shook out his hand-

kerchief: *C'est la lavande,*
une fleur mauve comme le ciel.

They gave us six fishhooks
and two blankets embroidered with smallpox.

Paul Muldoon, 'Meeting the British'

Godfather

Luciano Leggio, born January 6, 1925; died November 15, 1993.

It was a reminder of how little has changed in Italy after 18 months of tumult: the funeral on Wednesday of 'Don' Luciano Leggio, the real Godfather.

Leggio was the man who founded, built and brought to grim maturity the Mafia clan which controls the global empire of Cosa Nostra.

The Catholic Church complied, and full honours were granted; the Godfather's brother-in-law, a priest, pronounced himself 'blind with grief'; mourners attacked television cameras and accused 'you journalists' and the judges of wrongly blackening the name of 'Lucianeddu'.

Luciano Leggio lived the last 20 years of his life in the Sardinian jail where he died from a stroke last Monday, aged 68. He was the founder and boss of the infamous Corleone clan which now dominates the Sicilian Mafia, and which he directed from his prison cell. Corleone, a scrappy little village on the rocky plains above Palermo, gave its name to the family in Francis Ford Coppola's tasteless Mafia film, *The Godfather.*

Don Luciano is being credited across Italy's and the world's press with being the Man of Honour who created the octopus of crime syndicates, centred on Sicily, that ships, refines and deals the world's heroin and cocaine, so rich that it is among the planet's largest and most powerful international financial conglomerates. But he didn't, he stole it, through the bloodiest war in Cosa Nostra history, using a mix of stealth and violence that the Mafia has not known before or since.

Leggio was born in 1925 to an illiterate peasant family, but was rich by the age of 20. He was a cattle thief and had established a thriving ranch by the time he had killed the tin-pot Mafia boss in Corleone and the local labour leader. When a little boy witnessed the dumping of the latter's body, he was taken to hospital and killed with an injection.

Crafty Lucianeddu, a puffy-faced man with small wild eyes, was the most effective killer operating in the growing Corleone clan, over which he quickly established his authoritiy. Wanted by the authorities, he was obliged to move to Palmero – in hiding but enjoying the lifestyle of the coming Mafioso, driving a fleet of cars, accepted by the city's smart circles and enjoying a number of fleeting love affairs.

The ruling Mafia bosses were less enthusiastic. During the 1960s the clans under Stefano Bontate, Santo Inzerillo and Geatano Baladamenti, were building a formidable network of control over the drug syndicates in Italy, and in North and South America. Back home, they allegedly worked with the ruling Christian Democrat party, including, according to the current indictments, prime minister Guilio Andreotti.

They were also obliged to incorporate Leggio on to the 'Cupola', or high dome of the Mafia. Leggio had been carefully constructing his own clan. He had secured the loyalty of the Catania Mafia and the hinterland all around Palermo, thus tying a geographical noose around the establishment. He put his man, Francesco Di Carlo, in the United Kingdom to work with the Cuntrera family, based in South America and running the biggest heroin pipeline, and to keep an eye on Roberto Calvi's Banco Ambrosiano.

And he nurtured and recruited three lieutenants: Salvatore Riina and Bernardo Provezano, known as the Beasts, and Pipo Calo, who came to be called the Treasurer. He forged a far-sighed alliance with the Camorra of Naples and also opened up the runs from the fathomless morphine base suppliers in the Eastern Golden Triangle.

By the time he was arrested in 1974, Leggio had already been tried and acquitted for 11 murders. He had lived variously on the run or in detention since his first arrest in 1964, moving to Milan and changing his name to Baron Osvaldo Fatori, and betrayed by a phone call from one of the Mafia gang he built up in the Northern capital.

He developed a remarkable animosity with Italy's most extraordinary anti-Mafia judge of all, Cesare Terranova, who had warned in 1965 that 'The myth of the courageous and generous Man of Honour must be destroyed.' The Corleonesi were all acquitted at a trial in Bari by sending a circular to judge and jury threatening to kill all of them and their families.

Once in prison, Leggio's career began in earnest. After seven years he unleashed the Corleonesi against the rest of the Cupola with extraordinary ferocity. His men in prison had found out that Inzerillo and Bontate were keeping back some of the American heroin profits. Leggio's men also uncovered a plot to execute the Corleonesi's chief in the field, 'Toto' Riina. These offences against the criminal code gave Leggio just the spark he needed to ignite the Great Mafia War of 1981, during which a thousand of his adversaries were killed, the executions led by Riina and Provezano.

With two decades of homework behind him, Leggio and his men were triumphant, wiping out all the established families and bringing any stragglers into their fold. The murders crossed the Atlantic, and international connections in North America switched sides, happy to deal with the men in control, while the South American colonies had already been secured. Eleven members of Baladamenti's family were killed; Bontate lost 120 of his closest cohorts.

Asked to testify at the Mafia Mazxi-trial in 1986, Leggio said he did not know what the Mafia was. 'To all these charges, I have one answer,' he said, 'I was in jail.'

Ed Vulliamy, 'Man of Dishonour'

Guillotine

At about three o'clock in the morning I must have gone out for the tenth time into the street. The guillotine was ready. Its two beams, separated by about two feet, with the slanting line of the connecting blade, stood out dimly and strangely rather than terribly against the dark sky. For some reason I imagined that those beams ought to be more distant from each other; their proximity lent the whole machine a sort of sinister shapeliness, the shapeliness of a long, carefully stretched-out swan's neck. The large, dark-red wicker basket, looking like a suitcase, aroused a feeling of disgust in me. I knew that the executioners would throw the warm and still quivering dead body and the cut-off head into that basket . . . The mounted police (*garde municipale*), who had arrived a little earlier, took up their position in a large semicircle before the façade of the prison; from time to time the horses neighed, gnawed at their bits and tossed their heads; large drops of froth showed up white on the road between their forelegs. The riders dozed sombrely beneath their bearskins, pulled over their eyes. The lines of the soldiers, cutting across the square and holding back the crowds, fell back farther: now there were not two hundred but three hundred feet of empty space before the prison. I went up to one of those lines and gazed for a long time at the people crammed behind it; their shouting actually was elemental, that is, senseless. I still remember the face of a workman, a young fellow of about twenty: he stood there grinning, with his eyes fixed on the ground, just as though he were thinking of something amusing, then he would suddenly throw back his head, open his mouth wide and begin to shout in a drawn-out voice, without words, and then his head would again drop and he would start grinning again. What was going on inside that man? Why did he consign himself to such a painfully sleepless night, to an almost eight-hour long immobility? My ears did not catch any snatches of conversation; only occasionally there came through the unceasing uproar the piercing cry of a hawker selling a leaflet about Tropmann, about his life, his execution and even his 'last words' . . . Or, again, an argument broke out somewhere far away, or there would be a hideous burst of laughter, or some women would start screaming . . . This time I heard the Marseillaise, but it was sung only by five or six men, and that, too, with interruptions. The Marseillaise becomes significant only when thousands are singing it. *A bas Pierre Bonaparte!* someone shouted at the top of his voice . . . Oo–oo–ah—ah! the crowd responded in an incoherent roar. In one place the shouts assumed the measured rhythm of a polka: one – two – three – four! one – two – three – four – to the well-known tune of *Des lampions!* A heavy, rank breath of alcoholic fumes came from the crowd: a great deal of wine had been drunk by all those bodies; there were a great many drunken men there. It was not for nothing that the pot-houses glowed with red lights in the general background of this scene. The night had grown pitch-dark; the sky had become totally overcast and turned black. There were small clumps on the sparse trees, looming indistinctly out of the darkness like phantoms: those were street urchins who had climbed up on the trees and were sitting among the branches, whistling and screeching like birds. One of them had fallen down and, it is said, was fatally injured, having broken his spine, but he only aroused loud laughter, and that, too, for a short time.

On my way back to the prison governor's apartment, I passed the guillotine and saw on its platform the executioner surrounded by a small crowd of inquisitive people. He was carrying out a 'rehearsal' for them; threw down the hinged plank, to which the criminal was fastened and which, as it fell, touched with its end the semi-circular slot between the beams; he let fall the knife, which ran down heavily and smoothly with a rapid, hollow roar, and so on. I did not stop to watch this 'rehearsal', that is to say, I did not climb on to the platform: the feeling of some unknown transgression committed by myself, of some secret shame, was growing stronger inside me . . . It is perhaps to this feeling that I must ascribe in fact that the horses harnessed to the vans and calmly chewing the oats in their nosebags, seemed to me at that moment to be the only innocent creatures among us all.

Once more I went back to the solitude of my little sofa and once more I began to listen to the roar of the breakers on the sea-shore . . .

Contrary to what is generally asserted, the *last* hour of waiting passes much more quickly than the first and, more especially, than the second or third . . . So it happened this time. We were surprised at the news that it had struck six and that only one hour remained to the moment of execution. We had to go to Tropmann's cell in exactly half an hour: half past six. All traces of sleep at once disappeared from all the faces. I don't know what the others felt, but I felt terribly sick at heart. New figures appeared: a priest, a small grey-haired little man with a thin little face flashed by in his long, black cassock with the ribbon of the Légion d'Honneur and a low, wide-brimmed hat. The prison governor prepared a sort of breakfast for us, *une collation*; huge cups of chocolate appeared on the round table in the drawing-room . . . I did not even go near it, though our hospitable host advised me to fortify myself, 'because the morning air might be harmful'. To take food of that moment seemed – disgusting to me. Good Lord, a feast at such a time. 'I have no right,' I kept saying to myself for the hundredth time since the beginning of that night.

'Is *he* still asleep?' one of us asked, sipping his chocolate.

(They were all talking of Tropmann without referring to him by name: there could be no question of any other *him*.)

'Yes, he's asleep,' replied the prison governor.

'In spite of this terrible racket?'

(The noise had, in fact, grown extraordinarily loud and turned into a kind of hoarse roar; the menacing chorus, no longer crescendo, rumbled on victoriously, gaily.)

'His cell is behind three walls,' replied the prison governor.

M. Claude, whom the prison governor evidently treated as the most important person among us, looked at his watch and said: 'Twenty past six.'

We must, I expect, have all shuddered inwardly, but we just put on our hats and set off noisily after our guide.

'Where are you dining today?' a reporter asked in a loud voice.

But that struck us all as a little too unnatural.

We went into the large prison courtyard; and there, in the corner on the right before a half-closed door, a sort of roll-call took place; then we were shown into a tall, narrow and entirely empty room with a leather stool in the centre.

'It is here that *la toilette du condamné* takes place,' Du Camp whispered to me.

We did not all get in: there were only ten of us, including the prison governor, the priest, M. Claude and his assistant. During the next two or three minutes that we spent in that room (some kind of official documents were being signed there) the thought that we had no right to do what we were doing, that by being present with an air of hypocritical solemnity at the killing of a fellow human being, we were performing some odious, iniquitous farce – that thought flashed across my mind for the last time; as soon as we set off, again after M. Claude, along the wide stone corridor, dimly lit by two night-lights, I no longer felt anything except that now – now – this minute – this second . . . We rapidly climbed two staircases into another corridor, walked through it, went down a narrow spiral staircase and found ourselves before an iron door . . . Here!

The warder unlocked the door cautiously. It opened quietly – and we all went in quietly and in silence into a rather spacious room with yellow walls, a high barred window and a crumpled bed on which no one was lying . . . The steady light of a large night lamp lit up all the objects in the room quite clearly.

I was standing a little behind the rest and, I remember, screwed up my eyes involuntarily; however, I saw at once, diagonally opposite me, a young, black-haired, black-eyed face, which, moving slowly from left to right, gazed at us all with huge round eyes. That was Tropmann. He had woken up before our arrival. He was standing before the table on which he had just written a farewell (though rather trivial) letter to his mother. M. Claude took off his hat and went up to him.

'Tropmann,' he said in his dry, soft, but peremptory voice, 'we have come to inform you that your appeal for a reprieve has been dismissed and that the hour of retribution has come for you.'

Tropmann turned his eyes on him, but they were no longer 'huge'; he looked calmly, almost somnolently, and did not utter a word.

'My child,' the priest exclaimed dully, going up to him from the other side, '*du courage!*'

Tropmann looked at him exactly as he had looked at M. Claude.

'I knew he wouldn't be afraid,' said M. Claude in a confident tone, addressing us all. 'Now when he has got over the first shock (*le premier choc*), I can answer for him.'

(So does a schoolmaster, wishing to cajole his pupil, tell him beforehand that he is 'a clever fellow'.)

'Oh, I'm not afraid (*Oh! je n'ai pas peur!*),' said Tropmann, addressing M. Claude again, 'I'm not afraid!'

His voice, a pleasant, youthful baritone, was perfectly even.

The priest took a small bottle out of his pocket.

'Won't you have a drop of wine, my child?'

'Thank you, no,' Tropmann replied politely, with a slight bow.

M. Claude addressed him again.

'Do you insist that you are not guilty of the crime for which you've been condemned?'

'I did not strike the blow! (*Je n'ai pas frappé!*)'

'But – ?' the prison governor interjected.

'I did not strike the blow!'

(For some time past Tropmann, as everyone knows, had asserted, contrary to his former depositions, that he did take the Kink family to the place where they had been butchered, but that they were murdered by his associates, and that even the injury on his hand was due to his attempt to save one of the small children. However, he had told as many lies during his trial as very few criminals have done before him.)

'And do you still assert that you had accomplices?'

'Yes.'

'You can't name them, can you?'

'I can't and I won't. I won't!' Tropmann raised his voice and his face flushed. It seemed as though he were going to be angry.

'Oh, all right, all right,' M. Claude said hurriedly, as though implying that he had put his questions merely as a formality and that there was something else that had to be done now . . .

Tropmann had to undress.

Two warders went up to him and began taking off his prison strait-jacket (*camisole de force*), a kind of blouse of coarse bluish cloth, with belts and buckles behind, long sewn-up sleeves, to the ends of which strong pieces of tape were fastened near the thighs by the waist. Tropmann stood sideways, within two feet of me. Nothing prevented me from scrutinizing his face carefully. It could have been described as handsome but for the unpleasantly full lips, which made his mouth protrude a little too much and turn upwards funnel-like, just as with animals, and behind his lips were two rows of bad, sparse, fan-like teeth. He had thick, slightly wavy, dark hair, long eyebrows, expressive protruding eyes, a wide clear forehead, a regular, slightly aquiline nose, little curls of black down on his chin . . . If you happened to meet such a man outside prison and not in such surroundings, he would, no doubt, have made a good impression on you. Hundreds of such faces were to be seen among young factory workers, pupils of public institutions, etc. Tropmann was of medium height and of a youthfully thin and slender build. He looked to me like an overgrown boy, and, indeed, he was not yet twenty. He had a natural, healthy, slightly rosy complexion; he did not turn pale even at our entrance . . . There could be no doubt that he really had slept all night. He did not raise his eyes and his breathing was regular and deep, like a man walking up a steep hill. Once or twice he shook his hair as though wishing to dismiss a troublesome thought, tossed back his head, threw a quick glance at the ceiling and heaved a hardly perceptible sigh. With the exception of those, almost momentary, movements, nothing in him disclosed, I won't say fear, but even agitation or anxiety. We were all, I am sure, much paler and more agitated than he. When his hands were released from the sewn-up sleeves of the strait-jacket, he held up this strait-jacket in front of him, on his chest, with a pleased smile, while it was being undone at the back; little children behave like that when they are being undressed. Then he took off his shirt himself, put on another clean one, and carefully buttoned the neckband . . . It was strange to see the free sweeping movements of that naked body, those bare limbs against the yellowish background of the prison wall . . .

Then he bent down and put on his boots, knocking loudly with his heels and soles against the floor and the wall to make sure his feet got into them properly. All this he did cheerfully and without any sign of constraint – almost gaily, just as though he had been invited to go for a walk. He was silent and – we were silent. We merely exchanged glances, shrugging our shoulders involuntarily with surprise. We were all struck by the simplicity of his movements, a simplicity which, like any other calm and natural manifestation of life, amounted almost to elegance. One of our colleagues, who met me by accident later during that day, told me that all during our stay in Tropmann's cell, he had kept imagining that it was not 1870 but 1794, that we were not ordinary citizens but Jacobins, and that we were taking to his execution not a common murderer but a marquis-legitimist, *un ci-devant, un talon rouge, monsieur!*

It has been observed that when people sentenced to death have their sentences read out to them, they either lapse into complete insensibility and, as it were, die and decompose beforehand, or show off and brazen it out; or else give themselves up to despair, weep, tremble and beg for mercy . . . Tropmann did not belong to any of those categories – and that was why he puzzled even M. Claude himself. Let me say, by the way, that if Tropmann had begun to howl and weep, my nerves would certainly not have stood it and I should have run away. But at the sight of that composure, that simplicity and, as it were, modesty – all the feelings in me – the feelings of disgust for a pitiless murderer, a monster who cut the throats of little children while they were crying, *Maman! Maman!*, the feeling of compassion, finally, for a man whom death was about to swallow up, disappeared and dissolved in – a feeling of astonishment. What was sustaining Tropmann? Was it the fact that though he did not show off, he did 'cut a figure' before *spectators*, gave us his last performance? Or was it innate fearlessness or vanity aroused by M. Claude's words, the pride of the struggle that had to be kept up to the end – or something else, some still undivined feeling? . . . That was a secret he took to the grave with him. Some people are still convinced that Tropmann was not in his right mind. (I have mentioned earlier the lawyer in the white hat, whom, incidentally, I never saw again.) The aimlessness, one might almost say, the absurdity of the annihilation of the entire Kink family serves to a certain extent as a confirmation of that point of view.

But presently he finished with his boots and – straightened out, shook himself – ready! *Again* they put the prison jacket on him. M. Claude asked us to go out and – leave Tropmann alone with the priest. We did not have to wait even two minutes in the corridor before his small figure with his head held up fearlessly appeared among us. His religious feelings were not very strong and he probably carried out the last rite of confession before the priest absolving his sins, just as a rite. All of our group with Tropmann in the centre at once went up the narrow spiral staircase, which we had descended a quarter of an hour before, and – disappeared in pitch darkness: the night lamp on the staircase had gone out. It was an awful moment. We were all rushing upstairs, we could hear the rapid and harsh clatter of our feet on the iron steps, we trod on each other's heels, we knocked against each other's shoulders, one of us had his hat knocked off, someone behind me shouted angrily: '*Mais sacré dieu!* Light a candle! Let's have some light!' And there among us, together with us, in the pitch darkness was our victim, our prey – that unhappy man – and who of those who were pushing and scrambling upstairs was he? Would it not occur to him to take advantage of the darkness and with all his agility and the determination of despair to escape – where? Anywhere, to some remote corner of the prison – and just knock his head against a wall there! At least, he'd have killed himself . . .

I do not know whether these 'apprehensions' occurred to anyone else . . . But they appeared to be in vain. Our whole group with the small figure in the middle emerged from the inside recess of the staircase into the corridor. Tropmann evidently belonged to the guillotine – and the procession set off towards it.

This procession could be called a flight. Tropmann walked in front of us with quick, resilient, almost bounding steps; he was obviously in a hurry, and we all hurried after him. Some of us, anxious to have a look at his face once more, even ran ahead to the right and the left of him. So we rushed across the corridor and ran down the other staircase, Tropmann jumping two steps at a time, ran across another corridor, jumped over a few steps and, at last, we found ourselves in the tall room with the stool which I have mentioned and on which 'the toilet of the condemned man' was to be completed. We entered through one door, and from the other door there appeared, walking importantly in a white necktie and a black 'suit', the executioner, looking for all the world like a diplomat or a protestant pastor. He was followed by a short, fat old man in a black coat, his first assistant, the hangman of Beauvais. The old man held a small leather bag in his hand. Tropmann stopped at the stool. Everyone took up a position round him. The executioner and his old assistant stood to the right of him, the prison governor and M. Claude to the left. The old man turned the key of the bag, took out a few white raw-hide straps, some of them long and some short, and kneeling with difficulty behind Tropmann, began hobbling his legs. Tropman accidentally stepped on the end of one of those straps and the old man, trying to pull it out, muttered twice: '*Pardon, monsieur*' and, at last, touched Tropmann on the calf of the leg. Tropmann at once turned round and with his customary polite half-bow raised his foot and freed the strap. Meanwhile the priest was softly reading prayers in French out of a small book. Two other assistants came up, quickly removed the jacket from Tropmann, tied his hands behind him and began tying the straps round his whole body. The chief executioner gave orders, pointing here and there with a finger. It seemed that there were not enough holes in the straps for the tongues to go through: no doubt, the man who made the holes had a fatter man in mind. The old man at first searched in his bag, then fumbled about in all his pockets and, having felt everything carefully, at last drew out from one of them a small, crooked awl with which he bagan painfully to bore holes in the straps; his unskilful fingers, swollen with gout, obeyed him badly, and, besides, the hide was new and thick. He would make a hole, try it out – the tongue would not go through: he had to bore a little more. The priest evidently realized that things were not as they should be, and glancing stealthily once or twice over his shoulder, began to draw out the words of the prayers, so as to give the old man time to get things right. At last the operation during which, I frankly confess, I was covered with a cold sweat, was finished and all the tongues went in where required. But then another one started. Tropmann was asked to sit down on the stool, before which he was standing, and the same gouty old man began cutting his hair. He got out a pair of small scissors and, twisting his lips, carefully cut off at first the collar of Tropmann's shirt, the shirt he had only just put on and from which it would have been so easy to tear off the collar beforehand. But the cloth was coarse and all in pleats and it resisted the none too sharp blades. The chief executioner had a look and was dissatisfied: the space left by the cut-off piece was not big enough. He indicated with his hand how much more he wanted cut off and the gouty old man set to work again and cut out another big piece of cloth. The top and the back were uncovered – the shoulder-blades became visible. Tropman twitched them slightly: it was cold in the room. Then the old man started on the hair. Putting his puffy left hand on the head of Tropmann, who at once bent it down obediently, he began cutting the hair with his right. Thick strands of wiry, dark-brown hair slid over the shoulders and fell on the floor; one of them rolled up to my boot. Tropmann kept bending his head in the same obedient manner; the priest dragged out the words of the prayers even more slowly. I could not take my eyes off those hands, once stained with innocent blood, but now lying so helplessly one on top of the other – and particularly that slender, youthful neck. . . . In my imagination I could not help seeing a line cut straight across it . . . There, I thought, a five-hundred-pound axe would in a few moments pass, smashing the vertebrae and cutting through the veins and muscles, and yet the body did not seem to expect anything of the kind: it was so smooth, so white, so healthy . . .

I could not help asking myself what that so obediently bent head was thinking of at that moment. Was it holding on stubbornly and, as the saying is, with clenched teeth, to one and the same thought: 'I won't break down!' Were all sorts of memories of the past, probably quite unimportant ones, flashing through it at that moment? Was the memory of the face of one of the members of the Kink family, twisted in the agony of death, passing through it? Or was it simply trying not to think – that head, and was merely repeating to itself: 'That's nothing, that doesn't matter, we shall see, we shall see . . .' and would it go on repeating it till death came crashing down upon it – and there would be nowhere to recoil from it? . . .

And the little old man kept on cutting and cutting . . . The hair crunched as it was caught up by the scissors. . . . At last this operation, too, was at an end. Tropmann got up quickly, shook his head . . . Ordinarily, the condemned prisoners who are still able to speak at this moment address the governor of the prison with a last request, remind him of any money or debts they may leave behind, thank their warders, ask that a last note or a strand of hair should be sent to their relatives, send their regards for the last time – but Tropmann evidently was not an ordinary prisoner: he scorned such 'sentimentalities' and did not utter a single word. He was silent. He waited. A short tunic was thrown over his shoulders. The executioner grasped his elbow . . .

'Look here, Tropmann (*Voyons, Tropmann!*),' M. Claude's voice resounded in the death-like stillness, 'soon, in another minute, everything will be at an end. Do you still persist in claiming that you had accomplices?'

'Yes, sir, I do persist (*Oui, monsieur, je persiste*),' answered Tropmann in the same pleasant, firm baritone voice, and he bent forward slightly, as though courteously apologizing and even regretting that he could not answer otherwise.

'*Eh bien! Allons!*' said M. Claude, and we all set off; we went out into the large prison courtyard.

It was five to seven, but the sky hardly grew lighter and the same dull mist covered everything, concealing the contours of all objects. The roar of the crowd encompassed us by an unbroken, ear-splitting, thunderous wave as soon as we stepped over the threshold. Our small group, which had become thinner, for some of us had lagged behind, and I too, though walking with the others, kept myself a little apart, moved rapidly over the cobbled roadway of the courtyard straight to the gates. Tropmann minced along nimbly – his shackles interfered with his walk – and how small he suddenly appeared to me, almost a child! Suddenly the two halves of the gates, like some immense mouth of an animal, opened up slowly before us – and all at once, as though to the accompaniment of the great roar of the overjoyed crowd which had at last caught sight of what it had been waiting for, the monster of the guillotine stared at us with its two narrow black beams and its suspended axe.

I suddenly felt cold, so cold that I almost felt sick; it seemed to me that this cold, too, rushed at us into the courtyard through those gates; my legs gave way under me. However, I cast another glance at Tropmann. He suddenly recoiled, tossing back his head and bending his knees, as though someone hit him in the chest. 'He's going to faint,' someone whispered in my ear. . . . But he recovered himself immediately and went forward with a firm step. Those of us who wanted to see how his head would roll off rushed past him into the street . . . I had not enough courage for that; with a sinking heart I stopped at the gates . . .

I saw the executioner rise suddenly like a black tower on the left side of the guillotine platform; I saw Tropmann, separated from the huddle of people below, scrambling up the steps (there were ten of them – as many as ten!); I saw him stopping and turning round; I heard him say: '*Dites à Monsieur Claude!*'[1] I saw him appear above and two men pouncing on him from the right and left, like spiders on a fly; I saw him falling forward suddenly and his heels kicking . . .

But here I turned away and began to wait, the ground slowly rising and falling under my feet . . . And it seemed to me that I was waiting a terribly

1 I did not hear the rest of the sentence. His last words were: *Dites à Monsieur Claude que je persiste*, that is to say, tell M. Claude that I persist in claiming that I had accomplices. Tropmann did not want to deprive himself of this last pleasure, this last satisfaction: to leave the sting of doubt and reproach in the minds of his judges and the public.

long time.[1] I managed to notice that at Tropmann's appearance the roar of the crowd seemed suddenly to roll up into a ball and – a breathless hush fell over everything. . . . Before me stood a sentry, a young red-cheeked fellow . . . I just had time to see him looking intently at me with dull perplexity and horror . . . I even had time to think that that soldier probably hailed from some god-forsaken village and came from a decent, law-abiding family and – and the things he had to see now! At last I heard a light knocking of wood on wood – that was the sound made by the top part of the yoke with the slit for the passage of the knife as it fell round the murderer's head and kept it immobile . . . Then something suddenly descended with a hollow growl and stopped with an abrupt thud . . . Just as though a huge animal had retched . . . I cannot think of any better comparison. I felt dizzy. Everything swam before my eyes . . .

Someone seized me by the arm. I looked up: it was M. Claude's assistant, M. J. . . . , whom my friend Du Camp, as I learnt afterwards, had asked to keep an eye on me.

'You are very pale,' he said with a smile. 'Would you like a drink of water?'

But I thanked him and went back to the prison courtyard, which seemed to me like a place of refuge from the horrors on the other side of the gates.

Our group assembled in the guard-house by the gates to take leave of the prison governor and wait for the crowds to disperse. I, too, went in there and learnt that, while lying on the plank, Tropmann suddenly threw his head sideways convulsively so that it did not fit into the semi-circular hole. The executioners were forced to drag it there by the hair, and while they were doing it, Tropmann bit the finger of one of them – the chief one. I also heard that immediately after the execution, at the time when the body, thrown into the van, was being driven rapidly away, two men took advantage of the first moments of unavoidable confusion to force their way through the lines of the soldiers, and crawling under the guillotine, began wetting their handkerchiefs in the blood that had dripped through the chinks of the planks . . .

But I listened to all that talk as though in a dream. I felt very tired – and I was not the only one to feel like that. They all looked tired, though they all obviously felt relieved, just as if a load had been removed from their

1 As a matter of fact, only *twenty* seconds passed between the time Tropmann put his foot on the first step of the guillotine and the moment when his dead body was flung into the prepared basket.

backs. But not one of us, *absolutely no one looked like a man who realized that he had been present at the performance of an act of social justice:* everyone tried to turn away in spirit and, as it were, shake off the responsibility for this murder.

Ivan Turgenev, 'The Execution of Tropmann', trans. David Magarshack

Guilt

It was upon that dying Bed
  Where pale she laid, and cold as clay;
Dreading she knew not what to dread,
  And praying for a Heart to pray,
  I saw her in that gloomy day –
And spoke of Love divine; and Love
  Lent to the struggling Mind a Ray
Of Light! – and with her Terror strove.

It broke upon that horrid Cloud,
  And caused a plenteous flow of Tears;
She wept, and long she wept aloud;
  Wept, and laid open all her fears,
  And felt the mighty Storm that clears
The cloudy Mind! – The pains that prove
  There is a gracious Power, that hears
Such Cry! – The power of heavenly Love.

'Sit,' she began! 'and thou shalt hear,
  If I have strength! – and let me try
That I am, not what I appear.
  I would not in Deception die,
  Nor leave a spotless Name, a Lie.
For that would be the greater Sin –
  But is there none – Come near me! – by? –
O! Pride! – When I my Tale begin . . .

Was I not – Thou rememb'rest well,
  With all in Estimation high?
Even now, to my Reproach, they tell
  How lovely, how beloved was I:

The Cause they said of many a Sigh,
But kindly grieving for the Pain –
That fled! – it seems – when I was by,
If so – Alas! it came again.

They called me fair, and I could smile
Softly, as modest Maid behoved;
I wrote, and Men approved the Style,
And meekly I the Praise approved;
I heard of all my Charms unmoved:
That Fame had little Weight with me –
But I had Views, and dearly loved
To hear how wealthy I must be.

How strange to you it must appear,
An Infant Soul could have the Taint
Of Avarice – but I am Sincere,
And had I Words at will, could paint
That strong Corruption! But how faint
Are Words, that Evil to deplore –
How early was it my Complaint,
That, having much, I had no more.

This darling Sin was ever fed
By all that I observed or saw,
By all that I conceived or read:
It seemed an everlasting Law
That Riches kept Mankind in Awe –
I dreamed of Jewels, Garments, Gold:
All that admiring crowds would draw,
That they would with Desire behold!

I heard them speak of wealthy Men,
So close, so fond of what they gain,
That like a Lion in his Den
They in their District proudly reign,
And more than sovereign State maintain:
While thousands sigh, for but a Part
Of their vast Store! Alas, in vain
I strove! – the wish possessed my Heart.

I heard with eager Joy the Sum
  Bequeathed to me, a simple Child:
Mine would my Father's Wealth become;
  I heard! and (ah! deceit) reviled
  The Thought! And thus were they beguiled –
' 'Twas Joy, such Spirit to behold!' –
  And the Baby-Miser smiled
Who had (they thought) such Scorn of Gold.

Thus hard of Heart, of Spirits light,
  I seemed free, generous, and kind;
My Fortune ever in my Sight,
  The Means for ever in my Mind:
  My wealthy Friends were sure to find
Me all Attentive, but they knew
  No Ill in this; but all were blind
To that vile Love, and how it grew.

One who had more than All beside,
  Gained in the Still-productive East,
Was pleased with one so much allied
  In Thought, and my Desire increased:
  He taught me how my Soul to feast
On Bonds and Parchments, and would say:
  'My Wife, my Children, are deceased;
But thou . . .', then weeping turn Away.

I let him weep, and kindly sighed –
  Who could so young a Lass suspect?
'Thou hast a tender Heart' he cried,
  And for my Sake his Sorrow checked.
  His Life was hitherto correct –
A Man grave, prudent, thoughtful, still:
  Few Things his Passions could effect;
His Reason ever swayed his Will.

But he had Sin, and that was seen
  By a Domestic, shrewd and fly,
Light, and alluring, crafty-kind;
  With careless Air, with wanton Eye,

And Manner that would much imply
To him who doubted in his Mind;
That seemed to say, 'You can but try,
And you shall no Repulsion find.'

And none he found. – Then all of mine,
All that rejoiced my heart before,
All that I held, I must resign
To that unlawful Heir she bore:
Their Crime – not that I mourned, but sore
My Grief for my dear Prospects fled;
Those Bonds, those Lands were mine no more;
My Hopes were lost, were dying, dead.

My Uncle soothed me and was kind,
The Woman humble; so I went,
Sullen at first, but I designed
At their Entreaty to relent;
But secret kept the favour meant:
While he most bounteous Presents made,
Nor heeded what he largely spent,
Me into Kindness to persuade!

The Child was sick, nor seemed to love
The World to which he came of late;
And while the Mother fondly strove
T'avert, she met her Infant's fate:
As with the Wailing Boy she sate,
Languid and pale and faint she grew;
Ate not, slept ill, and mourned her State,
And from her daily Cares withdrew.

Then breathed with Labour and in Pain,
And bitter Tears, repenting shed;
And shunned with Fear, and with Disdain,
What to familiar Converse led:
She languished by her Boy, one bed
Held whom it seemed one Grave must hold –
And soon we saw the Mother dead,
And then the Infant's fate foretold!

Grieved I not then? I wept; the Child
  Of a sad Father seemed my Own!
Yet then a Thought, an Hope beguiled
  My Heart – a Hope I feared to own:
  From that hard Heart, ah! God! – was flown
All Woman's Nature! I caressed
  The Babe upon my Kindness thrown –
And what I felt? repelled, repressed!

You look, Alas!, with earnest Eye:
  What is it you can yet perceive?
'Have I confessed?', your Looks reply:
  But do not more than truth believe.
  'Tis not as you suppose – I grieve
For what it is; but come, attend –
  I cannot your Esteem retrieve
But, Man of God! my Soul befriend.

Ah! What Contention have I felt –
  'And will he leave it all?' I cried,
'It is his own – His Heart will melt,
  When he is by its pleadings tried.
Law and his Niece then set aside,
He to that Being, all will give –
  O! would that shivering Thing had died,
But he will pine and feed, and live.'

Your looks reprove me, yet indeed
  'Tis Nature – Now the Babe declined:
The Father said, 'It is decreed,
  I thus my Punishment shall find;
  It was my Sin, I am resigned –'
He was – Alas, so was not I.
  Nor in my Heart could Pity find
For One who would not quickly die.

Convulsed the pale cold boy became –
  'Gone! he is gone' the Father cried,
'O! bury with him Sin and Shame' –
  'Bury your Sorrow.' I replied,

Peevish! – for I the Life espied,
Rekindling – 'He your darling boy
Will by your Hoards and Lands be tried,
That He, not you, will then enjoy.'

And now returned the frequent Fit,
O'erpowering Sense, enduring long,
While I beside him bore to sit,
Indulging Thoughts a dreadful Throng;
But chief, of Riches gained by wrong!
And what is wrong, where all would gain?
And then I saw Life growing strong!
And sparkling in the Eye Again!

Thus was Vexation, Trouble, Pain,
Trial and Torment, wearing all
My Spirits, when I saw Again
The shake, the fit, the chilling call
Of Death – and then the creeping small
Reviving Pulse Again would beat:
Again to rise, Again to fall,
And my impatient Hope to cheat.

Then Nature made an Effort new,
The Life precarious to prolong;
The Father came the Child to view
And saw the misborn being strong:
Then sang he, fool he was, his Song
Of Thanks, that set my Soul a Snare –
'Niece! I must do my Boy no Wrong,
But thou shalt in the Savings share!'

Share! What? The Scraping of the Board?
Share of the Gleanings – and with One
Whom I have fondled, nursed, restored?
The nameless Thing he calls his Son?
Imprudent Care! but I must shun
Such Thoughts! and would my Mind were freed –
But come they will! I cannot run
From Thought! – but will not name the Deed.

Do I offend You, or affright?
  Alas, you look not now the Friend –
May we not wish ourselves a Right?
  And may we not our Rights defend?
  Heaven! Do not Men in Battle spend
Blood! – and destroy when they might save:
And do not all our Passions send
  Their groaning Myriads to the Grave?

Hope, when deferred too long, destroys;
  Fear, Sorrow and Despair will kill;
Love bears away our Girls and boys,
  And Hatred loves Men's blood to spill:
  Where is the Medicine, where the Skill
That can the Soul's Disorders tame?
  There lives within, the growing ill
That leads to Death, the wasting Frame –

Quickly their Way the Passions Win –
  And Reason's slumbering Guard destroy:
My Uncle's Folly sought the Inn –
  To talk of his recovered Boy
  And drench the Clowns in drunken Joy;
Him followed Men and Maids – I sate
  In Angry Silence: My Employ
To watch the Cause, and weep my Fate.

Sudden! the Bells with horrid Peal
  Rang out! Malicious Idiots, Why?
Wretches! Did I in Magic deal,
  The Ropes about your Necks should fly
  And every Dog be drawn on high,
That not one Hand a Rope should take
  To wake this Creature sleeping by –
Or fatal thoughts in me to wake.

They rang; my Head confused, my Heart
  Grew wrathful, and it grieved and bled,
And that pale Boy began to start! –
  And grew convulsed upon his Bed;

His Eye rolled wildly, and his head
Some strong spasmodic Force obeyed;
Then rested! – 'ah! and is he dead?
Is mine, is nature's Debt thus paid?'

Hope, Joy and Wonder forged a Chain
That bound my Soul! Within my Chair
I watched – 'He cannot come Again' –
I formed a selfish sinful Prayer:
I tried his Breath! the unmoved Air
Stirred not the Feather's Down; I drew
Near the Wan Life – 'No more despair'
I said in Joy! – 'vile Fears Adieu!'

Alas! – and must I now proceed?
I sat, and not a Being by –
Thoughts came – If asked who did the Deed?
'I did it not', I could reply.
Then should the boy breathe yet? – O! why
Could I not still without a Fear
Do that? And yet that done deny? . . .
O! mercy, look not so severe!

'Why, then suppose' – I thought – 'suppose
He had not died, and I had pressed? . . .'
You say I must the Truth disclose,
Locked like a fire within my Breast.
Suppose this Being's happy Rest
Had been by me! – Who would conceive
That I that Spirit dispossessed?
That I . . . no Creature could believe.

My Joy was still. I could not move,
But I indulged an eager Mind
With Sentiments of growing Love,
And gracious Deeds to all Mankind:
I would enjoy Delight refined,
I would all Tyranny oppose;
And had some twenty Plans designed,
For easing Pains and chasing Woes.

Self-soothed by this, th'accursèd deed
  Stole with my Boastings to my Breast;
As yet – for Strength, I saw no Need.
  None for Resistance. I had Rest;
  And all was good! – The Hour so blest
Its Quiet to the Bosom gives.
  Nay, Nay! That Clod is repossessed!
It moves! . . . It breathes, it looks! – It lives!

But wilt thou come Again, wilt thou
  Me of my Prospects dispossess?
Does Life rekindle thus, and how
  Can I with mockery acquiesce?
  There may – there must be – some Redress
For Spirits wrought like mine, I will –
  Strange Rival, let me view thee – Yes!
We must our Destiny fulfil.

I looked and saw no Creature nigh,
  And then again returned to view
The half unsealed and cloudy Eye,
  That shut again; for Life was new,
  Not perfect Life – I could not do
A Deed so foul; I had not planned
  To shut out Life, if fair and true:
But this . . . O! Why so drop my Hand?

In Pity spare me – I have felt
  Unintermitting, day and Night,
Remorse and Horror, God has dealt
  Me pangs for Sin! – 'tis just, 'tis right,
  Condemn not thou! but in his Sight
Thou, too, art faulty – let me live
As one whom her own thoughts affright:
  Sinner thyself, my Sins forgive.

O! it was vile, but Life indeed,
  Though kindling, was not come – the breast
Moved not – though Motion might succeed.
  'It will not die!' I said, and pressed –

My God forgive – and it had rest.
That I from that accursed time
  Never, in one sweet Hour, possessed:
So sure does Misery wait on Crime.

I gazed on that still Thing and cried
  'It is not Murder – he was dead
Or dying, nay he must have died.
  Then what have I for this to dread?'
  I turned me from th'accursèd Bed,
And the approaching Father saw!
  Then Comfort, and then Courage fled;
And Him I feared, and feared the Law.
  George Crabbe,'The Voluntary Insane'

Guitar

The only ways you could kill somebody with a guitar were to hit him with the sides of it or to bash him, mortar and pestle-like, with the fat tail-end of the sound box. One other method commonly used was to bore the victim to death by playing it. Such was not the case here, however. Nor, from the appearance of Barkin's guitar, was the mortar and pestle method employed. The killer I was looking for had used the most common approach to guitar murder – the Mickey Mantle method, in which the guitar is swung like a baseball bat in an effort to take the victim's head downtown. All this, I felt, was clearly indicated. Even the cops knew it.

The point of contact on Barkin's Gibson had been the top side of the sound box. I'd seen that in the dressing room. Some country singers tape cheat sheets on this part of their ax, with song titles, jokes, and maybe the name of the town they're in if they've been on the road for a long time. I never taped cheat sheets to my guitar. Always used the inside of my hat.

I took a few trial swings at the puppet head from the left-hand side. I held the guitar with both hands around the fingerboard. I held it close to the neck. Faceup. That was the way Barkin's attacker had probably done it. The guitar felt comfortable in my hands. I took a whack at the puppet head just for the hell of it, swinging from left to right. Sent it flying across the room. The cat jumped onto the desk. The cat detested violence of any sort.

'Relax,' I said. 'This is just a test.' I retrieved the puppet head and put it back on the table. Now came the crucial part of the experiment. I turned the guitar facedown and took a few trial swings from the right-hand side. The fingerboard felt awkward, nearly slipping from my grasp. The steel strings cut into my fingers. It was almost a chore to hold the guitar level because of the rounded shape of the guitar neck. It would be exceedingly difficult, I thought, to take a solid swing from the right side with the guitar in a facedown position. In other words, if a righty had croaked Barkin, he would have held the guitar faceup. But then the guitar would have been smashed on the bottom part of the sound box. The guitar was damaged on the top part of the sound box. Therefore, unless I'd missed my guess badly, Barkin's murderer was left-handed.

Kinky Friedman, *A Case of Lone Star*

Gunman

I do not think you know me.
I could be anyone
who comes from Atlanta or Athens,
Levittown or Babylon.

You probably know my girlfriend.
You've seen her on the screen
where light and shadow flicker
the Technicolor dreams.

She comes to me nightly –
Oh, yes she does – in sleep,
and says, 'Oh, how I love you,
you're beautiful and deep,

and no one can ever hurt you
as long as I am near,
but it's morning, I have to be going –
you mustn't fear.

I'll come again this evening.
I'll come again for more.
I'll come in by the window
and leave by the back door.'

She never stays for breakfast.
She never takes a meal.
The eggs look up like jaundice
by the talking cereal.

I have no mother or father,
no daughter and no son.
I have no past or future
but I have a little gun.

The handle's polished walnut,
the barrel's cold blue steel,
and six snug soldiers barrack
within the chambered wheel.

It has a shoulder holster
and a nasty trigger, too,
and six mad soldiers blossom
when I want them to.

You can see the holes in the ceiling
where I used to shoot at flies
and the holes in the television screen
where they tell lies,

because there won't be weather tomorrow
unless I want there to be.
There won't be any satellites
or any sea.

The sea's not blue in the darkness,
they say – but that can't be so.
What's blue is blue forever.
It's Death that won't let go.

Death's around every corner
though he can never be found.
That's why Death's so impressive –
he's the big man around.

I've seen them in the movies,
the killers and the killed.
They move like ballerinas.
They're elegant, they're skilled,

but they're only actors and actresses
and, then, aren't we all? —
waiting for the hour
we get the agent's call

and step out by the footlights
and bow to that applause
more delicious than truth or beauty
and louder than laws.

My girl never stays till daylight.
She lives in secrecy,
meeting I-don't-know-who, doing I-don't-know-what.
I want her to notice me

not just in the dark of the bedroom
where there's no light but the moon.
The moon is mad and lonely,
but he sings in tune,

singing, 'Where are all the lovers
from all years past?
Death and sleep sleep together
but love never lasts.

I remember Eden and Athens,
Paradise and Babylon.
Love would last forever
if you had a little gun.

Show your lover you love her.
Show her that you know
Death and sleep lie together.
She'll never let you go.'

I'm in a hotel waiting,
watching a man on t.v.
I can see him on three channels
but he can't see me.

Tomorrow I'll take a stroll
down by his hotel
where he'll be talking and talking
like a guy with a car to sell.

I'll wait for him on the corner.
I'll wait till he walks by,
where I can see in his empty eyes
the empty sky.

I have no mother or father,
no daughter and no son,
no past and no future,
but I have a little gun.

William Logan, 'The Shootist'

H

Hands

CASCA (*coming forward*): Speak hands for me.

They stab Caesar, Casca first, Brutus last

CAESAR: *Et tu, Brutè?* – Then fall Caesar.

He dies

William Shakespeare, *Julius Caesar*

'Murder,' said old Quong, ' – oblige me by passing my pipe – murder is one of the simplest things in the world to do. Killing a man is a much simpler matter than killing a duck. Not always so safe, perhaps, but simpler. But to certain gifted people it is both simple and entirely safe. Many minds of finer complexion than my own have discoloured themselves in seeking to name the identity of the author of those wholesale murders which took place last year. Who that man or woman really was, I know no more than you do, but I have a theory of the person it could have been; and if you are not pressed for time I will elaborate that theory into a little tale.'

As I had the rest of that evening and the whole of the next day for dalliance in my ivory tower, I desired that he would tell me the story; and, having reckoned up his cash register and closed the ivory gate, he told me – between then and the dawn – his story of the Mallon End murders. Paraphrased and condensed, it came out something like this:

At six o'clock of a January evening Mr Whybrow was walking home though the cobweb of London's East End. He had left the golden clamour of the great High Street to which the tram had brought him from the river and his daily work, and was now in the chess-board of byways that is called Mallon End. None of the rush and gleam of the High Street trickled into these byways. A few paces south – a flood-tide of life, foaming and beating. Here – only slow, shuffling figures and muffled pulses. He was in the sink of London, the last refuge of European vagrants.

As though in tune with the street's spirit, he too walked slowly, with head down. It seemed that he was pondering some pressing trouble, but he was not. He had no trouble. He was walking slowly because he had been on his feet all day, and he was bent in abstraction because he was wondering whether the Missis would have herrings for his tea, or haddock; and he was trying to decide which would be the more tasty on a night like this. A wretched night it was, of damp and mist, and the mist wandered into his throat and his eyes, and the damp had settled on pavement and roadway, and where the sparse lamplight fell it sent up a greasy sparkle that chilled one to look at. By contrast it made his speculations more agreeable, and made him ready for that tea – whether herring or haddock. His eye turned from the glum bricks that made his horizon, and went forward half a mile. He saw a gas-lit kitchen, a flamy fire and a spread tea-table. There was toast in the hearth and a singing kettle on the side and a piquant effusion of herrings, or maybe of haddock, or perhaps sausages. The vision gave his aching feet a throb of energy. He shook imperceptible damp from his shoulders, and hastened towards its reality.

But Mr Whybrow wasn't going to get any tea that evening – or any other evening. Mr Whybrow was going to die. Somewhere within a hundred yards of him another man was walking: a man much like Mr Whybrow and much like any other man, but without the only quality that enables mankind to live peaceably together and not as madmen in a jungle. A man with a dead heart eating into itself and bringing forth the foul organisms that arise from death and corruption. And that thing in man's shape, on a whim or a settled idea – one cannot know – had said within himself that Mr Whybrow should never taste another herring. Not that Mr Whybrow had injured him. Not that he had any dislike of Mr Whybrow. Indeed, he knew nothing of him save as a familiar figure about the streets. But, moved by a force that had taken possession of his empty cells, he had picked on Mr Whybrow with that blind choice that makes us pick one restaurant table that has nothing to mark it from four or five other tables, or one apple from a dish of half-a-dozen apples; or that drives Nature to send a cyclone upon one corner of this planet, and destroy five hundred lives in that corner, and leave another five hundred in the same corner unharmed. So this man had picked on Mr Whybrow, as he might have picked on you or me, had we been within his daily observation; and even now he was creeping through the blue-toned streets, nursing his large white hands, moving ever closer to Mr Whybrow's tea-table, and so closer to Mr Whybrow himself.

He wasn't, this man, a bad man. Indeed, he had many of the social and amiable qualities, and passed as a respectable man, as most successful criminals do. But the thought had come into his mouldering mind that he would like to murder somebody, and, as he held no fear of God or man, he was going to do it, and would then go home to *his* tea. I don't say that flippantly, but as a statement of fact. Strange as it may seem to the humane, murderers must and do sit down to meals after a murder. There is no reason why they shouldn't, and many reasons why they should. For one thing, they need to keep their physical and mental vitality at full bleat for the business of covering their crime. For another, the strain of their efforts makes them hungry, and satisfaction at the accomplishment of a desired thing brings a feeling of relaxation towards human pleasures. It is accepted among non-murderers that the murderer is always overcome by fear for his safety and horror at his act; but this type is rare. His own safety is, of course, his immediate concern, but vanity is a marked quality of most murderers, and that, together with the thrill of conquest, makes him confident that he can secure it, and when he has restored his strength with food he goes about securing it as a young hostess goes about the arranging of her first big dinner – a little anxious, but no more. Criminologists and detectives tell us that *every* murderer, however intelligent or cunning, always makes one slip in his tactics – one little slip that brings the affair home to him. But that is only half-true. It is true only of the murderers who are caught. Scores of murderers are not caught; therefore scores of murderers do not make any mistake at all. This man didn't.

As for horror or remorse, prison chaplains, doctors and lawyers have told us that of murderers they have interviewed under condemnation and the shadow of death, only one here and there has expressed any contrition for his act, or shown any sign of mental misery. Most of them display only exasperation at having been caught when so many have gone undiscovered, or indignation at being condemned for a perfectly reasonable act. However normal and humane they may have been before the murder, they are utterly without conscience after it. For what is conscience? Simply a polite nickname for superstition, which is a polite nickname for fear. Those who associate remorse with murder are, no doubt, basing their ideas on the world-legend of the remorse of Cain, or are projecting their own frail minds into the mind of the murderer, and getting false reactions. Peaceable folk cannot hope to make contact with this mind, for they are not merely different in mental type from the murderer: they are different in their personal chemistry and construction. Some men can and do kill, not one man, but two or three, and go calmly about their daily affairs. Other men could not, under the most agonizing provocation, bring themselves even to wound. It is men of this sort who imagine the murderer in torments of remorse and fear of the law, whereas he is actually sitting down to his tea.

The man with the large white hands was as ready for his tea as Mr Whybrow was, but he had something to do before he went to it. When he had done that something, and made no mistake about it, he would be even more ready for it, and would go to it as comfortably as he went to it the day before, when his hands were stainless.

Walk on, then, Mr Whybrow, walk on; and as you walk, look your last upon the familiar features of your nightly journey. Follow your jack-o'-lantern tea-table. Look well upon its warmth and colour and kindness; feed your eyes with it, and tease your nose with its gentle domestic odours; for you will never sit down to it. Within ten minutes' pacing of you a pursuing phantom has spoken in his heart, and you are doomed. There you go – you and phantom – two nebulous dabs of mortality, moving through green air along pavements of powder-blue, the one to kill, the other to be killed. Walk on. Don't annoy your burning feet by hurrying, for the more slowly you walk, the longer you will breath the green air of this January dusk, and see the dreamy lamplight and the little shops, and hear the agreeable commerce of the London crowd and the haunting pathos of the street-organ. These things are dear to you, Mr Whybrow. You don't know it now, but in fifteen minutes you will have two seconds in which to realize how inexpressibly dear they are.

Walk on, then, across this crazy chess-board. You are in Lagos Street now, among the tents of the wanderers of Eastern Europe. A minute or so, and you are in Loyal Lane, among the lodging-houses that shelter the useless and the beaten of London's camp-followers. The lane holds the smell of them, and its soft darkness seems heavy with the wail of the futile. But you are not sensitive to impalpable things, and you plod through it, unseeing, as you do every evening, and come to Blean Street, and plod through that. From basement to sky rise the tenements of an alien colony. Their windows slot the ebony of their walls with lemon. Behind those windows strange life is moving, dressed with forms that are not of London or of England, yet, in essence, the same agreeable life that you have been living, and tonight will live no more. From high above you comes a voice crooning *The Song of Katta*. Through a window you see a family keeping a religious rite. Through another you see a woman pouring out tea for her husband. You see a man mending a pair of boots; a mother bathing her baby. You have seen all these things before, and never noticed them. You do not notice them now, but if you knew that you were never going to see them again, you would notice them. You never *will* see them again, not because your life has run its natural course, but because a man whom you have often passed in the street has at his own solitary pleasure decided to usurp the awful authority of Nature, and destroy you. So perhaps it's as well that you don't notice them, for your part in them is ended. No more for you these pretty moments of our earthly travail; only one moment of terror, and then a plunging darkness.

Closer to you this shadow of massacre moves, and now he is twenty yards behind you. You can hear his footfall, but you do not turn your head. You are familiar with footfalls. You are in London, in the easy security of your daily territory, and footfalls behind you, your instinct tells you, are no more than a message of human company.

But can't you hear something in those footfalls – something that goes with a widdershins beat? Something that says: Look out look out! *Beware, beware!* Can't you hear the very syllables of *murd-er-er, murd-er-er*? No; there is nothing in footfalls. They are neutral. The foot of villainy falls with the same quiet note as the foot of honesty. But those footfalls, Mr Whybrow, are bearing on to you a pair of hands, and there *is* something in hands. Behind you that pair of hands is even now stretching its muscles in preparation for your end. Every minute of your days you have been seeing human hands. Have you ever realized the sheer horror of hands – those appendages that are a symbol for our moments of trust and affection and salutation? Have you thought of the sickening potentialities that lie within the scope of that five-tentacled member? No, you never have; for all the human hands that you have seen have been stretched to you in kindness or fellowship. Yet, though the eyes can hate, and the lips can sting, it is only that dangling member that can gather the accumulated essence of evil, and electrify it into currents of destruction. Satan may enter into man by many doors, but in the hands alone can he find the servants of his will.

Another minute, Mr Whybrow, and you will know all about the horror of human hands.

Thomas Burke, 'The Hands of Mr Ottermole'

Hanging

'What are the bugles blowin' for?' said Files-on-Parade.
'To turn you out, to turn you out,' the Colour-Sergeant said.
'What makes you look so white, so white?' said Files-on-Parade.
'I'm dreadin' what I've got to watch,' the Colour-Sergeant said.
For they're hangin' Danny Deever, you can hear the Dead March play,
The Regiment's in 'ollow square – they're hangin' him to-day;
They've taken of his buttons off an' cut his stripes away,
An' they're hangin' Danny Deever in the mornin'.

'What makes the rear-rank breathe so 'ard?' said Files-on-Parade.
'It's bitter cold, it's bitter cold,' the Colour-Sergeant said.
'What makes that front-rank man fall down?' said Files-on-Parade.
'A touch o' sun, a touch o' sun,' the Colour-Sergeant said.
They are hangin' Danny Deever, they are marchin' of 'im round,
They 'ave 'alted Danny Deever by 'is coffin on the ground;
An' 'e'll swing in 'arf a minute for a sneakin' shootin' hound –
O they're hangin' Danny Deever in the mornin'.

''Is cot was right-'and cot to mine,' said Files-on-Parade.
''E's sleepin' out an' far to-night,' the Colour-Sergeant said.
'I've drunk 'is beer a score o' times,' said Files-on-Parade.
''E's drinkin' bitter beer alone,' the Colour-Sergeant said.
They are hangin' Danny Deever, you must mark 'im to 'is place,
For 'e shot a comrade sleepin' – you must look 'im in the face;
Nine 'undred of 'is county an' the Regiment's disgrace,
While they're hangin' Danny Deever in the mornin'.

'What's that so black agin the sun?' said Files-on-Parade.
'It's Danny fightin' 'ard for life,' the Colour-Sergeant said.
'What's that that whimpers over'ead?' said Files-on-Parade.
'It's Danny's soul that's passin' now,' the Colour-Sergeant said.
For they're done with Danny Deever, you can 'ear the quickstep play,
The Regiment's in column, an' they're marchin' us away;
Ho! the young recruits are shakin', an' they'll want their beer to-day.
After hangin' Danny Deever in the mornin'!

Rudyard Kipling, 'Danny Deever'

John Price was indicted at the Old Bailey on the 24th of April, 1718, for the murder of Elizabeth, the wife of William White, on the 13th of the preceding month.

In the course of the evidence it appeared that Price met the deceased near ten at night in Moorfields, and attempted to ravish her; but the poor woman (who was the wife of a watchman, and sold gingerbread in the streets), doing all in her power to resist his villainous attacks, he beat her so cruelly that streams of blood issued from her eyes and mouth, broke one of her arms, beat out some of her teeth, bruised her head in a most dreadful manner, forced one of her eyes from the socket, and otherwise so ill-treated her that the language of decency cannot describe it.

Some persons, hearing the cries of the unhappy creature, repaired to the spot, took Price into custody, and lodged him in the watch-house; and conveyed the woman to a house where a surgeon and nurse were sent for to attend her. Being unable to speak, she answered the nurse's questions by signs, and in that manner described what had happened to her. She died after having languished four days.

The prisoner, on his trial, denied being guilty of the fact; and said that as he was crossing Moorfields he found something lying in his way; that he kicked at it, but discovering that it was a woman, he lifted her up, but she could not stand on her legs: and he said that he was taken into custody while he was thus employed. This defence, however, could not be credited, from what some former evidences had sworn; and the jury did not hesitate to find him guilty.

After sentence of death was passed on him he abandoned himself to the drinking of spiritous liquors to such a degree as rendered him totally incapable of all the exercises of devotion. He obstinately denied the fact till the day of his execution, when he confessed that he had been guilty of it; but said that the crime was perpetrated when he was in a state of intoxication. He was executed in Bunhill-Fields on the 31st of May, 1718, and, in his last moments, begged the prayers of the multitude, and hoped they would take warning by his untimely end. He was afterwards hung in chains near Holloway.

This offender was born in the parish of St Martin in the Fields, and while he was very young his father was blown up at the demolishing of Tangier. His mother being left in circumstances of distress, was not able to give him a proper education; but she put him apprentice to a dealer in rags. Having served about two years, his master died, and he soon afterwards ran away from his mistress, and got employment in loading waggons with rags for other dealers. After this he went to sea, and served on board several ships in the royal navy for the space of about eighteen years; but at length he was paid off, and discharged from service.

The place of public executioner becoming vacant by death, he accepted of it, and might have continued in it but for his own extravagance; for spending more money than his income, he ran in debt; and one day, as he was returning from an execution at Tyburn, he was arrested in Holborn for a trifling sum. However, he discharged this debt, and the costs, partly with a small sum of money he had in his pocket, and partly by the produce of three suits of cloaths, which he had taken from the bodies of poor wretches who had been that day executed.

Soon after this two other writs were taken out against him, when having no money, nor being able to procure bail, he was obliged to go to the Marshalsea Prison, where he continued till after the following sessions at the Old Bailey, when William Marvel was appointed executioner in his stead. Having continued some time longer in the Marshalsea, he and a fellow-prisoner broke a hole in the wall, through which they made their escape: and soon after this Price committed the horrid murder for which his life paid the forfeit.

One would imagine that the dreadful scenes of calamity to which this man had been witness, if they had not taught him humanity, would at least have given him wisdom enough not to have perpetrated a crime that must necessarily bring him to a similarly fatal end to what he had so often seen of others: but perhaps his profession tended rather to harden his mind than otherwise.

The murder of which Price was guilty appears to have been one of the most barbarous and unprovoked we ever remember to have read of: and his pretence that he was drunk when he perpetrated it was no sort of excuse; since drunkenness itself is a crime, and one which frequently leads to the commission of others.

The lesson to be learnt from the fate of this man is to moderate our passions of every kind; and to live by the rules of temperance and sobriety. We are told, from the best authority, that 'hands that shed innocent blood are an abomination to the Lord'.

'Jack Ketch' was the name applied by the public to every hangman, but there was a real Jack Ketch who attained to the dignity of an entry in the *Dictionary of National Biography*. He published a pamphlet to vindicate his conduct at the execution of Lord Russell in 1683, John Evelyn in the Diary having referred to the execution as being done in a 'butcherly manner'. Ketch was also the executioner at the death of Monmouth in 1685, and on the scaffold Monmouth spoke to him about the manner of Russell's execution. This appears to have unnerved Ketch altogether, so that, according to Macaulay, he was finally compelled to use a knife to sever the head. He also took part in the dreadful punishments of Titus Oates and his colleagues. There are many books and pamphlets about hangmen in general, and Jack Ketch in particular. On formal occasions he was referred to as 'John Ketch, Esq.,' and this title was claimed by all the hangmen who followed Brandon, the executioner of Charles the First, because Brandon had been granted a coat of arms. (Sir Norman Birkett, ed.)

Circumstances respecting the Trial and Execution of John Price, otherwise Jack Ketch, who was hanged for Murder, from *The Newgate Calendar*

Before the last Royal Commission that inquired into the whole subject of Capital Punishment, the late Chief Baron Kelly gave evidence that in the course of some forty years there were 22 persons sentenced to death who were afterwards *proved* to have been innocent of the crime for which they were sentenced. It is regrettable that such things should happen. They are bad for the honour of hanging.

Other cases could be cited of innocent men executed, though the official and correct view is 'out of sight, out of mind', and 'dead men tell no tales'. Hansard, of 1881, gives an account of a boy executed at Winchester. The prison chaplain rushed to London bearing a written confession made by a man for the very crime in question. This man was waiting to be hanged on another account. The chaplain could not find the Home Secretary in time; and so the poor boy was hanged. There is the much more spectacular and familiar case of Habron, who was found guilty of murder and afterwards proved innocent by the confession of the late Mr Charles Peace, before he passed away.[1] Earlier in this book I have already given instances of blunders on the part of hangmen, and, looking through Hansard, I find a few more cases which are too important to be missed. The first is that of Mathew Atkinson, a pitman, who took a couple of drops in the city of Durham. Hansard tells the story thus: From the moment Atkinson was sentenced to death, he diligently applied himself to a preparation for the happy life to come after the hangman had finished with him. At the ceremony, when the drop fell there was a rattle, a crash, a horrible thud, and the criminal had disappeared, and from the gallows was seen the broken end of a rope dangling in the wind. The half-strangled man, conscious of all that had taken place, was below the drop, bound

1 In the 'Thorne' murder trial, the evidence of *three* expert witnesses, including that of Dr R. M. Brontë – one of the most experienced pathologists living – was to the effect that the way in which the death of Elsie Cameron took place, as alleged by the prosecution, was impossible. Yet the jury decided that *probabilities* were of more cogency than possibilities. On this decision Thorne was hanged; and to this day the legal profession is divided in opinion as to his guilt.

hand and foot, his jaw horribly wrenched. Twenty-four minutes elapsed before the readjustments were made; and the official Parliamentary report concludes: 'The second hanging was successful.' That was bad enough, but there is on record the case of Brownless, whose life was taken by the late Mr Hangman Marwood; this also happened at Durham, and is reported in Hansard. The ceremony was very badly bungled and, when completed, it presented to the onlooker a spectacle so utterly gruesome and revolting that all intelligent advocates of the hangman's art trembled for its future. An onlooker reports:

On looking down into the pit where the body hung we observed that the feet were about within half an inch off the ground; the rope, which was about an inch and a half thick, was embedded in the neck; the blood was slowly trickling down the breast.

And so on. Hansard also gives the case of a criminal called Connor. Another bungled job. In this case the rope slipped. Connor turned philosophically to the hangman and, before the second attempt was begun, he asked, 'What do you call this? Murder?'

Charles Duff, *A Handbook on Hanging*

Head

Who hath not loitered in a green church-yard,
  And let his spirit, like a demon-mole,
Work through the clayey soil and gravel hard,
  To see skull, coffined bones, and funeral stole,
Pitying each form that hungry Death hath marred,
  And filling it once more with human soul?
Ah, this is holiday to what was felt
When Isabella by Lorenzo knelt.

She gazed into the fresh-thrown mould, as though
  One glance did fully all its secrets tell.
Clearly she saw, as other eyes would know
  Pale limbs at bottom of a crystal well.
Upon the murderous spot she seemed to grow,
  Like to a native lily of the dell –
Then with her knife, all sudden, she began
To dig more fervently than misers can.

Soon she turned up a soilèd glove, whereon
  Her silk had played in purple fantasies,
She kissed it with a lip more chill than stone,
  And put it in her bosom, where it dries
And freezes utterly unto the bone
  Those dainties made to still an infant's cries.
Then 'gan she work again, nor stayed her care,
But to throw back at times her veiling hair.

That old nurse stood beside her wondering,
  Until her heart felt pity to the core
At sight of such a dismal labouring,
  And so she kneelèd, with her locks all hoar,
And put her lean hands to the horrid thing –
  Three hours they laboured at this travail sore.
At last they felt the kernel of the grave,
And Isabella did not stamp and rave.

Ah, wherefore all this wormy circumstance?
  Why linger at the yawning tomb so long?
Oh, for the gentleness of old romance,
  The simple plaining of a minstrel's song!
Fair reader, at the old tale take a glance,
  For here, in truth, it doth not well belong
To speak – Oh, turn thee to the very tale,
And taste the music of that vision pale.

With duller steel than the Perséan sword
  They cut away no formless monster's head,
But one, whose gentleness did well accord
  With death, as life. The ancient harps have said,
Love never dies, but lives immortal Lord.
  If Love impersonate was ever dead,
Pale Isabella kissed it, and low moaned.
'Twas Love – cold, dead indeed, but not dethroned.

In anxious secrecy they took it home,
  And then the prize was all for Isabel.
She calmed its wild hair with a golden comb,
  And all around each eye's sepulchral cell

Pointed each fringèd lash. The smearèd loam
  With tears, as chilly as a dripping well,
She drenched away – and still she combed, and kept
Sighing all day – and still she kissed, and wept.

Then in a silken scarf – sweet with the dews
  Of precious flowers plucked in Araby,
And divine liquids come with odorous ooze
  Through the cold serpent-pipe refreshfully –
She wrapped it up, and for its tomb did choose
  A garden-pot, wherein she laid it by,
And covered it with mould, and o'er it set
Sweet basil, which her tears kept ever wet.

And she forgot the stars, the moon, and sun,
  And she forgot the blue above the trees,
And she forgot the dells where waters run,
  And she forgot the chilly autumn breeze.
She had no knowledge when the day was done,
  And the new morn she saw not, but in peace
Hung over her sweet basil evermore,
And moistened it with tears unto the core.

And so she ever fed it with thin tears,
  Whence thick and green and beautiful it grew,
So that it smelt more balmy than its peers
  Of basil-tufts in Florence, for it drew
Nurture besides, and life, from human fears,
  From the fast mouldering head there shut from view.
So that the jewel, safely casketed,
Came forth, and in perfumèd leafits spread.

O Melancholy, linger here awhile!
  O Music, Music, breathe despondingly!
O Echo, Echo, from some sombre isle,
  Unknown, Lethean, sigh to us – Oh, sigh!
Spirits in grief, lift up your heads, and smile.
  Lift up your heads, sweet spirits, heavily,
And make a pale light in your cypress glooms,
Tinting with silver wan your marble tombs.

Moan higher, all ye syllables of woe,
  From the deep throat of sad Melpomene!
Through bronzèd lyre in tragic order go,
  And touch the strings into a mystery.
Sound mournfully upon the winds and low,
  For simple Isabel is soon to be
Among the dead. She withers, like a palm
Cut by an Indian for its juicy balm.

Oh, leave the palm to wither by itself,
  Let not quick winter chill its dying hour!
It may not be – those Baälites of pelf,
  Her brethren, noted the continual shower
From her dead eyes, and many a curious elf,
  Among her kindred, wondered that such dower
Of youth and beauty should be thrown aside
By one marked out to be a noble's bride.

And, further, her brethren wondered much
  Why she sat drooping by the basil green,
And why it flourished, as by magic touch.
  Greatly they wondered what the thing might mean.
They could not surely give belief that such
  A very nothing would have power to wean
Her from her own fair youth, and pleasures gay,
And even remembrance of her love's delay.

Therefore they watched a time when they might sift
  This hidden whim, and long they watched in vain.
For seldom did she go to chapel-shrift,
  And seldom felt she any hunger-pain.
And when she left, she hurried back, as swift
  As bird on wing to breast its eggs again,
And, patient as a hen-bird, sat her there
Beside her basil, weeping through her hair.

Yet they contrived to steal the basil-pot,
  And to examine it in secret place.
The thing was vile with green and livid spot,
  And yet they knew it was Lorenzo's face.

The guerdon of their murder they had got,
 And so left Florence in a moment's space,
Never to turn again. Away they went,
With blood upon their heads, to banishment.
 John Keats, 'Isabella, or The Pot of Basil'

We came on them stretched out in a clearing,
feet and hands hacked off, privates in their mouths;
the gaudy shrieks beyond their blood-blocked hearing
with the echoes of their screams, the shots' aftermath –
I'd heard the loud black apparatus rise
and flap back, like the beating of giant moths
and bats that filled the ballroom with their cries
when Harry shouldered his way into a decade's
shuttered darkness at the Hotel de la Cruz –
the clapping hung, like flies on half-decayed
faces, in the still, hot blur of trees,
in thick green folds of forest . . . Then *OK, dickheads,*
keep your hands where I can see them. Freeze!
– the tone of the P.E. master's loutish sneer –
came from behind us, and in twos and threes
they loped from the bush, each a human snare
that bristled with knife, machete, automatic weapon;
jungle rig, stubble-shadowed face, a smear
of mud or blood on the cheekbones, sort of warpaint;
red-eyed, blank looks. I was sure we'd had it
there and then, but the tallish leader, wiping
sweat from his forehead, skull – he was shaven-headed
under the green képi – studied us in turn
through narrowed eyes; grim-mouthed, grave, he nodded
to the others, made a new sound (stern
but less sadistic than resigned), and trekked
with the slackly slouching gait of a Soho slattern
towards the thicket, the overgrown green track
out of that killing-ground. I was to follow,
I gathered from the goading of the gun at my back,
and so were Hugh and Harry; but Hugh, poor fellow,
whipped round with a reflex of anger – stupid, brave,
say what you like, both of them sound hollow –

and jabbed at his tormenter. Curses, brief
and terrible, rang out; a machete flashed, bright, cold;
Hugh's lean young body, come to grief,
fell forward, spurting blood; twitched and lolled;
and bouncing once, like a coconut at a fête,
mouth working soundlessly, his blond head rolled
in its own red carpet to my feet.

Alan Jenkins, 'Greenheart'

Heart

The Amphitheatre was a huge circular enclosure, with a notch at opposite extremities of its diameter north and south. From its sloping internal form it might have been called the spittoon of the Jötuns. It was to Casterbridge what the ruined Coliseum is to modern Rome, and was nearly of the same magnitude. The dusk of evening was the proper hour at which a true impression of this suggestive place could be received. Standing in the middle of the arena at that time there by degrees became apparent its real vastness, which a cursory view from the summit at noon-day was apt to obscure. Melancholy, impressive, lonely, yet accessible from every part of the town, the historic circle was the frequent spot for appointments of a furtive kind. Intrigues were arranged there; tentative meetings were there experimented after divisions and feuds. But one kind of appointment – in itself the most common of any – seldom had place in the Amphitheatre: that of happy lovers.

Why, seeing that it was pre-eminently an airy, accessible, and sequestered spot for interviews, the cheerfullest form of those occurrences never took kindly to the soil of the ruin, would be a curious inquiry. Perhaps it was because its associations had about them something sinister. Its history proved that. Apart from the sanguinary nature of the games originally played therein, such incidents attached to its past as these: that for scores of years the town-gallows had stood at one corner; that in 1705 a woman who had murdered her husband was half-strangled and then burnt there in the presence of ten thousand spectators. Tradition reports that at a certain stage of the burning her heart burst and leapt out of her body, to the terror of them all, and that not one of those ten thousand people ever cared particularly for hot roast after that.

Thomas Hardy, *The Mayor of Casterbridge*

Herod

Who's that knocking on the window,
Who's that standing at the door,
What are all those presents
Lying on the kitchen floor?

Who is the smiling stranger
With hair as white as gin,
What is he doing with the children
And who could have let him in?

Why has he rubies on his fingers,
A cold, cold crown on his head,
Why, when he caws his carol,
Does the salty snow run red?

Why does he ferry my fireside
As a spider on a thread,
His fingers made of fuses
And his tongue of gingerbread?

Why does the world before him
Melt in a million suns,
Why do his yellow, yearning eyes
Burn like saffron buns?

Watch where he comes walking
Out of the Christmas flame,
Dancing, double-talking:

Herod is his name.

Charles Causley, 'Innocent's Song'

Hitler

Adolf Hitler was one of history's greatest war criminals. In addition he may have murdered a young girl in 1931.

At the least, the circumstances invite suspicion. On 19 September 1931 Hitler's half-niece, the attractive 23-year-old Geli Raubal, was found dead in her bedroom in the Munich apartment she shared with Hitler, shot through the chest by a bullet from Hitler's 6.35 mm Walther pistol. On her desk lay a letter, broken off midway through a word, with the final 'd' of the *und* omitted. 'When I come to Vienna,' Geli was writing, 'hopefully very soon – we'll drive together to Semmering an . . .' There the letter ends.

Earlier that day, at lunch, Hitler and Geli had quarrelled violently over whether she could leave for Vienna. Only the previous week, she tried to escape from her claustrophobic life in Hitler's flat, reaching his cottage in Berchtesgaden before receiving orders to return.

Now Geli was dead and, whether it was murder or suicide, a corpse in Hitler's apartment constituted an embarrassment to his meteoric political career. Despite the damage limitation by Hitler's advisors, the periodical *Die Fanfare* ran the headline: 'Hitler's lover commits suicide: bachelors and homosexuals as leaders of the party.'

Long before then, over the weekend, Geli's corpse was spirited down the block's back stairs for a cursory medical examination. Then the sympathetic police hastily announced that Geli had taken her own life. The Bavarian Minister of Justice (already in Hitler's pocket and subsequently well promoted) put an end to any further investigation and the body was shipped to Vienna. There Geli was unaccountably buried on hallowed ground, a right normally denied to suicides.

Meanwhile a distraught Hitler went to earth at an isolated lakeside cottage on the Tegernesse where, in one version, Rudolf Hess snatched a gun out of his hand to prevent suicide. Scandal sheets printed rumours that Hitler had killed Geli; the *Müncher Post* said that 'the nose bone of the deceased was shattered and the corpse evidenced other serious injuries'.

But with the body buried, no police inquiries, and no coroner's report, the story lacked staying power. The only man to pursue it was journalist Fritz Gerlich, who, eighteen months later, was ready to reveal the truth in his paper, *Der Gerade Weg*. In March 1933, before he could publish, a squad of fifty stormtroopers burst into his newspaper office, smashed his face, burned his files and bundled him off to Dachau. A month later one of Gerlich's main sources, George Bell, was murdered. Gerlich himself perished during the Night of the Long Knives. But he reportedly smuggled out documentary proof that Hitler had ordered Geli's death; the recipient, Karl von Guttenberg, lodged this dangerous material in a numbered Swiss bank account and then took his secret to the grave as a participant in the July 1944 coup against Hitler.

Who killed Geli? At the heart of her fate is her relationship with 'Uncle Alfie'. It started shortly after his nine-month prison sentence in 1923 when Hitler summoned the 17-year-old Geli and her mother to Munich to act as live-in housekeepers. By 1925 Geli had blossomed: tall, vibrant, a golden girl who turned heads in the street. Hitler squired Geli around town, went riding with her, paid for her music lessons, mooned over her at the opera and, according to Fest (a party leader from Württemberg), turned in 'a very plausible imitation of adolescent infatuation'.

Of the seven women with whom Hitler had intimate relations, six committed suicide or seriously attempted it. Before her death in the Bunker in 1945, Eva Braun tried to take her own life in 1932 and 1935. Actress Renaté Mueller, later found dead beneath her Berlin hotel window, confided in her director that on her date with Hitler he 'fell on the floor and begged her to kick him . . . condemned himself as unworthy . . . and just grovelled in an agonising manner . . . She finally acceded to his wishes. As she continued to kick him he became more and more excited.'

Heiden, a respected writer on Hitler, calls the future Führer 'a man with masochistic–coprophil inclinations, bordering on what Havelock-Ellis calls undinism'. Geli confided in Otto Strasser, a one-time Nazi insider, on the way back from a Mardi Gras ball in 1931. Strasser recalls: 'Hitler made her undress while he would lie down on the floor. Then she would have to squat down over his face where he could examine her at close range, and this made him very excited. When the excitement reached its peak, he demanded that she urinate on him and that gave him his sexual pleasure.'

It is possible that Geli, trapped in a gilded cage with only Hitler for social and sexual recreation, took her own life. But her last, interrupted letter is the opposite of a suicide note; the girl is looking forward to life. But Geli constituted a serious threat to the future Führer. Two years before, in 1929, Hitler wrote her an explicit and degrading love letter which fell into the hands of his landlady's son. Hitler's fixers managed to buy the missive back. But it was clear that any future revelations by Geli could unleash deeply damaging press smears.

Perhaps Geli was carrying Hitler's child, and killed herself out of grief; for Hitler was just beginning to show an interest in Eva Braun. But if Geli was with child, it is most likely she had spurned Hitler's advances in favour of another admirer, either her suitor in Vienna or an art teacher from Linz, both Jews. Such an alliance would not have gone down well with the leader of the Master Race.

Perhaps Geli Raubal shot herself. Perhaps she was made to shoot herself. Perhaps she was shot on Hitler's orders. Perhaps Hitler shot her.

No one knows, and unless her body is exhumed from its zinc coffin in the featureless pauper's burial ground outside Vienna, it is unlikely that they ever will.

Oliver Cyriax, *Crime: an Encyclopedia*

Holocaust

Wir haben ein Gesetz,
Und nach dem Gesetz soll er sterben.[1]

The dowsed coals fume and hiss after your meal
Of grilled brook trout, and you saunter off for a walk
Down the fern trail, it doesn't matter where to,
Just so you're weeks and worlds away from home,
And among midsummer hills have set up camp
In the deep bronze glories of declining day.

You remember, peacefully, an earlier day
In childhood, remember a quite specific meal:
A corn roast and bonfire in summer camp.
That summer you got lost on a Nature Walk;
More than you dared admit, you thought of home;
No one else knows where the mind wanders to.

The fifth of August, 1942.
It was morning and very hot. It was the day
They came at dawn with rifles to The Home
For Jewish Children, cutting short the meal
Of bread and soup, lining them up to walk
In close formation off to a special camp.

How often you have thought about that camp,
As though in some strange way you were driven to,
And about the children, and how they were made to walk,
Yolek who had bad lungs, who wasn't a day
Over five years old, commanded to leave his meal
And shamble between armed guards to his long home.

1 We have a law,
And according to the law he should be killed.

We're approaching August again. It will drive home
The regulation torments of that camp
Yolek was sent to, his small, unfinished meal,
The electric fences, the numeral tattoo,
The quite extraordinary heat of the day
They all were forced to take that terrible walk.

Whether on a silent, solitary walk
Or among crowds, far off or safe at home,
You will remember, helplessly, that day,
And the smell of smoke, and the loudspeakers of the camp.
Wherever you are. Yolek will be there, too.
His unuttered name will interrupt your meal.

Prepare to receive him in your home some day.
Though they killed him in the camp they sent him to,
He will walk in as you're sitting down to a meal.

Anthony Hecht, 'The Book of Yolek'

Historical records in the public domain prove beyond any doubt that the Nazi extermination of the Jews, and concurrently of large numbers of gypsies, was intended as only the first step in a gigantic programme of genocide of all the so-called 'inferior races' of Europe. A beginning was made both in Russia, where the Nazis are said to have killed about seven million civilians between 1941 and 1944, and in Poland where the reported figures vary, depending on the source, from between 800,000 to 2,400,000 Poles other than Jews.

In view of these monstrous figures, and of the fact that genocide in one form or another has existed as long as human history is recorded – not least in our time, and also perpetrated by nations other than the Germans – it is not altogether surprising that the question 'What is so different about the Nazi murder of the Jews?' has been asked time and again, and often by enlightened people.

Perhaps because so much has been written, over so many years, about the highly emotive subject of the Nazis and the Jews, many people now manifest a weary – and wary – resistance to it. Hard facts have become blurred and some indeed have never been accepted.

Using – or misusing – the perspective of history, some chroniclers of the time will have us believe that the extermination of the Jews was almost an accidental development, somehow forced upon the Nazis by circumstances. Dieter Allers's 'Nobody here thought of extermination' has been said to me dozens of times in Germany, and by people far less implicated than Herr Allers.

But the truth is that the record does not bear out that defence. The ways and means towards achieving this enormous act of murder only evolved with time, but the intention was there almost from the start. On January 30, 1939, Hitler said in the course of a speech to the Reichstag: 'Today I will once more be a prophet. If the international Jewish financiers inside and outside Europe should again succeed in plunging the nations into a world war, the result will not be the bolshevization of the world and thus the victory of Jewry, but the annihilation [*Vernichtung*] of the Jewish race throughout Europe.'

It is true that the so-called 'Madagascar Plan' – conceived by the Poles in 1937 and briefly considered by the French as a solution to the voluntary resettlement of 10,000 of the many thousands of Jewish refugees who had been given sanctuary in France between 1936 and 1938 – was taken quite seriously by at least some of Nazi leadership for a short time. Eichmann is said to have been busy for a year working out the details. When the idea of eventually shipping four million people to Madagascar was defeated by its own lack of realism, the same faction of Nazi administrators who had entertained it as a possibility turned to the idea of setting up a Jewish reservation in the province of Lublin (Lublinland, it was to be called). But these were only pipe-dreams, quite possibly encouraged by those few really in Hitler's confidence in an effort to mislead the others.

On March 13, 1941, an ambiguous Führer order was communicated to the army command in Russia. 'By order of the Führer, the Reichsführer SS has been given special tasks, arising from the conclusive and decisive struggle between the two opposing political systems. Within the limits of the set tasks, the Reichsführer SS acts independently upon his own responsibility.' The fact that this Führer order, which was to cover the execution of a wide category of 'undesirable elements' in conquered Eastern territories, referred primarily to the Jews was never to be put into words, or on paper.

The Nazi plans for the 'Final Solution' in terms of mass murder had crystallized as the plans for invading Russia were made. The armies advancing into Russian territory in June 1941 were closely followed by the infamous *Einsatzgruppen* (Action Groups) who carried out faithfully the Führer order for the execution of 'Jews, gypsies, racial inferiors, asocials and Soviet political commissars'.

One of the SS signals concerning these 'actions' was found amongst

German army records after the war. Addressed to the security police, Riga, from the commander of the security police (and SD) Eastern zone, and entitled 'Executions', it requests 'immediate information regarding number of executions categorized as (*a*) Jews; (*b*) Communists; (*c*) Partisans; (*d*) Mentally ill; (*e*) Others. (The signals also requested the information: 'Of the total, how many women and children?')

The reply, addressed to Group A in Riga, states the executions up to February 1, 1942 (we do not know from when) were: (*a*) Jews, 136,421; (*b*) Communists, 1,064 (amongst then 1 Kommissar, 1 Oberpolitruck, 5 Politruck – presumably Communist Party titles); (*c*) Partisans, 56; (*d*) Mentally ill, 653; (*e*) Poles, 44; Russian POWs, 28; gypsies, 5; Armenian, 1. Total: 138,272; of which, women, 55,556; children, 34,464.

By early 1942, behind the front from Riga and Miusk to Kiev and the Crimea, they had killed well over 500,000 Jews – two-thirds of them, as we can see from the signal, women and children, and nearly all by shooting in previously dug mass graves.

Albert Hartl, the former chief of the Church Information Service at the Reich Security Office, who had been sent to Russia in January 1942 with a commission from Heydrich to 'report on the cultural and spiritual condition of the population', told me of the day he was invited to dine at the *dacha* – the weekend villa outside Kiev – of Brigadeführer (Major-General) Max Thomas, the higher SS the police leader who was his nominal superior. 'I was going with Standartenführer (Colonel) Blobel,' he said. 'I hardly knew him but he was invited to dinner too, so we went together. It was evening and just getting dark. At one moment – we were driving past a long ravine. I noticed strange movements of the earth: clumps of earth rose into the air as if by their own propulsion – and there was smoke: it was like a low-toned volcano: as if there was burning lava just beneath the earth. Blobel laughed, made a gesture with his arm, pointing back along the road and ahead of us, all along the ravine – the ravine of Babi Yar – and said, 'Here lie my 30,000 Jews."[1] (Hartl, a few months after that, had, or faked, a nervous breakdown, was first hospitalized in Kiev and then sent for six months to a convalescent home in the country. After this he was returned to Germany and, by request, invalided out of active, including administrative, service with the SS.)

But in spite of its hideous effectiveness in Russia, shooting was soon rejected as inefficient for what Himmler was to call 'the enormous task ahead' in Poland. It was also too dangerous, in that too many German

1 The movement of the earth was caused by the thaw releasing the gases from the corpses.

soldiers from the ranks of the Wehrmacht as well as from the SS had to be involved. New techniques were called for, and here the euthanasia personnel (some of whom had already been involved in the 'work' in Russia) found a new role.

What was different, and of unprecedented horror, in the Nazi genocide of the Jews as it now developed, was the concept and organization of the 'extermination camps'. Even today there is still widespread misunderstanding about the nature of these very special installations of which there were only four,[1] all of them on occupied Polish territory and all of them existing for only a short time.

Ever since the end of World War II these extermination camps have been confused in people's minds with 'concentration camps', of which there were literally dozens, spread all over Greater Germany and occupied Europe, and which have been the primary subject of descriptions in fiction and films.

There are two main reasons for the persistent confusion between these two kinds of Nazi installations; the first is that appallingly few people survived the extermination camps, and those who did are neither necessarily particularly articulate, nor anxious to relive their horrifying experiences. The second reason – far more subtle – is a universal reluctance to face the fact that these places really existed.

There is a somewhat similar confusion – in the sense of one concept being marginally more acceptable than the other – between 'War Crimes' and 'Nazi Crimes'. (Although the misinterpretation, or misapplication, of *these* two terms is far more deliberate and politically motivated.) For the truth is that 'Nazi Crimes' ('NS Crimes' in Germany), although their perpetration was facilitated by war, had in their origins nothing whatever to do with the war.

In *Mein Kampf*, written in 1923, Hitler had already committed himself to a concept of a new Europe based on racial theories according to which the whole of Eastern Europe was to become a 'service population' for the benefit of the 'superior races' (in addition to Germany: Scandinavia, Holland, some of France, and Britain). Even if there had been no war, or if Germany had won the war after the fall of France in 1940, the conditions under which this programme could have been implemented would have had to be created. It would still have been found necessary to

1 Five if we include Birkenau, the extermination section of Auschwitz – which, however, also functioned partly as a labour camp.

kill, or at best sterilize, all those in Eastern Europe most likely to resist: the intellectuals and the social and religious élite. Racially 'pure' children would still have been shipped to Germany in infancy and brought up by German foster-parents or in German institutions. (A beginning to this particular phase was in fact made during the war, when 200,000 Polish infants were forcibly removed from their parents. A large number of them were returned to Poland through the efforts of UNRRA in 1945–6, but by no means all of them were found.)

Hitler's new Europe was entirely based on this concept of superior and inferior peoples. Whether by annexation or by war, he was determined to create machinery for putting into practice the decimation of Eastern Europe. Equally, war or no war, as no other practical solution offered itself, he would eventually have had to find ways of physically exterminating the Jews; the only logical conclusion of the psychological defamation campaign on which most of his programme was built.

The 'concentration' camps were originally set up as extended prison services to deal with those resisting the New Order, and to eliminate them, with bogus legality, as 'traitors' or 'spies' if their 're-education' proved impossible. From 1941, most of these camps became vast slave-labour markets, but even then they still varied a good deal in severity, largely depending on the nationality of the prisoners they catered for. And even in the worst of them, however terrible the conditions, they offered at least a slim chance of survival.

The 'extermination' camps offered no such chance. They were created for the sole purpose of exterminating primarily the Jews of Europe, and also the Gypsies. There were four of these installations, planned *exclusively* for extermination; first, and as a testing ground, Chelmno (Kulmhof), set up in December 1941. Then, following the Wannsee Conference of January 1942 which, chaired by Reinhardt Heydrich, put the official seal of approval on the extermination programme, Belsec (March 1942), Sobibor (May 1942), and the largest of them, Treblinka (June 1942). All were within a two-hundred-mile radius of Warsaw.

The decision to place all of them on Polish soil has been attributed widely to the well-known anti-Semitism of large segments of the Polish population. Although this fact may have marginally influenced the choice, it is more reasonable to assume that it was mainly prompted by tactical considerations. Poland's railway system covered all of the country, with stations in even the smallest towns; while large tracts of the Polish countryside, densely forested and very thinly populated, made isolation possible. In this sense – and this sense only – the war did contribute to making this huge and sinister operation possible, for it is unlikely that it could have been attempted in any other region of Europe.

None of the extermination camps existed for longer than seventeen months when, one after the other, they were totally obliterated by the SS. The official Polish estimate – the most conservative, and not universally accepted – is that approximately 2,000,000 Jews and 52,000 gypsies (children made up at least one-third of this total) were killed in these four camps during that period.

The concentration camps too had gas-vans, gas chambers, crematoriums and mass graves. In them too people were shot, given lethal injections, gassed, and apart from being murdered, hundreds of thousands died of exhaustion, starvation and disease. But – even in Birkenau, the extermination section of Auschwitz (where 860,000 Jews are believed to have been killed) – there was in all of them a chance of life.

In the extermination camps, the only people who retained this chance from day to day were the pitifully few who were kept as 'work-Jews' to operate the camps. Eighty-two people – no children among them – survived the four Nazi death-camps in Poland.

But it was not only the policy behind the Nazi murder of the Jews which distinguished it from other instances of genocide. The methods employed, too, were unique and uniquely calculated. The killings were organized systematically to achieve the maximum humiliation and dehumanization of the victims before they died. This pattern was dictated by a distinct and careful purpose, not by 'mere' cruelty or indifference: the crammed airless freight-cars without sanitary provisions, food or drink, far worse than any cattle-transport; the whipped-up (literally so) hysteria of arrival; the immediate and always violent separation of men, women and children; the public undressing; the incredibly crude internal physical examinations for hidden valuables; the hair-cutting and shaving of the women; and finally the naked run to the gas chamber, under the lash of the whips.

'*What did you think at the time was the reason for the extermination of the Jews?*' I was to ask Stangl.

'They wanted their money,' he replied at once. 'Have you any idea of the fantastic sums that were involved? That's how the steel was bought, in Sweden.'

Perhaps he really did believe this, but I doubt it. Globocnik's final accounting disclosed that the *Aktion Reinhardt* (named after Heydrich) netted the Third Reich DM 178,745,960. To one man, in relation to his monthly wage, this may seem a lot of money. But what is it in the context of a nation's normal income and expenditure, in war or in peace? It is a trivial sum.

'*Why*,' I asked Stangl, '*if they were going to kill them anyway, what was the point of all the humiliation, why the cruelty?*'

'To condition those who actually had to carry out the policies,' he said. 'To make it possible for them to do what they did.' And this, I believe, was true.

To achieve the extermination of these millions of men, women and children, the Nazis committed not only physical but spiritual murder: on those they killed, on those who did the killing, on those who knew the killing was being done, and also, to some extent, for evermore, on all of us, who were alive and thinking beings at that time.

Gitta Sereny, *Into That Darkness*

The wind runs free across our plains,
The live sea beats for ever at our beaches.
Man makes earth fertile, earth gives him flowers and fruits.
He lives in toil and joy; he hopes, fears, begets sweet offspring.

. . . And you have come, our precious enemy,
Forsaken creature, man ringed by death.
What can you say now, before our assembly?
Will you swear by a god? What god?
Will you leap happily into the grave?
Or will you at the end, like the industrious man
Whose life was too brief for his long art,
Lament your sorry work unfinished,
The thirteen million still alive?

Oh son of death, we do not wish you death.
May you live longer than anyone ever lived.
May you live sleepless five million nights,
And may you be visited each night by the suffering of everyone who saw,
Shutting behind him, the door that blocked the way back,
Saw it grow dark around him, the air fill with death.

Primo Levi, 'For Adolf Eichmann', 20 July 1960,
trans. by Ruth Feldman and Brian Swann

I

Identity

It was the strangest murder trial I ever attended. They named it the Peckham murder in the headlines, though Northwood Street, where the old woman was found battered to death, was not strictly speaking in Peckham. This was not one of those cases of circumstantial evidence, in which you feel the jurymen's anxiety – because mistakes *have* been made – like domes of silence muting the court. No, this murderer was all but found with the body; no one present when the Crown counsel outlined his case believed that the man in the dock stood any chance at all.

He was a heavy stout man with bulging bloodshot eyes. All his muscles seemed to be in his thighs. Yes, an ugly customer, one you wouldn't forget in a hurry – and that was an important point because the Crown proposed to call four witnesses who hadn't forgotten him, who had seen him hurrying away from the little red villa in Northwood Street. The clock had just struck two in the morning.

Mrs Salmon in 15 Northwood Street had been unable to sleep; she heard a door click shut and thought it was her own gate. So she went to the window and saw Adams (that was his name) on the steps of Mrs Parker's house. He had just come out and he was wearing gloves. He had a hammer in his hand and she saw him drop it into the laurel bushes by the front gate. But before he moved away, he had looked up – at her window. The fatal instinct that tells a man when he is watched exposed him in the light of a street-lamp to her gaze – his eyes suffused with horrifying and brutal fear, like an animal's when you raise a whip. I talked afterwards to Mrs Salmon, who naturally after the astonishing verdict went in fear herself. As I imagine did all the witnesses – Henry MacDougall, who had been driving home from Benfleet late and nearly ran Adams down at the corner of Northwood Street. Adams was walking in the middle of the road looking dazed. And old Mr Wheeler, who lived next door to Mrs Parker, at no. 12, and was wakened by a noise – like a chair falling – through the thin-as-paper villa wall, and got up and looked out of the window, just as Mrs Salmon had done, saw Adams's back and, as he turned, those bulging eyes. In Laurel Avenue he had been seen by yet another witness – his luck was badly out; he might as well have committed the crime in broad daylight.

'I understand,' counsel said, 'that the defence proposes to plead mistaken identity. Adams's wife will tell you that he was with her at two in the morning on February 14, but after you have heard the witnesses for the Crown and examined carefully the features of the prisoner, I do not think you will be prepared to admit the possibility of a mistake.'

It was all over, you would have said, but the hanging.

After the formal evidence had been given by the policeman who had found the body and the surgeon who examined it, Mrs Salmon was called. She was the ideal witness, with her slight Scotch accent and her expression of honesty, care and kindness.

The counsel for the Crown brought the story gently out. She spoke very firmly. There was no malice in her, and no sense of importance at standing there in the Central Criminal Court with a judge in scarlet hanging on her words and the reporters writing them down. Yes, she said, and then she had gone downstairs and rung up the police station.

'And do you see the man here in court?'

She looked straight across at the big man in the dock, who stared hard at her with his pekingese eyes without emotion.

'Yes,' she said, 'there he is.'

'You are quite certain?'

She said simply, 'I couldn't be mistaken, sir.'

It was all as easy as that.

'Thank you, Mrs Salmon.'

Counsel for the defence rose to cross-examine. If you had reported as many murder trials as I have, you would have known beforehand what line he would take. And I was right, up to a point.

'Now, Mrs Salmon, you must remember that a man's life may depend on your evidence.'

'I do remember it, sir.'

'Is your eyesight good?'

'I have never had to wear spectacles, sir.'

'You are a woman of fifty-five?'

'Fifty-six, sir.'

'And the man you saw was on the other side of the road?'

'Yes, sir.'

'And it was two o'clock in the morning. You must have remarkable eyes, Mrs Salmon?'

'No, sir. There was moonlight, and when the man looked up, he had the lamplight on his face.'

'And you have no doubt whatever that the man you saw is the prisoner?'

I couldn't make out what he was at. He couldn't have expected any other answer than the one he got.

'None whatever, sir. It isn't a face one forgets.'

Counsel took a look round the court for a moment. Then he said: 'Do you mind, Mrs Salmon, examining again the people in court? No, not the prisoner. Stand up, please, Mr Adams,' and there at the back of the court, with thick stout body and muscular legs and a pair of bulging eyes, was the exact image of the man in the dock. He was even dressed the same – tight blue suit and striped tie.

'Now think very carefully, Mrs Salmon. Can you still swear that the man you saw drop the hammer in Mrs Parker's garden was the prisoner – and not this man, who is his twin brother?'

Of course she couldn't. She looked from one to the other and didn't say a word.

There the big brute sat in the dock with his legs crossed and there he stood too at the back of the court and they both stared at Mrs Salmon. She shook her head.

What we saw then was the end of the case. There wasn't a witness prepared to swear that it was the prisoner he'd seen. And the brother? He had his alibi, too; he was with his wife.

And so the man was acquitted for lack of evidence. But whether – if he did the murder and not his brother – he was punished or not, I don't know. That extraordinary day had an extraordinary end. I followed Mrs Salmon out of court and we got wedged in the crowd who were waiting, of course, for the twins. The police tried to drive the crowd away, but all they could do was keep the roadway clear for traffic. I learned later that they tried to get the twins to leave by a back way, but they wouldn't. One of them – no one knew which – said, 'I've been acquitted, haven't I?' and they walked bang out of the front entrance. Then it happened. I don't know how; though I was only six feet away. The crowd moved and somehow one of the twins got pushed on to the road right in front of a bus.

He gave a squeal like a rabbit and that was all; he was dead, his skull smashed just as Mrs Parker's had been. Divine vengeance? I wish I knew. There was the other Adams getting on his feet from beside the body and looking straight over at Mrs Salmon. He was crying, but whether he was the murderer or the innocent man, nobody will ever be able to tell. But if you were Mrs Salmon, could you sleep at night?

Graham Greene, 'The Case for the Defence'

Impulse

It was waiting for Roger to kiss me that I must have fallen in love with him. I never thought about making love in particular, nor what there might be in his trousers, nor if he would marry me nor anything like that: I was just waiting for a kiss, for some sign that he liked me, that somebody apart from Malcolm was paying me some attention, somebody intelligent and sensitive like Roger, and not a pig like Jonathan or Mr G who would have had your pants off even before they'd noticed the colour of your eyes. While I was waiting for him to kiss me and he was talking and talking, I watched him hard as I could for any sign he was noticing me, and so it was I grew familiar with the strong quick lines of his face, the close-set intense blue eyes, the straight, just slightly wide nose and the mouth that moved and moved and moved with a thick strong lower lip and a thin pale upper one and two front teeth that weren't quite perfectly straight. I dreamed those teeth.

And I grew familiar too with his gestures. While he spoke he would push his right hand into his hair and hold it there tight, gripping a handful of hair, so that when he took it out again it would stay standing up in a big shock of blond and he looked like a schoolboy. Then the other thing he did, if he was sitting at a table, was to prop up his chin on the palm of one hand with the elbow resting on the table and put his fingers in his mouth and lightly scratch those uneven teeth.

I liked these gestures. I liked the way he seemed so totally wrapped up in what he was saying that he didn't notice what he was doing with his hands. He didn't seem self-conscious at all. And he didn't seem particularly conscious of the room we were in either and never made any comment on all the rows of glass ornaments my mother had covered every horizontal surface with, so that dusting had become a sort of life sentence with picking them all up and wiping them one by one and trying to find enough room to put them all back again. Sometimes I think my mother needs to see a psychiatrist with all her whims and the way she says she's going upstairs to have a chat with Brian and goes and sits in his room for hours and hours and cries and laughs – only of course it's me most probably they'll be sending to a psychiatrist now, and I'm as right as rain, I know I am. I'm not even going to pretend I'm crazy or anything.

Before it happened he said, 'You're sick, you are. You're sick the way you draw everything into yourself, the way you never never never let be. You're sick because you can't adjust your trash literature expectations to the world as it is. To me as I am. And you eat your little heart out with that sickness and such blood out of everybody else.'

And I said, 'But I love you, Roger. You know I do. How can you say . . .'

'You love an idea of me,' he said. 'You don't love me as I really am. You don't love the me that's struggling, fighting and adventurous. You don't have a brave love. You want me as a failure, bled dry and white as a statue, posing traditionally by your side forever.'

'We're not in a play, Roger,' I said. 'You don't have to be so eloquent.' But he started to shout then and said, there I was again, there I was, always trying to pull him down to my level, and he started to laugh and shout together, almost in a frenzy, and he said, 'Going down, madam, third floor, second, first, ground, here we are, ground floor. Oh sorry, sorry, madam, it was the basement you wanted, was it? Here we are then, the basement, plastic flowers, romantic novels, all guaranteed over 600 pages, the very furthest pavilions, videos of the royal wedding, inflatable husbands to take to church with you.'

The baby was crying all through those last moments we had together and neither of us moved to comfort him, but that wild, unrestrained cry of his seemed to fill the room so full that we were pushed and pushed into a corner with no escape whatever.

I began to cry too.

'I do love you as you are, Roger. I love every inch of you. It's just that I'm tired of not knowing how things will be tomorrow, how I will manage.'

'You will never know exactly how things will be with me,' he said. 'Never, never, never. Because I'm not a statue. I'm alive. Got it? Alive. And that means I can't be pinned to any walls. Do you understand? I can't be made sense of.'

I was quiet a moment then and we both sat there all dressed up for work with the clock ticking on and on and the baby wailing and wailing and it was time to go almost.

'So leave, then,' I said. 'Leave. I don't want to see you again. I don't ever want to touch you or have anything to do with you again. Get your stuff and go.'

'No,' he said. 'That's stupid.' And then he said, 'You'd only come crying back to me after a couple of days anyway, like always.'

And it was true.

He was sitting at the table where we'd eaten breakfast with one hand clutched in his hair and the other twirling the bread knife round in his fingers. It seemed wherever he sat Roger always started to twirl the nearest thing to hand round and round in his fingers. Behind him was the new blue rug I'd bought to cover the floorboards in the corner and the TV with the lamp on top that had the bubbles rising and rising in its orange liquid.

I was weeping and furious and quite quite at the end, and I stood up and stumbled round the table and grabbed the knife from his hands so that it was pointing at him, at his chest.

'I'll kill you then,' I said, not meaning it at all.

And he said, 'Oh, I shouldn't do it with the knife, lovey.'

He looked into my eyes and his own were laughing. Our arguments didn't even seem to touch him any more. 'You're not strong enough for the knife. I'd use the shotgun, if I were you.' Because he had a shotgun, Roger did. He had shown it to me and it seemed he had made some kind of pact with himself that he would commit suicide the moment he was quite certain that he had failed in life. By putting the barrel in his mouth. That was how stupid he could be about his ambitions and things.

He looked into my eyes and looked away to gather the crumbs from his breakfast plate, as if I wasn't worth even a moment's more attention.

So I killed him.

I didn't know I was killing him. I just pushed the knife forward into his white work shirt as hard as I could and then let go of it at once, even before the blood came. I walked round him and picked up Bobby from his cot and walked out of the back door into the garden, rocking him from side to side to make him quiet. I must have closed my eyes and ears and heart to Roger, because all I saw was Bobby's pudgy face, too young to resemble anybody else's and all I heard were the baby's cries and whimpers and blubbering as he quietened down and I didn't see or hear anything of Roger at all.

Tim Parks, *Loving Roger*

Incarceration

Now I beheld two spirits by the ice
Pent in one hollow, that the head of one
Was cowl unto the other; and as bread

Is raven'd up through hunger, the uppermost
Did so apply his fangs to the other's brain,
Where the spine joins it. Not more furiously
On Menalippus' temples Tydeus gnawed,
Than on that skull and on its garbage he.
'Oh, thou! who show'st so beastly sign of hate
'Gainst him thou prey'st on, let me hear,' said I,
'The cause, on such condition, that if right
Warrant thy grievance, knowing who ye are,
And what the colour of his sinning was,
I may repay thee in the world above,
If that, wherewith I speak, be moist so long.'

His jaws uplifting from their fell repast
That sinner wiped them on the hairs o' the head,
Which he behind had mangled, then began:
'Thy will obeying, I call up afresh
Sorrow past cure; which, but to think of, wrings
My heart, or ere I tell on 't. But if words,
That I may utter, shall prove seed to bear
Fruit of eternal infamy to him,
The traitor whom I gnaw at, thou at once
Shalt see me speak and weep. Who thou mayst be
I know not, nor how here below art come:
But Florentine thou seemest of a truth,
When I do hear thee. Know, I was on earth
Count Ugolino, and the Archbishop he
Ruggieri. Why I neighbour him so close,
Now list. That through effect of his ill thoughts
In him my trust reposing, I was ta'en
And after murder'd, need is not I tell.
What therefore thou canst not have heard, that is,
How cruel was the murder, shalt thou hear,
And know if he have wrong'd me. A small grate
Within that mew, which for my sake the name
Of famine bears, where others yet must pine,
Already through its opening several moons
Had shown me, when I slept the evil sleep
That from the future tore the curtain off.

This one, methought, as master of the sport,
Rode forth to chase the gaunt wolf, and his whelps,
Unto the mountain which forbids the sight
Of Lucca to the Pisan. With lean braches
Inquisitive and keen, before him ranged
Lanfranchi with Sismondi and Gualandi.
After short course the father and the sons
Seem'd tired and lagging, and methought I saw
The sharp tusks gore their sides. When I awoke,
Before the dawn, amid their sleep I heard
My sons (for they were with me) weep and ask
For bread. Right cruel art thou, if no pang
Thou feel at thinking what my heart foretold;
And if not now, why use thy tears to flow?
Now had they waken'd; and the hour drew near
When they were wont to bring us food; the mind
Of each misgave him through his dream, and I
Heard, at its outlet underneath lock'd up
The horrible tower: whence, uttering not a word,
I look'd upon the visage of my sons.
I wept not: so all stone I felt within,
They wept: and one, my little Anselm, cried,
"Thou lookest so! Father, what ails thee?" Yet
I shed no tear, nor answer'd all that day
Nor the next night, until another sun
Came out upon the world. When a faint beam
Had to our doleful prison made its way,
And in four countenances I descried
The image of my own, on either hand
Through agony I bit; and they, who thought
I did it through desire of feeding, rose
O' the sudden, and cried, "Father, we should grieve
Far less, if thou wouldst eat of us: thou gavest
These weeds of miserable flesh we wear;
And do thou strip them off from us again."
Then, not to make them sadder, I kept down
My spirit in stillness. That day and the next
We all were silent. Ah, obdurate earth!
Why open'dst not upon us? When we came
To the fourth day, then Gaddo at my feet

Outstretch'd did fling him, crying, "Hast no help
For me, my father?" There he died; and e'en
Plainly as thou seest me, saw I the three
Fall one by one 'twixt the fifth day and sixth:
Whence I betook me, now grown blind, to grope
Over them all, and for three days aloud
Call'd on them who were dead. Then, fasting got
The mastery of grief.' Thus having spoke,
Once more upon the wretched skull his teeth
He fasten'd like a mastiff's 'gainst the bone,
Firm and unyielding. Oh, thou Pisa! shame
Of all the people, who their dwelling make
In that fair region, where the Italian voice
Is heard; since that thy neighbours are so slack
To punish, from their deep foundations rise
Capraia and Gorgona, and dam up
The mouth of Arno; that each soul in thee
May perish in the waters. What if fame
Reported that thy castles were betray'd
By Ugolino, yet no right hadst thou
To stretch his children on the rack. For them,
Brigata, Uguccione, and the pair
Of gentle ones, of whom my song hath told,
Their tender years, thou modern Thebes, did make
Uncapable of guilt. Onward we pass'd,
Where others, scarf'd in rugged folds of ice,
Not on their feet turn'd, but each reversed.

Dante Alighieri, *Inferno*, trans. Henry Francis Carey

Infanticide

'The Cruel Midvvife./ Being a True Account of a most Sad and La-/mentable Discovery that has been/ lately made in the Village of Poplar/ in the Parish of Stepney./ At the House of one Madame *Compton* alias/ *Norman* a Midwife, wherein has been discovered ma-/ny Children that have been Murdered. Particularly/ Two that were lately found in a Hand-Basket on a/ Shelf in the Sellar, whose Skins, Eyes, and part of their/ Flesh were eaten by Vermin: The Skelliton of Six/ others that were found buryed in the Sellar; with the/

design of digging for others in the Garden. With the/ manner of the Discovery./ Also/ an Account of the Seizing or Appre-/hending, Behaviour, and Commitment to/ Newgate, of Madam *Compton* alias/ *Norman*, the Midwife, on the Account of/ Murthering these Infants./ Licensed according to Order./ London,/ Printed for *R. Wier* at the *White Horse* in *Fleet-/ Street*, 1693./'

Summary of a pamphlet

I took my oath I would inquire,
  Without affection, hate, or wrath,
Into the death of Ada Wright –
  So help me God! I took that oath.

When I went out to see the corpse,
  The four months' babe that died so young,
I judged it was seven pounds in weight,
  And little more than one foot long.

One eye, that had a yellow lid,
  Was shut – so was the mouth, that smiled;
The left eye open, shining bright –
  It seemed a knowing little child.

For as I looked at that one eye,
  It seemed to laugh, and say with glee:
'What caused my death you'll never know –
  Perhaps my mother murdered me.'

When I went into court again,
  To hear the mother's evidence –
It was a love-child, she explained.
  And smiled, for our intelligence.

'Now, Gentlemen of the Jury,' said
  The coroner – 'this woman's child
By misadventure met its death.'
  'Aye, aye,' said we. The mother smiled.

And I could see that child's one eye
  Which seemed to laugh, and say with glee:
'What caused my death you'll never know –
  Perhaps my mother murdered me.'

W. H. Davies, 'The Inquest'

J

Jealousy

Enter Othello with a light. He draws back a curtain, revealing Desdemona asleep in her bed.

OTHELLO: It is the cause, it is the cause, my soul.
Let me not name it to you, you chaste stars.
It is the cause. Yet I'll not shed her blood,
Nor scar that whiter skin of hers than snow,
And smooth as monumental alabaster.
Yet she must die, else she'll betray more men.
Put out the light, and then put out the light.
If I quench thee, thou flaming minister,
I can again thy former light restore
Should I repent me; but once put out thy light,
Thou cunning'st pattern of excelling nature,
I know not where is that Promethean heat
That can thy light relume. When I have plucked thy rose
I cannot give it vital growth again.
It needs must wither. I'll smell thee on the tree.
(*He kisses her*)
O balmy breath, that dost almost persuade
Justice to break her sword! One more, one more.
Be thus when thou art dead, and I will kill thee
And love thee after. One more, and that's the last.
(*He kisses her*)
So sweet was ne'er so fatal. I must weep,
But they are cruel tears. This sorrow's heavenly,
It strikes where it doth love. She wakes.
DESDEMONA: Who's there? Othello?
OTHELLO: Ay, Desdemona.
DESDEMONA: Will you come to bed, my lord?
OTHELLO: Have you prayed tonight, Desdemon?

DESDEMONA: Ay, my lord.
OTHELLO: If you bethink yourself of any crime
Unreconciled as yet to heaven and grace,
Solicit for it straight.
DESDEMONA: Alack, my lord, what may you mean by that?
OTHELLO: Well, do it, and be brief. I will walk by.
I would not kill thy unprepared spirit.
No, heavens forfend! I would not kill thy soul.
DESDEMONA: Talk you of killing?
OTHELLO: Ay, I do.
DESDEMONA: Then heaven
Have mercy on me.
OTHELLO: Amen, with all my heart.
DESDEMONA: If you say so, I hope you will not kill me.
OTHELLO: Hum!
DESDEMONA: And yet I fear you, for you're fatal then
When your eyes roll so. Why I should fear I know not,
Since guiltiness I know not, but yet I feel I fear.
OTHELLO: Think on thy sins.
DESDEMONA: They are loves I bear to you.
OTHELLO: Ay, and for that thou diest.
DESDEMONA: That death's unnatural that kills for loving.
Alas, why gnaw you so your nether lip?
Some bloody passion shakes your very frame.
These are portents, but yet I hope, I hope
They do not point on me.
OTHELLO: Peace, and be still.
DESDEMONA: I will so. What's the matter?
OTHELLO: That handkerchief
Which I so loved and gave thee, thou gav'st to Cassio.
DESDEMONA: No, by my life and soul. Send for the man
And ask him.
OTHELLO: Sweet soul, take heed, take heed of perjury.
Thou art on thy deathbed.
DESDEMONA: Ay, but not yet to die.
OTHELLO: Presently.
Therefore confess thee freely of thy sin,
For to deny each article with oath
Cannot remove nor choke the strong conception
That I do groan withal. Thou art to die.

DESDEMONA: Then Lord have mercy on me.
OTHELLO: I say amen.
DESDEMONA: And have you mercy, too. I never did
Offend you in my life, never loved Cassio
But with such general warranty of heaven
As I might love. I never gave him token.
OTHELLO: By heaven, I saw my handkerchief in's hand.
O perjured woman! Thou dost stone my heart,
And makes me call what I intend to do
A murder, which I thought a sacrifice.
I saw the handkerchief.
DESDEMONA: He found it, then.
I never gave it him. Send for him hither.
Let him confess a truth.
OTHELLO: He hath confessed.
DESDEMONA: What, my lord?
OTHELLO: That he hath usèd thee.
DESDEMONA: How, unlawfully?
OTHELLO: Ay.
DESDEMONA: He will not say so.
OTHELLO: No, his mouth is stopped.
Honest Iago hath ta'en order for't.
DESDEMONA: O, my fear interprets! What, is he dead?
OTHELLO: Had all his hairs been lives, my great revenge
Had stomach for 'em all.
DESDEMONA (*weeping*): Alas, he is betrayed, and I undone.
OTHELLO: Out, strumpet! Weep'st thou for him to my face?
DESDEMONA: O, banish me, my lord, but kill me not.
OTHELLO (*attacking her*): Down, strumpet.
DESDEMONA: Kill me tomorrow; let me live tonight.
OTHELLO: Nay, an you strive –
DESDEMONA: But half an hour.
OTHELLO: Being done, there is no pause.
DESDEMONA: But while I say one prayer.
OTHELLO: It is too late.

He smothers her

DESDEMONA: O Lord, Lord, Lord!

Emilia at the door

EMILIA (*within*): My lord, my lord, what ho, my lord, my lord!
OTHELLO: What noise is this? Not dead? Not yet quite dead?

I that am cruel am yet merciful.
I would not have thee linger in thy pain.
So, so.

EMILIA (*within*): What ho, my lord, my lord!

OTHELLO: Who's there?

EMILIA (*within*): O, good my lord, I would speak a word with you.

OTHELLO (*calling*): Yes. – 'Tis Emilia. (*calling*) By and by! – She's dead.
'Tis like she comes to speak of Cassio's death.
The noise was high. Ha! No more moving.
Still as the grave. Shall she come in? Were't good?
I think she stirs again. No. What's best to do?
If she come in, she'll sure speak to my wife.
My wife, my wife! What wife? I ha' no wife.
O insupportable, O heavy hour!
Methinks it should be now a huge eclipse
Of sun and moon, and that th'affrighted globe
Should yawn at alteration.

EMILIA (*within*): I do beseech you
That I may speak with you. O, good my lord!

OTHELLO: I had forgot thee. – O, come in, Emilia. –
Soft, by and by. Let me the curtains draw.

He closes the bed-curtains

Where art thou?

He opens the door. Enter Emilia

What's the matter with thee now?

EMILIA: O my good lord, yonder's foul murder's done.

OTHELLO: What, now?

EMILIA: But now, my lord.

OTHELLO: It is the very error of the moon,
She comes more nearer earth than she was wont,
And makes men mad.

EMILIA: Cassio, my lord, hath killed a young Venetian
Called Roderigo.

OTHELLO: Roderigo killed
And Cassio killed?

EMILIA: No, Cassio is not killed.

OTHELLO: Not Cassio killed? Then murder's out of tune,
And sweet revenge grows harsh.

DESDEMONA: O, falsely, falsely murdered!

EMILIA: O Lord, what cry is that?

OTHELLO: That? What?

EMILIA: Out and alas, that was my lady's voice!

She opens the bed-curtains

Help, help, ho, help! O lady, speak again!
Sweet Desdemona, O sweet mistress speak!

DESDEMONA: A guiltless death I die.

EMILIA: O, who hath done this deed?

DESDEMONA: Nobody, I myself. Farewell.
Commend me to my kind lord. O, farewell!

She dies

OTHELLO: Why, how should she be murdered?

EMILIA: Alas, who knows?

OTHELLO: You heard her say herself it was not I.

EMILIA: She said so, I must needs report the truth.

OTHELLO: She's like a liar gone to burning hell.
'Twas I that killed her.

EMILIA: O, the more angel she, and you the blacker devil!

OTHELLO: She turned to folly, and she was a whore.

EMILIA: Thou dost belie her, and thou art a devil.

OTHELLO: She was false as water.

EMILIA: Thou art rash as fire
To say that she was false. O, she was heavenly true!

OTHELLO: Cassio did top her. Ask thy husband else.
O, I were damned beneath all depth in hell
But that I did proceed upon just grounds
To this extremity! Thy husband knew it all.

EMILIA: My husband?

OTHELLO: Thy husband.

EMILIA: That she was false to wedlock?

OTHELLO: Ay, with Cassio. Had she been true,
If heaven would make me such another world
Of one entire and perfect chrysolite
I'd not have sold her for it.

EMILIA: My husband?

OTHELLO: Ay, 'twas he that told me on her first.
An honest man he is, and hates the slime
That sticks on filthy deeds.

EMILIA: My husband?

OTHELLO: What needs this iterance? Woman, I say thy husband.

EMILIA: O mistress, villainy hath made mocks with love.
My husband say she was false?
OTHELLO: He, woman.
I say thy husband. Dost understand the word?
My friend, thy husband, honest, honest Iago.
EMILIA: If he say so, may his pernicious soul
Rot half a grain a day. He lies to th' heart.
She was too fond of her most filthy bargain.
OTHELLO: Ha?
EMILIA: Do thy worst.
This deed of thine is no more worthy heaven
Than thou wast worthy her.
OTHELLO: Peace, you were best.
EMILIA: Thou hast not half that power to do me harm
As I have to be hurt. O gull, O dolt,
As ignorant as dirt! Thou hast done a deed –
I care not for thy sword, I'll make thee known
Though I lost twenty lives. Help, help, ho! Help!
The Moor hath killed my mistress. Murder, murder!

William Shakespeare, *Othello*

Judith

Wondering how a good woman can murder
I enter the tent of Holofernes,
holding in one hand his long oiled hair
and in the other, raised above
his sleeping, wine-flushed face,
his fauchion with its unsheathed
curved blade. And I feel a rush
of tenderness, a longing
to put down my weapon, to lie
sheltered and safe in a warrior's
fumy sweat, under the emerald stars
of his purple and gold canopy,
to melt like a sweet on his tongue
to nothing. And I remember the glare
of the barley field; my husband
pushing away the sponge I pressed

to his burning head; the stubble
puncturing my feet as I ran,
flinging myself on a body
that was already cooling
and stiffening; and the nights
when I lay on the roof – my emptiness
like the emptiness of a temple
with the doors kicked in; and the mornings
when I rolled in the ash of the fire
just to be touched and dirtied
by something. And I bring my blade
down on his neck – and it's easy,
like slicing through fish.
And I bring it down again,
cleaving the bone.

Vicki Feaver, 'Judith'

Juries

The man who rose from behind his desk to receive them was in appearance the opposite of his clerk. He was a stocky, upright man in late middle age, dressed in a shabby but well tailored tweed suit, ruddy-faced and balding, his eyes keen under the spiky, restless eyebrows. He gave Dalgliesh a frankly appraising glance as he shook hands, as if deciding where exactly to place him in some private scheme of things, then nodded as if satisfied. He still looked more like a soldier than a solicitor, and Dalgliesh guessed that the voice with which he greeted them had acquired its loud authoritative bark across the parade-grounds and in the messes of the Second World War.

'Good morning, good morning. Please sit down, Commander. You come on tragic business. I don't think we have ever lost one of our clients by murder before.'

The clerk coughed. It was just such a cough as Dalgliesh would have expected, inoffensive but discreetly minatory and not to be ignored.

'There was Sir James Cummins, sir in 1923. He was shot by his neighbour, Captain Cartwright, because of the seduction of Mrs Cartwright by Sir James, a grievance aggravated by some unpleasantness over fishing rights.'

'Quite right, Mitching. But that was in my father's time. They hanged poor Cartwright. A pity, my father always thought. He had a good war record – survived the Somme and Arras and ended on the scaffold. Battle-scarred, poor devil. The jury would probably have made a recommendation to mercy if he hadn't cut up the body. He did cut up the body, didn't he, Mitching?'

'Quite right, sir. They found the head buried in the orchard.'

'That's what did for Cartwright. English juries won't stand for cutting up the body. Crippen would be alive today if he'd buried Belle Elmore in one piece.'

'Hardly, sir. Crippen was born in 1860.'

'Well he wouldn't have been long dead. It wouldn't surprise me if he'd reached his century. Only three years older than your father, Mitching, and much the same build, small, pop-eyed and wiry. They live for ever, that type.

P. D. James, *Death of an Expert Witness*

Justice

They turned and walked together towards the house. The girl said:

'Are you going to discover who killed Dr Lorrimer?'

'I hope so. I expect so.'

'And then what will happen to him, the murderer, I mean?'

'He'll appear before the magistrates. Then, if they think that the evidence is sufficient, they'll commit him to the Crown Court for trial.'

'And then?'

'If he's found guilty of murder, the judge will pass the statutory penalty, imprisonment for life. That means that he'll be in prison for a long time, perhaps ten years or more.'

'But that's silly. That won't put things right. It won't bring Dr Lorrimer back.'

'It won't put anything right, but it isn't silly. Life is precious to nearly all of us. Even people who have little more than life still want it to the last natural moment. No one has a right to take it away from them.'

'You talk as if life were like William's ball. If that's taken away he knows what he's lost. Dr Lorrimer doesn't know that he's lost anything.'

'He's lost the years he might have had.'

'That's like taking away the ball that William might have had. It doesn't mean anything. It's just words. Suppose he was going to die next week anyway. Then he'd only have lost seven days. You don't put someone in prison for ten years to repay seven lost days. They might not even have been happy days.'

'Even if he were a very old man with one day left to him, the law says that he has a right to live it. Wilful killing would still be murder.'

The girl said thoughtfully:

'I suppose it was different when people believed in God. Then the murdered person might have died in mortal sin and gone to hell. The seven days could have made a difference then. He might have repented and had time for absolution.'

Dalgliesh said:

'All these problems are easier for people who believe in God. Those of us who don't or can't have to do the best we can. That's what the law is, the best we can do. Human justice is imperfect, but it's the only justice we have.'

P. D. James, *Death of an Expert Witness*

Juvenile

These boys, fifteen, sixteen, seventeen, heeding
Not God nor social worker, being young the old therefore
Abjure. Her few pounds and her radio they care for

And steal, but do not care to leave her bleeding,
Nor break her flaky arms, nor black her eyes,
Nor crack with a brick her skull, though this is common.

Into her stair cupboard they scoop the little woman
Where, in her own damp and dark, at length she dies,
Of all deaths surely the most terrible.

What's to be done with such as these our children,
The untaught, the unfit, the unkind, the unnatural?
What right have we to pity or to pardon?

O bury them deep, deep in desolate places.
Stop eyes, ears, mouths with earth. My face is not these faces.
Each day somewhere the same, or worse disgraces.

John Whitworth, 'These Boys'

K

Kali

They began to eat. The Nawab ate seated on a carpet beside a roaring fire sixty feet from William's place. The fire was so big that its leaping flames turned the grove into an amphitheatre of red light. The clean boles of the bijasals stood up like pillars in the circle, red on one side, indigo blue on the other. The sound of crackling branches dominated the encampment. All the travellers ate, and the only voices to be heard were low and unhurried.

When he had finished, William washed the pans in the water, cleaned them with dirt from the stream bed and ashes from the fire, and squatted down as if talking to Hussein, but Hussein only looked at him with large, sad eyes, and moved his lips, but spoke no words.

The slow twang of a zither tinkled under the trees, carrying out to the travellers the tune of a northern love song. The Nawab reclined in a silk robe on his carpet, the pipe of a hookah to his mouth. The old body-servant squatted at his feet. To the right the Nawab's three wives showed as motionless, featureless shapes behind a screen of gold gauze hung between two trees. From every corner of the grove the travellers drifted across the grass toward the music and the light. William rose to his feet and looked at Hussein. Hussein nodded.

By the fire it was very like the scene in the grove near Kahari, where they had watched the murder of the Sikh and his son. Always at night on the road it was the same, because always travellers rested in these groves and lit fires, and sat around them. But there were more people here tonight, and William knew what would come, and feared it, but could not wish it away. He searched his mind and found no desire to warn the Nawab of his fate. He awaited the signal with gnawing eagerness.

It was the Jemadar who played the zither. The crowd thickened about the fire. Before squatting down, each new arrival made low salaam to the Nawab and in the direction of the gold curtain. The Nawab's eyes were half closed, and he nodded his head in time with the music. The Jemadar was singing softly:

Moon of the north, thy hands are lotus blossoms,
Moon of the north, thy lips are rose petals,
Petals stronger than steel,
Petals which touch the steel,
And bend it, and make it weak.
Moon of the north, dark-eyes, shine on me!
Moon of the north . . .

His voice wavered up and down the chromatic scale, sliding from note to note, slithering, holding. The zither twanged and twanged, the fire crackled. The audience relaxed in their places and sighed.

At the end they clapped their hands, beating them together at the wrists with low murmurs of appreciation. The Nawab said thickly, 'Play on! What is your name, haji? Khuda Baksh? A humble jeweller! You are a bulbul, and worthy of a perch by the King's ear at Delhi. Play on, sing on!'

The Jemadar began another song, low and muted in tone and sad.

The bird of the plains sings at dawn.
Who shall hear the lone bird in the morning?
But you, my love . . . ?

He sang a parable of the tragedy of love, despairing and endlessly long. Half the audience dozed off. Others closed their eyes and swayed gently on their heels in rhythms hardly distinguishable to William's ear. The singer sang softer and lower. In time, with the torpor of the song, men moved slowly, like sleepwalkers, about the grove. Two stood entranced behind the Nawab's carpet, three more at the sides of the gold cloth, but not so close that the old servitor would feel it necessary to tell them to keep their distance.

The singer sang so quietly that he could be heard only because there was otherwise utter silence. The fire was quiet. The nasal whine traditional to this music went out of the singer's voice. In the same low key, but in his ordinary speaking tone, he said, '*The stars are shining bright.*'

With the sudden brilliance of lightning the Deceivers struck. Around the fire the cloths flew out, the rumals William had seen consecrated. Men, singly or in pairs, jumped behind their victims. Beside William a small sleepy man leaned forward in a doze; and beyond, the ascetic gentleman who had invited the Nawab into the grove. The gentleman's delicate face froze in murder; he swung a rumal with his right hand. The weighted end, the rupee in it, whirled round the small man's neck into his left hand. The strangler's wrists were turned inward and pressed close together. With a savage explosion of effort he snapped his wrists inward and upward. The small man's head jerked back, a horrible panic mixed with the calm of sleep on his face. The face of the strangler tightened in the firelight, and he drew back his lips and bared his teeth. His wrists cracked with an audible force, his knee drove into the small man's back. A bone snapped, the small man's brown eyes bolted, and he was dead.

Across the fire the Nawab stared with bulging eyeballs into the flames, but he could not see anything, for he was dead. By his feet his servant writhed and heaved in colossal throes that threatened to upset Piroo, the strangler across his back. A knife flashed and blood spouted from Piroo's thigh, staining his loincloth and pouring down over the old servant's neck. The Jemadar called urgently, 'Wait! Hold him!' Stooping down he drove a dagger into the old man's side between the ribs.

The gold curtain heaved and bulged. The three men who had been standing beside it were gone from sight. Except for the Jemadar's cry there had been no sound. William squatted in his place, cold, turned to stone.

The Jemadar came across to him. 'You look amazed, Gopal.' He wiped his dagger on a leaf, dropped the leaf carefully in the fire, and clapped William's shoulder. 'It wasn't so neatly done as it should have been. Quick, to the grave!'

He snapped his fingers at the stranglers, who stood in groups around the fire with exultant, sweaty faces. In pairs and threes they lifted up the corpses and staggered with them across the grove and through the jungle to the clearing where the afternoon's ceremony had been held.

Piroo led the way with a hand lantern, limping slightly from his wound; already he had bound it up so that neither the wound nor the bandage showed beneath his loincloth. He walked across the clearing, under the solitary neem, past the abandoned idol, and stopped at the far bushes. He held up the lamp while the others pushed past him, groaning with suppressed pride at the weight of their loads, and forced through the thorns. In a few seconds the Jemadar stopped under a dense clump of prickly bamboo. William, close on his heels, saw that a circular pit surrounded the bamboo's multiple stems. The bamboo stood on a little island of earth, its murderous spines leaning out over the pit. The earth fill lay round the rim of the pit, and on the earth there were three sharpened bamboo stakes, a thick log, and a short rough-hewn club.

Piroo hurried up and set down the lantern. The men laid the bodies on the ground. Piroo and five others undressed down to the string about their loins and put their clothes carefully on one side. Then the six of them, working in pairs without a word spoken, began to break the victims' joints at knee and elbow. They laid each body over the log and with the club smashed the joints. When that was done they dragged the body to one side, picked up a stake, lifted together and drove it through and through the corpse's belly. They they lowered them one by one into the grave.

Stiff-jawed, William stared down at the disarray of the women's clothing; their wide eyes held the same mixed expressions that he had seen in the small man killed next to him. In each pasty brown face panic and disbelief mingled with the woman's last previous emotion. The rapt pleasure at the jeweller's song of love lingered on.

The pit filled and became a welter of bloody cloth, bursting entrails, and staring eyes. The flame of the lamp jumped as the Deceivers moved past it, each time lending the mangled pieces another jerky moment of life. William held to a tree for support and strained to keep down the vomit in his throat. Hussein, crouching the other side of the pit under the bamboo spines, watched him.

A party of stranglers returned to the encampment and came back with the belongings of the dead – the saddlebags and blankets and cooking pots, the Nawab's silk tent and carpet, the women's beautiful curtain, anything that was not worth taking or that might arouse inquiry. All went into the pit.

The Jemadar said, 'Finished? And ten bodies? That's all, isn't it?'

'Yes.'

The Jemadar gave a sign. Piroo threw the stakes, the club, and the log into the pit. Other men worked with their hands to push back the earth fill, covering the bodies and raising a low circular mound around the bamboo. Bending under the spines they stamped down the earth, then smoothed it and spread leaves and grass over it. When all was done they rubbed their hands on the ground, carefully picked up their clothes, and stood waiting.

The Jemadar said, 'O diggers, come forward.'

More men struggled through the bushes at the side, men William had never seen. The Jemadar said to one of them, 'It was well done. Difficult digging here under the bamboo, but an excellent place. We didn't hear a sound. When did you begin?'

'As soon as your prayers were finished, Jemadar-sahib.'

The Jemadar repeated, 'It was well done. We will check here in daylight, as usual. Move on now to Manikwal. Meet us there. I think – I am sure – that this merits a feast.

• • •

The Jemadar picked up the lamp and walked back to the grove; the band followed in a single file behind him. William walked among them, thinking. Hussein had told him earlier what would be done, and that it was at Kali's command. Why? Hussein did not know. Who could read the mind of the Destroyer-Goddess? But William saw that a broken body took less space than a whole one; that a ripped belly released the gases of decomposition to filter up through the earth, while a whole belly swelled and at last forced up the soil, and caused wandering dogs and jackals to scratch and dig and run away, carrying a woman's arm for all to see. Hussein said that Kali commanded the Deceivers to scatter the seeds of fleawort over the grave, as a sacrifice, but William knew no jackal would sniff twice where those peppery seeds stung his nostrils.

Back by the remains of the great fire the Jemadar turned and raised his arms. 'It is well enough done! Has Geb Khan's party come back yet?'

'No,' Yasin answered. 'I do not think we shall see them until morning. It depends when they found a chance with that fellow, the dealer in rats' droppings.' He laughed quietly. 'Our little Nawab had a sort of sulky wit.'

William realized they were talking about the man who had wanted to go on to the village. The three who had accompanied him were all Deceivers. That man would not reach the village. He, at least, would never report that a large party, including the Nawab-sahib of Dukwan, was coming up the road and might be momentarily expected. The goddess Kali gave her children a long sight as well as a strong hand.

John Masters, *The Deceivers*

Knife

Some vegetables
resist more vigorously
than others.

To vary things
she plays at cutting
herringbones and ovals,

teasing the skin
with her point before
penetrating the heart,

pictures a fingertip
nestling among peelings
on the spattered board,

and for the luxury
of granting him
a reprieve perhaps

imagines stepping
to where her husband sits
absorbed

and steering the knife
quite casually
into his side,

curious to see
his look of surprise, feel
how smoothly a blade can slide.

Ruth Sharman, 'Knife'

Hang everything! Mr Verloc reposed characteristically, clad in his outdoor garments. One side of his open overcoat was lying partly on the ground. Mr Verloc wallowed on his back. But he longed for a more perfect rest – for sleep – for a few hours of delicious forgetfulness. That would come later. Provisionally he rested. And he thought: 'I wish she would give over this damned nonsense. It's exasperating.'

There must have been something imperfect in Mrs Verloc's sentiment of regained freedom. Instead of taking the way of the door she leaned back, with her shoulders against the tablet of the mantelpiece, as a wayfarer rests against a fence. A tinge of wildness in her aspect was derived from the black veil hanging like a rag against her cheek, and from the fixity of her black gaze where the light of the room was absorbed and lost without the trace of a single gleam. This woman, capable of a bargain the mere suspicion of which would have been infinitely shocking to Mr Verloc's idea of love, remained irresolute, as if scrupulously aware of something wanting on her part for the formal closing of the transaction.

On the sofa Mr Verloc wriggled his shoulders into perfect comfort, and from the fullness of his heart emitted a wish which was certainly as pious as anything likely to come from such a source.

'I wish to goodness,' he growled, huskily, 'I had never seen Greenwich Park or anything belonging to it.'

The veiled sound filled the small room with its moderate volume, well adapted to the modest nature of the wish. The waves of air of the proper length, propagated in accordance with correct mathematical formulas, flowed around all the inanimate things in the room, lapped against Mrs Verloc's head as if it had been a head of stone. And incredible as it may appear, the eyes of Mrs Verloc seemed to grow still larger. The audible wish of Mr Verloc's overflowing heart flowed into an empty place in his wife's memory. Greenwich Park. A park! That's where the boy was killed. A park – smashed branches, torn leaves, gravel, bits of brotherly flesh and bone, all spouting up together in the manner of a firework. She remembered now what she had heard, and she remembered it pictorially. They had to gather him up with the shovel. Trembling all over with irrepressible shudders, she saw before her the very implement with its ghastly load scraped up from the ground. Mrs Verloc closed her eyes desperately, throwing upon that vision the night of her eyelids, where after a rainlike fall of mangled limbs the decapitated head of Stevie lingered suspended alone, and fading out slowly like the last star of a pyrotechnic display. Mrs Verloc opened her eyes.

Her face was no longer stony. Anybody could have noted the subtle change on her features, in the stare of her eyes, giving her a new and startling expression; an expression seldom observed by competent persons under the conditions of leisure and security demanded for thorough analysis, but whose meaning could not be mistaken at a glance. Mrs Verloc's doubts as to the end of the bargain no longer existed; her wits no longer disconnected, were working under the control of her will. But Mr Verloc observed nothing. He was reposing in that pathetic condition of optimism induced by excess of fatigue. He did not want any more trouble – with his wife, too – of all people in the world. He had been unanswerable in his vindication. He was loved for himself. The present phase of her silence he interpreted favourably. This was the time to make it up with her. The silence had lasted long enough. He broke it by calling to her in an undertone:

'Winnie.'

'Yes,' answered obediently Mrs Verloc the free woman. She commanded her wits now, her vocal organs; she felt herself to be in an almost preternaturally perfect control of every fibre of her body. It was all her own, because the bargain was at an end. She was clear sighted. She had become cunning. She chose to answer him so readily for a purpose. She did not wish that man to change his position on the sofa which was very suitable to the circumstances. She succeeded. The man did not stir. But after answering him she remained leaning negligently against the mantelpiece in the attitude of a resting wayfarer. She was unhurried. Her brow was smooth. The head and shoulders of Mr Verloc were hidden from her by the high side of the sofa. She kept her eyes fixed on his feet.

She remained thus mysteriously still and suddenly collected till Mr Verloc was heard with an accent of marital authority, and moving slightly to make room for her to sit on the edge of the sofa.

'Come here,' he said in a peculiar tone, which might have been the tone of brutality, but was intimately known to Mrs Verloc as the note of wooing.

She started forward at once, as if she were still a loyal woman bound to that man by an unbroken contract. Her right hand skimmed slightly at the end of the table, and when she had passed on towards the sofa the carving knife had vanished without the slightest sound from the side of the dish. Mr Verloc heard the creaky plank in the floor, and was content. He waited. Mrs Verloc was coming. As if the homeless soul of Stevie had flown for shelter straight to the breast of his sister, guardian and protector, the resemblance of her face with that of her brother grew at every step, even to the droop of the lower lip, even to the slight divergence of the eyes. But Mr Verloc did not see that. He was lying on his back and staring upwards. He saw partly on the ceiling and partly on the wall the moving shadow of an arm with a clenched hand holding a carving knife. It flickered up and down. Its movements were leisurely. They were leisurely enough for Mr Verloc to recognize the limb and the weapon.

They were leisurely enough for him to take in the full meaning of the portent, and to taste the flavour of death rising in his gorge. His wife had gone raving mad – murdering mad. They were leisurely enough for the first paralysing effect of this discovery to pass away before a resolute determination to come out victorious from the ghastly struggle with that armed lunatic. They were leisurely enough for Mr Verloc to elaborate a plan of defence, involving a dash behind the table, and the felling of the woman to the ground with a heavy wooden chair. But they were not leisurely enough to allow Mr Verloc the time to move either hand or foot. The knife was already planted in his breast. It met no resistance on its way. Hazard has such accuracies. Into that plunging blow, delivered over the side of the couch, Mrs Verloc had put all the inheritance of her immemorial and obscure descent, the simple ferocity of the age of caverns, and the unbalanced nervous fury of the age of bar-rooms. Mr Verloc, the secret agent, turning slightly on his side with the force of the blow, expired without stirring a limb, in the muttered sound of the word 'Don't' by way of protest.

Mrs Verloc had let go the knife, and her extraordinary resemblance to her late brother had faded, had become very ordinary now. She drew a deep breath, the first easy breath since Chief Inspector Heat had exhibited to her the labelled piece of Stevie's overcoat. She leaned forward on her folded arms over the side of the sofa. She adopted that easy attitude not in order to watch or gloat over the body of Mr Verloc, but because of the undulatory and swinging movements of the parlour, which for some time behaved as though it were at sea in a tempest. She was giddy but calm. She had become a free woman with a perfection of freedom which left her nothing to desire and absolutely nothing to do, since Stevie's urgent claim on her devotion no longer existed. Mrs Verloc, who thought in images, was not troubled now by visions, because she did not think at all. And she did not move. She was a woman enjoying her complete irresponsibility and endless leisure, almost in the manner of a corpse. She did not move, she did not think. Neither did the mortal envelope of the late Mr Verloc reposing on the sofa. Except for the fact that Mrs Verloc breathed these two would have been perfectly in accord: that accord of prudent reserve without superfluous words, and sparing of signs, which had been the foundation of their respectable home life. For it had been respectable, covering by a decent reticence the problems that may arise in the practice of a secret profession and the commerce of shady wares. To the last its decorum had remained undisturbed by unseemly shrieks and other misplaced sincerities of conduct. And after the striking of the blow, this respectability was continued in immobility and silence.

Nothing moved in the parlour till Mrs Verloc raised her head slowly and looked at the clock with inquiring mistrust. She had become aware of a ticking sound in the room. It grew upon her ear, while she remembered clearly that the clock on the wall was silent, had no audible tick. What did it mean by beginning to tick so loudly all of a sudden? Its face indicated ten minutes to nine. Mrs Verloc cared nothing for time, and the ticking went on. She concluded it could not be the clock, and her sullen gaze moved along the walls, wavered, and became vague, while she strained her hearing to locate the sound. Tic, tic, tic.

After listening for some time Mrs Verloc lowered her gaze deliberately on her husband's body. Its attitude of repose was so homelike and familiar that she could do so without feeling embarrassed by any pronounced novelty in the phenomena of her home life. Mr Verloc was taking his habitual ease. He looked comfortable.

By the position of the body the face of Mr Verloc was not visible to Mrs Verloc, his widow. Her fine, sleepy eyes, travelling downward on the track of the sound, became contemplative on meeting a flat object of bone which protruded a little beyond the edge of the sofa. It was the handle of the domestic carving knife with nothing strange about it but its position at right angles to Mr Verloc's waistcoat and the fact that something dripped from it. Dark drops fell on the floorcloth one after another, with a sound of ticking growing fast and furious like the pulse of an insane clock. At its highest speed this ticking changed into a continuous sound of trickling. Mrs Verloc watched that transformation with shadows of anxiety coming and going on her face. It was a trickle, dark, swift, thin. . . . Blood!

At this unforeseen circumstance Mrs Verloc abandoned her pose of idleness and irresponsibility.

With a sudden snatch at her skirts and a faint shriek she ran to the door, as if the trickle had been the first sign of a destroying flood. Finding the table in her way she gave it a push with both hands as though it had been alive, with such force that it went for some distance on its four legs, making a loud, scraping racket, whilst the big dish with the joint crashed heavily on the floor.

Then all became still. Mrs Verloc on reaching the door had stopped. A round hat disclosed in the middle of the floor by the moving of the table rocked slightly on its crown in the wind of her flight.

Joseph Conrad, *The Secret Agent*

Knight

A false knight wooed a maiden poor
& his high halls left he
To stoop in at her cottage door
When night left none to see

& welladay it is a tale
For pity too severe
A tale would melt the sternest eye
& wake the deafest ear

He stole her heart he stole her love
Twas all the wealth she had
Her truth & fame likewise stole he
& eke her maiden head

& he gave gold & promised more
That she his name should bear
That she should share his love for aye
& live his lady fair

But he never meant a maid so low
Should wear his haughty name
& much he feared his guilty love
Would work him mickle shame

So underneath the mask of love
He went to work her woe
& he did name the bridal day
& she prepared to go

He brought her silks unseen to wear
& a milk white steed to ride
& not a word was to be known
Till she was made a bride

He brought for her a milk white steed
& for himself a grey
& they are off none knoweth where
Three hours before the day

& as they rode she wished him speke
& not a word spoke he
You were not wont loved knight she said
To be this cold to me

& they rode on & they rode on
Far on this pair did ride
Till the maidens heart with fear & love
Beat quick against her side

& on they rode till rocks grew high
Sir knight what have we here
Unsaddle maid for here we stop
& deaths tongue smote her ear

Some ruffian rude she took him now
& wished she'd barred the door
Nor was it one that she could read
Of having heard before

Thou art not my true love she said
But some rude robber lown
Hed take me from the saddle bow
Nor leave me to get down

I neer was your true love said he
For Im more bold than true
Thou Im the knight that came at dark
To kiss & toy with you

I know youre not my love said she
That came at night & wooed
Although ye try to mock his speech
His ways was neer so rude

He neer said word but called me dear
& dear he is to me
Ye speke as ye neer knew the word
Rude ruffian as ye be

Ye never was my knight I trow
Ye pay me no regard
& he would take my arm in his
If we but went a yard

No matter whos truelove I am
Im more than true to you
For Ill neer wed a shepherd wench
Although I came to woo

& on to the rocks top they walked
Till they stood oer the salt seas brim
& there said he's your bridal bed
Where you may sink or swim

A moonbeam shone upon his face
The maid sank at his feet
For twas her own false love she saw
That once so fond did greet

& did ye promise love for this
Is the grave my priest to be
& did ye bring this silken dress
To wed me with the sea

O never mind your dress quoth he
Tis well to dress for sea
Mermaids will love to see you fine
Your bridemaids they will be

O let me cast this gown away
Its brought no good to me
& if my mother greets my clay
Tis wretched will she be

For she for my sad sake would keep
This guilty bridal dress
To break & tell her bursting heart
She had a daughter less

So off she threw her bridal gown
Likewise her gold clasped shoon
His looks frowned hard as any stone
Hers pale turned as the moon

O false false knight you've wrapt me warm
Ere I was cold before
& now you strip me unto death
Although Im out of door

O dash away those thistles rude
That crowd about the shore
Theyll wound my tender feet that neer
Went barefoot thus before

O dash those stinging nettles down
& cut away the briar
For deep they wound those lily arms
Which you did once admire

& he nor briars nor thistles cut
Allthough she grieved full sore
& he nor shed one single tear
Nor kiss took evermore

She shriekd & sank & is at rest
All in the deep deep sea
& home in base & scornful pride
With haunted heart rode he

Now oer that rock there hangs a tree
& chains doth creak thereon
& in those chains his memory hangs
Though all beside is gone

Anon., 'The False Knights Tragedy',
collected by John Clare

L

Locked Room

'H'mf! Ha! Now, here is your box with one door, one window, and solid walls. In discussing ways of escaping when both door and window are sealed, I shall not mention the low (and nowadays very rare) trick of having a secret passage to a locked room. This so puts a story beyond the pale that a self-respecting author scarcely needs even to mention that there is no such thing. We don't need to discuss minor variations of this outrage: the panel which is only large enough to admit a hand; or the plugged hole in the ceiling through which a knife is dropped, the plug replaced undetectably, and the floor of the attic above sprayed with dust so that no one seems to have walked there. This is only the same foul in miniature. The principle remains the same whether the secret opening is as small as a thimble or as big as a barn door . . . As to legitimate classification, you might jot some of these down, Mr Pettis . . .'

'Right,' said Pettis, who was grinning. 'Go on.'

'First! There is a crime committed in a hermetically sealed room which really is hermetically sealed, and from which no murderer has escaped because no murderer was actually in the room. Explanations:

'(1) It is not murder, but a series of coincidences ending in an accident which looks like murder. At an earlier time, before the room was locked, there has been a robbery, an attack, a wound, or a breaking of furniture which suggests a murder struggle. Later the victim is either accidentally killed or stunned in a locked room, and all these incidents are assumed to have taken place at the same time. In this case the means of death is usually a crack on the head – presumably by a bludgeon, but really from some piece of furniture. It may be from the corner of a table or the sharp edge of a chair, but the most popular object is an iron fender. The murderous fender, by the way, has been killing people in a way that looks like murder ever since Sherlock Holmes's adventure with the Crooked Man. The most thoroughly satisfying solution of this type of plot, which includes a murderer, is in Gaston Leroux's *The Mystery of the Yellow Room* – the best detective tale ever written.

'(2) It is murder, but the victim is impelled to kill himself or crash into an accidental death. This may be by the effect of a haunted room, by suggestion, or more usually by a gas introduced from outside the room. This gas or poison makes the victim go berserk, smash up the room as though there had been a struggle, and die of a knife-slash inflicted on himself. In other variations he drives the spike of the chandelier through his head, is hanged on a loop of wire, or even strangles himself with his own hands.

'(3) It is murder, by a mechanical device already planted in the room, and hidden undetectably in some innocent-looking piece of furniture. It may be a trap set by somebody long dead, and work either automatically or be set anew by the modern killer. It may be some fresh quirk of devilry from present-day science. We have, for instance, the gun-mechanism concealed in the telephone receiver, which fires a bullet into the victim's head as he lifts the receiver. We have the pistol with a string to the trigger, which is pulled by the expansion of water as it freezes. We have the clock that fires a bullet when you wind it; and (clocks being popular) we have the ingenious grandfather clock which sets ringing a hideously clanging bell on its top, so that when you reach up to shut off the din your own touch releases a blade that slashes open your stomach. We have the weight that swings down from the ceiling, and the weight that crashes out on your skull from the high back of a chair. There is the bed that exhales a deadly gas when your body warms it, the poisoned needle that leaves no trace, the –

'You see,' said Dr Fell, stabbing out with his cigar at each point, 'when we become involved with these mechanical devices we are rather in the sphere of the general "impossible situation" than the narrower one of the locked room. It would be possible to go on for ever, even on mechanical devices for electrocuting people. A cord in front of a row of pictures is electrified. A chess-board is electrified. Even a glove is electrified. There is death in every article of furniture, including a tea-urn. But these things seem to have no present application, so we go on to:

'(4) It is suicide, which is intended to look like murder. A man stabs himself with an icicle; the icicle melts; and, no weapon being found in the locked room, murder is presumed. A man shoots himself with a gun fastened on the end of an elastic – the gun, as he releases it, being carried up out of sight, into the chimney. Variations of this trick (not locked-room affairs) have been the pistol with a string attached to a weight, which is whisked over the parapet of a bridge into the water after the shot; and, in the same style, the pistol jerked out of a window into a snow-drift.

'(5) It is a murder which derives its problem from illusion and impersonation. Thus: the victim, still thought to be alive, is already lying murdered inside a room, of which the door is under observation. The murderer, either dressed as his victim or mistaken from behind for the victim, hurries in at the door. He whirls round, gets rid of his disguise, and instantly comes out of the room *as himself*. The illusion is that he has merely passed the other man in coming out. In any event, he has an alibi; since, when the body is discovered later, the murder is presumed to have taken place some time after the impersonated "victim" entered the room.

'(6) It is a murder which, although committed by somebody outside the room at the time, nevertheless seems to have been committed by somebody who must have been inside.

'In explaining this,' said Dr Fell, breaking off, 'I will classify this type of murder under the general name of the Long-Distance or Icicle Crime, since it is usually a variation of that principle. I've spoken of icicles; you understand what I mean. The door is locked, the window too small to admit a murderer; yet the victim has apparently been stabbed from inside the room and the weapon is missing. Well, the icicle has been fired as a bullet from outside – we will not discuss whether this is practical, any more than we have discussed the mysterious gases previously mentioned – and it melts without a trace.

• • •

'To continue with regard to the icicle: its actual use has been attributed to the Medici, and in one of the admirable Fleming Stone stories an epigram of Martial is quoted to show that it had its deadly origin in Rome in the first century AD. Variants of the same theme, a soluble missile, have been rock-salt bullets and even bullets made of frozen blood.

'But it illustrates what I mean in crimes committed inside a room by somebody who was outside. There are other methods. The victim may be stabbed by a thin sword-stick blade, passed between the twinings of a summer-house and withdrawn; or he may be stabbed with a blade so thin that he does not know he is hurt at all, and walks into another room before he suddenly collapses in death. Or he is lured into looking out of a window inaccessible from below; yet from above our old friend ice smashes down on his head, leaving him with a smashed skull but no weapon because the weapon has melted.

'Under this heading (although it might equally well go under head number 3) we might list murders committed by means of poisonous snakes or insects. Snakes can be concealed not only in chests and safes, but also deftly hidden in flower-pots, books, chandeliers, and walking-sticks. I even remember one cheerful little item in which the amber stem of a pipe, grotesquely carven as a scorpion, comes to life a real scorpion as the victim is about to put it into his mouth. But for the greatest long-range murder ever committed in a locked room, gents, I commend you to one of the most brilliant short detective stories in the history of detective fiction (In fact, it shares the honours for supreme untouchable top-notch excellence with Thomas Burke's *The Hands of Mr Ottermole*, Chesterton's *The Man in the Passage*, and Jacques Futrelle's *The Problem of Cell 13*.) This is Melville Davisson Post's, *The Doomdorf Mystery* – and the long-range assassin is the sun. The sun strikes through the window of the locked room, makes a burning-glass of a bottle of Doomdorf's own raw white wood-alcohol liquor on the table, and ignites through it the percussion cap of a gun hanging on the wall: so that the breast of the hated one is blown open as he lies in his bed. Then, again, we have –

'Steady! Harrumph. Ha. I'd better not meander; I'll round off this classification with the final heading:

'(7) This is a murder depending on an effect exactly the reverse of number 5. That is, the victim is presumed to be dead long before he actually is. The victim lies asleep (drugged but unharmed) in a locked room. Knockings on the door fail to rouse him. The murderer starts a foul-play scare; forces the door; gets in ahead and kills by stabbing or throat-cutting, while suggesting to other watchers that they have seen something they have not seen. The honour of inventing this device belongs to Israel Zangwill, and it has since been used in many forms. It has been done (usually by stabbing) on a ship, in a ruined house, in a conservatory, in an attic, and even in the open air – where the victim has first stumbled and stunned himself before the assassin bends over him.

• • •

'Chimneys, I regret to say,' Dr Fell pursued, his gusto returning as his abstraction left him, 'chimneys, I regret to say, are not favoured as a means of escape in detective fiction – except, of course, for secret passages. There they are supreme. There is the hollow chimney with the secret room behind; the back of the fire-place opening like a curtain; the fire-place that swings out; even the room under the hearthstone. Moreover, all kinds of things can be dropped *down* chimneys, chiefly poisonous things. But the murderer who makes his escape by climbing up is very rare. Besides being next to impossible, it is a much grimier business than monkeying with doors or windows. Of the two chief classifications, doors and windows, the door is by far the more popular, and we may list thus a few means of tampering with it so that it seems to be locked on the inside:

'(1) Tampering with the key which is still in the lock. This was the favourite old-fashioned method, but its variations are too well known nowadays for anybody to use it seriously. The stem of the key can be gripped and turned with pliers from outside; we did this ourselves to *open* the door of Grimaud's study. One practical little mechanism consists of a thin metal bar about two inches long, to which is attached a length of stout string. Before leaving the room, this bar is thrust into the hole at the head of the key, one end under and one end over, so that it acts as a lever; the string is dropped down and run under the door to the outside. The door is closed from outside. You have only to pull on the string, and the lever turns the lock; you then shake or pull out the loose bar by means of the string, and, when it drops, draw it under the door to you. There are various applications of this same principle, all entailing the use of string.

'(2) Simply removing the hinges of the door without disturbing lock or bolt. This is a neat trick, known to most schoolboys when they want to burgle a locked cupboard; but of course the hinges must be on the outside of the door.

'(3) Tampering with the bolt. String again: this time with a mechanism of pins and darning-needles, by which the bolt is shot from the outside by leverage of a pin stuck on the inside of the door, and the string is worked through the keyhole. Philo Vance, to whom my hat is lifted, has shown us this best application of the stunt. There are simpler, but not so effective, variations, using one piece of string. A "tomfool" knot, which a sharp jerk will straighten out, is looped in one end of a long piece of cord. This loop is passed round the knob of the bolt, down, and under the door. The door is then closed, and, by drawing the string along to the left or right, the bolt is shot. A jerk releases the knot from the knob, and the string drawn out. Ellery Queen has shown us still another method, entailing the use of the dead man himself – but a bald statement of this, taken out of its context, would sound so wild as to be unfair to that brilliant gentleman.

'(4) Tampering with a falling bar or latch. This usually consists in propping something under the latch, which can be pulled away after the door is closed from the outside, and let the bar drop. The best method by far is by the use of the ever-helpful ice, a cube of which is propped under the latch; and, when it melts, the latch falls. There is one case in which the mere slam of the door suffices to drop the bar inside.

'(5) An illusion, simple but effective. The murderer, after committing his crime, has locked the door from the outside and kept the key. It is assumed, however, that the key is still in the lock on the inside. The murderer, who is first to raise a scare and find the body, smashes the upper glass panel of the door, puts his hand through with the key concealed in it, and finds the key in the lock inside, by which he opens the door. This device has also been used with the breaking of a panel out of an ordinary wooden door.'

John Dickson Carr, *The Hollow Man*

Lodger

The household consisted of the following five persons: 1. Mr Williamson, its head, who was an old man above seventy, and was well fitted for his situation, being civil, and not at all morose, but, at the same time, firm in maintaining order; 2. Mrs Williamson, his wife, about ten years younger than himself; 3. a little granddaughter, about nine years old; 4. a housemaid, who was nearly forty years old; 5. a young journeyman, aged about twenty-six, belonging to some manufacturing establishment (of what class I have forgotten); neither do I remember of what nation he was. It was the established rule at Mr Williamson's, that, exactly as the clock struck eleven, all the company, without favour or exception, moved off. That was one of the customs by which, in so stormy a district, Mr Williamson had found it possible to keep his house free from brawls. On the present Thursday night everything had gone on as usual, except for one slight shadow of suspicion, which had caught the attention of more persons than one. Perhaps at a less agitating time it would hardly have been noticed; but now, when the first question and the last in all social meetings turned upon the Marrs, and their unknown murderer, it was a circumstance naturally fitted to cause some uneasiness, that a stranger, of sinister appearance, in a wide surtout, had flitted in and out of the room at intervals during the evening; had sometimes retired from the light into obscure corners; and, by more than one person, had been observed stealing into the private passages of the house. It was presumed in general that the man must be known to Williamson. And, in some slight degree, as an occasional customer of the house, it is not impossible that he *was*. But afterwards, this repulsive stranger, with his cadaverous ghastliness, extraordinary hair, and glazed eyes, showing himself intermittingly through the hours from 8 to 11 p.m., revolved upon the memory of all who had steadily observed him with something of the same freezing effect as belongs to the two assassins in *Macbeth*, who present themselves reeking from the murder of Banquo, and gleaming dimly, with dreadful faces, from the misty background, athwart the pomps of the regal banquet.

Meantime the clock struck eleven; the company broke up; the door of entrance was nearly closed; and at this moment of general dispersion the situation of the five inmates left upon the premises was precisely this: the three elders, viz., Williamson, his wife, and his female servant, were all occupied on the ground floor – Williamson himself was drawing ale, porter, etc., for those neighbours in whose favour the house-door had been left ajar, until the hour of twelve should strike; Mrs Williamson and her servant were moving to and fro between the back kitchen and the little parlour; the little granddaughter, whose sleeping-room was on the *first* floor (which term in London means always the floor raised by one flight of stairs above the level of the street), had been fast asleep since nine o'clock; lastly, the journeyman artisan had retired to rest for some time. He was a regular lodger in the house; and his bedroom was on the second floor. For some time he had been undressed, and had lain down in bed. Being, as a working man, bound to habits of early rising, he was naturally anxious to fall asleep as soon as possible. But, on this particular night, his uneasiness, arising from the recent murders at no. 29, rose to a paroxysm of nervous excitement which kept him awake. It is possible, that from somebody he had heard of the suspicious-looking stranger, or might even personally have observed him slinking about. But, were it otherwise, he was aware of several circumstances dangerously affecting this house; for instance, the ruffianism of this whole neighbourhood, and the disagreeable fact that the Marrs had lived within a few doors of this very house, which again argued that the murderer also lived at no great distance. These were matters of *general* alarm. But there were others peculiar to this house; in particular, the notoriety of Williamson's opulence; the belief, whether well or ill-founded, that he accumulated, in desks and drawers, the money continually flowing into his hands; and lastly, the danger so ostentatiously courted by that habit of leaving the house-door ajar through one entire hour – and that hour loaded with extra danger, by the well-advertised assurance that no collision need be feared with chance convivial visitors, since all such people were banished at eleven. A regulation, which had hitherto operated beneficially for the character and comfort of the house, now, on the contrary, under altered circumstances, became a positive proclamation of exposure and defencelessness, through one entire period of an hour. Williamson himself, it was said generally, being a large unwieldy man, past seventy, and signally inactive, ought, in prudence, to make the locking of his door coincident with the dismissal of his evening party.

Upon these and other grounds of alarm (particularly this, that Mrs Williamson was reported to possess a considerable quantity of plate), the journeyman was musing painfully, and the time might be within twenty-eight or twenty-five minutes of twelve, when all at once, with a crash, proclaiming some hand of hideous violence, the house door was suddenly shut and locked. Here, then, beyond all doubt, was the diabolic man, clothed in mystery, from no. 29 Ratcliffe Highway. Yes, that dreadful being, who for twelve days had employed all thoughts and all tongues, was now, too certainly, in this defenceless house, and would, in a few minutes, be face to face with every one of its inmates. A question still lingered in the public mind – whether at Marr's there might not have been *two* men at work. If so, there would be two at present; and one of the two would be immediately disposable for the upstairs work; since no danger could obviously be more immediately fatal to such an attack than any alarm given from an upper window to the passengers in the street. Through one half-minute the poor panic-stricken man sat up motionless in bed. But then he rose, his first movement being towards the door of his room. Not for any purpose of securing it against intrusion – too well he knew that there was no fastening of any sort – neither lock, nor bolt; nor was there any such moveable furniture in the room as might have availed to barricade the door, even if time could be counted on for such an attempt. It was no effect of prudence, merely the fascination of killing fear it was, that drove him to open the door. One step brought him to the head of the stairs; he lowered his head over the balustrade in order to listen; and at that moment ascended from the little parlour, this agonizing cry from the woman-servant, 'Lord Jesus Christ! we shall all be murdered!' What a Medusa's head must have lurked in those dreadful bloodless features, and those glazed rigid eyes, that seemed rightfully belonging to a corpse, when one glance at them sufficed to proclaim a death-warrant.

Three separate death-struggles were by this time over; and the poor petrified journeyman, quite unconscious of what he was doing, in blind, passive, self-surrender to panic, absolutely descended both flights of stairs. Infinite terror inspired him with the same impulse as might have been inspired by headlong courage. In his shirt, and upon old decaying stairs, that at times creaked under his feet, he continued to descend, until he had reached the lowest step but four. The situation was tremendous beyond any that is on record. A sneeze, a cough, almost a breathing, and the young man would be a corpse, without a chance or a struggle for his life. The murderer was at that time in the little parlour – the door of which parlour faced you in descending the stairs; and this door stood ajar; indeed, much more considerably open than what is understood by the term 'ajar'. Of that quadrant, or 90 degrees, which the door would describe in swinging so far open as to stand at right angles to the lobby, or to itself, in a closed position, 55 degrees at the least were exposed. Consequently, two out of three corpses were exposed to the young man's gaze. Where was the third? And the murderer – where was he? As to the murderer, he was walking rapidly backwards and forwards in the parlour, audible but not visible at first, being engaged with something or other in that part of the room which the door still concealed. What the something might be, the sound soon explained; he was applying keys tentatively to a cupboard, a closet, and a scrutoire, in the hidden part of the room. Very soon, however, he came into view; but, fortunately for the young man, at this critical moment, the murderer's purpose too entirely absorbed him to allow of his throwing a glance to the staircase, on which else the white figure of the journeyman, standing in motionless horror, would have been detected in one instant, and seasoned for the grave in the second. As to the third corpse, the missing corpse, viz., Mr Williamson's, *that* is in the cellar; and how its local position can be accounted for, remains as a separate question much discussed at the time, but never satisfactorily cleared up. Meantime, that Williamson was dead, became evident to the young man; since else he would have been heard stirring or groaning. Three friends, therefore, out of four, whom the young man had parted with forty minutes ago, were now extinguished; remained, therefore, 40 per cent (a large percentage for Williams to leave); remained, in fact, himself and his pretty young friend, the little granddaughter, whose childish innocence was still slumbering without fear for herself, or grief for her aged grandparents. If *they* are gone for ever, happily one friend (for such he will prove himself, indeed, if from such a danger he can save this child) is pretty near to her. But alas! he is still nearer to a murderer. At this moment he is unnerved for any exertion whatever; he has changed into a pillar of ice; for the objects before him, separated by just thirteen feet, are these: The housemaid had been caught by the murderer on her knees; she was kneeling before the fire-grate, which she had been polishing with black lead. That part of her task was finished; and she had passed on to another task, viz., the filling of the grate with wood and coals, not for kindling at this moment, but so as to have it ready for kindling on the next day. The appearances all showed that she must have been engaged in this labour at the very moment when the murderer entered; and perhaps the succession of the incidents arranged itself as follows: From the awful ejaculation and loud outcry to Christ, as overheard by the journeyman, it was clear that then first she had been alarmed; yet this was at least one and a-half or even two minutes after the door-slamming. Consequently the alarm which had so fearfully and seasonably alarmed the young man, must, in some unaccountable way, have been misinterpreted by the two women. It was said, at the time, that Mrs Williamson laboured under some dulness of hearing; and it was conjectured that the servant, having her ears filled with the noise of her own scrubbing, and her head half under the grate, might have confounded it with the street noises, or else might have imputed this violent closure to some mischievous boys. But, howsoever explained, the fact was evident, that, until the words of appeal to Christ, the servant had noticed nothing suspicious, nothing which interrupted her labours. If so, it followed that neither had Mrs Williamson noticed anything; for, in that case, she would have communicated her own alarm to the servant, since both were in the same small room. Apparently the course of things after the murderer had entered the room was this: Mrs Williamson had probably not seen him, from the accident of standing with her back to the door. Her, therefore, before he was himself observed at all, he had stunned and prostrated by a shattering blow on the back of her head; this blow, inflicted by a crowbar, had smashed in the hinder part of the skull. She fell; and by the noise of her fall (for all was the work of a moment) had first roused the attention of the servant; who then uttered the cry which had reached the young man; but before she could repeat it, the murderer had descended with his uplifted instrument upon *her* head, crushing the skull inwards upon the brain. Both the women were irrecoverably destroyed, so that further outrages were needless; and, moreover, the murderer was conscious of the imminent danger from delay; and yet, in spite of his hurry, so fully did he appreciate the fatal consequences to himself, if any of his victims should so far revive into consciousness as to make circumstantial depositions, that, by way of making this impossible, he had proceeded instantly to cut the throats of each. All this tallied with the appearances as now presenting themselves. Mrs Williamson had fallen backwards with her head to the door; the servant, from her kneeling posture, had been incapable of rising, and had presented her head passively to blows; after which, the miscreant had but to bend her head backwards so as to expose her throat, and the murder was finished. It is remarkable that the young artisan, paralysed as he had been by fear, and evidently fascinated for a time so as to walk right towards the lion's mouth, yet found himself able to notice everything important. The reader must suppose him at this point watching the murderer whilst hanging over the body of Mrs Williamson, and whilst renewing his search for certain important keys. Doubtless it was an anxious situation for the murderer; for, unless he speedily found the keys wanted, all this hideous tragedy would end in nothing but a prodigious increase of the public horror, in tenfold precautions therefore, and redoubled obstacles interposed between himself and his future game. Nay, there was even a nearer interest at stake; his own immediate safety might, by a probable accident, be compromised. Most of those who came to the house for liquor were giddy girls or children, who, on finding the house closed, would go off carelessly to some other; but, let any thoughtful woman or man come to the door now, a full quarter of an hour before the established time of closing, in that case suspicion would arise too powerful to be checked. There would be a sudden alarm given; after which, mere luck would decide the event. For it is a remarkable fact, and one that illustrates the singular inconsistency of this villain, who, being often so superfluously subtle, was in other directions so reckless and improvident, that at this very moment, standing amongst corpses that had deluged the little parlour with blood, Williams must have been in considerable doubt whether he had any sure means of egress. There were windows, he knew, to the back; but upon what ground they opened, he seems to have had no certain information; and in a neighbourhood so dangerous, the windows of the lower storey would not improbably be nailed down; those in the upper might be free, but then came the necessity of a leap too formidable. From all this, however, the sole practical inference was to hurry forward with the trial of further keys, and to detect the hidden treasure. This it was, this intense absorption in one overmastering pursuit, that dulled the murderer's perceptions as to all around him; otherwise, he must have heard the breathing of the young man, which to himself at times became fearfully audible. As the murderer stood once more over the body of Mrs Williamson, and searched her pockets more narrowly, he pulled out various clusters of keys, one of which dropping, gave a harsh jingling sound upon the floor. At this time it was that the secret witness, from his secret stand, noticed the fact of Williams's surtout being lined with silk of the finest quality. One other fact he noticed, which eventually became more immediately important than many stronger circumstances of incrimination; this was, that the shoes of the murderer, apparently new, and bought, probably, with poor Marr's money, creaked as he walked, harshly and frequently. With the new clusters of keys, the murderer walked off to the hidden section of the parlour. And here, at last, was suggested to the journeyman the sudden opening for an escape. Some minutes would be lost to a certainty in trying all these keys; and subsequently in searching the drawers, supposing that the keys answered – or in violently forcing them, supposing that they did *not*. He might thus count upon a brief interval of leisure, whilst the rattling of the keys might obscure to the murderer the creaking of the stairs under the re-ascending journeyman. His plan was now formed: on regaining his bedroom, he placed the bed against the door by way of a transient retardation to the enemy, that might give him a short warning, and in the worst extremity, might give him a chance for life by means of a desperate leap. This change made as quietly as was possible, he tore the sheets, pillow-cases, and blankets into broad ribbons; and after plaiting them into ropes, spliced the different lengths together. But at the very first he descries this ugly addition to his labours. Where shall he look for any staple, hook, or bar, or other fixture, from which his rope, when twisted, may safely depend? Measured from the window-*sill* – i.e., the lowest part of the window architrave – there count but twenty-two or twenty-three feet to the ground. Of this length ten or twelve feet may be looked upon as cancelled, because to that extent he might drop without danger. So much being deducted, there would remain, say, a dozen feet of rope to prepare. But, unhappily, there is no stout iron fixture anywhere about his window. The nearest, indeed the sole fixture of that sort, is not near to the window at all; it is a spike fixed (for no reason at all that is apparent) in the bed-tester; now, the bed being shifted, the spike is shifted; and its distance from the window, having always been four feet, is now seven. Seven entire feet, therefore, must be added to that which would have sufficed if measured from the window. But courage! God, by the proverb of all nations in Christendom, helps those that help themselves. This our young man thankfully acknowledges; he reads already, in the very fact of any spike at all being found where hitherto it has been useless, an earnest of providential aid. Were it only for himself that he worked, he could not feel himself meritoriously employed; but this is not so; in deep sincerity, he is now agitated for the poor child, whom he knows and loves; every minute, he feels, brings ruin nearer to *her*; and, as he passed her door, his first thought had been to take her out of bed in his arms, and to carry her where she might share his chances. But, on consideration, he felt that this sudden awaking of her, and the impossibility of even whispering any explanation, would cause her to cry audibly; and the inevitable indiscretion of one would be fatal to the two. As the Alpine avalanches, when suspended above the traveller's head, oftentimes (we are told) come down through the stirring of the air by a simple whisper, precisely on such a tenure of a whisper was now suspended the murderous malice of the man below. No; there is but one way to save the child; towards *her* deliverance, the first step is through his own. And he has made an excellent beginning; for the spike, which too fearfully he had expected to see torn away by any strain upon it from the half-carious wood, stands firmly when tried against the pressure of his own weight. He has rapidly fastened on to it three lengths of his new rope, measuring eleven feet. He plaits it roughly; so that only three feet have been lost in the intertwisting; he has spliced on a second length equal to the first; so that, already, sixteen feet are ready to throw out of the window; and thus, let the worst come to the worst, it will not be absolute ruin to swarm down the rope so far as it will reach, and then to drop boldly. All this has been accomplished in about six minutes; and the hot contest between above and below is still steadily but fervently proceeding. Murderer is working hard in the parlour; journeyman is working hard in the bedroom. Miscreant is getting on famously downstairs; one batch of banknotes he has already bagged; and is hard upon the scent of a second. He has also sprung a covey of golden coins. Sovereigns as yet were not; but guineas at this period fetched thirty shillings a-piece; and he has worked his way into a little quarry of these. Murderer is almost joyous; and if any creature is still living in this house, as shrewdly he suspects, and very soon means to know, with that creature he would be happy, before cutting the creature's throat, to drink a glass of something. Instead of the glass, might he not make a present to the poor creature of its throat? Oh no! impossible! Throats are a sort of thing that he never makes presents of; business – business must be attended to. Really the two men, considered simply as men of business, are both meritorious. Like chorus and semi-chorus, strophe and antistrophe, they work each against the other. Pull journeyman, pull murderer! Pull baker, pull devil! As regards the journeyman, he is now safe. To his sixteen feet, of which seven are neutralized by the distance of the bed, he has at last added six feet more, which will be short of reaching the ground by perhaps ten feet – a trifle which man or boy may drop without injury. All is safe, therefore, for him: which is more than one can be sure of for miscreant in the parlour. Miscreant, however, takes it coolly enough: the reason being, that, with all his cleverness, for once in his life miscreant has been over-reached. The reader and I know, but miscreant does not in the least suspect, a little fact of some importance, viz., that just now through a space of full three minutes he has been overlooked and studied by one, who (though reading in a dreadful book, and suffering under mortal panic) took accurate notes of so much as his limited opportunities allowed him to see, and will assuredly report the creaking shoes and the silk-mounted surtout in quarters where such little facts will tell very little to his advantage. But, although it is true that Mr Williams, unaware of the journeyman's having 'assisted' at the examination of Mrs Williamson's pockets, could not connect any anxiety with that person's subsequent proceedings, nor specially, therefore, with his having embarked in the rope-weaving line, assuredly he knew of reasons enough for not loitering. And yet he *did* loiter. Reading his acts by the light of such mute traces as he left behind him, the police became aware that latterly he must have loitered. And the reason which governed him is striking; because at once it records – that murder was not pursued by him simply as a means to an end, but also as an end for itself. Mr Williams had now been upon the premises for perhaps fifteen or twenty minutes; and in that space of time he had despatched, in a style satisfactory to himself, a considerable amount of business. He had done, in commercial language, 'a good stroke of business'. Upon two floors, viz., the cellar-floor and the ground-floor, he has 'accounted for' all the population. But there remained at least two floors more; and it now occurred to Mr Williams that, although the landlord's somewhat chilling manner had shut him out from any familiar knowledge of the household arrangements, too probably on one or other of those floors there must be some throats. As to plunder, he has already bagged the whole. And it was next to impossible that any arrear but the most trivial should still remain for a gleaner. But the throats – the throats – there it was that arrears and gleanings might perhaps be counted on. And thus it appeared that, in his wolfish thirst for blood, Mr Williams put to hazard the whole fruits of his night's work, and his life into the bargain. At this moment, if the murderer knew all, could he see the open window above stairs ready for the descent of the journeyman, could he witness the life-and-death rapidity with which that journeyman is working, could he guess at the almighty uproar which within ninety seconds will be maddening the population of this populous district – no picture of a maniac in flight of panic or in pursuit of vengeance would adequately represent the agony of haste with which he would himself be hurrying to the street-door for final evasion. That mode of escape was still free. Even at this moment, there yet remained time sufficient for a successful flight, and, therefore, for the following revolution in the romance of his own abominable life. He had in his pockets above a hundred pounds of booty; means, therefore, for a full disguise. This very night, if he will shave off his yellow hair, and blacken his eyebrows, buying, when morning light returns, a dark-coloured wig, and clothes such as may co-operate in personating the character of a grave professional man, he may elude all suspicions of impertinent policemen – may sail by any one of a hundred vessels bound for any port along the huge line of sea-board (stretching through 2,400 miles) of the American United States; may enjoy fifty years for leisurely repentance; and may even die in the odour of sanctity. On the other hand, if he prefer active life, it is not impossible that, with *his* subtlety, hardihood, and unscrupulousness, in a land where the simple process of naturalization converts the alien at once into a child of the family, he might rise to the president's chair; might have a statue at his death; and afterwards a life in three volumes quarto, with no hint glancing towards no. 29 Ratcliffe Highway. But all depends on the next ninety seconds. Within that time there is a sharp turn to be taken; there is a wrong turn, and a right turn. Should his better angel guide him to the right one, all may yet go well as regards this world's prosperity. But behold! in two minutes from this point we shall see him take the wrong one: and then Nemesis will be at his heels with ruin perfect and sudden.

Meanwhile, if the murderer allows himself to loiter, the ropemaker overhead does *not*. Well he knows that the poor child's fate is on the edge of a razor: for all turns upon the alarm being raised before the murderer reaches her bedside. And at this very moment, whilst desperate agitation is nearly paralysing his fingers, he hears the sullen stealthy step of the murderer creeping up through the darkness. It had been the expectation of the journeyman (founded on the clamorous uproar with which the street-door was slammed) that Williams, when disposable for his upstairs work, would come racing at a long jubilant gallop, and with a tiger roar; and perhaps, on his natural instincts, he would have done so. But this mode of approach, which was of dreadful effect when applied to a case of surprise, became dangerous in the case of people who might by this time have been placed fully upon their guard. The step which he had heard was on the staircase – but upon which stair? He fancied upon the lowest: and in a movement so slow and cautious, even this might make all the difference; yet might it not have been the tenth, twelfth, or fourteenth stair? Never, perhaps, in this world did any man feel his own responsibility so cruelly loaded and strained, as at this moment did the poor journeyman on behalf of the slumbering child. Lose but two seconds, through awkwardness or through the self-counteractions of panic, and for *her* the total difference arose between life and death. Still there is a hope: and nothing can so frightfully expound the hellish nature of him whose baleful shadow, to speak astrologically, at this moment darkens the house of life, than the simple expression of the ground on which his hope rested. The journeyman felt sure that the murderer would not be satisfied to kill the poor child whilst unconscious. This would be to defeat his whole purpose in murdering her at all. To an epicure in murder such as Williams, it would be taking away the very sting of the enjoyment, if the poor child should be suffered to drink off the bitter cup of death without fully apprehending the misery of the situation. But this luckily would require time: the double confusion of mind, first, from being roused up at so unusual an hour, and, secondly, from the horror of the occasion when explained to her, would at first produce fainting, or some mode of insensibility or distraction, such as must occupy a considerable time. The logic of the case, in short, all rested upon the *ultra* fiendishness of Williams. Were he likely to be content with the mere fact of the child's death, apart from the process and leisurely expansion of its mental agony – in that case there would be no hope. But, because our present murderer is fastidiously finical in his exactions – a sort of martinet in the scenical grouping and draping of the circumstances in his murders – therefore it is that hope becomes reasonable, since all such refinements of preparation demand time. Murders of mere necessity Williams was obliged to hurry; but, in a murder of pure voluptuousness, entirely disinterested, where no hostile witness was to be removed, no extra booty to be gained, and no revenge to be gratified, it is clear that to hurry would be altogether to ruin. If this child, therefore, is to be saved, it will be on pure aesthetical considerations.[1]

But all considerations whatever are at this moment suddenly cut short. A second step is heard on the stairs, but still stealthy and cautious; a third – and then the child's doom seems fixed. But just at that moment all is ready. The window is wide open; the rope is swinging free; the journeyman has launched himself; and already he is in the first stage of his

1 Let the reader, who is disposed to regard as exaggerated or romantic the pure fiendishness imputed to Williams, recollect that, except for the luxurious purpose of basking and revelling in the anguish of dying despair, he had no motive at all, small or great, for attempting the murder of this young girl. She had seen nothing, heard nothing – was fast asleep, and her door was closed; so that, as a witness against him, he knew that she was as useless as any one of the three corpses. And yet he *was* making preparations for her murder, when the alarm in the street interrupted him.

descent. Simply by the weight of his person he descended, and by the resistance of his hands he retarded the descent. The danger was, that the rope should run too smoothly through his hands, and that by too rapid an acceleration of pace he should come violently to the ground. Happily he was able to resist the descending impetus: the knots of the splicings furnished a succession of retardations. But the rope proved shorter by four or five feet than he had calculated: ten or eleven feet from the ground he hung suspended in the air; speechless for the present, through long-continued agitation; and not daring to drop boldly on the rough carriage pavement, lest he should fracture his legs. But the night was not dark, as it had been on occasion of the Marr murders. And yet, for purposes of criminal police, it was by accident worse than the darkest night that ever hid a murder or baffled a pursuit. London, from east to west, was covered with a deep pall (rising from the river) of universal fog. Hence it happened, that for twenty or thirty seconds the young man hanging in the air was not observed. His white shirt at length attracted notice. Three or four people ran up, and received him in their arms, all anticipating some dreadful annunciation. To what house did he belong? Even *that* was not instantly apparent; but he pointed with his finger to Williamson's door, and said in a half-choking whisper – '*Marr's murderer, now at work!*'

All explained itself in a moment: the silent language of the fact made its own eloquent revelation. The mysterious exterminator of no. 29 Ratcliffe Highway had visited another house; and, behold! one man only had escaped through the air, and in his night-dress, to tell the tale.

Thomas De Quincey, 'On Murder Considered as One of the Fine Arts'

Lovers

Charlotte Dymond, a domestic servant aged eighteen, was murdered near Rowtor Ford on Bodmin Moor on Sunday 14 April 1844 by her young man: a crippled farm-hand, Matthew Weeks, aged twenty-two. A stone marks the spot.

It was a Sunday evening
  And in the April rain
That Charlotte went from our house
  And never came home again.

Her shawl of diamond redcloth,
  She wore a yellow gown,
She carried the green gauze handkerchief
  She bought in Bodmin town.

About her throat her necklace
  And in her purse her pay:
The four silver shillings
  She had at Lady Day.

In her purse four shillings
  And in her purse her pride
As she walked out one evening
  Her lover at her side.

Out beyond the marshes
  Where the cattle stand,
With her crippled lover
  Limping at her hand.

Charlotte walked with Matthew
  Through the Sunday mist,
Never saw the razor
  Waiting at his wrist.

Charlotte she was gentle
  But they found her in the flood
Her Sunday beads among the reeds
  Beaming with her blood.

Matthew, where is Charlotte,
  And wherefore has she flown?
For you walked out together
  And now are come alone.

Why do you not answer,
  Stand silent as a tree,
Your Sunday worsted stockings
  All muddied to the knee?

Why do you mend your breast-pleat
  With a rusty needle's thread
And fall with fears and silent tears
  Upon your single bed?

Why do you sit so sadly
  Your face the colour of clay
And with a green gauze handkerchief
  Wipe the sour sweat away?

Has she gone to Blisland
  To seek an easier place,
And is that why your eye won't dry
  And blinds your bleaching face?

'Take me home!' cried Charlotte,
  'I lie here in the pit!
A red rock rests upon my breasts
  And my naked neck is split!'

Her skin was soft as sable,
  Her eyes were wide as day,
Her hair was blacker than the bog
  That licked her life away.

Her cheeks were made of honey,
  Her throat was made of flame
Where all around the razor
  Had written its red name.

As Matthew turned at Plymouth
  About the tilting Hoe,
The cold and cunning constable
  Up to him did go:

'I've come to take you, Matthew,
  Unto the magistrate's door.
Come quiet now, you pretty poor boy,
  And you must know what for.'

'She is as pure,' cried Matthew,
  'As is the early dew,
Her only stain it is the pain
  That round her neck I drew!

'She is as guiltless as the day
  She sprang forth from her mother.
The only sin upon her skin
  Is that she loved another.'

They took him off to Bodmin,
  They pulled the prison bell,
They sent him smartly up to heaven
  And dropped him down to hell.

All through the granite kingdom
  And on its travelling airs
Ask which of these two lovers
  The most deserves your prayers.

And your steel heart search, Stranger,
  That you may pause and pray
For lovers who come not to bed
  Upon their wedding day,

But lie upon the moorland
  Where stands the sacred snow
Above the breathing river,
  And the salt sea-winds go.

Charles Causley, 'The Ballad of Charlotte Dymond'

The rain set early in tonight,
  The sullen wind was soon awake,
It tore the elm-tops down for spite,
  And did its worst to vex the lake:
  I listened with heart fit to break.
When glided in Porphyria; straight
  She shut the cold out and the storm
And kneeled and made the cheerless grate
  Blaze up, and all the cottage warm;
  Which done, she rose, and from her form
Withdrew the dripping cloak and shawl,
  And laid her soiled gloves by, untied
Her hat and let the damp hair fall,
  And, last, she sat down by my side
  And called me. When no voice replied,
She put my arm about her waist,
  And made her smooth white shoulder bare,

And all her yellow hair displaced,
  And, stooping, made my cheek lie there,
  And spread, o'er all, her yellow hair,
Murmuring how she loved me – she
  Too weak, for all her heart's endeavour,
To set its struggling passion free
  From pride, and vainer ties dissever,
  And give herself to me for ever.
But passion sometimes would prevail,
  Nor could tonight's gay feast restrain
A sudden thought of one so pale
  For love of her, and all in vain:
  So, she was come through wind and rain.
Be sure I looked up at her eyes
  Happy and proud; at last I knew
Porphyria worshipped me; surprise
  Made my heart swell, and still it grew
  While I debated what to do.
That moment she was mine, mine, fair,
  Perfectly pure and good: I found
A thing to do, and all her hair
  In one long yellow string I wound
  Three times her little throat around,
And strangled her. No pain felt she;
    I am quite sure she felt no pain.
As a shut bud that holds a bee,
  I warily oped her lids: again
  Laughed the blue eyes without a stain.
And I untightened next the tress
  About her neck; her cheek once more
Blushed bright beneath my burning kiss:
  I propped her head up as before,
  Only, this time my shoulder bore
Her head, which droops upon it still:
  The smiling rosy little head,
So glad it has its utmost will,
  That all it scorned at once is fled,
  And I, its love, am gained instead!
Porphyria's love: she guessed not how
  Her darling one wish would be heard.

And thus we sit together now,
  And all night long we have not stirred,
  And yet God has not said a word!
  Robert Browning, 'Porphyria's Lover'

Victor was a little baby,
  Into this world he came;
His father took him on his knee and said:
  'Don't dishonour the family name.'

Victor looked up at his father
  Looked up with big round eyes:
His father said: 'Victor, my only son,
  Don't you ever ever tell lies.'

Victor and his father went riding
  Out in a little dog-cart;
His father took a Bible from his pocket and read,
  'Blessed are the pure in heart.'

It was a frosty December,
  It wasn't the season for fruits;
His father fell dead of heart disease
  While lacing up his boots.

It was a frosty December
  When into his grave he sank;
His uncle found Victor a post as cashier
  In the Midland Counties Bank.

It was a frosty December
  Victor was only eighteen,
But his figures were neat and his margins straight
  And his cuffs were always clean.

He took a room at the Peveril,
  A respectable boarding-house;
And Time watched Victor day after day
  As a cat will watch a mouse.

The clerks slapped Victor on the shoulder;
  'Have you ever had a woman?' they said,
'Come down town with us on Saturday night.'
  Victor smiled and shook his head.

The manager sat in his office,
  Smoked a Corona cigar:
Said: 'Victor's a decent fellow but
  He's too mousey to go far.'

Victor went up to his bedroom,
  Set the alarum bell;
Climbed into bed, took his Bible and read
  Of what happened to Jezebel.

It was the First of April,
  Anna to the Peveril came;
Her eyes, her lips, her breasts, her hips
  And her smile set men aflame.

She looked as pure as a schoolgirl
  On her First Communion day,
But her kisses were like the best champagne
  When she gave herself away.

It was the Second of April,
  She was wearing a coat of fur;
Victor met her upon the stairs
  And he fell in love with her.

The first time he made his proposal,
  She laughed, said: 'I'll never wed':
The second time there was a pause;
  Then she smiled and shook her head.

Anna looked into her mirror,
  Pouted and gave a frown:
Said: 'Victor's as dull as a wet afternoon
  But I've got to settle down.'

The third time he made his proposal,
  As they walked by the Reservoir:
She gave him a kiss like a blow on the head,
  Said: 'You are my heart's desire.'

They were married early in August,
  She said: 'Kiss me, you funny boy':
Victor took her in his arms and said:
  'O my Helen of Troy.'

It was the middle of September,
  Victor came to the office one day;
He was wearing a flower in his buttonhole,
  He was late but he was gay.

The clerks were talking of Anna,
  The door was just ajar:
One said: 'Poor old Victor, but where ignorance
  Is bliss, et cetera.'

Victor stood still as a statue,
  The door was just ajar:
One said: 'God, what fun I had with her
  In that Baby Austin car.'

Victor walked out into the High Street,
  He walked to the edge of the town;
He came to the allotments and the rubbish heap;
  And his tears came tumbling down.

Victor looked up at the sunset
  As he stood there all alone;
Cried: 'Are you in Heaven, Father?'
  But the sky said 'Address not known.'

Victor looked up at the mountains,
  The mountains all covered with snow;
Cried: 'Are you pleased with me, Father?'
  And the answer came back, 'No.'

Victor came to the forest,
  Cried: 'Father, will she ever be true?'
And the oaks and the beeches shook their heads
  And they answered: 'Not to you.'

Victor came to the meadow
  Where the wind went sweeping by:
Cried: 'O Father, I love her so',
  But the wind said: 'She must die.'

Victor came to the river
  Running so deep and so still:
Cried: 'O Father, what shall I do?'
  And the river answered: 'Kill.'

Anna was sitting at a table,
  Drawing cards from a pack;
Anna was sitting at table
  Waiting for her husband to come back.

It wasn't the Jack of Diamonds
  Nor the Joker she drew at first;
It wasn't the King or the Queen of Hearts
  But the Ace of Spades reversed.

Victor stood in the doorway,
  He didn't utter a word:
She said: 'What's the matter, darling?'
  He behaved as if he hadn't heard.

There was a voice in his left ear,
  There was a voice in his right,
There was a voice at the base of his skull
  Saying: 'She must die to-night.'

Victor picked up a carving-knife,
  His features were set and drawn,
Said: 'Anna, it would have been better for you
  If you had not been born.'

Anna jumped up from the table,
  Anna started to scream,
But Victor came slowly after her
  Like a horror in a dream.

She dodged behind the sofa,
  She tore down a curtain rod,
But Victor came slowly after her:
  Said; 'Prepare to meet thy God.'

She managed to wrench the door open,
  She ran and she didn't stop.
But Victor followed her up the stairs
  And he caught her at the top.

He stood there above the body,
He stood there holding the knife;
And the blood ran down the stairs and sang:
'I'm the Resurrection and the Life.'

They tapped Victor on the shoulder,
They took him away in a van;
He sat quiet as a lump of moss
Saying, 'I am the Son of Man.'

Victor sat in a corner
Making a woman of clay:
Saying: 'I am Alpha and Omega, I shall come
To judge the earth one day.'

W. H. Auden, 'Victor'

The following day was overcast, each street
A slow canal to float him to the place
Where he'd let fall the dear and staring face,
A funnel toward the thin reproachful tweet.

All day the starved canary called him back
In newsboy's whistle, crying of a tire,
Squeak of a squeegee, sirens finding fire,
Until the nightfall packed his head in black,

And he went back and climbed the stairs again,
Stepping across her body, freed the bird,
Which left its cage and out the window whirred
As a bad thought out of a cracked brain.

Richard Wilbur, 'Pity'

My true love breathed her latest breath
And I have closed her eyes in death.
It was a cold and windy day
In March, when my love went away.
She was not like other girls – rather diffident,
And that is how we had an accident.

Stevie Smith, 'The Murderer'

M

Macbeth

MACBETH (*to the Servant*): Go bid thy mistress, when my drink is ready,
She strike upon the bell. Get thee to bed. *Exit Servant*
Is this a dagger which I see before me,
The handle toward my hand? Come, let me clutch thee.
I have thee not, and yet I see thee still.
Art thou not, fatal vision, sensible
To feeling as to sight? Or art thou but
A dagger of the mind, a false creation
Proceeding from the heat-oppressèd brain?
I see thee yet, in form as palpable
As this which now I draw.
Thou marshall'st me the way that I was going,
And such an instrument I was to use.
Mine eyes are made the fools o'th' other senses,
Or else worth all the rest. I see thee still,
And on thy blade and dudgeon gouts of blood,
Which was not so before. There's no such thing.
It is the bloody business which informs
Thus to mine eyes. Now o'er the one half-world
Nature seems dead, and wicked dreams abuse
The curtained sleep. Witchcraft celebrates
Pale Hecate's offerings, and withered murder,
Alarumed by his sentinel the wolf,
Whose howl's his watch, thus with his stealthy pace,
With Tarquin's ravishing strides, towards his design
Moves like a ghost. Thou sure and firm-set earth,
Hear not my steps which way they walk, for fear
Thy very stones prate of my whereabout,
And take the present horror from the time,
Which now suits with it. Whiles I threat, he lives.

Words to the heat of deeds too cold breath gives.

A bell rings

I go, and it is done. The bell invites me.
Hear it not, Duncan; for it is a knell
That summons thee to heaven or to hell. *Exit*

Enter Lady Macbeth

LADY MACBETH: That which hath made them drunk hath made me bold.
What hath quenched them hath given me fire. Hark, peace! –
It was the owl that shrieked, the fatal bellman
Which gives the stern'st good-night. He is about it.
The doors are open, and the surfeited grooms
Do mock their charge with snores. I have drugged their possets
That death and nature do contend about them
Whether they live or die.

Enter Macbeth (above)

MACBETH: Who's there? What ho?

Exit

LADY MACBETH: Alack, I am afraid they have awaked,
And 'tis not done. Th'attempt and not the deed
Confounds us. Hark! – I laid their daggers ready;
He could not miss 'em. Had he not resembled
My father as he slept, I had done't.

(Enter Macbeth below)

My husband!

MACBETH: I have done the deed. Didst thou not hear a noise?
LADY MACBETH: I heard the owl scream and the crickets cry.
Did not you speak?
MACBETH: When?
LADY MACBETH: Now.
MACBETH: As I descended?
LADY MACBETH: Ay.
MACBETH: Hark! – Who lies i'th' second chamber?
LADY MACBETH: Donalbain.
MACBETH (*looking at his hands*): This is a sorry sight.
LADY MACBETH: A foolish thought, to say a sorry sight.
MACBETH: There's one did laugh in's sleep, and one cried 'Murder!'
That they did wake each other. I stood and heard them.
But they did say their prayers and addressed them
Again to sleep.
LADY MACBETH: They are two lodged together.

MACBETH: One cried 'God bless us' and 'Amen' the other,
As they had seen me with these hangman's hands.
List'ning their fear I could not say 'Amen'
When they did say 'God bless us.'
LADY MACBETH: Consider it not so deeply.
MACBETH: But wherefore could not I pronounce 'Amen'?
I had most need of blessing, and 'Amen'
Stuck in my throat.
LADY MACBETH: These deeds must not be thought
After these ways. So, it will make us mad.
MACBETH: Methought I heard a voice cry 'Sleep no more,
Macbeth does murder sleep' – the innocent sleep,
Sleep that knits up the ravelled sleave of care,
The death of each day's life, sore labour's bath,
Balm of hurt minds, great nature's second course,
Chief nourisher in life's feast –
LADY MACBETH: What do you mean?
MACBETH: Still it cried 'Sleep no more' to all the house,
'Glamis hath murdered sleep, and therefore Cawdor
Shall sleep no more, Macbeth shall sleep no more.'
LADY MACBETH: Who was it that thus cried? Why, worthy thane,
You do unbend your noble strength to think
So brain-sickly of things. Go get some water
And wash this filthy witness from your hand.
Why did you bring these daggers from the place?
They must lie there. Go, carry them, and smear
The sleepy grooms with blood.
MACBETH: I'll go no more.
I am afraid to think what I have done,
Look on't again I dare not.
LADY MACBETH: Infirm of purpose!
Give me the daggers. The sleeping and the dead
Are but as pictures. 'Tis the eye of childhood
That fears a painted devil. If he do bleed
I'll gild the faces of the grooms withal,
For it must seem their guilt. *Exit*

Knock within

MACBETH: Whence is that knocking? –
How is't with me when every noise appals me?
What hands are here! Ha, they pluck out mine eyes.

Will all great Neptune's ocean wash this blood
Clean from my hand? No, this my hand will rather
The multitudinous seas incarnadine,
Making the green one red.

Enter Lady Macbeth

LADY MACBETH: My hands are of your colour, but I shame
To wear a heart so white.

Knock within

I hear a knocking
At the south entry. Retire we to our chamber.
A little water clears us of this deed.
How easy it is then! Your constancy
Hath left you unattended.

Knock within

Hark, more knocking.
Get on your nightgown, lest occasion call us
And show us to be watchers. Be not lost
So poorly in your thoughts.

MACBETH: To know my deed 'twere best not know myself.

Knock within

Wake Duncan with thy knocking. I would thou couldst. *Exeunt*

William Shakespeare, *Macbeth*

From my boyish days I had always felt a great perplexity on one point in *Macbeth*. It was this: the knocking at the gate, which succeeds to the murder of Duncan, produced to my feelings an effect for which I never could account. The effect was, that it reflected back upon the murderer a peculiar awfulness and a depth of solemnity; yet, however obstinately I endeavoured with my understanding to comprehend this, for many years I never could see *why* it should produce such an effect.

Here I pause for one moment, to exhort the reader never to pay any attention to his understanding, when it stands in opposition to any other faculty of his mind. The mere understanding, however useful and indispensable, is the meanest faculty in the human mind, and the most to be distrusted; and yet the great majority of people trust to nothing else, which may do for ordinary life, but not for philosophical purposes. Of this out of ten thousand instances that I might produce, I will cite one. Ask of any person whatsoever, who is not previously prepared for the demand by a knowledge of the perspective, to draw in the rudest way the commonest appearance which depends upon the laws of that science; as, for instance, to represent the effect of two walls standing at right angles to each other, or the appearance of the houses on each side of a street, as seen by a person looking down the street from one extremity. Now in all cases, unless the person has happened to observe in pictures how it is that artists produce these effects, he will be utterly unable to make the smallest approximation to it. Yet why? For he has actually seen the effect every day of his life. The reason is – that he allows his understanding to overrule his eyes. His understanding, which includes no intuitive knowledge of the laws of vision, can furnish him with no reason why a line which is known and can be proved to be a horizontal line, should not *appear* a horizontal line; a line that made any angle with the perpendicular, less than a right angle, would seem to him to indicate that his houses were all tumbling down together. Accordingly, he makes the line of his houses a horizontal line, and fails, of course, to produce the effect demanded. Here, then, is one instance out of many, in which not only the understanding is allowed to overrule the eyes, but where the understanding is positively allowed to obliterate the eyes, as it were; for not only does the man believe the evidence of his understanding in opposition to that of his eyes, but (what is monstrous!) the idiot is not aware that his eyes ever gave such evidence. He does not know that he has seen (and therefore *quoad* his consciousness has *not* seen) that which he *has* seen every day of his life.

But to return from this digression, my understanding could furnish no reason why the knocking at the gate in *Macbeth* should produce any effect, direct or reflected. In fact, my understanding said positively that it could *not* produce any effect. But I knew better; I felt that it did; and I waited and clung to the problem until further knowledge should enable me to solve it. At length, in 1812, Mr Williams made his début on the stage of Ratcliffe Highway, and executed those unparalleled murders which have procured for him such a brilliant and undying reputation. On which murders, by the way, I must observe, that in one respect they have had an ill effect, by making the connoisseur in murder very fastidious in his taste, and dissatisfied by anything that has been since done in that line. All other murders look pale by the deep crimson of his; and, as an amateur once said to me in a querulous tone, 'There has been absolutely nothing *doing* since his time, or nothing that's worth speaking of.' But this is wrong; for it is unreasonable to expect all men to be great artists, and born with the genius of Mr Williams. Now it will be remembered, that in the first of these murders (that of the Marrs), the same incident (of a knocking at the door, soon after the work of extermination was complete) did actually occur, which the genius of Shakespeare has invented; and all good judges, and the most eminent dilettanti, acknowledged the felicity of Shakespeare's suggestion, as soon as it was actually realized. Here, then, was a fresh proof that I was right in relying on my own feeling, in opposition to my understanding; and I again set myself to study the problem; at length I solved it to my own satisfaction, and my solution is this. Murder, in ordinary cases, where the sympathy is wholly directed to the case of the murdered person, is an incident of coarse and vulgar horror; and for this reason, that it flings the interest exclusively upon the natural but ignoble instinct by which we cleave to life; an instinct which, as being indispensable to the primal law of self-preservation, is the same in kind (though different in degree) amongst all living creatures: this instinct, therefore, because it annihilates all distinctions, and degrades the greatest of men to the level of 'the poor beetle that we tread on', exhibits human nature in its most abject and humiliating attitude. Such an attitude would little suit the purposes of the poet. What then must he do? He must throw the interest on the murderer. Our sympathy must be with *him* (of course I mean a sympathy of comprehension, a sympathy by which we enter into his feelings, and are made to understand them, – not a sympathy of pity or approbation[1]). In the murdered person, all strife of thought, all flux and reflux of passion and of purpose, are crushed by one overwhelming panic; the fear of instant death smites him 'with its petrific mace'. But in the murderer, such a murderer as a poet will condescend to, there must be raging some great storm of passion – jealousy, ambition, vengeance, hatred – which will create a hell within him; and into this hell we are to look.

In *Macbeth*, for the sake of gratifying his own enormous and teeming faculty of creation, Shakespeare has introduced two murderers: and, as usual in his hands, they are remarkably discriminated: but, though in Macbeth the strife of mind is greater than in his wife, the tiger spirit not so awake, and his feelings caught chiefly by contagion from her, – yet, as both were finally involved in the guilt of murder, the murderous mind of necessity is finally to be presumed in both. This was to be expressed; and on its own account, as well as to make it a more proportionable antagonist to the unoffending nature of their victim, 'the gracious Duncan', and adequately to expound 'the deep damnation of his taking off', this was to

1 It seems almost ludicrous to guard and explain my use of a word, in a situation where it would naturally explain itself. But it has become necessary to do so, in consequence of the unscholarlike use of the word sympathy, at present so general, by which, instead of taking it in its proper sense, as the act of reproducing in our minds the feelings of another, whether for hatred, indignation, love, pity, or approbation, it is made a mere synonym of the word *pity*; and hence, instead of saying 'sympathy *with* another', many writers adopt the monstrous barbarism of 'sympathy *for* another'.

be expressed with peculiar energy. We were to be made to feel that the human nature, i.e. the divine nature of love and mercy, spread through the hearts of all creatures, and seldom utterly withdrawn from man – was gone, vanished, extinct; and that the fiendish nature had taken its place. And, as this effect is marvellously accomplished in the *dialogues* and *soliloquies* themselves, so it is finally consummated by the expedient under consideration; and it is to this that I now solicit the reader's attention. If the reader has ever witnessed a wife, daughter, or sister in a fainting-fit, he may chance to have observed that the most affecting moment in such a spectacle is *that* in which a sigh and a stirring announce the recommencement of suspended life. Or, if the reader has ever been present in a vast metropolis, on the day when some great national idol was carried in funeral pomp to his grave, and chancing to walk near the course through which it passed, has felt powerfully in the silence and desertion of the streets, and in the stagnation of ordinary business, the deep interest which at that moment was possessing the heart of man – if all at once he should hear the death-like stillness broken up by the sound of wheels rattling away from the scene, and making known that the transitory vision was dissolved, he will be aware that at no moment was his sense of the complete suspension and pause in ordinary human concerns so full and affecting, as at that moment when the suspension ceases, and the goings-on of human life are suddenly resumed. All action in any direction is best expounded, measured, and made apprehensible, by reaction. Now apply this to the case in *Macbeth*. Here, as I have said, the retiring of the human heart, and the entrance of the fiendish heart was to be expressed and made sensible. Another world has stepped in; and the murderers are taken out of the region of human things, human purposes, human desires. They are transfigured: Lady Macbeth is 'unsexed'; Macbeth has forgot that he was born of woman; both are conformed to the image of devils; and the world of devils is suddenly revealed. But how shall this be conveyed and made palpable? In order that a new world may step in, this world must for a time disappear. The murderers, and the murder must be insulated – cut off by an immeasurable gulf from the ordinary tide and succession of human affairs – locked up and sequestered in some deep recess; we must be made sensible that the world of ordinary life is suddenly arrested – laid asleep – tranced – racked into a dread armistice; time must be annihilated; relation to things without abolished; and all must pass self-withdrawn into a deep syncope and suspension of earthly passion. Hence it is, that when the deed is done, when the work of darkness is perfect, then the world of darkness passes away like a pageantry in the clouds: the knocking at the gate is heard; and it makes known audibly that the reaction has commenced; the human has made its reflux upon the fiendish; the pulses of life are beginning to beat again; and the re-establishment of the goings-on of the world in which we live, first makes us profoundly sensible of the awful parenthesis that had suspended them.

O mighty poet! Thy works are not as those of other men, simply and merely great works of art; but are also like the phenomena of nature, like the sun and the sea, the stars and the flowers; like frost and snow, rain and dew, hail-storm and thunder, which are to be studied with entire submission of our own faculties, and in the perfect faith that in them there can be no too much or too little, nothing useless or inert – but that, the further we press in our discoveries, the more we shall see proofs of design and self-supporting arrangement where the careless eye had seen nothing but accident!

Thomas De Quincey, 'On the Knocking at the Gate in *Macbeth*'

'It was a stupid mistake to make,' said the American woman I had met at my hotel in the English lake country, 'but it was on the counter with the other Penguin books – the little sixpenny ones, you know, with the paper covers – and I supposed of course it was a detective story. All the others were detective stories. I'd read all the others, so I brought this one without really looking at it carefully. You can imagine how mad I was when I found it was Shakespeare.' I murmured something sympathetically. 'I don't see why the Penguin-books people had to get out Shakespeare's plays in the same size and everything as the detective stories,' went on my companion. 'I think they have different-coloured jackets,' I said. 'Well, I didn't notice that,' she said. 'Anyway, I got real comfy in bed that night and all ready to read a good mystery story and here I had "The Tragedy of Macbeth" – a book for high-school students. Like "Ivanhoe".' 'Or "Lorna Doone",' I said. 'Exactly,' said the American lady. 'And I was just crazy for a good Agatha Christie, or something. Hercule Poirot is my favourite detective.' 'Is he the rabbity one?' I asked. 'Oh, no,' said my crime-fiction expert. 'He's the Belgian one. You're thinking of Mr Pinkerton, the one that helps Inspector Bull. He's good, too.'

Over her second cup of tea my companion began to tell the plot of a detective story that had fooled her completely – it seems it was the old family doctor all the time. But I cut in on her. 'Tell me,' I said; 'did you read "Macbeth"?' 'I *had* to read it,' she said. 'There wasn't a scrap of anything else to read in the whole room.' 'Did you like it?' I asked. 'No, I did not', she said, decisively. 'In the first place, I don't think for a moment that Macbeth did it.' I looked at her blankly. 'Did what?' I asked. 'I don't think for a moment that he killed the King,' she said. 'I don't think the Macbeth woman was mixed up in it, either. You suspect them the most, of course, but those are the ones that are never guilty – or shouldn't be, anyway.' 'I'm afraid,' I began, 'that I – ' 'But don't you see?' said the American lady. 'It would spoil everything if you could figure out right away who did it. Shakespeare was too smart for that. I've read that people never *have* figured out "Hamlet", so it isn't likely Shakespeare would have made "Macbeth" as simple as it seems.' I thought this over while I filled my pipe. 'Who do you suspect?' I asked, suddenly. 'Macduff,' she said, promptly. 'Good God!' I whispered, softly.

'Oh, Macduff did it, all right,' said the murder specialist. 'Hercule Poirot would have got him easily.' 'How did you figure it out?' I demanded. 'Well,' she said, 'I didn't right away. At first I suspected Banquo. And then, of course, he was the second person killed. That was good right in there, that part. The person you suspect of the first murder should always be the second victim.' 'Is that so?' I murmured. 'Oh, yes,' said my informant. 'They have to keep surprising you. Well, after the second murder I didn't know *who* the killer was for a while.' 'How about Malcolm and Donalbain, the King's sons?' I asked. 'As I remember it, they fled right after the first murder. That looks suspicious.' 'Too suspicious,' said the American lady. 'Much too suspicious. When they flee, they're never guilty. You can count on that.' 'I believe,' I said, 'I'll have a brandy,' and I summoned the waiter. My companion leaned toward me, her eyes bright, her teacup quivering. 'Do you know who discovered Duncan's body?' she demanded. I said I was sorry, but I had forgotten. 'Macduff discovers it,' she said, slipping into the historical present. 'Then he comes running downstairs and shouts, "Confusion has broke open the Lord's anointed temple" and "Sacrilegious murder has made his masterpiece" and on and on like that.' The good lady tapped me on the knee. 'All that stuff was *rehearsed*,' she said. 'You wouldn't say a lot of stuff like that, offhand, would you – if you had found a body?' She fixed me with a glittering eye. 'I – ' I began. 'You're right!' she said. 'You wouldn't! Unless you had practised it in advance. "My God, there's a body in there!" is what an innocent man would say.' She sat back with a confident glare.

I thought for a while. 'But what do you make of the Third Murderer?' I asked. 'You know, the Third Murderer has puzzled "Macbeth" scholars for three hundred years.' 'That's because they never thought of Macduff,' said the American lady. 'It was Macduff, I'm certain. You couldn't have one of the victims murdered by two ordinary thugs – the murderer always has to be somebody important.' 'But what about the banquet scene?' I asked, after a moment. 'How do you account for Macbeth's guilty actions there, when Banquo's ghost came in and sat in his chair?' The lady leaned forward and tapped me on the knee again. 'There wasn't any ghost,' she said. 'A big, strong man like that doesn't go around seeing ghosts – especially in a brightly lighted banquet hall with dozens of people around. Macbeth was *shielding somebody*!' 'Who was he shielding?' I asked. 'Mrs Macbeth, of course,' she said. 'He thought she did it and he was going to take the rap himself. The husband always does that when the wife is suspected.' 'But what,' I demanded, 'about the sleepwalking scene, then?' 'The same thing, only the other way around,' said my companion. 'That time *she* was shielding *him*. She wasn't asleep at all. Do you remember where it says, "Enter Lady Macbeth with a taper"?' 'Yes,' I said. 'Well, people who walk in their sleep *never carry lights*!' said my fellow-traveller. 'They have second sight. Did you ever hear of a sleepwalker carrying a light?' 'No,' I said, 'I never did.' 'Well, then, she wasn't asleep. She was acting guilty to shield Macbeth.' 'I think,' I said, 'I'll have another brandy,' and I called the waiter. When he brought it, I drank it rapidly and rose to go. 'I believe,' I said, 'that you have got hold of something. Would you lend me that "Macbeth"? I'd like to look it over tonight. I don't feel, somehow, as if I'd ever really read it.' 'I'll get it for you,' she said. 'But you'll find that I am right.'

I read the play over carefully that night, and the next morning, after breakfast, I sought out the American woman. She was on the putting green, and I came up behind her silently and took her arm. She gave an exclamation. 'Could I see you alone?' I asked, in a low voice. She nodded cautiously and followed me to a secluded spot. 'You've found out something?' she breathed. 'I've found out,' I said, triumphantly, 'the name of the murderer!' 'You mean it wasn't Macduff?' she said. 'Macduff is as innocent of those murders,' I said, 'as Macbeth and the Macbeth woman.' I opened the copy of the play, which I had with me, and turned to Act II, Scene 2. 'Here,' I said, 'you will see where Lady Macbeth says, "I laid their daggers ready. He could not miss 'em. Had he not resembled my father as he slept, I had done it." Do you see?' 'No,' said the American woman, bluntly, 'I don't.' 'But it's simple!' I exclaimed. 'I wonder I didn't see it years ago. The reason Duncan resembled Lady Macbeth's father as he slept is that *it actually was her father*!' 'Good God!' breathed my companion, softly. 'Lady Macbeth's father killed the King,' I said, 'and, hearing someone coming, thrust the body under the bed and crawled into the bed himself.' 'But,' said the lady, 'you can't have a murderer who only appears in the story once. You can't have that.' 'I know that,' I said, and turned to Act II, Scene 4. 'It says here, "Enter Ross with an old Man." Now, that old man is never identified and it is my contention he was old Mr Macbeth, whose ambition it was to make his daughter Queen. There you have your motive.' 'But even then,' cried the American lady, 'he's still a minor character!' 'Not,' I said, gleefully, 'when you realize that he was also *one of the weird sisters in disguise*!' 'You mean one of the three witches?' 'Precisely,' I said. 'Listen to this speech of the old man's. "On Tuesday last, a falcon towering in her pride of place, was by a mousing owl hawk'd at and kill'd." Who does that sound like?' 'It sounds like the way the three witches talk,' said my companion, reluctantly. 'Precisely!' I said again. 'Well,' said the Amrican woman, 'maybe you're right, but – ' 'I'm sure I am,' I said. 'And do you know what I'm going to do now?' 'No,' she said. 'What?' 'Buy a copy of "Hamlet",' I said, 'and solve *that*!' My companion's eyes brightened. 'Then,' she said, 'you don't think Hamlet did it?' 'I am,' I said, 'absolutely positive he didn't.' 'But who,' she demanded, 'do you suspect?' I looked at her cryptically. 'Everybody,' I said, and disappeared into a small grove of trees as silently as I had come.

James Thurber, 'The Macbeth Murder Mystery'

Maniac

Some days later Paul entered on another phase of his reclamation. When he came into the prison-square for his afternoon exercise he found that his companion's place had been taken by a burly man of formidable aspect. He had red hair and beard, and red-rimmed eyes, and vast red hands which twirled convulsively at his sides. He turned his ox-like eyes on Paul and gave a slight snarl of welcome.

'Your new pal,' said the warder. 'Get on with it.'

'How do you do?' said Paul politely. 'Are you here for long?'

'Life,' said the other. 'But it doesn't matter much. I look daily for the Second Coming.'

They marched on in silence.

'Do you think that this a good plan of the Governor's?' asked Paul.

'Yes,' said his companion. They walked on in silence, once round, twice round, three times round.

'Talk, you two,' shouted the warder. 'That's your instructions. Talk.'

'It makes a change,' said the big man.

'What are you here for?' asked Paul. 'You don't mind my asking, do you?'

'It's all in the Bible,' said the big man. 'You should read about it there. Figuratively, you know,' he added. 'It wouldn't be plain to you, I don't suppose, not like it is to me.'

'It's not an easy book to understand, is it?'

'It's not understanding that's needed. It's vision. Do you ever have visions?'

'No, I'm afraid I don't.'

'Nor does the Chaplain. He's no Christian. It was a vision brought me here, an angel clothed in flame, with a crown of flame on his head, crying "Kill and spare not. The Kingdom is at hand." Would you like to hear about it? I'll tell you. I'm a carpenter by profession, or at least I was, you understand.' He spoke with a curious blend of cockney and Biblical English. 'Not a joiner – a cabinet-maker. Well, one day I was just sweeping out the shop before shutting up when the angel of the Lord came in. I didn't know who it was at first. "Just in time," I said. "What can I do for you?" Then I noticed that all about him there was a red flame and a circle of flame over his head, same as I've been telling you. Then he told me how the Lord had numbered His elect and the day of tribulation was at hand. "Kill and spare not," he says. I'd not been sleeping well for some time before this. I'd been worrying about my soul and whether I was saved. Well, all that night I thought of what the angel had told me. I didn't see his meaning, not at first, same as you wouldn't. Then it all came to me in a flash. Unworthy that I am, I am the Lord's appointed,' said the carpenter. 'I am the sword of Israel; I am the lion of the Lord's elect.'

'And did you kill anybody?' asked Paul.

'Unworthy that I am, I smote the Philistine; in the name of the Lord of hosts, I struck off his head. It was for a sign of Israel. And now I am gone into captivity, and the mirth is turned into weeping, but the Lord shall deliver me in His appointed time. Woe unto the Philistine in that day! woe unto the uncircumcised! It were better that a stone were hanged about his neck and he were cast into the depths of the sea.'

The warder rang his bell. 'Inside, you two!' he shouted.

'Any complaints?' asked the Governor on his rounds.

'Yes, sir,' said Paul.

The Governor looked at him intently. 'Are you the man I put under special treatment?'

'Yes, sir.'

'Then it's ridiculous to complain. What is it?'

'I have reason to believe that the man I have to take exercise with is a dangerous lunatic.'

'Complaints by one prisoner about another can only be considered when substantiated by the evidence of a warder or of two other prisoners,' said the Chief Warder.

'Quite right,' said the Governor. 'I never heard a more ridiculous complaint. All crime is a form of insanity. I myself chose the prisoner with whom you exercise. I chose him for his peculiar suitability. Let me hear no more on this subject, please.'

That afternoon Paul spent another disquieting half-hour on the square.

'I've had another vision,' said the mystical homicide. 'But I don't yet know quite what it portends. No doubt I shall be told.'

'Was it a very beautiful vision?' asked Paul.

'No words can describe the splendour of it. It was all crimson and wet like blood. I saw the whole prison as if it were carved of ruby, hard and glittering and the warders and the prisoners creeping in and out like little red ladybirds. And then as I watched all the ruby became soft and wet, like a great sponge soaked in wine, and it was dripping and melting into a great lake of scarlet. Then I woke up. I don't know the meaning of it yet, but I feel that the hand of the Lord is hanging over this prison. D'you ever feel like that, as though it were built in the jaws of a beast? I sometimes dream of a great red tunnel like the throat of a beast and men running down it, sometimes one by one and sometimes in great crowds, running down the throat of the beast, and the breath of the beast is like the blast of a furnace. D'you ever feel like that?'

'I'm afraid not,' said Paul. 'Have they given you an interesting library book?'

'*Lady Almina's Secret*,' said the lion of the Lord's elect. 'Pretty soft stuff, old-fashioned, too. But I keep reading the Bible. There's a lot of killing in that.'

'Dear me, you seem to think about killing a great deal.'

'I do. It's my mission, you see,' said the big man simply.

Sir Wilfred Lucas-Dockery felt very much like Solomon at ten o'clock every morning of the week except Sunday. It was then that he sat in judgement upon the cases of misconduct among the prisoners that were brought to his notice. From his chair Colonel MacAdder had delivered sentence in undeviating accordance with the spirit and the letter of the Standing Orders Concerning the Government of Her Majesty's Prisons, dispensing automatic justice like a slot machine: in went the offence; out came the punishment. Not so Wilfred Lucas-Dockery. Never, he felt, was his mind more alert or resourceful or his vast accumulation of knowledge more available than at his little court of summary justice. 'No one knows what to expect,' complained warders and prisoners alike.

'Justice,' said Sir Wilfred, 'is the capacity for regarding each case as an entirely new problem.' After a few months of his administration, Sir Wilfred was able to point with some pride to a marked diminution in the number of cases brought before him.

One morning, soon after Paul began on his special *régime* of reclamation, his companion was called up before the Governor.

'God bless my soul!' said Sir Wilfred; 'that's the man I put on special treatment. What is he here for?'

'I was on night duty last night between the hours of 8 p.m. and 4 a.m.,' testified the warder in a sing-song voice, 'when my attention was attracted by sounds of agitation coming from the prisoner's cell. Upon going to the observation hole I observed the prisoner pacing up and down his cell in a state of high excitement. In one hand he held his Bible, and in the other a piece of wood which he had broken from his stool. His eyes were staring; he was breathing heavily, and at times muttering verses of the Bible. I remonstrated with the prisoner when he addressed me in terms prejudicial to good discipline.'

'What are the words complained of?' asked the Chief Warder.

'He called me a Moabite, an abomination of Moab, a wash-pot, an unclean thing, an uncircumcised Moabite, an idolater, and a whore of Babylon, sir.'

'I see. What do you advise, officer?'

'A clear case of insubordination, sir,' said the Chief Warder. 'Try him on No. 1 diet for a bit.'

But when he asked the Chief Warder's opinion, Sir Wilfred was not really seeking advice. He liked to emphasize in his own mind, and perhaps that of the prisoner's, the difference between the official view and his own.

'What would you say was the most significant part of the evidence?' he asked.

The Chief Warder considered. 'I think whore of Babylon, on the whole, sir.'

Sir Wilfred smiled as a conjurer may who has forced the right card.

'Now I,' he said, 'am of different opinion. It may surprise you, but I should say that the *significant* thing about this case was the fact that the prisoner held a piece of the stool.'

'Destruction of prison property,' said the Chief Warder. 'Yes, that's pretty bad.'

'Now what was your profession before conviction?' asked the Governor, turning to the prisoner.

'Carpenter, sir.'

'*I knew it*,' said the Governor triumphantly. 'We have another case of the frustrated creative urge. Now listen, my man. It is very wrong of you to insult the officer, who is clearly none of the things you mentioned. He symbolizes the just disapproval of society and is, like all the prison staff, a member of the Church of England. But I understand your difficulty. You have been used to creative craftsmanship, have you not, and you find prison life deprives you of the means of self-expression, and your energies find vent in these foolish outbursts? I will see to it that a bench and a set of carpenter's tools are provided for you. The first thing you shall do is to mend the piece of furniture you so wantonly destroyed. After that we will find other work for you in your old trade. You may go. Get to the cause of the trouble,' Sir Wilfred added when the prisoner was led away; 'your Standing Orders may repress the symptoms; they do not probe to the underlying cause.'

Two days later the prison was in a state of intense excitement. Something had happened. Paul woke as the bell rang at the usual time, but it was nearly half an hour before the doors were unlocked. He heard the warder's 'Slops outside!' getting nearer and nearer, interjected with an occasional 'Don't ask questions', 'Mind your own business', or a sinister 'You'll know soon enough', in reply to the prisoner's questions. They, too, had sensed something unusual. Perhaps it was an outbreak of some disease – spotted fever, Paul thought, or a national disaster in the world outside – a war or revolution. In their enforced silence the nerves of all the men were tightened to an acuteness of perception. Paul read wholesale massacres in the warder's face.

'Anything wrong?' he asked.

'I should bleeding well say there was,' said the warder, 'and the next man as asks me a question is going to cop it hot.'

Paul began scrubbing out his cell. Dissatisfied curiosity contended in his thoughts with irritation at this interruption of routine. Two warders passed his door talking.

'I don't say I'm not sorry for the poor bird. All I says is, it was time the Governor had a lesson.'

'It might have been one of us,' said the other warder in a hushed voice.

Breakfast arrived. As the hand appeared at his door Paul whispered: 'What's happened?'

'Why, ain't you 'eard? There's been a murder, shocking bloodthirsty.'

'Get on there,' roared the warder in charge of the landing.

So the Governor had been murdered, thought Paul; he had been a mischievous old bore. Still, it was very disturbing, for the news of a murder which was barely noticed in the gay world of trams and tubes and boxing-matches caused an electric terror in this community of silent men. The interval between breakfast and chapel seemed interminable. At last the bell went. The doors were opened again. They marched in silence to the chapel. As it happened, Philbrick was in the next seat to Paul. The warders sat on raised seats, watchful for any attempt at conversation. The hymn was the recognized time for the exchange of gossip. Paul waited for it impatiently. Clearly it was not the Governor who had been murdered. He stood on the chancel steps, Prayerbook in hand. Mr Prendergast was nowhere to be seen. The Governor conducted the service. The Medical Officer read the lessons, stumbling heavily over the longer words. Where was Mr Prendergast?

At last the hymn was announced. The organ struck up, played with great feeling by a prisoner who until his conviction had been assistant organist at a Welsh cathedral. All over the chapel the men filled their chests for a burst of conversation.

'O God, our help in ages past,' sang Paul.
  'Where's Prendergast today?'
'What, ain't you 'eard? 'e's been done in.'
  'And our eternal home.'

'Old Prendy went to see a chap
  What said he'd seen a ghost;
Well, he was dippy, and he'd got
  A mallet and a saw.'

'Who let the madman have the things?'
  'The Governor; who d'you think?
He asked to be a carpenter,
  He sawed off Prendy's head.

'A pal of mine what lives next door,
  'E 'eard it 'appening;
The warder must 'ave 'eard it too,
  'E didn't interfere.'

'Time, like an ever-rolling stream,
  Bears all its sons away.'
'Poor Prendy 'ollered fit to kill
  For nearly 'alf an hour.

'Damned lucky it was Prendergast,
  Might 'ave been you or me!
The warder says – and I agree –
  It serves the Governor right.'

'Amen'

From all points of view it was lucky that the madman had chosen Mr Prendergast for attack. Some people even suggested that the choice had been made in a more responsible quarter. The death of a prisoner or warder would have called for a Home Office inquiry which might seriously have discouraged the Lucas-Dockery reforms and also reflected some discredit upon the administration of the Chief Warder. Mr Prendergast's death passed almost unnoticed. His assassin was removed to Broadmoor, and the life of the prison went on smoothly. It was observed, however, that the Chief Warder seemed to have more influence with his superior than he had had before. Sir Wilfred concentrated his attention upon the statistics, and the life of the prison was equitably conducted under the Standing Orders. It was quite like it had been in old MacAdder's day, the warders observed. But Paul did not reap the benefits of this happy reversion to tradition, because some few days later he was removed with a band of others to the Convict Settlement at Egdon Heath.

Evelyn Waugh, *Decline and Fall*

There can be little question but that in the majority of cases in which persons have been acquitted of offences on the ground of insanity, they knew perfectly that they were committing acts forbidden by law; they knew, also, the difference between right and wrong, but they acted under the influence of impressions more powerful than those which are sufficient, under ordinary circumstances, to deter from the commission of great crimes. They probably, in some cases, persuaded themselves that although the acts they meditated were wrong generally, they were justifiable in those particular cases, or under those peculiar circumstances, which they believed at the time to exist: but in many others they were clearly satisfied that they were wrong, and that, being contrary to law, they entailed that punishment which the law awarded to such offences; but yet they could not restrain the insane impulse which, contrary to their wish and inclination, drove them to commit crimes from which their nature recoiled with horror. If the mind is sufficiently disturbed to create impressions which have no other foundation than the disordered working of the brain, who can say how powerful may be those impressions, or to what extent the individual is able or powerless to direct his acts, in opposition to such a controlling power?

Several cases of the most conclusive nature are quoted in Taylor's excellent work on Medical Jurisprudence, to show how frequently great crimes have been committed, which the offender has evidently known were illegal; amongst others is that of [Richard] Dadd, which is sufficiently interesting and to the point, to merit some passing notice.

Some few years ago, at my request that he would write out for me a little history of his case, he very good-naturedly furnished me with a long and rambling account of the ideas that had, from time to time, occurred to him, and that still occupied his mind. The part in which he explained his views in reference to his crime, was summed up in a few lines. The following are his own words: 'On my return from travel,[1] I was roused to a consideration of subjects which I have previously never dreamed of, or thought about, connected with self; and I had such ideas that, had I spoken of them openly, I must, if answered in the world's fashion, have been told I was unreasonable. I concealed, of course, these secret admonitions. I knew not whence they came, although I could not question their propriety, nor could I separate myself from what appeared my fate. My religious opinions varied and do vary from the vulgar; I was inclined to fall in with the views of the ancients, and to regard the substitution of modern ideas thereon as not for the better. These and the like, coupled with the idea of a descent from the Egyptian God Osiris, induced me to put a period to the existence of him whom I had always regarded as a parent, but whom the secret admonishings I had, counselled me was the author of the ruin of my race. I enveigled him, by false pretences, into Cobham Park,[2] and slew him with a knife, with which I stabbed him,

1 An extensive tour of the Middle East, including Egypt
2 28 August 1843

after having vainly endeavoured to cut his throat. Now the author of this act is unknown to me, although, as being the cat's-paw, I am held responsible. I do not extenuate my act: but as men are reasonable, or *capable of reason*, I think I have said enough to prove that I have no other concerns than with an act of volition, blindly, it is true, but, as I thought, rightly accorded.'

So well acquainted was Dadd with the consequences that would follow such an act, that some time before committing it he procured a passport, and made arrangements for his immediate escape to France, and this he actually accomplished as soon as he had killed his father.

It is manifest that this individual knew perfectly well, at the time of committing the crime, that he was acting contrary to law, and therefore, according to the interpretation of the judges, was punishable according to the nature of the crime, although it was committed under the influence of insane delusion; but it is equally clear that the court by which the prisoner was tried felt it impossible to apply the legal test; it was obvious that he was not morally responsible, and it was properly determined that he was not legally so, notwithstanding that this determination was arrived at in direct opposition to what was laid down as the established law.

William Wood, MD, Medical Officer of Bethlem Hospital, 'Remarks on the Plea of Insanity and on the Management of Criminal Lunatics'

The *Kentish Independent* of 1843
carried his pictures of his father, himself
and the scene of his crime. The first photo-journalist:
fairy-painter, father-slayer, poor, bad, mad Richard Dadd.

His extended Grand Tour took in the Holy Land
and ended in Bethlem Hospital, with its long panoptical
galleries, spider-plants, whippets and double-gaslights.
He had outlived himself at twenty-six . . .

There was one day he seemed to catch sunstroke.
He fancied the black, scorched beard of a sheik
would furnish him with some 'capital paintbrushes'.
Sailing up the Nile, on the *Hecate*,

they spent Christmas Day eating boiled eggs
and plum pudding, and playing cards for the captain's soul.
The temples at Luxor stood under a full moon, lightly boiled.
Sir Thomas got off to try and bag a crocodile.

The route up from Marseille went as the crow flies –
precipitately, a dash from ear to ear.
A fellow-traveller let him play with his collar and tie,
until he pulled out 'an excellent English razor'.

There was his watercolour, 'Dead Camel',
and a series of drawings of his friends,
all with their throats cut,
Frith, Egg, Dadd, Phillip and O'Neill.

He saw himself as a catspaw, Osiris's right-hand man
on earth. His digs in Newman Street
contained three hundred eggs, and the earth
cracked when he walked on it.

Michael Hofmann, 'The Late Richard Dadd, 1817–1886'

Marlowe

Once again we are drawn back to the inquest: to what it says, to what it does not say. We look at the story told to Coroner Danby and his sixteen stout jurors, and we wonder about it. How well does it hang together? At some point on the evening of 30 May 1593, after a long 'quiet' day together in Deptford, Frizer and Marlowe start to argue about who should pay the 'sum of pence' owed to Mistress Bull. There is nothing implausible about this – one can see the components: the money-maker's stinginess, the poet's quick temper – but there is nothing certain about it either. The only evidence for it is the testimony of a pair of professional deceivers, Nicholas Skeres and Robert Poley. This argument may never have happened.

Then comes the fight. Marlowe climbs off the bed, whips out Frizer's dagger and strikes him. He attacks from behind, 'on a sudden', with surprise on his side. Frizer is sitting on a bench, 'with the front part of his body towards the table'. He is hemmed in tight by Poley and Skeres either side of him. The advantage is clearly Marlowe's, but despite this Frizer receives only a couple of minor scalp-wounds, and manages to drive the dagger into Marlow's face with such force that it penetrates his brain to a depth of two inches.

What are Skeres and Poley up to while this happens? They are, we are told, sitting either side of Frizer in such a way that he 'could in no wise take flight'. They are there as the two men argue, as Marlowe clambers to his feet, as the dagger is drawn, as Frizer is wounded, as the fighters wrestle for control of the knife, and *still* they are tight in there, so that at the very moment when Frizer makes the fatal thrust, he is still physically unable to 'get away from' Marlowe. The coroner is quite clear about this: it is a vital point in Frizer's plea of self-defence. Skeres and Poley are oddly motionless figures during the last moments of Marlowe's life. No strangers to violence, a soldier for Essex and a spy for the Queen, they prove inept in this particular crisis. They seem to have made no effort to restrain or separate the fighters. They are close enough to impede, but not to intervene.

This kind of questioning will never get an answer, never recover the logic of that moment. We can only listen to the coroner's narrative, the story given by the witnesses, and say once again that what actually happened might have been different – or indeed that it might have been the same except for one vital thing: *it was the other way round.* It was not Marlowe who was the aggressor, but Frizer. It was not Frizer who was pinioned between Skeres and Poley, so that he could not 'get away', but Marlowe. The shallow slashes on Frizer's head were not inflicted by a man standing over him, but by a victim flailing and lunging for his life. The killing of Christopher Marlowe was not self-defence but murder.

All the physical evidence could point to this, just as well as it could point to the story told in the coroner's inquest. In some senses, it is a better deduction from the evidence. There was only one knife used in the affray at Mistress Bull's house: the twelvepenny dagger of Ingram Frizer. This is, prima facie, an awkward point in his plea of self-defence. Frizer needs this story, this particular reconstruction of the event, to explain away a more obvious deduction. He has killed an unarmed man with his dagger, but by virtue of this story it is not his fault.

It is sometimes said, in defence of the inquest's account, that the wound Marlowe received is more suggestive of a chaotic struggle than a planned attack, but I do not think this is so. The face, and particularly the eye, was regarded as a prime target. The manuals of swordsmanship described the thrust *alla revolta*, whose precise purpose was to skewer your opponent's eye-ball. Nashe transfers this to mental combat: Harvey's style is an unwieldy 'two-hand sword', and he cannot 'make one straight thrust at his enemy's face'. In another fight, another inquest, we hear of the actor Gabriel Spenser driving his rapier, scabbard and all, into the face of a man called Feake. The blade went 'between the pupil of the right eye and the eyebrows, penetrating to the brain'. Like Frizer, Spenser claimed he stabbed in self-defence, but in one famous case a man was murdered in this way. This was Thomas Arden, killed by two men in his house at Faversham in 1551. A contemporary account describes the attack:

Black Will stepped forth and cast a towel about his neck, so to stop his breath and strangle him. Then Mosby, having at his girdle a pressing-iron of 14 pound weight, struck him on the head with the same, so that he fell down and gave a great groan, insomuch that they thought he had been killed. Then they bare him away to lay him in the counting-house, and as they were about to lay him down, the pangs of death coming on him, he gave a great groan and stretched himself. And then Black Will gave him a great gash in the face, and so killed him out of hand.

In this case too, the *coup de grâce* is a 'gash in the face'. It is not a premeditated stroke, exactly, but it is the one chosen for its effectiveness: to kill him 'out of hand'.

Another frequent statement about the inquest version is that it agrees with what we already know, from other sources, about Marlowe's physical aggressiveness. One of the chief sources cited is Thomas Kyd, who describes Marlowe as 'intemperate', and speaks of his 'rashness in attempting sudden privy injuries to men'. This is always taken to mean that Marlowe physically attacked people, but again I am unsure about this. In Elizabethan usage to 'injure' almost always means to insult, to abuse verbally. This is closer to the root-meaning of the word, which is connected with injustice, and it is the invariable meaning of modern French *injurier*. Kyd's particular phrase, 'privy injuries', is similar to a term in Puttenham's influential *Art of English Poesy*, published in 1589, where a certain kind of insult is called the 'privy nip'. From Puttenham's definition, it sounds like what we call sarcasm: 'when ye give a mock under smooth and lowly words,' he says, 'we may call it the privy nip, or a mild and appeasing mockery.' Kyd is not being quite so specific, but I am sure that his general meaning is to do with Marlowe as a scoffer, not as a brawler. This certainly is the context in which the phrase appears. Kyd is writing about Marlowe's dreadful blasphemies and dangerous opinions. He mentions this 'rashness' against people because it is part of the same general accusation. He is talking about the violence of language, not of the dagger.

This does not, of course, mean that Marlowe is innocent of the charge, only that Kyd was not actually making it when he wrote those words. There is plenty of independent evidence that Marlowe was as quick on the draw as any other young Elizabethan. In 1589 he was imprisoned after a swordfight in Shoreditch which resulted in the death of William Bradley, an innkeeper's son. In 1592, again in Shoreditch, he was bound over by the local constabulary to 'keep the peace'. A few months later, on a street corner in Canterbury, he fought a tailor named Corkine 'with a staff and a dagger'. These are part of the lurid side of Marlowe's reputation, but what really do they show?

They show that he was no stranger to violence, but they do not prove much about him as an *aggressor*. There is no evidence that he started the fight with Bradley. In fact, he did not actually inflict any wound on Bradley at all – Bradley was killed by another man – and he was bailed and acquitted shortly afterwards. His later breach of the peace in Shoreditch may well be another case of verbal rather than physical rowdiness. His attack on the tailor Corkine is, on the face of it, a clear instance of aggression (and quite possibly entailed the embarrassing situation of being arrested by his father, who was then serving as a constable) but once again there are extenuating factors. When Corkine sued him for assault, Marlowe's response was to file a counter-suit, claiming that it was not he but Corkine who was the assailant. The tailor had 'beat, wounded and maltreated' him to his 'grave damage'. What the truth was we do not know. By the time it came to court the two men had patched up their differences, and the case was dismissed. Twenty years later, a William Corkine published a lute accompaniment to Marlowe's famous lyric 'Come Live With Me'. This was almost certainly the tailor's son.

On the basis of Marlowe's police record – perhaps known to the coroner, perhaps not – we can say that he had twice been involved in violent clashes, in public, though in neither case can we be sure that he was the aggressor, and in neither case was he subsequently charged with any crime. The story of his assault on Ingram Frizer is plausible – we know that anyway – but these earlier events do not really add weight to it, as they are usually thought to, and the 'privy injuries' mentioned by Kyd add nothing at all.

Charles Nicholl, *The Reckoning*

Rain filled the gutters and splashed knee-high off the pavement. Big cops in slickers that shone like gun barrels had a lot of fun carrying giggling girls across the bad places. The rain drummed hard on the roof of the car and the burbank top began to leak. A pool of water formed on the floorboards for me to keep my feet in. It was too early in the fall for that kind of rain. I struggled into a trench coat and made a dash for the nearest drugstore and bought myself a pint of whisky. Back in the car I used enough of it to keep warm and interested. I was long overparked, but the cops were too busy carrying girls and blowing whistles to bother about that.

In spite of the rain, or perhaps even because of it, there was business done at Geiger's. Very nice cars stopped in front and very nice-looking people went in and out with wrapped parcels. They were not all men.

He showed about four o'clock. A cream-coloured coupé stopped in front of the store and I caught a glimpse of the fat face and the Charlie Chan moustache as he dodged out of it and into the store. He was hatless and wore a belted green leather raincoat. I couldn't see his glass eye at that distance. A tall and very good-looking kid in a jerkin came out of the store and rode the coupé off around the corner and came back walking, his glistening black hair plastered with rain.

Another hour went by. It got dark and the rain-clouded lights of the stores were soaked up by the black street. Streetcar bells jangled crossly. At around five-fifteen the tall boy in the jerkin came out of Geiger's with an umbrella and went after the cream-coloured coupé. When he had it in front Geiger came out and the tall boy held the umbrella over Geiger's bare head. He folded it, shook it off and handed it into the car. He dashed back into the store. I started my motor.

The coupé went west on the boulevard, which forced me to make a left turn and a lot of enemies, including a motor-man who stuck his head out into the rain to bawl me out. I was two blocks behind the coupé before I got in the groove. I hoped Geiger was on his way home. I caught sight of him two or three times and then made him turning north into Laurel Canyon Drive. Half-way up the grade he turned left and took a curving ribbon of wet concrete which was called Laverne Terrace. It was a narrow street with a high bank on one side and a scattering of cabin-like houses built down the slope on the other side, so that their roofs were not very much above road level. Their front windows were masked by hedges and shrubs. Sodden trees dripped all over the landscape.

Geiger had his lights on and I hadn't. I speeded up and passed him on a curve, picked a number off a house as I went by and turned at the end of the block. He had already stopped. His car lights were tilted in at the garage of a small house with a square box hedge so arranged that it masked the front door completely. I watched him come out of the garage with his umbrella up and go in through the hedge. He didn't act as if he expected anybody to be tailing him. Light went on in the house. I drifted down to the next house above it, which seemed empty but had no signs out. I parked, aired out the convertible, had a drink from my bottle, and sat. I didn't know what I was waiting for, but something told me to wait. Another army of sluggish minutes dragged by.

Two cars came up the hill and went over the crest. It seemed to be a very quiet street. At a little after six more bright lights bobbed through the driving rain. It was pitch-black by then. A car dragged to a stop in front of Geiger's house. The filaments of its lights glowed dimly and died. The door opened and a woman got out. A small slim woman in a vagabond hat and a transparent raincoat. She went in through the box maze. A bell rang faintly, light through the rain, a closing door, silence.

I reached a flash out of my car pocket and went down-grade and looked at the car. It was a Packard convertible, maroon or dark brown. The left window was down. I felt for the licence holder and poked light at it. The registration read: Carmen Sternwood, 3765 Alta Brea Crescent, West Hollywood. I went back to my car again and sat and sat. The top dripped on my knees and my stomach burned from the whisky. No more cars came up the hill. No lights went on in the house before which I was parked. It seemed like a nice neighbourhood to have bad habits in.

At seven-twenty a single flash of hard white light shot out of Geiger's house like a wave of summer lightning. As the darkness folded back on it and ate it up a thin tinkling scream echoed out and lost itself among the rain-drenched trees. I was out of the car and on my way before the echoes died.

There was no fear in the scream. It had a sound of half-pleasurable shock, an accent of drunkenness, an overtone of pure idiocy. It was a nasty sound. It make me think of men in white and barred windows and hard narrow cots with leather wrist and ankle straps fastened to them. The Geiger hideaway was perfectly silent again when I hit the gap in the hedge and dodged around the angle that masked the front door. There was an iron ring in a lion's mouth for a knocker. I reached for it, I had hold of it. At that exact instant, as if somebody had been waiting for the cue, three shots boomed in the house. There was a sound that might have been a long harsh sigh. Then a soft messy thump. And then rapid footsteps in the house – going away.

The door fronted on a narrow run, like a footbridge over a gully, that filled the gap between the house wall and the edge of the bank. There was no porch, no solid ground, no way to get around to the back. The back entrance was at the top of a flight of wooden steps that rose from the alley-like street below. I knew this because I heard a clatter of feet on the steps, going down. Then I heard the sudden roar of a starting car. It faded swiftly into the distance. I thought the sound was echoed by another car, but I wasn't sure. The house in front of me was as silent as a vault. There wasn't any hurry. What was in there was in there.

I straddled the fence at the side of the runway and leaned far out to the draped but unscreened French window and tried to look in at the crack where the drapes came together. I saw lamplight on a wall and one end of a bookcase. I got back on the runway and took all of it and some of the hedge and gave the front door the heavy shoulder. This was foolish. About the only part of a California house you can't put your foot through is the front door. All it did was hurt my shoulder and make me mad. I climbed over the railing again and kicked the French window in, used my hat for a glove and pulled out most of the lower small pane of glass. I could now reach in and draw a bolt that fastened the window to the sill. The rest was easy. There was no top bolt. The catch gave. I climbed in and pulled the drapes off my face.

Neither of the two people in the room paid any attention to the way I came in, although only one of them was dead.

It was a wide room, the whole width of the house. It had a low beamed ceiling and brown plaster walls decked out with strips of Chinese embroidery, and Chinese and Japanese prints in grained wood frames. There were low bookshelves, there was a thick pinkish Chinese rug in which a gopher could have spent a week without showing his nose above the nap. There were floor cushions, bits of odd silk tossed around, as if whoever lived there had to have a piece he could reach out and thumb. There was a broad low divan of old rose tapestry. It had a wad of clothes on it, including lilac-coloured silk underwear. There was a big carved lamp on a pedestal, two other standing lamps with jade-green shades and long tassels. There was a black desk with carved gargoyles at the corners and behind it a yellow satin cushion on a polished black chair with carved arms and back. The room contained an odd assortment of odours, of which the most emphatic at the moment seemed to be the pungent aftermath of cordite and the sickish aroma of ether.

On a sort of low dais at one end of the room there was a high-backed teakwood chair in which Miss Carmen Sternwood was sitting on a fringed orange shawl. She was sitting very straight, with her hands on the arms of the chair, her knees close together, her body stiffly erect in the pose of an Egyptian goddess, her chin level, her small bright teeth shining between her parted lips. Her eyes were wide open. The dark slate colour of the iris had devoured the pupil. They were mad eyes. She seemed to be unconscious, but she didn't have the pose of unconsciousness. She looked as if, in her mind, she was doing something very important and making a fine job of it. Out of her mouth came a tinny chuckling noise which didn't change her expression or even move her lips.

She was wearing a pair of long jade earrings. They were nice earrings and had probably cost a couple of hundred dollars. She wasn't wearing anything else.

She had a beautiful body, small, lithe, compact, firm, rounded. Her skin in the lamplight had the shimmering lustre of a pearl. Her legs didn't quite have the raffish grace of Mrs Regan's legs, but they were very nice. I looked her over without either embarrassment or ruttishness. As a naked girl she was not there in that room at all. She was just a dope. To me she was always just a dope.

I stopped looking at her, and looked at Geiger. He was on his back on the floor, beyond the fringe of the Chinese rug, in front of a thing that looked like a totem pole. It had a profile like an eagle and its wide round eye was a camera lens. The lens was aimed at the naked girl in the chair. There was a blackened flash bulb clipped to the side of the totem pole. Geiger was wearing Chinese slippers with thick felt soles, and his legs were in black satin pyjamas and the upper part of him wore a Chinese embroidered coat, the front of which was mostly blood. His glass eye shone brightly up at me and was by far the most lifelike thing about him. At a glance none of the three shots I heard had missed. He was very dead.

The flash bulb was the sheet lightning I had seen. The crazy scream was the doped and naked girl's reaction to it. The three shots had been somebody else's idea of how the proceedings might be given a new twist. The idea of the lad who had gone down the back steps and slammed into a car and raced away. I could see merit in his point of view.

Raymond Chandler, *The Big Sleep*

Massacre

Avenge O Lord thy slaughtered saints, whose bones
 Lie scattered on the Alpine mountains cold,
 Even them who kept thy truth so pure of old
 When all our fathers worshipped stocks and stones,
Forget not: in thy book record their groans
 Who were thy sheep and in their ancient fold
 Slain by the bloody Piedmontese that rolled
 Mother with infant down the rocks. Their moans
The vales redoubled to the hills, and they
 To heaven. Their martyred blood and ashes sow
 O'er all the Italian fields where still doth sway
The triple Tyrant: that from these may grow
 A hundredfold, who having learnt thy way
 Early may fly the Babylonian woe.

John Milton, 'On the Late Massacre in Piedmont'

[The Idumaeans] were furious and insulted at their exclusion from the City, and the failure of the Zealots, who seemed to be in a strong position, to give them any assistance so bewildered them that many were sorry they had come. But the disgrace of going home with nothing whatever accomplished outweighed their regrets, and they stayed where they were before the wall, encamped in the greatest discomfort. During the night a devastating storm broke; a hurricane raged, rain fell in torrents, lightning flashed continuously, the thunderclaps were terrifying, and the earth quaked with deafening roars. Disaster to the human race was plainly foreshadowed by this collapse of the whole framework of things, and no one could doubt that the omens portended a catastrophe without parallel.

The Idumaeans and the people in the City drew the same conclusion. The former felt that God was angry about the expedition and that they would not escape punishment for bearing arms against the Capital; Ananus and his friends were sure that they had gained a victory without a battle and that God was championing their cause. But this guess was wide of the mark – they were predicting for their enemies the fate that awaited their friends. For the Idumaeans pressing close together kept each other warm, and by making a roof overhead with their long shields were little the worse for the downpour; and the Zealots, more anxious about them than about the danger to themselves, met to discuss the possibility of helping them. The hotheads favoured using their weapons to force a way through the lines of guards, and then charging into the middle of the City and defiantly opening the gates to their allies. The guards would fall back confused by their unexpected move, especially as most of them were unarmed and had seen no fighting, while the citizen army could not easily be mustered, as they were confined to their own houses by the storm. If this meant danger, it was their duty to put up with anything rather than stand by while such a huge army perished miserably because of them. The more sensible people on the other hand opposed the use of force, seeing not only that the guards encircling them were at full strength, but that because of the Idumaeans the City wall was carefully guarded. They assumed also that Ananus was everywhere, visiting the guards at all hours. On other nights such was indeed the case, but on this night it was omitted, not through neglect on Ananus' part, but because Fate was determined that he should perish and all his guards with him. It was she who as the night advanced and the storm reached its height put to sleep the sentries guarding the colonnade, and gave the Zealots the idea of borrowing some of the Temple saws and cutting through the bars of the gates. The noise was not heard, thanks to the roar of the wind and the continuous crash of thunder.

They stole out of the Temple and made for the wall; then plying the same saws they opened the gate in front of the Idumaeans. The latter panicked at first, thinking that Ananus and his men were making an attack, and every man grasped his sword to defend himself; but they soon realized who had come, and passed through the gateway. If they had flung themselves on the City, nothing could have prevented the citizens from perishing to a man, such was their fury; but they were anxious to free the Zealots from their confinement first, as the men who had admitted them implored them not to forget that those they had come to assist were in dire peril, or involve them in greater danger. When they had overwhelmed the guards, they could easily attack the City; but if they once roused the City, they would never overcome the guards; for as soon as they realized the situation, the citizens would form up and block every way to the Temple.

Convinced by this reasoning, the Idumaeans passed through the City and up the slope to the Temple. When they appeared inside, the Zealots, who had been on tenterhooks till they arrived, emerged full of confidence from the inner courts, and mingling with the Idumaeans attacked the pickets, knifing some of the advanced sentries in their sleep. The shouts of those who were awake roused the whole force. Completely taken aback they snatched their weapons and rallied to the defence. As long as they thought that only the Zealots were attacking them they fought confidently, hoping to win by weight of numbers, but when they saw others streaming in from outside, they grasped the fact of the Idumaean irruption. Most of them lost hope, flung away their arms, and gave themselves up to lamentation; but some of the younger men, putting up a wall of shields, fought the Idumaeans tooth and nail and for a long time sheltered the feebler folk. Their cries informed the people in the City of the disastrous situation; but none of these ventured to help them when they learnt that the Idumaeans had broken in; they merely replied with futile shouts and groans, and loud shrieks went up from the women who all had relations in danger among the guards. The Zealots echoed the war-cry of the Idumaeans, and the din from every side was made more terrifying by the tempest. No one was spared by the Idumaeans, by nature most barbarous and bloodthirsty, and so knocked about by the storm that they vented their rage on the men who had shut them out, making no distinction between those who cried for mercy and those who fought. Many who reminded them of the ties of blood and begged them to reverence the Temple they shared were run through with swords. There was no room for flight, no hope of safety; they were crushed together and cut down until most of them, driven back, with no way of retreat left, relentlessly assailed by their murderous foes and, in a hopeless position, flung themselves headlong into the City, choosing for themselves a fate more pitiable, it seems to me, than the one they were fleeing from. The entire outer court of the Temple was deluged with blood, and 8,500 corpses greeted the rising sun.

This holocaust did not satisfy the Idumaean appetite for blood. Turning to the City they plundered every house and killed anyone they met. Then thinking the common people not worth bothering about they went after the high priests. It was against them that the main rush was made, and they were soon caught and killed. The murderers, standing on their dead bodies, ridiculed Ananus for his devotion to the people and Jeshua for his speech from the wall. So devoid of decency were they that they threw out the dead bodies without burial, though the Jews pay so much regard to obsequies that even those found guilty and crucified are taken down and buried before sunset. I should not be far wrong if I said that the fall of the City began with Ananus' death, and that the overthrow of the wall and the destruction of the Jewish state dated from the day when they saw the high priest, the champion of their cause, assassinated in the middle of the City. For he was a man looked up to on every account and entirely honest, and although so distinguished by birth, position, and reputation, he loved to treat even the humblest as equals. Utterly devoted to liberty and with a passion for democracy, he always made his own interests take second place to the public advantage and made peace the aim of his life; for he knew that Rome was invincible. But when he had no option he made careful preparations for war, in order that, if the Jews would not end hostilities, they might carry on the fight efficiently. In short, had Ananus lived, hostilities would indeed have ended; for he was an eloquent speaker who could mould public opinion and had already silenced his opponents: if war it was to be, the Jews would have held up the Roman advance a very long time under such a general.

His yoke-fellow was Jeshua, not on his level perhaps, but far above the rest. But I think God had sentenced this polluted city to destruction and willed that the Sanctuary should be purged by fire, and so cut off those who clung to them and loved them so dearly. Thus men who a little while before had been clad in the sacred vestments, had conducted the worship renowned through the world and had been revered by visitors from every land on earth, were thrown out naked, to be devoured by dogs and wild beasts before all eyes. Virtue herself wept for these splendid men, I believe, lamenting her total defeat at the hands of Vice. Yet such was the end of Ananus and Jeshua.

With these two out of the way, the Zealots and a solid mass of Idumaeans fell upon the population and butchered them like a herd of unclean animals. Ordinary people were killed where they were caught; the young nobles were arrested, fettered, and locked up in prison: in the hope that some would join the rebels, their execution was delayed. But not a man did so – rather than align themselves with scoundrels against their own country they all chose death. For this refusal they paid a terrible price; they were flogged and racked, and only when their bodies could endure no more torture were they allowed to die by the sword. Those arrested in the morning were finished off at night, and the bodies brought up and thrown out to make room for the next batch. The people were so petrified with fear that no one dared either to be seen weeping for a dead kinsman or to bury him, but they kept their tears secret behind locked doors, and made sure that none of their enemies could hear them before they uttered a groan; for the mourner promptly received the same treatment as the mourned. By night they took up a little dust in their hands and sprinkled it on the bodies – or by day, if a man was exceptionally bold. Twelve thousand of the young nobles died in this way.

Disgusted now with haphazard slaughter, the Zealots set up sham courts and faked trials. They had decided to liquidate one of the most distinguished citizens, Zachariah, son of Baruch, as they were annoyed by his burning hatred of wrong and love of freedom, and his wealth made them hope not only to plunder his property but also to get rid of a man capable of destroying them. They therefore issued a categorical order, summoning seventy men in public positions to the Temple, where they turned them into a stage jury with no authority. Then they charged Zachariah with trying to betray their country to Rome and sending an offer of treason to Vespasian. There was no proof of the charges, no evidence at all, but they said that they themselves were quite convinced of his guilt and claimed that that should satisfy anyone. Zachariah realized that his fate was sealed: he had been treacherously summoned to a prison, not a court. But certain death was not going to deprive him of free speech – he stood up, scoffed at the incredibility of the charges, and in a few words disposed of the whole indictment. Then, turning the tables on his accusers, he methodically detailed all their illegalities and mercilessly exposed their mismanagement of affairs. The Zealots howled with rage and could hardly keep their hands off their swords, determined as they were to play out this farce, this sham trial to the end, and eager also to find out whether the jurors would risk their own lives in the cause of justice. But the seventy brought in a unanimous verdict of Not Guilty, choosing to die with the defendant rather than bear the responsibility for his destruction. The Zealots greeted this acquittal with shouts of indignation, and were all enraged with the jury for not realizing that the authority bestowed on them was a mere sham. Two of the most unscrupulous fell upon Zachariah, murdered him in the middle of the Temple, and jested over his dead body: 'Now you have got our verdict too, and your trials are over.' With that they threw him out of the Temple and into the valley beneath. Then they showed their contempt for the jurors by belabouring them with the backs of their swords and driving them from the precincts. For one purpose only they refrained from murdering them – that they might go into every part of the City and let all the citizens know that they were slaves.

The Idumaeans now felt sorry they had come and were disgusted with the goings-on. One of the Zealots came to them privately and held a meeting at which he denounced the excesses they had committed jointly with those who had called them in, and listed the damage done to the Capital. They had taken up arms on the ground that the high priests were betraying the Capital to the Romans, yet they had found no evidence of treason whatever. But her defenders so-called were all out for war and personal domination. The right time to stop all this had been at the outset;

but having once formed a partnership to shed their country's blood, they ought at least to set a limit to their misdeeds and not go on assisting the destroyers of all they held dear. If some of them were vexed at the closing of the gates and the refusal to let them enter at once with their weapons, those responsible had certainly paid for their opposition. Ananus was dead, and in a single night the population had been almost wiped out. This had produced an unmistakable revulsion of feeling in many of their own people, but those who had called them in displayed unparalleled savagery and not a trace of respect for their deliverers. Before the very eyes of their allies they perpetrated the vilest atrocities, and their excesses would be laid at the Idumaeans' door until someone either ended or repudiated what was going on. And so, as the allegation of treason had been exploded and there was no Roman invasion on the horizon, while the City was at the mercy of a caucus that could not be dislodged, their right course was to go back home and have nothing more to do with these contemptible people, and so blot out the memory of all the crimes in which they had been tricked into playing a part.

Accepting his advice the Idumaeans first released from prison about 2,000 citizens who at once left the City and fled to Simon, of whom we shall speak by and by; then turning their backs on Jerusalem they went home. Their departure had a paradoxical effect on both sides: the citizens, unaware of the revulsion of feeling, recovered their spirits for a time as if rid of an enemy, while the Zealots became more arrogant still, not as if they were deserted by allies, but as if relieved of men who frowned upon and interfered with their excesses. No longer was there any hesitation or circumspection about their outrages: they reached all their decisions with the utmost speed and executed them more quickly still. Chief objects of their lust for blood were the brave and the nobly born, the former being victims of their fear, the latter of their envy: they felt that their whole safety depended on their leaving no one who counted alive. Along with many others they murdered Gurion, a man with a reputation and of good family, but democratic and passionately devoted to liberty, if ever a Jew was. He owned his ruin mainly to his plain speaking, as well as the advantages he enjoyed. Niger the Peraean did not escape their clutches. He had shown amazing courage in the campaigns against the Romans; but now, protesting loudly and displaying his scars, he was dragged through the middle of the City. When pulled outside the gates he despaired of life and pleaded for burial; but they made it brutally clear that the grave he so desired would never be his, and then did the foul deed. As he died, Niger called down on their heads the vengeance of Rome, famine and pestilence, battle and slaughter, and as a final disaster, a death-grapple with their fellow-citizens. All these things heaven visited on the godless wretches; and the retribution was most just, for through their party-strife they were to taste before long the mad fury of their fellow-citizens.

Josephus, *The Jewish War*, trans. G. A. Williamson

Most were naked but for the locked tin masks
which stop them sucking the cane they harvest.
We could see they had been made tigerish

by their whippings. Our sabres stuck in bone,
our saddle-girths were slashed by their children,
crones tore shot from the mouths of primed cannon

while our powder-monkeys fumbled and wept.
But we have laid them up in lavender.
They think their dead will wake in Africa.

Ian Duhig, 'Croix-des-Bouquets, Haiti'

Mitigation

As o'er my latest book I pored,
  Enjoying it immensely
I suddenly exclaimed 'Good Lord!'
  And gripped the volume tensely.
'Golly!' I cried. I writhed in pain.
'They've done it on me once again!'
  And furrows creased my brow.
I'd written (which I thought quite good)
'Ruth, ripening into womanhood,
Was now a girl who knocked men flat
And frequently got whistled at,'
And some vile, careless, casual gook
Had spoiled the best thing in the book
  By printing 'not'
  (Yes, 'not', great Scott!)
    When I had written 'now'.

On murder in the first degree
  The Law, I knew, is rigid:
Its attitude, if A kills B,
  To A is always frigid.
It counts it not a trivial slip
If on behalf of authorship
You liquidate compositors.
This kind of conduct it abhors
  And seldom will allow.
Nevertheless, I deemed it best
And in the public interest
To buy a gun, to oil it well,
Inserting what is called a shell,
  And go and pot
    With sudden shot
    This printer who had printed 'not'
      When I had written 'now'.
I tracked the bounder to his den
  Through private information:
I said 'Good afternoon' and then
  Explained the situation:
'I'm not a fussy man,' I said.
'I smile when you put "rid" for "red"
And "bad" for "bed" and "hoad" for "head"
  And "bolge" instead of "bough".
When "wone" appears in lieu of "wine"
Or if you alter "Cohn" to "Schine",
  I never make a row.
I know how easy errors are.
But this time you have gone too far
By printing "not" when you knew what
  I really wrote was "now".
Prepare,' I said, 'to meet your God
Or, as you'd say, your Goo or Bod
  Or possibly your Gow.'

A few weeks later into court
  I came to stand my trial.
The Judge was quite a decent sort,
  He said 'Well, cocky, I'll

Be passing sentence in a jiff,
And so, my poor unhappy stiff,
If you have anything to say,
Now is the moment. Fire away.
   You have?'
      I said 'And how!
Me lud, the facts I don't dispute.
I did, I own it freely, shoot
This printer through the collar stud.
What else could I have done, me lud?
   He's printed "not" . . .'
   The Judge said '*What!*
      When you had written "now"?
God bless my soul! Gadzooks!' said he.
'The blighters did that once to me.
   A dirty trick, I trow.
I hereby quash and override
The jury's verdict. Gosh!' he cried.
'Give me your hand. Yes, I insist,
You splendid fellow! Case dismissed.'
   (Cheers, and a Voice 'Wow-wow!')

A statue stands against the sky,
   Lifelike and rather pretty.
'Twas recently erected by
   The P.E.N. committee.
And many a passer-by is stirred,
For on the plinth, if that's the word,
In golden letters you may read
'This is the man who did the deed.
   His hand set to the plough,
He did not sheathe the sword, but got
A gun at great expense and shot
The human blot who'd printed "not"
   When he had written "now".
He acted with no thought of self,
Not for advancement, not for pelf,
But just because it made him hot
To think the man had printed "not"
   When he had written "now".'

P. G. Wodehouse, 'Printer's Error'

Mob

Jack leapt on to the sand.

'Do our dance! Come on! Dance!'

He ran stumbling through the thick sand to the open space of rock beyond the fire. Between the flashes of lightning the air was dark and terrible; and the boys followed him, clamorously. Roger became the pig, grunting and charging at Jack, who side-stepped. The hunters took their spears, the cooks took spits, and the rest clubs of fire-wood. A circling movement developed and a chant. While Roger mimed the terror of the pig, the littluns ran and jumped on the outside of the circle. Piggy and Ralph, under the threat of the sky, found themselves eager to take a place in this demented but partly secure society. They were glad to touch the brown backs of the fence that hemmed in the terror and made it governable.

'*Kill the beast! Cut his throat! Spill his blood!*'

The movement became regular while the chant lost its first superficial excitement and began to beat like a steady pulse. Roger ceased to be a pig and became a hunter, so that the centre of the ring yawned emptily. Some of the littluns started a ring on their own; and the complementary circles went round and round as though repetition would achieve safety of itself. There was the throb and stamp of a single organism.

The dark sky was shattered by a blue-white scar. An instant later the noise was on them like the blow of a gigantic whip. The chant rose a tone in agony.

'*Kill the beast! Cut his throat! Spill his blood!*'

Now out of the terror rose another desire, thick, urgent, blind.

'*Kill the beast! Cut his throat! Spill his blood!*'

Again the blue-white scar jagged above them and the sulphurous explosion beat down. The littluns screamed and blundered about, fleeing from the edge of the forest, and one of them broke the ring of biguns in his terror.

'Him! Him!'

The circle became a horseshoe. A thing was crawling out of the forest. It came darkly, uncertainly. The shrill screaming that rose before the beast was like a pain. The beast stumbled into the horseshoe.

'*Kill the beast! Cut his throat! Spill his blood!*'

The blue-white scar was constant, the noise unendurable. Simon was crying out something about a dead man on a hill.

'Kill the beast! Cut his throat! Spill his blood! Do him in!'

The sticks fell and the mouth of the new circle crunched and screamed. The beast was on its knees in the centre, its arms folded over its face. It was crying out against the abominable noise something about a body on the hill. The beast struggled forward, broke the ring, and fell over the steep edge of the rock to the sand by the water. And once the crowd surged after it, poured down the rock, leapt on to the beast, screamed, struck, bit, tore. There were no words, and no movements but the tearing of teeth and claws.

Then the clouds opened and let down the rain like a waterfall. The water bounded from the mountain-top, tore leaves and branches from the trees, poured like a cold shower over the struggling heap on the sand. Presently the heap broke up and figures staggered away. Only the beast lay still, a few yards from the sea. Even in the rain they could see how small a beast it was; and already its blood was staining the sand.

Now a great wind blew the rain sideways, cascading the water from the forest trees. On the mountain-top the parachute filled and moved; the figure slid, rose to its feet, spun, swayed down through a vastness of wet air and trod with ungainly feet the tops of the high trees; falling, still falling, it sank towards the beach and the boys rushed screaming into the darkness. The parachute took the figure forward, furrowing the lagoon, and bumped it over the reef and out to sea.

Towards midnight the rain ceased and the clouds drifted away, so that the sky was scattered once more with the incredible lamps of stars. Then the breeze died too and there was no noise save the drip and trickle of water that ran out of clefts and spilled down, leaf by leaf, to the brown earth of the island. The air was cool, moist, and clear; and presently even the sound of the water was still. The beast lay huddled on the pale beach and the stains spread, inch by inch.

The edge of the lagoon became a streak of phosphorescence which advanced minutely, as the great wave of the tide flowed. The clear water mirrored the clear sky and the angular bright constellations. The line of phosphorescence bulged about the sand grains and little pebbles; it held them each in a dimple of tension, then suddenly accepted them with an inaudible syllable and moved on.

Along the shoreward edge of the shallows the advancing clearness was full of strange, moonbeam-bodied creatures with fiery eyes. Here and there a larger pebble clung to its own air and was covered with a coat of pearls. The tide swelled in over the rain-pitted sand and smoothed everything with a layer of silver. Now it touched the first of the stains that seeped from the broken body and the creatures made a moving patch of light as they gathered at the edge. The water rose further and dressed Simon's coarse hair with brightness. The line of his cheek silvered and the turn of his shoulder became sculptured marble. The strange, attendant creatures, with their fiery eyes and trailing vapours, busied themselves round his head. The body lifted a fraction of an inch from the sand and a bubble of air escaped from the mouth with a wet plop. Then it turned gently in the water.

Somewhere over the darkened curve of the world the sun and moon were pulling; and the film of water on the earth planet was held, bulging slightly on one side while the solid core turned. The great wave of the tide moved further along the island and the water lifted. Softly, surrounded by a fringe of inquisitive bright creatures, itself a silver shape beneath the steadfast constellations, Simon's dead body moved out towards the open sea.

• • •

Piggy eyed the advancing figure carefully. Nowadays he sometimes found that he saw more clearly if he removed his glasses and shifted the one lens to the other eye; but even through the good eye, after what had happened, Ralph remained unmistakably Ralph. He came now out of the coconut trees, limping, dirty, with dead leaves hanging from his shock of yellow hair. One eye was a slit in his puffy cheek and a great scab had formed on his right knee. He paused for a moment and peered at the figure on the platform.

'Piggy? Are you the only one left?'

'There's some littluns.'

'They don't count. No biguns?'

'Oh – Samneric. They're collecting wood.'

'Nobody else?'

'Not that I know of.'

Ralph climbed on to the platform carefully. The coarse grass was still worn away where the assembly used to sit; the fragile white conch still gleamed by the polished seat. Ralph sat down in the grass facing the Chief's seat and the conch. Piggy knelt at his left, and for a long minute there was silence.

At last Ralph cleared his throat and whispered something.

Piggy whispered back.

'What you say?'

Ralph spoke up.

'Simon.'

Piggy said nothing but nodded, solemnly. They continued to sit, gazing with impaired sight at the chief's seat and the glittering lagoon. The green light and the glossy patches of sunshine played over their befouled bodies.

At length Ralph got up and went to the conch. He took the shell caressingly with both hands and knelt, leaning against the trunk.

'Piggy.'

'Uh?'

'What we going to do?'

Piggy nodded at the conch.

'You could – '

'Call an assembly?'

Ralph laughed sharply as he said the word and Piggy frowned.

'You're still Chief.'

Ralph laughed again.

'You are. Over us.'

'I got the conch.'

'Ralph! Stop laughing like that. Look there ain't no need, Ralph! What's the others going to think?'

At last Ralph stopped. He was shivering.

'Piggy.'

'Uh?'

'That was Simon.'

'You said that before.'

'Piggy.'

'Uh?'

'That was murder.'

'You stop it!' said Piggy, shrilly. 'What good're you doing talking like that?'

He jumped to his feet and stood over Ralph.

'It was dark. There was that – that bloody dance. There was lightning and thunder and rain. We was scared!'

'I wasn't scared,' said Ralph slowly, 'I was – I don't know what I was.'

'We was scared!' said Piggy excitedly. 'Anything might have happened. It wasn't – what you said.'

He was gesticulating, searching for a formula.

'Oh, Piggy!'

Ralph's voice, low and stricken, stopped Piggy's gestures. He bent down and waited. Ralph, cradling the conch, rocked himself to and fro.

'Don't you understand, Piggy? The things we did – '

'He may still be – '

'No.'

'P'raps he was only pretending – '

Piggy's voice tailed off at the sight of Ralph's face.

'You were outside. Outside the circle. You never really came in. Didn't you see what we – what they did?'

There was loathing, and at the same time a kind of feverish excitement in his voice.

'Didn't you see, Piggy?'

'Not all that well. I only got one eye now. You ought to know that, Ralph.'

Ralph continued to rock to and fro.

'It was an accident,' said Piggy suddenly, 'that's what it was. An accident.' His voice shrilled again. 'Coming in the dark – he hadn't no business crawling like that out of the dark. He was batty. He asked for it.' He gesticulated widely again. 'It was an accident.'

'You didn't see what they did – '

'Look, Ralph. We got to forget this. We can't do no good thinking about it, see?'

'I'm frightened. Of us. I want to go home. O God, I want to go home.'

'It was an accident,' said Piggy stubbornly, 'and that's that.'

He touched Ralph's bare shoulder and Ralph shuddered at the human contact.

'And look, Ralph,' Piggy glanced round quickly, then leaned close – 'don't let on we was in that dance. Not to Samneric.'

'But we were! All of us!'

Piggy shook his head.

'Not us till last. They never noticed in the dark. Anyway you said I was only on the outside – '

'So was I,' muttered Ralph, 'I was on the outside too.'

Piggy nodded eagerly.

'That's right. We was on the outside. We never done nothing, we never seen nothing.'

Piggy paused, then went on.

'We'll live on our own, the four of us – '

'Four of us. We aren't enough to keep the fire burning.'

'We'll try. See? I lit it.'

Samneric came dragging a great log out of the forest. They dumped it by the fire and turned to the pool. Ralph jumped to his feet.

'Hi! You two!'

The twins checked a moment, then walked on.

'They're going to bathe, Ralph.'

'Better get it over.'

The twins were very surprised to see Ralph. They flushed and looked past him into the air.

'Hullo. Fancy meeting you, Ralph.'

'We just been in the forest – '

' – to get wood for the fire – '

' – we got lost last night.'

Ralph examined his toes.

'You got lost after the . . .'

Piggy cleaned his lens.

'After the feast,' said Sam in a stifled voice. Eric nodded. 'Yes, after the feast.'

'We left early,' said Piggy quickly, 'because we were tired.'

'So did we – '

' – very early – '

' – we were very tired.'

Sam touched a scratch on his forehead and then hurriedly took his hand away. Eric fingered his split lip.

'Yes. We were very tired,' repeated Sam, 'so we left early. Was it a good – '

The air was heavy with unspoken knowledge. Sam twisted and the obscene word shot out of him. ' – dance?'

Memory of the dance that none of them had attended shook all four boys convulsively.

'We left early.'

William Golding, *The Lord of the Flies*

Mousetrap

PLAYER QUEEN: Nor earth to me give food, nor heaven light,
Sport and repose lock from me day and night,
Each opposite that blanks the face of joy
Meet what I would have well and it destroy,
Both here and hence pursue me lasting strife
If, once a widow, ever I be wife.

HAMLET: If she should break it now!

PLAYER KING (*to Player Queen*): 'Tis deeply sworn. Sweet, leave me here a while.
My spirits grow dull, and fain I would beguile
The tedious day with sleep.

PLAYER QUEEN: Sleep rock thy brain,
And never come mischance between us twain.

Player King sleeps. Player Queen exits

HAMLET (*to Gertrude*): Madam, how like you this play?

QUEEN GERTRUDE: The lady protests too much, methinks.

HAMLET: O, but she'll keep her word.

KING CLAUDIUS: Have you heard the argument? Is there no offence in't?

HAMLET: No, no, they do but jest, poison in jest. No offence i'th' world.

KING CLAUDIUS: What do you call the play?

HAMLET: *The Mousetrap*. Marry, how? Tropically. This play is the image of a murder done in Vienna. Gonzago is the Duke's name, his wife Baptista. You shall see anon. 'Tis a knavish piece of work; but what o' that? Your majesty, and we that have free souls, it touches us not. Let the galled jade wince, our withers are unwrung.

Enter Player Lucianus

This is one Lucianus, nephew to the King.

OPHELIA: You are as good as a chorus, my lord.

HAMLET: I could interpret between you and your love if I could see the puppets dallying.

OPHELIA: You are keen, my lord, you are keen.

HAMLET: It would cost you a groaning to take off mine edge.

OPHELIA: Still better, and worse.

HAMLET: So you mis-take your husbands. (*To Lucianus*)
Begin, murderer. Pox, leave thy damnable faces and begin. Come: 'the croaking raven doth bellow for revenge'.

PLAYER LUCIANUS: Thoughts black, hands apt, drugs fit, and time agreeing,
Confederate season, else no creature seeing;
Thou mixture rank of midnight weeds collected,
With Hecate's ban thrice blasted, thrice infected,
Thy natural magic and dire property
On wholesome life usurp immediately.

He pours the poison in the Player King's ear

HAMLET: A poisons him i'th' garden for 's estate. His name's Gonzago. The story is extant, and writ in choice Italian. You shall see anon how the murderer gets the love of Gonzago's wife.

OPHELIA: The King rises.
HAMLET: What, frighted with false fire?
QUEEN GERTRUDE (*to Claudius*): How fares my lord?
POLONIUS: Give o'er the play.
KING CLAUDIUS: Give me some light. Away.
(COURTIERS): Lights, lights, lights!

William Shakespeare, *Hamlet*

N

Nail

And Sisera gathered together all his chariots, even nine hundred chariots of iron, and all the people that were with him, from Harosheth of the Gentiles unto the river of Kishon.

And Deborah said unto Barak, Up; for this is the day in which the LORD hath delivered Sisera into thine hand: is not the LORD gone out before thee? So Barak went down from mount Tabor, and ten thousand men after him.

And the LORD discomfited Sisera, and all his chariots, and all his host, with the edge of the sword before Barak; so that Sisera lighted down off his chariot, and fled away on his feet.

But Barak pursued after the chariots, and after the host, unto Harosheth of the Gentiles: and all the host of Sisera fell upon the edge of the sword; and there was not a man left.

Howbeit Sisera fled away on his feet to the tent of Jael the wife of Heber the Kenite: for there was peace between Jabin the king of Hazor and the house of Heber the Kenite.

And Jael went out to meet Sisera, and said unto him, Turn in, my lord, turn in to me; fear not. And when he had turned in unto her into the tent, she covered him with a mantle.

And he said unto her, Give me, I pray thee, a little water to drink; for I am thirsty. And she opened a bottle of milk, and gave him drink, and covered him.

Again he said unto her, Stand in the door of the tent; and it shall be, when any man doth come and enquire of thee, and say, Is there any man here? that thou shalt say, No.

Then Jael 'Heber's wife' took a nail of the tent, and took an hammer in her hand, and went softly unto him, and smote the nail into his temples, and fastened it into the ground: for he was fast asleep and weary. So he died.

And, behold, as Barak pursued Sisera, Jael came out to meet him, and said unto him, Come, and I will shew thee the man whom thou seekest. And when he came into her tent, behold, Sisera lay dead, and the nail was in his temples.

Judges: 4:13–22

Nero

Claudius was the first victim of his murderous career: because, though Nero may not have been actually responsible for the poisoning of his adoptive father, he knew all about it, as he later admitted by appreciatively quoting a Greek proverb which calls mushrooms (the cause of this death and deification) 'the food of the gods'. And he did his utmost to insult Claudius's memory, accusing him either of stupidity or of cruelty. It was a favourite joke of his that Claudius could no longer 'play the fool on earth', lengthening the initial syllable of *morari*, 'to linger on', so that it meant 'to play the fool'. Nero annulled many of Claudius's decrees and edicts, on the ground that he had been a doddering old idiot; and enclosed the place where he had been cremated with nothing better than a low rubble wall.

He tried to poison Britannicus, being not merely jealous of his voice, which was far more musical than his own, but afraid that the common people might be less attached to Claudius's adopted son than to his real one. The drug came from an expert poisoner named Locusta, and when its action was not so rapid as he expected – the effect was violently laxative – he called for her, complaining that she had given him medicine instead of poison, and flogged her with his own hands. Locusta explained that she had reduced the dose to make the crime less obvious. 'Oho!' he said. 'So you think that I am afraid of the Julian law against poisoning?' Then he led Locusta into his bedroom and stood over her while she concocted the fastest-working poison in her pharmacopoeia. This he administered to a kid, but when it took five hours to die he made her boil down the brew again and again. At last he tried it on a pig, which died on the spot; and that night at dinner had what remained poured into Britannicus's cup. Britannicus dropped dead at the very first taste, but Nero lyingly assured the guests that the poor boy had 'long been subject to these epileptic seizures'. Britannicus was buried hastily and without ceremony on the following day during a heavy shower of rain, and Nero rewarded Locusta generously for her services with a free pardon – she had been condemned to death as a poisoner even before Agrippina employed her to murder Claudius – and actually supplied her with students.

The over-watchful, over-critical eye that Agrippina kept on whatever Nero said or did proved more than he could stand. He first tried to embarrass her by frequent threats to abdicate and go into retirement in Rhodes. Then, having deprived her of all power, and even of her Roman and German bodyguard, he expelled her from his Palace; after which he did everything possible to annoy her, sending people to pester her with law-suits while she stayed in Rome, and when she took refuge on her riverside estate, making them constantly drive or sail past the windows, disturbing her with jeers and cat-calls. In the end her threats and violent behaviour terrified him into deciding that she must die. He tried to poison her three times, but she had always taken the antidote in advance; so he rigged up a machine in the ceiling of her bedroom which would dislodge the panels and drop them on her while she slept. However, someone gave the secret away. Then he had a collapsible cabin-boat designed which would either sink or fall in on top of her. Under pretence of a reconciliation, he sent the most friendly note inviting her to celebrate the Feast of Minerva with him at Baiae, and on her arrival made one of his captains stage an accidental collision with the galley in which she had sailed. Then he protracted the feast until a late hour, and when at last she said: 'I really must get back to Rome,' offered her his collapsible boat instead of the damaged galley. Nero was in a very happy mood as he led Agrippina down to the quay, and even kissed her breasts before she stepped aboard. He sat up all night, on tenterhooks of anxiety, waiting for news of her death. At dawn Lucius Agermus, her freedman, entered joyfully to report that although the ship had foundered, his mother had swum to safety, and he need have no fears on her account. For want of a better plan, Nero ordered one of his men to drop a dagger surreptitiously beside Agermus, whom he arrested at once on a charge of attempted murder. After this he arranged for Agrippina to be killed, and made it seem as if she had sent Agermus to assassinate him but committed suicide on hearing that the plot had miscarried. Other more gruesome details are supplied by reliable authorities: it appears that Nero rushed off to examine Agrippina's corpse, handling her legs and arms critically and, between drinks, discussing their good and bad points. Though encouraged by the congratulations which poured in from the Army, the Senate and the people, he was never thereafter able to free his conscience from the guilt of this crime. He often admitted that the Furies were pursuing him with whips and burning torches; and set Persian mages at work to conjure up the ghost and make her stop haunting him. During his tour of Greece he came to Athens, where the Eleusinian Mysteries were being held, but dared not participate when a herald ordered all criminals present to withdraw before the ceremonies began.

Having disposed of his mother, Nero proceeded to murder his aunt Domitia Lepida. He found her confined to bed with severe constipation. The old lady stroked his downy beard affectionately – he was already full-grown – murmuring: 'Whenever you celebrate your coming-of-age and present me with this, I shall die happy.' Nero turned to his courtiers and said laughingly: 'In that case I must shave at once' – which he did. Then he ordered the doctors to give her a laxative of fatal strength, seized her property before she was quite dead, and avoided all legal complications by tearing up the will.

After getting rid of Octavia, he took two more wives – first Poppaea Sabina, a quaestor's daughter, at that time married to a knight, and Statilia Messalina, great-great-grand-daughter of Augustus's general Statilius who had twice been Consul and won a triumph. To marry Statilia he was obliged to murder her husband, a consul. Life with Octavia had soon bored him, and when his friends criticized his treatment of her, he retorted: 'Being an emperor's wife ought surely to be enough to make her happy?' He tried to strangle her on several occasions, but finally pronounced that she was barren, and divorced her. This act made him so unpopular and caused so great a scandal that he banished Octavia and later had her executed on a charge of adultery. Her innocence was proved by the refusal of the witnesses called by him to testify against her even under torture; so he bribed his old tutor Anicetus[1] to confess (falsely) that he had tricked her into infidelity. Though he doted on Poppaea, whom he married twelve days after this divorce, he kicked her to death while she was pregnant and feeling very ill, because she dared complain that he came home late from the races. Poppaea had borne him a daughter, Claudia Augusta, who died in infancy.

There was no family relationship which Nero did not criminally abuse. When Claudius's daughter Antonia refused to take Poppaea's place, he had her executed on a charge of attempted rebellion and destroyed every other member of his family, including relatives by marriage, in the same way. He committed an indecent assault on young Aulus Plautius and then put him to death, remarking: 'Now Mother may come and kiss my successor'; he explained that Agrippina had been in love with Aulus and induced him to make a bid for the throne. There was also his step-son,

1 Anicetus, the freedman who had designed the collapsible boat, was now commanding the fleet at Misenum.

Rufrius Crispinus, Poppaea's child by her former husband. Nero had the boy's own slaves drown him on a fishing expedition simply because he was said to have played at being a general and an emperor. He banished Tuscus, the son of his foster-mother and now Procurator of Egypt, for daring to use the baths which he had built in preparation for the Imperial visit to Alexandria. When his tutor Seneca repeatedly asked leave to retire, and offered to surrender all his estates, Nero swore that he had no cause to suspect the old man, whom he would rather die than harm; but drove him to commit suicide nevertheless. He promised Burrus, the Guards' commander, a cough mixture, but sent poison instead; also poisoning the food and drink of the rich old freedmen who had originally arranged for him to be adopted as Claudius's heir, and were now acting as his Privy Councillors.

Nero was no less cruel to strangers than to members of his family. A comet,[1] popularly supposed to herald the death of some person of outstanding importance, appeared several nights running and greatly disturbed him. His astrologer Balbillus observed that monarchs usually avoided portents of this kind by executing their most prominent subjects and thus directing the wrath of heaven elsewhere; so Nero resolved on a wholesale massacre of the nobility. What fortified him in this decision, and seemed to justify it, was that he had discovered two plots against his life. The earlier and more important one of the two was Piso's conspiracy in Rome; the other, detected at Beneventum, had been headed by Vinicius. When brought up for trial the conspirators were loaded with three sets of chains. Some, while admitting their guilt, claimed that by destroying a man so thoroughly steeped in evil as Nero, they would have been doing him the greatest possible service. All children of the condemned men were banished from Rome, and then starved to death or poisoned.

After this, nothing could restrain Nero from murdering anyone he pleased, on whatever pretext. Here are a few instances only: Salvidienus Orfitus was charged with leasing three shops, which formed part of his house, close to the Forum, as offices for the representatives of certain allied States; and a blind lawyer, Cassius Longinus, with keeping a mask of Gaius Cassius, one of Julius Caesar's murderers, attached to the family-tree; and Paetus Thrasea for looking like a cross old schoolmaster. Those whom he ordered to commit suicide were never given more than an hour's grace. To insure against delays he made doctors 'take care' of any

1 One is recorded in AD 60; the other in AD 64.

who were found still alive – which, in Nero's vocabulary, meant opening their veins. He was eager, it is said, to get hold of a certain Egyptian – a sort of ogre who would eat raw flesh and practically anything else he was given – and watch him tear live men to pieces and then devour them. These 'successes', as Nero called them, went to his head and he boasted that no previous sovereign had ever realized the extent of his power. Often he hinted broadly that it was not his intention to spare the remaining senators, but would one day wipe out the entire Senatorial Order, and let knights and freedmen govern the provinces and command the armies, instead. He certainly never gave senators the kisses they expected when he set out on a journey, or returned from one, and never bothered to answer their greetings. In his announcement of the Isthmus Canal project, to a huge crowd, he loudly voiced the hope that it might benefit himself and the Roman people, but made no mention of the Senate.

Nero showed no greater mercy to the common folk, or to the very walls of Rome. Once, in the course of a general conversation, someone quoted the line:

When I am dead, may fire consume the earth

but Nero said that the first part of the line should read: 'While I yet live', and soon converted this fancy into fact. Pretending to be disgusted by the drab old buildings and narrow, winding streets of Rome, he brazenly set fire to the City; and though a group of ex-consuls caught his attendants, armed with oakum and blazing torches, trespassing on their property, they dared not interfere. He also coveted the sites of several granaries, solidly built in stone, near the Golden House; having knocked down their walls with siege-engines, he set the interiors ablaze. This terror lasted for six days and seven nights, causing many people to take shelter in the tombs. Nero's men destroyed not only a vast number of tenements, but mansions which had belonged to famous generals and were still decorated with their triumphal trophies; temples, too, dating back to the time of the kingship, and others dedicated during the Punic and Gallic wars – in fact, every ancient monument of historical interest that had hitherto survived. Nero watched the conflagration from the Tower of Maecenas, enraptured by what he called 'the beauty of the flames'; then put on his tragedian's costume and sang *The Fall of Ilium* from beginning to end. He offered to remove corpses and rubble free of charge, but allowed nobody to search among the ruins even of his own mansion; he wanted to collect as much loot as possible himself. Then he opened a Fire Relief Fund and insisted on contributions, which bled the provincials white and practically beggared all private citizens.

Gaius Suetonius Tranquillus, *The Twelve Caesars*, trans. Robert Graves

Nero . . . was an amateur, and an enthusiastic amateur, of murder. But, as this taste, in the most ingenious hands, is limited and monotonous in its modes of manifestation, it would be tedious to run through the long Suetonian roll-call of his peccadilloes in this way. One only we shall cite, to illustrate the amorous delight with which he pursued any murder which happened to be seasoned highly to his taste by enormous atrocity, and by almost unconquerable difficulty. It would really be pleasant, were it not for the revolting consideration of the persons concerned, and their relation to each other, to watch the tortuous pursuit of the hunter, and the doubles of the game, in this obstinate chase. For certain reasons of state, as Nero attempted to persuade himself, but in reality because no other crime had the same attractions of unnatural horror about it, he resolved to murder his mother Agrippina. This being settled, the next thing was to arrange the mode and the tools. Naturally enough, according to the custom then prevalent in Rome, he first attempted the thing by poison. The poison failed: for Agrippina, anticipating tricks of this kind, had armed her constitution against them, like Mithridates, and daily took potent antidotes and prophylactics. Or else (which is more probable) the Emperor's agent in such purposes, fearing his sudden repentance and remorse on first hearing of his mother's death, or possibly even witnessing her agonies, had composed a poison of inferior strength. This had certainly occurred in the case of Britannicus, who had thrown off with ease the first dose administered to him by Nero. Upon which he had summoned to his presence the woman employed in the affair, and, compelling her by threats to mingle a more powerful potion in his own presence, had tried it successively upon different animals, until he was satisfied with its effects; after which, immediately inviting Britannicus to a banquet, he had finally despatched him. On Agrippina, however, no changes in the poison, whether of kind or strength, had any effect; so that, after various trials, this mode of murder was abandoned, and the Emperor addressed himself to other plans. The first of these was some curious mechanical device by which a false ceiling was to have been suspended by bolts above her bed, and in the middle of the night, the bolt being suddenly drawn, a vast weight would have descended with a ruinous destruction to all below. This scheme, however, taking air from the indiscretion of some amongst the accomplices, reached the ears of Agrippina; upon which the old lady looked about her too sharply to leave much hope in that scheme: so *that* also was abandoned. Next, he conceived the idea of an artificial ship, which, at the touch of a few springs, might fall to pieces in deep water. Such a ship was prepared, and stationed at a suitable point. But the main difficulty remained; which was to persuade the old lady to go on board. Not that she knew in this case *who* had been the ship-builder, for that would have ruined all; but it seems that she took it ill to be hunted in this murderous spirit, and was out of humour with her son; besides that any proposal coming from him, though previously indifferent to her, would have instantly become suspected. To meet this difficulty, a sort of reconciliation was proposed, and a very affectionate message sent, which had the effect of throwing Agrippina off her guard, and seduced her to Baiæ for the purpose of joining the Emperor's party at a grand banquet held in commemoration of a solemn festival. She came by water in a sort of light frigate, and was to return in the same way. Meantime Nero tampered with the commander of her vessel, and prevailed upon him to wreck it. What was to be done? The great lady was anxious to return to Rome, and no proper conveyance was at hand. Suddenly it was suggested, as if by chance, that a ship of the Emperor's, new and properly equipped, was moored at a neighbouring station. This was readily accepted by Agrippina: the Emperor accompanied her to the place of embarkation, took a most tender leave of her, and saw her set sail. It was necessary that the vessel should get into deep water before the experiment could be made; and with the utmost agitation this pious son awaited news of the result. Suddenly a messenger rushed breathless into his presence, and horrified him by the joyful information that his august mother had met with an alarming accident, but, by the blessing of Heaven, had escaped safe and sound, and was now on her road to mingle congratulations with her affectionate son. The ship, it seems, had done its office; the mechanism had played admirably; but who can provide for everything? The old lady, it turned out, could swim like a duck; and the whole result had been to refresh her with a little sea-bathing. Here was worshipful intelligence. Could any man's temper be expected to stand such continued sieges? Money, and trouble, and infinite contrivance, wasted upon one old woman, who absolutely would not, upon any terms, be murdered! Provoking it certainly was; and of a man like Nero it could not be expected that he should any longer dissemble his disgust, or put up with such repeated affronts. He rushed upon his simple congratulating friend, swore that he had come to murder him; and, as nobody could have suborned him but Agrippina, he ordered her off to instant execution. And, unquestionably, if people will not be murdered quietly and in a civil way, they must expect that such forbearance is not to continue for ever, and obviously have themselves only to blame for any harshness or violence which they may have rendered necessary.

Thomas De Quincey, from 'The Caesars'

Net

The palace doors swing open and reveal CLYTEMNESTRA *standing over the bodies of* AGAMEMNON *and* CASSANDRA.

CLYTEMNESTRA: I've spoken many words to serve the moment
which I've no compunction now to contradict.
How else but by lying and seeming so loving
could I have plotted my enemy's downfall?
How rig the net so it can't be leapt out of?
This is the bloodgrudge, the grudge's fruition
something I've brooded on quite a long time.
I've done what I meant to. I wouldn't deny it.
Over his head I cast a vast trammel
the sort that hauls in whole shoals at each casting.
He couldn't get out of his rich, flowing doom-robe.
Twice I struck him. He screamed twice, then crumpled.
Once he'd fallen I struck him a third blow,
one struck for Zeus in his role as corpse-keeper.
He lay there gasping and splurting his blood out
spraying me with dark blood-dew, dew I delight in
as much as the graincrop in the fresh gloss of rainfall
when the wheatbud's in labour and swells into birthpang.

So that's how it is, old men of Argos.
Cheer if you want to. I revel in glory.
He's had his libation, spurts from his bloodvein.
He poured woe and bitterness into our winebowl.
He's got the last goblet and laps up the leas!

CHORUS: Your words revolt me. How can you trumpet,
so unlike a woman, over your manlord?

CLYTEMNESTRA: Still you can treat me like a woman who's witless?
My heart's made of steel, and as I have stated,

whether you like it or not, there's Agamemnon.
This is the swordhand that brought him to bloodright.
I hacked down my husband. That's how it is.

Tony Harrison, *The Oresteia*

Not Proven

Henry got me with child,
Knowing that I could not bring forth life
Without losing my own.
In my youth therefore I entered the portals of dust.
Traveler, it is believed in the village where I lived
That Henry loved me with a husband's love,
But I proclaim from the dust
That he slew me to gratify his hatred.

Edgar Lee Masters, 'Amanda Barker'

O

Oedipus

Enter TIRESIAS

OEDIPUS: O thou whose universal thought commands
All knowledge and all mysteries, in Heaven
And on the earth beneath, thy mind perceives,
Tirésias, though thine outward eye be dark,
What plague is wasting Thebè, who in thee,
Great Sir, finds her one saviour, her sole guide.
Phoebus (albeit the messengers perchance
Have told thee this) upon our sending sent
This answer back, that no release might come
From this disaster, till we sought and found
And slew the murderers of king Laïus,
Or drave them exiles from our land. Thou, then,
Withhold nor any word of augury
Or other divination which thou knowest,
But rescue Thebè, and thyself, and me,
And purge the stain that issues from the dead.
On thee we lean: and 'tis a noble thing
To use what power one hath in doing good.
TIRESIAS: Ah! terrible is knowledge to the man
Whom knowledge profits not. This well I knew,
But had forgotten. Else I ne'er had come.
OEDIPUS: Why dost thou bring a mind so full of gloom?
TIRESIAS: Let me go home. Thy part and mine to-day
Will best be borne, if thou obey me in that.
OEDIPUS: Disloyal and ungrateful! to deprive
The state that reared thee of thine utterance now.
TIRESIAS: Thy speech, I see, is foiling thine intent;
And I would shield me from the like mishap. (*Going*)

OEDIPUS: Nay, if thou knowest, turn thee not away:
All here with suppliant hands importune thee.
TIRESIAS: Yea, for ye all are blind. Never will I
Reveal my woe; – mine, that I say not, thine.
OEDIPUS: So, then, thou hast the knowledge of the crime
And wilt not tell, but rather wouldst betray
This people, and destroy thy fatherland!
TIRESIAS: You press me to no purpose. I'll not pain
Thee, nor myself. Thou wilt hear nought from me.
OEDIPUS: How? Miscreant! Thy stubbornness would rouse
Wrath in a breast of stone. Wilt thou yet hold
That silent, hard, impenetrable mien?
TIRESIAS: You censure me for my harsh mood. Your own
Dwells unsuspected with you. Me you blame!
OEDIPUS: Who can be mild and gentle, when thou speakest
Such words to mock this people?
TIRESIAS It will come:
Although I bury it in silence here.
OEDIPUS: Must not the King be told of what will come?
TIRESIAS: No word from me. At this, an if thou wilt,
Rage to the height of passionate vehemence.
OEDIPUS: Ay, and my passion shall declare my thought.
'Tis clear to me as daylight, thou hast been
The arch-plotter of this deed; yea, thou hast done
All but the actual blow. Hadst thou thy sight,
I had proclaimed thee the sole murderer.
TIRESIAS: Ay, say'st thou so? – I charge thee to abide
By thine own ordinance; and from this hour
Speak not to any Theban nor to me.
Thou art the vile polluter of the land.
OEDIPUS: O void of shame! What wickedness is this?
What power will give thee refuge for such guilt?
TIRESIAS: The might of truth is scatheless. I am free.
OEDIPUS: Whence came the truth to thee? Not from thine art.
TIRESIAS: From thee, whose rage impelled my backward tongue.
OEDIPUS: Speak it once more, that I may know the drift.
TIRESIAS: Was it so dark? Or wouldst thou tempt me further?
OEDIPUS: I cannot say 'twas clear. Speak it again.
TIRESIAS: I say thou art the murderer whom thou seekest.
OEDIPUS: Again that baleful word! But thou shalt rue.

TIRESIAS: Shall I add more, to aggravate thy wrath?
OEDIPUS: All is but idleness. Say what thou wilt.
TIRESIAS: I tell thee thou art living unawares
In shameful commerce with thy near'st of blood,
Ignorant of the abyss wherein thou liest.
OEDIPUS: Think you to triumph in offending still?
TIRESIAS: If Truth have power.
OEDIPUS: She hath, but not for thee,
Blind as thou art in eyes and ears and mind.
TIRESIAS: O miserable reproach, which all who now
Behold thee, soon shall thunder forth on thee!
OEDIPUS: Nursed in unbroken night, thou canst not harm
Or me, or any man who seëth the day.
TIRESIAS: No, not from me proceeds thy fall; the God,
Who cares for this, is able to perform it.
OEDIPUS: Came this device from Creon or thyself?
TIRESIAS: Not Creon: thou art thy sole enemy.

Sophocles, *Oedipus Rex*, trans. Lewis Campbell

Offence

KING CLAUDIUS: O, my offence is rank! It smells to heaven.
It hath the primal eldest curse upon't,
A brother's murder. Pray can I not.
Though inclination be as sharp as will,
My stronger guilt defeats my strong intent,
And like a man to double business bound
I stand in pause where I shall first begin,
And both neglect. What if this cursèd hand
Were thicker than itself with brother's blood,
Is there not rain enough in the sweet heavens
To wash it white as snow? Whereto serves mercy
But to confront the visage of offence?
And what's in prayer but this twofold force,
To be forestallèd ere we come to fall,
Or pardoned being down? Then I'll look up.
My fault is past – but O, what form of prayer
Can serve my turn? 'Forgive me my foul murder'?
That cannot be, since I am still possessed

Of those effects for which I did the murder –
My crown, mine own ambition, and my queen.
May one be pardoned and retain th'offence?
In the corrupted currents of this world
Offence's gilded hand may shove by justice,
And oft 'tis seen the wicked prize itself
Buys out the law. But 'tis not so above.
There is no shuffling, there the action lies
In his true nature, and we ourselves compelled
Even to the teeth and forehead of our faults
To give in evidence. What then? What rests?
Try what repentance can. What can it not?
Yet what can it when one cannot repent?
O wretched state, O bosom black as death,
O limèd soul that, struggling to be free,
Art more engaged! Help, angels! Make assay.
Bow, stubborn knees; and heart with strings of steel,
Be soft as sinews of the new-born babe.
All may be well.

He kneels.

Enter PRINCE HAMLET *behind him*

HAMLET: Now might I do it pat, now a is praying,
And now I'll do't,

(*He draws his sword*)

and so a goes to heaven,
And so am I revenged. That would be scanned.
A villain kills my father, and for that
I, his sole son, do this same villain send
To heaven.
O, this is hire and salary, not revenge!
A took my father grossly, full of bread,
With all his crimes broad blown, as flush as May;
And how his audit stands, who knows save heaven?
But in our circumstance and course of thought
'Tis heavy with him. And am I then revenged
To take him in the purging of his soul,
When he is fit and seasoned for his passage?
No.

He sheathes his sword

Up, sword, and know thou a more horrid hint.

When he is drunk asleep, or in his rage,
Or in th'incestuous pleasure of his bed,
At gaming, swearing, or about some act
That has no relish of salvation in't,
Then trip him that his heels may kick at heaven,
And that his soul may be as damned and black
As hell whereto it goes. My mother stays.
This physic but prolongs thy sickly days. *Exit*

William Shakespeare, *Hamlet*

Oracle

Okonkwo sat in his *obi* crunching happily with Ikemefuna and Nwoye, and drinking palm-wine copiously, when Ogbuefi Ezeudu came in. Ezeudu was the oldest man in his quarter of Umuofia. He had been a great and fearless warrior in his time, and was now accorded great respect in all the clan. He refused to join in the meal, and asked Okonkwo to have a word with him outside. And so they walked out together, the old man supporting himself with his stick. When they were out of ear-shot, he said to Okonkwo:

'That boy calls you father. Do not bear a hand in his death.' Okonkwo was surprised, and was about to say something when the old man continued:

'Yes, Umuofia has decided to kill him. The Oracle of the Hills and the Caves has pronounced it. They will take him outside Umuofia as is the custom, and kill him there. But I want you to have nothing to do with it. He calls you his father.'

The next day a group of elders from all the nine villages of Umuofia came to Okonkwo's house early in the morning, and before they began to speak in low tones Nwoye and Ikemefuna were sent out. They did not stay very long, but when they went away Okonkwo sat still for a very long time supporting his chin in his palms. Later in the day he called Ikemefuna and told him that he was to be taken home the next day. Nwoye overheard it and burst into tears, whereupon his father beat him heavily. As for Ikemefuna, he was at a loss. His own home had gradually become very faint and distant. He still missed his mother and his sister and would be very glad to see them. But somehow he knew he was not going to see them. He remembered once when men had talked in low tones with his father; and it seemed now as if it was happening all over again.

Later, Nwoye went to his mother's hut and told her that Ikemefuna was going home. She immediately dropped the pestle with which she was grinding pepper, folded her arms across her breast and sighed, 'Poor child.'

The next day, the men returned with a pot of wine. They were all fully dressed as if they were going to a big clan meeting or to pay a visit to a neighbouring village. They passed their cloths under the right armpit, and hung their goatskin bags and sheathed matchets over their left shoulders. Okonkwo got ready quickly and the party set out with Ikemefuna carrying the pot of wine. A deathly silence descended on Okonkwo's compound. Even the very little children seemed to know. Throughout that day Nwoye sat in his mother's hut and tears stood in his eyes.

At the beginning of their journey the men of Umuofia talked and laughed about the locusts, about their women, and about some effeminate men who had refused to come with them. But as they drew near to the outskirts of Umuofia silence fell upon them too.

The sun rose slowly to the centre of the sky, and the dry, sandy footway began to throw up the heat that lay buried in it. Some birds chirruped in the forests around. The men trod dry leaves on the sand. All else was silent. Then from the distance came the faint beating of the *ekwe*. It rose and faded with the wind – a peaceful dance from a distant clan.

'It is an *ozo* dance,' the men said among themselves. But no one was sure where it was coming from. Some said Ezimili, others Abame or Aninta. They argued for a short while and fell into silence again, and the elusive dance rose and fell with the wind. Somewhere a man was taking one of the titles of his clan, with music and dancing and a great feast.

The footway had now become a narrow line in the heart of the forest. The short trees and sparse undergrowth which surrounded the men's village began to give way to giant trees and climbers which perhaps had stood from the beginning of things, untouched by the axe and the bush-fire. The sun breaking through their leaves and branches threw a pattern of light and shade on the sandy footway.

Ikemefuna heard a whisper close behind him and turned round sharply. The man who had whispered now called out aloud, urging the others to hurry up.

'We still have a long way to go,' he said. Then he and another man went before Ikemefuna and set a faster pace.

Thus the men of Umuofia pursued their way, armed with sheathed matchets, and Ikemefuna, carrying a pot of palm-wine on his head, walked in their midst. Although he had felt uneasy at first, he was not afraid now. Okonkwo walked behind him. He could hardly imagine that Okonkwo was not his real father. He had never been fond of his real father, and at the end of three years he had become very distant indeed. But his mother and his three-year-old sister . . . of course she would not be three now, but six. Would he recognize her now? She must have grown quite big. How his mother would weep for joy, and thank Okonkwo for having looked after him so well and for bringing him back. She would want to hear everything that had happened to him in all these years. Could he remember them all? He would tell her about Nwoye and his mother, and about the locusts. . . . Then quite suddenly a thought came upon him. His mother might be dead. He tried in vain to force the thought out of his mind. Then he tried to settle the matter the way he used to settle such matters when he was a little boy. He still remembered the song:

Eze elina, elina!
Sala
Eze ilikwa ya
Ikwaba akwa oligholi
Ebe Danda nechi eze
Ebe Uzuzu nete egwu
Sala

He sang it in his mind, and walked to its beat. If the song ended on his right foot, his mother was alive. If it ended on his left, she was dead. No, not dead, but ill. It ended on the right. She was alive and well. He sang the song again, and it ended on the left. But the second time did not count. The first voice gets to Chukwu, or God's house. That was a favourite saying of children. Ikemefuna felt like a child once more. It must be the thought of going home to his mother.

One of the men behind him cleared his throat. Ikemefuna looked back, and the man growled at him to go on and not stand looking back. The way he said it sent cold fear down Ikemefuna's back. His hands trembled vaguely on the black pot he carried. Why had Okonkwo withdrawn to the rear? Ikemefuna felt his legs melting under him. And he was afraid to look back.

As the man who had cleared his throat drew up and raised his matchet, Okonkwo looked away. He heard the blow. The pot fell and broke in the sand. He heard Ikemefuna cry, 'My father, they have killed me!' as he ran towards him. Dazed with fear, Okonkwo drew his matchet and cut him down. He was afraid of being thought weak.

Chinua Achebe, *Things Fall Apart*

Orderly

A table had been set up under a tree, and there the slim lieutenant stood, importantly busy. Then the Captain summoned himself to an act of courage. He called his orderly.

The flame leapt into the young soldier's throat as he heard the command, and he rose blindly, stifled. He saluted, standing below the officer. He did not look up. But there was the flicker in the Captain's voice.

'Go to the inn and fetch me . . .' the officer gave his commands. 'Quick!' he added.

At the last word, the heart of the servant leapt with a flash, and he felt the strength come over his body. But he turned in mechanical obedience, and set off at a heavy run downhill, looking almost like a bear, his trousers bagging over his military boots. And the officer watched this blind, plunging run all the way.

But it was only the outside of the orderly's body that was obeying so humbly and mechanically. Inside had gradually accumulated a core into which all the energy of that young life was compact and concentrated. He executed his commission, and plodded quickly back uphill. There was a pain in his head, as he walked, that made him twist his features unknowingly. But hard there in the centre of his chest was himself, himself, firm, and not to be plucked to pieces.

The Captain had gone up into the wood. The orderly, plodded through the hot, powerfully smelling zone of the company's atmosphere. He had a curious mass of energy inside him now. The Captain was less real than himself. He approached the green entrance to the wood. There, in the half-shade, he saw the horse standing, the sunshine and the flickering shadow of leaves dancing over his brown body. There was a clearing where timber had lately been felled. Here, in the gold-green shade beside the brilliant cup of sunshine, stood two figures, blue and pink, the bits of pink showing out plainly. The Captain was talking to his lieutenant.

The orderly stood on the edge of the bright clearing, where great trunks of trees, stripped and glistening, lay stretched like naked, brown-skinned bodies. Chips of wood littered the trampled floor, like splashed light, and the bases of the felled trees stood here and there, with their raw, level tops. Beyond was the brilliant, sunlit green of a beech.

'Then I will ride forward,' the orderly heard his Captain say. The lieutenant saluted and strode away. He himself went forward. A hot flash passed through his belly, as he tramped towards his officer.

The Captain watched the rather heavy figure of the young soldier stumble forward, and his veins, too, ran hot. This was to be man to man between them. He yielded before the solid, stumbling figure with bent head. The orderly stooped and put the food on a level-sawn tree-base. The Captain watched the glistening, sun-inflamed, naked hands. He wanted to speak to the young soldier, but could not. The servant propped a bottle against his thigh, pressed open the cork, and poured out the beer into the mug. He kept his head bent. The Captain accepted the mug.

'Hot!' he said, as if amiably.

The flame sprang out of the orderly's heart, nearly suffocating him.

'Yes, sir,' he replied, between shut teeth.

And he heard the sound of the Captain's drinking, and he clenched his fists, such a strong torment came into his wrists. Then came the faint clang of the closing pot-lid. He looked up. The Captain was watching him. He glanced swiftly away. Then he saw the officer stoop and take a piece of bread from the tree-base. Again the flash of flame went through the young soldier, seeing the stiff body stoop beneath him, and his hands jerked. He looked away. He could feel the officer was nervous. The bread fell as it was being broken. The officer ate the other piece. The two men stood tense and still, the master laboriously chewing his bread, the servant staring with averted face, his fist clenched.

Then the young soldier started. The officer had pressed open the lid of the mug again. The orderly watched the lid of the mug, and the white hand that clenched the handle, as if he were fascinated. It was raised. The youth followed it with his eyes. And then he saw the thin, strong throat of the elder man moving up and down as he drank, the jaw working. And the instinct which had been jerking at the young man's wrists suddenly jerked free. He jumped, feeling as if it were rent in two by a strong flame.

The spur of the officer caught in a tree-root, he went down backwards with a crash, the middle of his back thudding sickeningly against a sharp-edged tree-base, the pot flying away. And in a second the orderly, with serious, earnest young face, and underlip between his teeth, had got his knee in the officer's chest and was pressing the chin backward over the farther edge of the tree-stump, pressing, with all his heart behind in a passion of relief, the tension of his wrists exquisite with relief. And with the base of his palms he shoved at the chin, with all his might. And it was pleasant, too, to have that chin, that hard jaw already slightly rough with beard, in his hands. He did not relax one hair's breadth, but, all the force of all his blood exulting in his thrust, he shoved back the head of the other man, till there was a little 'cluck' and a crunching sensation. Then he felt as if his head went to vapour. Heavy convulsions shook the body of the officer, frightening and horrifying the young soldier. Yet it pleased him, too, to repress them. It pleased him to keep his hands pressing back the chin, to feel the chest of the other man yield in expiration to the weight of his strong, young knees, to feel the hard twitchings of the prostrate body jerking his own whole frame, which was pressed down on it.

But it went still. He could look into the nostrils of the other man, the eyes he could scarcely see. How curiously the mouth was pushed out, exaggerating the full lips, and the moustache bristling up from them. Then, with a start, he noticed the nostrils gradually filled with blood. The red brimmed, hesitated, ran over, and went in a thin trickle down the face to the eyes.

It shocked and distressed him. Slowly, he got up. The body twitched and sprawled there, inert. He stood and looked at it in silence. It was a pity *it* was broken. It represented more than the thing which had kicked and bullied him. He was afraid to look at the eyes. They were hideous now, only the whites showing, and the blood running to them. The face of the orderly was drawn with horror at the sight. Well, it was so. In his heart he was satisfied. He had hated the face of the Captain. It was extinguished now. There was a heavy relief in the orderly's soul. That was as it should be. But he could not bear to see the long, military body lying broken over the tree-base, the fine fingers crisped. He wanted to hide it away.

Quickly, busily, he gathered it up and pushed it under the felled tree-trunks, which rested their beautiful, smooth length either end on logs. The face was horrible with blood. He covered it with the helmet. Then he pushed the limbs straight and decent, and brushed the dead leaves off the fine cloth of the uniform. So, it lay quite still in the shadow under there. A little strip of sunshine ran along the breast, from a chink between the logs. The orderly sat by it for a few moments. Here his own life also ended.

Then, through his daze, he heard the lieutenant, in a loud voice, explaining to the men outside the wood, that they were to suppose the bridge on the river below was held by the enemy. Now they were to march to the attack in such and such a manner. The lieutenant had no gift of expression. The orderly, listening from habit, got muddled. And when the lieutenant began it all again he ceased to hear.

He knew he must go. He stood up. It surprised him that the leaves were glittering in the sun, and the chips of wood reflecting white from the ground. For him a change had come over the world. But for the rest it had not – all seemed the same. Only he had left it. And he could not go back. It was his duty to return with the beer-pot and the bottle. He could not. He had left all that. The lieutenant was still hoarsely explaining. He must go, or they would overtake him. And he could not bear contact with anyone now.

He drew his fingers over his eyes, trying to find out where he was. Then he turned away. He saw the horse standing in the path. He went up to it and mounted. It hurt him to sit in the saddle. The pain of keeping his seat occupied him as they cantered through the wood. He would not have minded anything, but he could not get away from the sense of being divided from the others. The path led out of the trees. On the edge of the wood he pulled up and stood watching. There in the spacious sunshine of the valley soldiers were moving in a little swarm. Every now and then, a man harrowing on a strip of fallow shouted to his oxen, at the turn. The village and the white-towered church was small in the sunshine. And he no longer belonged to it – he sat there, beyond, like a man outside in the dark. He had gone out from everyday life into the unknown, and he could not, he even did not want to go back.

Turning from the sun-blazing valley, he rode deep into the wood. Tree-trunks, like people standing grey and still, took no notice as he went. A doe, herself a moving bit of sunshine and shadow, went running through the flecked shade. There were bright green rents in the foliage. Then it was all pine wood, dark and cool. And he was sick with pain, he had an intolerable great pulse in his head, and he was sick. He had never been ill in his life. He felt lost, quite dazed with all this.

Trying to get down from the horse, he fell, astonished at the pain and his lack of balance. The horse shifted uneasily. He jerked its bridle and sent it cantering jerkily away. It was his last connection with the rest of things.

D. H. Lawrence, *The Prussian Officer*

Overboard

Later he whispers to me take care of my girl don't let him do it to her get her away before he does her too, do I have your promise? I promise, I tell him in the first act of mercy in my life. For now the engine is idling and the tug rocks wildly in the wash of the ocean waves, I never knew they made a point of being out here too even bigger more ferocious with their own life in the middle of nowhere. Irving comes down the ladder and Bo and I both watch him in the economy of his movements swing open the double doors at the rear of the cabin and step outside and hook them fast. Suddenly the clean rage of air has blown out the smell of the oil and cigar, we are outdoors in here, I see the height of the heavy seas like gigantic black throats in the dim cast of our cabin light and Irving is at the stern rail, which he unhooks and lifts and stows neatly to the side. The boat is yawing in such a wallow that I have gone back to my position on the side bench, which I affix myself to by bracing my heels against a steel deck plate and clutching the bulkheads on either side of me. Irving is a true sailor mindless of the rising and falling deck and no less of the splashing he has taken about the legs of his pants. He is back inside, his thin gaunt face is splotched with sea spittle, his thin hair glistens on his shining scalp, and methodically without asking my help he jimmies up one end of the galvanized tin tub and jams a dolly under it and shoves and bangs the dolly further and further under the tub to where he can use the leverage of his whole weight to hold down the dolly with one foot and pull the tub up on it, an oddly dry scraping sound reminding me that if it were a sandpail and nobody's feet were in it, it could be turned over and tapped and leave whole a perfect cement sculpture of an overturned laundry tub perhaps even showing the embossed letters of the manufacturer. Bo's knees are now raised to a painful angle and his head is even lower, he is just about folded in half, but Irving fixes that next, after he jams wood shivs under the four rubber wheels of the dolly, he opens a steel tool kit and removes a fisherman's knife and cuts Bo's ropes, and lassoes them off and helps Bo up off the kitchen chair and stands him up in the tub on the dolly on the deck of the tugboat here at the very top of the Atlantic Ocean. Bo is shaky, he moans, his legs are buckling he lacks circulation and Irving calls to me, tells me to support Bo's other side, and oh this is just what I prefer not to do in my criminal training, exactly this, feeling Bo's palsy arm around me, smelling his hot breath, the sweat under his arm all the way through his black jacket on my neck, his hand fluttering grabbing my head like a claw, clutching my hair, his elbow drilling into the flesh of my shoulder, the man in his heat and animation resting his weight on me moaning over my head and his whole body in tremors. Here I am supporting the man I am helping to kill, we are his sole support, he holds on for dear life, and Irving says it's all right Bo, it's okay, and as calm and encouraging as a nurse, he kicks out the right stern shiv, we are facing the open deck you see, and commands me to do likewise with the shiv on my side, which I do quickly and accurately and we roll Bo on the dolly quite easily with the sea's help to the open hatch, where he lets go of us and grabs the framework standing now there alone his cement tub vehicle shooting back and forth like roller skates he can't quite manage yelling *ohh ohhoooooo*, his body twisting from the waist as he struggles to keep himself vertical and Irving and I stand back and watch this and all at once Bo learns the control, and manages to diminish the roll of the rubber wheels and with his legs locks his cement tub in some relatively governable slightness of motion and he trusts himself to look up and finds himself facing an open deck and a sea higher than he is and then lower than he is in a night of raging black wind, and his straining arms are being pulled out of the sockets and he takes great deep breaths of this awful wind and night and I see the back of his head moving and his shoulders and his head is up facing into this world of inexplicable terror and though I can't hear it for the wind I know he is singing and though I can't hear it I know the song, it is blown away by sea wind, his farewell chant, the song in his mind, all anybody ever has, and so Bo Weinberg was on his own in catastrophic solitude when the pilot engaged the engine and the boat suddenly shot forward and Mr Schultz in his shirtsleeves and suspenders appeared and came up behind him and lifted one stockinged foot and shoved it in the small of Bo's back, and the hands broken from their grasp and the body's longing lunge for balance where there was none, careening leaning backward he went over into the sea and the last thing I saw were the arms which had gone up, and the shot white cuffs and the pale hands reaching for heaven.

E. L. Doctorow, *Billy Bathgate*

Overheard

Anthony said he only killed Mrs Proudie off because he was writing away at the book in the long drawing-room at the Athenaeum one morning and overheard two clergymen complaining about the way he reintroduced the same characters in his novels, with special reference to Mrs Proudie. 'I got up, and standing between them, I acknowledged myself to be the culprit. "As to Mrs Proudie," I said, "I will go home and kill her before the week is over." And so I did.'

Victoria Glendinning, *Trollope*

Overstayed

Which reminds me. He appeared
at noon, asking for water. He'd walked from town
after losing his job, leaving a note for his wife and his brother
and locking his dog in the coal bunker.
We made him a bed

and he slept till Monday.
A week went by and he hung up his coat.
Then a month, and not a stroke of work, a word of thanks,
a farthing of rent or a sign of him leaving.
One evening he mentioned a recipe

for smooth, seedless gooseberry sorbet
but by then I was tired of him: taking pocket money
from my boy at cards, sucking up to my wife and on his last night
sizing up my daughter. He was smoking my pipe
as we stirred his supper.

Where does the hand become the wrist?
Where does the neck become the shoulder? The watershed
and then the weight, whatever turns up and tips us over that razor's edge
between something and nothing, between
one and the other.

I could have told him this
but didn't bother. We ran him a bath
and held him under, dried him off and dressed him
and loaded him into the back of the pick-up.
Then we drove without headlights

to the county boundary,
dropped the tailgate, and after my boy
had been through his pockets we dragged him like a mattress
across the meadow and on the count of four
threw him over the border.

This is not general knowledge, except
in gooseberry season, which reminds me, and at the table
I have been known to raise an eyebrow, or scoop the sorbet

into five equal portions, for the hell of it.
I mention this for a good reason.
Simon Armitage, 'Gooseberry Season'

It was with a vast relief that Mr Treadwell finally decided to pay a visit to the Society of Gerontology. He knew what he would find there: a dingy room or two, a couple of underpaid clerical workers, the musty odour of a piddling charity operation – all of which would restore matters to their proper perspective again. He went so strongly imbued with this picture that he almost walked past the gigantic glass and aluminium tower which was the address of the Society, rode its softly humming elevator in confusion, and emerged in the ante-room of the Main Office in a daze.

And it was still in a daze that he was ushered through a vast and seemingly endless labyrinth of rooms by a sleek, long-legged young woman, and saw, as he passed, hosts of other young women, no less sleek and long-legged, multitudes of brisk, square-shouldered young men, rows of streamlined machinery clicking and chuckling in electronic glee, mountains of stainless-steel card indexes, and, over all, the bland reflection of modern indirect lighting on plastic and metal – until finally he was led into the presence of Bunce himself, and the door closed behind him.

'Impressive, isn't it?' said Bunce, obviously relishing the sight of Mr Treadwell's stupefaction.

'Impressive?' croaked Mr Treadwell hoarsely. 'Why. I've never seen anything like it. It's a ten-million-dollar outfit!'

'And why not? Science is working day and night like some Frankenstein, Mr Treadwell, to increase longevity past all sane limits. There are fourteen million people over sixty-five in this country right now. In twenty years their number will be increased to twenty-one million. Beyond that no one can even estimate what the figures will rise to!

'But the one bright note is that each of these aged people is surrounded by many young donors or potential donors to our Society. As the tide rises higher, we, too, flourish and grow stronger to withstand it.'

Mr Treadwell felt a chill of horror penetrate him. 'Then it's true, isn't it?'

'I beg your pardon?'

'This Blessington Method you're always talking about,' said Mr Treadwell wildly. 'The whole idea is just to settle things by getting rid of old people!'

'Right!' said Bunce. 'That is the exact idea. And not even J. G. Blessington himself ever phrased it better. You have a way with words, Mr Treadwell. I always admire a man who can come to the point without sentimental twaddle.'

'But you can't get away with it!' said Mr Treadwell incredulously. 'You don't really believe you can get away with it, do you?'

Bunce gestured toward the expanses beyond the closed door. 'Isn't that sufficient evidence of the Society's success?'

'But all those people out there! Do they realize what's going on?'

'Like all well-trained personnel, Mr Treadwell,' said Bunce reproachfully, 'they know only their own duties. What you and I are discussing here happens to be upper echelon.'

Mr Treadwell's shoulders drooped. 'It's impossible,' he said weakly. 'It can't work.'

'Come, come,' Bunce said not unkindly, 'you mustn't let yourself be overwhelmed. I imagine that what disturbed you most is what J. G. Blessington sometimes referred to as the Safety Factor. But look at it this way, Mr Treadwell: isn't it perfectly natural for old people to die? Well, our Society guarantees that the deaths will appear natural. Investigations are rare – not one has ever caused us any trouble.

'More than that, you would be impressed by many of the names on our list of donors. People powerful in the political world as well as the financial world have been flocking to us. One and all, they could give glowing testimonials as to our efficiency. And remember that such important people make the Society for Gerontology invulnerable, no matter at what point it may be attacked, Mr Treadwell. And such invulnerability extends to every single one of our sponsors, including you, should you choose to place your problem in our hands.'

'But I don't have the right,' Mr Treadwell protested despairingly. 'Even if I wanted to, who am I to settle things this way for anybody?'

'Aha.' Bunce leaned forward intently. 'But you do want to settle things?'

'Not this way.'

'Can you suggest any other way?'

Mr Treadwell was silent.

'You see,' Bunce said with satisfaction, 'the Society for Gerontology offers the one practical answer to the problem. Do you still reject it, Mr Treadwell?'

'I can't see it,' Mr Treadwell said stubbornly. 'It's just not right.'

'Are you sure of that?'

'Of course I am!' snapped Mr Treadwell. 'Are you going to tell me that it's right and proper to go around killing people just because they're old?'

'I am telling you that very thing, Mr Treadwell, and I ask you to look at it this way. We are living today in a world of progress, a world of producers and consumers, all doing their best to improve our common lot. The old are neither producers nor consumers, so they are only barriers to our continued progress.

'If we want to take a brief, sentimental look into the pastoral haze of yesterday we may find that once they did serve a function. While the young were out tilling the fields, the old could tend to the household. But even that function is gone today. We have a hundred better devices for tending the household, and they come far cheaper. Can you dispute that?'

'I don't know,' Mr Treadwell said doggedly. 'You're arguing that people are machines, and I don't go along with that at all.'

'Good heavens,' said Bunce, 'don't tell me that you see them as anything else! Of course we are machines, Mr Treadwell, all of us. Unique and wonderful machines, I grant, but machines nevertheless. Why, look at the world around you. It is a vast organism made up of replaceable parts, all striving to produce and consume, produce and consume until worn out. Should one permit the worn-out part to remain where it is? Of course not! It must be cast aside so that the organism will not be made inefficient. It is the whole organism that counts, Mr Treadwell, not any of its individual parts. Can't you understand that?'

'I don't know,' said Mr Treadwell uncertainly. 'I've never thought of it that way. It's hard to take in all at once.'

'I realize that, Mr Treadwell, but it is part of The Blessington Method that the sponsor fully appreciate the great value of his contribution in all ways – not only as it benefits him, but also in the way it benefits the entire social organism. In signing a pledge to our society a man is truly performing the most noble act of his life.'

'Pledge?' said Mr Treadwell. 'What kind of pledge?'

Bunce removed a printed form from a drawer of his desk and laid it out carefully for Mr Treadwell's inspection. Mr Treadwell read it and sat up sharply.

'Why, this says that I'm promising to pay you two thousand dollars in a month from now. You never said anything about that kind of money!'

'There has never been any occasion to raise the subject before this,' Bunce replied. 'But for some time now a committee of the Society has been examining your financial standing, and it reports that you can pay this sum without stress or strain.'

'What do you mean, stress or strain?' Mr Treadwell retorted. 'Two thousand dollars is a lot of money, no matter how you look at it.'

Bunce shrugged. 'Every pledge is arranged in terms of the sponsor's ability to pay, Mr Treadwell. Remember, what may seem expensive to you would certainly seem cheap to many other sponsors I have dealt with.'

'And what do I get for this?'

'Within one month after you sign the pledge, the affair of your father-in-law will be disposed of. Immediately after that you will be expected to pay the pledge in full. Your name is then enrolled on our list of sponsors, and that is all there is to it.'

'I don't like the idea of my name being enrolled on anything.'

'I can appreciate that,' said Bunce. 'But may I remind you that a donation to a charitable organization such as the Society for Gerontology is tax-deductible?'

Mr Treadwell's fingers rested lightly on the pledge. 'Now just for the sake of argument,' he said, 'suppose someone signs one of these things and then doesn't pay up. I guess you know that a pledge like this isn't collectible under the law, don't you?'

'Yes,' Bunce smiled, 'and I know that a great many organizations cannot redeem pledges made to them in apparently good faith. But the Society for Gerontology has never met that difficulty. We avoid it by reminding all sponsors that the young, if they are careless, may die as unexpectedly as the old . . . No, no,' he said, steadying the paper, 'just your signature at the bottom will do.'

When Mr Treadwell's father-in-law was found drowned off the foot of East Sconsett pier three weeks later (the old man fished regularly although he had often been told by various local authorities that the fishing was poor there), the event was duly entered into the East Sconsett records as Death By Accidental Submersion, and Mr Treadwell himself made the arrangements for an exceptionally elaborate funeral.

Stanley Ellin, *The Blessington Method*

Night was falling and Jean could barely distinguish old Fouan sitting on the stone bench. He was just coming up to the kitchen door in which there was a lighted candle when Buteau recognized him and rushed out to block the way.

'Christ Almighty, it's you again. What do you want?'

'I want my coat and my two pairs of trousers.'

A furious quarrel arose. Jean stood his ground and wanted to look inside the wardrobe cupboard while Buteau picked up a bill-hook and was swearing he would slit his throat if he tried to come in. In the end Lise's voice was heard shouting inside the house:

'Oh, go on, let him have his old rags. You'll never wear them, he's contaminated them!'

The two men stopped shouting. Jean stood waiting and at that very moment, behind his back, he heard old Fouan, dreaming to himself and rambling in his mind, mumble out loud:

'Get away quick! They'll be after your blood just as they were after the girl's.'

In a blinding flash, Jean understood everything, Françoise's death as well as her obstinate silence. He already had his suspicions and now he no longer had any doubt that she had saved her family from the guillotine. His hair stood on end and he could find nothing to say or do when Lise flung his coat and trousers straight at his face through the open door.

'Here, take your filthy rags! They're so foul they'd've stunk the place out!'

He picked them up and went off. And not until he was out of the yard and on the street did he wave his fist at the house, shattering the silence with one single word: 'Murderers!'

Then he disappeared into the darkness. Buteau was shaken to the core. He had heard old Fouan muttering and rambling and Jean's last word struck home like a bullet. What now? Were the police going to start interfering just when he thought that the affair had been buried with Françoise's dead body? He had been breathing freely ever since he had seen her disappearing into the earth that morning and now the old man knew everything! Was he just pretending to be stupid in order to keep them under observation? This thought added the final drop to Buteau's cup of bitterness and made him feel so ill that he left half his supper, and when he told Lise, she started shivering too and could not eat anything either.

They had both been looking forward to their first night of their newly won home, but it turned out to be a night of horror and misery. They had put Laure and Jules to bed on a mattress in front of the chest of drawers, until such time as they could find somewhere else, and had gone to bed and blown out their candle before the children were asleep. But they could not sleep a wink themselves and lay tossing and turning as though on hot coals. Finally they started talking in an undertone. What a burden this old father of theirs had become since he'd fallen into his second childhood! A real burden who could ruin them with what he cost to keep. You couldn't imagine the amount of bread he ate and a real glutton as well, picking his meat up in his fingers, spilling his wine all over his beard and so filthy it made you sick to look at him. And now he always went about with his trousers undone, he'd been caught exposing himself to little girls like a worn-out, half-dead animal. What a disgusting obsession for an old man who in his youth hadn't been any filthier than anyone else in his habits. Really, it was enough to make you want to pole-axe him, for he didn't seem ready to go of his own accord.

'When you think that he'd topple over if you blew on him,' muttered Buteau. 'And he won't give up, he doesn't care a damn about mucking us up! Those old buggers, the less they work and the less they earn, the harder they cling on! He's never going to kick the bucket.'

Lying on her back, Lise added:

'It's a bad thing for him to have come back here. He'll be too comfortable, he'll take on a new lease of life. If I'd had anything to say about it, I'd've prayed God not to let him sleep a single night here.'

Neither of them mentioned their real concern, the thought that their father knew everything and could give them away, quite innocently. This was the last straw. The fact that he cost them money, that he was an encumbrance, that he was preventing them from freely enjoying the stolen bonds, was something they had been putting up with for a long time. But the thought that one word from him could bring them to the guillotine, that was really going too far. They'd have to do something about it.

'I'm going to see if he's asleep,' Lise said suddenly.

She relit the candle, made sure that Jules and Laure were sound asleep and slipped along in her shift to the room where they stored the beetroot and where they had set up the old man's iron bedstead again. When she came back she was shivering, her feet frozen by the tiled floor. She slid under the blanket again and snuggled up to her husband, who held her in his arms to warm her.

'Well?'

'Well, he's sleeping with his mouth wide open like a trap-door because he can't breathe properly.'

Silence fell but, although they said nothing as they lay in each other's arms, they could sense their thoughts in the beating of their hearts. This old man who always had difficulty in breathing would be so easy to finish off, some little thing pushed gently into his throat, a handkerchief or just fingers, and they'd be rid of him. They'd even be doing him a favour.

Wouldn't he be better sleeping peacefully in the churchyard than being a burden to everyone, himself included?

Buteau was still hugging Lise in his arms. Now they were both burning hot as if desire had set their blood on fire. Suddenly he let go of her and sprang out onto the tiled floor in his bare feet.

'I'm going to take a look myself.'

He disappeared, candle in hand, while she held her breath and listened wide-eyed in the dark. But minutes went by and no sound came from the room next door. In the end, she heard him come back without a light, his feet padding softly on the floor, his breath coming in gasps. He came up to the bed and reached for her, whispering:

'You come, too, I'm afraid to do it by myself.'

Lise followed Buteau, holding her arms out in front in order not to bump into him. They no longer noticed the cold and felt uncomfortable in their nightclothes. The candle standing on the ground in the corner of the old man's room showed him lying on his back with his head beside the pillow. He was so stiff and gaunt with age that but for the painful rasping breath issuing from his gaping mouth you might have thought he was dead. He was toothless and his mouth looked like a black hole into which his lips seemed to be falling; and the two of them bent over and peered into it as if to see how much life remained at the bottom. For a long time, they stood looking side by side, with their hips touching. But their arms had lost their strength; it was so easy and yet so difficult to pick something up and stuff it into that hole. They walked away and came back again. Their mouths were too dry to say anything, they could speak only with their eyes. She was staring at the pillow as though to say: Go on! What are you waiting for? But he stood there, blinking and pushing her into his place. In exasperation, Lise suddenly caught hold of the pillow and clapped it down on her father's face.

'What a skunk you are! Why has it always got to be a woman?'

At this, Buteau ran forward and pressed with all his might on the pillow while Lise climbed on to the bed and sat her bare rump down with all her weight like some dropsical old carthorse. As though demented, they leant on him with their hands and thighs and shoulders. Their father gave a violent jerk and his legs shot up with a sound like a breaking spring; he looked like a fish squirming about on the grass. But not for long. They were holding on to him too tightly and they could feel him subsiding underneath them as his life ebbed away. A long shudder, a final quiver and all that was left was a piece of limp rag.

'I think that's it,' grunted Buteau breathlessly.

Lise stopped bouncing up and down and remained sitting hunched up, waiting to see if she could feel any quiver of life underneath her.

'That's it, he's not moving.'

She slid to one side, her shift rolled up round her hips, and lifted off the pillow. But then they gave a grunt of terror.

'Christ Almighty! He's gone all black, we're sunk!'

Indeed, it would have been impossible for him to have got into such a state by himself. They had pounded away at him so savagely that his nose had been pushed right down into the back of his mouth; and he was all purple, like a real black man. For a second, they could feel the ground swaying beneath their feet, they could hear the thundering hooves of the gendarmes, the clink of handcuffs, the thud of the guillotine. The sight of their botched handiwork filled them with horror and remorse. What could they do about it now? It would be no good washing his face with soap, they'd never succeed in making him white. And this terrifying, sooty hue gave them an inspiration.

'Suppose we set fire to him?' muttered Lise.

Buteau heaved a sigh of relief:

'That's right, we can say he set light to himself.'

Then he thought of the bonds and he clapped his hands as his face lit up and he gave an exultant laugh.

'By Christ, that's it! We'll make them think that the papers went up in flames with him. There'll be no accounts to settle!'

He quickly rushed over to fetch the candle but she was afraid of setting everything alight and at first refused to let him bring it too close to the bed. In the corner behind the beetroot there were some straw ties; she picked one up, lit it and began by setting fire to her father's hair and his long white beard. There was a sizzling sound, with little yellow flames and a smell of spilt fat. Suddenly they recoiled in horror, open-mouthed, as if some icy hand had pulled them back by their hair. Under the dreadful pain of his burns, their father, not completely smothered, had opened his eyes and this hideous black countenance, with its big broken nose and blazing beard, was staring at them. It took on a fearsome expression of pain and hatred and then collapsed. The old man was dead.

Buteau was panic-stricken, but at this moment he uttered a yell of fury as he heard sobbing at the doorway. It was the two children, Laure and Jules, in their nightclothes, who had been woken up by the noise and had come in through the open bedroom door, attracted by the glare of the flames. They had seen what was happening and were screaming with fright.

'You blasted little vermin,' shouted Buteau, rushing towards them. 'If you ever say a word, I'll strangle you. And here's something to remind you.'

He gave them both a clout that sent them sprawling. They picked themselves up, dry-eyed, and ran away, to curl up on their mattress, where they did not stir again.

Now anxious to finish, Buteau, despite his wife's objections, set light to the palliasse. Fortunately the room was so damp that the straw burned slowly. Big clouds of smoke swirled up and they opened the skylight, half asphyxiated. Then it began to flare up until the flames reached the ceiling. In the middle their father was crackling and the unbearable stench, the stench of burning flesh, grew stronger. The old house would all have gone up in flames like a haystack if the straw had not started smoking again, damped down by the bubbles dripping from the body. All that remained on the cross-pieces of the iron bedstead was a half-charred corpse, disfigured and unrecognizable. One corner of the straw mattress was still intact, with a tiny corner of cloth hanging down.

'Let's go,' said Lise, who was shivering again, despite the tremendous heat.

'Wait a minute,' Buteau replied. 'Got to make things look all right.'

Placing a chair beside the bedhead, he knocked the old man's candle off it, to make it seem as if it had fallen onto the palliasse. He was even artful enough to set light to some paper on the ground. They would find the ashes and he would explain that the day before the old man had found his bonds and kept them by him.

'That's that, let's get to bed!'

Buteau and Lise left the room, jostling each other in their haste and hurry back to bed. But the sheets were icy cold and so they once more clung desperately to each other to warm themselves up. Dawn came and still they could not sleep. They said nothing, but shudders ran through them and they could hear the pounding of their hearts. They had left the door of the next room open and it was this that so troubled them; but the thought of closing it disturbed them even more. They dozed off, still clasped in each other's arms.

Next morning, hearing the Buteaus' desperate calls, the neighbours hurried round and Frimat's wife and the other women were able to see the upset candle, the half-burnt straw mattress, the papers reduced to ashes. They all exclaimed that it was bound to happen, they'd predicted it dozens of times before, because the old man was in his second childhood. And what a stroke of luck that the house hadn't burnt down as well!

Emile Zola, *The Earth*, trans. Douglas Parmée

P

Parrot

'May I ask a question?' Mason inquired.

The coroner nodded assent.

Mason stepped forward and said in a low, kindly voice, 'I don't wish to subject your nerves to any undue strain, Miss Monteith, but I'm going to ask you to try and bring yourself to look at this parrot. I'm going to ask you to study it carefully, and I'm going to ask you whether this *is* the parrot which your husband brought home to you.'

Helen Monteith made an effort at self-control. She turned and looked down at the lifeless parrot in the cage, then quickly averted her head. 'I c-c-can't,' she said, in a quavering voice, 'but the parrot my husband brought home had one claw missing. I think it was from his right foot. My husband said he's caught the foot in a rat trap, and . . .'

'*This* parrot has no claws missing,' Mason said.

'Then it isn't the same parrot.'

'Just a moment,' Mason said; 'I'm going to ask you to make another identification.'

He nodded a signal to Paul Drake, who, in turn, passed the word to an operative who was waiting in the corridor. The operative came through the door carrying a caged parrot.

Amid a silence so tense that the steps of the detective could be heard as he walked down the carpeted aisle, the caged parrot suddenly broke into shrill laughter.

Helen Monteith's lips quivered. Apparently she was restraining herself from hysteria by a supreme effort.

Mason took the caged parrot from the operative. 'Hush, Polly,' he said.

The parrot twisted its head first to one side, then the other, leered about him at the courtroom with twinkling, wicked little eyes; then, as Mason set the cage on the table, the bird hooked its beak on the cross-wires of the cage, and completely circled it, walking over the top, head downward, to return to the perch as though proud of the accomplishment.

'Nice Polly,' Mason said.

The parrot shuffled its feet on the perch.

Helen Monteith turned to regard the parrot. 'Why,' she said, 'that's Casanova . . . The Sheriff told me he'd been killed.'

The parrot, tucking its head slightly to one side, said in a low, throaty voice, 'Come in and sit down, won't you? Come in and sit down down, take that chair . . . *Squawk* . . . *Squawk* . . . Put down that gun, Helen . . . don't shoot . . . *Squawk* . . . *Squawk* . . . My God, you've shot me.'

The spectators stared wide-eyed at the drama of the parrot apparently accusing the witness.

'*That's* Casanova!' Helen Monteith exclaimed.

The district attorney said dramatically, 'I want the words of this parrot in the record. The parrot is accusing the witness. I want the record to show it.'

Mason regarded the district attorney with a half smile twisting his lips. 'Do I understand,' he inquired, 'that you're adopting this parrot as your witness?'

'The parrot has made a statement. I want it in the record,' the district attorney insisted.

'But the parrot hasn't been sworn as a witness,' Mason observed.

The district attorney appealed to the coroner. 'The parrot has made a statement. It was a plainly audible statement.'

'I would like to know,' Mason said, 'whether the district attorney is making the parrot his witness.'

'I'm not talking about witnesses,' Sprague countered. 'I'm talking about parrots. This parrot made a statement. I want it in the record.'

'If the parrot is to be a witness,' Mason said, 'I should have *some* right of cross-examination.'

'Well,' the coroner ruled, 'a parrot can't be a witness, but the parrot *did* say something. What these words were can be put in the record for what they're worth. I think the coroner's jury understands the situation thoroughly. I never did believe in putting things in a record, and then striking them out. When jurors hear things, they've heard them, and that's that. Now, go on with the inquest.'

'I think that's all the questions I have,' Mason said.

'That's all,' Sprague said, 'except . . . wait a minute . . . Miss Monteith, if this parrot is Casanova, then where did the parrot come from that was killed?'

'I don't know,' she said.

'It was in your house.'

'I can't help that.'

'You must have had something to do with it.'

'I didn't.'

'But you're certain this is Casanova?'

'Yes. I can identify him by that claw that's missing, and by what he said about dropping the gun.'

'Oh, you've heard *that* before, have you?'

'Yes. My husband commented on it when he brought the bird home with him.'

The district attorney said, 'Miss Monteith, I'm not satisfied that your violent emotional reaction when this dead parrot was brought before you is purely the result of a nervous condition. Now I'm going to insist that you look at this parrot and . . .'

Mason got to his feet and said, 'You don't need to look at that parrot, Miss Monteith.'

Sprague flushed and said, 'I insist that she does.'

'And I insist that she doesn't,' Mason said. 'Miss Monteith is not going to answer any more questions. She's been a witness. She's under a great emotional strain. I think the jury will understand my position as her attorney in announcing that she has now completed her testimony. She has given the district attorney and the coroner an opportunity to ask her all reasonable questions. I am not going to have the examination unduly prolonged.'

'He can't do that,' Sprague said to the coroner.

'I've already done it,' Mason told him.

Erle Stanley Gardner, *The Case of the Perjured Parrot*

Pirate

Philip Roche was born in Ireland, and from his youth had been bred up to the sea. He was a brisk, genteel fellow of thirty years of age at the time of his death; one whose black and savage nature did no ways answer the comeliness of his person, his life being almost one continued scene of villainy before he was discovered to have committed the horrid murders we are now speaking of.

This inhuman monster had been concerned, with others, in insuring ships to a great value and then destroying them; by which means and other rogueries he had got a little money, and being mate of a ship, was diligent enough in trading for himself between Ireland and France, so that he was in a way of getting himself a comfortable livelihood. But, as he was resolved to be rich, and finding fair dealing brought in wealth but slowly, he contrived to put other things in execution and certainly had murdered several innocent persons in the prosecution of his abominable schemes. But as I have now forgot the particular circumstances of those relations, I shall confine myself at present to the fact for which he suffered.

Roche, getting acquainted with one Neal, a fisherman at Cork, whom he found ready for any villainous attempt, he imparted his design to him, who, being pleased with the project, brings one Pierce Cullen and his brother into the confederacy, together with one Wise, who at first was very unwilling to come into their measures and, indeed, had the least hand in the perpetration of what follows.

They pitched upon a vessel in the harbour, belonging to Peter Tartoue, a Frenchman, to execute their cruel intentions upon, because it was a small one and had not a great number of hands on board, and 'twas easy afterwards to exchange it for one more fit for piracy. And therefore they applied themselves to the master of her for a passage to Nantes, whereto the ship was bound. And accordingly, the beginning of November, 1721, they went aboard; and when at sea, Philip Roche, being an experienced sailor, the master of the vessel readily trusted him with the care of her at times, while he and the mate went to rest.

The 15th of November, at night, was the time designed for the tragedy. But Francis Wise relented and appeared desirous to divert them from their bloody purposes. Roche (sometimes called Captain) told him *That as Cullen and he had sustained great losses at sea, unless every Irishman present would assist in repairing their losses by murdering all the French rogues and running away with their ship, he should suffer the same fate with the Frenchmen; but if all would assist all should have a share in the booty.* Upon this they all resolved alike, and Captain Roche ordered three Frenchmen and a boy to hand the topsails, the master and mate being then asleep in their cabins. The two first that came down, they beat out their brains and threw them overboard. The other two, seeing what was done, ran to the topmast-head; but Cullen followed them and taking the boy by the arm, tossed him into the sea; then driving down the man, those below knocked him on the head and threw him overboard.

Those who were asleep, being awakened by the dismal shrieks and groans of dying men, ran upon the deck in confusion, to enquire into the cause of such unusual noises; but the same cruelty was immediately acted towards them e'er they could be sensible of the danger that threatened them.

They were now (as Roche himself afterwards confessed), *All over as wet with blood that had been spilt as if they had been dipped in water or stood in a shower of rain, nor did they regard it any more.* Roche said [that] Captain Tartoue used many words for mercy and asked them if he had not used them with civility and kindness; if they were not of the same Christian religion and owned the same blessed Jesus and the like? But they, not regarding what he said, took cords and bound the poor master and his mate back to back; and while this was doing both of them begged with the utmost earnestness, and used the most solemn entreaties, that they would at least allow them a few minutes to say their prayers and beg mercy of God for the various slips and offences of their lives. But it did not move them (though all the rest were dead and no danger could be apprehended from them two alone) for the bound persons were hurried up and thrown into the sea.

The massacre being finished, they washed themselves a little from the blood and searched the chests and lockers and all places about the ship, and then sat down in the captain's cabin and refreshed themselves with some rum they found there, and (as Roche confessed) were never merrier in their lives. They invested Roche with the command of the ship and, calling him Captain, talked over their liquor what rare actions they would perform about Cape Breton, Sable Island, and the Banks of Newfoundland, whither they designed to go as soon as they had recruited their company and got a better ship, which they proposed speedily to do.

Roche taking upon himself the command of the vessel, Andrew Cullen was to pass for a merchant or supercargo; but then they bethought themselves that they were in danger of being discovered by the papers of the ship relating to the cargo, as bills of lading etc; therefore they erase and take out the name of the French master and, instead thereof, insert the name of Roche, so that it stood in the ship's papers, Peter Roche, master; that then, having so few hands on board, they contrived, if they should meet any ships, to give out that they had lost some hands in a storm, and by that means screen themselves from being suspected of having committed such wicked acts, by reason of the fewness of their hands on board; and also might prevail with some ships to spare them some in consideration of their pretended disaster.

In going to Cadiz they were in distress by the weather; and being near Lisbon, they made complaint to a ship, but obtained no assistance. They were then obliged to sail back for England and put into the port of Dartmouth. But then they were in fear lest they might be discovered, therefore, to prevent that, they resolved to alter the ship; and getting workmen, they took down the mizenmast and built a spar-deck and made rails (on pretence that the sailors had been washed overboard) to secure the men. Then they took down the image of St Peter at the head of the ship and put up a Lion in its place, and painted over the stern of the ship with red and named her the *Mary Snow*. The ship being thus altered that they thought it could not be known, they fancied themselves pretty secure; but wanting money to defray the charges of these alterations, Roche, as master of the vessel, and Andrew Cullen, as merchant, applied themselves to the officers of the Customs for liberty to dispose of some of the cargo, in order to pay the workmen; which they having obtained, they sold fifty-eight barrels of beef. And having hired three more hands, they set sail for Ostend, and there, having sold more barrels of beef, they steered their course to Rotterdam, disposed of the rest of the cargo and took in one Mr Annesly, who freighted the ship for England. But in their passage, in a stormy night, it being very dark, they took up Mr Annesly their passenger, and threw him into the sea, who swam about the ship a pretty while, calling out for life, and telling them they should have all his goods if they would receive him again into the vessel. But in vain were his cries!

After this they were obliged to put into several ports, and by contrary winds came to the coast of France. And hearing there was an enquiry made after the ship, Roche quits her at Havre de Grace and leaves the management to Cullen and the rest; who, having shipped other men, sailed away to Scotland and there quitted the vessel, which was afterwards seized and brought into the river of Thames.

Some time after this, Philip Roche came to London, and making some claim for money he had made insurance of in the name of John Eustace, the officer was apprised of the fraud and he [was] arrested and flung into the compter; from whence directing a letter to his wife, she showed it to a friend, who discovered by it that he was the principal villain concerned in the destruction of Peter Tartoue and the crew. Upon this, an information was given to my Lord Carteret that the person who went by the name of John Eustace was Philip Roche, as aforesaid; and being brought down by his lordship's warrant, he stiffly denied it for some time, notwithstanding a letter was found in his pocket directed to him by the name of Roche. But, being confronted by a captain of a ship who knew him well, he confessed it, but prevaricated in several particulars. Whereupon he was committed to Newgate, upon violent suspicion, and the next day was brought down again at his own request, confessed the whole, desired to be made an evidence, and promised to convict three men worse than himself. Two were discovered by him, who died miserably in the Marshalsea, and

Roche himself was afterwards tried (no more being taken), found Guilty of the piracy, and executed.

Captain Charles Johnson, *Lives of the Most Notorious Pirates*

Poirot

Poirot rapped gently on a table and cleared his throat significantly.

'The board meeting's going to begin,' said Flora. 'M. Poirot hints that we mustn't talk. But just tell me one thing. Where is Ralph? You must know if anyone does.'

'But I don't,' cried Ursula, almost in a wail. 'That's just it, I don't.'

'Isn't he detained at Liverpool?' asked Raymond. 'It said so in the paper.'

'He is not at Liverpool,' said Poirot shortly.

'In fact,' I remarked, 'no one knows where he is.'

'Excepting Hercule Poirot, eh?' said Raymond.

Poirot replied seriously to the other's banter.

'Me, I know everything. Remember that.'

Geoffrey Raymond lifted his eyebrows.

'Everything?' He whistled. 'Whew! that's a tall order.'

'Do you mean to say you can really guess where Ralph Paton is hiding?' I asked incredulously.

'You call it guessing. I call it knowing, my friend.'

'In Cranchester?' I hazarded.

'No,' replied Poirot gravely, 'not in Cranchester.'

He said no more, but at a gesture from him the assembled party took their seats. As they did, the door opened once more and two other people came in and sat down near the door. They were Parker and the housekeeper.

'The number is complete,' said Poirot. 'Everyone is here.'

There was a ring of satisfaction in his tone. And with the sound of it I saw a ripple of something like uneasiness pass over all those faces grouped at the other end of the room. There was a suggestion in all this as of a trap – a trap that had closed.

Poirot read from a list in an important manner.

'Mrs Ackroyd, Miss Flora Ackroyd, Major Blunt, Mr Geoffrey Raymond, Mrs Ralph Paton, John Parker, Elizabeth Russell.'

He laid the paper down on the table.

'What's the meaning of all this?' began Raymond.

'The list I have just read,' said Poirot, 'is a list of suspected persons. Every one of you present had the opportunity to kill Mr Ackroyd – '

With a cry Mrs Ackroyd sprang up, her throat working.

'I don't like it,' she wailed. 'I don't like it. I would much prefer to go home.'

'You cannot go home, madame,' said Poirot sternly, 'until you have heard what I have to say.'

He paused a moment, then cleared his throat.

'I will start at the beginning. When Miss Ackroyd asked me to investigate the case, I went up to Fernly Park with the good Doctor Sheppard. I walked with him along the terrace, where I was shown the footprints on the window-sill. From there Inspector Raglan took me along the path which leads to the drive. My eye was caught by a little summer-house, and I searched it thoroughly. I found two things – a scrap of starched cambric and an empty goose quill. The scrap of cambric immediately suggested to me a maid's apron. When Inspector Raglan showed me his list of the people in the house, I noticed at once that one of the maids – Ursula Bourne, the parlourmaid – had no real alibi. According to her own story, she was in her bedroom from nine-thirty until ten. But supposing that instead she was in the summer-house? If so, she must have gone there to meet someone. Now we know from Dr Sheppard that someone from outside *did* come to the house that night – a stranger whom he met just by the gate. At first glance it would seem that our problem was solved, and that the stranger went to the summer-house to meet Ursula Bourne. It was fairly certain that he *did* go to the summer-house because of the goose quill. That suggested at once to my mind a taker of drugs – and one who had acquired the habit on the other side of the Atlantic where sniffing 'snow' is more common than in this country. The man whom Dr Sheppard met had an American accent, which fitted in with that supposition.

'But I was held up by one point. *The times did not fit.* Ursula Bourne could certainly not have gone to the summer-house before nine-thirty, whereas the man must have got there by a few minutes past nine. I could, of course, assume that he waited there for half an hour. The only alternative supposition was that there had been two separate meetings in the summer-house that night. *Eh bien*, as soon as I went into that alternative I found several significant facts. I discovered that Miss Russell, the housekeeper, had visited Dr Sheppard that morning, and had displayed a good deal of interest in cures for victims of the drug habit. Taking that in conjunction with the goose quill, I assumed that the man in question came to Fernly to meet the housekeeper, and not Ursula Bourne. Who, then, did Ursula Bourne come to the rendezvous to meet? I was not long in doubt. First I found a ring – a wedding ring – with 'From R.' and a date inside it. Then I learnt that Ralph Paton had been seen coming up the path which led to the summer-house at twenty-five minutes past nine, and I also heard of a certain conversation which had taken place in the wood near the village that very afternoon – a conversation between Ralph Paton and some unknown girl. So I had my facts succeeding each other in a neat and orderly manner. A secret marriage, an engagement announced on the day of the tragedy, the stormy interview in the wood, and the meeting arranged for the summer-house that night.

'Incidentally this proved to me one thing, that both Ralph Paton and Ursula Bourne (or Paton) had the strongest motives for wishing Mr Ackroyd out of the way. And it also made one other point unexpectedly clear. It could not have been Ralph Paton who was with Mr Ackroyd in the study at nine-thirty.

'So we come to another and most interesting aspect of the crime. Who was it in the room with Mr Ackroyd at nine-thirty? Not Ralph Paton, who was in the summer-house with his wife. Not Charles Kent, who had already left. Who, then? I posed my cleverest – my most audacious question: *Was anyone with him?*'

Poirot leaned forward and shot the last words triumphantly at us, drawing back afterwards with the air of one who has made a decided hit.

Raymond, however, did not seem impressed, and lodged a mild protest.

'I don't know if you're trying to make me out a liar, M. Poirot, but the matter does not rest on my evidence alone – except perhaps as to the exact words used. Remember, Major Blunt also heard Mr Ackroyd talking to someone. He was on the terrace outside, and couldn't catch the words clearly, but he distinctly heard the voices.'

Poirot nodded.

'I have not forgotten,' he said quietly. 'But Major Blunt was under the impression that it was *you* to whom Mr Ackroyd was speaking.'

For a moment Raymond seemed taken aback. Then he recovered himself.

'Blunt knows now that he was mistaken,' he said.

'Exactly,' agreed the other man.

'Yet there must have been some reason for his thinking so,' mused Poirot. 'Oh! no,' he held up his hand in protest. 'I know the reason you will give – but it is not enough. We must seek elsewhere. I will put it this way.

From the beginning of the case I have been struck by one thing – the nature of those words which Mr Raymond overheard. It has been amazing to me that no one has commented on them – has seen anything odd about them.'

He paused a minute, and then quoted softly:

'. . . *the calls on my purse have been so frequent of late that I fear it is impossible for me to accede to your request.* Does nothing strike you as odd about that?'

'I don't think so,' said Raymond. 'He has frequently dictated letters to me, using almost exactly those same words.'

'Exactly,' cried Poirot. 'That is what I seek to arrive at. Would any man use such a phrase in *talking* to another? Impossible that that should be part of a real conversation. Now, if he had been dictating a letter – '

'You mean he was reading a letter aloud,' said Raymond slowly. 'Even so, he must have been reading to someone.'

'But why? We have no evidence that there was anyone else in the room. No other voice but Mr Ackroyd's was heard, remember.'

'Surely a man wouldn't read letters of that type aloud to himself – not unless he was – well – going balmy.'

'You have all forgotten one thing,' said Poirot softly: 'the stranger who called at the house the preceding Wednesday.'

They all stared at him.

'But yes,' said Poirot nodding encouragingly, 'on Wednesday. The young man was not of himself important. But the firm he represented interested me very much.'

'The Dictaphone Company,' gasped Raymond. 'I see it now. A dictaphone. That's what you think?'

Poirot nodded.

'Mr Ackroyd had promised to invest in a dictaphone, you remember. Me, I had the curiosity to inquire of the company in question. Their reply is that Mr Ackroyd *did* purchase a dictaphone from their representative. Why he concealed the matter from you, I do not know.'

'He must have meant to surprise me with it,' murmured Raymond. 'He had quite a childish love of surprising people. Meant to keep it up his sleeve for a day or so. Probably was playing with it like a new toy. Yes, it fits in. You're quite right – no one would use quite those words in casual conversation.'

'It explains, too,' said Poirot, 'why Major Blunt thought it was you who were in the study. Such scraps as came to him were fragments of dictation, and so his subconscious mind deduced that you were with him. His conscious mind was occupied with something quite different – the white figure he had caught a glimpse of. He fancied it was Miss Ackroyd. Really, of course, it was Ursula Bourne's white apron he saw as she was stealing down to the summer-house.'

Raymond had recovered from his first surprise.

'All the same,' he remarked, 'this discovery of yours, brilliant though it is (I'm quite sure I should never have thought of it), leaves the essential position unchanged. Mr Ackroyd was alive at nine-thirty, since he was speaking into the dictaphone. It seems clear that the man Charles Kent was really off the premises by then. As to Ralph Paton – ?'

He hesitated, glancing at Ursula.

Her colour flared up, but she answered steadily enough.

'Ralph and I parted just before a quarter to ten. He never went near the house, I am sure of that. He had no intention of doing so. The last thing on earth he wanted was to face his stepfather. He would have funked it badly.'

'It isn't that I doubt your story for a moment,' explained Raymond. 'I've always been quite sure Captain Paton was innocent. But one has to think of a court of law – and the questions that would be asked. He is in a most unfortunate position, but if he were to come forward – '

Poirot interrupted.

'That is your advice, yes? That he should come forward?'

'Certainly. If you know where he is – '

'I perceive that you do not believe that I do know. And yet I have told you just now that I know everything. The truth of the telephone call, of the footprints on the window-sill, of the hiding-place of Ralph Paton – '

'Where is he?' said Blunt sharply.

'Not very far away,' said Poirot, smiling.

'In Cranchester?' I asked.

Poirot turned towards me.

'Always you ask me that. The idea of Cranchester it is with you an *idée fixé*. No, he is not in Cranchester. He is – *there*!'

He pointed a dramatic forefinger. Everyone's head turned.

Ralph Paton was standing in the doorway.

Agatha Christie, *The Murder of Roger Ackroyd*

Poison

Trulie this poisoning art called *Veneficium*, of all others is most abhominable; as whereby murthers maie be committed, where no suspicion maie be gathered, nor anie resistance can be made; the strong cannot avoid the weake, the wise cannot prevent the foolish, the godlie cannot be preserved from the hands of the wicked; children maie hereby kill their parents, the servant the maister, the wife hir husband, so privilie, so inevitablie, and so incurablie, that of all other it hath beene thought the most odious kind of murther; according to the saieng of *Ovid*
[Englished by Abraham Fleming]:

The travelling ghest opprest
Dooth stand in danger of his host, the host eke of his ghest:
The father of his sonne in lawe, yea rare is seene to rest
Twixt brethren love and amitie, and kindness void of strife;
The husband seekes the goodwifes death, and his againe the wife.
Ungentle stepdames grizlie poison temper and doo give:
The sonne too soone dooth ask how long the father is to live.

The monke that poisoned king *John*, was a right *Veneficus*; to wit, both a witch and a murtherer: for he killed the king with poison, and persuaded the people with lies, that he had doone a good and a meritorious act: and doubtlesse, manie were so bewitched, as they thought and he did verie well therein. *Antonius Sabellicus* writeth of a horrible poisoning murther, committed by women at *Rome*, where were executed (after due conviction) 170 women at one time; besides 20 women of that consort, who were poisoned with the poison which they had prepared for others.

Reginald Scot, *The Discovery of Witchcraft*

King John is brought in, with Lord Bigot attending

KING JOHN: Ay marry, now my soul hath elbow-room;
It would not out at windows nor at doors.
There is so hot a summer in my bosom
That all my bowels crumble up to dust;
I am a scribbled form, drawn with a pen
Upon a parchment, and against this fire
Do I shrink up.

PRINCE HENRY: How fares your majesty?

KING JOHN: Poisoned, ill fare! Dead, forsook, cast off;
And none of you will bid the winter come
To thrust his icy fingers in my maw,
Nor let my kingdom's rivers take their course
Through my burned bosom, nor entreat the north
To make his bleak winds kiss my parchèd lips
And comfort me with cold. I do not ask you much;
I beg cold comfort, and you are so strait
And so ingrateful you deny me that.
PRINCE HENRY: O, that there were some virtue in my tears
That might relieve you!
KING JOHN: The salt in them is hot.
Within me is a hell, and there the poison
Is, as a fiend, confined to tyrannize
On unreprievable condemnèd blood.

Enter the Bastard

BASTARD: O, I am scalded with my violent motion
And spleen of speed to see your majesty!
KING JOHN: O cousin, thou art come to set mine eye.
The tackle of my heart is cracked and burnt,
And all the shrouds wherewith my life should sail
Are turnèd to one thread, one little hair;
My heart hath one poor string to stay it by,
Which holds but till thy news be utterèd,
And then all this thou seest is but a clod
And module of confounded royalty.
BASTARD: The Dauphin is preparing hitherward,
Where God He knows how we shall answer him;
For in a night the best part of my power,
As I upon advantage did remove,
Were in the Washes all unwarily
Devourèd by the unexpected flood.

King John dies

SALISBURY: You breathe these dead news in as dead an ear.
(*To King John*) My liege, my lord! – But now a king, now thus.

William Shakespeare, *King John*

'O where hae ye been, Lord Randal, my son?
O where hae ye been my handsome young man?'
'I hae been to the wild wood; mother, make my bed soon,
For I'm weary wi' hunting, and fain wald lie down.'

'Where gat ye your dinner, Lord Randal, my son?
Where gat ye your dinner, my handsome young man?
'I dined wi' my true-love; mother, make my bed soon,
For I'm weary wi' hunting, and fain wald lie down.'

'What gat ye to your dinner, Lord Randal, my son?
What gat ye to your dinner, my handsome young man?'
'I gat eels boiled in broo; mother, make my bed soon,
For I'm weary wi' hunting, and fain wald lie down.'

'What became of your bloodhounds, Lord Randal, my son?'
What became of your bloodhounds, my handsome young man?'
'O they swelled and they died; mother, make my bed soon,
For I'm weary wi' hunting, and fain wald lie down.'

'O I fear ye are poisoned, Lord Randal, my son!
O I fear ye are poisoned, my handsome young man!'
'O yes, I am poisoned, mother, make my bed soon,
For I'm sick at the heart, and I fain wald lie down.'

Anon., 'Lord Randal'

Inspector Blount picked up a ruler from the desk, and sighted along it with one eye screwed up. Then he suddenly sat up straight, speaking with remarkable incisiveness.

'George Rattery was poisoned by strychnine: can't enlarge upon that till after the autopsy – be finished by midday. He, Mrs Rattery, Lena Lawson, old Mrs Rattery, his mother, and his son Philip – a wee boy, had dinner together. They all ate the same food. The deceased and his mother took whisky with their food, the rest water. None of the others suffered any ill effects. They left the dinner table about quarter past eight, the women and the wee boy first, the deceased following them in a minute's time. They all repaired to the drawing-room with the exception of Master Philip. George Rattery was seized with severe pains between ten and fifteen minutes later. The women-folk, poor souls, were helpless; they gave him a mustard-emetic, but that only aggravated the seizure; the symptoms, of course, are very horrifying. Their own medical man, whom they rang up first, was out to a road accident; and by the time they had got hold of another, it was too late. Dr Clarkson arrived a little before ten – he'd been out on a maternity case – and applied the usual chloroform treatment: but Rattery was too far gone then. He died five or ten minutes later. I'll not bother you with the details: I've assured myself, however, that the poison could not have been introduced through any of the food or drink taken at dinner. The symptoms of strychnine poisoning, moreover, rarely take longer than an hour to supervene; the company sat down to dinner at quarter past seven; therefore Rattery could not likely have taken the poison before dinner. There remains the interval of one minute between the time the others left the dining-room and the time Rattery rejoined them in the drawing-room.'

'Coffee? Port? No, of course it couldn't have been in the port. Nobody gulps that down; and strychnine's got such a bitter taste, anyone'd spit it out at once unless he was expecting a bitter taste.'

'Just so. And the family did not take coffee on Saturday night – the parlourmaid had broken the percolator.'

'It sounds to me like suicide, then.'

Inspector Blount's face betrayed a slight impatience. 'My dear Mr Strangeways,' he said, 'a suicide does not take poison and then walk into the drawing-room – into the bosom of his family – so that they can all watch the poison taking effect. In the second place, Colesby could find no trace of *how* he took it.'

'Had the dinner things been washed up?'

'The glass and silver: not all the crockery, though. Mind you, Colesby – he's the local chap – may have missed something: I didn't get down here till this morning myself; but – '

'You know that Cairnes did not return to this house after he left it in the early afternoon?'

'Indeed? Have you proof of that?'

'Well, no,' said Nigel, taken rather aback. 'At the moment, I haven't. He told me that, after the show-down in the dinghy, Rattery refused to let him come back here, even to pack his things. It can be verified, anyway.'

'Maybe,' said Blount cautiously. He drummed his fingers on the desk. 'I think – ye-es, I think we might take another peek at the dining-room.'

Nicholas Blake, *The Beast Must Die*

Power

It should be noted that when he seizes a state the new ruler ought to determine all the injuries that he will need to inflict. He should inflict them once for all, and not have to renew them every day, and in that way he will be able to set men's minds at rest and win them over to him when he confers benefits. Whoever acts otherwise, either through timidity or bad advice, is always forced to have the knife ready in his hand and he can never depend on his subjects because they, suffering fresh and continuous violence, can never feel secure with regard to him. Violence should be inflicted once for all; people will then forget what it tastes like and so be less resentful.

Niccolò Machiavelli, *The Prince*, trans. George Bull

Preamble

BOSOLA: I am come to make thy tomb.

DUCHESS: Ha! my tomb?
Thou speak'st as if I lay upon my death-bed,
Gasping for breath: dost thou perceive me sick?

BOSOLA: Yes, and the more dangerously, since thy sickness is insensible.

DUCHESS: Thou art not mad, sure; dost know me?

BOSOLA: Yes.

DUCHESS: Who am I?

BOSOLA: Thou art a box of worm seed, at best, but a salvatory of green mummy: what's this flesh? a little cruded milk, fantastical puff-paste: our bodies are weaker than those paper prisons boys use to keep flies in: more contemptible; since ours is to preserve earth-worms: didst thou ever see a lark in a cage? such is the soul in the body: this world is like her little turf of grass, and the heaven o'er our heads, like her looking-glass, only gives us a miserable knowledge of the small compass of our prison.

DUCHESS: Am not I thy Duchess?

BOSOLA: Thou art some great woman, sure; for riot begins to sit on thy forehead (clad in grey hairs) twenty years sooner than on a merry milkmaid's. Thou sleep'st worse, than if a mouse should be forc'd to take up her lodging in a cat's ear: a little infant, that breeds its teeth, should it lie with thee, would cry out, as if thou wert the more unquiet bedfellow.

DUCHESS: I am Duchess of Malfi still.

BOSOLA: That makes thy sleeps so broken:
Glories, like glow-worms, afar off shine bright,
But look'd to near, have neither heat nor light.

DUCHESS: Thou art very plain.

BOSOLA: My trade is to flatter the dead, not the living;
I am a tomb-maker.

DUCHESS: And thou com'st to make my tomb?

BOSOLA: Yes.

DUCHESS: Let me be a little merry;
Of what stuff wilt thou make it?

BOSOLA: Nay, resolve me first, of what fashion?

DUCHESS: Why, do we grow fantastical in our death-bed?
Do we affect fashion in the grave?

BOSOLA: Most ambitiously. Princes' images on their tombs
Do not lie as they were wont, seeming to pray
Up to Heaven: but with their hands under their cheeks,
As if they died of the tooth-ache; they are not carved
With their eyes fix'd upon the stars; but as
Their minds were wholly bent upon the world,
The self-same way they seem to turn their faces.

DUCHESS: Let me know fully therefore the effect
Of this thy dismal preparation,
This talk, fit for a charnel.

BOSOLA: Now I shall;

Enter EXECUTIONERS *with a coffin, cords, and a bell*

Here is a present from your princely brothers,
And may it arrive welcome, for it brings
Last benefit, last sorrow.

DUCHESS: Let me see it.
I have so much obedience, in my blood,
I wish it in their veins, to do them good.

BOSOLA: This is your last presence chamber.

CARIOLA: O my sweet lady!

DUCHESS: Peace; it affrights not me.

BOSOLA: I am the common bellman,
That usually is sent to condemn'd persons,
The night before they suffer.

DUCHESS: Even now thou said'st
Thou wast a tomb-maker?
BOSOLA: 'Twas to bring you
By degrees to mortification. Listen: (*rings the bell*)
Hark, now every thing is still,
The screech-owl and the whistler shrill
Call upon our Dame, aloud,
And bid her quickly don her shroud.
Much you had of land and rent,
Your length in clay's now competent.
A long war disturb'd your mind,
Here your perfect peace is sign'd.
Of what is't fools make such vain keeping?
Sin their conception, their birth, weeping:
Their life, a general mist of error,
Their death, a hideous storm of terror.
Strew your hair with powders sweet:
Don clean linen, bath your feet,
And the foul fiend more to check,
A crucifix let bless your neck.
'Tis now full tide 'tween night and day,
End your groan, and come away.
(EXECUTIONERS *approach*)
CARIOLA: Hence villains, tyrants, murderers. Alas!
What will you do with my lady? Call for help.
DUCHESS: To whom, to our next neighbours? They are mad-folks.
BOSOLA: Remove that noise.
(EXECUTIONERS *seize* CARIOLA, *who struggles*)
DUCHESS: Farewell Cariola
In my last will I have not much to give;
A many hungry guests have fed upon me,
Thine will be a poor reversion.
CARIOLA: I will die with her.
DUCHESS: I pray thee look thou giv'st my little boy
Some syrup for his cold and let the girl
Say her prayers, ere she sleep.
(CARIOLA *is forced off*)
Now what you please,
What death?
BOSOLA: Strangling: here are your executioners.

DUCHESS: I forgive them:
    The apoplexy, catarrh, or cough o'th' lungs
    Would do as much as they do.
BOSOLA: Doth not death fright you?
DUCHESS: Who would be afraid on't?
    Knowing to meet such excellent company
    In th'other world.
BOSOLA: Yet, methinks,
    The manner of your death should much afflict you,
    This cord should terrify you?
DUCHESS: Not a whit:
    What would it pleasure me, to have my throat cut
    With diamonds? or to be smothered
    With cassia? Or to be shot to death, with pearls?
    I know death hath ten thousand several doors
    For men to take their *Exits*: and 'tis found
    They go on such strange geometrical hinges,
    You may open them both ways: any way, for Heaven sake,
    So I were out of your whispering. Tell my brothers
    That I perceive death, now I am well awake,
    Best gift is, they can give, or I can take.
    I would fain put off my last woman's fault,
    I'll'd not be tedious to you.
EXECUTIONERS: We are ready.
DUCHESS: Dispose my breath how please you, but my body
    Bestow upon my women, will you?
EXECUTIONERS: Yes.
DUCHESS: Pull, and pull strongly, for your able strength
    Must pull down heaven upon me:
    Yet stay, heaven's gates are not so highly arch'd
    As princes' palaces: they that enter there
    Must go upon their knees. Come violent death,
    Serve for mandragora to make me sleep;
    Go tell my brothers, when I am laid out,
    They then may feed in quiet.

(*They strangle her*)

BOSOLA: Where's the waiting woman?
    Fetch her. Some other strangle the children.

John Webster, *The Duchess of Malfi*

Premonition

A windy night was blowing on Rome,
The cressets guttered on Cæsar's home,
The fish-boats, moored at the bridge, were breaking
The rush of the river to yellow foam.

The hinges whined to the shutters shaking,
When clip-clop-clep came a horse-hoof raking
The stones of the road at Cæsar's gate;
The spear-butts jarred at the guard's awaking.

'Who goes there?' said the guard at the gate.
'What is the news, that you ride so late?'
'News most pressing, that must be spoken
To Cæsar alone, and that cannot wait.'

'The Cæsar sleeps; you must show a token
That the news suffice that he be awoken.
What is the news, and whence do you come?
For no light cause may his sleep be broken.'

'Out of the dark of the sands I come,
From the dark of death, with news for Rome.
A word so fell that it must be uttered
Though it strike the soul of the Cæsar dumb.'

Cæsar turned in his bed and muttered,
With a struggle for breath the lamp-flame guttered;
Calpurnia heard her husband moan:
    'The house is falling,
The beaten men come into their own.'

'Speak your word,' said the guard at the gate;
'Yes, but bear it to Cæsar straight,
Say, "Your murderer's knives are honing,
Your killer's gang is lying in wait."

'Out of the wind that is blowing and moaning,
Through the city palace and the country loaning,
I cry, "For the world's sake, Cæsar, beware,
And take this warning as my atoning.

‘ “Beware of the Court, of the palace stair,
Of the downcast friend who speaks so fair,
Keep from the Senate, for Death is going
On many men’s feet to meet you there.”

‘I, who am dead, have ways of knowing
Of the crop of death that the quick are sowing.
I, who was Pompey, cry it aloud
From the dark of death, from the wind blowing.

‘I, who was Pompey, once was proud,
Now I lie in the sand without a shroud;
I cry to Cæsar out of my pain,
“Cæsar, beware, your death is vowed.” ’

The light grew grey on the window-pane,
The windcocks swung in a burst of rain,
The window of Cæsar flung unshuttered,
The horse-hoofs died into wind again.

Cæsar turned in his bed and muttered,
With a struggle for breath the lamp-flame guttered:
Calpurnia heard her husband moan:
‘The house is falling,
The beaten men come into their own.’

John Masefield, ‘The Rider at the Gate’

Prisoner

He did not wear his scarlet coat,
For blood and wine are red,
And blood and wine were on his hands
When they found him with the dead,
The poor dead woman whom he loved,
And murdered in her bed.

He walked amongst the Trial Men
In a suit of shabby grey;
A cricket cap was on his head,
And his step seemed light and gay;

But I never saw a man who looked
  So wistfully at the day.

I never saw a man who looked
  With such a wistful eye
Upon that little tent of blue
  Which prisoners call the sky,
And at every drifting cloud that went
  With sails of silver by.

I walked, with other souls in pain,
  Within another ring,
And was wonderfing if the man had done
  A great or little thing,
When a voice behind me whispered low,
  '*That fellow's got to swing.*'

Dear Christ! the very prison walls
  Suddenly seemed to reel,
And the sky above my head became
  Like a casque of scorching steel;
And, though I was a soul in pain,
  My pain I could not feel.

I only knew what hunted thought
  Quickened his step, and why
He looked upon the garish day
  With such a wistful eye;
The man had killed the thing he loved,
  And so he had to die.

Yet each man kills the thing he loves,
  By each let this be heard,
Some do it with a bitter look,
  Some with a flattering word,
The coward does it with a kiss,
  The brave man with a sword!

Some kill their love when they are young,
  And some when they are old;
Some strangle with the hands of Lust,
  Some with the hands of Gold:

The kindest use a knife, because
  The dead so soon grow cold.

Some love too little, some too long,
  Some sell, and others buy;
Some do the deed with many tears,
  And some without a sigh:
For each man kills the thing he loves,
  Yet each man does not die.

He does not die a death of shame
  On a day of dark disgrace,
Nor have a noose about his neck,
  Nor a cloth upon his face,
Nor drop feet foremost through the floor
  Into an empty space.

He does not sit with silent men
  Who watch him night and day;
Who watch him when he tries to weep,
  And when he tries to pray;
Who watch him lest himself should rob
  The prison of its prey.

He does not wake at dawn to see
  Dread figures throng his room,
The shivering Chaplain robed in white,
  The Sheriff stern with gloom,
And the Governor all in shiny black,
  With the yellow face of Doom.

He does not rise in piteous haste
  To put on convict-clothes,
While some coarse-mouthed Doctor gloats, and notes
  Each new and nerve-twitched pose,
Fingering a watch whose little ticks
  Are like horrible hammer-blows.

He does not know that sickening thirst
  That sands one's throat, before
The hangman with his gardener's gloves
  Slips through the padded door,

And binds one with three leathern thongs,
  That the throat may thirst no more.

He does not bend his head to hear
  The Burial Office read,
Nor, while the terror of his soul
  Tells him he is not dead,
Cross his own coffin, as he moves
  Into the hideous shed.

He does not stare upon the air
  Through a little roof of glass:
He does not pray with lips of clay
  For his agony to pass;
Nor feel upon his shuddering cheek
  The kiss of Caiaphas.

Oscar Wilde, 'The Ballad of Reading Gaol'

Q

Quality

GENTLEMEN, I have had the honour to be appointed by your committee to the trying task of reading the Williams' Lecture on Murder, considered as one of the Fine Arts; a task which might be easy enough three or four centuries ago, when the art was little understood, and few great models had been exhibited; but in this age, when masterpieces of excellence have been executed by professional men, it must be evident, that in the style of criticism applied to them, the public will look for something of a corresponding improvement. Practice and theory must advance *pari passu*. People begin to see that something more goes to the composition of a fine murder than two blockheads to kill and be killed – a knife – a purse – and a dark lane. Design, gentlemen, grouping, light and shade, poetry, sentiment, are now deemed indispensable to attempts of this nature. Mr Williams has exalted the ideal of murder to all of us; and to me, therefore, in particular, has deepened the arduousness of my task. Like Æschylus or Milton in poetry, like Michael Angelo in painting, he has carried his art to a point of colossal sublimity; and, as Mr Wordsworth observes, has in a manner 'created the taste by which he is to be enjoyed'. To sketch the history of the art, and to examine its principles critically, now remains as a duty for the connoisseur, and for judges of quite another stamp from his Majesty's Judges of Assize.

Before I begin, let me say a word or two to certain prigs, who affect to speak of our society as if it were in some degree immoral in its tendency. Immoral! Jupiter protect me, gentlemen, what is it that people mean? I am for morality, and always shall be, and for virtue, and all that; and I do affirm, and always shall (let what will come of it), that murder is an improper line of conduct, highly improper; and I do not stick to assert, that any man who deals in murder, must have very incorrect ways of thinking, and truly inaccurate principles; and so far from aiding and abetting him by pointing out his victim's hiding-place, as a great moralist[1] of Germany declared it to be every good man's duty to do, I would subscribe one shilling and sixpence to have him apprehended, which is more by eighteenpence than the most eminent moralists have hitherto subscribed for that purpose. But what then? Everything in this world has two handles. Murder, for instance, may be laid hold of by its moral handle (as it generally is in the pulpit, and at the Old Bailey); and *that*, I confess, is its weak side; or it may also be treated *aesthetically*, as the Germans call it – that is, in relation to good taste.

To illustrate this, I will urge the authority of three eminent persons; viz., S. T. Coleridge, Aristotle, and Mr Howship the surgeon. To begin with S. T. C. One night, many years ago, I was drinking tea with him in Berners Street (which, by the way, for a short street, has been uncommonly fruitful in men of genius). Others were there besides myself; and, amidst some carnal considerations of tea and toast, we were all imbibing a dissertation on Plotinus from the attic lips of S. T. C. Suddenly a cry arose of, 'Fire – fire!' upon which all of us, master and disciples, Plato and ὁι περὶ τον Πλάτωνα, rushed out, eager for the spectacle. The fire was in Oxford Street, at a pianoforte-maker's; and, as it promised to be a conflagration of merit, I was sorry that my engagements forced me away from Mr Coleridge's party, before matters had come to a crisis. Some days after, meeting with my Platonic host, I reminded him of the case, and begged to know how that very promising exhibition had terminated. 'Oh, sir,' said he, 'it turned out so ill that we damned it unanimously.' Now, does any man suppose that Mr Coleridge – who, for all he is too fat to be a person of active virtue, is undoubtedly a worthy Christian – that this good S. T. C., I say, was an incendiary, or capable of wishing any ill to the poor man and his pianofortes (many of them, doubtless, with the additional keys)? On the contrary, I know him to be that sort of man, that I durst stake my life upon it, he would have worked an engine in a case of necessity, although rather of the fattest for such fiery trials of his virtue. But how stood the case? Virtue was in no request. On the arrival of the fire-engines, morality had devolved wholly on the insurance office. This being the case, he had a right to gratify his taste. He had left his tea. Was he to have nothing in return?

1 Kant – who carried his demands of unconditional veracity to so extravagant a length as to affirm, that, if a man were to see an innocent person escape from a murderer, it would be his duty, on being questioned by the murderer, to tell the truth, and to point out the retreat of the innocent person, under any certainty of causing murder. Lest this doctrine should be supposed to have escaped him in any heat of dispute, on being taxed with it by a celebrated French writer, he solemnly re-affirmed it, with his reasons.

I contend that the most virtuous man, under the premises stated, was entitled to make a luxury of the fire, and to hiss it, as he would any other performance that raised expectations in the public mind which afterwards it disappointed. Again, to cite another great authority, what says the Stagirite? He (in the Fifth Book, I think it is, of his Metaphysics) describes what he calls κλεπτὴν τέλειον – i.e., a *perfect thief*; and, as to Mr Howship, in a work of his on Indigestion, he makes no scruple to talk with admiration of a certain ulcer which he had seen, and which he styles 'a beautiful ulcer'. Now, will any man pretend, that, abstractedly considered, a thief could appear to Aristotle a perfect character, or that Mr Howship could be enamoured of an ulcer? Aristotle, it is well known, was himself so very moral a character, that, not content with writing his Nichomachéan Ethics, in one volume octavo, he also wrote another system, called *Magna Moralia*, or Big Ethics. Now, it is impossible that a man who composes any ethics at all, big or little, should admire a thief *per se*; and as to Mr Howship, it is well known that he makes war upon all ulcers, and, without suffering himself to be seduced by their charms, endeavours to banish them from the County of Middlesex. But the truth is, that, however objectionable *per se*, yet, relatively to others of their class, both a thief and an ulcer may have infinite degrees of merit. They are both imperfections, it is true; but, to be imperfect being their essence, the very greatness of their imperfection becomes their perfection. *Spartam nactus es, hanc exorna*. A thief like Autolycus or the once famous George Barrington, and a grim phagedænic ulcer, superbly defined, and running regularly through all its natural stages, may no less justly be regarded as ideals after *their* kind, than the most faultless moss-rose amongst flowers, in its progress from bud to 'bright consummate flower'; or, amongst human flowers, the most magnificent young female, apparelled in the pomp of womanhood. And thus not only the ideal of an inkstand may be imagined (as Mr Coleridge illustrated in his celebrated correspondence with Mr Blackwood), in which, by the way, there is not so much, because an inkstand is a laudable sort of thing, and a valuable member of society; but even imperfection itself may have its ideal or perfect state.

Really, gentlemen, I beg pardon for so much philosophy at one time; and now let me apply it.

When a murder is in the paulo-post-futurum tense – not done, not even (according to modern purism) *being* done, but only going to be done – and a rumour of it comes to our ears, by all means let us treat it morally. But suppose it over and done, and that you can say of it, Τετέλεςαι, It is finished, or (in that adamantine molossus of Medea) εἴργαςαι,

Done it is: it is a *fait accompli*; suppose the poor murdered man to be out of his pain, and the rascal that did it off like a shot, nobody knows whither; suppose, lastly, that we have done our best, by putting out our legs, to trip up the fellow in his flight, but all to no purpose – 'abiit, evasit, excessit, erupit', etc. – why, then, I say, what's the use of any more virtue? Enough has been given to morality; now comes the turn of Taste and the Fine Arts. A sad thing it was, no doubt, very sad; but *we* can't mend it. Therefore let us make the best of a bad matter; and, as it is impossible to hammer anything out of it for moral purposes, let us treat it aesthetically, and see if it will turn to account in that way. Such is the logic of a sensible man, and what follows? We dry up our tears, and have the satisfaction, perhaps, to discover that a transaction, which, morally considered, was shocking, and without a leg to stand upon, when tried by principles of Taste, turns out to be a very meritorious performance. Thus all the world is pleased; the old proverb is justified, that it is an ill wind which blows nobody good; the amateur, from looking bilious and sulky, by too close an attention to virtue, begins to pick up his crumbs; and generally hilarity prevails. Virtue has had her day; and henceforward, *Virtu*, so nearly the same thing as to differ only by a single letter (which surely is not worth haggling or higgling about) – *Virtu*, I repeat, and Connoisseurship, have leave to provide for themselves.

Thomas De Quincey, 'Murder Considered as One of the Fine Arts'

It is Sunday afternoon, preferably before the war. The wife is already asleep in the armchair, and the children have been sent out for a nice long walk. You put your feet up on the sofa, settle your spectacles on your nose, and open the *News of the World*. Roast beef and Yorkshire, or roast pork and apple sauce, followed up by suet pudding and driven home, as it were, by a cup of mahogany-brown tea, have put you in just the right mood. Your pipe is drawing sweetly, the sofa cushions are soft underneath you, the fire is well alight, the air is warm and stagnant. In these blissful circumstances, what is it that you want to read about?

Naturally, about a murder. But what kind of murder? If one examines the murders which have given the greatest amount of pleasure to the British public, the murders whose story is known in its general outline to almost everyone and which have been made into novels and rehashed over and over again by the Sunday papers, one finds a fairly strong family resemblance running through the greater number of them. Our great period in murder, our Elizabethan period, so to speak, seems to have been between roughly 1850 and 1925, and the murderers whose reputation has stood the test of time are the following: Dr Palmer of Rugeley, Jack the Ripper, Neill Cream, Mrs Maybrick, Dr Crippen, Seddon, Joseph Smith, Armstrong, and Bywaters and Thompson. In addition, in 1919 or thereabouts, there was another very celebrated case which fits into the general pattern but which I had better not mention by name, because the accused man was acquitted.

Of the above-mentioned nine cases, at least four have had successful novels based on them, one has been made into a popular melodrama, and the amount of literature surrounding them, in the form of newspaper write-ups, criminological treatises and reminiscences by lawyers and police officers, would make a considerable library. It is difficult to believe that any recent English crime will be remembered so long and so intimately, and not only because the violence of external events has made murder seem unimportant, but because the prevalent type of crime seems to be changing. The principal *cause célèbre* of the war years was the so-called Cleft Chin Murder, which has now been written up in a popular booklet;[1] the verbatim account of the trial was published some time last year by Messrs Jarrolds with an introduction by Mr Bechhofer-Roberts. Before returning to this pitiful and sordid case, which is only interesting from a sociological and perhaps a legal point of view, let me try to define what it is that the readers of Sunday papers mean when they say fretfully that 'you never seem to get a good murder nowadays'.

In considering the nine murders I named above, one can start by excluding the Jack the Ripper case, which is in a class by itself. Of the other eight, six were poisoning cases, and eight of the ten criminals belonged to the middle class. In one way or another, sex was a powerful motive in all but two cases, and in at least four cases respectability – the desire to gain a secure position in life, or not to forfeit one's social position by some scandal such as a divorce – was one of the main reasons for committing murder. In more than half the cases, the object was to get hold of a certain known sum of money such as a legacy or an insurance policy, but the amount involved was nearly always small. In most of the cases the crime only came to light slowly, as the result of careful investigation which started off with the suspicions of neighbours or relatives; and in nearly every case there was some dramatic coincidence, in which the finger of Providence could be clearly seen, or one of those episodes that no novelist would dare to make up, such as Crippen's flight across the Atlantic with

1 *The Cleft Chin Murder* by R. Alwyn Raymond

his mistress dressed as a boy, or Joseph Smith playing 'Nearer, my God, to Thee' on the harmonium while one of his wives was drowning in the next room. The background of all these crimes, except Neill Cream's, was essentially domestic; of twelve victims, seven were either wife or husband of the murderer.

With all this in mind one can construct what would be, from a *News of the World* reader's point of view, the 'perfect' murder. The murderer should be a little man of the professional class – a dentist or a solicitor, say – living an intensely respectable life somewhere in the suburbs, and preferably in a semi-detached house, which will allow the neighbours to hear suspicious sounds through the wall. He should be either chairman of the local Conservative Party branch, or a leading Nonconformist and strong Temperance advocate. He should go astray through cherishing a guilty passion for his secretary or the wife of a rival professional man, and should only bring himself to the point of murder after long and terrible wrestles with his conscience. Having decided on murder, he should plan it all with the utmost cunning, and only slip up over some tiny, unforeseeable detail. The means chosen should, of course, be poison. In the last analysis he should commit murder because this seems to him less disgraceful, and less damaging to his career, than being detected in adultery. With this kind of background, a crime can have dramatic and even tragic qualities which make it memorable and excite pity for both victim and murderer. Most of the crimes mentioned above have a touch of this atmosphere, and in three cases, including the one I referred to but did not name, the story approximates to the one I have outlined.

Now compare the Cleft Chin Murder. There is no depth of feeling in it. It was almost chance that the two people concerned committed that particular murder, and it was only by good luck that they did not commit several others. The background was not domesticity, but the anonymous life of the dance halls and the false values of the American film. The two culprits were an eighteen-year-old ex-waitress named Elizabeth Jones, and an American army deserter, posing as an officer, named Karl Hulten. They were only together for six days, and it seems doubtful whether, until they were arrested, they even learned one another's true names. They met casually in a teashop, and that night went out for a ride in a stolen army truck. Jones described herself as a strip-tease artist, which was not strictly true (she had given one unsuccessful performance in this line), and declared that she wanted to do something dangerous, 'like being a gun-moll'. Hulten described himself as a big-time Chicago gangster, which was also untrue. They met a girl bicycling along the road, and to show how tough he was Hulten ran over her with his truck, after which the pair robbed her of the few shillings that were on her. On another occasion they knocked out a girl to whom they had offered a lift, took her coat and handbag and threw her into a river. Finally, in the most wanton way, they murdered a taxi-driver who happened to have £8 in his pocket. Soon afterwards they parted. Hulten was caught because he had foolishly kept the dead man's car, and Jones made spontaneous confessions to the police. In court each prisoner incriminated the other. In between crimes, both of them seem to have behaved with the utmost callousness: they spent the dead taxi-driver's £8 at the dog races.

Judging from her letters, the girl's case has a certain amount of psychological interest, but this murder probably captured the headlines because it provided distraction amid the doodle-bugs and the anxieties of the Battle of France. Jones and Hulten committed their murder to the tune of V1, and were convicted to the tune of V2. There was also considerable excitement because – as has become usual in England – the man was sentenced to death and the girl to imprisonment. According to Mr Raymond, the reprieving of Jones caused widespread indignation and streams of telegrams to the Home Secretary: in her native town, 'She should hang' was chalked on the walls beside pictures of a figure dangling from a gallows. Considering that only ten women have been hanged in Britain in this century, and that the practice has gone out largely because of popular feeling against it, it is difficult not to feel that this clamour to hang an eighteen-year-old girl was due partly to the brutalizing effects of war. Indeed, the whole meaningless story, with its atmosphere of dance-halls, movie palaces, cheap perfume, false names and stolen cars, belongs essentially to a war period.

Perhaps it is significant that the most talked-of English murder of recent years should have been committed by an American and an English girl who had become partly Americanized. But it is difficult to believe that this case will be so long remembered as the old domestic poisoning dramas, product of a stable society where the all-prevailing hypocrisy did at least ensure that crimes as serious as murder should have strong emotions behind them.

George Orwell, 'Decline of the English Murder'

Quits

Enter Titus Andronicus with a knife, and Lavinia with a basin

TITUS: Come, come, Lavinia. Look, thy foes are bound.
Sirs, stop their mouths. Let them not speak to me,
But let them hear what fearful words I utter.
O villains, Chiron and Demetrius!
Here stands the spring whom you have stained with mud,
This goodly summer with your winter mixed.
You killed her husband, and for that vile fault
Two of her brothers were condemned to death,
My hand cut off and made a merry jest,
Both her sweet hands, her tongue, and that more dear
Than hands or tongue, her spotless chastity,
Inhuman traitors, you constrained and forced.
What would you say if I should let you speak?
Villains, for shame. You could not beg for grace.
Hark, wretches, how I mean to martyr you.
This one hand yet is left to cut your throats,
Whiles that Lavinia 'tween her stumps doth hold
The basin that receives your guilty blood.
You know your mother means to feast with me,
And calls herself Revenge, and thinks me mad.
Hark, villains, I will grind your bones to dust,
And with your blood and it I'll make a paste,
And of the paste a coffin I will rear,
And make two pasties of your shameful heads,
And bid that strumpet, your unhallowed dam,
Like to the earth swallow her own increase.
This is the feast that I have bid her to,
And this the banquet she shall surfeit on;
For worse than Philomel you used my daughter,
And worse than Progne I will be revenged.
And now, prepare your throats. Lavinia, come.
Receive the blood, and when that they are dead
Let me go grind their bones to powder small,
And with this hateful liquor temper it,
And in that paste let their vile heads be baked.
Come, come, be everyone officious

To make this banquet, which I wish may prove
More stern and bloody than the Centaurs' feast.

He cuts their throats

So, now bring them in, for I'll play the cook
And see them ready against their mother comes.

Exeunt carrying the bodies

William Shakespeare, *Titus Andronicus*

R

Race

Scene: Montgomery County, Kentucky, July 1911

Kentucky water, clear springs: a boy fleeing
   To water under the dry Kentucky sun,
   His four little friends in tandem with him, seeing

Long shadows of grapevine wriggle and run
   Over the green swirl; mullein under the ear
   Soft as Nausicaä's palm; sullen fun

Savage as childhood's thin harmonious tear:
   O fountain, bosom source undying-dead
   Replenish me the spring of love and fear

And give me back the eye that looked and fled
   When a thrust idling in the tulip tree
   Unwound the cold dream of the copperhead.

– Along the creek the road was winding; we
   Felt the quicksilver sky. I see again
   The shrill companions of that odyssey:

Bill Eaton, Charlie Watson, 'Nigger' Layne
   The doctor's son, Harry Duèsler who played
   The flute; and Tate, with water on the brain.

Dog-days: the dusty leaves where rain delayed
   Hung low on poison-oak and scuppernong,
   And we were following the active shade

Of water, that bells and bickers all night long.
   'No more'n a mile,' Layne said. All five stood still.
   Listening, I heard what seemed at first a song;

Peering, I heard the hooves come down the hill.
  The posse passed, twelve horse; the leader's face
  Was worn as limestone on an ancient sill.

Then, as sleepwalkers shift from a hard place
  In bed, and rising to keep a formal pledge
  Descend a ladder into empty space,

We scuttled down the bank below a ledge
  And marched stiff-legged in our common fright
  Along a hog-track by the riffle's edge:

Into a world where sound shaded the sight
  Dropped the dull hooves again; the horsemen came
  Again, all but the leader: it was night

Momently and I feared: eleven same
  Jesus-Christers unmembered and unmade,
  Whose Corpse had died again in dirty shame.

The bank then levelling in a speckled glade,
  We stopped to breathe above the swimming-hole;
  I gazed at its reticulated shade

Recoiling in blue fear, and felt it roll
  Over my ears and eyes and lift my hair
  Like seaweed tossing on a sunk atoll.

I rose again. Borne on the copper air
  A distant voice green as a funeral wreath
  Against a grave: 'That dead nigger there.'

The melancholy sheriff slouched beneath
  A giant sycamore; shaking his head
  He plucked a sassafras twig and picked his teeth:

'We come too late.' He spoke to the tired dead
  Whose ragged shirt soaked up the viscous flow
  Of blood in which It lay discomfited.

A butting horse-fly gave one ear a blow
  And glanced off, as the sheriff kicked the rope
  Loose from the neck and hooked it with his toe

Away from the blood – I looked back down the slope:
  The friends were gone that I had hoped to greet –
  A single horseman came at a slow lope

And pulled up at the hanged man's horny feet;
  The sheriff noosed the feet, the other end
  The stranger tied to his pommel in a neat

Slip-knot. I saw the Negro's body bend
  And straighten, as a fish-line cast transverse
  Yields to the current that it must subtend.

The sheriff's Goddamn was a murmured curse
  Not for the dead but for the blinding dust
  That boxed the cortège in a cloudy hearse

And dragged it towards our town. I knew I must
  Not stay till twilight in that silent road;
  Sliding my bare feet into the warm crust,

I hopped the stonecrop like a panting toad
  Mouth open, following the heaving cloud
  That floated to the court-house square its load

Of limber corpse that took the sun for shroud.
  There were three figures in the dying sun
  Whose light were company where three was crowd.

My breath crackled the dead air like a shotgun
  As, sheriff and the stranger disappearing,
  The faceless head lay still. I could not run

Or walk, but stood. Alone in the public clearing
  This private thing was owned by all the town,
  Though never claimed by us within my hearing.

Allen Tate, 'The Swimmers'

Moving his three acres with a tractor,
a man notices something ahead – a mannequin –
he thinks someone threw it from a car. Closer
he sees it is the body of a black woman.

The medics come and turn her with pitchforks.
Her gaze shoots past him to nothing. Nothing
is explained. How many black women
have been turned up to stare at us blankly,

in weedy fields, off highways,
pushed out in plastic bags,
shot, knifed, unclothed partially, raped,
their wounds sealed with a powdery crust.

Last week on TV, a gruesome face, eyes bloated shut.
No one will say, 'She looks like she's sleeping,' ropes
of blue-black slashes at the mouth. Does anybody
know this woman? Will anyone come forth? Silence

like a backwave rushes into that field
where, just the week before, four other black girls
had been found. The gritty image hangs in the air
just a few seconds, but it strikes me,

a black woman, there is a question being asked
about my life. How can I
protect myself? Even if I lock my doors,
walk only in the light, someone wants me dead.

It is any wonder I walk over these bodies
pretending they are not mine, that I do not know
the killer, that I am just like any women –
if not wanted, at least tolerated.

Part of me wants to disappear, to pull
the earth on top of me. Then there is this part
that digs me up with this pen
and turns my sad black face to the light.

Toi Derricotte,
'On the Turning Up of Unidentified Black Female Corpses'

Reasons of State

(*The* KNIGHTS, *having completed the murder, advance to the front of the stage and address the audience.*)

FIRST KNIGHT: We beg you to give us your attention for a few moments. We know that you may be disposed to judge unfavourably of our action. You are Englishmen, and therefore you believe in fair play: and when you see one man being set upon by four, then your sympathies are all with the under dog. I respect such feelings, I share them. Nevertheless, I appeal to your sense of honour. You are Englishmen, and therefore will not judge anybody without hearing both sides of the case. That is in accordance with our long-established principle of Trial by Jury. I am not myself qualified to put our case to you. I am a man of action and not of words. For that reason I shall do no more than introduce the other speakers, who, with their various abilities, and different points of view, will be able to lay before you the merits of this extremely complex problem. I shall call upon our eldest member to speak first, my neighbour in the country: Baron William de Traci.

THIRD KNIGHT: I am afraid I am not anything like such an experienced speaker as my old friend Reginald Fitz Urse would lead you to believe. But there is one thing I should like to say, and I might as well say it at once. It is this: in what we have done, and whatever you may think of it, we have been perfectly disinterested. (*The other* KNIGHTS: 'Hear! hear!') *We* are not getting anything out of this. We have much more to lose than to gain. We are four plain Englishmen who put our country first. I dare say that we didn't make a very good impression when we came in just now. The fact is that we knew we had taken on a pretty stiff job; I'll only speak for myself, but I had drunk a good deal – I am not a drinking man ordinarily – to brace myself up for it. When you come to the point, it does go against the grain to kill an Archbishop, especially when you have been brought up in good Church traditions. So if we seemed a bit rowdy, you will understand why it was; and for my part I am awfully sorry about it. We realized this was our duty, but all the same we had to work ourselves up to it. And, as I said, *we* are not getting a penny out of this. We know perfectly well how things will turn out. King Henry – God bless him – will have to say, for reasons of state, that he never meant this to happen; and there is going to be an awful row; and at the best we shall have to spend the rest of our lives abroad. And even when reasonable people come to see that the Archbishop *had* to be put out of the way – and personally I had a tremendous admiration for him – you must have noted what a good show he put up at the end – they won't give *us* any glory. No, we have done for ourselves, there's no mistake about that. So, as I said at the beginning, please give us at least the credit for being completely disinterested in this business. I think that is about all I have to say.

FIRST KNIGHT: I think we will all agree that William de Traci has spoken well and has made a very important point. The gist of his argument is this: that we have been completely disinterested. But our act itself needs more justification than that; and you must hear our other speakers. I shall next call upon Hugh de Morville, who has made a special study of statecraft and constitutional law. Sir Hugh de Morville.

SECOND KNIGHT: I should like first to recur to a point that was very well put by our leader, Reginald Fitz Urse: that you are Englishmen, and therefore your sympathies are always with the under dog. It is the English spirit of fair play. Now the worthy Archbishop, whose good qualities I very much admired, has throughout been presented as the under dog. But is this really the case? I am going to appeal not to your emotions but to your reason. You are hard-headed sensible people, as I can see, and not to be taken in by emotional clap-trap. I therefore ask you to consider soberly: what were the Archbishop's aims? and what are King Henry's aims? In the answer to these questions lies the key to the problem.

The King's aim has been perfectly consistent. During the reign of the late Queen Matilda and the irruption of the unhappy usurper Stephen, the kingdom was very much divided. Our King saw that the one thing needful was to restore order: to curb the excessive powers of local government, which were usually exercised for selfish and often for seditious ends, and to reform the legal system. He therefore intended that Becket, who had proved himself an extremely able administrator – no one denies that – should unite the offices of Chancellor and Archbishop. Had Becket concurred with the King's wishes, we should have had an almost ideal State: a union of spiritual and temporal administration, under the central government. I knew Becket well, in various official relations; and I may say that I have never known a man so well qualified for the highest rank of the Civil Service. And what happened? The moment that Becket, at the

King's instance, had been made Archbishop, he resigned the office of Chancellor, he became more priestly than the priests, he ostentatiously and offensively adopted an ascetic manner of life, he affirmed immediately that there was a higher order than that which our King, and he as the King's servant, had for so many years striven to establish; and that – God knows why – the two orders were incompatible.

You will agree with me that such interference by an Archbishop offends the instincts of a people like ours. So far, I know that I have your approval: I read it in your faces. It is only with the measures we have had to adopt, in order to set matters to rights, that you take issue. No one regrets the necessity for violence more than we do. Unhappily, there are times when violence is the only way in which social justice can be secured. At another time, you would condemn an Archbishop by vote of Parliament and execute him formally as a traitor, and no one would have to bear the burden of being called murderer. And at a later time still, even such temperate measures as these would become unnecessary. But, if you have now arrived at a just subordination of the pretensions of the Church to the welfare of the State, remember that it is we who took the first step. We have been instrumental in bringing about the state of affairs that you approve. We have served your interests; we merit your applause; and if there is any guilt whatever in the matter, you must share it with us.

FIRST KNIGHT: Morville has given us a great deal to think about. It seems to me that he has said almost the last word, for those who have been able to follow his very subtle reasoning. We have, however, one more speaker, who has I think another point of view to express. If there are any who are still unconvinced, I think that Richard Brito, coming as he does of a family distinguished for its loyalty to the Church, will be able to convince them. Richard Brito.

FOURTH KNIGHT: The speakers who have preceded me, to say nothing of our leader, Reginald Fitz Urse, have all spoken very much to the point. I have nothing to add along their particular lines of argument. What I have to say may be put in the form of a question: *Who killed the Archbishop?* As you have been eye-witnesses of this lamentable scene, you may feel some surprise at my putting it in this way. But consider the course of events. I am obliged, very briefly, to go over the ground traversed by the last speaker. While the late Archbishop was Chancellor, no one, under the King, did more to weld the country together, to give it the unity, the stability, order, tranquillity, and justice that it so badly needed. From the moment he became Archbishop, he completely reversed his policy; he showed himself to be utterly indifferent to the fate of the country, to be, in fact, a monster of egotism. This egotism grew upon him, until it became at last an undoubted mania. I have unimpeachable evidence to the effect that before he left France he clearly prophesied, in the presence of numerous witnesses that he has not long to live, and that he would be killed in England. He used every means of provocation; from his conduct, step by step, there can be no inference except that he had determined upon a death by martyrdom. Even at the last, he could have given us reason: you have seen how he evaded our questions. And when he had deliberately exasperated us beyond human endurance, he could still have easily escaped; he could have kept himself from us long enough to allow our righteous anger to cool. That was just what he did not wish to happen; he insisted, while we were still inflamed with wrath, that the doors should be opened. Need I say more? I think, with these facts before you, you will unhesitatingly render a verdict of Suicide while of Unsound Mind. It is the only charitable verdict you can give, upon one who was, after all, a great man.

FIRST KNIGHT: Thank you, Brito, I think that there is no more to be said; and I suggest that you now disperse quietly to your homes. Please be careful not to loiter in groups at street corners, and do nothing that might provoke any public outbreak.

(*Exeunt* KNIGHTS)

T. S. Eliot, *Murder in the Cathedral*

Responsibilities

And they said: If a man commit murder
  Should his father protect him, and hide him?
And Kung said:
  He should hide him.

Ezra Pound, *The Cantos*

Retribution

There were four of us about that bed;
  The mass-priest knelt at the side,
I and his mother stood at the head,
  Over his feet lay the bride;
We were quite sure that he was dead,
  Though his eyes were open wide.

He did not die in the night,
  He did not die in the day,
But in the morning twilight
  His spirit passed away,
When neither sun nor moon was bright,
  And the trees were merely grey.

He was not slain with the sword,
  Knight's axe, or the knightly spear,
Yet spoke he never a word
  After he came in here;
I cut away the cord
  From the neck of my brother dear.

He did not strike one blow,
  For the recreants came behind,
In a place where the hornbeams grow,
  A path right hard to find,
For the hornbeam boughs swing so,
  That the twilight makes it blind.

They lighted a great torch then,
  When his arms were pinioned fast.
Sir John the knight of the Fen,
  Sir Guy of the Dolorous Blast,
With knights threescore and ten,
  Hung brave Lord Hugh at last.

I am threescore and ten,
  And my hair is all turned grey,
But I met Sir John of the Fen
  Long ago on a summer day,

And am glad to think of the moment when
  I took his life away.

I am threescore and ten,
  And my strength is mostly passed,
But long ago I and my men,
  When the sky was overcast,
And the smoke rolled over the reeds of the fen,
  Slew Guy of the Dolorous Blast.

And now, knights all of you,
  I pray you pray for Sir Hugh,
A good knight and a true,
  And for Alice, his wife, pray too.

William Morris, 'Shameful Death'

A winter pass'd since Peter saw the town,
And summer-lodgers were again come down;
These, idly curious, with their glasses spied
The ships in bay as anchor'd for the tide, –
The river's craft, – the bustle of the quay, –
And sea-port views, which landmen love to see.
One, up the river, had a man and boat
Seen day by day, now anchor'd, now afloat;
Fisher he seem'd, yet used no net nor hook;
Of sea-fowl swimming by no heed he took,
But on the gliding waves still fix'd his lazy look:
At certain stations he would view the stream,
As if he stood bewilder'd in a dream,
Or that some power had chain'd him for a time,
To feel a curse or meditate on crime.
This known, some curious, some in pity went,
And others question'd – 'Wretch, dost thou repent?'
He heard, he trembled, and in fear resign'd
His boat: new terror fill'd his restless mind;
Furious he grew, and up the country ran,
And there they seized him – a distemper'd man: –
Him we received, and to a parish-bed,
Follow'd and cursed, the groaning man was led.

Here when they saw him, whom they used to shun,
A lost, lone man, so harass'd and undone;
Our gentle females, ever prompt to feel,
Perceived compassion on their anger steal;
His crimes they could not from their memories blot,
But they were grieved, and trembled at his lot.
A priest too came, to whom his words are told;
And all the signs they shudder'd to behold.
'Look! look!' they cried; 'his limbs with horror shake,
And as he grinds his teeth, what noise they make!
How glare his angry eyes, and yet he's not awake:
See! what cold drops upon his forehead stand,
And how he clenches that broad bony hand.'
The priest attending, found he spoke at times
As one alluding to his fears and crimes:
'It was the fall,' he mutter'd, 'I can show
The manner how – I never struck a blow:' –
And then aloud – 'Unhand me, free my chain;
On oath, he fell – it struck him to the brain: –
Why ask my father? – that old man will swear
Against my life; besides, he wasn't there: –
What, all agreed? – Am I to die today? –
My Lord, in mercy, give me time to pray.'
Then, as they watch'd him, calmer he became,
And grew so weak he couldn't move his frame,
But murmuring spake, – while they could see and hear
The start of terror and the groan of fear;
See the large dew-beads on his forehead rise,
And the cold death-drop glaze his sunken eyes;
Nor yet he died, but with unwonted force
Seem'd with some fancied being to discourse:
He knew not us, or with accustom'd art
He hid the knowledge, yet exposed his heart;
'Twas part confession and the rest defence,
A madman's tale, with gleams of waking sense.
'I'll tell you all,' he said, 'the very day
When the old man first placed them in my way:
My father's spirit – he who always tried
To give me trouble, when he lived and died –
When he was gone, he could not be content

To see my days in painful labour spent,
But would appoint his meetings, and he made
Me watch at these, and so neglect my trade.
''Twas one hot noon, all silent, still, serene,
No living being had I lately seen;
I paddled up and down and dipp'd my net,
But (such his pleasure) I could nothing get, –
A father's pleasure, when his toil was done,
To plague and torture thus an only son!
And so I sat and look'd upon the stream,
How it ran on, and felt as in a dream:
But dream it was not; no! – I fix'd my eyes
On the mid stream and saw the spirits rise;
I saw my father on the water stand,
And hold a thin pale boy in either hand;
And there they glided ghastly on the top
Of the salt flood, and never touch'd a drop:
I would have struck them, but they knew th' intent,
And smiled upon the oar, and down they went.
'Now, from that day, whenever I began
To dip my net, there stood the hard old man –
He and those boys: I humbled me and pray'd
They would be gone; – they heeded not, but stay'd:
Nor could I turn, nor would the boat go by,
But gazing on the spirits, there was I:
They bade me leap to death, but I was loth to die:
And every day, as sure as day arose,
Would these three spirits meet me ere the close;
To hear and mark them daily was my doom,
And "Come," they said, with weak, sad voices, "come."
To row away with all my strength I try'd,
But there were they, hard by me in the tide,
The three unbodied forms – and "Come," still "come," they cried.
'Fathers should pity – but this old man shook
His hoary locks, and froze me by a look:
Thrice, when I struck them, through the water came
A hollow groan, that weaken'd all my frame:
"Father!" said I, "have mercy:" – He replied,
I know not what – the angry spirit lied, –
"Didst thou not draw thy knife?" said he? – 'Twas true,

But I had pity and my arm withdrew:
He cried for mercy which I kindly gave,
But he has no compassion in his grave.
'There were three places, where they ever rose, –
The whole long river has not such as those, –
Places accursed, where, if a man remain,
He'll see the things which strike him to the brain;
And there they made me on my paddle lean,
And look at them for hours; – accursed scene.
When they would glide to that smooth eddy-space,
Then bid me leap and join them in the place;
And at my groans each little villain sprite
Enjoy'd my pains and vanish'd in delight.
'In one fierce summer-day, when my poor brain
Was burning hot and cruel was my pain,
Then came this father-foe, and there he stood
With his two boys again upon the flood;
There was more mischief in their eyes, more glee
In their pale faces when they glared at me:
Still did they force me on the oar to rest,
And when they saw me fainting and oppress'd,
He, with his hand, the old man, scoop'd the flood,
And there came flame about him mix'd with blood;
He bade me stoop and look upon the place,
Then flung the hot-red liquor in my face;
Burning it blazed, and then I roar'd for pain,
I thought the demons would have turn'd my brain.
'Still there they stood, and forced me to behold
A place of horrors – they cannot be told –
Where the flood open'd, there I heard the shriek
Of tortured guilt – no earthly tongue can speak:
"All days alike! for ever!" did they say,
"And unremitted torments every day" –
Yes, so they said:' – But here he ceased and gazed
On all around, affrighten'd and amazed;
And still he tried to speak, and look'd in dread
Of frighten'd females gathering round his bed;
Then dropp'd exhausted and appear'd at rest,
Till the strong foe the vital powers possess'd:

Then with an inward, broken voice he cried,
'Again they come,' and mutter'd as he died.

George Crabbe, 'Peter Grimes'

O Jellon Grame sat in Silverwood,
He sharp'd his broadsword lang;
And he has call'd his little foot-page
An errand for to gang.

'Win up, my bonny boy,' he says,
'As quickly as ye may;
For ye maun gang for Lillie Flower
Before the break of day.' –

The boy has buckled his belt about,
And through the green-wood ran;
And he came to the ladye's bower
Before the day did dawn.

'O sleep ye, wake ye, Lillie Flower?
The red sun's on the rain;
Ye're bidden come to Silverwood,
But I doubt ye'll never win hame.'

She hadna ridden a mile, a mile,
A mile but barely three,
Ere she came to a new-made grave
Beneath a green aik tree.

O then up started Jellon Grame
Out of a bush thereby;
'Light down, light down, now, Lillie Flower,
For it's here that ye maun lye.'

She lighted aff her milk-white steed,
And kneel'd upon her knee;
'O mercy, mercy, Jellon Grame,
For I'm no prepared to die!

'Your bairn, that stirs between my sides,
Maun shortly see the light;
But to see it weltering in my blood
Would be a piteous sight.' –

'O should I spare your life,' he says,
'Until that bairn were born,
Full weel I ken your auld father
Would hang me on the morn.' –

'O spare my life now, Jellon Grame!
My father ye needna dread!
I'll keep my babe in gude green-wood,
Or wi' it I'll beg my bread.' –

He took nae pity on Lillie Flower,
Though she for life did pray;
But pierced her through the fair body
As at his feet she lay.

He felt nae pity for Lillie Flower,
Where she was lying dead;
But he felt some for the bonny bairn
That lay weltering in her bluid.

Up has he ta'en that bonny boy,
Given him to nurses nine;
Three to sleep, and three to wake,
And three to go between.

And he bred up that bonny boy,
Call'd him his sister's son;
And he thought nae eye could ever see
The deed that had been done.

O so it fell upon a day,
When hunting they might be,
They rested them in Silverwood,
Beneath that green aik tree.

And many were the green-wood flowers
Upon that grave that grew,
And marvell'd much that bonny boy
To see their lovely hue.

'What's paler than the primrose wan?
What's redder than the rose?
What's fairer than the lilye flower
On this wee know that grows?' –

O out and answer'd Jellon Grame,
  And he spak hastilie:
'Your mother was a fairer flower,
  And lies beneath this tree.

'More pale she was, when she sought my grace,
  Than primrose pale and wan;
And redder than rose her ruddy heart's blood,
  That down my broadsword ran.' –

Wi' that the boy has bent his bow,
  It was baith stout and lang;
And thro' and thro' him, Jellon Grame,
  He gar'd an arrow gang.

Says, – 'Lie ye there, now, Jellon Grame!
  My malisoun gang you wi'!
The place that my mother lies buried in
  Is far too good for thee.'

Anon., 'Jellon Grame'

Review

Who kill'd John Keats?
  'I,' says the Quarterly,
So savage and Tartarly;
  ''Twas one of my feats.'

Who shot the arrow?
  'The poet-priest Milman
(So ready to kill man),
  Or Southey, or Barrow.'

George Gordon, Lord Byron, 'John Keats'

Reviewer

I discovered that if I were going to review books I should need to do battle with a certain phantom. And the phantom was a woman, and when I came to know her better I called her after the heroine of a famous poem, The Angel in the House. It was she who used to come between me and my paper when I was writing reviews. It was she who bothered me and wasted my time and so tormented me that at last I killed her. You who come of a younger and happier generation may not have heard of her – you may not know what I mean by the Angel in the House. I will describe her as shortly as I can. She was intensely sympathetic. She was immensely charming. She was utterly unselfish. She excelled in the difficult arts of family life. She sacrificed herself daily. If there was chicken, she took the leg; if there was a draught she sat in it – in short she was so constituted that she never had a mind or a wish of her own, but preferred to sympathize always with the minds and wishes of others. Above all – I need not say it – she was pure. Her purity was supposed to be her chief beauty – her blushes, her great grace. In those days – the last of Queen Victoria – every house had its Angel. And when I came to write I encountered her with the very first words. The shadow of her wings fell on my page; I heard the rustling of her skirts in the room. Directly, that is to say, I took my pen in my hand to review that novel by a famous man, she slipped behind me and whispered: 'My dear, you are a young woman. You are writing about a book that has been written by a man. Be sympathetic; be tender; flatter; deceive; use all the arts and wiles of our sex. Never let anybody guess that you have a mind of your own. Above all, be pure.' And she made as if to guide my pen. I now record the one act for which I take some credit to myself, though the credit rightly belongs to some excellent ancestors of mine who left me a certain sum of money – shall we say five hundred pounds a year? – so that it was not necessary for me to depend solely on charm for my living. I turned upon her and caught her by the throat. I did my best to kill her. My excuse, if I were to be had up in a court of law, would be that I acted in self-defence.

Had I not killed her she would have killed me. She would have plucked the heart out of my writing. For, as I found, directly I put pen to paper, you cannot review even a novel without having a mind of your own, without expressing what you think to be the truth about human relations, morality, sex. And all these questions, according to the Angel of the House, cannot be dealt with freely and openly by women; they must charm, they must conciliate, they must – to put it bluntly – tell lies if they are to succeed. Thus, whenever I felt the shadow of her wing or the radiance of her halo upon my page, I took up the inkpot and flung it at her. She died hard. Her fictitious nature was of great assistance to her. It is far harder to kill a phantom than a reality. She was always creeping back when I thought I had despatched her. Though I flatter myself that I killed her in the end, the struggle was severe; it took much time that had better have been spent upon learning Greek grammar; or in roaming the world in search of adventures. But it was a real experience; it was an experience that was found to befall all women writers at that time. Killing the Angel in the House was part of the occupation of a woman writer.

Virginia Woolf, from 'Professions for Women'

S

Sacrifice

Human sacrifices were adopted by the Aztecs early in the fourteenth century, about two hundred years before the Conquest. Rare at first, they became more frequent with the wider extent of their empire; till, at length, almost every festival was closed with this cruel abomination. These religious ceremonials were generally arranged in such a manner as to afford a type of the most prominent circumstances in the character or history of the deity who was the object of them. A single example will suffice.

One of their most important festivals was that in honour of the god Tezcatlipoca, whose rank was inferior only to that of the Supreme Being. He was called 'the soul of the world', and supposed to have been its creator. He was depicted as a handsome man, endowed with perpetual youth. A year before the intended sacrifice, a captive, distinguished for his personal beauty, and without a blemish on his body, was selected to represent this deity. Certain tutors took charge of him, and instructed him how to perform his new part with becoming grace and dignity. He was arrayed in a splendid dress, regaled with incense, and with a profusion of sweet-scented flowers, of which the ancient Mexicans were as fond as their descendants at the present day. When he went abroad, he was attended by a train of the royal pages, and, as he halted in the streets to play some favourite melody, the crowd prostrated themselves before him, and did him homage as the representative of their good deity. In this way he led an easy, luxurious life, till within a month of his sacrifice. Four beautiful girls, bearing the names of the principal goddesses, were then selected to share the honours of his bed; and with them he continued to live in idle dalliance, feasted at the banquets of the principal nobles, who paid him all the honours of a divinity.

At length the fatal day of sacrifice arrived. The term of his short-lived glories was at an end. He was stripped of his gaudy apparel, and bade adieu to the fair partners of his revelries. One of the royal barges transported him across the lake to a temple which rose on its margin, about a league from the city. Hither the inhabitants of the capital flocked, to witness the consummation of the ceremony. As the sad procession wound up the sides of the pyramid, the unhappy victim threw away his gay chaplet of flowers, and broke in pieces the musical instruments with which he had solaced the hours of captivity. On the summit he was received by six priests, whose long and matted locks flowed disorderly over their sable robes, covered with hieroglyphic scrolls of mystic import. They led him to the sacrificial stone, a huge block of jasper, with its upper surface somewhat convex. On this the prisoner was stretched. Five priests secured his head and his limbs; while the sixth, clad in a scarlet mantle, emblematic of his bloody office, dexterously opened the breast of the wretched victim with a sharp razor of *itztli* – a volcanic substance hard as flint – and, inserting his hand in the wound, tore out the palpitating heart. The minister of death, first holding this up towards the sun, an object of worship throughout Anahuac, cast it at the feet of the deity to whom the temple was devoted, while the multitudes below prostrated themselves in humble adoration. The tragic story of this prisoner was expounded by the priests as the type of human destiny, which, brilliant in its commencement, too often closes in sorrow and disaster.

Such was the form of human sacrifice usually practised by the Aztecs. It was the same that often met the indignant eyes of the Europeans, in their progress through the country, and from the dreadful doom of which they themselves were not exempted. There were, indeed, some occasions when preliminary tortures, of the most exquisite kind – with which it is unnecessary to shock the reader – were inflicted, but they always terminated with the bloody ceremony above described. It should be remarked, however, that such tortures were not the spontaneous suggestions of cruelty, as with the North American Indians; but were all rigorously prescribed in the Aztec ritual, and doubtless were often inflicted with the same compunctious visitings which a devout familiar of the Holy Office might at times experience in executing its sterm decrees. Women, as well as the other sex, were sometimes reserved for sacrifice. On some occasions, particularly in seasons of drought, at the festival of the insatiable Tlaloc, the god of rain, children, for the most part infants, were offered up. As they were borne along in open litters, dressed in their festal robes, and decked with the fresh blossoms of spring, they moved the hardest heart to pity, though their cries were drowned in the wild chant of the priests, who read in their tears a favourable augury for their petition. These innocent victims were generally bought by the priests of parents who were poor, but who stifled the voice of nature, probably less at the suggestions of poverty than of a wretched superstition.

The most loathsome part of the story, the manner in which the body of the sacrificed captive was disposed of, remains yet to be told. It was delivered to the warrior who had taken him in battle, and by him, after being dressed, was served up in an entertainment to his friends. This was not the coarse repast of famished cannibals, but a banquet teeming with delicious beverages and delicate viands, prepared with art, and attended by both sexes, who, as we shall see hereafter, conducted themselves with all the decorum of civilized life. Surely, never were refinement and the extreme of barbarism brought so closely in contact with each other!

Human sacrifices have been practised by many nations, not excepting the most polished nations of antiquity; but never by any, on a scale to be compared with those in Anahuac. The amount of victims immolated on its accursed altars would stagger the faith of the least scrupulous believer. Scarcely any author pretends to estimate the yearly sacrifices throughout the empire at less than twenty thousand, and some carry the number as high as fifty!

On great occasions, as the coronation of a king, or the consecration of a temple, the number becomes still more appalling. At the dedication of the great temple of Huitzilopotchli, in 1486, the prisoners, who for some years had been reserved for the purpose, were drawn from all quarters to the capital. They were ranged in files, forming a procession nearly two miles long. The ceremony consumed several days, and seventy thousand captives are said to have perished at the shrine of this terrible deity! But who can believe that so numerous a body would have suffered themselves to be led, unresistingly, like sheep to the slaughter? Or how could their remains, too great for consumption in the ordinary way, be disposed of, without breeding a pestilence in the capital? Yet the event was of recent date, and is unequivocally attested by the best informed historians. One fact may be considered certain. It was customary to preserve the skulls of the sacrificed, in buildings appropriated to the purpose. The companions of Cortés counted one hundred and thirty-six thousand in one of these edifices! Without attempting a precise calculation, therefore, it is safe to conclude that thousands were yearly offered up, in the different cities of Anahuac, on the bloody altars of the Mexican divinities . . .

In reflecting on the revolting usages recorded in the preceding pages, one finds it difficult to reconcile their existence with anything like a regular form of government, or an advance in civilization. Yet the Mexicans had many claims to the character of a civilized community. One may, perhaps, better understand the anomaly, by reflecting on the condition of some of the most polished countries in Europe, in the sixteenth century, after the establishment of the modern Inquisition; an institution which yearly destroyed its thousands by a death more painful than the Aztec sacrifices;

which armed the hand of brother against brother, and, setting its burning seal upon the lip, did more to stay the march of improvement than any other scheme ever devised by human cunning.

Human sacrifice, however cruel, has nothing in it degrading to its victim. It may be rather said to ennoble him, by devoting him to the gods. Although so terrible with the Aztecs, it was sometimes voluntarily embraced by them, as the most glorious death, and one that opened a sure passage into paradise. The Inquisition, on the other hand, branded its victims with infamy in this world, and consigned them to everlasting perdition in the next.

One detestable feature of the Aztec superstition, however, sunk it far below the Christian. This was its cannibalism; though, in truth, the Mexicans were not cannibals, in the coarsest acceptation of the term. They did not feed on human flesh merely to gratify a brutish appetite, but in obedience to their religion. Their repasts were made of the victims whose blood had been poured out on the altar of sacrifice. This is a distinction worthy of notice. Still, cannibalism, under any form, or whatever sanction, cannot but have a fatal influence on the nation addicted to it. It suggests ideas so loathsome, so degrading to man, to his spiritual and immortal nature, that it is impossible the people who practise it should make any great progress in moral or intellectual culture. The Mexicans furnish no exception to this remark. The civilization which they possessed descended from the Toltecs, a race who never stained their altars, still less their banquets, with the blood of man. All that deserved the name of science in Mexico came from this source; and the crumbling ruins of edifices, attributed to them, still extant in various parts of New Spain, show a decided superiority in their architecture over that of the later races of Anahuac. It is true, the Mexicans made great proficiency in many of the social and mechanic arts, in that material culture – if I may so call it – the natural growth of increasing opulence, which ministers to the gratification of the senses. In purely intellectual progress, they were behind the Tezcucans, whose wise sovereigns came into the abominable rites of their neighbours with reluctance, and practised them on a much more moderate scale.

W. H. Prescott, *The Conquest of Mexico*

Scene of the Crime

We did not care muchly who, in the murder,
we turned out to be, providing whoever
used to inhabit the white chalk figure
frozenly pawing the blood-stained sofa
was not one of us but a different dier.

Dazzled colonel, distracted lover,
meddling couple of the library whisper,
cook unpoisoned or ponderous super,
sleuth, inheritor, innocent, actual
killer detected or undetected – it

didn't matter, but not that ended
individual manning the hour
he died in, as we would all one *dies*
man one hour, one mo, one jiffy.
Let us be Anybody other than Body!

But then we'd go on with the game all summer:
the three allowed queries on the hot verandah,
the fib in the gazebo, the starlit rumour,
the twitching curtain and the dim unhelpful
gardener's boy: it would all be explicable

soon in the lounge, and we didn't mind waiting.
No, what we minded was the hairless stranger
who wasn't invited and wouldn't answer
and had no secrets or skeletons either,
and got up later than us, then later

than even the bodies, and never turned in,
or blamed or suspected or guessed the outcome
but always was exiting, vanishing, going,
seen on the lawn – then there were more of them
massing, unarmed, parting when followed,

combing the country but not for a weapon
or corpse or clue, then halting and singing
unknown thunderous hymns to a leader
new on us all at our country party he'd
caught in the act of an act of murder.

Glyn Maxwell, 'The Uninvited'

No butler, no second maid, no blood upon the stair.
No eccentric aunt, no gardener, no family friend
Smiling among the bric-à-brac and murder.
Only a suburban house with the front door open

And a dog barking at a squirrel, and the cars
Passing. The corpse quite dead. The wife in Florida.

Consider the clues: the potato masher in a vase,
The torn photograph of a Wesleyan basketball team,
Scattered with check stubs in the hall;
The unsent fan letter to Shirley Temple,
The Hoover button on the lapel of the deceased,
The note: 'To be killed this way is quite all right with me.'

Small wonder that the case remains unsolved,
Or that the sleuth, Le Roux, is now incurably insane,
And sits alone in a white room in a white gown,
Screaming that all the world is mad, that clues
Lead nowhere, or to walls so high their tops cannot be seen;
Screaming all day of war, screaming that nothing can be solved.

Weldon Kees, 'Crime Club'

Frances. You were the favoured son
they never had – a tomboy, Frankie-boy,
collar and tie through the garden gates
each early morning. *Not too far though –*

be careful. Your father's voice was the ghost
of the terrace roses, his uniform smudged
behind slithering leaves. *I promise . . .*
only as far as the road. If he could hear

he would think you meant Cairo Road,
and hopscotch in sight of the settlers'.
At eight, when his sluggish official car
ferried him down to Government House

any old chalky grid was a sign of you,
your fist-clenched, stammering dance
flicking and juddering round in his head
like a handkerchief waving goodbye.

Or so you imagine it now. Or so you say,
when you're telling me late in bed,
and sleepy enough to confuse what was
with what you're beginning to dream.

All Africa knew how the settlers behaved.
Why should he think I was safe with them?
'Cut them in half, you'll find mostly gin'
– I can hear him still – 'They're out and outers.'

What did they find when the Earl was killed,
I wonder? What kind of blood did he bleed?
You were going to smile, but a sigh
catches you out, and as simply as that

you're asleep, quickly swivelling round in my arms
so it seems you are trying to shake yourself free.
I click off the light, and at once, with my eyes shut
I can see you again, crouching close at my side

when we stop on a stretch of moonlit road
and discover the Earl, whoever he was, with his head
crammed through his knees on the floor of a car,
his evening dress speckled with glass. Listen:

that's the Savoy Orpheans, foxtrotting out
from a wireless dumped on his passenger seat,
and the car itself is climbing a sandstone rock
like a toy someone pretended could dance.

It might be bad luck, we are hoping –
he's drunk. But an accident wouldn't explain
this gooey hole in the core of his ear
where you show me a bullet went in.

Not that you're with me for long. When you say
I'll go for some help. Stay put, you've already gone,
your tie like a tongue flipped over your shoulder,
leaving me wandering stupidly round and round

on worn-out grass by the car. I am guessing
There must be evidence here. Footprints?
A cartridge case? but each step I take
explodes and disperses a cloud of dust

until I can scarcely be sure which footprints
are innocent: which ones are mine,
which yours, and which, supposing any are his,
might be the killer's – and whether or not

I should pay any heed to this hoarse emphatic whisper
which says out of nowhere *Don't look in the car*
Don't look at the Earl. It's as if I were dreaming
and could not control what I saw. As if I might find

his face had been changed into one that I know,
or into my own, and could never be altered back
to a stranger's again – not even by half sitting up
in the bed beside you like this, reminding myself

I am home, completely awake, and seeing you still
with your beautiful boyish face on the pillow
masked by your hair, but clearly smiling at something
you will not remember tomorrow, which I cannot share.

Andrew Motion, 'Dangerous Play'

Second Thoughts

The Farr family ate in a briskly competitive, albeit communal style. No one spoke while eating; all that was to be heard was grunting and wheezing until the last crisp, the last drop of tea and orange juice and the last fragments of white icing had disappeared down one or other of the Farr family throats.

Someone was prodding Henry in the ribs. Looking down he noticed that it was Elinor. Her mouth full of crumbs, she said, 'What are all those books on poison doing in your study?'

Henry belched and looked at his boots. 'What books on poison?' he said.

'Oh,' said Elinor, '*Great Poisoners of the World, Death Was Their Business, Encyclopedia of Murder, Forensic Medicine, Exit a Poisoner, The Life of "Apple Pip" Kelly the Strychnine Killer, Six Hundred Toxic Deaths* – '

'Oh, those,' said Henry, 'I – '

'*Strong Poison, A Life of William Palmer, the Notorious Staffordshire Poisoner, Hyoscine; Its Uses in Toxicology* by Adolf Gee Smith, *Some Applications of Arsenic in Industry* by – '

She broke off and peered at him. 'Are you trying to poison me, Henry?' she said, and then, looking round the café, in a humorous voice – 'I say, everybody – Henry wants to poison me!'

Then, because it was such a ridiculous idea, she threw back her head and gave a booming, confident laugh.

'I couldn't do that, darling,' said Henry, 'I love you!'

Elinor's eyes narrowed. 'Do you?' she said.

'You're the sun and the moon and the stars to me,' said Henry, 'you're the reason why I get up in the morning and go to bed at night. You give meaning to my every breath. You are my rationale!'

Elinor folded her arms. She looked, Henry thought, like an off-duty policeman listening to some suspect political opinions in his local pub.

'Am I?' she said.

'Yes, yes,' said Henry, 'deep down. You know. Really deep down. Of course you are.'

She didn't look very convinced by this. Did she, he wondered, really suspect him? And if she did, was it the kind of thing she might mention to Detective Inspector Rush, assuming that she and Rush were . . .

'Actually,' Henry found himself saying, 'I just got really interested in poisons. It became a bit of a . . . well . . . a . . . hobby. You know?'

'Well, I always said,' said Elinor, 'that you should have more interests.'

Henry gulped. 'That's right!' he said. 'And I was trying to look at our relationship in the light of that. To make it, you know, grow . . .'

She still did not look entirely convinced. Henry talked more rapidly. 'Did you know,' he said, 'that alkaloids of pomegranate are a deadly poison? Or that the poisoner Neil Cream handed out strychnine to young girls for no apparent motive!'

Elinor's brow furrowed. 'Actually,' she said, 'I am very interested in food additives of any kind.'

'Precisely!' said Henry wildly. 'This is all part of it, you see. I've been trying to . . .' He groped for the word. 'Rethink my attitudes!'

She shook her hair out and for a moment looked like someone he remembered liking, years ago. Why was it that they no longer had a common language?

Henry blundered on, trying to use the words she used. 'I've been thinking about poison as . . . as a mode of communication!'

She looked a little doubtful about this. Picking at the crumbs on the table, she said, 'It is odd though, isn't it?'

'What is?'

'Those deaths. All those people at Donald's funeral. And the punch . . .'

'What about the punch?' said Henry.

She didn't answer this question but continued to trace little circles on the damp plastic of the table.

'I was talking about it all to John Rush,' she said, 'I think he knows something. But isn't saying. You know?'

'I know!' said Henry.

'Mind you – ' said Elinor, 'the police never do, do they?'

'No, no . . .' said Henry.

What was all this about *John* Rush?

'They could,' said Elinor, 'be biding their time.'

'I know!' said Henry.

There was a long silence. Henry filled it with a boyishly enthusiastic speech about Mrs Greve, who had poisoned her husband with ground glass in Dublin in the early 1920s. Elinor watched him as he spoke with a kind of sadness he did not understand.

'Actually,' she said, 'it's nice to see you excited about something. There were times when I thought you'd . . . you know . . . given up. There were times when I thought . . .'

She laughed, a little nervously. 'You know . . . you'd . . . poisoned the chicken or something . . .'

Then she clasped his hand, firmly. 'But you wouldn't do a thing like that. You're a confused man. You're a sad man in many ways. But you're not a bad man, are you?'

Henry tried, not very successfully, to look deep into her eyes. 'No,' he said, 'not really!'

'Why would you ever want to poison me anyway?' went on Elinor wistfully. 'What have I ever done to you? You'd be lost without me. Wouldn't you?'

And, with those words, she took Maisie's hand and walked out to the rain-soaked car park.

Indeed.

What, when you thought about it, had she actually done to him? Why was he trying to poison her? Didn't this approach to their marriage need a complete re-think?

As they trudged across the common towards the village, Henry realized that few, if any advantages, financial or social, would accrue to him on her death. He would have to get an au pair – some Swedish or German floozy who went out till four in the morning and brought men back to her room. He would have to do even more domestic work than he did at the moment. There would be another funeral to organize. He might even have to speak at it (Henry shuddered slightly at this thought).

Then there was her mother. She would want to help. She would take the train down from Cumbria and sit in the front room and want to talk about her daughter. She would hold Henry's hand and look deep into Henry's eyes and say 'Let's talk about Elinor!' She would go on about how wonderful her daughter was, she would probably describe her talent for opera singing and gourmet cuisine. She might even – Henry started to shake uncontrollably – ask to stay.

There was quite a lot to be said for leaving Elinor alive. From the administrative point of view alone. Where, now he thought about it, was the salt kept for the dishwasher? How often did you have to put salt in it? When you put salt in it – where did it go? Did you just chuck it over the dishes like seasoning, or what?

How would he tell Maisie about periods?

They stopped outside a bookshop in the village High Street. Maisie pressed her nose to the glass. Elinor did the same. Then they squashed their lips against its cold, clean surface. They started to laugh.

'Can I buy a book?' said Maisie.

'Of course, darling!' said Elinor.

She wasn't all bad, thought Henry. When the three of them were like this, it almost felt good to be part of a family, knowing you were going back to a warm house, a well-tuned piano, a decent, ordered existence. Didn't married men stand less chance of getting heart attacks than bachelors?

Let's be reasonable, he told himself, as he followed Elinor and Maisie into the bookshop, you're not going to find another woman anyway. You're one of those people who looked interesting but turned out not to be. You didn't show much early promise, but what promise you showed you didn't fulfil. You're just another little Englishman who gets a laugh at parties. That's what you are. The one interesting thing you've ever done is try and murder your wife. Even if you did end up murdering your doctor and your dentist and –

Oh my God, thought Henry, I'm a murderer. I am actually a murderer. He felt suddenly very cold. Why? Why did he feel something that was almost guilt but not quite? As he stood watching Elinor and Maisie he realised it was something very simple. It was the urge to tell someone what had happened, coupled with the realization that he would never be able to do so. That what he had done was a totally private act, that it condemned him to an awful isolation, a world in which every remark or approach, however natural-seeming, was false. 'You are a poisoner!' an unpleasant, small voice in his head began to say.

And this was worse than anything he had felt before. It was worse, precisely because he now knew that he didn't want to poison his wife. With that realization came an inexpressible relief. He felt like a man who has just been told his brain scan is clear. He wanted to rush up to her and tell her the good news (although in that negative way women had she would probably brood over the implications of his original intention). But at the same time as this relief came this stinging, nagging ache. This feeling of isolation that threatened to overwhelm him, and lead him to shout out the truth here, in the shop, on a cold October afternoon.

Hang on, hang on, Henry. This is England, not Russia. For Christ's sake! You've tried to poison your wife. It was something people did. In the heat of the moment. No jury would convict. You had a tiff – you went out and got a shotgun or some strychnine and let off steam. You couldn't have love without hate as that man on *Stars on Sunday* had pointed out. Think positive, Henry.

I have become tougher, he said to himself, I have become more independent. I am better read. I know a lot more about chemistry. Yes, I have lost a valued friend and several neighbours, but for God's sake, if people can't learn from their mistakes and become useful citizens once more, what is the hope for any of us? Crime does not necessarily imply punishment these days – if it ever did. We are more, not less Christian than we were in Dostoevsky's day.

As they approached number 54, he linked his arm into hers. She started at first. Elinor was not used to him touching her. Her therapy group had apparently decided that Henry had something called 'touch taboo'. And, indeed, the pressure of her arm on his felt, at first, a little alarming. But as they turned in through the gateway Henry realized, to his surprise, that he was not actually gritting his teeth. She felt warm and, yes, comforting.

It was amazing how, when you had decided not to poison a person who probably deserved it, the world suddenly seemed a better, more decent, cleaner place. Maybe that was it. Maybe he had been suffering from whatever it was Raskolnikov had had, and hadn't realized it. He had had bad thoughts. He had acted on them. He had been mean and small-minded and thought only about himself and his problems. And look what had happened to him as a result! Years of negative thinking had turned him into a quadruple murderer. But, thought Henry as he let them in to the hall, he wasn't going to lie down under that stereotype. No sirree!

He had been full of spite and bitterness towards the world that lay outside Wimbledon. But now he was going to learn to be generous. Some people flew all over the world and had themselves profiled in colour magazines and had hundreds of women and as much Jack Daniels as they could drink while other people were fat and lived in Wimbledon. That was life! Some people sat up till four in the morning talking about the imagination and the sunset on the north face of the Eiger, while other people watched *News at Ten* and went to bed. That was life. The people with yachts and penthouses and as much sex as they wanted and shares and private beaches and planes constantly at their disposal and suntans and fantastic digestions were not, most of them, happy. Were they! Oh no. Happiness was a more complex emotion than that.

Would he, for example, when it came down to it, swap Maisie and Elinor and 54 Maple Drive for some villa with a swimming pool in Marbella complete with leggy blonde with a first in physics and an insatiable appetite for sex in strange positions with Henry? Would he?

Henry felt a momentary twinge of doubt and pushed it aside. He wouldn't.

Would he exchange his life of struggle, of patient, unrewarded research on a subject that was, possibly, of no interest to anyone anyway? Would he swap his *Complete History of Wimbledon* for some quick, easy, Nobel Prize-winning piece of crap about the state of play in Third World gaols? Would he exchange all that lived experience, the forty years of actually being Henry Farr for the cushy way out – I mean, said Henry to himself, who do you want to be? Henry Farr or Graham Greene?

For the briefest of brief moments he thought he was going to scream 'GRAHAM FUCKING GREENE!' and, running from the room, sink the coal shovel into Elinor's neck, but such was the power of positive thinking that the moment passed. He looked round at the sitting-room and, his heart growing bigger and bigger, more and more human with each glance, he reached for pencil and paper. He found himself writing:

Pluses
1. I have not been found out.
2. I have not killed anyone on purpose.
3. I have come to terms with my marriage.

Minuses

But, when it came to it, he could not think of any minuses. From where Henry was sitting, poisoning had been a challenging, bracing way of getting to grips with a mid-life crisis. The *Reader's Digest* would have been proud of him. He was already thinking of Henry the murderer in the past tense. Something along the lines of 'When I Tried my Hand at Poisoning . . .' or 'My Wife-murdering Phase'. He was entering a new world in which he might learn all those basic skills that had for so long been denied him. For Christ's sake, thought Henry, women are just people. People have problems, don't they?

The awesome thought came to him that, on his own, without any artificial aids or any money changing hands, he, Henry Farr, was experiencing Therapy.

'Open up, Henry,' said a voice within him, 'you are not all bad! You are businessman, father, cook, raconteur! You are murderer, socialite, good neighbour. A murderer is, in many ways, a very positive thing to be. Quite a lot of people would like to be in your shoes. Go with the flow, Henry. Accept the changes in your life! Be well, husband, commuter, solicitor, unapprehended poisoner!'

He was actually grinning to himself when Elinor came into the room. She looked, he thought, almost triumphant.

'John Rush!' she said, in the tones of a butler announcing a celebrity at a party. Then she flung the door wide open. 'He says he wants to see you about something!'

Henry goggled at her as Rush came into the room, bowing slightly as if to acknowledge the importance of his appearance. Before she retired, Elinor, still in larky mood, waved her hand towards him, as if she was proud to have a representative of Law and Order on the premises.

'Detective Inspector Rush,' she said, 'all the way from Wimbledon CID!'

Nigel Williams, *The Wimbledon Poisoner*

Sex

For one, the sudden fantastic grimace
Above, the red clown's-grin ripping the chalk sad sky,
Hailstones hatched out of midsummer, a face
Blanched with love's vile reversal.

The spirit died
First – such blank amazement took away its breath,
And let the body cry
Through the short scuffle and infamy of death.
For the other, who knows what nice proportion of loathing
And lust conjured the deep devil, created
That chance of incandescence? Figures here prove nothing.

One step took him through the roaring waterfall
That closed like a bead-curtain, left him alone with the writhing
Of what he loved or hated.
His hands leapt out: they took vengeance for all
Denials and soft answers. There was one who said
Long since, 'rough play will end in tears'. There was Cain
In the picture-book. Forgotten. Here is one dead,
And one could never be whole again.

The news
Broke a Sunday inertia: ring after ring
Across that smug mirror went echoing
And fainting out to the dim margins of incredulity.
A few raw souls accuse
Themselves of this felony and find not guilty –
Acquitted on a mere álibi or technical point.
Most see it as an island eruption, viewed
From the safe continent; not dreaming the same fire pent
Within their clay that warps
The night with fluent alarm, their own wrath spewed
Through the red craters of that undistinguished corpse.
All that has reached them is the seismic thrill:
The ornaments vibrate on the shelf; then they are still.
Snugly we settle down
Into our velvet and legitimate bed,
While news-sheets are yet falling all over the town
Like a white ash. Falling on one dead
And one can never be whole again.

You watch him
Pulpited in the dock, preaching repentance
While the two professionals in fancy dress
Manœuvre formally to score off him or catch him.
But grief has her conventions –
The opaque mask of misery will confess
Nothing, nor plead moving extenuations.
But you who crowd the court-room, will you never be called
To witness for the defence?

Accomplices
All of you, now – though now it is still too late –
Bring on the missing evidence! Reveal the coiled
Venom, the curse that needs
Only a touch to be articulate.
You, Judge, strip off! Show us the abscess boiling
Beneath your scarlet. Oh point, someone, to where it spreads
On every hand – the red, collusive stain . . .
All too well you have done your work: for one is dead,
And the other will not be whole again.

C. Day Lewis, 'Sex-Crime'

'I know a girl who went to a guy's flat. He was very respectable-looking – when a man goes out to do a woman in, he always wears a nice suit. This man hit her, stripped her and tied her up with a noose round her neck, which he pulled very tight. She lost consciousness, and when she came to he was in a drunken stupor. The police went round and found a body cut up in pieces in bin-liners. That would have stopped me – but she still works.'

Melanie McFadyean, 'Helen's Story'

SWEENEY WAUCHOPE HORSFALL KLIPSTEIN
KRUMPACKER SWARTS SNOW DORIS DUSTY

SWEENEY: I'll carry you off
To a cannibal isle.
DORIS: You'll be the cannibal!
SWEENEY: You'll be the missionary!
You'll be my little seven stone missionary!
I'll gobble you up. I'll be the cannibal.
DORIS: You'll carry me off? To a cannibal isle?
SWEENEY: I'll be the canibal.
DORIS: I'll be the missionary.
I'll convert you!
SWEENEY: I'll convert *you*!
Into a stew.
A nice little, white little, missionary stew.
DORIS: You wouldn't eat me!

SWEENEY: Yes I'd eat you!
In a nice little, white little, soft little, tender little,
Juicy little, right little, missionary stew.
You see this egg
You see this egg
Well that's life on a crocodile isle.
There's no telephones
There's no gramophones
There's no motor cars
No two-seaters, no six-seaters,
No Citroën, no Rolls-Royce.
Nothing to eat but the fruit as it grows.
Nothing to see but the palmtrees one way
And the sea the other way,
Nothing to hear but the sound of the surf.
Nothing at all but three things.
DORIS: What things?
SWEENEY: Birth, and copulation and death.
That's all, that's all, that's all, that's all,
Birth, and copulation, and death.
DORIS: I'd be bored.
SWEENEY: You'd be bored.
Birth, and copulation, and death.
DORIS: I'd be bored.
SWEENEY: You'd be bored.
Birth, and copulation, and death.
That's all the facts when you come to brass tacks:
Birth, and copulation, and death.
I've been born, and once is enough.
You don't remember, but I remember,
Once is enough.

Song by WAUCHOPE *and* HORSFALL
SWARTS *as* TAMBO. SNOW *as* BONES

Under the bamboo
Bamboo bamboo
Under the bamboo tree
Two live as one
One live as two

Two live as three
Under the bam
Under the boo
Under the bamboo tree.

Where the breadfruit fall
And the penguin call
And the sound is the sound of the sea
Under the bam
Under the boo
Under the bamboo tree

Where the Gauguin maids
In the banyan shades
Wear palmleaf drapery
Under the bam
Under the boo
Under the bamboo tree.
Tell me in what part of the wood
Do you want to flirt with me?
Under the breadfruit, banyan, palmleaf
Or under the bamboo tree?
Any old tree will do for me
Any old wood is just as good
Any old isle is just my style
Any fresh egg
Any fresh egg
And the sound of the coral sea.

DORIS: I don't like eggs; I never liked eggs;
And I don't like life on your crocodile isle.

Song by KLIPSTEIN and KRUMPACKER
SNOW *and* SWARTS *as before*

My little island girl
My little island girl
I'm going to stay with you
And we won't worry what to do
We won't have to catch any trains
And we won't go home when it rains
We'll gather hibiscus flowers

For it won't be minutes but hours
For it won't be hours but years

diminuendo
And the morning
And the evening
And noontide
And night
Morning
Evening
Noontime
Night

DORIS: That's not life, that's no life
Why I'd just as soon be dead.
SWEENEY: That's what life is. Just is
DORIS: What is?
What's that life is?
SWEENEY: Life is death
I knew a man once did a girl in –
DORIS: Oh Mr Sweeney, please don't talk,
I cut the cards before you came
And I drew the coffin
SWARTS: *You* drew the coffin?
DORIS: I drew the COFFIN very last card.
I don't care for much conversation
A woman runs a terrible risk.
SNOW: Let Mr Sweeney continue his story.
I assure you, Sir, we are very interested.
SWEENEY: I knew a man once did a girl in.
Any man might do a girl in
Any man has to, needs to, wants to
Once in a lifetime, do a girl in
Well he kept her there in a bath
With a gallon of lysol in a bath
SWARTS: These fellows always get pinched in the end.
SNOW: Excuse me, they don't all get pinched in the end.
What about them bones on Epsom Heath?
I seen that in the papers
You seen it in the papers
They *don't* all get pinched in the end.
DORIS: A woman runs a terrible risk.
SNOW: Let Mr Sweeney continue his story.

SWEENEY: This one didn't get pinched in the end
But that's another story too.
This went on for a couple of months
Nobody came
And nobody went
But he took in the milk and he paid the rent.
SWARTS: What did he do?
All that time, what did he do?
SWEENEY: What did he do! what did he do?
That don't apply.
Talk to live men about what they do.
He used to come and see me sometimes
I'd give him a drink and cheer him up.
DORIS: Cheer him up?
DUSTY: Cheer him up?
SWEENEY: Well here again that don't apply
But I've gotta use words when I talk to you.
But here's what I was going to say.
He didn't know if he was alive
and the girl was dead
He didn't know if the girl was alive
and he was dead
He didn't know if they were both alive
or both were dead
If he was alive then the milkman wasn't
and the rent-collector wasn't
And if they were alive then he was dead.
There wasn't any joint
There wasn't any joint
For when you're alone
When you're alone like he was alone
You're either or neither
I tell you again it don't apply
Death or life or life or death
Death is life and life is death
I gotta use words when I talk to you
But if you understand or if you don't
That's nothing to me and nothing to you
We all gotta do what we gotta do
We're gona sit here and drink this booze

We're gona sit here and have a tune
We're gona stay and we're gona go
And somebody's gotta pay the rent
DORIS: I know who
SWEENEY: But that's nothing to me and nothing to you.

Full chorus: WAUCHOPE, HORSEFALL, KLIPSTEIN, KRUMPACKER

When you're alone in the middle of the night and
you wake in a sweat and a hell of a fright
When you're alone in the middle of the bed and
you wake like someone hit you in the head
You've had a cream of a nightmare dream and
you've got the hoo-ha's coming to you.

T. S. Eliot, 'Fragment of an Agon'

We dropped the swine and he crashed to the floor. Sir Edmund, Simone, and myself were coldly animated by the same determination, together with an incredible excitement and levity. The priest lay there with a limp cock, his teeth digging into the floor with rage and shame. Now that his balls were drained, his abomination appeared to him in all its horror. He audibly sighed:

'Oh miserable sacrileges . . .'

And muttering other incomprehensible laments.

Sir Edmund nudged him with his foot; the monster leaped up and drew back, bellowing with such ludicrous fury that we burst out laughing.

'Get on your feet,' Sir Edmund ordered him, 'you're going to fuck this girl.'

'Wretches . . .' Don Aminado threatened in a choking voice, 'Spanish police . . . prison . . . the garrotte . . .'

'But you are forgetting that is your sperm,' observed Sir Edmund.

A ferocious grimace, a trembling like that of a cornered beast, and then: 'The garrotte for me too. But you three . . . first.'

'Poor fool,' smirked Sir Edmund. '*First!* Do you think I am going to let you wait that long? *First!*'

The imbecile gaped dumbstruck at the Englishman: an extremely silly expression darted across his handsome face. Something like an absurd joy began to open his mouth, he crossed his arms over his naked chest and finally gazed at us with ecstatic eyes. 'Martyrdom . . .' he uttered in a voice that was suddenly feeble and yet tore out like a sob. 'Martyrdom . . .' A bizarre hope of purification had come to the wretch, illuminating his eyes.

'First I am going to tell you a story,' Sir Edmund said to him sedately. 'You know that men who are hanged or garrotted have such stiff cocks the instant their respiration is cut off, that they ejaculate. You are going to have the pleasure of being martyred while fucking this girl.'

And when the horrified priest rose to defend himself, the Englishman brutally knocked him down, twisting his arm.

Next, Sir Edmund, slipping under his victim, pinioned his arms behind his back while I gagged him and bound his legs with a belt. The Englishman, gripping his arms from behind in a strangle-hold, disabled the priest's legs in his own. Kneeling behind, I kept the man's head immobile between my thighs.

'And now,' said Sir Edmund to Simone, 'mount this little padre.'

Simone removed her dress and squatted on the belly of this singular martyr, her cunt next to his flabby cock.

'Now,' continued Sir Edmund, 'squeeze his throat, the pipe just behind the Adam's apple: a strong, gradual pressure.'

Simone squeezed, a dreadful shudder ran through that mute, fully immobilized body, and the cock stood on end. I took it into my hands and had no trouble fitting it into Simone's vulva, while she continued to squeeze the throat.

The utterly intoxicated girl kept wrenching the big cock in and out with her buttocks, atop the body whose muscles were cracking in our formidable strangleholds.

At last, she squeezed so resolutely that an even more violent thrill shot through her victim, and she felt the come shooting inside her cunt. Now she let go, collapsing backwards in a tempest of joy.

Simone lay on the floor, her belly up, her thigh still smeared by the dead man's sperm which had trickled from her vulva. I stretched out at her side to rape and fuck her in turn, but all I could do was squeeze her in my arms and kiss her mouth, because of a strange inward paralysis ultimately caused by my love for the girl and the death of the unspeakable creature. I have never been so content.

I didn't even stop Simone from pushing me aside and going to view her work. She straddled the naked cadaver again, scrutinizing the purplish face with the keenest interest, she even sponged the sweat off the forehead and obstinately waved away a fly buzzing in a sunbeam and endlessly flitting back to alight on the face. All at once, Simone uttered a soft cry.

Something bizarre and quite baffling had happened: this time, the insect had perched on the corpse's eye and was agitating its long nightmarish legs on the strange orb. The girl took her head in her hands and shook it, trembling, then she seemed to plunge into an abyss of reflections.

Georges Bataille, *Story of the Eye*, trans. Joachim Neugroschel

This is pure essence, human wickedness,
This blind crustacean scuttling from a van
Between two constables in burberries,
This vicious, stupid, ignorant old man,
Caretaker of a lifetime and a kettle,
A smell, a shuffle and a smoker's cough.
He longs to loll on banks of pink rose petal
With a pretty little boy to suck him off.
As man born into joy lives on and grieves,
Lips that forget to kiss must learn to pray.
The little boy lies swaddled in wet leaves
And a bin-liner beside the motorway.
But not so deep his father cannot find
Him.
Pity for this, pity for humankind.

John Whitworth, 'The Pure Essence'

Shrubbery

Mr Ponderby-Wilkins was a man so rich, so ugly, so cross, and so old, that even the stupidest reader could not expect him to survive any longer than Chapter 1. Vulpine in his secretiveness, he was porcine in his habits, saturnine in his appearance, and ovine in his unconsciousness of doom. He was the kind of man who might easily perish as early as paragraph two.

Little surprise, therefore, was shown by Police-Inspector Blowhard of Nettleby Parva when a message reached him on the telephone:

'You are wanted immediately at the Towers. Mr Ponderby-Wilkins has been found dead.'

The inspector was met at the gate by the deceased's secretary, whom he knew and suspected on the spot.

'Where did it happen, Mr Porlock?' he asked. 'The lake, the pigeon-loft, or the shrubbery?'

'The shrubbery,' answered Porlock quietly, and led the way to the scene.

Mr Ponderby-Wilkins was suspended by means of an enormous woollen muffler to the bough of a tree, which the police-officer's swift eye noticed at once to be a sycamore.

'How long has that sycamore tree been in the shrubbery?' he inquired suspiciously.

'I don't know,' answered Porlock, 'and I don't care.'

'Tell me precisely what happened,' went on the inspector.

'Four of us were playing tennis, when a ball was hit out into the bushes. On going to look for it at the end of the set, I found Mr Wilkins as you see him, and called the attention of the other players to the circumstances at once. Here they all are.'

And pushing aside the boughs of a laurel, he showed the police-officer two young women and a young man. They were standing quietly in the middle of the tennis-court, holding their tennis-racquets soberly in their hands.

'Do you corroborate Mr Porlock's account of the affair?' inquired Blowhard.

'We do,' they answered quietly in one breath.

'Hum!' mused the inspector, stroking his chin. 'By the way,' he continued, 'I wonder whether life is extinct?'

He went and looked at the body. It was.

'A glance showed us that life was extinct when we found it,' said the four, speaking together, 'and we thought it better to go on playing tennis as reverently as possible until you arrived.'

'Quite right,' said Blowhard. 'I shall now examine the whole household *viva voce*. Kindly summon them to the drawing-room.'

They went together into the large, white-fronted mansion, and soon the notes of a gong, reverberating through the house and all over the grounds, had summoned the whole house-party, including the servants, to the Louis-Seize *salon* overlooking the tennis lawn. The gathering consisted, as the inspector had foreseen, of the usual types involved in a country house murder, namely, a frightened stepsister of the deceased, a young and beautiful niece, a major, a doctor, a chaperon, a friend, Mr Porlock himself, an old butler with a beard, a middle-aged gardener with whiskers, an Irish cook, and two servants who had only come to the place the week before. Every one of them had a bitter grudge against the deceased. He had been about to dismiss his secretary, had threatened to disinherit his niece, sworn repeatedly at his stepsister, thrown a port decanter at the butler's head, insulted the guests by leaving *Bradshaws* in their bedrooms, pulled up the gardener's antirrhinums, called the cook a good-for-nothing, and terrified the housemaids by making noises at them on the stairs. In addition, he had twice informed the major that his regiment had run away at Balaclava, and had put a toad in the doctor's bed.

Blowhard felt instinctively that this was a case for Bletherby Marge, the famous amateur, and sent him a telegram at once. Then he ordered the body to be removed, walked round the grounds, ate a few strawberries, and went home.

Bletherby Marge was a man of wide culture and sympathy. In appearance he was fat, red-faced, smiling, and had untidy hair. He looked stupid and wore spats. In fact, whatever the inexperienced reader supposes to be the ordinary appearance of a detective, to look like that was the very reverse of Bletherby Marge. He was sometimes mistaken for a business man, more often for a billiard-marker or a baboon. But whenever Scotland Yard was unable to deal with a murder case – that is to say, whenever a murder case happened at a country house – Bletherby Marge was called in. The death of an old, rich, and disagreeable man was like a clarion call to him. He packed his pyjamas, his tooth-brush, and a volume of *Who's Who*, and took the earliest train.

As soon as he had seen the familiar newsbill:

HOST OF COUNTRY HOUSE-PARTY
INEXPLICABLY SLAIN

he had expected his summons to The Towers. Telegraphing to the coroner's jury to return an open verdict at Nettleby Parva, he finished off the case of the Duke of St Neots, fragments of whom had mysteriously been discovered in a chaff-cutting machine, and made all haste to the scene of the new affair. It was his forty-ninth mystery, and in every previous affair he had triumphantly slain his man. A small silver gallows had been presented to him by Scotland Yard as a token of esteem.

'We are in deep waters, Blowhard – very deep,' he said, as he closely scrutinized the comforter which had been wrapped round Mr Ponderby-Wilkins's throat. 'Just tell me once more about these alibis.'

'Every one of them is perfect,' answered the police inspector, 'so far as I can see. The butler, the cook, and the two housemaids were all together playing poker in the pantry. Miss Brown, the deceased's stepsister, was giving instructions to the gardener, and the doctor was with her, carrying her trowel and her pruning scissors. The chaperon and the friend were playing tennis with Mr Porlock and the major, and the niece was rowing herself about on the lake, picking water-lilies.'

A gleam came into Bletherby Marge's eyes.

'Alone?' he queried.

'Alone. But you forget that the lake is in full view of the tennis-court. It almost seems as if it must have been constructed that way on purpose,' added the inspector rather crossly. 'This girl was seen the whole time during which the murder must have occurred, either by one pair of players or the other.'

'Tut, tut,' said Bletherby Marge. 'Now take me to the scene of the crime.'

Arrived at the sycamore tree, he studied the bark with a microscope, and the ground underneath. This was covered with dead leaves. There was no sign of a struggle.

'Show me exactly how the body was hanging,' he said to Blowhard.

Police-Inspector Blowhard tied the two ends of the comforter to the bough and wrapped the loop several times round Bletherby Marge's neck, supporting him, as he did so, by the feet.

'Don't let go,' said Bletherby Marge.

'I won't,' said Blowhard, who was used to the great detective's methods in reconstructing a crime.

'Have you photographed the tree from every angle?' went on Bletherby.

'Yes.'

'Were there any finger-prints on it?'

'No,' replied Blowhard. 'Nothing but leaves.'

Then together they wandered round the grounds, eating fruit and discussing possible motives for the murder. No will had been discovered.

From time to time one or other of the house-party would flit by them, humming a song, intent on a game of tennis, or a bathe in the lake. Now and then a face would look haggard or strained, at other times the same face would be merry and wreathed with smiles.

'Do you feel baffled?' asked Blowhard.

Bletherby Marge made no reply.

The house-party were having a motor picnic at Dead Man's Wood, ten miles from The Towers. The festivity had been proposed by Bletherby Marge, who was more and more endearing himself, by his jokes and wide knowledge of the world, to his fellow-guests. Many of them had already begun to feel that a house-party without a detective in it must be regarded as a literary failure.

'Bless my soul!' said Marge suddenly, when the revelry was at its height, turning to Blowhard, who was out of breath, for he had been carrying the champagne across a ploughed field. 'I ask you all to excuse me for a moment. I have forgotten my pipe.'

They saw him disappear in a two-seater towards The Towers. In little more than an hour he reappeared again and delighted the company by singing one or two popular revue songs in a fruity baritone. But, as the line of cars went homeward in the dusk, Bletherby Marge said to Blowhard, seated beside him, 'I want to see you again in the shrubbery tomorrow at ten-thirty prompt. Don't begin playing clock-golf!'

Inspector Blowhard made a note of the time in his pocket-book.

'Perhaps you wonder why I went away in the middle of our little outing?' questioned Marge, as they stood together under the fatal sycamore tree.

'I suspected,' answered Blowhard, without moving a muscle of his face, except the ones he used for speaking, 'that it was a ruse.'

'It was,' replied Marge.

Without another word he took a small folding broom from his pocket and brushed aside the dead leaves which strewed the ground of the shrubbery.

The dark mould was covered with footprints, large and small.

'What do you deduce from this?' cried Blowhard, his eyes bulging from his head.

'When I returned from the picnic,' explained the great detective, 'I first swept the ground clear as you see it now. I then hastily collected all the outdoor shoes in the house.'

'All?'

'Every one. I brought them to the shrubbery on a wheelbarrow. I locked the servants, as though by accident, in the kitchen and the gardener in the tool-shed. I then compared the shoes with these imprints, and found that every one of them was a fit.'

'Which means?'

'That every one of them was here when the murder took place. I have reconstructed the scene exactly. The marks of the shoes stretch in a long line, as you will observe, from a point close to the tree almost to the edge of the tennis-lawn. The heels are very deeply imprinted; the mark of the toes is very light indeed.'

He paused and looked at Blowhard.

'I suppose you see now how the murder was done?' he barked loudly.

'No,' mewed the inspector quietly.

'Ponderby-Wilkins,' said Marge, 'had the comforter twisted once round his neck, and one end was tie to the tree. Then – at a signal, I imagine – the whole house-party, including the servants, pulled together on the other end of the comforter until he expired. You see here the imprints of the butler's feet. As the heaviest man, he was at the end of the rope. Porlock was in front, with the second housemaid immediately behind him. Porlock, I fancy, gave the word to pull. Afterwards they tied him up to the tree as you found him when you arrived.'

'But the alibis?'

'All false. They were all sworn to by members of the household, by servants or by guests. That was what put me on the scent.'

'But how is it there were no finger-prints?'

'The whole party,' answered Bletherby, 'wore gloves. I collected all the gloves in the house and examined them carefully. Many of them had hairs from the comforter still adhering to them. Having concluded my investigations, I rapidly replaced the boots and gloves, put the leaves back in their original position, unlocked the kitchen and the tool-house, and came back to the picnic again.'

'And sang comic songs!' said Blowhard.

'Yes,' replied Marge. 'A great load had been taken off my mind by the discovery of the truth. And I felt it necessary to put the murderers off their guard.'

'Wonderful!' exclaimed Blowhard, examining the footprints minutely. 'There is now only one difficulty, Mr Marge, so far as I can see.'

'And that is?'

'How am I going to convey all these people to the police station?'

'How many pairs of manacles have you about you?'

'Only two,' confessed Blowhard, feeling in his pocket.

'You had better telephone,' said Bletherby, 'for a motor-omnibus.'

The simultaneous trial of twelve prisoners on a capital charge, followed by their joint condemnation and execution, thrilled England as no sensation had thrilled it since the death of William II. The Sunday papers were never tired of discussing the psychology of the murderers and publishing details of their early life and school careers. Never before, it seemed, had a secretary, a stepsister, a niece, an eminent KC, a major, a chaperon, a friend, a cook, a butler, two housemaids, and a gardener gone to the gallows on the same day for the murder of a disagreeable old man.

On a morning not long after the excitement had died away, Bletherby

Marge and a house agent went together to The Towers, which for some reason or other was still 'To Let'. As they looked at the library, Bletherby Marge tapped a panel in the mantelpiece.

'It sounds hollow,' he said.

Finding the spring, he pressed it. The wood shot back and revealed a small cavity. From this he drew a dusty bundle of papers, tied together with a small dog-collar.

It was Ponderby-Wilkins's will. On the first page was written:

I am the most unpopular man in England, and I am about to commit suicide by hanging myself in the shrubbery. If Bletherby Marge can make it a murder I bequeath him all my possessions in honour of his fiftieth success.

'Extraordinary!' ejaculated the house agent.

Mr Bletherby Marge smiled.

E. V. Knox, 'The Murder at the Towers'

Spit

Berkeley Castle

Enter MATREVIS *and* GURNEY

MATREVIS: Gurney, I wonder the king dies not,
Being in a vault up to the knees in water,
To which the channels of the castle run,
From whence a damp continually ariseth
That were enough to poison any man,
Much more a king, brought up so tenderly.

GURNEY: And so do I, Matrevis. Yesternight
I open'd but the door to throw him meat,
And I was almost stifled with the savour.

MATREVIS: He hath a body able to endure
More than we can inflict, and therefore now
Let us assail his mind another while.

GURNEY: Send for him out thence, and I will anger him.

MATREVIS: But stay; who's this?

Enter LIGHTBORN

LIGHTBORN: My Lord Protector greets you.

Gives letter

GURNEY: What's here? I know not how to conster it.

MATREVIS: Gurney, it was left unpointed for the nonce:
Edwardum occidere nolite timere,
That's his meaning.
LIGHTBORN: Know you this token? I must have the king.
Gives token
MATREVIS: Ay, stay a while; thou shalt have answer straight.
This villain's sent to make away the king.
GURNEY: I thought as much.
MATREVIS: And, when the murder's done,
See how he must be handled for his labour,
Pereat iste! Let him have the king;
What else? Here is the keys, this is the lake.
Do as you are commanded by my lord.
LIGHTBORN: I know what I must do. Get you away:
Yet be not far off, I shall need your help.
See that in the next room I have a fire,
And get me a spit, and let it be red-hot.
MATREVIS: Very well.
GURNEY: Need you anything besides?
LIGHTBORN: What else? A table and a feather-bed.
GURNEY: That's all?
LIGHTBORN: Ay, ay: so, when I call you, bring it in.
MATREVIS: Fear not you that.
GURNEY: Here's a light to go into the dungeon.
Gives light to LIGHTBORN, *and then exit with* MATREVIS
LIGHTBORN: So, now.
Must I about this gear: ne'er was there any
So finely handled as this king shall be.
Foh, here's a place indeed, with all my heart!
KING EDWARD: Who's there? What light is that?
Wherefore comes thou?
LIGHTBORN: To comfort you, and bring you joyful news.
KING EDWARD: Small comfort finds poor Edward in thy looks.
Villain, I know thou com'st to murder me.
LIGHTBORN: To murder you, my most gracious lord?
Far is it from my heart to do you harm.
The queen sent me to see how you were us'd,
For she relents at this your misery:
And what eye can refrain from shedding tears,
To see a king in this most piteous state?

KING EDWARD: Weep'st thou already? List a while to me,
And when thy heart, were it as Gurney's is,
Or as Matrevis', hewn from the Caucasus,
Yet will it melt ere I have done my tale.
This dungeon where they keep me is the sink
Wherein the filth of all the castle falls.
LIGHTBORN: O villains!
KING EDWARD: And there, in mire and puddle, have I stood
This ten days' space; and, lest that I should sleep,
One plays continually upon a drum.
They give me bread and water, being a king;
So that, for want of sleep and sustenance,
My mind's distemper'd and my body's numb'd,
And whether I have limbs or no I know not.
O, would my blood dropp'd out from every vein,
As doth this water from my tatter'd robes!
Tell Isabel the queen, I look'd not thus,
When for her sake I ran at tilt in France,
And there unhors'd the Duke of Cleremont.
LIGHTBORN: O, speak no more my lord! This breaks my heart.
Lie on this bed, and rest yourself a while.
KING EDWARD: These looks of thine can harbour naught but death;
I see my tragedy written in thy brows.
Yet stay a while; forbear thy bloody hand,
And let me see the stroke before it comes,
That even then when I shall lose my life,
My mind may be more steadfast on my God.
LIGHTBORN: What means your highness to mistrust me thus?
KING EDWARD: What mean'st thou to dissemble with me thus?
LIGHTBORN: These hands were never stain'd with innocent blood,
Nor shall they now be tainted with a king's.
KING EDWARD: Forgive my thought for having such a thought.
One jewel have I left; receive thou this.

Giving jewel

Still fear I, and I know not what's the cause,
But every joint shakes as I give it thee.
O, if thou harbour'st murder in thy heart,
Let this gift change thy mind, and save thy soul!
Know that I am a king: O, at that name

I feel a hell of grief! Where is my crown?
Gone, gone! And do I remain alive?
LIGHTBORN: You're overwatch'd, my lord: lie down and rest.
KING EDWARD: But that grief keeps me waking, I should sleep;
For not these ten days have these eyes' lids clos'd.
Now, as I speak, they fall; and yet with fear
Open again. O, wherefore sitt'st thou here?
LIGHTBORN: If you mistrust me, I'll be gone, my lord.
KING EDWARD: No, no; for, if thou mean'st to murder me,
Thou wilt return again; and therefore stay.

Sleeps

LIGHTBORN: He sleeps.
KING EDWARD (*waking*): O, let me not die yet! Stay, O, stay a while!
LIGHTBORN: How now, my lord!
KING EDWARD: Something still buzzeth in mine ears,
And tells me, if I sleep, I never wake.
This fear is that which makes me tremble thus;
And therefore tell me, wherefore art thou come?
LIGHTBORN: To rid thee of thy life, Matrevis, come!

Enter MATREVIS *and* GURNEY

KING EDWARD: I am too weak and feeble to resist.
Assist me, sweet God, and receive my soul!
LIGHTBORN: Run for the table.
KING EDWARD: O, spare me, or despatch me in a trice!

MATREVIS *brings in a table*

LIGHTBORN: So, lay the table down, and stamp on it,
But not too hard, lest that you bruise his body.

KING EDWARD *is murdered*

MATREVIS: I fear me that this cry will raise the town,
And therefore let us take horse and away.
LIGHTBORN: Tell me, sirs, was it not bravely done?
GURNEY: Excellent well: take this for thy reward.

Stabs LIGHTBORN *who dies*

Come, let us cast the body in the moat,
And bear the king's to Mortimer our lord:
Away!

Exeunt with the bodies

Christopher Marlowe, *Edward II*

Spot

Mrs Brooks, the lady who was the householder at The Herons, and owner of all the handsome furniture, was not a person of an unusually curious turn of mind. She was too deeply materialized, poor woman, by her long and enforced bondage to that arithmetical demon Profit-and-Loss, to retain much curiosity for its own sake, and apart from possible lodgers' pockets. Nevertheless, the visit of Angel Clare to her well-paying tenants, Mr and Mrs d'Urberville, as she deemed them, was sufficiently exceptional in point of time and manner to reinvigorate the feminine proclivity which had been stifled down as useless save in its bearings on the letting trade.

Tess had spoken to her husband from the doorway, without entering the dining-room, and Mrs Brooks, who stood within the partly-closed door of her own sitting-room at the back of the passage, could hear fragments of the conversation – if conversation it could be called – between those two wretched souls. She heard Tess re-ascend the stairs to the first floor, and the departure of Clare, and the closing of the front door behind him. Then the door of the room above was shut, and Mrs Brooks knew that Tess had re-entered her apartment. As the young lady was not fully dressed, Mrs Brooks knew that she would not emerge again for some time.

She accordingly ascended the stairs softly, and stood at the door of the front room – a drawing-room, connected with the room immediately behind it (which was a bedroom) by folding doors in the common manner. This first floor, containing Mrs Brooks's best apartments, had been taken by the week by the d'Urbervilles. The back room was now in silence; but from the drawing-room there came sounds.

All that she could at first distinguish of them was one syllable, continually repeated in a low note of moaning, as if it came from a soul bound to some Ixionian wheel –

'O – O – O!'

Then a silence, then a heavy sigh, and again –

'O – O – O!'

The landlady looked through the keyhole. Only a small space of the room inside was visible, but within that space came a corner of the breakfast table, which was already spread for the meal, and also a chair beside. Over the seat of the chair Tess's face was bowed, her posture being a kneeling one in front of it; her hands were clasped over her head, the skirts of her dressing-gown and the embroidery of her night-gown flowed upon the floor behind her, and her stockingless feet, from which the slippers had fallen, protruded upon the carpet. It was from her lips that came the murmur of unspeakable despair.

Then a man's voice from the adjoining bedroom –

'What's the matter?'

She did not answer, but went on, in a tone which was a soliloquy rather than an exclamation, and a dirge rather than a soliloquy. Mrs Brooks could only catch a portion:

'And then my dear, dear husband came home to me . . . and I did not know it! . . . And you had used your cruel persuasion upon me . . . you did not stop using it – no – you did not stop! My little sisters and brothers and my mother's needs – they were the things you moved me by . . . and you said my husband would never come back – never; and you taunted me, and said what a simpleton I was to expect him! . . . And at last I believed you and gave way! . . . And then he came back! Now he is gone. Gone a second time, and I have lost him now for ever . . . and he will not love me the littlest bit ever any more – only hate me! . . . O yes, I have lost him now – again because of – you!' In writhing, with her head on the chair, she turned her face towards the door, and Mrs Brooks could see the pain upon it; and that her lips were bleeding from the clench of her teeth upon them, and that the long lashes of her closed eyes stuck in wet tags to her cheeks. She continued: 'And he is dying – he looks as if he is dying! . . . And my sin will kill him and not kill me! . . . O, you have torn my life all to pieces . . . made me be what I prayed you in pity not to make me be again! . . . My own true husband will never, never – O God – I can't bear this! – I cannot!'

There were more and sharper words from the man; then a sudden rustle; she had sprung to her feet. Mrs Brooks, thinking that the speaker was coming to rush out of the door, hastily retreated down the stairs.

She need not have done so, however, for the door of the sitting-room was not opened. But Mrs Brooks felt it unsafe to watch on the landing again, and entered her own parlour below.

She could hear nothing through the floor, although she listened intently, and thereupon went to the kitchen to finish her interrupted breakfast. Coming up presently to the front room on the ground floor she took up some sewing, waiting for her lodgers to ring that she might take away the breakfast, which she meant to do herself, to discover what was the matter if possible. Overhead, as she sat, she could now hear the floor-boards slightly creak, as if some one were walking about, and presently the movement was explained by the rustle of garments against the banisters, the opening and the closing of the front door, and the form of Tess passing to the gate on her way into the street. She was fully dressed now in the walking costume of a well-to-do young lady in which she had arrived, with the sole addition that over her hat and black feathers a veil was drawn.

Mrs Brooks had not been able to catch any word of farewell, temporary or otherwise, between her tenants at the door above. They might have quarrelled, or Mr d'Urberville might still be asleep, for he was not an early riser.

She went into the back room which was more especially her own apartment, and continued her sewing there. The lady lodger did not return, nor did the gentleman ring his bell. Mrs Brooks pondered on the delay, and on what probable relation the visitor who had called so early bore to the couple upstairs. In reflecting she leant back in her chair.

As she did so her eyes glanced casually over the ceiling till they were arrested by a spot in the middle of its white surface which she had never noticed there before. It was about the size of a wafer when she first observed it, but it speedily grew as large as the palm of her hand, and then she could perceive that it was red. The oblong white ceiling, with this scarlet blot in the midst, had the appearance of a gigantic ace of hearts.

Mrs Brooks had strange qualms of misgiving. She got upon the table, and touched the spot in the ceiling with her fingers. It was damp, and she fancied that it was a blood stain.

Descending from the table, she left the parlour, and went upstairs, intending to enter the room overhead, which was the bedchamber at the back of the drawing-room. But, nerveless woman as she had now become, she could not bring herself to attempt the handle. She listened. The dead silence within was broken only by a regular beat.

Drip, drip, drip.

Mrs Brooks hastened downstairs, opened the front door, and ran into the street. A man she knew, one of the workmen employed at an adjoining villa, was passing by, and she begged him to come in and go upstairs with her; she feared something had happened to one of her lodgers. The workman assented, and followed her to the landing.

She opened the door of the drawing-room, and stood back for him to pass in, entering herself behind him. The room was empty; a breakfast – a substantial repast of coffee, eggs, and a cold ham – lay spread upon the table untouched, as when she had taken it up, excepting that the carving knife was missing. She asked the man to go through the folding doors into the adjoining room.

He opened the doors, entered a step or two, and came back almost instantly with a rigid face. 'My good God, the gentleman in bed is dead! I think he has been hurt with a knife – a lot of blood has run down upon the floor!'

The alarm was soon given, and the house which had lately been so quiet resounded with the tramp of many footsteps, a surgeon among the rest. The wound was small, but the point of the blade had touched the heart of the victim, who lay on his back, pale, fixed, dead, as if he had scarcely moved after the infliction of the blow. In a quarter of an hour the news that a gentleman who was a temporary visitor to the town had been stabbed in his bed, spread through every street and villa of the popular watering-place.

Thomas Hardy, *Tess of the D'Urbervilles*

LADY MACBETH: Yet here's a spot.

DOCTOR: Hark, she speaks. I will set down what comes from her to satisfy my remembrance the more strongly.

LADY MACBETH: Out, damned spot; out, I say. One, two, – why, then 'tis time to do't. Hell is murky. Fie, my lord, fie, a soldier and afeard? What need we fear who knows it when none can call our power to account? Yet who would have thought the old man to have had so much blood in him?

DOCTOR: Do you mark that?

LADY MACBETH: The Thane of Fife had a wife. Where is she now? What, will these hands ne'er be clean? No more o' that, my lord, no more o' that. You mar all with this starting.

DOCTOR: Go to, go to. You have known what you should not.

GENTLEWOMAN: She has spoke what she should not, I am sure of that. Heaven knows what she has known.

LADY MACBETH: Here's the smell of the blood still. All the perfumes of Arabia will not sweeten this little hand. O, O, O!

DOCTOR: What a sigh is there! The heart is sorely charged.

GENTLEWOMAN: I would not have such a heart in my bosom for the dignity of the whole body.

DOCTOR: Well, well, well.

GENTLEWOMAN: Pray God it be, sir.

DOCTOR: This disease is beyond my practice. Yet I have known those which have walked in their sleep who have died holily in their beds.

LADY MACBETH: Wash your hands, put on your night-gown, look not so pale. I tell you yet again, Banquo's buried. He cannot come out on's grave.

DOCTOR: Even so?

LADY MACBETH: To bed, to bed. There's knocking at the gate. Come, come, come, come, give me your hand. What's done cannot be undone. To bed, to bed, to bed.

William Shakespeare, *Macbeth*

Stories

When weary of the dance one reads a tale
Tho puzzled oft to spell a lengthy word
Storys though often read yet never stale
But gaining interest every time theyre heard
With morts of wonderment that neer occurred
Yet simple souls their faith it knows no stint
Things least to be believed are most preferred
All counterfiets as from truths sacred mint
Are readily believed if once put down in print

Bluebeard & all his murders dread parade
Are listened to & mourned for & the tear
Drops from the blue eye of the listening maid
Warm as it fell upon her lovers bier
None in the circle doubt of what they hear
It were a sin to doubt oer tales so true
So say the old whose wisdom all revere
& unto whom such reverence may be due
For honest good intents praise that belongs to few

John Clare, from 'St Martin's Eve'

Sometimes they would tell stories: the story of the Black Pig who kept guard over a treasure with a red key in his jaws; or the Beast of Orléans who had a man's face, bat's wings, hair reaching to the ground, two horns and two tails, one to catch and the other to kill you; and this monster had eaten a man from Rouen and left only his hat and his boots. At other times, they would launch into endless tales about wolves, the devouring wolves which ravaged Beauce for centuries. Formerly, when Beauce, which is so bare and treeless at the present time, had still a few coppices left from original forests, countless bands of wolves, impelled by hunger, used to come out in the winter to prey on the flocks. They devoured women and children, and the old people of the district could remember that in times of heavy snow the wolves would come into the towns. In Cloyes you could hear them howling on the Place Saint-Georges; in Rognes they would push their noses under the loose doors of cowsheds and sheep pens. Then, one after the other, the same old stories would be told: the miller ambushed by wolves who put them to flight by striking a match; the little girl who ran for two hours pursued by a she-wolf which ate her up when she fell down just as she reached the door of her home; and still more stories, legends of werewolves, of men changed into beasts leaping out on to the shoulders of belated passers-by or running them to death.

But what made the blood of the girls run cold as they sat round in the pale candlelight, and sent them running off to peer wildly into the darkness, was the story of the famous band of criminals from Orgères called the Roasters, whose exploits still made the district shudder with horror sixty years later. There were hundreds of them, beggars, tramps, deserters and pretended hawkers, men, women and children living from theft, murder and vice. They were descended from the old bands of organized armed bandits, who took advantage of the troubles arising out of the Revolution by systematically attacking isolated houses which they burst into by breaking down the doors with battering rams. At nightfall they would come like wolves out of the forest of Dourdan, the scrubland of La Conie, from the dens where they lurked in the woods; and as dusk fell, terror descended on the farms of Beauce, from Étampes to Châteaudun and from Chartres to Orléans. Amongst their legendary atrocities the one most frequently spoken of in Rognes was the sacking of the Millouard farm, only a score of miles away, in the canton of Orgères. On that night, their celebrated leader, Beau François, who had succeeded May Blossom, had with him his lieutenant, Red Auneau, the Big Dragoon, Breton-dry-arse, Longjumeau, One-thumb Jean and fifty more, all with blackened faces. First, they forced all the workers on the farm, the maids, the carters and the shepherd, down the cellar at bayonet-point; then they 'roasted' old Fousset the farmer, whom they had kept separate from the rest. Having stretched his feet out over the glowing embers of the fire, they set light to his beard and all the hair on his body with lighted wisps of straw; then they went back to his feet which they slashed with the point of a knife so that they would cook better. When the old man had been persuaded to reveal the whereabouts of his money, they eventually let him go and made off with an immense amount of loot; Fousset had the strength to crawl to a neighbouring house and did not die until some time later. And the tale invariably ended with the trial and execution in Chartres of the band of the Roasters who had been betrayed by One-eyed Jacques: a mass trial for which it took eighteen months to collect the evidence and in the course of which sixty-four of the accused died in prison from a plague caused by their own filth; a trial which brought one hundred and fifteen prisoners before the assize court (thirty-three of them *in absentia*), which required the jury to answer seven thousand eight hundred questions and led to twenty-three death sentences. On the night of the execution, the executioners of Chartres and Dreux came to blows underneath the blood-stained scaffold while sharing out the condemned men's effects.

Émile Zola, *The Earth*, trans. Douglas Parmée

There are not many places that I find it more agreeable to revisit when I am in an idle mood, than some places to which I have never been. For, my acquaintance with those spots is of such long standing, and has ripened into an intimacy of so affectionate a nature, that I take a particular interest in assuring myself that they are unchanged.

• • •

When I was in Dullborough one day, revisiting the associations of my childhood as recorded in previous pages of these notes, my experience in this wise was made quite inconsiderable and of no account, by the quantity of places and people – utterly impossible places and people, but none the less alarmingly real – that I found I had been introduced to by my nurse before I was six years old, and used to be forced to go back to at night without at all wanting to go. If we all knew our own minds (in a more enlarged sense than the popular acceptation of that phrase), I suspect we should find our nurses responsible for most of the dark corners we are forced to go back to, against our wills.

The first diabolical character who intruded himself on my peaceful youth (as I called to mind that day at Dullborough) was a certain Captain Murderer. This wretch must have been an offshoot of the Blue Beard family, but I had no suspicion of the consanguinity in those times. His warning name would seem to have awakened no general prejudice against him, for he was admitted into the best society and possessed immense wealth. Captain Murderer's mission was matrimony, and the gratification of a cannibal appetite with tender brides. On his marriage morning, he always caused both sides of the way to church to be planted with curious flowers; and when his bride said, 'Dear Captain Murderer, I never saw flowers like these before: what are they called?' he answered, 'They are called Garnish for house-lamb,' and laughed at his ferocious practical joke in a horrid manner, disquieting the minds of the noble bridal company, with a very sharp show of teeth, then displayed for the first time. He made love in a coach and six, and married in a coach and twelve, and all his horses were milk-white horses with one red spot on the back which he caused to be hidden by the harness. For, the spot *would* come there, though every horse was milk-white when Captain Murderer bought him. And the spot was young bride's blood. (To this terrific point I am indebted for my first personal experience of a shudder and cold beads on the forehead.) When Captain Murderer had made an end of feasting and revelry, and had dismissed the noble guests, and was alone with his wife on the day month after their marriage, it was his whimsical custom to produce a golden rolling-pin and a silver pie-board. Now, there was this special feature in the Captain's courtship, that he always asked if the young lady could make pie-crust; and if she couldn't by nature or education, she was taught. Well. When the bride saw Captain Murderer produce the golden rolling-pin and silver pie-board, she remembered this, and turned up her lace-silk sleeves to make a pie. The Captain brought out a silver pie-dish of immense capacity, and the Captain brought out flour and butter and eggs and all things needful, except the inside of the pie; of materials for the staple of the pie itself, the Captain brought out none. Then said the lovely bride, 'Dear Captain Murderer, what pie is this to be?' He replied, 'A meat pie.' Then said the lovely bride, 'Dear Captain Murderer, I see no meat.' The Captain humorously retorted, 'Look in the glass.' She looked in the glass, but still she saw no meat, and then the Captain roared with laughter, and suddenly frowning and drawing his sword, bade her roll out the crust. So she rolled out the crust, dropping large tears upon it all the time because he was so cross, and when she had lined the dish with crust and had cut the crust all ready to fit the top, the Captain called out, '*I* see the meat in the glass!' And the bride looked up at the glass, just in time to see the Captain cutting her head off; and he chopped her in pieces, and peppered her, and salted her, and put her in the pie, and sent it to the bakers, and ate it all, and picked the bones.

Captain Murderer went on in this way, prospering exceedingly, until he came to choose a bride from two twin sisters, and at first didn't know which to choose. For, though one was fair and the other dark, they were both equally beautiful. But the fair twin loved him, and the dark twin hated him, so he chose the fair one. The dark twin would have prevented the marriage if she could, but she couldn't; however, on the night before it, much suspecting Captain Murderer, she stole out and climbed his garden wall, and looked in at his window through a chink in the shutter, and saw him having his teeth filed sharp. Next day she listened all day, and heard him make his joke about the house-lamb. And that day month, he had the paste rolled out, and cut the fair twin's head off, and chopped her in pieces, and peppered her, and salted her, and put her in the pie, and sent it to the baker's, and ate it all, and picked the bones.

Now, the dark twin had had her suspicions much increased by the filing of the Captain's teeth, and again by the house-lamb joke. Putting all things together when he gave out that her sister was dead, she divined the truth, and determined to be revenged. So, she went up to Captain Murderer's house, and knocked at the knocker and pulled at the bell, and when the Captain came to the door, said: 'Dear Captain Murderer, marry me next, for I always loved you and was jealous of my sister.' The Captain took it as a compliment, and made a polite answer, and the marriage was quickly arranged. On the night before it, the bride again climbed to his window, and again saw him having his teeth filed sharp. At this sight she laughed such a terrible laugh at the chink in the shutter, that the Captain's blood curdled, and he said: 'I hope nothing has disagreed with me!' At that, she laughed again, a still more terrible laugh, and the shutter was opened and search made, but she was nimbly gone, and there was no one. Next day they went to church in a coach and twelve, and were married. And that day month, she rolled the pie-crust out, and Captain Murderer cut her head off, and chopped her in pieces, and peppered her, and salted her, and put her in the pie, and sent it to the baker's, and ate it all, and picked the bones.

But before she began to roll out the paste she had taken a deadly poison of a most awful character, distilled from toads' eyes and spiders' knees; and Captain Murderer had hardly picked her last bone, when he began to swell, and to turn blue, and to be all over spots, and to scream. And he went on swelling and turning bluer, and being more all over spots and screaming, until he reached from floor to ceiling and from wall to wall; and then, at one o'clock in the morning, he blew up with a loud explosion. At the sound of it, all the milk-white horses in the stables broke their halters and went mad, and then they galloped over everybody in Captain

Murderer's house (beginning with the family blacksmith who had filed his teeth) until the whole were dead, and then they galloped away.

Hundreds of times did I hear this legend of Captain Murderer, in my early youth, and hundreds of times was there a mental compulsion upon me in bed, to peep in at his window as the dark twin peeped, and to revisit his horrible house, and look at him in his blue and spotty and screaming stage, as he reached from floor to ceiling and from wall to wall. The young woman who brought me acquainted with Captain Murderer had a fiendish enjoyment of my terrors, and used to begin, I remember – as a sort of introductory overture – by clawing the air with both hands, and uttering a long low hollow groan. So acutely did I suffer from this ceremony in combination with this infernal Captain, that I sometimes used to plead I thought I was hardly strong enough and old enough to hear the story again just yet. But, she never spared me one word of it, and indeed commended the awful chalice to my lips as the only preservative known to science against 'The Black Cat' – a weird and glaring-eyed supernatural Tom, who was reputed to prowl about the world by night, sucking the breath of infancy, and who was endowed with a special thirst (as I was given to understand) for mine.

Charles Dickens, *The Uncommercial Traveller*

Stranglers

Bhurtote: A strangler.

Bhurtotee: The office or duty of strangler. Thugs seldom attain this rank or office till they have been on many expeditions, and acquired the requisite courage or insensibility by slow degrees. At first they are almost always shocked and frightened; but after a time they say they lose all sympathy with the victims. A Thug leader, of most polished manners and great eloquence, being asked one day in my presence by a native gentleman, whether he never felt compunction in murdering innocent people, replied with a smile, 'Does any man feel compunction in following his trade; and are not all our trades assigned us by providence.' The native gentleman said, 'How many people have you in the course of your life killed with your own hands at a rough guess?' 'I have killed none.' 'Have you not been just describing to me a number of murders?' 'Yes; but do you suppose I could have committed them. Is any man killed from man's killing? *Admee ke marne se koe murta*. Is it not the hand of God that kills him? and are we not mere instruments in the hand of God?' They are first employed as scouts; then as sextons; then as *shumseeas* or holders of hands; and lastly as *Bhurtotes*. When a man feels that he has sufficient courage and insensibility for the purpose, he solicits the oldest and most renowned Thug of the gang to make him his *cheyla*, or disciple. The Thug agrees to become his *gooroo*, or spiritual preceptor and when the gang falls in with a man of respectability but not much strength, fitted for the purpose, he tells the gooroo that he is prepared, with his permission, to try his hands upon him. While the traveller is asleep with the gang at their quarters, the gooroo takes his disciple into a neighbouring field followed by three or four old members of the gang. On reaching the spot chosen, they all face to the direction the gang intends to move, and the gooroo says, '*Oh Kalee, Kunkalee, Bhudkalee. Oh Kalee, Mahakalee, Calcutta Walee.* If it seemeth to thee fit that the traveller now at our lodging should die by the hands of this thy slave, vouchsafe us the *Thibaoo*.' If they get the auspice on the right within a certain time (half an hour), it signifies her sanction; but if they have no sign or the *dhilhaoo*, (or sign on the left) some other Thug must put the traveller to death, and the candidate for honor wait for another time.

W. H. Sleeman, General Superintendent for the suppression of Thug Associations, *Ramseeana, or A Vocabulary of the Peculiar Language Used by the Thugs*

Suicide Club

Mr Malthus looked at the Colonel curiously, and then requested him to take a seat upon his right.

'You are a new-comer,' he said, 'and wish information? You have come to the proper source. It is two years since I first visited this charming Club.'

The Colonel breathed again. If Mr Malthus had frequented the place for two years there could be little danger for the Prince in a single evening. But Geraldine was none the less astonished, and began to suspect a mystification.

'What!' cried he, 'two years! I thought – but indeed I see I have been made the subject of a pleasantry.'

'By no means,' replied Mr Malthus mildly. 'My case is peculiar. I am not, properly speaking, a suicide at all; but, as it were, an honorary member. I rarely visit the Club twice in two months. My infirmity and the kindness of the President have procured me these little immunities, for which besides I pay at an advanced rate. Even as it is my luck has been extraordinary.'

'I am afraid,' said the Colonel, 'that I must ask you to be more explicit. You must remember that I am still most imperfectly acquainted with the rules of the Club.'

'An ordinary member who comes here in search of death like yourself,' replied the paralytic, 'returns every evening until fortune favours him. He can even, if he is penniless, get board and lodging from the President: very fair, I believe, and clean, although, of course, not luxurious; that could hardly be, considering the exiguity (if I may so express myself) of the subscription. And then the President's company is a delicacy in itself.'

'Indeed!' cried Geraldine, 'he has not greatly prepossessed me.'

'Ah!' said Mr Malthus, 'you do not know the man: the drollest fellow! What stories! What cynicism! He knows life to admiration, and between ourselves, is probably the most corrupt rogue in Christendom.'

'And he also,' asked the Colonel, 'is a permanency – like yourself, if I may say so without offence?'

'Indeed, he is a permanency in a very different sense from me,' replied Mr Malthus. 'I have been graciously spared, but I must go at last. Now he never plays. He shuffles and deals for the Club, and makes the necessary arrangements. That man, my dear Mr Hammersmith, is the very soul of ingenuity. For three years he has pursued in London his useful, and, I think I may add, his artistic calling; and not so much as a whisper of suspicion has been once aroused. I believe him myself to be inspired. You doubtless remember the celebrated case, six months ago, of the gentleman who was accidentally poisoned in a chemist's shop? That was one of the least rich, one of the least racy, of his notions; but then, how simple! and how safe!'

'You astound me,' said the Colonel. 'Was that unfortunate gentleman one of the – ' He was about to say 'victims'; but bethinking himself in time, he substituted – 'members of the Club?'

In the same flash of thought it occurred to him that Mr Malthus himself had not at all spoken in the tone of one who is in love with death; and he added hurriedly:

'But I perceive I am still in the dark. You speak of shuffling and dealing; pray for what end? And since you seem rather unwilling to die than otherwise, I must own that I cannot conceive what brings you here at all.'

'You say truly that you are in the dark,' replied Mr Malthus with more animation. 'Why, my dear sir, this Club is the temple of intoxication. If my enfeebled health could support the excitement more often, you may depend upon it I should be more often here. It requires all the sense of duty engendered by a long habit of ill-health and careful regimen, to keep me from excess in this, which is, I may say, my last dissipation. I have tried them all, sir,' he went on, laying his hand on Geraldine's arm, 'all without exception, and I declare to you, upon my honour, there is not one of them that has not been grossly and untruthfully overrated. People trifle with love. Now, I deny that love is a strong passion. Fear is the strong passion; it is with fear that you must trifle, if you wish to taste the intensest joys of living. Envy me – envy me, sir,' he added with a chuckle, 'I am a coward!'

Geraldine could scarcely repress a movement of repulsion for this deplorable wretch; but he commanded himself with an effort, and continued his inquiries.

'How, sir,' he asked, 'is the excitement so artfully prolonged? and where is there any element of uncertainty?'

'I must tell you how the victim for every evening is selected,' returned Mr Malthus; 'and not only the victim, but another member, who is to be the instrument in the Club's hands, and death's high priest for that occasion.'

'Good God!' said the Colonel, 'do they then kill each other?'

'The trouble of suicide is removed in that way,' returned Malthus with a nod.

'Merciful Heavens!' ejaculated the Colonel, 'and may you – may I – may the – my friend I mean – may any of us be pitched upon this evening as the slayer of another man's body and immortal spirit? Can such things be possible among men born of women? Oh! infamy of infamies!'

He was about to rise in his horror, when he caught the Prince's eye. It was fixed upon him from across the room with a frowning and angry stare. And in a moment Geraldine recovered his composure.

'After all,' he added, 'why not? And since you say the game is interesting, *vogue la galère* – I follow the Club!'

Mr Malthus had keenly enjoyed the Colonel's amazement and disgust. He had the vanity of wickedness; and it pleased him to see another man give way to a generous movement, while he felt himself, in his entire corruption, superior to such emotions.

'You now, after your first moment of surprise,' said he, 'are in a position to appreciate the delights of our society. You can see how it combines the excitement of a gaming-table, a duel, and a Roman amphitheatre. The Pagans did well enough; I cordially admire the refinement of their minds; but it has been reserved for a Christian country to attain this extreme, this quintessence, this absolute of poignancy. You will understand how vapid are all amusements to a man who has acquired a taste for this one. The game we play,' he continued, 'is one of extreme simplicity. A full pack – but I perceive you are about to see the thing in progress. Will you lend me the help of your arm? I am unfortunately paralysed.'

Indeed, just as Mr Malthus was beginning his description, another pair of folding doors was thrown open, and the whole Club began to pass, not without some hurry, into the adjoining room. It was similar in every respect to the one from which it was entered, but somewhat differently furnished. The centre was occupied by a long green table, at which the President sat shuffling a pack of cards with great particularity. Even with the stick and the Colonel's arm, Mr Malthus walked with so much difficulty that every one was seated before this pair and the Prince, who had waited for them, entered the apartment; and in consequence, the three took seats close together at the lower end of the board.

'It is a pack of fifty-two,' whispered Mr Malthus. 'Watch for the ace of spades, which is the sign of death, and the ace of clubs, which designates the official of the night. Happy, happy young men!' he added. 'You have good eyes, and can follow the game. Alas! I cannot tell an ace from a deuce across the table.'

And he proceeded to equip himself with a second pair of spectacles.

'I must at least watch the faces,' he explained.

The Colonel rapidly informed his friend of all that he had learned from the honorary member, and of the horrible alternative that lay before them. The Prince was conscious of a deadly chill and a contraction about his heart; he swallowed with difficulty, and looked from side to side like a man in a maze.

'One bold stroke,' whispered the Colonel, 'and we may still escape.'

But the suggestion recalled the Prince's spirits.

'Silence!' said he. 'Let me see that you can play like a gentleman for any stake, however serious.'

And he looked about him, once more to all appearance at his ease, although his heart beat quickly, and he was conscious of an unpleasant heat in his bosom. The members were all very quiet and intent; every one was pale, but none so pale as Mr Malthus. His eyes protruded; his head kept nodding involuntarily upon his spine; his hands found their way, one after the other, to his mouth, where they made clutches at his tremulous and ashen lips. It was plain that the honorary member enjoyed his membership on very startling terms.

'Attention, gentlemen!' said the President.

And he began slowly dealing the cards about the table in the reverse direction, pausing until each man had shown his card. Every one hesitated; and sometimes you would see a player's finger stumble more than once before he could turn over the momentous slip of pasteboard. As the Prince's turn drew nearer, he was conscious of a growing and almost suffocating excitement; but he had somewhat of the gambler's nature, and recognized almost with astonishment that there was a degree of pleasure in his sensations. The nine of clubs fell to his lot; the three of spades was dealt to Geraldine; and the queen of hearts to Mr Malthus, who was unable to suppress a sob of relief. The young man of the cream tarts almost immediately afterwards turned over the ace of clubs, and remained frozen with horror, the card still resting on his finger; he had not come there to kill, but to be killed; and the Prince in his generous sympathy with his position almost forgot the peril that still hung over himself and his friend.

The deal was coming round again, and still Death's card had not come out. The players held their respiration, and only breathed by gasps. The Prince received another club; Geraldine had a diamond; but when Mr Malthus turned up his card a horrible noise, like that of something breaking, issued from his mouth; and he rose from his seat and sat down again, with no sign of his paralysis. It was the ace of spades. The honorary member had trifled once too often with his terrors.

Conversation broke out again almost at once. The players relaxed their rigid attitudes, and began to rise from the table and stroll back by twos and threes into the smoking-room. The President stretched his arms and yawned, like a man who has finished his day's work. But Mr Malthus sat in his place, with his head in his hands, and his hands upon the table, drunk and motionless – a thing stricken down.

The Prince and Geraldine made their escape at once. In the cold night air their horror of what they had witnessed was redoubled.

'Alas!' cried the Prince, 'to be bound by an oath in such a matter! to allow this wholesale trade in murder to be continued with profit and impunity! If I but dared to forfeit my pledge!'

'That is impossible of your Highness,' replied the Colonel, 'whose honour is the honour of Bohemia. But I dare, and may with propriety, forfeit mine.'

'Geraldine,' said the Prince, 'if your honour suffers in any of the adventures into which you follow me, not only will I never pardon you, but – what I believe will much more sensibly affect you – I should never forgive myself.'

'I receive your Highness's commands,' replied the Colonel. 'Shall we go from this accursed spot?'

'Yes,' said the Prince. 'Call a cab in Heaven's name, and let me try to forget in slumber the memory of this night's disgrace.'

But it was notable that he carefully read the name of the court before he left it.

The next morning, as soon as the Prince was stirring, Colonel Geraldine brought him a daily newspaper, with the following paragraph marked:

MELANCHOLY ACCIDENT

This morning, about two o'clock, Mr Bartholomew Malthus, of 16 Chepstow Place, Westbourne Grove, on his way home from a party at a friend's house, fell over the upper parapet in Trafalgar Square, fracturing his skull and breaking a leg and an arm. Death was instantaneous. Mr Malthus, accompanied by a friend, was engaged in looking for a cab at the time of the unfortunate occurrence. As Mr Malthus was paralytic, it is thought that his fall may have been occasioned by another seizure. The unhappy gentleman was well known in the most respectable circles, and his loss will be widely and deeply deplored.

'If ever a soul went straight to hell,' said Geraldine solemnly, 'it was that paralytic man's.'

The Prince buried his face in his hands and remained silent.

'I am almost rejoiced,' continued the Colonel, 'to know that he is dead. But for our young man of the cream tarts I confess my heart bleeds.'

'Geraldine,' said the Prince, raising his face, 'that unhappy lad was last night as innocent as you and I, and this morning the guilt of blood is on his soul. When I think of the President, my heart grows sick within me. I do not know how it shall be done, but I shall have that scoundrel at my mercy as there is a God in Heaven. What an experience, what a lesson, was that game of cards!'

'One,' said the Colonel, 'never to be repeated.'

The Prince remained so long without replying that Geraldine grew alarmed.

'You cannot mean to return,' he said. 'You have suffered too much and seen too much horror already. The duties of your high position forbid the repetition of the hazard.'

'There is much in what you say,' replied Prince Florizel, 'and I am not altogether pleased with my own determination. Alas! in the clothes of the greatest potentate, what is there but a man? I never felt my weakness more acutely than now, Geraldine, but it is stronger than I. Can I cease to interest myself in the fortunes of the unhappy young man who supped with us some hours ago? Can I leave the President to follow his nefarious career unwatched? Can I begin an adventure so entrancing, and not follow it to an end? No, Geraldine: you ask of the Prince more than the man is able to perform. Tonight, once more, we take our places at the table of the Suicide Club.'

Robert Louis Stevenson, 'The Suicide Club'

Symmetry

Gentlemen, you will please wear a tie
while peeing. And in the criss-cross corridors
you will pass without touching,
as you journey to and from the dining-room
under the portraits of Prime Ministers
(except for the woman). You will sit
equally spaced apart, four facing four,
with one (each of you in turn) facing me
down the long, driftwood table.
While eating, you needn't call me Sir.

Two legs of lamb must be carved
simultaneously. Decide among yourselves.
And eat as much or as little as you like
but eat the same. Your weights
must match at the end as at the start;
must be half of mine. And no glass
can go empty of blood-red wine
till the clock-hands cross at midnight
when I will retire. Leaving nine.
Gentlemen, you will please set that right.

Matthew Sweeney, 'Symmetry'

T

Taboo

Since taboos are mainly expressed in prohibitions, the underlying presence of a *positive* current of desire may occur to us as something quite obvious and calling for no lengthy proofs based on the analogy of the neuroses. For, after all, there is no need to prohibit something that no one desires to do, and a thing that is forbidden with the greatest emphasis must be a thing that is desired. If we were to apply this plausible thesis to our primitive peoples, we should be led to the conclusion that some of their strongest temptations were to kill their kings and priests, to commit incest, to maltreat the dead, and so on – which seems scarcely probable. And we should be met with the most positive contradiction if we were to apply the same thesis to instances in which we ourselves seem most clearly to hear the voice of conscience. We should maintain with the most absolute certainty that we feel not the slightest temptation to violate any of these prohibitions – the commandment to 'do no murder', for instance – and that we feel nothing but horror at the notion of violating them.

If, however, we were to admit the claims thus asserted by our conscience, it would follow, on the one hand, that these prohibitions would be superfluous – both taboo and our own moral prohibitions – and, on the other hand, the fact of conscience would remain unexplained and no place would be left for the relations between conscience, taboo and neurosis. In other words, we should be back in the state of knowledge we were in before we approached the problem from the psychoanalytic angle.

Suppose, on the other hand, that we were to take into account the finding arrived at by psychoanalysis from the dreams of normal people, to the effect that we ourselves are subject, more strongly and more often that we suspect, to a temptation to kill someone and that that temptation produces psychical effects even though it remains out of sight of our consciousness. Suppose, again, that we were to recognize the compulsive observances of certain neurotics as being guarantees against an intensified impulse to murder or as being self-punishments on account of it. In that case we should have to attach still greater importance to our thesis that where there is a prohibition there must be an underlying desire. We should have to suppose that the desire to murder is actually present in the unconscious and that neither taboos nor moral prohibitions are psychologically superfluous but that on the contrary they are explained and justified by the existence of an ambivalent attitude towards the impulse to murder.

Sigmund Freud, *Totem and Taboo*, trans. James Strachey

Terrorism

I had come to the edge of the water,
soothed by just looking, idling over it
as if it were a clear barometer

or a mirror, when his reflection
did not appear but I sensed a presence
entering into my concentration

on not being concentrated as he spoke
my name. And though I was reluctant
I turned to meet his face and the shock

is still in me at what I saw. His brow
was blown open above the eye and blood
had dried on his neck and cheek. 'Easy now,'

he said, 'it's only me. You've seen men as raw
after a football match . . . What time it was
when I was wakened up I still don't know

but I heard this knocking, knocking, and it
scared me, like the phone in the small hours,
so I had the sense not to put on the light

but looked out from behind the curtain.
I saw two customers on the doorstep
and an old landrover with the doors open

parked on the street so I let the curtain drop;
but they must have been waiting for it to move
for they shouted to come down into the shop.

She started to cry then and roll round the bed,
lamenting and lamenting to herself,
not even asking who it was. "Is your head

astray, or what's come over you?" I roared, more
to bring myself to my senses
than out of any real anger at her

for the knocking shook me, the way they kept it up,
and her whingeing and half-screeching made it worse.
All the time they were shouting, "Shop!

Shop!" so I pulled on my shoes and a sportscoat
and went back to the window and called out,
"What do you want? Could you quieten the racket

or I'll not come down at all." "There's a child not well.
Open up and see what you have got – pills
or a powder or something in a bottle,"

one of them said. He stepped back off the footpath
so I could see his face in the street lamp
and when the other moved I knew them both.

But bad and all as the knocking was, the quiet
hit me worse. She was quiet herself now,
lying dead still, whispering to watch out.

At the bedroom door I switched on the light.
"It's odd they didn't look for a chemist.
Who are they anyway at this time of the night?"

she asked me, with the eyes standing in her head.
"I know them to see," I said, but something
made me reach and squeeze her hand across the bed

before I went downstairs into the aisle
of the shop. I stood there, going weak
in the legs. I remember the stale smell

of cooked meat or something coming through
as I went to open up. From then on
you know as much about it as I do.'

'Did they say nothing?' 'Nothing. What would they say?'
'Were they in uniform? Not masked in any way?'
'They were barefaced as they would be in the day,

shites thinking they were the be-all and the end-all.'
'Not that it is any consolation,
but they were caught,' I told him, 'and got jail.'

Big-limbed, decent, open-faced, he stood
forgetful of everything now except
whatever was welling up in his spoiled head,

beginning to smile. 'You've put on weight
since you did your courting in that big Austin
you got the loan of on a Sunday night.'

Through life and death he had hardly aged.
There always was an athlete's cleanliness
shining off him and except for the ravaged

forehead and the blood, he was still that same
rangy midfielder in a blue jersey
and starched pants, the one stylist on the team,

the perfect, clean, unthinkable victim.
'Forgive the way I have lived indifferent –
forgive my timid circumspect involvement,'

I surprised myself by saying. 'Forgive
my eye,' he said, 'all that's above my head.'
And then a stun of pain seemed to go through him

and he trembled like a heatwave and faded.

Seamus Heaney, *Station Island*

Now take these golf balls, scattered all around the place, which since
The reproduction's blurred, you'd easily misconstrue as ping-pong –
You can't make out the dimples. But they're different as chalk and
 cheese:
Ever get hit by a golf ball? You'd know all about it. And perhaps
The golf club in the bottom corner is no give-away. People have been
 known
To mistake it for a gun. And the disembodied plus-fours

Might be army surplus. No, all these things are dangerous enough,
According to whose rules you play. Which is maybe why they're put there,
Where you'd least expect them, floating against the façade of the Europa.

Hotel, that is. You know it? Looks as if it's taken from a photograph,
Down to the missing *E* of the logo, the broken windows, which they only got
Around to fixing last week. Things drift off like that, or people drift in.
Like Treacy, who it's all about, according to the guy who painted it.
This splash of red here: not blood, but a port-wine stain or strawberry mark
That Treacy carried all his life, just here, above the wrist-watch. Any time
You saw him sitting, he would have his right hand over it. Like this.
Too easily recognised, he didn't like. This is where the black gloves
Come in, gripping the revolving foyer doors. Or maybe one of them
Is raised, like saying *Power* – to the people, to himself, whatever.

Billiard balls? Well, maybe. Certainly these random scratches on the canvas
Suggest the chalk-marks on a green baize, a faded diagram from which
You'd try to piece together what the action was. Like trying to account
For Treacy's movements. Though on the night in question, according to the barman
In The Beaten Docket, he'd staggered in from some win on the horses,
Slaps a tenner on the counter, and orders a 'Blue Angel'. Blue what?
Says the barman. Angel, Treacy says, Blue Bols, vodka, ice, a drop of sugar.
Oh, and top it up with whipped cream. I say this just to show the sort
Of him, like someone who a year or two ago would not have known cocktail
From a hen's arse. You're sure, the barman says, you wouldn't like a straw?

The staircase is important. The zig-zag is like taking one step forward.
Two steps back. For who would take the stairs up thirteen floors, when
He could take the lift? The reason why, the power had gone that night.
So only one way in, and one way out. As sure as meeting your own shadow.

This, I think, is what the mirror represents. Like, everybody knew
about the split,
And what side Treacy ended up on. Of course, the detail's lost;
You have to see it like it is, original. The colours, the dimensions.
Even the frame, like someone spying through binoculars, is saying
something:
I'm watching you; but you, you can't see me. Ping-pong. Yin-yang.

So here is Treacy, at the wrong end of the telescope, diminishing.
He was seen in this bar, that bar. Like what I'm saying is, that anybody
Might have fingered him. So the man on the thirteenth floor sits pat.
He draws back the curtain. He stares through the kaleidoscope of snow
And sees what's coming next. Treacy's footsteps. Game, set and
match.
They found him in the empty room. The face was blown off. They
rolled down
One black glove. A Rorschach blot. The Red Hand, as he called
himself.
Me? I knew him like a brother. Once. But then our lives grew parallel,
if
Parallel is never meeting. He started dressing up and talking down.
What
He would and wouldn't do. And people don't go shooting off their
mouths like that.

Ciaran Carson, 'Narrative in Black and White'

Si señor, sure we har claiming the
bomb as Glorious Blow by
Forces of Liberate Dark
Dictate Oppression. Too long

far have we, fathers and hrandfathers
forced to Slavery lifes hwich
Army of Liberate fight
struggles till all mens are dead!

Down with the generalísimo!
(not the present or last hwon,
only the hwon pefore last),
Viva la Muerte! señor,

Viva el excelentísimo
Señor conde de Torre-
    gamberro! Yes sirs my friend,
    what is the matter that some

dies for the Cause of the hwons that is
thinking right in this matters?
    This she's Political's War.
    Sure what are some person lifes?

We not Guerrillas amigo but
Counter-Anti-Guerrilla
    them was our Leaders but now –
    those is our Enemy, si,

ow you say por favor now they has
showed False Ideologics.
    Terrorist Actions too bad;
    this why we take such Campaigns!

This very Positive Actions she
may have kill some who have no
    doings with Rebels but so?
    Bombs she not go off for fun.

Don't say amigo you not with the
understandings of why we
    fights in montañas of South?
    This are the struggles to death!

OK so 20 am dead and some
shrapnels goes to some peoples –
    we har of People's own blood!
    This is of why we shall fight!

Last bomb was not our bomb *that* was bomb
blown hwen Traitor who carries
    gets it hexplosure too soon
    killing himself and some mans.

Somehow you get mix up, señor, you
see we Neutral in all thing
    this hwy the reasons hwe fights!
    Freedoms to Govermans Farce!

Same Costa Rica but also with
Nicaraguan Border!
  Now you mus hunderstand well
  which why this bombs must hexplode.

Peter Reading, *Going On*

Theatre

As to women, he had once already been drawn headlong by impetuous folly, which he meant to be final, since marriage at some distant period would of course not be impetuous. For those who want to be acquainted with Lydgate it will be good to know what was that case of impetuous folly, for it may stand as an example of the fitful swerving of passion to which he was prone, together with the chivalrous kindness which helped to make him morally lovable. The story can be told without many words. It happened when he was studying in Paris, and just at the time when, over and above his other work, he was occupied with some galvanic experiments. One evening, tired with his experimenting, and not being able to elicit the facts he needed, he left his frogs and rabbits to some repose under their trying and mysterious dispensation of unexplained shocks, and went to finish his evening at the theatre of the Porte Saint Martin, where there was a melodrama which he had already seen several times; attracted, not by the ingenious work of the collaborating authors, but by an actress whose part it was to stab her lover, mistaking him for the evil-designing duke of the piece. Lydgate was in love with this actress, as a man is in love with a woman whom he never expects to speak to. She was a Provençale, with dark eyes, a Greek profile, and rounded majestic form, having that sort of beauty which carries a sweet matronliness even in youth, and her voice was a soft cooing. She had but lately come to Paris, and bore a virtuous reputation, her husband acting with her as the unfortunate lover. It was her acting which was 'no better than it should be', but the public was satisfied. Lydgate's only relaxation now was to go and look at this woman, just as he might have thrown himself under the breath of the sweet south on a bank of violets for a while, without prejudice to his galvanism, to which he would presently return. But this evening the old drama had a new catastrophe. At the moment when the heroine was to act the stabbing of her lover, and he was to fall gracefully, the wife veritably stabbed her husband, who fell as death willed. A wild shriek pierced the house, and the Provençale fell swooning: a shriek and a swoon were demanded by the play, but the swooning too was real this time. Lydgate leaped and climbed, he hardly knew how, on to the stage, and was active in help, making the acquaintance of his heroine by finding a contusion on her head and lifting her gently in his arms. Paris rang with the story of this death: was it a murder? Some of the actress's warmest admirers were inclined to believe in her guilt, and liked her the better for it (such was the taste of those times); but Lydgate was not one of these. He vehemently contended for her innocence, and the remote impersonal passion for her beauty which he had felt before, had passed now into personal devotion, and tender thought of her lot. The notion of murder was absurd; no motive was discoverable, the young couple being understood to dote on each other; and it was not unprecedented that an accidental slip of the foot should have brought these grave consequences. The legal investigation ended in Madame Laure's release. Lydgate by this time had had many interviews with her, and found her more and more adorable. She talked little; but that was an additional charm. She was melancholy, and seemed grateful; her presence was enough, like that of the evening light. Lydgate was madly anxious about her affection, and jealous lest any other man than himself should win it and ask her to marry him. But instead of re-opening her engagement at the Porte Saint Martin, where she would have been all the more popular for the fatal episode, she left Paris without warning, forsaking her little court of admirers. Perhaps no one carried inquiry far except Lydgate, who felt that all science had come to a stand-still while he imagined the unhappy Laure, stricken by ever-wandering sorrow, herself wandering, and finding no faithful comforter. Hidden actresses, however, are not so difficult to find as some other hidden facts, and it was not long before Lydgate gathered indications that Laure had taken the route to Lyons. He found her at last acting with great success at Avignon under the same name, looking more majestic than ever as a forsaken wife carrying her child in her arms. He spoke to her after the play, was received with the usual quietude which seemed to him beautiful as clear depths of water, and obtained leave to visit her the next day; when he was bent on telling her that he adored her, and on asking her to marry him. He knew that this was like the sudden impulse of a madman – incongruous even with his habitual foibles. No matter! It was the one thing which he was resolved to do. He had two selves within him apparently, and they must learn to accommodate each other and bear reciprocal impediments. Strange, that some of us, with quick alternate vision, see beyond our infatuations, and even while we rave on the heights, behold the wide plain where our persistent self pauses and awaits us.

To have approached Laure with any suit that was not reverentially tender would have been simply a contradition of his whole feeling towards her.

'You have come all the way from Paris to find me?' she said to him the next day, sitting before him with folded arms, and looking at him with eyes that seemed to wonder as an untamed ruminating animal wonders. 'Are all Englishmen like that?'

'I came because I could not live without trying to see you. You are lonely; I love you; I want you to consent to be my wife: I will wait, but I want you to promise that you will marry me – no one else.'

Laure looked at him in silence with a melancholy radiance from under her grand eyelids, until he was full of rapturous certainty, and knelt close to her knees.

'I will tell you something,' she said, in her cooing way, keeping her arms folded. 'My foot really slipped.'

'I know, I know,' said Lydgate deprecatingly. 'It was a fatal accident – a dreadful stroke of calamity that bound me to you the more.'

Again Laure paused a little and then said, slowly, '*I meant to do it.*'

Lydgate, strong man as he was, turned pale and trembled: moments seemed to pass before he rose and stood at a distance from her.

'There was a secret, then,' he said at last, even vehemently. 'He was brutal to you: you hated him.'

'No! he wearied me; he was too fond: he would live in Paris, and not in my country; that was not agreeable to me.'

'Great God!' said Lydgate, in a groan of horror. 'And you planned to murder him?'

'I did not plan: it came to me in the play – *I meant to do it.*'

Lydgate stood mute, and unconsciously pressed his hat on while he looked at her. He saw this woman – the first to whom he had given his young adoration – amid the throng of stupid criminals.

'You are a good young man,' she said. 'But I do not like husbands. I will never have another.'

George Eliot, *Middlemarch*

I entered with a torch before me
And cast my shadow on the backcloth
Momentarily: a handful of words,
One bullet with my initials on it –
And that got stuck in a property tree.

I would have caught it between my teeth
Or, a true professional, stood still
While the two poetic murderers
Pinned my silhouette to history
In a shower of accurate daggers.

But as any illusionist might
Unfasten the big sack of darkness,
The ropes and handcuffs, and emerge
Smoking a nonchalant cigarette,
I escaped – only to lose myself.

It took me a lifetime to explore
The dusty warren beneath the stage
With its trapdoor opening on to
All that had happened above my head
Like noises-off or distant weather.

In the empty auditorium I bowed
To one preoccupied caretaker
And, without removing my make-up,
Hurried back to the digs where Banquo
Sat up late with a hole in his head.

Michael Longley, 'Fleance'

Towel

Golubev drowsed off and awoke when someone's hand pulled the blanket from his face. (Golubev always slept camp fashion, covering his head, attempting above all to keep it warm and to protect it.) A very pretty head with a small mustache and hair cut square in back was suspended above his own. In a word, the head was not at all the head of a convict, and when Golubev opened his eyes, his first thought was that this was some sort of recollection of yogis or a dream – perhaps a nightmare, perhaps not.

'Not an honest crook, not a human being in the whole place,' the man wheezed in a disappointed fashion and covered Golubev's face again with the blanket.

But Golubev pulled down the blanket with feeble fingers and looked at the man. The man knew Golubev and Golubev knew him. There was no mistaking it. But he mustn't rush, rush to recognize him. He had to remember. Remember everything. And Golubev remembered. The man with the hair cut square in back was . . . Now the man would take off his shirt, and Golubev would see a cluster of intertwining snakes on his chest . . . The man turned around, and the cluster of intertwining snakes appeared before Golubev's eyes. It was Kononenko, a criminal who had been in the same transit prison with Golubev several months earlier. A murderer with multiple sentences, he played a prominent role among the camp criminals and had been 'braking' for several years in pretrial prisons. As soon as he was about to be sent off to a forced-labor camp, he would kill someone in the transit prison. He didn't care whom he killed as long as it was not a fellow criminal. He strangled his victims with a towel. A towel, a regulation-issue towel was his favorite murder instrument, his 'authorial style'. They would arrest him, start up a new case, try him again, and add a new twenty-five-year term to the hundreds of years he already had to serve. After the trial Kononenko would try to be hospitalized to 'rest up', and then he would kill again. And everything would begin from the beginning. At that time, execution of common criminals had been abolished. Only 'enemies of the people' convicted under Article 58 could be shot.

'Kononenko's in the hospital now,' Golubev thought calmly, and every cell in his body sang joyously, fearing nothing and confident of success. Kononenko's in the hospital now. He's passing through his hospital 'cycle' – one of the sinister phases of his metamorphoses. Tomorrow, or perhaps the day after tomorrow, Kononenko's program would demand the usual victim. Perhaps all Golubev's efforts had been in vain – the operation, the fearful straining of the will? Now he, Golubev, would be strangled by Kononenko as his latest victim. Perhaps it was a mistake to evade being sent to a hard-labor camp where they gave you a striped uniform and affixed a six-digit number to your back like an ace of diamonds? But at least you don't get beaten there, and there aren't a lot of Kononenkos running around.

Golubev's bed was under the window. Opposite him lay Kononenko. Next to the door, his feet almost touching Kononenko's, lay a third man, and Golubev could see his face well without having to turn his body. Golubev knew this patient too. It was Podosenov, an eternal resident of the hospital.

The door opened, and the orderly came in with medicine.

'Kazakov!' he shouted.

'Here,' shouted Kononenko, getting up.

'There's a note for you.' The orderly handed him a folded piece of paper.

'Kazakov?' The name pulsed through Golubev's mind. 'He's Kononenko, not Kazakov.' Suddenly Golubev comprehended the situation, and a cold sweat formed on his body.

It was much worse than he had thought. None of the three was in error. It was Kononenko under another's name, Kazakov's name and with Kazakov's crimes, and he had been sent to the hospital as a 'stand-in'. This was even worse, even more dangerous. If Kononenko was Kononenko, Golubev might or might not be his victim. In such a case there was an element of chance, of choice, the opportunity to be saved. But if Kononenko was Kazakov, then there was no chance for Golubev. If Kononenko nursed only the slightest suspicion that Golubev had recognized him, Golubev would die.

'Have you met me before? Why do you keep staring at me like a python at a rabbit? Or maybe like a rabbit at a python? How do you educated people say it?'

Kononenko sat on the stool before Golubev's bed, shredding the note with his fingers and scattering the fragments on Golubev's blanket.

'No, I never laid eyes on you before.' Golubev's face was colorless, and his voice hoarse.

'It's a good thing too,' said Kononenko, taking a towel from the nail driven in the wall above the bed and shaking the towel before Golubev's face. 'I was going to strangle this "doctor" yesterday.' He nodded in the direction of Podosenov whose face was a picture of infinite horror. 'Look what the bastard is doing,' Kononenko said cheerfully, pointing with the towel in the direction of Podosenov. 'See the jar under his cot? He's mixing his own blood with his piss . . . He scratches his finger and drips in a little blood. Knows what he's doing. No worse than any doctor. And the lab analysis shows he has blood in his urine. Our "doctor" stays in the hospital. Tell me, is a man like that worthy to live in this world?'

'I don't know.'

'You don't know? Yes you do. But yesterday they brought you in. We were together in the transit prison, right? Before my last trial. Then I went under the name of Kononenko.'

'I never saw you before,' said Golubev.

'Yes you did. That's when I decided. Better I do you in than the "doctor". It's not his fault.' Kononenko pointed at Podosenov, whose circulation was slowly, very slowly returning to normal. 'It's not his fault. He's only saving his own skin. Just like you or me . . .'

Varlem Shalamov, 'The Criminal World', trans. John Glad

Tragedy

ALCMAEON CHORUS

CHORUS: O suitably attired in leather boots
Head of a traveller, wherefore seeking whom
Whence by what way how purposed art thou come
To this well-nightingaled vicinity?
My object in inquiring is to know.
But if you happen to be deaf and dumb
And do not understand a word I say,
Nod with your hand to signify as much.
ALCMAEON: I journeyed hither a Boeotian road.
CHORUS: Sailing on horseback or with feet for oars?
ALCMAEON: Plying by turns my partnership of legs.
CHORUS: Beneath a shining or a rainy Zeus?
ALCMAEON: Mud's sister, not himself, adorns my shoes.
CHORUS: To learn your name would not displease me much.
ALCMAEON: Not all that men desire do they obtain.
CHORUS: Might I then hear at what your presence shoots?
ALCMAEON: A shepherd's questioned mouth informed me that –
CHORUS: What? for I know not yet what you will say.
ALCMAEON: Nor will you ever, if you interrupt.
CHORUS: Proceed, and I will hold my speechless tongue.
ALCMAEON: – This house was Eriphyla's, no one's else.
CHORUS: Nor did he shame his throat with hateful lies.
ALCMAEON: May I then enter, passing through the door?
CHORUS: Go, chase into the house a lucky foot.
And, O my son, be, on the one hand, good,
And do not, on the other hand, be bad;
For that is very much the safest plan.
ALCMAEON: I go into the house with heels and speed.

Strophe

CHORUS: In speculation
I would not willingly acquire a name
For ill-digested thought,
But after pondering much
To this conclusion I at last have come:
Life is uncertain.
This truth I have written deep

In my reflective midriff
On tablets not of wax,
Nor with a pen did I inscribe it there
For many reasons: *Life*, I say, *is not*
A stranger to uncertainty.
Not from the flight of omen-yelling fowls
This fact did I discover,
Nor did the Delphic tripod bark it out,
Nor yet Dodona.
Its native ingenuity sufficed
My self-taught diaphragm.

Why should I mention *Antistrophe*
The Inachean daughter, loved of Zeus?
Her whom of old the gods,
More provident than kind,
Provided with four hoofs, two horns, one tail,
A gift not asked for,
And sent her forth to learn
The unfamiliar science
Of how to chew the cud.
She therefore, all above the Argive fields,
Went cropping pale green grass and nettle-tops,
Nor did they disagree with her.
Yet, howsoe'er nutritious, such repasts
I do not hanker after.
Never may Cypris for her seat select
My dappled liver!
Why should I mention Io? Why indeed?
I have no notion why.

But now does my boding heart *Epode*
Unhired, unaccompanied, sing
A strain not meet for the dance.
Yea, even the palace appears
To my yoke of circular eyes
(The right, nor omit I the left)
Like a slaughterhouse, so to speak,
Garnished with woolly deaths
And many shipwrecks of cows.

I therefore in a Cissian strain lament,
And to the rapid,
Loud, linen-tattering thumps upon my chest
Resounds in concert
The battering of my unlucky head.

ERIPHYLA (*within*): O, I am smitten with a hatchet's jaw;
And that in deed and not in word alone.
CHORUS: I thought I heard a sound within the house
Unlike the voice of one that jumps for joy.
ERIPHYLA: He splits my skull, not in a friendly way,
Once more: he purposes to kill me dead.
CHORUS: I would not be reputed rash, but yet
I doubt if all be gay within the house.
ERIPHYLA: O! O! another stroke! That makes the third.
He stabs me to the heart against my wish.
CHORUS: If that be so, thy state of health is poor;
But thine arithmetic is quite correct.

A. E. Housman, 'Fragment of a Greek Tragedy'

Trois

So I sit here, in a comfortable chair, waiting
for the three bangs on the head with a wooden mallet
that will auction me, as it were, to Eternity.
I wear my long nightcap (nearly a bottle of whisky)
each night – and, later, a conventional Counsel
will call me a *mari complaisant*, something not very nice.
But really I neither know nor care what they get up to.
I was successful, and now I'm very depressed.

We get on well enough, with friendliness.
The times are bad (the times are always bad),
I sleep downstairs. We drink a bit – that's true.
I'm 67, she's 38, and he's 18.
These are all dangerous ages. Hypocrites in wigs
will make us ogres, who prove the power of love.

Gavin Ewart, 'Sonnet: At the Villa Madeira'

He rides his 1,000 cc vaulting horse hell for leather
to the waxworks, and buys her a souvenir
– geraniums, rooting thickly in skullpowder.
He will smear all the album photographs
with a deadly fume. And the conjuror?
He will deceive him into eating fireworks
at an intimate supper – just the three of them –
and taunt him, minutes before they explode,
while his lungs burst and his face blackens.

She watches a death tumbling through the saltcellar,
the conjuror's arms tight at her naked waist;
she whispers lullabies to his enchantments,
their discreet trespass void of symbolic dreams.
She has poisoned his visor, and in the saltcellar
watches a rider's hands fly from his handlebars
at a hundred and twenty. 'The future's secure,'
murmurs the conjuror, as florid blooms settle
over the limp corpse strewn on the roadway.
The salt grains turn sepia like old photographs.

John Gohorry, 'Jacobean'

Two

We're not together any more.
After Bobby Baxter followed us home,
drank our pop and ate our mini pork pies
(he had five) our whole life

changed. We kept him in our room
upstairs; taught him our special tongue,
watched him flash up on television.
Missing three days, four days, six, seven.

On the last day at ninety degrees fahrenheit,
Robert James Baxter looked out our high window
and waved. He had been warned. Bad Bobby.
And some ugly nosy Parker looked

up, some pain-in-the-neck village golfer.
Put Put Put. 999. A hole in one.
Next thing: the policemen at our door;
our mum there in her brassiere,

the loose language of gin, opening
and closing her mouth; her eyes narrow
and fierce as a bird's; a seagull's fury,
calling us down, calling us down,

Hannah and Helen. Never Helen and Hannah,
we dressed in the same black patent leather
shoes, shining like mirrors. Our checked
gingham dress, its pink and green square.

Our jet black hair parted in the same centre;
our east-coast identical accents, *wellspoken*.
The village plodder held the picture in the air.
'Have you seen this boy?'

'No Sir.' We said together. Pause. 'No Sir.'
Big boys in blue searched our room,
but Bobby Baxter, beautiful Bobby Baxter,
wasn't found till five days later.

Jackie Kay, 'Pork Pies'

'You think people should just do as they like.'

'I think they always do. But I should like them to like the purely individual thing in themselves, which makes them act in singleness. And they only like to do the collective thing.'

'And I,' said Gerald grimly, 'shouldn't like to be in a world of people who acted individually and spontaneously, as you call it. – We should have everybody cutting everybody's else's throat in five minutes.'

'That means *you* would like to be cutting everybody's throat,' said Birkin.

'How does that follow?' asked Gerald crossly.

'No man,' said Birkin, 'cuts another man's throat unless he wants to cut it, and unless the other man wants it cut. This is a complete truth. It takes two people to make a murder: a murderer and a murderee. And a murderee is a man who is murderable. And a man who is murderable is a man who in a profound, if hidden lust, desires to be murdered.'

'Sometimes you talk pure nonsense,' said Gerald to Birkin. 'As a matter of fact, none of us wants our throat cut, and most other people would like to cut it for us – some time or other – '

'It's a nasty view of things, Gerald,' said Birkin, 'and no wonder you are afraid of yourself and your own unhappiness.'

'How am I afraid of myself?' said Gerald; 'and I don't think I am unhappy.'

'You no doubt have a lurking desire to have your gizzard slit, and imagine every man has his knife up his sleeve for you,' Birkin said.

'How do you make that out?' said Gerald.

'From you,' said Birkin.

D. H. Lawrence, *Women in Love*

Every fear is a desire. Every desire is fear.
The cigarettes are burning under the trees
Where the Staffordshire murderers wait for their accomplices
And victims. Every victim is an accomplice.

It takes a lifetime to stroll to the carpark
Stopping at the footbridge for reassurance,
Looking down at the street, observing
(With one eye) the mallard's diagonal progress backwards.

You could cut and run, now. It is not too late.
But your fear is like a long-case clock
In the last whirring second before the hour,
The hammer drawn back, the heart ready to chime.

Fear turns the ignition. The van is unlocked.
You may learn now what you ought to know:
That every journey begins with a death,
That the suicide travels alone, that the murderer needs company.

And the Staffordshire murderers, nervous though they are,
Are masters of the conciliatory smile.
A cigarette? A tablet in a tin?
Would you care for a boiled sweet from the famous poisoner

Of Rugely? These are his own brand.
He has never had any complaints.

He speaks of his victims as a sexual braggart
With a tradesman's emphasis on the word 'satisfaction'.

You are flattered as never before. He appreciates
So much, the little things – you willingness for instance
To bequeath your body at once to his experiments.
He sees the point of you as no one else does.

Large parts of Staffordshire have been undermined.
The trees are in it up to their necks. Fish
Nest in their branches. In one of the Five Towns
An ornamental pond disappeared overnight

Dragging the ducks down with it, down to the old seams
With a sound as of a gigantic bath running out,
Which is in turn the sound of ducks in distress.
Thus History murders mallards, while we hear nothing

Or what we hear we do not understand.
It is heard as the tramp's rage in the crowded precinct:
'Woe to the bloody city of Lichfield.'
It is lost in the enthusiasm of the windows

From which we are offered on the easiest terms
Five times over in colour and once in monochrome
The first reprisals after the drill-sergeant's coup.
How speedily the murder detail makes its way

Along the green beach, past the pink breakers,
And binds the whole cabinet to the oil-drums,
Where death is a preoccupied tossing of the head,
Where no decorative cloud lingers at the gun's mouth.

At the Dame's School dust gathers on the highwayman,
On Sankey and Moody, Wesley and Fox,
On the snoring churchwarden, on Palmer the Poisoner
And Palmer's house and Stanfield Hall.

The brilliant moss has been chipped from the Red Barn.
They say that Cromwell played ping-pong with the cathedral.
We train roses over the arches. In the Minster Pool
Crayfish live under carved stones. Every spring

The rats pick off the young mallards and
The good weather brings out the murderers
By the Floral Clock, by the footbridge,
The pottery murderers in jackets of prussian blue.

'Alack, George, where are thy shoes?'
He lifted up his head and espied the three
Steeple-house spires, and they struck at his life.
And he went by his eye over hedge and ditch

And no one laid hands on him, and he went
Thus crying through the streets, where there seemed
To be a channel of blood running through the streets,
And the market-place appeared like a pool of blood.

For this field of corpses was Lichfield
Where a thousand Christian Britons fell
In Diocletian's day, and 'much could I write
Of the sense that I had of the blood – '

That winter Friday. Today it is hot.
The cowparsley is so high that the van cannot be seen
From the road. The bubbles rise in the warm canal.
Below the lock-gates you can hear mallards.

A coot hurries along the tow-path, like a Queen's Messenger.
On the heli-pad, an arrival in blue livery
Sends the water-boatmen off on urgent business.
News of a defeat. Keep calm. The cathedral chimes.

The house by the bridge is the house in your dream.
It stares through new frames, unwonted spectacles,
And the paint, you can tell, has been weeping.
In the yard, five striped oil-drums. Flowers in a tyre.

This is where the murderer works. But it is Sunday.
Tomorrow's bank holiday will allow the bricks to set.
You see? he has thought of everything. He shows you
The snug little cavity he calls 'your future home'.

And 'Do you know,' he remarks, 'I have been counting my victims.
Nine hundred and ninety nine, the Number of the Beast!
That makes you . . .' But he sees he has overstepped the mark:
'I'm sorry, but you cannot seriously have thought you were the first?'

A thousand preachers, a thousand poisoners,
A thousand martyrs, a thousand murderers –
Surely these preachers are poisoners, these martyrs murderers?
Surely this is all a gigantic mistake?

But there has been no mistake. God and the weather are glorious.
You have come as an anchorite to kneel at your funeral.
Kneel then and pray. The blade flashes a smile.
This is your new life. This murder is yours.

James Fenton, 'A Staffordshire Murderer'

U

Uncommon

'You've just come back from Adelaide's funeral, haven't you?' said Sir Lulworth to his nephew; 'I suppose it was very like most other funerals?'

'I'll tell you all about it at lunch', said Egbert.

'You'll do nothing of the sort. It wouldn't be respectful either to your great-aunt's memory or to the lunch. We begin with Spanish olives, then a borsch, then more olives and a bird of some kind, and a rather enticing Rhenish wine, not at all expensive as wines go in this country, but still quite laudable in its way. Now there's absolutely nothing in that menu that harmonizes in the least with the subject of your great-aunt Adelaide or her funeral. She was a charming woman, and quite as intelligent as she had any need to be, but somehow she always reminded me of an English cook's idea of a Madras curry.'

'She used to say you were frivolous,' said Egbert. Something in his tone suggested that he rather endorsed the verdict.

'I believe I once considerably scandalized her by declaring that clear soup was a more important factor in life than a clear conscience. She had very little sense of proportion. By the way, she made you her principal heir, didn't she?'

'Yes,' said Egbert, 'and executor as well. It's in that connection that I particularly want to speak to you.'

'Business is not my strong point at any time,' said Sir Lulworth, 'and certainly not when we're on the immediate threshold of lunch.'

'It isn't exactly business,' explained Egbert, as he followed his uncle into the dining-room. 'It's something rather serious. Very serious.'

'Then we can't possibly speak about it now,' said Sir Lulworth; 'no one could talk seriously, during a borsch. A beautifully constructed borsch, such as you are going to experience presently, ought not only to banish conversation but almost to annihilate thought. Later on, when we arrive at the second stage of olives, I shall be quite ready to discuss that new book on Borrow, or, if you prefer it, the present situation in the Grand Duchy of

Luxemburg. But I absolutely decline to talk anything approaching business till we have finished with the bird.'

For the greater part of the meal Egbert sat in an abstracted silence, the silence of a man whose mind is focused on one topic. When the coffee stage had been reached he launched himself suddenly athwart his uncle's reminiscences of the Court of Luxemburg.

'I think I told you that great-aunt Adelaide had made me her executor. There wasn't very much to be done in the way of legal matters, but I had to go through her papers.'

'That would be a fairly heavy task in itself. I should imagine there were reams of family letters.'

'Stacks of them, and most of them highly uninteresting. There was one packet, however, which I thought might repay a careful perusal. It was a bundle of correspondence from her brother Peter.'

'The Canon of tragic memory,' said Lulworth.

'Exactly, of tragic memory, as you say; a tragedy that has never been fathomed.'

'Probably the simplest explanation was the correct one,' said Sir Lulworth; 'he slipped on the stone staircase and fractured his skull in falling.'

Egbert shook his head. 'The medical evidence all went to prove that the blow on the head was struck by someone coming up behind him. A wound caused by violent contact with the steps could not possibly have been inflicted at that angle of the skull. They experimented with a dummy figure falling in every conceivable position.'

'But the motive?' exclaimed Sir Lulworth; 'no one had any interest in doing away with him, and the number of people who destroy Canons of the Established Church for the mere fun of killing must be extremely limited. Of course there are individuals of weak mental balance who do that sort of thing, but they seldom conceal their handiwork; they are more generally inclined to parade it.'

'His cook was under suspicion,' said Egbert shortly.

'I know he was,' said Sir Lulworth, 'simply because he was about the only person on the premises at the time of the tragedy. But could anything be sillier than trying to fasten a charge of murder on to Sebastien? He had nothing to gain in fact, a good deal to lose, from the death of his employer. The Canon was paying him quite as good wages as I was able to offer him when I took him over into my service. I have since raised them to something a little more in accordance with his real worth, but at the time he was glad to find a new place without troubling about an increase of wages. People were fighting rather shy of him, and he had no friends in this country. No; if any one in the world was interested in the prolonged life and unimpaired digestion of the Canon it would certainly be Sebastien.'

'People don't always weigh the consequences of their rash acts,' said Egbert, 'otherwise there would be very few murders committed. Sebastien is a man of hot temper.'

'He is a southerner,' admitted Sir Lulworth; 'to be geographically exact I believe he hails from the French slopes of the Pyrenees. I took that into consideration when he nearly killed the gardener's boy the other day for bringing him a spurious substitute for sorrel. One must always make allowances for origin and locality and early environment; "Tell me your longitude and I'll know what latitude to allow you," is my motto.'

'There, you see,' said Egbert, 'he nearly killed the gardener's boy.'

'My dear Egbert, between nearly killing a gardener's boy and altogether killing a Canon there is a wide difference. No doubt you have often felt a temporary desire to kill a gardener's boy; you have never given way to it, and I respect you for your self-control. But I don't suppose you have ever wanted to kill an octogenarian Canon. Besides, as far as we know, there had never been any quarrel or disagreement between the two men. The evidence at the inquest brought that out very clearly.'

'Ah!' said Egbert, with the air of a man coming at last into a deferred inheritance of conversational importance, 'that is precisely what I want to speak to you about.'

He pushed away his coffee cup and drew a pocket-book from his inner breast-pocket. From the depths of the pocket-book he produced an envelope, and from the envelope he extracted a letter, closely written in a small, neat handwriting.

'One of the Canon's numerous letters to Aunt Adelaide,' he explained, 'written a few days before his death. Her memory was already failing when she received it, and I dare say she forgot the contents as soon as she had read it; otherwise, in the light of what subsequently happened, we should have heard something of this letter before now. If it had been produced at the inquest I fancy it would have made some difference in the course of affairs. The evidence, as you remarked just now, choked off suspicion against Sebastien by disclosing an utter absence of anything that could be considered a motive or provocation for the crime, if crime there was.'

'Oh, read the letter,' said Sir Lulworth impatiently.

'It's a long rambling affair, like most of his letters in his later years,' said Egbert. 'I'll read the part that bears immediately on the mystery.

' "I very much fear I shall have to get rid of Sebastien. He cooks divinely, but he has the temper of a fiend or an anthropoid ape, and I am really in bodily fear of him. We had a dispute the other day as to the correct sort of lunch to be served on Ash Wednesday, and I got so irritated and annoyed at his conceit and obstinacy that at last I threw a cupful of coffee in his face and called him at the same time an impudent jackanapes. Very little of the coffee went actually in his face, but I have never seen a human being show such deplorable lack of self-control. I laughed at the threat of killing me that he spluttered out in his rage, and thought the whole thing would blow over, but I have several times since caught him scowling and muttering in a highly unpleasant fashion, and lately I have fancied that he was dogging my footsteps about the grounds, particularly when I walk of an evening in the Italian Garden."

'It was on the steps in the Italian Garden that the body was found,' commented Egbert, and resumed reading.

' "I dare say the danger is imaginary; but I shall feel more at ease when he has quitted my service." '

Egbert paused for a moment at the conclusion of the extract; then, as his uncle made no remark, he added: 'If lack of motive was the only factor that saved Sebastien from prosecution I fancy this letter will put a different complexion on matters.'

'Have you shown it to any one else?' asked Sir Lulworth, reaching out his hand for the incriminating piece of paper.

'No,' said Egbert, handing it across the table, 'I thought I would tell you about it first. Heavens, what are you doing?'

Egbert's voice rose almost to a scream. Sir Lulworth had flung the paper well and truly into the glowing centre of the grate. The small, neat handwriting shrivelled into black flaky nothingness.

'What on earth did you do that for?' gasped Egbert. 'That letter was our one piece of evidence to connect Sebastien with the crime.'

'That is why I destroyed it,' said Sir Lulworth.

'But why should you want to shield him?' cried Egbert; 'the man is a common murderer.'

'A common murderer, possibly, but a very uncommon cook.'

'Saki', 'The Blind Spot'

Unpremeditated

At three o'clock, Emil felt that he could stand it no longer. He slipped out under cover of 'The Holy City', followed by Malvina's wistful eye, and went to the stable for his mare. He was at that height of excitement from which everything is foreshortened, from which life seems short and simple, death very near, and the soul seems to soar like an eagle. As he rode past the graveyard he looked at the brown hole in the earth where Amédée was to lie, and felt no horror. That, too, was beautiful, that simple doorway into forgetfulness. The heart, when it is too much alive, aches for that brown earth, and ecstasy has no fear of death. It is the old and the poor and the maimed who shrink from that brown hole; its wooers are found among the young, the passionate, the gallant-hearted. It was not until he had passed the graveyard that Emil realized where he was going. It was the hour for saying good-bye. It might be the last time that he would see her alone, and today he could leave her without rancor, without bitterness.

Everywhere the grain stood ripe and the hot afternoon was full of the smell of the ripe wheat, like the smell of bread baking in an oven. The breath of the wheat and the sweet clover passed him like pleasant things in a dream. He could feel nothing but the sense of diminishing distance. It seemed to him that his mare was flying, or running on wheels, like a railway train. The sunlight, flashing on the window-glass of the big red barns, drove him wild with joy. He was like an arrow shot from the bow. His life poured itself out along the road before him as he rode to the Shabata farm.

When Emile alighted at the Shabatas' gate, his horse was in a lather. He tied her in the stable and hurried to the house. It was empty. She might be at Mrs Hiller's or with Alexandra. But anything that reminded him of her would be enough, the orchard, the mulberry tree . . . When he reached the orchard the sun was hanging low over the wheatfield. Long fingers of light reached through the apple branches as through a net; the orchard was riddled and shot with gold; light was the reality, the trees were merely interferences that reflected and refracted light. Emil went softly down between the cherry trees toward the wheatfield. When he came to the corner, he stopped short and put his hand over his mouth. Marie was lying on her side under the white mulberry tree, her face half hidden in the grass, her eyes closed, her hands lying limply where they had happened to fall. She had lived a day of her new life of perfect love, and it had left her like this. Her breast rose and fell faintly, as if she were asleep. Emil threw himself down beside her and took her in his arms. The blood came back to her cheeks, her amber eyes opened slowly, and in them Emil saw his own face and the orchard and the sun. 'I was dreaming this,' she whispered, hiding her face against him, 'don't take my dream away!'

• • •

When Frank Shabata got home that night, he found Emil's mare in his stable. Such an impertinence amazed him. Like everybody else, Frank had had an exciting day. Since noon he had been drinking too much, and he was in a bad temper. He talked bitterly to himself while he put his own horse away, and as he went up the path and saw that the house was dark he felt an added sense of injury. He approached quietly and listened on the doorstep. Hearing nothing, he opened the kitchen door and went softly from one room to another. Then he went through the house again, upstairs and down, with no better result. He sat down on the bottom step of the box stairway and tried to get his wits together. In that unnatural quiet there was no sound but his own heavy breathing. Suddenly an owl began to hoot out in the fields. Frank lifted his head. An idea flashed into his mind, and his sense of injury and outrage grew. He went into his bedroom and took his murderous 405 Winchester from the closet.

When Frank took up his gun and walked out of the house, he had not the faintest purpose of doing anything with it. He did not believe that he had any real grievance. But it gratified him to feel like a desperate man. He had got into the habit of seeing himself always in desperate straits. His unhappy temperament was like a cage; he could never get out of it; and he felt that other people, his wife in particular, must have put him there. It had never more than dimly occurred to Frank that he made his own unhappiness. Though he took up his gun with dark projects in his mind, he would have been paralyzed with fright had he known that there was the slightest probability of his ever carrying any of them out.

Frank went slowly down to the orchard gate, stopped and stood for a moment lost in thought. He retraced his steps and looked through the barn and the hayloft. Then he went out to the road, where he took the footpath along the outside of the orchard hedge. The hedge was twice as tall as Frank himself, and so dense that one could see through it only by peering closely between the leaves. He could see the empty path a long way in the moonlight. His mind traveled ahead to the stile, which he always thought of as haunted by Emil Bergson. But why had he left his horse?

At the wheatfield corner, where the orchard hedge ended and the path led across the pasture to the Bergsons', Frank stopped. In the warm, breathless night air he heard a murmuring sound, perfectly inarticulate, as low as the sound of water coming from a spring, where there is no fall, and where there are no stones to fret it. Frank strained his ears. It ceased. He held his breath and began to tremble. Resting the butt of his gun on the ground, he parted the mulberry leaves softly with his fingers and peered through the hedge at the dark figures on the grass, in the shadow of the mulberry tree. It seemed to him that they must feel his eyes, that they must hear him breathing. But they did not. Frank, who had always wanted to see things blacker than they were, for once wanted to believe less than he saw. The woman lying in the shadow might so easily be one of the Bergsons' farm-girls . . . Again the murmur, like water welling out of the ground. This time he heard it more distinctly, and his blood was quicker than his brain. He began to act, just as a man who falls into the fire begins to act. The gun sprang to his shoulder, he sighted mechanically and fired three times without stopping, stopped without knowing why. Either he shut his eyes or he had vertigo. He did not see anything while he was firing. He thought he heard a cry simultaneous with the second report, but he was not sure. He peered again through the hedge, at the two dark figures under the tree. They had fallen a little apart from each other, and were perfectly still – No, not quite; in a white patch of light, where the moon shone through the branches, a man's hand was plucking spasmodically at the grass.

Suddenly the woman stirred and uttered a cry, then another, and another. She was living! She was dragging herself toward the hedge! Frank dropped his gun and ran back along the path, shaking, stumbling, gasping. He had never imagined such horror. The cries followed him. They grew fainter and thicker, as if she were choking. He dropped on his knees beside the hedge and crouched like a rabbit, listening; fainter, fainter; a sound like a whine; again – a moan – another – silence. Frank scrambled to his feet and ran on, groaning and praying. From habit he went toward the house, where he was used to being soothed when he had worked himself into a frenzy, but at the sight of the black, open door, he started back. He knew that he had murdered somebody, that a woman was bleeding and moaning in the orchard, but he had not realized before that it was his wife. The gate stared him in the face. He threw his hands over his head. Which way to turn? He lifted his tormented face and looked at the sky. 'Holy Mother of God, not to suffer! She was a good girl – not to suffer!'

Frank had been wont to see himself in dramatic situations; but now, when he stood by the windmill, in the bright space between the barn and the house, facing his own black doorway, he did not see himself at all. He stood like the hare when the dogs are approaching from all sides. And he ran like a hare, back and forth about that moonlit space, before he could make up his mind to go into the dark stable for a horse. The thought of going into a doorway was terrible to him. He caught Emil's horse by the bit and led it out. He could not have buckled a bridle on his own. After two or three attempts, he lifted himself into the saddle and started for Hanover. If he could catch the one o'clock train, he had money enough to get as far as Omaha.

While he was thinking dully of this in some less sensitized part of his brain, his acuter faculties were going over and over the cries he had heard in the orchard. Terror was the only thing that kept him from going back to her, terror that she might still be she, that she might still be suffering. A woman, mutilated and bleeding in his orchard – it was because it was a woman that he was so afraid. It was inconceivable that he should have hurt a woman. He would rather be eaten by wild beasts than see her move on the ground as she had moved in the orchard. Why had she been so careless? She knew he was like a crazy man when he was angry. She had more than once taken that gun away from him and held it, when he was angry with other people. Once it had gone off while they were struggling over it. She was never afraid. But, when she knew him, why hadn't she been more careful? Didn't she have all summer before her to love Emil Bergson in, without taking such chances? Probably she had met the Smirka boy, too, down there in the orchard. He didn't care. She could have met all the men on the Divide there, and welcome, if only she hadn't brought this horror on him.

There was a wrench in Frank's mind. He did not honestly believe that of her. He knew that he was doing her wrong. He stopped his horse to admit this to himself the more directly, to think it out the more clearly. He knew that he was to blame. For three years he had been trying to break her spirit. She had a way of making the best of things that seemed to him a sentimental affectation. He wanted his wife to resent that he was wasting his best years among these stupid and unappreciative people; but she had seemed to find the people quite good enough. If he ever got rich he meant to buy her pretty clothes and take her to California in a Pullman car, and treat her like a lady; but in the mean time he wanted her to feel that life was as ugly and as unjust as he felt it. He had tried to make her life ugly. He had refused to share any of the little pleasures she was so plucky about making for herself. She could be gay about the least thing in the world; but she must be gay! When she first came to him, her faith in him, her adoration – Frank struck the mare with his fist. Why had Marie made him do this thing; why had she brought this upon him? He was overwhelmed by sickening misfortune. All at once he heard her cries again – he had forgotten for a moment. 'Maria,' he sobbed aloud, 'Maria!'

When Frank was halfway to Hanover, the motion of his horse brought on a violent attack of nausea. After it had passed, he rode on again, but he could think of nothing except his physical weakness and his desire to be comforted by his wife. He wanted to get into his own bed. Had his wife been at home, he would have turned and gone back to her meekly enough.

• • •

When old Ivar climbed down from his loft at four o'clock the next morning, he came upon Emil's mare, jaded and lather-stained, her bridle broken, chewing the scattered tufts of hay outside the stable door. The old man was thrown into a fright at once. He put the mare in her stall, threw her a measure of oats, and then set out as fast as his bow legs could carry him on the path to the nearest neighbor.

'Something is wrong with that boy. Some misfortune has come upon us. He would never have used her so, in his right senses. It is not his way to abuse his mare,' the old man kept muttering, as he scuttled through the short, wet pasture grass on his bare feet.

While Ivar was hurrying across the fields, the first long rays of the sun were reaching down between the orchard boughs to those two dew drenched figures. The story of what had happened was written plainly on the orchard grass, and on the white mulberries that had fallen in the night and were covered with dark stain. For Emil the chapter had been short. He was shot in the heart, and had rolled over on his back and died. His face was turned up to the sky and his brows were drawn in a frown, as if he had realized that something had befallen him. But for Marie Shabata it had not been so easy. One ball had torn through her right lung, another had shattered the carotid artery. She must have started up and gone toward the hedge, leaving a trail of blood. There she had fallen and bled. From that spot there was another trail, heavier than the first, where she must have dragged herself back to Emil's body. Once there, she seemed not to have struggled any more. She had lifted her head on her lover's breast, taken his hand in both her own, and bled quietly to death. She was lying on her right side in an easy and natural position, her cheek on Emil's shoulder. On her face there was a look of ineffable content. Her lips were parted a little; her eyes were lightly closed, as if in a day-dream or a light slumber. After she lay down there, she seemed not to have moved an eyelash. The hand she held was covered with dark stains, where she had kissed it.

But the stained, slippery grass, the darkened mulberries, told only half the story. Above Marie and Emil, two white butterflies from Frank's alfalfa field were fluttering in and out among the interlacing shadows; diving and soaring, now close together, now far apart; and in the long grass by the fence the last wild roses of the year opened their pink hearts to die.

When Ivar reached the path by the hedge, he saw Shabata's rifle lying in the way. He turned and peered through the branches, falling upon his knees as if his legs had been mowed from under him. 'Merciful God!' he groaned; 'merciful, merciful God!'

Alexandra, too, had risen early that morning, because of her anxiety about Emil. She was in Emil's room upstairs when, from the window, she saw Ivar coming along the path that led from the Shabatas'. He was running like a spent man, tottering and lurching from side to side. Ivar never drank, and Alexandra thought at once that one of his spells had come upon him, and that he must be in a very bad way indeed. She ran downstairs and hurried out to meet him, to hide his infirmity from the eyes of her household. The old man fell in the road at her feet and caught her hand, over which he bowed his shaggy head. 'Mistress, mistress,' he sobbed, 'it has fallen! Sin and death for the young ones! God have mercy upon us!'

Willa Cather, *O Pioneers!*

Unreported

My husband eats with a good appetite. But I don't think he's really hungry. He chews, arms on the table, and stares at something across the room. He looks at me and looks away. He wipes his mouth on the napkin. He shrugs, and goes on eating.

'What are you staring at me for?' he says. 'What is it?' he says and lays down his fork.

'Was I staring?' I say, and shake my head.

The telephone rings.

'Don't answer it,' he said.

'It might be your mother,' I say.

'Watch and see,' he says.

I pick up the receiver and listen. My husband stops eating.

'What did I tell you?' he says when I hang up. He starts to eat again. Then throws his napkin on his plate. He says, 'Goddamn it, why can't people mind their own business? Tell me what I did wrong and I'll listen! I wasn't the only man there. We talked it over and we all decided. We couldn't just turn around. We were five miles from the car. I won't have you passing judgment. Do you hear?'

'You know,' I say.

He says, 'What do I know, Claire? Tell me what I'm supposed to know. I don't know anything except one thing.' He gives me what he thinks is a meaningful look. 'She was dead,' he says. 'And I'm so sorry as anyone else. But she was dead.'

'That's the point,' I say.

He raises his hands. He pushes his chair away from the table. He takes out his cigarettes and goes out to the back with a can of beer. I see him sit in the lawn chair and pick up the newspaper again.

His name is in there on the first page. Along with the names of his friends.

I close my eyes and hold on to the sink. Then I rake my arm across the drainboard and send the dishes to the floor.

He doesn't move. I know he's heard. He lifts his head as if still listening. But he doesn't move otherwise. He doesn't turn around.

He and Gordon Johnson and Mel Dorn and Vern Williams, they play poker and bowl and fish. They fish every spring and early summer before visiting relatives can get in the way. They are decent men, family men, men who take care of their jobs. They have sons and daughters who go to school with our son, Dean.

Last Friday these family men left for the Naches River. They parked the car in the mountains and hiked to where they wanted to fish. They carried their bedrolls, their food, their playing cards, their whiskey.

They saw the girl before they set up camp. Mel Dorn found her. No clothes on her at all. She was wedged into some branches that stuck out over the water.

He called the others and they came to look. They talked about what to do. One of the men – my Stuart didn't say which – said they should start back at once. The others stirred the sand with their shoes, and they didn't feel inclined that way. They pleaded fatigue, the late hour, the fact that the girl wasn't going anywhere.

In the end they went ahead and set up the camp. They built a fire and drank their whiskey. When the moon came up, they talked about the girl. Someone said they should keep the body from drifting away. They took their flashlights and went back to the river. One of the men – it might have been Stuart – waded in and got her. He took her by the fingers and pulled her into shore. He got some nylon cord and tied it to her wrist and then looped the rest around a tree.

The next morning they cooked breakfast, drank coffee, and drank whiskey, and then split up to fish. That night they cooked fish, cooked potatoes, drank coffee, drank whiskey, then took their cooking things and eating things back down to the river and washed them where the girl was.

They played some cards later on. Maybe they played until they couldn't see them anymore. Vern Williams went to sleep. But the others told stories. Gordon Johnson said the trout they'd caught were hard because of the terrible coldness of the water.

The next morning they got up late, drank whiskey, fished a little, took down their tents, rolled their sleeping bags, gathered their stuff, and hiked out. They drove until they got to a telephone. It was Stuart who made the call while the others stood around in the sun and listened. He gave the sheriff their names. They had nothing to hide. They weren't ashamed. They said they'd wait until someone could come for better directions and take down their statements.

I was asleep when he got home. But I woke up when I heard him in the kitchen. I found him leaning against the refrigerator with a can of beer. He put his heavy arms around me and rubbed his big hands on my back. In bed he put his hands on me again and then waited as if thinking of something else. I turned and opened my legs. Afterwards, I think he stayed awake.

He was up that morning before I could get out of bed. To see if there was something in the paper, I suppose.

The telephone began ringing right after eight.

'Go to hell!' I heard him shout.

The telephone rang right again.

'I have nothing to add to what I already said to the sheriff!'

He slammed the receiver down.

'What is going on?' I said.

It was then that he told me what I just told you.

I sweep up the broken dishes and go outside. He is lying on his back on the grass now, the newspaper and can of beer within reach.

'Stuart, could we go for a drive?' I say.

He rolls over and looks at me. 'We'll pick up some beer,' he says. He gets to his feet and touches me on the hip as he goes past. 'Give me a minute,' he says.

We drive through town without speaking. He stops at a roadside market for beer. I notice a great stack of papers just inside the door. On the top step a fat woman in a print dress holds out a licorice stick to a little girl. Later on, we cross Everson Creek and turn into the picnic grounds. The creek runs under the bridge and into a large pond a few hundred yards away. I can see the men out there. I can see them out there fishing.

So much water so close to home.

I say, 'Why did you have to go miles away?'

'Don't rile me,' he says.

We sit on a bench in the sun. He opens us cans of beer. He says, 'Relax, Claire.'

'They said they were innocent. They said they were crazy.'

He says, 'Who?' He says, 'What are you talking about?'

'The Maddox brothers. They killed a girl named Arlene Hubly where I grew up. They cut off her head and threw her into the Cle Elum River. It happened when I was a girl.'

'You're going to get me riled,' he says.

I look at the creek. I'm right in it, eyes open, face down, staring at the moss on the bottom, dead.

'I don't know what's wrong with you,' he says on the way home. 'You're getting me more riled by the minute.'

There is nothing I can say to him.

He tries to concentrate on the road. But he keeps looking into the rear-view mirror.

He knows.

Stuart believes he is letting me sleep this morning. But I was awake long before the alarm went off. I was thinking, lying on the far side of the bed away from his hairy legs.

He gets Dean off for school, and then he shaves, dresses, and leaves for work. Twice he looks in and clears his throat. But I keep my eyes closed.

In the kitchen I find a note from him. It's signed 'Love'.

I sit in the breakfast nook and drink coffee and leave a ring on the note. I look at the newspaper and turn it this way and that on the table. Then I skid it close and read what it says. The body has been identified, claimed. But it took some examining it, some putting things into it, some cutting, some weighing, some measuring, some putting things back again and sewing them in.

I sit for a long time holding the newspaper and thinking. Then I call up to get a chair at the hairdresser's.

I sit under the dryer with a magazine on my lap and let Marnie do my nails.

'I am going to a funeral tomorrow,' I say.

'I'm sorry to hear that,' Marie says.

'It was a murder,' I say.

'That's the worst kind,' Marnie says.

'We weren't all that close,' I say. 'But you know.'

'We'll get you fixed up for it,' Marnie says.

That night I make my bed on the sofa, and in the morning I get up first. I put on coffee and fix breakfast while he shaves.

He appears in the kitchen doorway, towel over his bare shoulder, appraising.

'Here's coffee,' I say. 'Eggs'll be ready in a minute.'

I wake Dean, and the three of us eat. Whenever Stuart looks at me, I ask Dean if he wants more milk, more toast, etc.

'I'll call you today,' Stuart says as he opens the door.

I say, 'I don't think I'll be home today.'

'All right,' he says. 'Sure.'

I dress carefully. I try on a hat and look at myself in the mirror. I write out a note for Dean.

Honey, Mommy has things to do this afternoon, but will be back later. You stay in or be in the backyard until one of us comes home.

Love, Mommy

I look at the word 'Love' and then I underline it. Then I see the word 'backyard'. Is it one word or two?

I drive through farm country, through fields of oats and sugar beets and past apple orchards, cattle grazing in pastures. Then everything changes, more like shacks than farmhouses and stands of timber instead of orchards. Then mountains, and on the right, far below, I sometimes see the Naches River.

A green pickup comes up behind me and stays behind me for miles.

I keep slowing at the wrong times, hoping he will pass. Then I speed up. But this is at the wrong times, too. I grip the wheel until my fingers hurt.

On a long clear stretch he goes past. But he drives along beside for a bit, a crewcut man in a blue workshirt. We look each other over. Then he waves, toots his horn, and pulls on up ahead.

I slow down and find a place. I pull over and shut off the motor. I can hear the river down below the trees. Then I hear the pickup coming back.

I lock the doors and roll up the windows.

'You all right?' the man says. He raps on the glass. 'You okay?' He leans his arms on the door and brings his face to the window.

I stare at him. I can't think what else to do.

'Is everything all right in there? How come you're all locked up?'

I shake my head.

'Roll down your window.' He shakes his head and looks at the highway and then back at me. 'Roll it down now.'

'Please,' I say, 'I have to go.'

'Open the door,' he says as if he isn't listening. 'You're going to choke in there.'

He looks at my breasts, my legs. I can tell that's what he's doing.

'Hey, sugar,' he says. 'I'm just here to help is all.'

The casket is closed and covered with floral sprays. The organ starts up the minute I take a seat. People are coming in and finding chairs. There's a boy in flared pants and a yellow short-sleeved shirt. A door opens and the family comes in in a group and moves over to a curtained place off to one side. Chairs creak as everybody gets settled. Directly, a nice blond man in a nice dark suit stands and asks us to bow our heads. He says a prayer for us, the living, and when he finishes, he says a prayer for the soul of the departed.

Along with the others I go past the casket. Then I move out onto the front steps and into the afternoon light. There's a woman who limps as she goes down the stairs ahead of me. On the sidewalk she looks around. 'Well, they got him,' she says. 'If that's any consolation. They arrested him this morning. I heard it on the radio before I come. A boy right here in town.'

We move a few steps down the hot sidewalk. People are starting cars. I put out my hand and hold on to a parking meter. Polished hoods and polished fenders. My head swims.

I say, 'They have friends, these killers. You can't tell.'

'I have known that child since she was a little girl,' the woman says. 'She used to come over and I'd bake cookies for her and let her eat them in front of the TV.'

Back home, Stuart sits at the table with a drink of whiskey in front of him. For a crazy instant I think something's happened to Dean.

'Where is he?' I say. 'Where is Dean?'

'Outside,' my husband says.

He drains his glass and stands up. He says, 'I think I know what you need.'

He reaches an arm around my waist and with his other hand he begins to unbutton my jacket and then he goes on to the buttons of my blouse.

'First things first,' he says.

He says something else. But I don't need to listen. I can't hear a thing with so much water going.

'That's right,' I say, finishing the buttons myself. 'Before Dean comes. Hurry.'

Raymond Carver, 'So Much Water So Close to Home'

V

Valentine

I tried to put in what I really felt.
I really tried to put in what I felt.
I really felt – what I tried to put.
I put it really feelingly, or tried.
I felt it really tried to put it in.
What I put in I tried to really feel.
Really I felt I'd tried to put it in.
I really tried to feel what I put in.

It cost £5 in WH Smith's.
£5 it cost – WH Smith's ain't cheap.
£5 ain't cheap, not for a thing like that.
It costs, a thing like that – £5 ain't cheap.
It wasn't a cheap thing – £5 it cost.
A thing like that ain't cheap in WH Smith's.
In WH Smith's a thing like that comes costly.
A lot to pay, £5, for a thing like that.

The heart was scarlet satin, sort of stuffed.
I sort of felt it was me own heart, like.
SHE TORE THE STUFFING OUT OF THE SCARLET HEART.
I sort of stuffed and tore her sort of scarlet.
I stuffed her, like, and felt her sort of satin.
I sort of felt she'd tore out all me stuffing.
I felt her stuff like satin sort of scarlet
her stuff felt sore, torn satin whorlet scar
I liked her score felt stiffed her scar lick hurt
I tore her satin felt her stuffed her scarlet
tore out her heart stuff scarred her Satan har
I licked her stiff tore scarf her harlot hair
tied scarf tore stabbed scar whore sin sat tit star

stuffed finger scar ha ha ha ha ha ha
felt stiff scarf tight tore scarlet heart her scare
her scare stare stabbed heart scarlet feel torn mur

Peter Reading, '15th February'

Verities

Whoso sheddeth man's blood, by man shall his blood be shed: for in the image of God made he man.

Genesis 9: 6

And the LORD spake unto Moses, saying,

Speak unto the children of Israel, and say unto them, When ye be come over Jordan into the land of Canaan;

Then ye shall appoint you cities to be cities of refuge for you; that the slayer may flee thither, which killeth any person at unawares.

And they shall be unto you cities for refuge from the avenger; that the manslayer die not, until he stand before the congregation in judgment.

And of these cities which ye shall give six cities shall ye have for refuge.

Ye shall give three cities on this side Jordan, and three cities shall ye give in the land of Canaan, which shall be cities of refuge.

These six cities shall be a refuge, both for the children of Israel, and for the stranger, and for the sojourner among them: that every one that killeth any person unawares may flee thither.

And if he smite him with an instrument of iron, so that he die, he is a murderer: the murderer shall surely be put to death.

And if he smite him with throwing a stone, wherewith he may die, and he die, he is a murderer: the murderer shall surely be put to death.

Or if he smite him with an hand weapon of wood, wherewith he may die, and he die, he is a murderer: the murderer shall surely be put to death.

The revenger of blood himself shall slay the murderer: when he meeteth him, he shall slay him.

Numbers 35: 9–19

Mr Marybone (for that was the gentleman's name to whom he applied) readily agreed to the robbery, but he hesitated at the murder. He said, as to robbery, he had, on much weighing and considering the matter, very well reconciled his conscience to it; for, though that noble kind of robbery which was executed on the highway was, from the cowardice of mankind, less frequent, yet the baser and meaner species, sometimes called cheating, but more commonly known by the name of robbery within the law, was in a manner universal. He did not, therefore, pretend to the reputation of being so much honester than other people; but could by no means satisfy himself in the commission of murder, which was a sin of the most heinous nature, and so immediately prosecuted by God's judgement that it never passed undiscovered or unpunished.

Wild, with the utmost disdain in his countenance, answered as follows: 'Art thou he whom I have selected out of my whole gang for this glorious undertaking, and dost thou cant of God's revenge against murder? You have, it seems, reconciled your conscience (a pretty word) to robbery, from its being so common. Is it then the novelty of murder which deters you? Do you imagine that guns, and pistols, and swords, and knives, are the only instruments of death? Look into the world and see the numbers whom broken fortunes and broken hearts bring untimely to the grave. To omit those glorious heroes who, to their immortal honour, have massacred whole nations, what think you of private persecution, treachery, and slander, by which the very souls of men are in a manner torn from their bodies? Is it not more generous, nay, more good-natured, to send a man to his rest, than, after having plundered him of all he hath, or from malice or malevolence deprived him of his character, to punish him with a languishing death, or, what is worse, a languishing life? Murder, therefore, is not so uncommon as you weakly conceive it, though, as you said of robbery, that more noble kind which lies within the paw of the law may be so. But this is the most innocent in him who doth it, and the most eligible to him who is to suffer it. Believe me, lad, the tongue of a viper is less hurtful than that of a slanderer, and the gilded scales of a rattlesnake less dreadful than the purse of the oppressor. Let me, therefore, hear no more of your scruples; but consent to my proposal without further hesitation, unless, like a woman, you are afraid of blooding your clothes, or, like a fool, are terrified with the apprehensions of being hanged in chains. Take my word for it, you had better be an honest man than half a rogue. Do not think of continuing in my gang without abandoning yourself absolutely to my pleasure; for no man shall ever receive a favour at my hands who sticks at anything, or is guided by any other law than that of my will.'

Wild then ended his speech, which had not the desired effect on

Marybone: he agreed to the robbery, but would not undertake the murder, as Wild (who feared that, by Marybone's demanding to search the gentleman's coat, he might hazard suspicion himself) insisted. Marybone was immediately entered by Wild in his black-book, and was presently after impeached and executed as a fellow on whom his leader could not place sufficient dependence; thus falling, as many rogues do, a sacrifice, not to his roguery, but to his conscience.

Henry Fielding, *Jonathan Wild the Great*

Let us deign for a moment to illumine our spirit by philosophy's sacred flame; what other than Nature's voice suggests to us personal hatreds, revenges, wars, in a word, all those causes of perpetual murder? Now, if she incites us to murderous acts, she has need of them; that once grasped, how may we suppose ourselves guilty in her regard when we do nothing more than obey her intentions?

But that is more than what is needed to convince any enlightened reader, that for murder ever to be an outrage to Nature is impossible.

Is it a political crime? We must avow, on the contrary, that it is, unhappily, merely one of policy's and politics' greatest instruments. Is it not by dint of murders that France is free today? Needless to say, here we are referring to the murders occasioned by war, not to the atrocities committed by plotters and rebels; the latter, destined to the public's execration, have only to be recollected to arouse forever general horror and indignation. What study, what science, has greater need of murder's support than that which tends only to deceive, whose sole end is the expansion of one nation at another's expense? Are wars, the unique fruit of this political barbarism, anything but the means whereby a nation is nourished, whereby it is strengthened, whereby it is buttressed? And what is war if not the science of destruction? A strange blindness in man, who publicly teaches the art of killing, who rewards the most accomplished killer, and who punishes him who for some particular reason does away with his enemy! Is it not high time errors so savage be repaired?

Is murder then a crime against society? But how could that reasonably be imagined? What difference does it make to this murderous society, whether it have one member more, or less? Will its laws, its manners, its customs be vitiated? Has an individual's death ever had any influence upon the general mass? And after the loss of the greatest battle, what am I saying? after the obliteration of half the world – or, if one wishes, of the entire world – would the little number of survivors, should there be any, notice even the faintest difference in things? No, alas. Nor would Nature notice any either, and the stupid pride of man, who believes everything created for him, would be dashed indeed, after the total extinction of the human species, were it to be seen that nothing in Nature had changed, and that the stars' flight had not for that been retarded. Let us continue.

What must the attitude of a warlike and republican state be toward murder?

Dangerous it should certainly be, either to cast discredit upon the act, or to punish it. Republican mettle calls for a touch of ferocity: if he grows soft, if his energy slackens in him, the republican will be subjugated in a trice. A most unusual thought comes to mind at this point, but if it is audacious it is also true, and I will mention it. A nation that begins by governing itself as a republic will only be sustained by virtues because, in order to attain the most, one must always start with the least. But an already old and decayed nation which courageously casts off the yoke of its monarchical government in order to adopt a republican one, will only be maintained by many crimes; for it is criminal already, and if it were to wish to pass from crime to virtue, that is to say, from a violent to a pacific, benign condition, it should fall into an inertia whose result would soon be its certain ruin. What happens to the tree you would transplant from a soil full of vigor to a dry and sandy plain? All intellectual ideas are so greatly subordinate to Nature's physical aspect that the comparisons supplied us by agriculture will never deceive us in morals.

Savages, the most independent of men, the nearest to Nature, daily indulge in murder which amongst them goes unpunished. In Sparta, in Lacedaemon, they hunted Helots, just as we in France go on partridge shoots. The freest of people are they who are most friendly to murder: in Mindanao, a man who wishes to commit a murder is raised to the rank of warrior brave, he is straightway decorated with a turban; amongst the Caraguos, one must have killed seven men to obtain the honors of this headdress: the inhabitants of Borneo believe all those they put to death will serve them when they themselves depart life; devout Spaniards made a vow to St James of Galicia to kill a dozen Americans every day; in the kingdom of Tangut, there is selected a strong and vigorous young man: on certain days of the year he is allowed to kill whomever he encounters! Was there ever a people better disposed to murder than the Jews? One sees it in every guise, upon every page of their history.

Now and again, China's emperor and mandarins take measures to stir up a revolt amongst the people, in order to derive, from these maneuvers, the right to transform them into horrible slaughters. May that soft and effeminate people rise against their tyrants; the latter will be massacred in their turn, and with much greater justice; murder, adopted always, always necessary, will have but changed its victims; it has been the delight of some, and will become the felicity of others.

An infinite number of nations tolerates public assassinations; they are freely permitted in Genoa, Venice, Naples, and throughout Albania; at Kachoa on the San Domingo River, murderers, undisguised and unashamedly, upon your orders and before your very eyes cut the throat of the person you have pointed out to them; Hindus take opium to encourage themselves to murder; and then, rushing out into the street, they butcher everyone they meet; English travelers have found this idiosyncracy in Batavia, too.

What people were at once greater and more bloodthirsty than the Romans, and what nation longer preserved its splendor and freedom? The gladiatorial spectacles fed its bravery, it became warlike through the habit of making a game of murder. Twelve or fifteen hundred victims filled the circus' arena every day, and there the women, crueler than the men, dared demand that the dying fall gracefully and be sketched while still in death's throes. The Romans moved from that to the pleasures of seeing dwarfs cut each other to pieces; and when the Christian cult, then infecting the world, came to persuade men there was evil in killing one another, the tyrants immediately enchained that people, and everyone's heroes became their toys.

Everywhere, in short, it was rightly believed that the murderer – that is to say, the man who stifled his sensibilities to the point of killing his fellow man, and of defying public or private vengeance – everywhere, I say, it was thought such a man could only be very courageous, and consequently very precious to a warlike or republican community.

• • •

Must murder be repressed by murder? Surely not. Let us never impose any other penalty upon the murderer than the one he may risk from the vengeance of the friends or family of him he has killed. 'I grant you pardon,' said Louis XV to Charolais who, to divert himself, had just killed a man; 'but I also pardon whoever will kill you.' All the bases of the law against murderers may be found in that sublime motto.[1]

Briefly, murder is a horror, but an often necessary horror, never

1 The Salic Law only punished murder by exacting a simple fine, and as the guilty one easily found ways to avoid payment, Childebert, king of Austrasia, decreed, in a writ published at Cologne, the death penalty, not against the murderer, but against him who would shirk the murderer's fine.

criminal, which it is essential to tolerate in a republican State. I have made it clear the entire universe has given an example of it; but ought it be considered a deed to be punished by death? They who respond to the following dilemma will have answered the question:

Is it or is it not a crime?

If it is not, why make laws for its punishment? And if it is, by what barbarous logic do you, to punish it, duplicate it by another crime?

The Marquis de Sade, *Philosophy in the Bedroom*,
trans. Richard Seaver and Austryn Wainhouse

The element of truth . . . which people are so ready to disavow, is that men are not gentle creatures who want to be loved, and who at the most can defend themselves if they are attacked; they are, on the contrary, creatures among whose instinctual endowments is to be reckoned a powerful share of aggressiveness. As a result, their neighbour is for them not only a potential helper or sexual object, but also someone who tempts them to satisfy their aggressiveness on him, to exploit his capacity for work without compensation, to use him sexually without his consent, to seize his possessions, to humiliate him, to cause him pain, to torture and to kill him. *Homo homini lupus.*[1] Who, in the face of all his experience of life and of history, will have the courage to dispute this assertion? As a rule this cruel aggressiveness waits for some provocation or puts itself at the service of some other purpose, whose goal might also have been reached by milder measures. In circumstances that are favourable to it, when the mental counter-forces which ordinarily inhibit it are out of action, it also manifests itself spontaneously and reveals man as a savage beast to whom consideration towards his own kind is something alien. Anyone who calls to mind the atrocities committed during the racial migrations or the invasions of the Huns, or by the people known as Mongols under Jenghiz Khan and Tamerlane, or at the capture of Jerusalem by the pious Crusaders, or even, indeed, the horrors of the recent World War – anyone who calls these things to mind will have to bow humbly before the truth of this view.

Sigmund Freud, *Civilization and its Discontents*, trans. Joan Riviere

---

Ripuarian Law similarly ordained no more against this act than a fine proportionate to the individual killed. A priest was extremely costly: a leaden tunic, cut to his measurements, was tailored for the assassin, and he was obliged to produce the equivalent of this tunic's weight in gold; in default of which the guilty one and his family remained slaves of the Church.

1 'Man is a wolf to man.' Derived from Plautus, *Asinaria* II, iv, 88.

Victim

'Tell me about Lorrimer. What was he like?'

This was the question which lay at the heart of every murder investigation; and yet he knew its absurdity before he asked it. It was the strangest part of a detective's job, this building up of a relationship with the dead, seen only as a crumpled corpse at the scene of crime or naked on the mortuary table. The victim was central to the mystery of his own death. He died because of what he was. Before the case was finished Dalgliesh would have received a dozen pictures of Lorrimer's personality, transferred like prints from other men's minds. From these amorphous and uncertain images he would create his own imaginings, superimposed and dominant, but essentially just as incomplete, just as distorted – as were the others – by his own preconceptions, his own personality. But the question had to be asked. And at least he could rely on Freeborn to answer it without initiating a philosophical discussion about the basis of the self. But their minds must for a moment have flowed together, for Freeborn said:

'It's odd how you always have to ask that question, that you'll only see him through other men's eyes. Aged about forty. Looks like John the Baptist without his beard and is about as uncompromising. Single. Lives with an elderly father in a cottage just outside the village. He is – was – an extremely competent forensic biologist, but I doubt whether he would have gone any higher. Obsessional, edgy, uncomfortable to be with.'

P. D. James, *Death of an Expert Witness*

Knowing our desire for details,
the evening news tells us
how the man died, and even a little
of how he lived, his work, and whom he loved.

He worked in an office downtown.
At night he rode the train home.
There's the point of entry: the broken window.
There, the bed where he was sleeping

when he heard the intruder. Now
the camera hurries through the house,

like a reader skimming pages,
to the room where his life

is outlined in chalk
and the knife is held up to the lights.

Richard Jones, 'Desire'

Who killed Cock Robin?
  I, said the Sparrow,
  With my bow and arrow,
I killed Cock Robin.

Who saw him die?
  I, said the Fly,
  With my little eye,
I saw him die.

Who caught his blood?
  I, said the Fish,
  With my little dish,
I caught his blood.

Who'll make his shroud?
  I, said the Beetle,
  With my thread and needle,
I'll make the shroud.

Who'll dig his grave?
  I, said the Owl,
  With my pick and shovel,
I'll dig his grave.

Who'll be the parson?
  I, said the Rook,
  With my little book,
I'll be the parson.

Who'll be the clerk?
  I, said the Lark,
  If it's not in the dark,
I'll be the clerk.

Who'll carry the link?
  I, said the Linnet,
  I'll fetch it in a minute,
I'll carry the link.

Who'll be chief mourner?
  I, said the Dove
  I mourn for my love,
I'll be chief mourner.

Who'll carry the coffin?
  I, said the Kite,
  If it's not through the night,
I'll carry the coffin.

Who'll bear the pall?
  We, said the Wren,
  Both the cock and the hen,
We'll bear the pall.

Who'll sing a psalm?
  I, said the Thrush,
  As she sat on a bush,
I'll sing a psalm.

Who'll toll the bell?
  I, said the Bull,
  Because I can pull,
So Cock Robin, farewell.

All the birds of the air
  Fell a-sighing and a-sobbing,
When they heard the bell toll
  For poor Cock Robin.

Anon., 'Who Killed Cock Robin?'

Village

Soon after the First World War a violent event took place in the village which drew us together in a web of silence and cut us off for a while almost entirely from the outside world. I was too young at the time to be surprised by it, but I knew those concerned and learned the whole story early. Though it was seldom discussed – and never with strangers – the facts of that night were familiar to us all, and common consent buried the thing down deep and raked out the tracks around it. So bloody, raw, and sudden it was, it resembled an outbreak of family madness which we took pains to conceal, out of shame and pride, and for the sake of those infected.

The crime occurred a few days before Christmas, on a night of deep snow and homecoming; the time when the families called in their strays for an annual feast of goose. The night was as cold as Cotswold cold can be, with a wind coming straight from the Arctic. We children were in bed blowing hard on our knees; wives toasted their feet by the fires; while the men and youths were along at the pub, drinking hot-pokered cider, cutting cards for crib, and watching their wet boots steam.

But few cards were dealt or played that night. An apparition intervened. The door blew open to a gust of snow and a tall man strode into the bar. He seemed to the drinkers both unknown and familiar; he had a sharp tanned face, a nasal twang, and convinced of his welcome he addressed everyone by name, while they lowered their eyes and nodded. Slapping the bar, he ordered drinks all round, and then he began to talk.

Everyone, save the youths, remembered this man; now they studied the change within him. Years ago, as a pale and bony lad, he had been packed off to one of the Colonies, sent by subscription and the prayers of the Church, as many a poor boy before him. Usually they went, and were never heard from again, and their existence was soon forgotten. Now one of them had returned like a gilded ghost, successful and richly dressed, had come back to taunt the stay-at-homes with his boasting talk and money.

He had landed that morning, he said, at Bristol, from an Auckland mutton-boat. The carriage he'd hired had broken down in the snow, so he was finishing his journey on foot. He was on his way to his parents' cottage to give them a Christmas surprise; another mile up the valley, another mile in the snow – he couldn't pass the old pub, now, could he?

He stood feet apart, his back to the bar, displaying himself to the company. Save for his yelping voice, the pub was silent, and the drinkers watched him closely. He'd done pretty well out there, he said, raised cattle, made a heap of money. It was easy enough if you just had the guts and weren't stuck in the bogs like some . . . The old men listened, and the young men watched, with the oil lamps red in their eyes . . .

He sent round more drinks and the men drank them down. He talked of the world and its width and richness. He lectured the old ones for the waste of their lives and the youths for their dumb contentment. They slogged for the Squire and the tenant-farmers for a miserable twelve bob a week. They lived on potatoes and by touching their caps, they hadn't a sovereign to rub between them, they saw not a thing save muck and each other – and perhaps Stroud on a Saturday night. Did they know what he'd done? what he'd seen? what he'd made? His brown face was aglow with whisky. He spread a sheaf of pound notes along the bar and fished a fat gold watch from his pocket. That's nothing, he said, that's only a part of it. They should see his big farm in New Zealand – horses, carriages, meat every day, and he never said 'sir' to no one.

The old men kept silent, but drank their free drinks and sniggered every so often. The youths in the shadows just gazed at the man, and gazed at his spinning watch, and as he grew more drunk they looked at each other, then stole away one by one . . .

The weather outside had suddenly hardened into a blizzard of cutting snow; the night shut down to the blinding cold and the village curled up in its sheets. When the public house closed and turned down its lamps, the New Zealander was the last to leave. He refused a lantern, said he was born here, wasn't he? and paid for his bill with gold. Then he buttoned his coat, shouted goodnight, and strode up the howling valley. Warm with whisky and nearing home, he went singing up the hill. There were those in their beds who heard his last song, pitched wailing against the storm.

When he reached the stone-cross the young men were waiting, a bunched group, heads down in the wind.

'Well, Vincent?' they said; and he stopped, and stopped singing.

They hit him in turn, beat him down to his knees, beat him bloodily down in the snow. They beat and kicked him for the sake of themselves, as he lay there face down, groaning. Then they ripped off his coat, emptied his pockets, threw him over a wall, and left him. He was insensible now from his wounds and the drink; the storm blew all night across him. He didn't stir again from the place where he lay; and in the morning he was found frozen to death.

The police came, of course, but discovered nothing. Their inquiries were met by stares. But the tale spread quickly from mouth to mouth, was deliberately spread amongst us, was given to everyone, man and child, that we might learn each detail and hide it. The police left at last with the case unsolved; but neither we nor they forgot it . . .

About ten years later an old lady lay dying, and towards the end she grew light-headed. The subject of her wandering leaked out somehow: she seemed to be haunted by a watch. 'The watch,' she kept mumbling, 'they maun find the watch. Tell the boy to get it hid.' A dark-suited stranger, with a notebook in his hand, appeared suddenly at her bedside. While she tossed and muttered, he sat and waited, head bent to her whispering mouth. He was patient, anonymous, and never made any fuss; he just sat by her bed all day, his notebook open, his pencil poised, the blank pages like listening ears.

The old lady at last had a lucid moment and saw the stranger sitting beside her. 'Who's this?' she demanded of her hovering daughter. The girl leaned over the bed. 'It's all right, Mother,' said the daughter distinctly. 'It's only a police-station gentleman. He hasn't come to make any trouble. He just wants to hear about the watch.'

The old lady gave the stranger a sharp clear look and uttered not another word; she just leaned back on the pillow, closed her lips and eyes, folded her hands, and died. It was the end of the weakness that had endangered her sons; and the dark-suited stranger knew it. He rose to his feet, put his notebook in his pocket, and tiptoed out of the room. This old and wandering dying mind had been their final chance. No other leads appeared after that, and the case was never solved.

But the young men who had gathered in that winter ambush continued to live among us. I saw them often about the village: simple jokers, hard-working, mild – the solid heads of families. They were not treated as outcasts, nor did they appear to live under any special stain. They belonged to the village and the village looked after them. They are all of them dead now anyway.

Laurie Lee, *Cider with Rosie*

The murder story has often been told, but incorrectly. What happened was that Lawrence on his way to Syria had bought a copper watch at Paris for ten francs. By constant use the case had been polished till it shone. In a Turkman village near the banks of the Euphrates where he was collecting Hittite antiquities he took out this watch one morning; the villagers murmured 'Gold'. A villager stalked Lawrence all day as he went on his journey and towards evening ran ahead and met him, as if accidentally.

Lawrence asked the way to a certain village. The Turkman showed him a short cut across country; where he sprang upon Lawrence, knocked him down, snatched his Colt revolver, put it to his head and pulled the trigger. Though loaded it did not go off: the villager did not understand the mechanism of the safety catch, which was raised. He tried the trigger again and then in anger threw it away and battered Lawrence about the head with stones. The appearance of a shepherd fortunately frightened him off before he had succeeded in cracking Lawrence's skull. Lawrence got up, crossed the Euphrates to the nearest town (Birejik) where he could find Turkish policemen. There he presented the order that he had from the Turkish Ministry of the Interior requiring all local governors to afford him every help, and collected a hundred and ten men. With this force, whose ferry-fare he had to pay across the river, he re-entered the village. Contrary to the usual story of a desperate fight and the burning of the village, there was no violence. Lawrence, with fever heavy on him, went to sleep while the usual day-long argument went on between the police and the villagers. At night the village elders gave up the stolen property and the thief. The true version of the story is better if only because it has this more satisfactory ending that the thief afterwards worked in the diggings at Carchemish under Lawrence; not too well, but Lawrence was easy with him.

Robert Graves, *Lawrence and the Arabs*

W

War

NORTHUMBERLAND: Now bind my brows with iron, and approach
The ragged'st hour that time and spite dare bring
To frown upon th'enraged Northumberland!
Let heaven kiss earth! Now let not nature's hand
Keep the wild flood confined! Let order die!
And let this world no longer be a stage
To feed contention in a ling'ring act;
But let one spirit of the first-born Cain
Reign in all bosoms, that each heart being set
On bloody courses, the rude scene may end,
And darkness be the burier of the dead!

William Shakespeare, *2 Henry IV*

All was prepared – the fire, the sword, the men
To wield them in their terrible array.
The army, like a lion from his den,
March'd forth with nerve and sinews bent to slay, –
A human Hydra, issuing from its fen
To breathe destruction on its winding way,
Whose heads were heroes, which, cut off in vain,
Immediately in others grew again.

History can only take things in the gross;
But could we know them in detail, perchance
In balancing the profit and the loss,
War's merit it by no means might enhance,

To waste so much gold for so little dross,
  As hath been done, mere conquest to advance.
The drying up a single tear has more
Of honest fame, than shedding seas of gore.

And why? – because it brings self-approbation;
  Whereas the other, after all its glare,
Shouts, bridges, arches, pensions from a nation,
  Which (it may be) has not much left to spare,
A higher title, or a loftier station,
  Though they may make corruption gape and stare,
Yet, in the end, except in freedom's battles,
Are nothing but a child of Murder's rattles.

George Gordon, Lord Byron, *Don Juan*

So Abram rose, and clave the wood, and went,
And took the fire with him, and a knife.
And as they sojourned both of them together,
Isaac the first-born spake and said, 'My Father,
Behold the preparations, fire and iron,
But where the lamb for this burnt-offering?
Then Abram bound the youth with belts and straps,
And builded parapets and trenches there,
And stretchèd forth the knife to slay his son.
When lo! an angel called him out of heaven,
Saying, Lay not thy hand upon the lad,
Neither do anything to him. Behold,
A ram, caught in a thicket by its horns;
Offer the Ram of Pride instead of him.
But the old man would not so, but slew his son,
And half the seed of Europe, one by one.

Wilfred Owen, 'The Parable of the Old Man and the Young'

I am a Socialist, and so hold in all sincerity that the life and personality of every man is sacred, and that there is something of divinity in every human being, irrespective of the nation to which he belongs. I cannot betray my belief in the brotherhood of all men. To me, war is murder and will only become impossible when an increasing number of those who share this conviction remain true to their beliefs and refuse to take part in warfare, whatever be the pretext for which it is waged.

Clifford Allen, Claim for Absolute Exemption, Local Tribunal, Battersea, 14 March 1916

Wedding Night

Laurent closed the door carefully behind him and stayed leaning against it for a while, looking around the room with an anxious, embarrassed expression on his face.

A fire was burning brightly in the grate, casting swathes of dancing yellow light on to the ceiling and walls and illuminating the room with a strong, flickering glow which made the lamp on the table seem feeble by comparison. Madame Raquin had wanted to arrange the room prettily, and it was all perfumed and decked out in white, like a nest for young, innocent love; she had taken particular pleasure in adding a few pieces of lace around the bed and filling the vases on the mantelpiece with great bouquets of roses. The room was full of gentle warmth and lingering scents, and bathed in a calm, reposeful atmosphere redolent of relaxed sensuality. From time to time the crackling of the fire broke into the silence of trembling anticipation. It was like some delightful wilderness, a warm and sweet-scented hideaway shut off from the bustle of the outside world, one of those secret places which form the perfect background to passion and sensual pleasure, providing the sense of mystery that is their necessary accompaniment.

Thérèse was sitting on a low chair to the right of the fireplace, her chin cupped in her hand, staring fixedly into the flames. She did not look round when Laurent came in. Her lace-trimmed petticoat and bodice stood out stark white in the brilliant light of the fire. The bodice had slipped down, revealing a pink patch of shoulder half hidden by a lock of her black hair.

Laurent moved a few steps forward, without speaking. He took off his tail-coat and jacket. When he was in his shirt-sleeves he looked again at Thérèse, who had not moved. Then he caught sight of her exposed shoulder and bent down, trembling, to press his lips to the piece of bare flesh. But she turned abruptly round, withdrawing her shoulder, and gave Laurent such a strange look of revulsion and fear that he backed away, disconcerted and ill at ease, as if himself smitten with fear and loathing.

He sat down opposite Thérèse, on the other side of the fireplace, and there they remained, silent and motionless, for a whole five minutes. Now and again jets of reddish flame would shoot forth from the burning wood, casting blood-red reflections over the faces of the murderers.

It was almost two years since the lovers had found themselves in the same bedroom together, without witnesses and able to give themselves up entirely to each other. They had not had a single amorous assignation since the day when Thérèse had come round to the Rue Saint-Victor, bringing with her the idea of murdering Camille. As a prudent calculation they had weaned their bodies off each other, scarcely even allowing themselves an occasional hand-clasp or furtive kiss. After the murder of Camille, when new desires had seized them, they had contained their lust and decided to await their wedding night, promising themselves extraordinary pleasures once they could enjoy them with impunity. Now that the great night had finally arrived, they just sat there face to face, suddenly overcome with panic and unease. They only had to stretch out their arms to fall together in a passionate embrace, but their arms felt limp, as though they were already tired out and satiated with love. The torpor of the day's events weighed more and more heavily on them and they looked at each other without any desire, afraid, embarrassed, and upset at their own frigid, silent behaviour. Thus their passionate dreams had led them into a peculiar situation in which, having succeeded in killing Camille and getting married to each other, all it had taken to cool their lust to the point of horror and disgust was for Laurent's lips to have brushed against Thérèse's shoulder.

They started desperately searching within themselves for a little of the passion that had burned in their hearts long ago. Their bodies no longer seemed to contain either muscles or nerves, and their embarrassment and worry grew until they became horribly ashamed of just sitting, glum and silent, opposite each other. They wished they could find the strength to throw themselves into a crushing embrace, so as not to appear as complete fools in their own eyes. After all, they belonged to each other, didn't they? They had killed a man and played out a gruesome comedy so as to be free to wallow in constant sensual gratification, and now there they were, sitting stiffly on opposite sides of the fireplace, exhausted, troubled in mind, and utterly lethargic of body. After a while, they both began to feel that such an outcome was just too ridiculously horrible and cruel. So Laurent tried to speak of love and conjure up memories of the past, calling upon his imagination to revive their former tender feelings.

'Thérèse,' he said, leaning over to the young woman, 'do you remember our afternoons in this room . . . I used to come in through that door . . .

Today, I came in through this one here . . . We are free now, and we'll be able to love each other in peace.'

He spoke hesitantly and without conviction. Thérèse, hunched up in her low chair, was still staring absently into the flames, not listening. Laurent continued:

'Do you remember that dream of mine? I used to dream I was going to spend a whole night with you, and fall asleep in your arms and be woken in the morning by your kisses. Now I'm going to make the dream come true.'

Thérèse started, as if surprised by a voice muttering in her ear, and turned towards Laurent, on whose face the fire was at that moment casting a reddish glow; at the sight of this bloody visage, a shiver ran through her.

He went on, disconcerted now and even more anxious:

'We have done it, Thérèse, we have removed all the obstacles between us and we belong to each other . . . The future is all ours, isn't it? A future full of peace and happiness, and contented love . . . Camille isn't there any more . . .'

He stopped short, his throat dry, gasping for air, unable to carry on. The name of Camille had come as a blow to Thérèse, hitting her in the pit of her stomach. The two murderers stared dumbfounded at each other, pale and shaking. The yellow light of the fire still danced across the walls and ceiling, a warm scent of roses hung in the air, and the fire crackled away in the silence.

Now their memories had been let loose, the ghost of Camille had been invoked, and it had come to seat itself between the newly-weds, in front of the blazing fire. Thérèse and Laurent smelt again the same cold, damp stench of the drowned man in the warm air that they were breathing; they both sensed the presence of a corpse there with them, and gazed at each other, not daring to move. Then the whole appalling story of their crime unfolded once more before their mind's eye. The victim's name was enough to bring the past flooding back and force them to relive the anguish of the murder all over again. Without opening their lips they stared at each other, and both experienced the same nightmare and read the start of the same cruel story in each other's eyes. This exchange of terrified looks, and the wordless narrative of the murder which they were about to recount to each other, filled them both with intolerably acute apprehension. With their nerves thus stretched to breaking-point, they were on the verge of screaming and coming to blows. In an attempt to drive away the memories, Laurent wrenched himself out of the terrified fascination which held him transfixed in Thérèse's gaze and moved a few steps away, taking off his boots and putting slippers on; then he went back to sit down by the fireplace and tried to make trivial conversation.

Thérèse understood what he wanted to do, and made herself respond to his questions. They chatted about this and that, trying to force themselves to make small talk. Laurent declared that it was hot in the bedroom, and Thérèse replied that nevertheless a draught was coming in under the door to the back stairs; and they both turned towards the little door with a sudden shudder. So Laurent quickly changed the subject, talking about the roses, the fire, and anything else he could see in the room; with a great effort, she found monosyllabic replies to keep the conversation going. They had moved further apart and assumed an air of unconcern; they were trying to forget who they were, and to behave towards each other like strangers thrown together purely by chance.

Yet oddly, despite all their efforts to exchange empty nothings, each could guess the thoughts that the other was hiding beneath the banality of his or her speech. They were quite unable to stop thinking about Camille, and their eyes carried on telling the story from the past as they conversed silently but insistently in glances beneath the aimless conversation they were holding out loud. The occasional words they spoke were meaningless, disconnected, and contradictory, for their whole being was straining towards a silent exchange of terrifying memories. When Laurent spoke of the roses, or the fire, or whatever else, Thérèse understood perfectly that he was reminding her of the struggle in the boat and the muted splash made by Camille, and, whenever she replied to a trivial question with a yes or a no, Laurent understood that she was saying she did or did not remember a particular detail of the crime. And in this way they discussed what was on their minds, with no need of words, and while talking about something else. Moreover, they were not really aware of what they were saying, for they were busy following the train of their secret thoughts, one idea after another; had they suddenly carried on with their confidences aloud, they would have understood perfectly well what each other was talking about. Gradually, this kind of mind-reading, caused by their memory's stubborn insistence on constantly forcing upon them the image of Camille, began to drive them frantic; they realized they could each see what the other was thinking and that, if they did not keep quiet, words would come unbidden into their mouths to name the drowned man and retell the story of the murder out loud. Whereupon they brought the conversation to an end and kept their lips sealed.

But in the dreadful silence that followed, the two murderers still went on conversing about their victim. Each felt as if the other's gaze were piercing his or her flesh with sharp, pointed phrases. Sometimes they thought they heard each other speaking out loud; their senses were becoming distorted, their vision turning into a strange, delicate kind of hearing; they could read each other's faces so clearly that the very thoughts acquired a peculiar, strident sound of their own which shook their organisms to the core. They could not have understood each other better if they had both screamed in heart-rending tones: 'We killed Camille, and his body is still here between us, turning our limbs to ice.' And the terrible confessions went on flowing between them, more visible and resounding than ever, in the calm, damp air of the room.

Laurent and Thérèse had begun communicating their unspoken story to each other by recounting the day of their first meeting, in the shop. Then other memories had come back one by one, in order; the hours of ecstasy, the moments of hesitation and anger, and the terrible instant of the murder. It was at that point that they had sealed up their lips and stopped their small talk, for fear of suddenly naming Camille without meaning to. Yet their thoughts did not stop there, but took them on through the panic and the fearful waiting that had followed the murder. And so into their minds came thoughts of the drowned man's corpse stretched out on a slab in the Morgue. With one look, Laurent told Thérèse all about the horror he had felt, and Thérèse, pushed beyond endurance and forced by a hand of iron to unseal her lips, suddenly took up the conversation out loud:

'So you saw him at the Morgue?' she asked Laurent, without naming Camille.

Laurent seemed to be expecting this question; he had aleady been reading it for a while on the young woman's blanched face.

'Yes,' he replied in a choked voice.

A shudder ran through the murderers; they moved closer to the fire and held their hands out to the flames, as if an icy draught had suddenly whistled through the hot room. They remained silent for a while as they huddled there together in the warmth. Then Thérése continued in an undertone:

'Did he look as though he had suffered much pain?'

Laurent was unable to answer, but made a shocked gesture, as if to ward off some revolting vision. Then he jumped up and went over to the bed, before coming back over to Thérèse with his arms open in a violent gesture.

'Give me a kiss,' he said, stretching out his neck to her.

Thérèse had risen to her feet, looking terribly pale in her night attire, and was leaning back with one elbow on the marble of the fireplace. She looked at Laurent's neck. Amid the white of the flesh she could see a pink blotch, which a rush of blood was now enlarging and turning a fiery red.

'Kiss me, kiss me,' he said again, with his face and neck aflame.

She leaned even further back to avoid kissing him, then, pressing a finger-tip to Camille's bite-mark, she asked her husband:

'What's that? I didn't know you had hurt yourself.'

Thérèse's finger felt as if it were boring a hole in his throat; the contact made him pull away, wincing in pain.

'That,' he stammered, 'it's . . .'

He hesitated, but found he could not lie and had to admit the truth.

'It's Camille; you see, he bit me, in the boat. It's nothing, it's all right now . . . Kiss me, kiss me!'

Then the wretched fellow held out his smarting neck once more. He wanted Thérèse to kiss him on the scar in the hope that it would soothe the thousand stings which were torturing his flesh. Chin held up and neck thrust forward, he offered himself again, but Thérèse, by now almost lying along the fireplace, made a gesture of utter repugnance and cried out in a beseeching voice:

'No, no, not there . . . it's all bloody.'

She slumped down trembling on to the low chair and held her head in her hands. Laurent stood there, not knowing what had happened. He lowered his chin and looked uncomprehendingly at Thérèse. Then, all of a sudden, he seized her head between his great hands in an animal-like embrace and forced her lips towards his neck, down on to the bite. He held her head there for a few seconds, crushed against his skin. Thérèse had given up resisting and was emitting muffled moans, unable to breathe against his neck. When she managed to escape from his clutches, she wiped her mouth violently and spat in the fire. She had not said a word.

Ashamed at his brutality, Laurent began to walk slowly up and down between the bed and the window. It was pain alone, that terrible smarting, that had made him demand a kiss from Thérèse, and when her cold lips had pressed against the burning scar the pain had been ever greater. This kiss obtained by violence had shattered him; nothing in the world could have made him wish for another one, so painful had the shock been. And as he looked at the woman with whom he was now obliged to live, trembling and hunched up in front of the fire, with her back to him, he told himself over and again that he no longer loved her and she did not love him. For nearly an hour Thérèse sat slumped in her chair while

Laurent paced silently up and down. They were each facing up to the terrifying fact that their passion was now dead, and that in killing Camille they had also killed off their own desire. The fire was slowly dying down, leaving a great mass of glowing embers. The heat in the room had gradually become stifling; the flowers were drooping, thickening the air with their heavy, drowsy scents.

Suddenly Laurent thought he had had a hallucination. As he was turning round to walk back from the window to the bed, he saw Camille in a shadowy corner, between the fireplace and the wardrobe. His victim's face was all green and contorted, just as he had seen it on the slab at the Morgue. He stood there rooted to the spot, weak at the knees, leaning against a piece of furniture. Hearing his low gasp of terror, Thérèse looked up.

'There, over there,' he groaned.

With arm outstretched, he pointed to the shadowy corner where he could see the ghastly face of Camille. Thérèse, caught up in his fear, ran over and clung to him.

'It's his portrait,' she whispered, as if the painted figure of her former husband could hear her.

'His portrait?' Laurent repeated, his hair by now standing on end.

'Yes, you know, the painting you did of him. My aunt was going to move it into her room today; she must have forgotten to take it down.'

'Of course . . . his portrait . . .'

For some time the murderer did not recognize the canvas. In his fear and confusion, he had forgotten that he himself had drawn the crude features and daubed on the muddy colours which so terrified him now. Panic made him see the painting as it really was, repulsive, ill-composed, and murky, a grimacing death's head on a black background. He was astounded and overwhelmed by the unspeakable ugliness of his own creation; above all there were the two white eyes swimming in their spongy, yellowish sockets which exactly reminded him of the decomposing eyes of the drowned man at the Morgue. He stood there for a while panting for breath, thinking that Thérèse was lying in order to reassure him. Then he made out the frame, and began to calm down.

'Go and take it down,' he said to her in a whisper.

'Oh no! I'm scared!' she replied with a shudder.

Laurent started shaking again. At times the frame seemed to disappear and he saw only the two white eyes staring hard at him.

'Please,' he begged his wife, 'will you take it down?'

'No, I can't.'

'We'll turn it round to face the wall, then it won't be able to scare us any more.'

The murderer, craven and cringing, pushed Thérèse towards the canvas, hiding behind her to avoid the drowned man's stare. However, she freed herself, so he decided to take the risk himself and went up to the picture with arm raised, fumbling for the hook. But the portrait gave him such a long, hideous, crushing look that, having tried to out-stare it, Laurent was overwhelmed and forced to admit defeat, backing away and muttering:

'No, you're right, Thérèse, we can't . . . Your aunt can take it down tomorrow.'

Head bowed, he resumed his pacing up and down, feeling sure that the portrait was still staring at him, following him around with its eyes. He could not stop himself from casting a furtive glance at the painting now and again, and each time he saw the drowned man's blank, lifeless stare emerging from the shadows. The thought that Camille was there in the corner, spying on him, observing his wedding night, scrutinizing Thérèse and himself, drove him utterly crazy with fear and desperation.

A small thing which would have made anyone else smile caused him to lose his head altogether. As he was by the fireplace, he heard a sort of scratching sound. He turned pale, convinced that it was coming from the portrait and imagining that Camille was getting down from his frame. Then he realized that it was actually coming from the door to the back stairs. He looked at Thérèse, who was again gripped by panic.

'There's someone at the top of the stairs,' he hissed. 'Who could it be, coming in that way?'

She made no reply. Their minds both turned to the drowned man, and an icy sweat broke out on their foreheads. They fled to the far side of the room, expecting the door to fly open and Camille's corpse to fall in on the floor. As the scratching continued, louder and more erratic, they imagined their victim tearing at the wood with his nails in an attempt to get in. For almost five minutes they did not dare to move. Then at last there came a miaow, and, as Laurent went over to look, he realized that it was Madame Raquin's tabby cat, which had been shut in the bedroom by mistake and was trying to get out by rattling the door with his claws. François was frightened by Laurent; in a single bound he leapt up on to a chair and, with fur bristling and legs out rigid, he stared straight at his new master with a hard, cruel look in his eye. Laurent did not like cats, and François was close to frightening him, for in this overwrought atmosphere of fear he thought the cat was about to leap at his face to avenge Camille. The creature must know everything; there were thoughts going on behind its round, strangely dilated eyes. Faced with the fixity of this animal stare, Laurent had to look away. He was on the point of giving François a kick when Thérèse cried out:

'Don't hurt him!'

Her shout affected him strangely and brought an absurd idea into his head.

'Camille has entered that cat's body,' he thought. 'I shall have to kill it . . . It looks so human.'

He did not deliver the kick, for fear of hearing François speak to him with Camille's voice. Then he remembered the jokes Thérèse used to make in the days of their great passion, when the cat had been a witness to all their embraces, and he told himself that the creature knew too much and would have to be thrown out of the window. But he lacked the courage to go through with his plan. François was still ready for battle: with claws out and back arched in aggravation, he followed his enemy's every movement with superb detachment. Laurent was disconcerted by the steely glint in his eye; he hastened to open the door into the dining-room and the cat fled with a high-pitched miaow.

Thérèse had resumed her seat by the hearth, where the fire had now gone out; Laurent went back to pacing up and down between the bed and the window; and thus they waited for dawn. They had no thoughts of going to bed; the life had quite gone out of their hearts and their bodies, and they had one desire only, to get out of that suffocating room. Being shut up together and having to breathe the same air made them feel utterly sick; they would have liked someone else there to interrupt their intimacy and rescue them from the cruel embarrassment of being in each other's presence, unable to utter a word and quite incapable of resurrecting their passion. Their prolonged silences, heavy with bitter, despairing recriminations and unspoken accusations, which they could nevertheless hear quite distinctly in the calm air, were a torture to them.

Daylight came at last, dirty and grey, bringing with it a biting chill.

Once the room was filled with pale light, Laurent shivered but felt rather calmer. He looked squarely at Camille's portrait and saw it as it really was, trivial and childish; with a shrug he took it down, thinking how silly he had been. Thérèse stood up and went to unmake the bed, so as to deceive her aunt into thinking they had spent a blissful night together.

'Now look here,' said Laurent harshly, 'I hope we'll get a bit more sleep tonight. This kind of childishness just can't go on.'

Thérèse gave him a deep, serious look.

'You must realize,' he said, 'I didn't get married for sleepless nights . . . We're behaving like children . . . It's your fault; when you put on your graveyard expression like that, it flusters me. Do try and be a bit more cheerful tonight and not scare me to death.'

He gave a forced laugh, for no particular reason.

'I'll try,' she replied in an undertone.

Such was their wedding night.

Emile Zola, *Thérèse Raquin*, trans. Andrew Rothwell

Whitechapel

31 August 1888 to 9 November 1888

I said a shilling, since it was a smart carriage
and he did me on the floor of it then pushed me out
with my skirt round my ears, drove off without paying.

Mary Ann had her skirt up too and a knife mark
jagged from rib to pelvis; throat cut to the spine.

Tinker, tailor,

I had my monthly health next and couldn't work –
didn't get the fourpence for the lodging house,
had to sleep the night in a doorway.
I was glad to see it though. He stole Annie's uterus.

Tinker, tailor,
Foreign Sailor,

The next was too drunk –
champagne and best claret at two and six a bottle –
only talked and talked and talked.

Two that night – Lizzie and Cathy.
He cut their ears off.

Tinker, tailor,
Foreign Sailor,
Surgeon, butcher,

Then I had five in a mews. It was November and cold
and I had the stench of horse piss in my nose.

But they were good boys, sailors from the docks,
and filled me with beer and gin and themselves.

Afterwards, I rested inside.
A hansom nag nuzzled my face like a kiss.
Mary Kelly was the last, that night.
Everything: head, arm, nose, skin.

Tinker, tailor,
Foreign Sailor,
Surgeon, butcher,
Royal Duke.

Call him Tom, Dick, Harry, Jack –
He takes everything.

Susan Kelly, 'Whitechapel Nights'

Armchair detectives hoping to identify Jack the Ripper face a clear choice. One route is to follow hunches, attributing the means, motive and opportunity to a likely Victorian. A hundred years after the event, very few suspects can be excluded with complete confidence: hence the steady proliferation of 'final solutions'.

The alternative is to be guided by the police officers charged with the original investigation. We now know who they suspected although, tantalizingly, we do not know why. There are two pieces of evidence, the Macnaghten Memorandum and the Swanson Marginalia.

Sir Melville Macnaghten was the Assistant Chief Constable from 1889 to 1890, and in 1894 he recorded his views on the Ripper case, first setting out his reasons for believing that a man called Cutbush was not the culprit, and then discussing his three preferred suspects, now identified as Druitt, Kosminski and Ostrog. In the early 1930s Macnaghten's memorandum was copied by his youngest daughter, Lady Christabel Aberconway, who typed out seven quarto sheets, the existence of which only came to public attention in 1959.

In his memorandum, Macnaghten concludes: 'I am inclined to exonerate the last two' – Kosminski and Ostrog – 'but I have always held strong opinions about No 1' – Druitt – 'and the more I think the matter over, the stronger these opinions become. The truth, however, will never be known.' Serious historical work on Jack the Ripper's identity started with the Macnaghten Memorandum.

Of the three suspects, Druitt was a barrister who committed suicide in December 1888 shortly after the last of the murders, leaving a note to the effect that 'since Friday I felt that I was going to be like Mother, and it would be best for all concerned if I were to die'. Druitt had recently been dismissed from Valentine's school at Blackheath for an unspecified but serious offence; according to Macnaghten he was 'sexually insane and from private information I have little doubt but that his family believed him to have been the murderer'. Macnaghten continued: 'The Whitechapel murderer in all probability put an end to himself soon after the Dorset Street affair in November 1888 . . . Certain facts, pointing to this conclusion, were not in possession of the police till some years after I became a police officer.'

No one knows what these 'certain facts' were; the only certainty is that Macnaghten, a sensible, reliable man who knew everything about the case, believed that Druitt was his man and put his suspicions on file.

Michael Ostrog proved the most difficult suspect to track down since he operated under at least thirty aliases. Macnaghten characterized him as 'a mad Russian doctor and convict and unquestionably a homicidal maniac. This man was said to have been habitually cruel to women and carried about with him surgical knives and other instruments.' A Russian or Polish Jew born in 1833, Ostrog traded as a confidence trickster. The year before the murders, in September 1887, he appeared at the Old Bailey accused of stealing a metal tankard. Ostrog pleaded insanity, but was sentenced to six months; he was discharged from Surrey Pauper Lunatic Asylum on 10 March 1888. Thereafter he failed to report to the police and his later movements, including his whereabouts during and after the vital period of six months later, are vague, although Macnaghten notes he 'was subsequently detained in a lunatic asylum'.

Finally there is suspect Number Three: Aaron Kosminski, the Man Who Died of Masturbation. Kosminski was a Polish Jew, a bootmaker who arrived in Britain in 1882 at the age of seventeen. He lived at 15 Black Lion Yard in Whitechapel, and was diagnosed as syphilitic on 24 March 1888. According to the Macnaghten Memorandum, he inhabited the heart of the district where the murders were committed. He became 'insane owing to many years of indulgence in solitary vices. He had a great hatred of women with strong homicidal tendencies. He was and I believe is detained in a lunatic asylum about March 1889 . . . There were many circumstances connected with this man which made him a strong "suspect".'

At this stage the Swanson Marginalia come into play. These are the recently discovered pencil notes made by Chief Inspector Donald Swanson in his personal copy of Sir Robert Anderson's memoirs, *The Lighter Side of My Official Life*. Anderson had early charge of the Ripper investigation; his book says: 'The conclusion we came to was that he and his people were certain low class Polish Jews; for it is remarkable that the people of that class in the East End will not give up one of their number to Gentile justice. And the result proved that our diagnosis was right on every point. I will merely add that the only person who ever had a good view of the murder unhesitatingly identified the suspect the instant he was confronted with him, but he refused to give evidence against him. In saying that he was a Polish Jew I am merely stating a definitely ascertained fact. And my words are meant to specify race, not religion.'

For many decades these sentences were believed to refer to a suspect known as 'Leather Apron', or John Pizer. But Anderson's predecessor at the Yard, Chief Inspector Donald Swanson, owned a copy of Anderson's book, which he read and annotated. On Swanson's death, it passed to his daughter, and on her death it was inherited by his nephew who, in 1987, ninety-nine years after the murders, stumbled upon his grandfather's marginal notes.

The jottings identify Anderson's man as Kosminski, and explain the refusal of the eyewitness to confirm his identification thus: 'because the suspect was also a Jew and also because his evidence would convict the suspect'. Swanson commented that after Kosminski's identification the killings came to an end, 'and very shortly afterwards the suspect with his hands tied behind his back was sent to Stepney Workhouse and thence to Colney Hatch; poor Polish Jews from Whitechapel, had a home to go to wash and people to shield him. Redischarged after three days, readmitted 4 Feb 1891. He took up a knife and threatened his sister.'

Kosminski died in confinement in 1919. Unlikely though it may be that the police allowed their prime suspect to go free from 1888 to 1891, the fact remains that the only candidates on a shortlist compiled by the handful of men versed in the full details of the police inquiry were Druitt, Osgood and Kosminski.

This trail is lukewarm at best. Macnaghten clearly knew little about Druitt, putting his age at forty-one instead of thirty-one and describing him as a doctor not a barrister; and cricket enthusiasts point out that Druitt's fixtures show him taking wickets only a few hours after the killings, turning out on Blackheath's Rectory Field on the morning of 8 September 1888. But if the Ripper's identity is to be revealed, it is by reliance on the written record through documentary research. A cold trail is better than no trail at all, and there is no reason why the murderer should have come to public attention in any other context. Who would have heard of Ramirez, or DeSalvo, or Bianchi, but for their killings?

The 1993 'Ripper diary' designates James Maybrick as the culprit, but pre-publication doubts have focused on the handwriting, which bears no overt resemblence to Maybrick's known script.

Oliver Cyriax, *Crime: An Encyclopedia*

To my astonishment I cannot believe I have not been caught. My heart felt as if it had left my body. Within my fright I imagined my heart bounding along the street with I in desperation following it. I would have dearly loved to have cut the head of the damned horse off and stuff it as far as it would go down the whores throat. I had no time to rip the bitch wide, I curse my bad luck. I believe the thrill of being caught thrilled me more than cutting the whore herself. As I write I find it impossible to believe he did not see me, in my estimation I was less than a few feet from him. The fool panicked, it is what saved me. My satisfaction was far from complete, damn the bastard, I cursed him and cursed him, but I was clever, they could not out do me. *No one* ever will. Within the quarter of the hour I found another dirty bitch willing to sell her wares. The whore like all the rest was only too willing. The thrill she gave me was unlike the others, I cut deep deep deep. Her nose annoyed me so I cut it off, had a go at her eyes, left my mark, could not get the bitch's head off. I believe now it is impossible to do so. The whore never screamed. I took all I could away with me. I am saving it for a rainy day *ha ha*.

• • •

With a rose to match the red
I tried to cut off the head.
Damn it I cried,
the horse went and shied
hence forth I did hide,
but I could still smell
her sweet scented breath

One whore no good, decided Sir Jim strike another.
I showed no fright, and indeed no light.
Damn it, the tin box was empty

Sweet sugar and tea
could have paid my small fee
But instead I did flee and by way showed my glee
by eating cold kidney for supper

Oh, Mr Abberline he is a clever little man,
he keeps back all that he can.
For do I not know better, Indeed I do,
did I not leave him a very good clue
Nothing is mentioned of this I know sure,
ask clever Abberline, could tell you more

He believes I will trip over,
but I have no fear.
For I could not possibly
redeem it here.
Of this certain fact I could send them poste haste
If he requested that be the case

• • •

Soon, I trust I shall be laid beside my dear mother and father. I shall seek their forgiveness when we are reunited. God I pray will allow me at least that privilege, although I know only too well I do not deserve it. My thoughts will remain in tact, for a reminder to all how love does destroy. I place this now in a place were it shall be found. I pray whoever should read this will find it in their heart to forgive me. Remind all, whoever you may be, that I was once a gentle man. May the good lord have mercy on my soul, and forgive me for all I have done.

I give my name that all know of me, so history do tell, what love can do to a gentle man born
Yours truly
Jack the Ripper
Dated this third day of May 1889

The Diary of Jack the Ripper, ed. Shirley Harrison

Why?

'It was like this: I asked myself one day this question – what if Napoleon, for instance, had happened to be in my place, and if he had not had

Toulon nor Egypt nor the passage of Mont Blanc to begin his career with, but instead of all those picturesque and monumental things there had simply been some ridiculous old hag, a pawnbroker, who had to be murdered too to get money from her trunk (for his career, you understand). Well, would he have brought himself to that if there had been no other means? Wouldn't he have felt a pang at its being so far from monumental and . . . and sinful, too? Well, I must tell you that I worried myself fearfully over that "question" so that I was awfully ashamed when I guessed at last (all of a sudden, somehow) that it would not have given him the least pang, that it would not even have struck him that it was not monumental . . . that he would not have seen that there was anything in it to pause over, and that, if he had had no other way, he would have strangled her in a minute without thinking about it! Well, I too . . . left off thinking about it . . . murdered her, following his example. And that's exactly how it was! Do you think it funny? Yes, Sonia, the funniest thing of all is that perhaps that's just how it was.'

Sonia did not think it at all funny.

'You had better tell me straight out . . . without examples,' she begged, still more timidly and scarcely audibly.

He turned to her, looked sadly at her, and took her hands.

'You are right again, Sonia. Of course that's all nonsense, it's almost all talk! You see, you know of course that my mother has scarcely anything, my sister happened to have a good education and was condemned to drudge as a governess. All their hopes were centred on me. I was a student, but I couldn't keep myself at the university and was forced for a time to leave it. Even if I had lingered on like that, in ten or twelve years I might (with luck) hope to be some sort of teacher or clerk with a salary of a thousand roubles' – he repeated it as though it were a lesson – 'and by that time my mother would be worn out with grief and anxiety and I could not succeed in keeping her in comfort, while my sister . . . well, my sister might well have fared worse! And it's a hard thing to pass everything by all one's life, to turn one's back upon everything, to forget one's mother and decorously accept the insults inflicted on one's sister. Why should one? When one has buried them, to burden oneself with others – wife and children – and to leave them again without a farthing? So I resolved to gain possession of the old woman's money and to use it for my first years without worrying my mother, to keep myself at the university and for a little while after leaving it – and to do this all on a broad, thorough scale, so as to build up a completely new career and enter upon a new life of independence

. . . Well . . . that's all . . . Well, of course in killing the old woman I did wrong . . . Well, that's enough.'

He struggled to the end of his speech in exhaustion and let his head sink.

'Oh, that's not it, that's not it,' Sonia cried in distress. 'How could one . . . no, that's not right, not right.'

'You see yourself that it's not right. But I've spoken truly, it's the truth.'

'As though that could be the truth! Good God!'

'I've only killed a louse, Sonia, a useless, loathsome, harmful creature.'

'A human being – a louse!'

'I too know it wasn't a louse,' he answered, looking strangely at her. 'But I am talking nonsense, Sonia,' he added. 'I've been talking nonsense a long time . . . That's not it, you are right there. There were quite, quite other causes for it! I haven't talked to anyone for so long, Sonia . . . My head aches dreadfully now.'

His eyes shone with feverish brilliance. He was almost delirious; an uneasy smile strayed on his lips. His terrible exhaustion could be seen through his excitement. Sonia saw how he was suffering. She too was growing dizzy. And he talked so strangely: it seemed somehow comprehensible, but yet . . . 'But how, how? Good God!' And she wrung her hands in despair.

'No, Sonia, that's not it,' he began again suddenly, raising his head as though a new and sudden train of thought had struck and as it were roused him, 'that's not it! Better . . . imagine – yes, it's certainly better – imagine that I am vain, envious, malicious, base, vindictive, and . . . well, perhaps with a tendency to insanity. (Let's have it all out at once! They've talked of madness already, I noticed.) I told you just now I could not keep myself at the university. But do you know that perhaps I might have done? My mother would have sent me what I needed for the fees and I could have earned enough for clothes, boots, and food, no doubt. Lessons had turned up at half a rouble. Razumihin works! But I turned sulky and wouldn't. (Yes, sulkiness, that's the right word for it!) I sat in my room like a spider. You've been in my den, you've seen it . . . And do you know, Sonia, that low ceilings and tiny rooms cramp the soul and the mind? Ah, how I hated that garret! And yet I wouldn't go out of it! I wouldn't on purpose! I didn't go out for days together, and I wouldn't work, I wouldn't even eat, I just lay there doing nothing. If Nastasya brought me anything I ate it, if she didn't I went all day without; I wouldn't ask, on purpose, from sulkiness! At night I had no light, I lay in the dark and I wouldn't earn money for candles. I ought to have studied, but I sold my books; and the dust lies an inch thick on the note-books on my table. I preferred lying still and thinking. And I kept thinking . . . And I had dreams all the time, strange dreams of all sorts, no need to describe! Only then I began to fancy that . . . No, that's not it! Again I am telling you wrong! You see, I kept asking myself then: why am I so stupid, that if others are stupid – and I know they are – yet I won't be wiser? Then I saw, Sonia, that if one waits for everyone to get wiser it will take too long . . . Afterwards I understood that that would never come to pass, that men won't change and that nobody can alter it and that it's not worth wasting effort over it. Yes, that's so. That's the law of their nature, Sonia . . . that's so! And I know now, Sonia, that whoever is strong in mind and spirit will have power over them. Anyone who is greatly daring is right in their eyes. He who despises most things will be a law-giver among them and he who dares most of all will be most in the right! So it has been till now and so it will always be. A man must be blind not to see it!'

Though Raskolnikov looked at Sonia as he said this, he no longer cared whether she understood or not. The fever had complete hold of him; he was in a sort of gloomy ecstasy (he certainly had been too long without talking to anyone). Sonia felt that this gloomy creed had become his faith and code.

'I divined then, Sonia,' he went on eagerly, 'that power is only vouchsafed to the man who dares to stoop and pick it up. There is only one thing, one thing needful: one has only to dare! Then for the first time in my life an idea took shape in my mind which no one had ever thought of before me, no one! I saw clear as daylight how strange it is that not a single person living in this mad world has had the daring to go straight for it all and send it flying to the devil! I . . . I wanted *to have the daring* . . . and I killed her. I only wanted to have the daring, Sonia! That was the whole cause of it!'

'Oh, hush, hush!' cried Sonia, clasping her hands. 'You turned away from God and God has smitten you, has given you over to the devil!'

'Then, Sonia, when I used to lie there in the dark and all this became clear to me, was it a temptation of the devil, eh?'

'Hush, don't laugh, blasphemer! You don't understand, you don't understand! Oh, God! He won't understand!'

'Hush, Sonia! I am not laughing. I know myself that it was the devil leading me. Hush, Sonia, hush!' he repeated with gloomy insistence. 'I know it all, I have thought it all over and over and whispered it all over to myself, lying there in the dark . . . I've argued it all over with myself, every point of it, and I know it all, all! And how sick, how sick I was then of going over it all! I kept wanting to forget it and make a new beginning, Sonia, and leave off thinking. And you don't suppose that I went into it headlong like a fool? I went into it like a wise man, and that was just my destruction. And you mustn't suppose that I didn't know, for instance, that if I began to question myself whether I had the right to gain power – I certainly hadn't the right – or that if I asked myself whether a human being is a louse it proved that it wasn't so for me, though it might be for a man who would go straight to his goal without asking questions . . . If I worried myself all those days, wondering whether Napoleon would have done it or not, I felt clearly, of course, that I wasn't Napoleon. I had to endure all the agony of that battle of ideas, Sonia, and I longed to throw it off: I wanted to murder without casuistry, to murder for my own sake, for myself alone! I didn't want to lie about it even to myself. It wasn't to help my mother I did the murder – that's nonsense – I didn't do the murder to gain wealth and power and to become a benefactor of mankind. Nonsense! I simply did it; I did the murder for myself, for myself alone, and whether I became a benefactor to others, or spent my life like a spider catching men in my web and sucking the life out of men, I couldn't have cared at that moment . . . And it was not the money I wanted, Sonia, when I did it. It was not so much the money I wanted, but something else . . . I know it all now . . . Understand me! Perhaps I should never have committed a murder again. I wanted to find out something else; it was something else led me on. I wanted to find out then and quickly whether I was a louse like everybody else or a man. Whether I can step over barriers or not, whether I dare stoop to pick up or not, whether I am a trembling creature or whether I have the *right* . . .'

'To kill? Have the right to kill?' Sonia clasped her hands.

'Ach, Sonia!' he cried irritably and seemed about to make some retort, but was contemptuously silent. 'Don't interrupt me, Sonia. I want to prove one thing only, that the devil led me on then and he has shown me since that I had not the right to take that path, because I am just such a louse as all the rest. He was mocking me and here I've come to you now! Welcome your guest! If I were not a louse should I have come to you? Listen: when I went then to the old woman's I only went to *try* . . . You may be sure of that!'

'And you murdered her!'

'But how did I murder her? Is that how men do murders? Do men go to commit a murder as I went then? I will tell you some day how I went! Did I murder the old woman? I murdered myself, not her! I crushed myself once for all, for ever . . . But it was the devil that killed that old woman, not I. Enough, enough, Sonia, enough! Let me be!' he cried in a sudden spasm of agony, 'let me be!'

Fyodor Dostoyevsky, *Crime and Punishment*, trans. Constance Garnett

Wishful Thinking

It struck out, like the lash of a new clause
On a curse thought dead and buried, when he wished
His little girl of four goodnight, sleep well: –
He'd never speak with innocence again
To anyone; nor would his wishes work.

*

Kicking eventually the shallow hour's
Puddle of sleep his own face wobbled in
Disturbed this dream: the same shawled grandmother
That formerly he'd easily managed to kill
Was helpless, backed against a bathroom wall;

But every time he walloped the axe-blade
At the joint of her head and neck, the rubber head
Bounced from the impact, bounced against the wall
Like a patient rubber ball. When the rubber
Weapon sagged in failure from his wrist

The head, rebounding on its springy neck,
Addressed him freely, in familiar terms:
'But *please*, before you wake – wish me goodnight;
With kisses, please – ain't I your little girl?'
(He'll strain towards the lacey punchbag). BOING!

Mick Imlah, 'Crime and Punishment'

The selfishness of the riparian proprietor grows with every year. If these men had their way they would close the River Thames altogether. They actually do this along the minor tributary streams and in the backwaters. They drive posts into the bed of the stream, and draw chains across from bank to bank, and nail huge notice-boards on every tree. The sight of those notice-boards rouses every evil instinct in my nature. I feel I want to tear each one down, and hammer it over the head of the man who put it up, until I have killed him, and then I would bury him, and put the board up over the grave as a tombstone.

I mentioned these feelings of mine to Harris, and he said he had them worse than that. He said he not only felt he wanted to kill the man who caused the board to be put up, but that he should like to slaughter the whole of his family and all his friends and relations, and then burn down his house. This seemed to me to be going too far, and I said so to Harris; but he answered: 'Not a bit of it. Serve 'em all jolly well right, and I'd go and sing comic songs on the ruins.'

Jerome K. Jerome, *Three Men in a Boat*

LEAR: It were a delicate stratagem to shoe
A troop of horse with felt. I'll put't in proof,
And when I have stol'n upon these son-in-laws,
Then kill, kill, kill, kill, kill, kill!

William Shakespeare, *King Lear*

To Robert Conquest,
28 October 1958

Dear Bob,

My God yes about the ponce of Hessle – you'll never bloody well credit it, but that sodding recording was a flop: outside noise getting into the recording – I TOLD them TWICE I was being practically deafened by music and feet, but the stupid digitally-impaled sods said it would be 'all right' aha aha aha ha ha h ~~Is shit~~ I'll give them all right RIGHT IN THE GOOLIES. Upshot is I have to do it again, but quick. Probably next weekend – but the visit will be so quick I doubt if I'll have time to kill. Give you a buzz if I do. God I'm so angry I could kick sodding little G. from here to Hessle Market Cross and then stick him on top of it. Then I'd go and pelt sodding HMV with napalm bombs, machine-gunning the sprinting torches that emerged.

Philip Larkin, *Selected Letters*

Thinking of new ways to kill you
and bring you back from the dead,
I try drowning you in the lily pond –

holding your head down
until every bubble of breath
is squeezed from your lungs

and the flat leaves and spiky flowers
float over you like a wreath.
I sit on the stones until I'm numb,

until, among reflections of sky,
water-buttercups, spears of iris,
your face rises to the surface –

a face that was always puffy
and pale, so curiously unchanged.
A wind rocks the waxy flowers, curls

the edges of the leaves. Blue dragonflies
appear and vanish like ghosts.
I part the mats of yellow weed

and drag you to the bank, covering
your green algae-stained corpse
with a white sheet. Then, I lift the edge

and climb underneath –
thumping your chest,
breathing into your mouth.

Vicki Feaver, 'Lily Pond'

Witch

For if a malitious minded Witch intends to consume and pine away the Life or Estate of any miserable Man or Woman, she makes his Image of wax in such an ominous aspect as may conduce to her design, making several magical Characters upon the sides of the head, describing the character of the hour or Planetary time upon the breast of the Image; the name of the party on his forehead; the intended effect to be wrought upon him upon his back. When they cause aches, pains, and violent pangs in the sinews and the flesh, they stick thorns and pins in divers places of their arms, breasts, and legs. When they cast them into Feavers and Consumptions, they spend an hour in every day to warm and turn the Image before a doleful and lingring fire, composed of divers exotick Gums, and magical Ingredients of sweet Odours, and strange Roots of shrubs, efficient for their purpose . . .

Their *Needles* are made of Hedge-hog prickles . . . Their *Writing-pens* are of Owls or Ravens, their *Ink* of Mans blood: their *Oyntments* Mans fat, Blood, Usnea, Hoggs-grease, Oyl of Whales. Their Characters are ancient *Hebrew* or *Samaritan*: Their *Speech* is *Hebrew* or *Latine*. Their *Paper* must be of the Membranes of Infants, which they call *Virgin-parchment*, or the skins of Cats, or Kids. Besides, they compose their *Fires* of sweet Wood, Oyl or Rosin: And their *Candles* of the Fatt or Marrow of Men or Children: Their *Vessels* are Earthen, their *Candlesticks* with three feet, of dead mens bones: Their *Swords* are steel, without Guards, the poynts being reversed. These are their Materials, which they do particularly choose for the Magical qualities whereof they are composed.

Reginald Scot, *The Discovery of Witchcraft*

Wood

The day passed on. Noon, afternoon, evening. Sunset.

At that serene and peaceful time two men, riding in a gig, came out of the city by a road not much frequented. It was the day on which Mr Pecksniff had agreed to dine with Montague. He had kept his appointment, and was now going home. His host was riding with him for a short distance; meaning to return by a pleasant track, which Mr Pecksniff had engaged to show him, through some fields. Jonas knew their plans. He had hung about the inn-yard while they were at dinner and had heard their orders given.

They were loud and merry in their conversation, and might have been heard at some distance: far above the sound of their carriage wheels or horses' hoofs. They came on noisily, to where a stile and footpath indicated their point of separation. Here they stopped.

'It's too soon. Much too soon,' said Mr Pecksniff. 'But this is the place, my dear sir. Keep the path, and go straight through the little wood you'll come to. The path is narrower there, but you can't miss it. When shall I see you again? Soon, I hope?'

'I hope so,' replied Montague.

'Good night!'

'Good night. And a pleasant ride!'

So long as Mr Pecksniff was in sight, and turned his head at intervals to salute him, Montague stood in the road smiling, and waving his hand. But when his new partner had disappeared, and this show was no longer necessary, he sat down on the stile with looks so altered, that he might have grown ten years older in the meantime.

He was flushed with wine, but not gay. His scheme had succeeded, but he showed no triumph. The effort of sustaining his difficult part before his late companion had fatigued him, perhaps, or it may be that the evening whispered to his conscience, or it may be (as it *has* been) that a shadowy veil was dropping round him, closing out all thoughts but the presentiment and vague foreknowledge of impending doom.

If there be fluids, as we know there are, which, conscious of a coming wind, or rain, or frost, will shrink and strive to hide themselves in their glass arteries; may not that subtle liquor of the blood perceive, by properties within itself, that hands are raised to waste and spill it; and in the veins of men run cold and dull as his did, in that hour!

So cold, although the air was warm: so dull, although the sky was bright: that he rose up shivering from his seat, and hastily resumed his walk. He checked himself as hastily: undecided whether to pursue the footpath, which was lonely and retired, or to go back by the road.

He took the footpath.

The glory of the departing sun was on his face. The music of the birds was in his ears. Sweet wild flowers bloomed about him. Thatched roofs of poor men's homes were in the distance; and an old grey spire, surmounted by a Cross, rose up between him and the coming night.

He had never read the lesson which these things conveyed; he had ever mocked and turned away from it; but, before going down into a hollow place, he looked round, once, upon the evening prospect, sorrowfully. Then he went down, down, down, into the dell.

It brought him to the wood; a close, thick, shadowy wood, through which the path went winding on, dwindling away into a slender sheep-track. He paused before entering; for the stillness of this spot almost daunted him.

The last rays of the sun were shining in, aslant, making a path of golden light along the stems and branches in its range, which, even as he looked, began to die away, yielding gently to the twilight that came creeping on. It was so very quiet that the soft and stealthy moss about the trunks of some old trees, seemed to have grown out of the silence, and to be its proper offspring. Those other trees which were subdued by blasts of wind in winter time, had not quite tumbled down, but being caught by others, lay all bare and scathed across their leafy arms, as if unwilling to disturb the general repose by the crash of their fall. Vistas of silence opened everywhere, into the heart and innermost recesses of the wood; beginning with the likeness of an aisle, a cloister, or a ruin open to the sky; then tangling off into a deep green rustling mystery, through which gnarled trunks and twisted boughs, and ivy-covered stems, and trembling leaves, and bark-stripped bodies of old trees stretched out at length, were faintly seen in beautiful confusion.

As the sunlight died away, and evening fell upon the wood, he entered it. Moving, here and there, a bramble or a drooping bough which stretched across his path, he slowly disappeared. At intervals a narrow opening showed him passing on, or the sharp cracking of some tender branch denoted where he went; then he was seen or heard no more.

Never more beheld by mortal eye or heard by mortal ear: one man excepted. That man, parting the leaves and branches on the other side, near where the path emerged again, came leaping out soon afterwards.

What had he left within the wood, that he sprang out of it as if it were a hell!

The body of a murdered man. In one thick solitary spot, it lay among the last year's leaves of oak and beech, just as it had fallen headlong down. Sopping and soaking in among the leaves that formed its pillow; oozing down into the boggy ground, as if to cover itself from human sight; forcing its way between and through the curling leaves, as if those senseless things rejected and forswore it, and were coiled up in abhorrence; went a dark, dark stain that dyed the whole summer night from earth to heaven.

The doer of this deed came leaping from the wood so fiercely, that he cast into the air a shower of fragments of young boughs, torn away in his passage, and fell with violence upon the grass. But he quickly gained his feet again, and keeping underneath a hedge with his body bent, went running on towards the road. The road once reached, he fell into a rapid walk and set on towards London.

And he was not sorry for what he had done. He was frightened when he thought of it – when did he not think of it! – but he was not sorry. He had had a terror and dread of the wood when he was in it; but being out of it, and having committed the crime, his fears were now diverted, strangely, to the dark room he had left shut up at home. He had a greater horror, infinitely greater, of that room than of the wood. Now that he was on his return to it, it seemed beyond comparison more dismal and more dreadful than the wood. His hideous secret was shut up in the room, and all its terrors were there; to his thinking it was not in the wood at all.

• • •

He tried – he had never left off trying – not to forget it was there, for that was impossible, but to forget to weary himself by drawing vivid pictures of it in his fancy: by going softly about it and about it among the leaves, approaching it nearer and nearer through a gap in the boughs, and startling the very flies that were thickly sprinkled all over it, like heaps of dried currants. His mind was fixed and fastened on the discovery, for intelligence of which he listened intently to every cry and shout; listened when any one came in or went out; watched from the window the people who passed up and down the street; mistrusted his own looks and words. And the more his thoughts were set upon the discovery, the stronger was the fascination which attracted them to the thing itself: lying alone in the wood. He was for ever showing and presenting it, as it were, to every creature whom he saw. 'Look here! Do you know of this? Is it found? Do you suspect *me*?' If he had been condemned to bear the body in his arms, and lay it down for recognition at the feet of every one he met, it could not have been more constantly with him, or a cause of more monotonous and dismal occupation than it was in this state of his mind.

Still he was not sorry. It was no contrition or remorse for what he had done that moved him; it was nothing but alarm for his own security. The vague consciousness he possessed of having wrecked his fortune in the murderous venture, intensified his hatred and revenge, and made him set the greater store by what he had gained. The man was dead; nothing could undo that. He felt a triumph yet, in the reflection.

Charles Dickens, *Martin Chuzzlewit*

Wragg

'A shocking child murder has just been committed at Nottingham. A girl named Wragg left the workhouse there on Saturday morning with her young illegitimate child. The child was soon afterwards found dead on Mapperly Hills, having been strangled. Wragg is in custody.'

Nothing but that; but, in juxtaposition with the absolute euologies of Sir Charles Adderley and Mr Roebuck, how eloquent, how suggestive are those few lines! 'Our old Anglo-Saxon breed, the best in the whole world!' – how much that is harsh and ill-favoured there is in this best! *Wragg!* If we are to talk of ideal perfection, of 'the best in the whole world', has any one reflected what a touch of grossness in our race, what an original shortcoming in the more delicate spiritual perceptions, is shown by the natural growth amongst us of such hideous names, – Higginbottom, Stiggins, Bugg! In Ionia and Attica they were luckier in this respect than 'the best race in the world'; by the Ilissus there was no Wragg, poor thing! And 'our unrivalled happiness'; – what an element of grimness, bareness, and hideousness mixes with it and blurs it? the workhouse, the dismal Mapperly Hills, – how dismal those who have seen them will remember; – the gloom, the smoke, the cold, the strangled illegitimate child! 'I ask you whether the world over or in past history, there is anything like it?' Perhaps not, one is inclined to answer; but at any rate, in that case, the world is very much to be pitied. And the final touch, – short, bleak and inhuman: *Wragg is in custody*. The sex lost in the confusion of our unrivalled happiness; or (shall I say?) the superfluous Christian name lopped off by the straightforward vigour of our old Anglo-Saxon breed!

Matthew Arnold, 'The Function of Criticism at the Present Time'

X

It is not every day that one makes the acquaintance of a skeleton; and with regard to such a thing – thing, shall one say, or person? – there is a favourable presumption from beforehand; which is this: – As he is of no use, neither profitable nor ornamental, to any person whatever, absolutely *de trop* in good society, what but distinguished merit of some kind or other could induce any man to interfere with that gravitating tendency that by an eternal *nisus* is pulling him below ground? Lodgings are dear in England. True it is that, according to the vile usage on the Continent, one room serves a skeleton for bedroom and sitting-room; neither is his expense heavy, as regards wax-lights, fire, or 'bif-steck'. But still, even a skeleton is chargeable; and, if any dispute should arise about his maintenance, the parish will do nothing. Mr White's skeleton, therefore, being costly, was presumably meritorious, before we had seen him or heard a word in his behalf. It was, in fact, the skeleton of an eminent robber, or perhaps of a murderer. But I, for my part, reserved a faint right of suspense. And, as to the profession of robber in those days exercised on the roads of England, it was a liberal profession, which required more accomplishments than either the bar or the pulpit; from the beginning it presumed a most bountiful endowment of heroic qualifications – strength, health, agility, and exquisite horsemanship, intrepidity of the first order, presence of mind, courtesy, and a general ambidexterity of powers for facing all accidents, and for turning to a good account all unlooked-for contingencies. The finest men in England, physically speaking, throughout the eighteenth century, the very noblest specimens of man, considered as an animal, were beyond a doubt the mounted robbers who cultivated their profession on the great leading roads – viz., on the road from London to York (technically known as 'the Great North Road'); on the road west to Bath, and thence to Exeter and Plymouth; north-westwards from London to Oxford, and thence to Chester; eastwards to Tunbridge; southwards by east to Dover; then inclining westwards to Portsmouth; more so still, through Salisbury to Dorsetshire and Wilts. These great roads were farmed out as so many Roman provinces amongst proconsuls. Yes, but with a difference, you will say, in respect of moral principles. Certainly with a difference: for the English highwayman had a sort of conscience for gala-days, which could not often be said of the Roman governor or procurator. At this moment we see that the opening for the forger of banknotes is brilliant; but practically it languishes, as being too brilliant: it demands an array of talent for engraving, &c., which, wherever it exists, is sufficient to carry a man forward upon principles reputed honourable. Why then should *he* court danger and disreputability? But in that century the special talents which led to distinction upon the high road had oftentimes no career open to them elsewhere. The mounted robber on the highways of England, in an age when all gentlemen travelled with firearms, lived in an element of danger and adventurous gallantry; which, even from those who could least allow him any portion of their esteem, extorted sometimes a good deal of their unwilling admiration. By the necessities of the case, he brought into his perilous profession some brilliant qualities – intrepidity, address, promptitude of decision; and if to these he added courtesy, and a spirit (native or adopted) of forbearing generosity, he seemed almost a man that merited public encouragement: since very plausibly it might be argued that his profession was sure to exist; that, if he were removed, a successor would inevitably arise, and that successor might or might *not* carry the same liberal and humanizing temper into his practice. The man whose skeleton was now before us had ranked amongst the most chivalrous of his order, and was regarded by some people as vindicating the national honour in a point where not very long before it had suffered a transient eclipse. In the preceding generation, it had been felt as throwing a shade of disgrace over the public honour, that the championship of England upon the high road fell for a time into French hands: upon French prowess rested the burden of English honour, or, in Gallic phrase, of English *glory*. Claude Duval, a Frenchman of undeniable courage, handsome, and noted for his chivalrous devotion to women, had been honoured, on his condemnation to the gallows, by the tears of many ladies who attended his trial, and by their sympathizing visits during his imprisonment. But the robber represented by the skeleton in Mr White's museum (whom let us call *X*, since his true name has perished), added to the same heroic qualities a person far more superb. Still it was a dreadful drawback from his pretensions, if he had really practised as a murderer. Upon what ground did that suspicion arise? In candour (for candour is due even to a skeleton) it ought to be mentioned that the charge, if it amounted to so much, arose with a lady from some part of Cheshire – the district of Knutsford, I believe; – but, wherever it was, in the same district, during the latter part of his career, had resided our *X*. At first he was not suspected even as a robber – as yet not so much as suspected of being suspicious: in a simple rustic neighbourhood, amongst good-natured peasants, for a long time he was regarded with simple curiosity, rather than suspicion; and even the curiosity pointed to his horse more than to himself. The robber had made himself popular amongst the kind-hearted rustics by his general courtesy. Courtesy and the spirit of neighbourliness go a great way amongst country people; and the worst construction of the case was, that he might be an embarrassed gentleman from Manchester or Liverpool, hiding himself from his creditors, who are notoriously a very immoral class of people. At length, however, a violent suspicion broke loose against him; for it was ascertained that on certain nights, when perhaps he had *extra* motives for concealing the fact of having been abroad, he drew woollen stockings over his horse's feet, with the purpose of deadening the sound in riding up a brick-paved entry, common to his own stable and that of a respectable neighbour. Thus far there was a reasonable foundation laid for suspicion: but suspicion of what? Because a man attends to the darning of his horse's stockings, why must he be meditating murder? The fact is – and known from the very first to a select party of amateurs – that *X*, our superb-looking skeleton, *did*, about three o'clock on a rainy Wednesday morning, in the dead of winter, ride silently out of Knutsford; and about forty-eight hours afterwards, on a rainy Friday, silently and softly did that same superb blood-horse, carrying that same blood-man – viz., our friend the superb skeleton – pace up the quiet brick entry, in a neat pair of socks, on his return.

During that interval of forty-eight hours, an atrocious murder was committed in the ancient city of Bristol. By whom? That question is to this day unanswered. The scene of it was a house on the west side of the College Green; which is in fact that same quadrangle, planted with trees, and having on its southern side the Bristol Cathedral, up and down which, early in the reign of George III, Chatterton walked in jubilant spirits with fair young women of Bristol; up and down which, some thirty years later, Robert Southey and S. T. C. walked with young Bristol belles from a later generation. The subjects of the murder were an elderly lady, bearing some such name as Rusborough, and her female servant. Mystery there was none as to the motive of the murder – manifestly it was a hoard of money that had attracted the assassin: but there was great perplexity as to the agent or agents concerned in the atrocious act, and as to the mode by which an entrance, under the known precautions of the lady, could have been effected. Because a thoroughbred horse could easily have accomplished the distance to and fro (say 300 miles) within the forty-eight hours, and because the two extreme dates of this forty-eight hours' absence tallied with the requisitions of the Bristol tragedy, it did not follow that *X* must have had a hand in it. And yet, had these coincidences *then* been observed, they would certainly – now that strong suspicions had been directed to the man from the extraordinary character of his nocturnal precautions – not have passed without investigation. But the remoteness of Bristol, and the rarity of newspapers in those days, caused these indications to pass unnoticed. Bristol knew of no such Knutsford highwayman; Knutsford knew of no such Bristol murder. It is singular enough that these earlier grounds of suspicion against *X* were not viewed as such by anybody, until they came to be combined with another and final ground. Then the presumptions seemed conclusive. But by that time *X* himself had been executed for a robbery, had been manufactured into a skeleton by the famous surgeon, Cruickshank,[1] assisted by Mr White and other pupils. All interest in the case had subsided in Knutsford that could now have cleared up the case satisfactorily: and thus it happened that to this day the riddle, which was read pretty decisively in a northern county, still remains a riddle in the south. When I saw the College Green house in 1809–10, it was apparently empty, and, as I was told, had always been empty since the murder: forty years had not cicatrized the bloody remembrance; and, to this day, perhaps, it remains amongst the gloomy traditions of Bristol.

But whether the Bristol house has or has not shaken off that odour of blood which offended the nostrils of tenants, it is, I believe, certain that the city annals have not shaken off the mystery: which yet to certain people in Knutsford, as I have said, and to us the spectators of the skeleton, immediately upon hearing one damning fact from the lips of Mr White, seemed to melt away and evaporate as convincingly as if we had heard the explanation issuing in the terms of a confession from the mouth of the skeleton itself. What, then, *was* the fact? With pain, and reluctantly, we felt its force, as we looked at the royal skeleton, and reflected on the many evidences which he had given of courage, and perhaps of other noble qualities. The ugly fact was this: – In a few weeks after the College Green tragedy, Knutsford, and the whole neighbourhood as far as Warrington

1 William Cruickshank, anatomist, born 1746, died 1800.

(the half-way town between Liverpool and Manchester), were deluged with gold and silver coins, moidores and dollars, from the Spanish mint of Mexico, &c. These, during the frequent scarcities of English silver currency, were notoriously current in England. Now, it is an unhappy fact, and subsequently became known to the Bristol and London police, that a considerable part of poor Mrs Rusborough's treasure lay in such coins, gold and silver, from the Spanish colonial mints.

Thomas De Quincey, *Autobiography from 1785 to 1803*

The Audubon Ballroom between Broadway and St Nicholas Avenue, on the south side of West 166th Street, is a two-story building frequently rented for dances, organizational functions, and other affairs. A dark, slender, pretty young lady, occupationally a receptionist and avocationally a hardworking OAAU assistant to Malcolm X, has since told me that she arrived early, about 1.30 p.m., having some preliminary work to do. Entering, she saw that the usual 400 wooden chairs had been set up, with aisles on either side, but no center aisle; the young lady (she wishes to be nameless) noticed that several people were already seated in the front rows, but she gave it no thought since some always came early, liking to get seats up close to the stage, to savor to the fullest the dramatic orator Malcolm X. On the stage, behind the speaker's stand were eight straight brown chairs arranged in a row and behind them was the stage's painted backdrop, a mural of a restful country scene. The young lady's responsibilities for this day had included making arrangements and subsequent confirmations with the scheduled co-speaker, the Reverend Milton Galamison, the militant Brooklyn Presbyterian who in 1964 had led the two one-day Negro boycotts in New York City public schools, protesting 'racial imbalance'. She had similarly made arrangements with some other prominent Negroes who were due to appeal to the audience for their maximum possible contributions to aid the work of Malcolm X and his organization.

The people who entered the ballroom were not searched at the door. In recent weeks, Malcolm X had become irritable about this, saying 'It makes people uncomfortable' and that it reminded him of Elijah Muhammad. 'If I can't be safe among my own kind, where can I be?' he had once said testily. For this day, also, he had ordered the press – as such – barred, white or black. He was angry at what he interpreted as 'slanted' press treatment recently; he felt especially that the newspapers had not taken seriously his statements of the personal danger he was in. United

Press International reporter Stanley Scott, a Negro, had been admitted, he later said, when a Malcolm lieutenant decided, 'As a Negro, you will be allowed to enter as a citizen if you like, but you must remove your press badge.' The same criterion had applied to WMCA newsman Hugh Simpson. Both he and Scott came early enough so that they obtained seats up near the stage.

Malcolm X entered the ballroom at shortly before two o'clock, trudging heavily instead of with his usual lithe strides, his young lady assistant has told me. By this time several other of his assistants were filtering in and out of the small anteroom alongside the stage. He sat down sideways on a chair, his long legs folded around its bottom, and he leaned one elbow on a kind of counter before a rather rickety makeup mirror that entertainers used when dances were held in the ballroom. He wore a dark suit, white shirt and narrow dark tie. He said to a little group of his assistants that he wasn't going to talk about his personal troubles, 'I don't want that to be the reason for anyone to come to hear me.' He stood up and paced about the little room. He said he was going to state that he had been hasty to accuse the Black Muslims of bombing his home. 'Things have happened since that are bigger than what they can do. I know what they can do. Things have gone beyond that.'

Those in the anteroom could hear the sounds of the enlarging audience outside taking seats. 'The way I feel, I ought not to go out there at all today,' Malcolm X said. 'In fact, I'm going to ease some of this tension by telling the black man not to fight himself – that's all a part of the white man's big maneuver, to keep us fighting among ourselves, against each other. I'm not fighting anyone, that's not what we're here for.' He kept glancing at his wrist watch, anticipating the arrival of Reverend Galamison. 'Whenever you make any appointment with a minister,' he said to his young lady assistant, 'you have to call them two or three hours before time, because they will change their mind. This is typical of ministers.'

'I felt bad, I felt that it was my fault,' the young lady told me. 'It was time for the meeting to start, too.' She turned to Malcolm X's stalwart assistant Benjamin X, known as a highly able speaker himself. 'Brother, will you speak?' she asked – then, turning to Malcolm X, 'Is it all right if he speaks? And maybe he could introduce you.' Malcolm X abruptly whirled on her, and barked, 'You know you shouldn't ask me right in front of him!' Then, collecting himself quickly, he said 'Okay.' Brother Benjamin X asked how long he should speak. Malcolm X said, glancing again at his wrist watch, 'Make it half an hour.' And Brother Benjamin X went through the door leading onto the stage. They heard him expertly exhorting the audience about what is needed today by 'the black man here in these United States'.

The Reverend Galamison and other notables due hadn't arrived by three o'clock. 'Brother Malcolm looked so disappointed,' the young lady says. 'He said to me "I don't think any of them are coming either." I felt so terrible for him. It did seem as if no one cared. I told him "Oh, don't worry, they're just late, they'll be here." ' (It was also reported by another source that Galamison, unable to come to the meeting, did telephone earlier, and that Malcolm X was told of this before he went out to speak.)

Then Brother Benjamin X's half-hour was up, and the young lady and Malcolm X, alone back there in the anteroom could hear him entering the introduction: 'And now, without further remarks, I present to you one who is willing to put himself on the line for you, a man who would give his life for you – I want you to hear, listen, to understand – one who is a *trojan* for the black man!'

Applause rose from the audience; at the anteroom door, Malcolm X turned and looked back at his young lady assistant. 'You'll have to forgive me for raising my voice to you – I'm just about at my wit's end.'

'Oh, don't *mention* it!' she said quickly, 'I understand.'

His voice sounded far away, 'I wonder if anybody *really* understands – ' And he walked out onto the stage, into the applause, smiling and nodding at Brother Benjamin X who passed him en route to the anteroom.

The young lady had picked up some paperwork she had to do when Benjamin X came in, perspiring. She patted his hand, saying, 'That was good!' Through the anteroom door, just ajar, she and Benjamin X heard the applause diminishing, then the familiar ringing greeting, '*Asalaikum*, brothers and sisters!'

'Asalaikum salaam!' some in the audience responded.

About eight rows of seats from the front, then, a disturbance occurred. In a sudden scuffling, a man's voice was raised angrily, 'Take your hand out of my pocket!' The entire audience was swiveling to look. 'Hold it! Hold it! Don't get excited,' Malcolm X said crisply, 'Let's cool, it, brothers – '

With his own attention distracted, it is possible that he never saw the gunmen. One woman who was seated near the front says, 'The commotion back there diverted me just for an instant, then I turned back to look at Malcolm X just in time to see at least three men in the front row stand and take aim and start firing simultaneously. It looked like a firing squad.' Numerous persons later said they saw two men rushing toward the stage, one with a shotgun, the other with two revolvers. Said UPI reporter Stanley Scott: 'Shots rang out. Men, women and children ran for cover. They stretched out on the floor and ducked under tables.' Radio Station WMCA reporter Hugh Simpson said, 'Then I heard this muffled sound, I saw Malcolm hit with his hands still raised, then he fell back over the chairs behind him. Everybody was shouting. I saw one man firing a gun from under his coat behind me as I hit it [the floor], too. He was firing like he was in some Western, running backward toward the door and firing at the same time.'

The young lady who was in the backstage anteroom told me, 'It sounded like an army had taken over. Somehow, I knew. I wouldn't go and look. I wanted to remember him as he was.'

Malcolm X's hand flew to his chest as the first of sixteen shotgun pellets or revolver slugs hit him. Then the other hand flew up. The middle finger of the left hand was bullet-shattered, and blood gushed from his goatee. He clutched his chest. His big body suddenly fell back stiffly, knocking over two chairs; his head struck the stage floor with a thud.

In the bedlam of shouting, screaming, running people, some ran toward the stage. Among them Sister Betty scrambled up from where she had thrown her body over her children, who were shrieking; she ran crying hysterically, 'My husband! They're killing my husband!' An unidentified photographer snapped shots of Malcolm X prone on the stage floor with people bent over him snatching apart his bloody shirt, loosening his tie, trying to give him mouth-to-mouth artificial respiration, first a woman, then a man. Said the woman, who identified herself only as a registered nurse, 'I don't know how I got up on the stage, but I threw myself down on who I thought was Malcolm – but it wasn't. I was willing to die for the man, I would have taken the bullets myself; then I saw Malcolm, and the firing had stopped, and I tried to give him artificial respiration.' Then Sister Betty came through the people, herself a nurse, and people recognizing her moved back; she fell on her knees looking down on his bare, bullet-pocked chest, sobbing, 'They killed him!'

Patrolman Thomas Hoy, 22, was stationed outside the Audubon Ballroom entrance. 'I heard the shooting and the place exploded.' He rushed inside, he saw Malcolm X lying on the stage, and then some people chasing a man. Patrolman Hoy 'grabbed the suspect'.

Louis Michaux, the owner of the National Memorial Bookstore at 125th Street and Seventh Avenue in Harlem, said 'I was arriving late at the meeting where Malcolm X had invited me, I met a large number of people rushing out.'

Sergeant Alvin Aronoff and Patrolman Louis Angelos happened to be cruising by in their radio car when they heard shots. 'When we got there,' said Aronoff, 'the crowds were pushing out and screaming "Malcolm's been shot!" and "Get 'im, get 'im, don't let him go!" ' The two policemen grabbed by the arms a Negro who was being kicked as he tried to escape. Firing a warning shot into the air, the policemen pushed the man into their police car, not wanting the angry crowd to close in, and drove him quickly to the police station.

Someone had run up to the Columbia-Presbyterian Hospital's Vanderbilt Clinic emergency entrance at 167th Street and grabbed a poles-and-canvas stretcher and brought it back to the Audubon Ballroom stage. Malcolm X was put on the stretcher and an unidentified photographer got a macabre picture of him, with his mouth open and his teeth bared, as men rushed him up to the hospital clinic emergency entrance. A hospital spokesman said later that it was about 3.15 p.m. when Malcolm X reached a third-floor operating room. He was 'either dead, or in a death-appearing state,' said the spokesman.

A team or surgeons cut through his chest to attempt to massage the heart. The effort was abandoned at 3.30 p.m.

Reporters who had descended upon the hospital office fired questions at the spokesman, who kept saying brusquely, 'I don't know.' Then he took the elevator upstairs to the emergency operating room. A small crowd of friends and Sister Betty had also pushed into the hospital office when the hospital spokesman returned. Collecting himself, he made an announcement: 'The gentleman you know as Malcolm X is dead. He died from gun-shot wounds. He was apparently dead before he got here. He was shot in the chest several times, and once in the cheek.'

The group filed out of the hospital office. The Negro men were visibly fighting their emotions; one kept smashing his fist into the other cupped palm. Among the women, many were openly crying.

Moments after the news flashed throughout Harlem (and throughout the entire world), a crowd began to gather outside the Hotel Theresa where Malcolm X's OAAU had its headquarters. They learned over transistor radios that the man whom the two policemen had taken from the murder scene initially identified himself as Thomas Hagan, 22 (he was later identified as Talmadge Hayer), in whose right trousers pocket the policeman had found a ·45 caliber cartridge clip containing four unused cartridges, and then at Jewish Memorial Hospital doctors had reported that Hayer had been shot in the left thigh, his forehead was bruised and his body was beaten. 'If we hadn't gotten him away, they would have kicked him to death,' Sergeant Aronoff had said, and Hayer had been taken to the Bellevue Hospital Prison Ward.

By 5 p.m., the crowd in front of the Theresa Hotel had been quietly, carefully dispersed, and the Black Muslim Mosque Number 7 and its restaurant around the corner, at 116th Street and Lenox Avenue, had been ordered closed as a precautionary measure, on the orders of the local 28th Precinct's Captain Lloyd Sealy, New York City's first Negro to command a precinct. When reporters telephoned the Black Muslim restaurant, a man's voice stated, 'No one is available to make any statement.' When the OAAU office in the Theresa Hotel was tried, the telephone kept ringing, unanswered. Precinct Captain Sealy soon appeared, walking by himself along 125th Street, swinging his nightstick and conversing with people he met.

At the 28th Precinct station house on West 123rd Street, the forty policemen who were to have gone off duty at 4 p.m. had been told they must remain on duty, and two full busloads of the highly trained New York City Police Tactical Patrol Force had arrived at the precinct. Various high police officials made press statements. A Tactical Patrol Force Captain, Harry Kaiser, said no unusual occurrences had been noted, and he anticipated no trouble. Deputy Police Commissioner Walter Arm said that 'hundreds' of extra policemen would be put into the Harlem area, including some members of the Bureau of Special Services. An Assistant Chief Inspector, Harry Taylor, speculated that the assassins had not rushed from the ballroom among the crowd, but had kept running past the stage and escaped on 165th Street. In the early evening, the police department's Chief of Detectives Philip J. Walsh quit a vacation he was on to join the hunt for the killers, and he said he looked forward to 'a long-drawn-out investigation'. Police and reporters at the shooting scene had pictures taken of the stage, with white chalk marks now circling five bullet holes in the speaker's stand; there were other holes in the stage's mural backdrop, indicating slugs or shotgun pellets which had either missed Malcolm X or passed through him. Police declined to discuss a rumor sweeping Harlem that they had some motion pictures which had been taken in the Audubon Ballroom as the murder took place. Another rumor that gained swift momentum was that when Sister Betty had leaned over her husband's body, she had removed from his coat pocket a paper on which he had written the names of those he had supposedly learned were assigned to execute him.

Deputy Police Commissioner Walter Arm stressed that the department had made efforts to protect Malcolm X. Twenty different times the department had offered protection to Malcolm X or to some of his assistants, and the protection was refused, said Commissioner Arm, and seventeen times uniformed police guards had been offered for the OAAU meetings at the Audubon Ballroom, the most recent time being 'last Sunday'. Asked about the pistol permit that Malcolm X had said publicly he planned to request, Commissioner Arm said that as far as he knew, Malcolm X had never actually filed a request.

A number of questions have been raised. The 'suspect' arrested by Patrolman Hoy as he was being chased from the meeting has, at present writing, not been identified publicly. Deputy Police Commissioner Walter Arm's statement that Malcolm X refused police protection conflicts directly with the statements of many of his associates that during the week preceding his assassination Malcolm X complained repeatedly that the police would not take his requests for protection seriously. Finally, although police sources said that a special detail of twenty men had been assigned to the meeting and that it had even been attended by agents of the Bureau of Special Services, these men were nowhere in evidence during or after the assassination, and Talmadge Hayer, rescued from the crowd and arrested as a suspect immediately after the assassination, was picked up by two patrolmen in a squad car cruising by.

On long-distance telephones, reporters reached the Chicago mansion headquarters of Elijah Muhammad. He would not come to the telephone, but a spokesman of his said that Muhammad 'has no comment today, but he might have something to say tomorrow'. No statement could be obtained either from Malcolm X's oldest brother, Wilfred X, the Black Muslim minister of Mosque Number 1 in Detroit. At his home, a woman told reporters that Minister Wilfred X was not there, that he had not gone to New York, and she didn't believe he had any plans to do so. (Minister Wilfred X, reached later, said that he anticipated attending the Black Muslim convention in Chicago on the following Sunday, and regarding his brother, 'My brother is dead and there is nothing we can do to bring him back.')

As dark fell, many Negro men and women assembled before Louis Michaux's bookstore, where most of Harlem's Black Nationalist activity centered. A small group of OAAU members opened their Hotel Theresa headquarters and sat in the room and would not make any statements to reporters.

The New York *Daily News* came onto the newsstands with its cover page devoted to 'Malcolm X murdered' over the photograph of him being borne away on the stretcher, and a subcaption, 'Gunned Down at Rally'. In Long Island, where she had been taken just after her father's murder, six-year-old Attilah carefully wrote a letter to him, 'Dear Daddy, I love you so. O dear, O dear, I wish you wasn't dead.'

The Autobiography of Malcolm X, with the assistance of Alex Haley

X-Ray

I was only thirty-five when I had the sort of case every young pathologist dreams of, 'the case of a lifetime', Molly Lefebure called it. It certainly had all the ingredients, and, but for the heavy shadow of a war that still hung desperately in the balance, it would have hit the news headlines as Crippen did in Spilsbury's younger days.

On 17 July 1942, a workman helping to demolish a bombed Baptist church premises in Vauxhall Road, South London, drove his pick under a heavy stone slab set on the floor of a cellar under the vestry and prised it up. Underneath lay a skeleton with a few tags of flesh clinging to it, which he assumed to be the remains of another victim of the Blitz. He put his shovel under the skeleton and lifted it out. The head stayed on the ground.

Detective Inspectors Hatton and Keeling, who were called in to investigate, wrapped the bones in a brown paper parcel and took them to the public mortuary at Southwark, where I inspected them the next morning. The sight of a dried-up womb tucked down in the remains of the trunk established the sex. There was a yellowish deposit on the head and neck. Fire had blackened parts of the skull, the hip, and the knees.

Could she have been the victim of a bomb explosion? Hardly likely, considering she had been lying neatly buried under a slab of stone, neatly set in the floor of a cellar; this was no bomb crater. The detectives told me there had been an ancient cemetery on the site: could the body have been there fifty years? I shook my head. Soft tissues do not last so long. I thought the body was only about twelve to eighteen months dead. The church had been blitzed in August 1940, almost two years before.

Who was it? How had it got there? Was it murder? These questions were obviously going to take a lot of answering, and neither the cellar nor an old-fashioned mortuary was a suitable place for a scientific reconstruction. I asked the Coroner, Hervey Wyatt, for permission to take it to my laboratory at Guy's to sort it out in the only way possible – a slow step-by-step laboratory reconstruction.

The head had not broken off when the workman had shovelled up the skeleton, as he had thought. It had been cut off. Further, both arms had been cut off at the elbow, and both legs at the knee. Bomb blast could do strange things, I knew from experience, but not as strange as that. Someone had dismembered the body.

Pieces of the limbs were missing, and the first job was to try to find them. I spent two afternoons with the police sifting nearly three tons of earth from under the floor of the cellar. We found animal bones but nothing human. However, I noted two interesting things in the cellar: a yellowish powder on the earth where the body had been buried, and a wooden chest slightly less than five feet long.

John Ryffel, the Home Office analyst and Head of the Department of Clinical Chemistry at Guy's, analysed both the powder from the cellar and the yellowish deposit on the body, and reported that she had been buried in slaked lime.

I reassembled the body and measured it. After making due allowance for missing bones and soft tissues, I calculated the height as 5 feet ½ inch. I checked this by reference to the well-known 'Pearson's formulae' and also the less reliable Rollet's tables, both of which give estimates of height based on one of the long bones of the limbs. I had one long bone, the left humerus. Pearson and Rollet differed slightly, but the mean was 5 feet ½ inch.

The woman's neck was bent at a fairly sharp angle upon the trunk, and if she had been like that in life she would have been a conspicuous figure. I had X-ray photographs taken to see if there had been any disease to cause curvature of the spine. Nothing was found, and I concluded the neck had been bent after death. Why? Perhaps, at some stage, to cram the body into a space that was a little too small for it. As it was, it would have just fitted into the wooden chest. I examined this for bloodstains, but all the tests were negative.

How old was she? I had X-ray photographs taken of the skull plates, which join together at pretty constant periods between the teens and old age. Her brow plates were completely fused, fusion was in progress between the top plates, and there was no fusion between the two groups. That put her age between forty and fifty.

The person who had dismembered the body had evidently tried to make her utterly unidentifiable. The scalp and hair, face, eyes, hands and feet had all gone. No, not quite all: I found a fragment of hair sticking to the back of her skull. It was dark brown, going grey.

The uterus was enlarged. Another X-ray photograph, in case there was a pregnancy. No foetal bones. Instead, the swelling proved to be a fibroid tumour, three to four inches in diameter, for which she might well have sought medical attention.

Teeth? Her lower jaw had gone completely, but in the upper jaw I found as much dental information as a portrait, if her dentist could ever be found. Three molars on the right, two of them filled; the first molar on the left also filled. Marks from the metal claws of a dental plate. A high palate, and considerable thickening of the bone in the region of the back teeth. It was a mine of information. 'If you trace her dentist, and he has kept proper records, you'll identify her beyond doubt,' I told the police.

Inspector Keeling thought he might have found her. Working through the lists of missing persons, he discovered that Rachel Dobkin, the wife of the fire-watcher to the bombed Baptist Church premises, had disappeared after setting out to visit him to collect arrears of maintenance fifteen months previously. Her sister, Polly Dubinski, had reported her disappearance to the police.

Rachel was forty-seven, Polly said. Height about 5 feet 1 inch, 'the same height as me'. Dark hair going grey. She had been going to hospital about 'something internal'. Her dentist was Mr Kopkin – a strangely close spelling! – of Stoke Newington. Polly gave the police a photograph of Rachel.

Yes, said Dr Marie Watson, of the Mildmay Mission Hospital, Bethnal Green, she had examined Mrs Rachel Dobkin in October 1939, and found fibroid growths of the uterus. Yes, confirmed another doctor, at the London Hospital, fibroid growths of the uterus: an operation had been advised, but Mrs Dobkin had refused.

Yes, said Barnett Kopkin, the dental surgeon, recognizing Rachel Dobkin from the photograph – yes, she had been his patient for six years. From April 1934 to March 1940, to be precise; and Kopkin could be very precise, for his records were the most comprehensive that Inspector Keeling had ever seen.

'From these cards,' he asked, 'could you draw a picture of her upper jaw as it was when you saw her last?'

Kopkin sat down in his consulting room and drew the diagram. At Keeling's request he signed and dated it: 3 August 1942, at 11 a.m. Then Keeling brought him to my laboratory at Guy's where the skull of Rachel Dobkin lay upside down on the bench.

'That's my patient!' he burst out excitedly, before I had time to greet him. 'That's Mrs Dobkin! Those are my fillings!'

It was as dramatic a moment as I can remember. Molly Lefebure nearly fell off her lab stool.

Inspector Keeling produced the diagram the dental surgeon had made. It was an exact replica of the upper jaw from the cellar – teeth in the right positions, fillings just so, gap for the denture, claw marks – but also a couple of possible extra: tiny fragments of the roots of the first and second pre-molars on the left side that Kopkin thought he might have left in the jaw when extracting those teeth in April 1934. These did not appear on our X-ray photographs.

We had the jaw X-rayed again, this time by Guy's own senior dental surgeon, the famous Sir William Kelsey Fry. He found the fragments.

Meanwhile I had been feeling my way in photography myself, with the help of Mary Newman, who was in charge of the Photographic Department of Guy's. Now that we had a photograph of the missing woman, a full-face portrait, I wanted to try to superimpose it on a similar photograph of the skull. This identification technique had been used first in 1936, by Professors Glaister and Brash, in the famous case of Buck Ruxton, the Indian doctor who had murdered his wife and her maid and thrown their dismembered bodies into a ravine. Having the jumbled remains of two bodies, Glaister and Brash had been concerned with sorting out the pieces. I had only one head and one photograph, and I wanted to see how far they matched.

Miss Newman photographed the skull and photographed the portrait, and enlarged the latter to the same size. Then she made fresh photographs on X-ray film, a negative of the skull and a positive of the portrait, and placed them together superimposed. We found no dissimilarities whatever. The portrait fitted the skull like a mask.

Keeping was so pleased you would think he had caught the murderer. And in a sense he had; at least, he had him half in the bag.

Murderer? It is all very well to say you do not find yourself in several pieces under a slab of stone in the floor of a Baptist Church cellar unless something sinister has been going on, but that is not enough for a charge of murder. What evidence was there that she had been killed?

Probably there would have been none, but for a very important contribution by the murderer himself. In sprinkling slaked lime over the body he had no doubt intended to keep down the smell of decomposition and perhaps to destroy the soft tissues. Lime has a reputation for burning human flesh. But slaked lime has little or no destructive action; on the contrary, by killing maggots and beetles it acts as a preservatives. Thanks to the lime, certain injuries to the throat, in part to the voice box, had been preserved in this way.

It was another dramatic moment, later in the evening, when I was alone in my laboratory and dissected out the voice box and saw that the upper horn of the thyroid cartilage on the right side was fractured. There was a little blood clot round it, so the workmen had not done the damage with their picks and shovels. It had occurred in life.

Now this little bone never gets broken, alone, except when the neck is gripped tight by a strangling hand. It is the pressure of a finger tip or thumb that does it.

'Are you quite sure, doctor?' Could I really say it was strangling without the classic signs, the imprint of fingers, the asphyxia? Both Hatton and Keeling were very tense.

'I'm certain. This means strangling. This little bone gets broken in no other way. I am quite prepared to say so in court. And if any other pathologist wants to confirm the injury for himself, well, there it is. We'll keep it and I'll have microscopic sections made to confirm the bruising.'

I found another possible bruise on the back of the head. It could have followed upon the throat being gripped and the head bashed against the ground, but it might equally have followed upon a fall. This was a much less significant injury, and as there were no tissues left for microscopical examination I could not be so sure it had occurred before death.

My work was done. I had, I thought, enough evidence to convince a jury that the skeleton was Rachel Dobkin, and that she had been murdered by strangling some fifteen months previously. It was for the police to show who had killed her.

Professor Keith Simpson, *Forty Years of Murder*

Yellow Book

Do you see this square old yellow Book, I toss
I' the air, and catch again, and twirl about
By the crumpled vellum covers, – pure crude fact
Secreted from a man's life when hearts beat hard,
And brains, high-blooded, ticked two centuries since?

• • •

'*Romana Homicidiorum*' – nay,
Better translate – 'A Roman murder-case:
Position of the entire criminal cause
Of Guido Franceschini, nobleman,
With certain Four the cutthroats in his pay,
Tried, all five, and found guilty and put to death
By heading or hanging as befitted ranks,
At Rome on February Twenty Two,
Since our salvation Sixteen Ninety Eight:
Wherein it is disputed if, and when,
Husbands may kill adulterous wives, yet 'scape
The customary forfeit.'

Word for word,
So ran the title-page: murder, or else
Legitimate punishment of the other crime,
Accounted murder by mistake, – just that
And no more, in a Latin cramp enough
When the law had her eloquence to launch,
But interfilleted with Italian streaks
When testimony stooped to mother-tongue, –
That, was this old square yellow book about.

• • •

A solitary villa stood
In a lone garden-quarter: it was eve,
The second of the year, and oh so cold!
Ever and anon there flittered through the air
A snow-flake, and a scanty couch of snow
Crusted the grass-walk and the garden-mould.
All was grave, silent, sinister, – when, ha?
Glimmeringly did a pack of were-wolves pad
The snow, those flames were Guido's eyes in front,
And all five found and footed it, the track,
To where a threshold-streak of warmth and light
Betrayed the villa-door with life inside,
While an inch outside were those blood-bright eyes,
And black lips wrinkling o'er the flash of teeth,
And tongues that lolled – Oh God that madest man!
They parleyed in their language. Then one whined –
That was the policy and master-stroke –
Deep in his throat whispered what seemed a name –
'Open to Caponsacchi!' Guido cried:
'Gabriel!' cried Lucifer at Eden-gate.
Wide as a heart, opened the door at once,
Showing the joyous couple, and their child
The two-weeks' mother, to the wolves, the wolves
To them. Close eyes! And when the corpses lay
Stark-stretched, and those the wolves, their wolf-work done,
Were safe-embosomed by the night again,
I knew a necessary change in things;
As when the worst watch of the night gives way,
And there comes duly, to take cognisance,
The scrutinizing eye-point of some star –
And who despairs of a new daybreak now?
Lo, the first ray protruded on those five!
It reached them, and each felon writhed transfixed.

• • •

[COUNT GUIDO FRANCESCHINI *speaks*]
'That is a way, thou whisperest in my ear!
I doubt, I will decide, then act,' said I –
Then beckoned my companions: 'Time is come!'

And so, all yet uncertain save the will
To do right, and the daring aught save leave
Right undone, I did find myself at last
I' the dark before the villa with my friends,
And made the experiment, the final test,
Ultimate chance that ever was to be
For the wretchedness inside. I knocked – pronounced
The name, the predetermined touch for truth,
'What welcome for the wanderer? Open straight – '
To the friend, physician, friar upon his rounds,
Traveller belated, beggar lame and blind? –
No, but – 'to Caponsacchi!' And the door
Opened.
And then, – why, even then, I think,
I' the minute that confirmed my worst of fears,
Surely, – I pray God that I think aright! –
Had but Pompilia's self, the tender thing
Who once was good and pure, was once my lamb
And lay in my bosom, had the well-known shape
Fronted me in the door-way, – stood there faint
With the recent pang, perhaps, of giving birth
To what might, though by miracle, seem my child, –
Nay more, I will say, had the aged fool
Pietro, the dotard, in whom folly and age
Wrought, more than enmity or malevolence,
To practice and conspire against my peace, –
Had either of these but opened, I had paused.
But it was she the hag, she that brought hell
For a dowry with her to her husband's house,
She the mock-mother, she had made the match
And married me to perdition, spring and source
O' the fire inside me that boiled up from heart
To brain and hailed the Fury gave it birth, –
Violante Comparini, she it was,
With the old grin amid the wrinkles yet,
Opened: as if in turning from the Cross,
With trust to keep the sight and save my soul,
I had stumbled, first thing, on the serpent's head
Coiled with a leer at foot of it.
There was the end!

Then was I rapt away by the impulse, one
Immeasurable everlasting wave of a need
To abolish that detested life. 'T was done:
You know the rest and how the folds o' the thing,
Twisting for help, involved the other two
More or less serpent-like: how I was mad,
Blind, stamped on all, the earth-worms with the asp,
And ended so.
You came on me that night,
Your officers of justice, – caught the crime
In the first natural frenzy of remorse?
Twenty miles off, sound sleeping as a child
On a cloak i' the straw which promised shelter first,
With the bloody arms beside me, – was it not so?
Wherefore not? Why, how else should I be found?
I was my own self, had my sense again,
My soul safe from the serpents. I could sleep.'

Robert Browning, *The Ring and the Book*

Z

Zarathustra

You do not intend to kill, you judges and sacrificers, before the beast has bowed its neck? Behold, the pale criminal has bowed his neck: from his eye speaks the great contempt.

'My Ego is something that should be overcome: my Ego is to me the great contempt of man': that is what this eye says.

He judged himself – that was his supreme moment: do not let the exalted man relapse again into his lowly condition!

There is no redemption for him who thus suffers from himself, except it be a quick death.

Your killing, you judges, should be a mercy and not a revenge. And since you kill, see to it that you yourselves justify life!

It is not sufficient that you should be reconciled with him you kill. May your sorrow be love for the Superman: thus will you justify your continuing to live!

You should say 'enemy', but not 'miscreant'; you should say 'invalid', but not 'scoundrel'; you should say 'fool', but not 'sinner'.

And you, scarlet judge, if you would speak aloud all you have done in thought, everyone would cry: 'Away with this filth and poisonous snake!'

But the thought is one thing, the deed is another, and another yet is the image of the deed. The wheel of causality does not roll between them.

An image made this pale man pale. He was equal to his deed when he did it: but he could not endure its image after it was done.

Now for evermore he saw himself as the perpetrator of one deed. I call this madness: in him the exception has become the rule.

The chalk-line charmed the hen; the blow he struck charmed his simple mind – I call this madness *after* the deed.

Listen, you judges! There is another madness as well; and it comes *before* the deed. Ah, you have not crept deep enough into this soul!

Thus says the scarlet judge: 'Why did this criminal murder? He wanted to steal.' But I tell you: his soul wanted blood not booty: he thirsted for the joy of the knife!

But his simple mind did not understand this madness and it persuaded him otherwise. 'What is the good of blood?' it said. 'Will you not at least commit a theft too? Take a revenge?'

And he hearkened to his simple mind: its words lay like lead upon him – then he robbed as he murdered. He did not want to be ashamed of his madness.

And now again the lead of his guilt lies upon him, and again his simple mind is so numb, so paralysed, so heavy.

If only he could shake his head his burden would roll off: but who can shake this head?

What is this man? A heap of diseases that reach out into the world through the spirit: there they want to catch their prey.

What is this man? A knot of savage serpents that are seldom at peace among themselves – thus they go forth alone to seek prey in the world.

Behold this poor body! This poor soul interpreted to itself what this body suffered and desired – it interpreted it as lust for murder and greed for the joy of the knife.

The evil which is now evil overtakes him who now becomes sick: he wants to do harm with that which harms him. But there have been other ages and another evil and good.

Once doubt and the will to Self were evil. Then the invalid became heretic and witch: as heretic and witch he suffered and wanted to cause suffering.

But this will not enter your ears: you tell me it hurts your good people. But what are your good people to me?

Much about your good people moves me to disgust, and it is not their evil I mean. How I wish they possessed a madness through which they could perish, like this pale criminal.

Truly, I wish their madness were called truth or loyalty or justice: but they possess their virtue in order to live long and in a miserable ease.

I am a railing beside the stream: he who can grasp me, let him grasp me! I am not, however, your crutch.

Thus spoke Zarathustra.

Friedrich Nietzsche, *Thus Spake Zarathustra*, trans. R. J. Hollingdale

Zembla

Line 1000: [= Line 1: I was the shadow of the waxwing slain]

Through the back of John's thin cotton shirt one could distinguish patches of pink where it stuck to the skin above and around the outline of the funny little garment he wore under the shirt as all good Americans do. I see with such awful clarity one fat shoulder rolling, the other rising; his gray mop of hair, his creased nape; the red bandanna handkerchief limply hanging out of one hip pocket, the wallet bulge of the other; the broad deformed pelvis; the grass stains on the seat of his old khaki pants, the scuffed back seams of his loafers; and I hear his delightful growl as he looks back at me, without stopping, to say something like: 'Be sure not to spill anything – this is not a paper chase,' or [wincing] 'I'll have to write again to Bob Wells [the town mayor] about those damned Tuesday night trucks.'

We had reached the Goldsworth side of the lane, and the flagged walk that scrambled along a side lawn to connect with the gravel path leading up from Dulwich road to the Goldsworth front door, when Shade remarked: 'You have a caller.'

In profile to us on the porch a short thickset, dark-haired man in a brown suit stood holding by its ridiculous strap a shabby and shapeless briefcase, his curved forefinger still directed toward the bell button he had just pressed.

'I will kill him,' I muttered. Recently a bonneted girl had made me accept a bunch of religious tracts and had told me that her brother, whom for some reason I had pictured to myself as a fragile neurotic youth, would drop in to discuss with me God's Purpose, and explain anything I had not understood in the tracts. Youth, indeed!

'Oh, I will kill him,' I repeated under my breath – so intolerable was it to think that the rapture of the poem might be delayed. In my fury and hurry to dismiss the intruder, I outstripped John who until then had been in front of me, heading at a good shamble for the double treat of revel and revelation.

Had I ever seen Gradus before? Let me think. Had I? Memory shakes her head. Nevertheless the killer affirmed to me later that once from my tower, overlooking the Palace orchard, I had waved to him as he and one of my former pages, a boy with hair like excelsior, were carrying cradled glass from the hothouse to a horse-drawn van; but, as the caller now veered toward us and transfixed us with his snake-sad, close-set eyes, I felt such a tremor of recognition that had I been in bed dreaming I would have awoken with a groan.

His first bullet ripped a sleeve button off my black blazer, another sang past my ear. It is evil piffle to assert that he aimed not at me (whom he had just seen in the library – let us be consistent, gentlemen, ours is a rational world after all), but at the gray-locked gentleman behind me. Oh, he was aiming at me all right but missing me every time, the incorrigible bungler, as I instinctively backed, bellowing and spreading my great strong arms (with my left hand still holding the poem, 'still clutching the inviolable shade', to quote Matthew Arnold, 1822–1888), in an effort to halt the advancing madman and shield John, whom I feared he might, quite accidentally, hit, while he, my sweet awkward old John, kept clawing at me and pulling me after him, back to the protection of his laurels, with the solemn fussiness of a poor lame boy trying to get his spastic brother out of the range of the stones hurled at them by schoolchildren, once a familiar sight in all countries. I felt – I still feel – John's hand fumbling at mine, seeking my fingertips, finding them, only to abandon them at once as if passing to me, in a sublime relay race, the baton of life.

One of the bullets that spared me struck him in the side and went through his heart. His presence behind me abruptly failing me caused me to lose my balance, and, simultaneously, to complete the farce of fate, my gardener's spade dealt gunman Jack from behind the hedge a tremendous blow on the pate, felling him and sending his weapon flying from his grasp. Our savior retrieved it and helped me to my feet. My coccyx and right wrist hurt badly but the poem was safe. John, though, lay prone on the ground, with a red spot on his white shirt. I still hoped he had not been killed. The madman sat on the porch step, dazedly nursing with bloody hands a bleeding head. Leaving the gardener to watch over him I hurried into the house and concealed the invaluable envelope under a heap of girls' galoshes, furred snowboots and white wellingtons heaped at the bottom of a closet, from which I exited as if it had been the end of the secret passage that had taken me all the way out of my enchanted castle and right from Zembla to *this* Arcady. I then dialed 11111 and returned with a glass of water to the scene of the carnage. The poor poet had now been turned over and lay with open dead eyes directed up at the sunny evening azure. The armed gardener and the battered killer were smoking side by side on the steps. The latter, either because he was in pain, or because he had decided to play a new role, ignored me as completely as if I were a stone king on a stone charger in the Tessera Square of Onhava; but the poem was safe.

The gardener took the glass of water I had placed near the flowerpot beside the porch steps and shared it with the killer, and then accompanied him to the basement toilet, and presently the police and the ambulance arrived, and the gunman gave his name as Jack Grey, no fixed abode, except the Institute for the Criminal Insane, *ici*, good dog, which of course should have been his permanent address all along, and which the police thought he had just escaped from.

'Come along, Jack, we'll put something on that head of yours,' said a calm but purposeful cop stepping over the body, and then there was the awful moment when Dr Sutton's daughter drove up with Sybil Shade.

In the course of that chaotic night I found a moment to transfer the poem from under the booties of Goldsworth's four nymphets to the austere security of my black valise, but only at daybreak did I find it safe enough to examine my treasure.

We know how firmly, how stupidly I believed that Shade was composing a poem, a kind of *romaunt*, about the King of Zembla. We have been prepared for the horrible disappointment in store for me. Oh, I did not expect him to devote himself *completely* to that theme! It might have been blended of course with some of his own life stuff and sundry Americana – but I was sure his poem would contain the wonderful incidents I had described to him, the characters I had made alive for him and all the unique *atmosphere* of my kingdom. I even suggested to him a good title – the title of the book in me whose pages he was to cut: *Solus Rex*; instead of which I saw *Pale Fire*, which meant to me nothing. I started to read the poem. I read faster and faster. I sped through it, snarling, as a furious young heir through an old deceiver's testament. Where were the battlements of my sunset castle? Where was Zembla the Fair? Where her spine of mountains? Where her long thrill through the mist? And my lovely flower boys, and the spectrum of the stained windows, and the Black Rose Paladins, and the whole marvelous tale? Nothing of it was there! The complex contribution I had been pressing upon him with a hypnotist's patience and a lover's urge was simply not there. Oh, but I cannot express the agony! Instead of the wild glorious romance – what did I have? An autobiographical, eminently Appalachian, rather old-fashioned narrative in a neo-Popian prosodic style – beautifully written of course – Shade could not write otherwise than beautifully – but void of my magic, of that special rich streak of magical madness which I was sure would run through it and make it transcend its time.

Vladimir Nabokov, *Pale Fire*

Zone

From beyond the ocean there had arrived one of those creatures as a symbol of victory, friendship, and something else.

Three hundred men felt boundless envy toward the prisoner sitting at the wheel of the American tractor – Grinka Lebedev. There were better tractor operators than Lebedev among the convicts, but they had all been convicted according to Article 58 of the Criminal Code (political prisoners). Grinka Lebedev was a common criminal, a parricide to be precise. Each of the three hundred witnessed his earthly joy: to roar over to the logging area sitting at the wheel of a well-lubricated tractor.

The logging area kept moving back. Felling the taller trees suitable for building materials in Kolyma takes place along the stream banks where deep ravines force the trees to reach upward from their wind-protected havens toward the sun. In windy spots, in bright light, on marshy mountain slopes stand dwarfs – broken, twisted, tormented from eternally turning after the sun, from their constant struggle for a piece of thawed ground. The trees on the mountain slopes don't look like trees, but like monsters fit for a sideshow. Felling trees is similar to mining gold in those same streams in that it is just as rushed: the stream, the pan, the launder, the temporary barracks, the hurried predatory leap that leaves the stream and area without forest for three hundred years and without gold – forever.

Somewhere there exists the science of forestry, but what kind of forestry can there be in a three-hundred-year-old larch forest in Kolyma during the war when the response to Lend-Lease is a hurried plunge into gold fever, harnessed, to be sure, by the guard towers of the 'zones'.

Many tall trees and even prepared, sectioned firelogs were abandoned. Many thick-ended logs disappeared into the snow, falling to the ground as soon as they had been hoisted onto the sharp, brittle shoulders of the prisoners. Weak prisoner hands, tens of hands cannot lift onto a shoulder (there exists no such shoulder!) a two-meter log, drag its iron weight for tens of meters over shrubs, potholes, and pits. Many logs had been abandoned because of the impossibility of the job, and the bulldozer was supposed to help us.

But for its first trip in the land of Kolyma, on Russian land, it had been assigned a totally different job.

We watched the chugging bulldozer turn to the left and begin to climb the terrace to where there was a projection of rock and where we had been taken to work hundreds of times along the old road that led past the camp cemetery.

I hadn't given any thought to why we were led to work for the last few weeks along a new road instead of the familiar path indented from the boot heels of the guards and the thick rubber galoshes of the prisoners. The new road was twice as long as the old one. Everywhere there were hills and dropoffs, and we exhausted ourselves just getting to the job. But no one asked why we were being taken by a new path.

That was the way it had to be; that was the order; and we crawled on all fours, grabbing at stones that ripped open the skin of the fingers till the blood ran.

Only now did I see and understand the reason for all of this, and I thank God that He gave me the time and strength to witness it.

The logging area was just ahead, the slope of the mountain had been laid bare, and the shallow snow had been blown away by the wind. The stumps had all been rooted out; a charge of ammonal was placed under the larger ones, and the stump would fly into the air. Smaller stumps were uprooted with long bars. The smallest were simply pulled out by hand like the shrubs of dwarf cedar . . .

The mountain had been laid bare and transformed into a gigantic stage for a camp mystery play.

A grave, a mass prisoner grave, a stone pit stuffed full with undecaying corpses of 1938 was sliding down the side of the hill, revealing the secret of Kolyma.

In Kolyma, bodies are not given over to earth, but to stone. Stone keeps secrets and reveals them. The permafrost keeps and reveals secrets. All of our loved ones who died in Kolyma, all those who were shot, beaten to death, sucked dry by starvation, can still be recognized even after tens of years. There were no gas furnaces in Kolyma. The corpses wait in stone, in the permafrost.

In 1938 entire work gangs dug such graves, constantly drilling, exploding, deepening the enormous gray, hard, cold stone pits. Digging graves in 1938 was easy work; there was no 'assignment', no 'norm' calculated to kill a man with a fourteen-hour working day. It was easier to dig graves than to stand in rubber galoshes over bare feet in the icy waters where they mined gold – the 'basic unit of production', the 'first of all metals'.

These graves, enormous stone pits, were filled to the brim with corpses. The bodies had not decayed; they were just bare skeletons over which stretched dirty, scratched skin bitten all over by lice.

The north resisted with all its strength this work of man, not accepting the corpses into its bowels. Defeated, humbled, retreating, stone promised to forget nothing, to wait and preserve its secret. The severe winters, the hot summers, the winds, the six years of rain had not wrenched the dead men from the stone. The earth opened, baring its subterranean storerooms, for they contained not only gold and lead, tungsten and uranium, but also undecaying human bodies.

These human bodies slid down the slope, perhaps attempting to arise. From a distance, from the other side of the creek, I had previously seen these moving objects that caught up against branches and stones; I had seen them through the few trees still left standing and I thought that they were logs that had not yet been hauled away.

Now the mountain was laid bare, and its secret was revealed. The grave 'opened', and the dead men slid down the stony slope. Near the tractor road an enormous new common grave was dug. Who had dug it? No one was taken from the barracks for this work. It was enormous, and I and my companions knew that if we were to freeze and die, place would be found for us in this new grave, this housewarming for dead men.

The bulldozer scraped up the frozen bodies, thousands of bodies of thousands of skeleton-like corpses. Nothing had decayed: the twisted fingers, the pus-filled toes which were reduced to mere stumps after frostbite, the dry skin scratched bloody and eyes burning with a hungry gleam.

With my exhausted, tormented mind I tried to understand: How did there come to be such an enormous grave in this area? I am an old resident of Kolyma, and there hadn't been any gold mine here as far as I knew. But then I realized that I knew only a fragment of that world surrounded by a barbed-wire zone and guard towers that reminded one of the pages of tent-like Moscow architecture. Moscow's taller buildings are guard towers keeping watch over the city's prisoners. That's what those buildings look like. And what served as models for Moscow architecture – the watchful towers of the Moscow Kremlin or the guard towers of the camps? The guard towers of the camp 'zone' represent the main concept advanced by their time and brilliantly expressed in the symbolism of architecture.

I realized that I knew only a small bit of that world, a pitifully small part, that twenty kilometers away there might be a shack for geological explorers looking for uranium or a gold mine with thirty thousand prisoners. Much can be hidden in the folds of the mountain.

And then I remembered the greedy blaze of the fireweed, the furious blossoming of the taiga in summer when it tried to hide in the grass and foliage any deed of man – good or bad. And if I forget, the grass will forget. But the permafrost and stone will not forget.

Grinka Lebedev, parricide, was a good tractor driver, and he controlled the well-oiled foreign tractor with ease. Grinka Lebedev carefully carried out his job, scooping the corpses toward the grave with the gleaming bulldozer knife-shield, pushing them into the pit and returning to drag up more.

The camp administration had decided that the first job for the bulldozer received from Lend-Lease should not be work in the forest, but something far more important.

The work was finished. The bulldozer heaped a mound of stones and gravel on the new grave, and the corpses were hidden under stone. But they did not disappear.

The bulldozer approached us. Grinka Lebedev, common criminal and parricide, did not look at us, prisoners of Article 58. Grinka had been entrusted with a task by the government, and he had fulfilled that task. On the stone face of Grinka Lebedev were hewn pride and a sense of having accomplished his duty.

The bulldozer roared past us; on the mirror-like blade there was no scratch, not a single spot.

Varlem Shalamov, 'The American Connection', trans. John Glad

Acknowledgements

CHINUA ACHEBE, from *Things Fall Apart*. © Chinua Achebe 1958. Reprinted by permission of William Heinemann Ltd.

FERGUS ALLEN, from *Brown Parrots of Providencia*. © Fergus Allen 1993. Reprinted by permission of Faber and Faber Ltd.

KINGSLEY AMIS, from *The Riverside Villas Murder*. © Kingsley Amis 1973 (Cape, 1973/Penguin, 1984). Reprinted by permission of Jonathan Clowes Ltd, Random Century Group Ltd.

SIMON ARMITAGE, from *Kid*. © Simon Armitage 1992. Reprinted by permission of Faber and Faber Ltd.

W. H. AUDEN, extracts from *The Dyer's Hand and Other Essays* © W. H. Auden 1963; 'Victor' from *Collected Shorter Poems 1927–57*. 'Paid On Both Sides' from *The English Auden: Poems Essays and Dramatic Writings 1927–1939* © 1977 by Edward Mendelson, William Meredith and Munro K. Spears, Executors of the Estate of W. H. Auden. Reprinted by permission of Faber and Faber Ltd and Random House, Inc.

GEORGES BATAILLE, from *Story of the Eye*, translated by Joachim Neugroschel, © J-J. Pauvert 1967, translation © Urizen Books 1977. First published in Great Britain by Marion Boyars Publishers 1979.

NICHOLAS BLAKE, from *The Beast Must Die*. © The Estate of C. D. Lewis 1938. First published in Great Britain by Collins, 1938.

JOHN DICKSON CARR, from *The Locked Room Lecture*. Reprinted by permission of David Higham Associates Ltd.

CIARAN CARSON, from *Belfast Confetti* © Ciaran Carson 1989, 1990 (Bloodaxe Books Ltd 1990). First published 1989 by The Gallery Press.

RAYMOND CARVER, from *Furious Seasons* © Raymond Carver 1977. Reprinted by permission of Capra Pree, Santa Barbara.

CHARLES CAUSLEY, from *Collected Poems* © Charles Causley 1992 (Macmillan London Ltd) Reprinted by permission David Higham Associates Ltd.

RAYMOND CHANDLER, from *The Simple Art of Murder*, © Raymond Chandler 1950 (Hamish Hamilton); from *The Big Sleep* (Hamish Hamilton). Reprinted by permission of Hamish Hamilton Ltd.

AGATHA CHRISTIE, from *The Murder of Roger Ackroyd*, © Agatha Christie 1926. Reprinted by permission of Hughes Massie Ltd.

DIANA COOPER CLARKE, extracts from *Designs of Darkness: Interviews with Detective Novelists*. © Diana Cooper Clarke.

OLIVER CYRIAX, from *Crime: An Encyclopaedia*. © Oliver Cyriax 1993 (André Deutsch Ltd).

TOI DERRICOTE, from *Captivity*. © Toi Derricote 1989 (University of Pittsburgh).

From *The Diary of Jack the Ripper*, narrative by Shirley Harrison. Original diary and facsimile and transcript of the diary, Smith Gryphon Ltd 1993. © Narrative and commentary Shirley Harrison and Michael Barrett 1993.

E. L. DOCTOROW, from *Billy Bathgate*, © E. L. Doctorow 1989. Reprinted by permission of Macmillan London Ltd.

IAN DUHIG, from *The Bradford Count*. © Ian Duhig 1991 (Bloodaxe Books Ltd).

T. S. ELIOT, from *The Complete Poems and Plays of T. S. Eliot*. © Valerie Eliot 1969. Reprinted by permission of Faber and Faber Ltd.

STANLEY ELLIN, *The Blessington Method*. © Stanley Ellin.

GAVIN EWART, 'Sonnet: At The Villa Madeira' from *The Collected Ewart 1933–1980*. © Gavin Ewart 1980 (Hutchinson); 'The Owl Writes A Detective Story' from *Collected Poems 1980–1990*. © Gavin Ewart 1991 (Hutchinson). Reprinted by permission of Random House UK, Ltd.

VICKI FEAVER, 'Judith' from the *Independent on Sunday* 1.11.92. © Vicki Feaver 1992; also 'Lily Pond' from the *Independent on Sunday* (n.d.). Used with permission.

JAMES FENTON, from *The Memory of War: Poems 1968–1982*. © James Fenton, 1972, 1978, 1980, 1981, 1982. Published by The Salamander Press, Edinburgh 1982.

JAMES FOX, from *White Mischief*. © James Fox 1982 (Jonathan Cape Ltd). Reprinted by permission of Random House UK, Ltd.

SIGMUND FREUD, from *Totem and Taboo*, English translation first published in *The Standard Edition of the Complete Psychological Works of Sigmund Freud*, Vol XII, 1955 by The Hogarth Press and the Institute of Psycho-Analysis, London. Translation © Angela Richards and The Institute of Psycho-Analysis, 1953, 1959, 1962, 1964. Used with permission; from *Civilisation and Its Discontents* (The Hogarth Press), translated by Joan Riviere, translation © The Institute of Psycho-Analysis and Angela Richards 1963. Used by permission.

KINKY FRIEDMAN, 'A Case of Lone Star' in *The Kinky Friedman Crime Club*. © Kinky Friedman 1986, 1987, 1988, 1992. First published in UK by Faber and Faber Ltd 1992 and in USA by William Morrow & Co Inc. 1987.

ERLE STANLEY GARDNER, from *The Case of the Perjured Parrot*. First published 1939. First published by Penguin Books Ltd. 1959.

VICTORIA GLENDINNIG, from *Trollope*. © Victoria Glendinnig 1992 (Hutchinson). Reprinted by permission of Random Century Group Ltd.

JOHN GOHORRY, from *A Voyage Round The Moon*. © John Gohorry 1984. Reprinted by permission of Peterloo Poets.

WILLIAM GOLDING, from *Lord of the Flies*. © William Golding 1954. Reprinted by permission of Faber and Faber Ltd.

ROBERT GRAVES, from *The Twelve Caesars*. Translation © Robert Graves 1957. Reprinted by permission of A. P. Watt; extract from *Lawrence and the Arabs* (Jonathan Cape Ltd., 1927). © The Estate of Robert Graves.

GRAHAM GREENE, 'The Case for the Defence' from *Collected Stories*. © Graham Greene 1954, 1972, and from *Collected Short Stories*. © 1947, © renewed 1975 by Graham Greene. From *The Third Man*. © 1950 Graham Greene. Reprinted by permission of David Higham Associates Ltd.

THOMAS HARRIS, from *The Silence of the Lambs*. © 1988 by Yazoo Inc (William Heinemann Ltd.).

TONY HARRISON, from 'The Oresteia' reprinted in *Theatre Works 1973–1985*. © Tony Harrison, 1985. Reprinted by permission of the Peters Fraser & Dunlop Group Ltd.

SEAMUS HEANEY, from *Station Island*. © Seamus Heaney 1984. Reprinted by permission of Faber and Faber Ltd and Farrar, Straus and Giroux, Inc.

ANTHONY HECHT, from *The Transparent Man*. © Anthony Hecht 1980, 1981, 1982, 1986, 1987, 1990. Reprinted by permission of Oxford University Press.

PATRICIA HIGHSMITH, *Ripley's Game* reprinted in *The Mysterious Mr Ripley*. © Patricia Highsmith 1974. Reprinted by permission of William Heinemann Ltd and Diogenes Verlag AG on behalf of the author.

DARYL HINE, from *Minutes*. © by Daryl Hine 1967. Reprinted by permission of Simon & Schuster.

MICHAEL HOFMANN, from *Corona Corona*. © Michael Hofmann 1993. Reprinted by permission of Faber and Faber Ltd.

TED HUGHES, from *Gaudete*. © Ted Hughes 1977. Reprinted by permission of Faber and Faber Ltd.

ALDOUS HUXLEY, from *Point Counter Point*. Reprinted by permission of Chatto & Windus Ltd, and HarperCollins Publishers Inc.

MICK IMLAH, from *Birthmarks*. © Mick Imlah 1988 (Chatto & Windus Ltd).

P. D. JAMES, from *A Taste For Death*. © P. D. James 1986 (Faber and Faber Ltd); from *Death of an Expert Witness*, © P. D. James 1977 (Faber and Faber Ltd). Reprinted by permission of Elaine Greene Ltd.

ALAN JENKINS, from *Greenheart*. © Alan Jenkins 1990. Reprinted by permission of Chatto & Windus Ltd.

CAPTAIN CHARLES JOHNSON, from *The Lives of the Most Notorious Pirates*. Text by kind permission of Routledge & Kegan Paul Ltd.

JOSEPHUS, from *The Jewish War*, translated by G. A. Williamson, revised by E. Mary Smallwood (Penguin Classics, 1959) © E. M. Smallwood, 1981.

JACKIE KAY, 'Pork Pies'. © Jackie Kay.

WELDON KEES, 'Crime Club'. © Weldon Kees.

E. V. KNOX, 'The Murder at the Towers' from *This Other Eden* (Methuen). © The Estate of E. V. Knox.

PHILIP LARKIN, from *Selected Letters of Philip Larkin 1940–85*. © the Estate of Philip Larkin, 1992. Reprinted by permission of Faber and Faber Ltd.

LAURIE LEE, from *Cider with Rosie*. Reprinted by permission of The Hogarth Press.

PRIMO LEVI, from *Collected Poems*. Translated by Ruth Feldman and Brian Swann. © Ruth Feldman and Brian Swann 1988. Reprinted by permission of Faber and Faber Ltd.

C. DAY LEWIS, from *Collected Poems 1954* (Jonathan Cape Ltd 1954) reprinted by permission of A. M. Heath Ltd.

WILLIAM LOGAN, from *Difficulty*. © William Logan, 1984. First published by The Salamander Press, 1984.

MICHAEL LONGLEY, from *Poems 1963–1983* published by Secker and Warburg. Reprinted by permission of Reed Consumer Books Ltd and the Peters Fraser & Dunlop Group Ltd.

NICCOLO MACHIAVELLI, from *The Prince*, translated by George Bull. Translation © George Bull 1961. First published Penguin Books Ltd.

JIM MARRS, from *Crossfire*. © Jim Marrs 1989. First published in Great Britain by Pocket Books 1993, an imprint of Simon & Schuster, and in the USA by Carroll & Graf Publishers, Inc. Used with permission.

JOHN MASEFIELD, 'No Man Takes the Farm' and 'The Rider At The Gate'. Reprinted by permission of The Society of Authors as the literary representative of the Estate of John Masefield.

EDGAR LEE MASTERS, 'Amanda Barker' from *Spoon River Anthology* (1915). © The Estate of Edgar Lee Masters.

IAN McEWAN, from *The Innocent*. © Ian McEwan 1989. Reprinted by permission of Random House UK, Bantam Doubleday and Key Porter Books.

MELANIE McFADYEAN, 'Helen's Story' from *Independent on Sunday*, 13.9.92. © Melanie McFadyean 1992. Used with permission.

ROGER McGOUGH, from *Defying Gravity*. © Roger McGough 1991, 1992. Reprinted by permission of the Peters Fraser & Dunlop Group Ltd.

MALCOLM X, from *The Autobiography of Malcolm X*, with the assistance of Alex Haley. © Alex Haley and Malcolm X 1964. Reprinted by permission of Random House UK.

JOHN MASTERS, from *The Deceivers*, © John Masters 1952 (Michael Joseph, 1952/Penguin Books Ltd., 1955, reprinted 1957, 1959, 1962). Used with permission.

GLYN MAXWELL, from *Out Of The Rain*. © Glyn Maxwell 1992 (Bloodaxe Books Ltd).

TIMOTHY MO, from *Sour Sweet*. © Timothy Mo 1982 (André Deutsch Ltd).

ANDREW MOTION, from *Dangerous Play: Poems 1974–1984*. Reprinted by permission of the author and the Peters Fraser and Dunlop Group Ltd.

PAUL MULDOON, from *Meeting The British*. © Paul Muldoon 1987. Reprinted by permission of Faber and Faber Ltd.

LES MURRAY, from *Dog Fox Field*. © Les Murray 1990, 1991. Published in Australia by Collins Angus & Robertson Publ. Pty. Ltd 1990. First published in UK Carcanet Press Ltd 1991.

VLADIMIR NABOKOV, from *Pale Fire*. © Vladimir Nabokov 1962.

OGDEN NASH, from *I Wouldn't Have Missed It*. Reprinted by permission of Curtis Brown, New York and Little Brown.

CHARLES NICHOLL, from *The Reckoning: The Murder of Christopher Marlowe*. © Charles Nicholl 1992. Reprinted by permission of Jonathan Cape Ltd.

GEORGE ORWELL, from *Decline of the English Murder*. © Sonia Brownell Orwell 1968. Reprinted by permission of A. M. Heath on behalf of the estate of the late Sonia Brownell Orwell and Martin Secker & Warburg, and Harcourt Brace Jovanovich.

TIM PARKS, from *Loving Roger*. © Tim Parks 1986. Reprinted by permission of Watson Little Ltd.

MERVYN PEAKE, from *Titus Groan*. © The Estate of Mervyn Peake 1968. Reprinted by permission of David Higham Associates Ltd and The Overlook Press.

MARCO POLO, from *The Travels of Marco Polo*. Translation © 1958 R. E. Latham (Penguin Books Ltd, 1958).

EZRA POUND, from *The Cantos of Ezra Pound*. © 1937 by Ezra Pound. Reprinted by permission of Faber and Faber Ltd and New Directions Publishing Corporation.

PETER READING, '15th February' from *Essential Reading*. © Peter Reading 1986; 'Going On' from *Ukulele Music*. © Peter Reading 1985. Reprinted by permission of the author.

WILLIAM RUSHTON, from *W. G. Grace's Last Case*. © William Rushton 1984. (Methuen London Ltd).

MARQUIS DE SADE, 'Philosophy in the Bedroom', reprinted in *The Marquis de Sade*, translated by Richard Seaver and Austryn Wainhouse. © 1965 by Richard Seaver and Austryn Wainhouse (Grove Press, Inc.).

DOROTHY L. SAYERS, from *Have His Carcase*. © The Estate of Dorothy L. Sayers 1932. Reprinted by permission of David Higham Associates Ltd.

VERNON SCANNELL, 'A Case of Murder'. Reprinted by permission of the author.

GITTA SERENY, from *Into That Darkness*. © Gitta Sereny 1984 (André Deutsch Ltd).

VARLEM SHALAMOV, from *Kolyma Tales*, translated by John Glad. Translation © John Glad 1980. Reprinted by permission of W. W. Norton & Company Inc., and Penguin Books Ltd.

RUTH SHARMAN. Reprinted by permission of the author.

KEITH SIMPSON, from *Forty Years of Murder*. © Keith Simpson 1978 (George G. Harrap Ltd, 1978).

HARRY SMART, from *Pierrot*. © Harry Smart 1991. Reprinted by permission of Faber and Faber Ltd.

STEVIE SMITH, from *The Collected Poems of Stevie Smith*. © 1972 by Stevie Smith. Reprinted by permission of James MacGibbon and New Directions Publishing Corporation.

PATRICK SUSKIND, from *Perfume*, translated by John E. Woods. Translation © John E. Woods, 1986 (Hamish Hamilton). First published as *Das Parfum* by Diogenes Verlag AG, Zurich. © Diogenes Verlag, 1985. Used by permission.

ALLEN TATE, from *Collected Poems 1919–1972*. © Allen Tate 1977. Reprinted by permission of Faber and Faber Ltd and Farrar, Straus and Giroux, Inc.

JAMES THURBER, 'The Macbeth Murder Mystery' from *My World and Welcome To It*. © 1970 Helen Thurber and Rosemary Thurber. Reprinted by permission of Rosemary A. Thurber.

IVAN TURGENEV, from *Literary Reminiscences and Autobiographical Fragments*, translated by David Magarshack. © Farrar, Straus & Giroux, Inc. 1958.

ED VULLIAMY, 'Luciano Leggio: Man of Dishonour', from the *Guardian*, 20.11.93. © the *Guardian* 1993. Reprinted by permission.

EVELYN WAUGH, from *Decline and Fall*. © the Estate of Evelyn Waugh 1928. Reprinted by permission of the Peters Fraser & Dunlop Group Ltd.

JOHN WHITWORTH, 'The Pure Essence' from *Tennis and Sex and Death* © John Whitworth 1989. Used by permission of Peterloo Poets 1989. 'These Boys' from *Lovely Day for a Wedding*. © John Whitworth 1985 (Secker & Warburg Ltd). 'Home Entertainments' and 'Blood Ties' both © John Whitworth.

RICHARD WILBUR, from *New and Collected Poems*. © Richard Wilbur 1988. First published in USA by Harcourt Brace Jovanovich, Inc. and in UK by Faber and Faber Ltd.

NIGEL WILLIAMS, from *The Wimbledon Poisoner*. © Nigel Williams 1990. Reprinted by permission of Faber and Faber Ltd.

P. G. WODEHOUSE, from *The Parrot*. © The Estate of P. G. Wodehouse. (Hutchinson).

EMILE ZOLA, from *Thérèse Raquin*. Translation © Andrew Rothwell 1992. Reprinted by permission of Oxford University Press. From *The Earth*. Translation © Douglas Parmee 1980 (Penguin Books Ltd, 1980).

Faber and Faber Limited apologize for any errors or omissions in the above list and would be grateful to be notified of any corrections that should be incorporated in the next edition or reprint of this volume.

Index of Authors